WITHDRAWAL

MAGILL'S
LEGAL GUIDE

MAGILL'S LEGAL GUIDE

Volume 3

Prison system — Zoning laws

EDITOR

Timothy L. Hall
University of Mississippi Law School

PROJECT EDITOR

R. Kent Rasmussen

SALEM PRESS, INC.
PASADENA, CALIFORNIA   HACKENSACK, NEW JERSEY

Managing Editor: Christina J. Moose
Project Editor: R. Kent Rasmussen
Copy Editor: Robert Michaels
Research Supervisor: Jeffry Jensen
Photograph Editor: Karrie Hyatt
Editorial Secretary: Andrea E. Miller
Acquisitions Editor: Mark Rehn
Production Editor: Yasmine A. Cordoba
Layout: William Zimmerman

Copyright © 2000, by SALEM PRESS, INC.
All rights in this book are reserved. No part of this work may be used or reproduced in any manner whatsoever or transmitted in any form or by any means, electronic or mechanical, including photocopy, recording, or any information storage and retrieval system, without written permission from the copyright owner except in the case of brief quotations embodied in critical articles and reviews. For information address the publisher, Salem Press, Inc., P.O. Box 50062, Pasadena, California 91115.

∞ The paper used in these volumes conforms to the American National Standard for Permanence of Paper for Printed Library Materials, Z39.48-1992(R1997).

Note to Readers

The material presented in *Magill's Legal Guide* is intended for broad informational and educational purposes. Although the articles in these volumes have been prepared to provide accurate and authoritative information, they should not be used as substitutes for professional legal advice. Readers needing legal assistance are advised to consult competent licensed legal professionals.

Library of Congress Cataloging-in-Publication Data

Magill's legal guide / editor, Timothy L. Hall ; project editor, R. Kent Rasmussen.
  p. cm.
  Includes bibliographical references and index.
  1. Law—United States. I. Hall, Timothy L. II. Rasmussen, R. Kent.
KF385.M35 2000
349.73—dc21   99-35385
ISBN 0-89356-165-7 (set)   CIP
ISBN 0-89356-168-1 (vol. 3)

First Printing

PRINTED IN THE UNITED STATES OF AMERICA

Table of Contents

Prison system 691
Prisoners' rights 695
Privacy rights 699
Private investigators 701
Privileged communication 702
Pro bono legal work 703
Probable cause 705
Probate 707
Probation, adult 710
Probation, juvenile 713
Product liability law 716
Property liability 717
Property rights 718
Property taxes 720
Property types 724
Prosecutors 725
Prostitution 728
Proximate cause 730
Public accommodations 731
Public defenders 733
Public domain 736
Public interest law 737
Public nuisance 740

Quitclaim deed 741

Race and the law 742
Rape 745
Real estate law 749
Real estate listing agreements . . . 753
Real property 754
Reasonable doubt 755
Reckless endangerment 755
Rehabilitative support 756
Release 756
Religious institutions 756
Rent control 760
Rental agreements 761
Renters' rights 764
Repossession 766
Restraining order, temporary 767
Retainers 767
Retirement planning 768
Retirement plans 770
Right to die 771
Robbery 773

Sales taxes 775
School law 776
Search and seizure, illegal 781
Search warrant 782
Secured transaction 783
Self-defense 785
Self-employment taxes 785
Sentencing 787
Service contracts 789
Sexual battery 790
Sexual harassment 791
Shareholder suit 794
Sheriffs 795
Shoplifting 797
Slander 798
Small businesses 798
Small claims court 802
Smoking and tobacco use 803
Smuggling 806
Social Security 808
Solicitation of legal clients 811
Space law 812
Speedy-trial requirement 813
Spousal abuse 813
Stakeout 816
Stalking 816
State judicial systems 817
State police 818
Statute 822
Statute of limitations 822
Statutory fee ceilings 823
Stepparents 824
Stock certificate 825
Stockholders 826
Stop and frisk 828
Study-abroad programs 829
Subleases 829
Subpoena 830
Subrogation 831
Substantive law 831
Summary judgment 832
Summer clerkships 832
Summons 833
Superfund litigation 833
Supreme Court, U.S. 834
Surrogate parenting 837
Suspect 838

Tax law	840
Telephone law	844
Television courtroom programs	846
Television dramas about the legal profession	848
Tenancy in common	851
Test case	851
Testimony	852
Theft	853
Three-strikes laws	855
Title	855
Title companies	856
Title search	857
Torts	857
Trade secret	862
Trademarks	863
Traffic court	865
Traffic law	866
Traffic schools	868
Treason	870
Trespass	871
Trial publicity	871
Trial transcript	872
Trials	873
Truancy	876
Trustees	877
Trusts	877
Trusts, charitable	881
Unauthorized practice of law	882
Unconscionable contracts	882
Undergraduate preparation for law school	883
Unemployment insurance	885
Unethical conduct of attorneys	887
Uniform laws	889
Unwed parents and rights of children	890
Usury	892
Vagrancy	894
Vandalism	894
Vehicle licenses and registration	895
Venue, change of	896
Verdict	896
Victims' rights	897
Visas, foreign	900
Visas, U.S.	902
Voting rights	906
Warranties	909
Whistle-blowing	910
White-collar crime	911
Wills	913
Wills, holographic	917
Wiretap	918
Witness protection programs	918
Witnesses	920
Witnesses, expert	923
Women in legal professions	924
Workers' compensation	927
World Court	928
Wrongful death	929
Zoning laws	932
Important Federal Laws	934
Important U.S. Supreme Court Cases	944
Legal Assistance Organizations	959
Legal Resources	968
State Bar Associations	977
Federal Law-Enforcement Agencies	981
Filmography	989
Glossary	997
Bibliography	1011
Topics by Subject Category	XXIII
Index	XXXI

Magill's
Legal Guide

Prison system

The U.S. prison system is the complex of correctional institutions and facilities for incarcerating persons serving sentences for felony convictions

The United States has the world's highest per capita incarceration rate, and the world's largest prison system. Prisons, unlike jails or detention facilities, are correctional institutions designed for long term incarceration of persons convicted of serious crimes—felonies. The system of prisons in the U.S. is composed of both federal prisons, run by the U.S. government for persons convicted of crimes in federal court, and state prisons located in each U.S. state, which incarcerate persons convicted of state offenses. Federal prisons are run by the U.S. Bureau of Prisons, an agency which is part of the U.S. Justice Department. In 1995 the U.S. Justice Department counted 1,196 state and federal "confinement facilities" and 304 "community-based" facilities, which held pretrial detainees and persons in noncustodial work programs.

Although the United States was initially renowned for its modern and enlightened approach to corrections in the nineteenth century, it is now the industrialized world's leader in constructing larger and harsher prison facilities. This development, as well as the expanded use of privately operated correctional facilities, has made the imprisonment of persons very big business in the United States. The U.S. Justice Department estimates that in 1993 states spent a total of about $14.2 billion on correctional institutions, a ten-year increase of 270 percent. While the federal prison system is much smaller than its state counterpart, the federal government spent slightly over $1 billion on correctional institutions in 1993. This spending has generated a large, and in some smaller communities a critically important, industry. Nationwide, nearly 600,000 people were employed in corrections in the United States in 1993.

Progressive, Humane Approaches. Many prisons in the early American republic were among the most modern and progressive in the world. In the early nineteenth century new "penitentiaries," in which silent inmates might find reform and rehabilitation through hard labor and solitude, were constructed in New York and Pennsylvania. These facilities, which aimed to replace the brutal and filthy conditions of eighteenth century prisons and the practice of whipping and beating prisoners with enlightened and "scientific" approaches, were praised by European visitors. They so impressed the French social observer Alexis de Tocqueville that he wrote a book about them. Later in the nineteenth century U.S. reformers developed such innovations as probation, parole (early conditional release of inmates), "good-time" (which provided inmates credits that reduced their sentences for appropriate behavior while imprisoned), and indeterminate sentences (under which persons convicted of crimes were incarcerated until they were "reformed" rather than for a set period of years).

Throughout the nineteenth and most of the twentieth centuries, the U.S. prison system underwent successive periods of reform, in which various techniques were tried and then abandoned. The most recent period occurred in the 1970's, following a four-day riot by inmates at the New York State prison in Attica. The Attica uprising ended with the deaths of forty-three people during an assault by the state police to regain control of the prison. A subsequent state investigation placed much of the blame for the incident on the lack of educational and vocational opportunities for inmates, overcrowding, inadequate and insufficiently trained personnel, and a climate of racism. The report concluded that the remedy for such incidents would require

> major efforts to train officers to understand and deal with the new breed of inmates, to eliminate the petty harassments and root out the racist attitudes which these inmates will never tolerate, and accelerate programs to make prisons—as long as they must exist—more humane environments for men to live in.

Incidents such as the Attica uprising led authorities to conclude that more aggressive reform efforts, including expanded vocational and educational opportunities for inmates, greater access to legal resources, better training of personnel, and less crowding were necessary to avoid future violent episodes.

Modern, More Punitive Approach. While the 1970's saw a reform movement in American prisons, a backlash in the 1980's reversed this trend. A combination of political and social movements,

Police herd inmates into a yard during a prison rebellion in Attica, New York, in 1971. Forty-three people were killed during an assault by the state police to regain control of the prison. (AP/Wide World Photos)

including the ascendancy of harsher criminal justice policies nationally under President Ronald Reagan, the "War on Drugs," and increased public concern about violent crime, led to a much more punitive approach to corrections. The principal purpose of incarceration was seen as punishment, and reform or rehabilitation of offenders was viewed at best as an unintended—and at worst as a largely impossible—effect. This change in thinking led to a great increase in the rate and length of incarceration during the 1980's and 1990's.

As of mid-1997, according to the U.S. Justice Department, 1.7 million people were incarcerated in state and federal prisons and in jails awaiting trials or serving shorter sentences. This incarceration rate is more than triple that of 1980, when less than half a million persons were incarcerated. The high growth rate in the number of persons in prison during the 1980's and 1990's was not the result of an increase in crime or prosecutions. U.S. Justice Department figures show that between 1973 and 1992 the number of crimes actually fell slightly and that the number of violent crimes was virtually unchanged.

The increase in the prison population has been due almost exclusively to the lengthening of sentences or to the increasing severity of punishments. The most significant part of this increase in the federal prison system has been in the area of drug offenses. Much of the increase in the size of the prison population has been the result of much more severe penalties for drug offenses and changes in sentencing laws that require minimum mandatory prison terms for certain offenses. In 1970, according to the U.S. Bureau of Prisons, drug offenders represented about 16.3 percent of all inmates. In 1995 drug offenders represented 60.6 percent of federal inmates. Drug offenses have become the most common and among the most severely punished offenses in federal court. A study by the U.S. Justice Department's Bureau of Justice Statistics found that in an eighteen-month period in 1989-1990, 95 percent of those convicted of drug trafficking offenses in federal court were sentenced to prison. The Bureau of Justice Statistics reported in 1995 that only 46 percent of state prison inmates were incarcerated for violent offenses. Meanwhile, 24 percent of state prison inmates were incarcerated for property offenses and 23 percent for drug offenses. The National Criminal Justice Commission, a group of thirty-four academics, law-enforcement and corrections personnel, and attorneys concluded in a 1996 study that the vast majority of crime in America is not violent, that the vast majority of people filling the prisons are nonviolent property and drug offenders.

Security, Technology, and "Supermax" Prisons. As the numbers of inmates have increased, so has the burden on prison staff of effectively managing the inmate population. Security classifications, under which inmates are divided according to how dangerous or likely to misbehave they are, have been used for decades to maintain control. Federal correctional facilities include eight penitentiaries, all classified as "high security," and fifty federal correctional institutions, classified as "medium security," "low security" or "administrative" (for inmates needing special protection or supervision). A dozen minimum security federal "prison camps," six metropolitan correctional facilities in major cities, five federal medical centers, two detention centers (principally for aliens seeking admission), and a transportation facility complete the federal complement of correctional facilities.

Technology is an important aid in maintaining control and enabling fewer corrections personnel to effectively and safely manage larger populations. Computer-operated gates allow prison personnel to minimize direct contact with inmates, and remote video cameras provide surveillance without the need for more guards. The newest, highest security facilities are designed for exclusively solitary confinement, with showers in each cell to minimize the need for inmates to ever be removed from their cells.

A new approach to corrections management involves the concentration of a single security classification or type of inmate in a single facility. This eliminates the need to handle a range of inmate classifications. This concentration approach has been used most notably in high-security and administrative classifications, in which inmates who are management or discipline problems or who require special protection, are grouped in a single facility. The federal penitentiary at Marion, Illinois, was for years the federal government's highest-security facility. It housed inmates sent from other federal and some state facilities because they created management or discipline problems. In this "supermax" facility, inmates are on "lock down," or restricted to their cells, twenty-three hours a day. They have virtually no contact with other inmates and very little with guards. Inmates are shackled before any movement from their cells and are moved individually by teams of guards. This extensive use of "lock down" is controversial because of the long-term psychological effects isolation can have, but prison authorities contend it is necessary to maintain discipline. In 1995 the federal government opened a new administrative maximum security facility in Florence, Colorado.

Development of the Private Prison Industry. In the 1980's a combination of factors led to the growth in the United States of private companies that managed and operated correctional facilities. First, taxpayers in many states were opposed to spending money on many public projects, and government at all levels was required to do more with less revenue. Second, the United States (and other countries) began experimenting during this period with "privatization"—the delivery of services by private companies that had previously been provided only through the government. Third, the state prison systems in several states had come under federal court control because of inmate lawsuits challenging poor conditions, and states sought quick ways to efficiently improve their prison systems. Fourth, increases in the numbers of persons sentenced to prison and the lengths of prison terms led to a demand for more prison capacity. Although many states needed more and higher quality correctional facilities, the public was often unwilling to fund them. Thus, a new industry responded to this demand with the promise of cheaper, more efficient, privately operated prisons.

These privatization arrangements took various forms. In the early 1980's thirty-eight U.S. states had some form of contract with private correctional service providers. A 1991 study of private correctional facilities in the United States showed that fourteen companies operating forty-four facilities housed approximately 13,400 inmates. The expanded use of private facilities, in which the government pays a daily rate for each inmate, is controversial. Private corrections companies must make a profit, and some believe that the profit motive may negatively affect the quality of operations. Others believe that profit should not be made from the deprivation of persons' liberty, which imprisonment requires. Whether privately operated prisons actually provide cheaper incarceration is still unclear, and data as of the late 1990's left the matter open to question.

Disproportionate Imprisonment of Minorities. In terms of gender, race, ethnicity, and economic status the composition of the prison population generally is very different from that of the U.S. population as a whole. Prison inmates in the United States are overwhelmingly male. According to the U.S. Justice Department *Sourcebook of Criminal Justice Statistics*, women accounted for only about 65,000 of more than 1.2 million state and federal inmates. In 1998 the U.S. Bureau of Prisons reported that 93 percent of its inmates were male.

While the prison population in the U.S. has historically been overwhelmingly male, its racial and ethnic composition had changed dramatically by the 1980's and 1990's. Incarcerated persons were disproportionately members of racial or ethnic minority groups. Approximately 40 percent of inmates in federal prison in 1997 were African American. Nearly 30 percent of federal prison inmates were Hispanic. In 1996 the National Criminal Justice Commission compared U.S. Justice Department statistics from 1930 and 1992 for admissions to state and federal prisons. The racial and ethnic breakdown of new prison admissions has virtually been reversed over the fifty-year period, from 75 percent white and 25 percent African American in 1930 to 29 percent white, 51 percent African American and 20 percent Hispanic in 1992. Ninety percent of those imprisoned for drug offenses were either African Americans or Hispanics.

The racial and ethnic composition of the prison population reflects what many observers have noted is the disproportionate impact of both crime and the criminal justice system on racial and ethnic minorities. Many prisons are sited in rural or outlying areas, where there may be few racial or ethnic minority residents. Prisons are large, stable employers, which often bring badly needed jobs and a concentrated demand for goods and services to remote communities. These economic factors, however, mean that the inmate population, disproportionately composed of racial and ethnic minorities who often come from large urban centers, is principally guarded and supervised by rural, often nonminority personnel. This can create frictions between staff and inmates beyond those inherent in a correctional environment.

Moreover, prison facilities are not evenly distributed throughout the United States; they are clustered in particular regions. Justice Department figures from 1995 show that about 40 percent of the nation's state and federal prisons and nearly 40 percent of the nation's prison capacity are located in the South. Given the demand for prison space and the high rate of admissions of minority inmates from large, urban centers, many inmates find themselves housed far from family and friends. This can make maintaining ties to those outside difficult, and the loss of family and emotional ties during incarceration can dramatically worsen an inmate's prospects for successful reintegration into society upon release.

Suggested Readings. Annual statistical information on the total number of persons in prisons and jails nationwide and on the numbers of those under correctional supervision through parole or probation is available in the U.S. Department of Justice publication *Correctional Populations in the United States* (Washington, D.C.: Bureau of Justice Statistics, published annually) and its *Sourcebook of Criminal Justice Statistics*, edited by Kathleen Maguire and Ann L. Pastore (Washington, D.C.: Bureau of Justice Statistics, published annually). A comprehensive account of national crime policy, including prisons and privatization, is *The Real War on Crime: The Report of the National Criminal Justice Commission*, edited by Steven R. Donziger (New York: Harper-Collins, 1996). Particularly articulate and thoughtful accounts of the personal experiences of former inmates include Sol Wachtler's *After the Madness: A Judge's Own Prison Memoir* (New York: Random House, 1997), written by a former state supreme court justice, and Jean Harris's *They Always Call Us Ladies: Stories from Prison* (New York: Scribner's, 1988), written by the former headmistress of an exclusive private school. For general histories of U.S. prisons see *Encyclopedia of American Prisons*, edited by Marilyn D. McShane and Frank P. Williams III (New York: Garland, 1996) and *The Oxford History of the Prison: The Practice of Punishment in Western Society*, edited by Norval Morris and David J. Rothman (New York: Oxford University Press, 1995). The official account of the inmate uprising at the New York State prison in Attica is *Attica: The Official Report of the New York State Special Commission* *on Attica* (New York: Praeger, 1972). An interesting account by a journalist who participated in the mediation efforts is Tom Wicker's *A Time to Die* (New York: Quadrangle/New York Times, 1975). Overviews of the privatization movement include *Punishment for Profit: Private Prisons/Public Concerns* by David Shichor (Thousand Oaks, Calif.: Sage Publications, 1995) and *Private Prisons and the Public Interest*, edited by Douglas C. McDonald (New Brunswick, N.J.: Rutgers University Press, 1990). A survey of private correctional facilities is C. W. Thomas and S. L. Foard's *Private Correctional Facility Census* (Gainesville: Center for Studies in Criminology and Law, University of Florida, 1991). A survey of prison overcrowding is *America's Correctional Crisis: Prison Populations and Public Policy*, edited by Stephen D. Gottfredson (New York: Greenwood Press, 1987). —David M. Siegel

See also Criminal justice system; Drugs, illegal; Felony; Parole; Parole officers; Prisoners' rights; Probation, adult; Sentencing.

Prisoners' rights

Although the large and rapidly growing population of U.S. prisons and jails poses serious problems for the criminal justice system and U.S. society, prisoners have certain basic rights that must be protected.

On any given day there are well over a million prison inmates and well over a half million jail inmates in the United States, not counting juveniles. The vast majority of prison inmates are in state institutions, having been convicted of state felonies after arrest and prosecution at the local level. The vast majority of the jail inmates are incarcerated on misdemeanor charges. However, about half of all jail inmates still face trial, and this population includes a number of felons who will ultimately find their way into the prison system.

The total correctional caseload also includes several million probationers, both felons and misdemeanants, who are typically supervised locally by state agencies, and a considerably smaller number of parolees. Some jurisdictions, including the federal government, have abolished parole but have often been forced by the pressures of the escalating prison population to revive it under other names or auspices. Most wardens favor parole as an incentive to inmates to demonstrate good behavior.

Prison Demographics. Several demographic groups are statistically overrepresented in the inmate population. Most markedly, 90 percent of inmates in almost all jurisdictions are males. Moreover, ethnic minorities make up about half of the total. Young African American males from economically and culturally impoverished urban areas are the single most overrepresented group among inmates, and in many cities the majority of such persons experience correctional supervision before they reach the age of twenty-five.

Inmate populations have increased rapidly in almost all jurisdictions, despite the leveling off or even decrease in crime rates in the late 1990's. This is due largely to citizens' and politicians' continuing willingness to expend public resources on punishment for the sake of retribution and incapacitation, despite mounting evidence that neither deterrence nor institutionally based rehabilitation has worked very well. Institutional overcrowding is generally conceded to be the largest and fastest-growing single problem of the U.S. correctional system. However, in some experts' opinions probation caseloads, well over one hundred in almost all jurisdictions, contrasts with the American Correctional Association's recommendation of fifty, constituting an equal or even greater problem than overcrowding. The entire correctional system suffers from an immense crisis of overwork and undersupport to a much greater extent than the rest of the American criminal justice system.

Prison Overcrowding. Overcrowding causes daily and cumulative pressures on inmates that exceed those intended by incarceration. The U.S. Supreme Court ruled in the landmark cases of *Bell v. Wolfish* (1979) and *Rhodes v. Chapman* (1981) that double-bunking of two jail or prison inmates in a cell designed for one person was constitutionally permissible provided that the institution was relatively clean, modern, and safe and that good faith efforts were under way to relieve overcrowding. Such a cell is typically 60 to 80 square feet in size and contains a bunk bed, a chair, a desk, a dresser, a stool, and a basin that take up most of the space. The typical cell costs at least $25,000 to $50,000 to build.

Since wardens and sheriffs rarely have sufficient control over their own purse strings to initiate construction programs with any degree of timeliness, double-bunking is permitted as long as good faith efforts exist to find and deploy resources for cell construction. Almost every jurisdiction is under severe population pressure, with double-bunking providing the most frequent safety valve.

Even the federal prison system with its immense resources has been forced to house increasing numbers of its inmates in local jails on the basis of daily fee contracts with sheriffs, while the jails have become less able to absorb the inmate overload. One reason for this problem is the rapidly increasing number of federal inmates serving mandatory sentences on drug-related charges. Generalizing upon this theme, the jurisdictions with the greatest problems of inmate population management tend to be those with the strictest programs of mandatory or determinate sentencing, while those that have maintained significant aspects of the less politically fashionable indeterminate sentencing are better able to manage their total caseloads through the effective use of probation, parole, and diversions as alternatives to incarceration.

Racial Tensions and Health Problems. In addition to overcrowding and double-bunking, several other systemic stresses impinge upon the daily lives

---

Selected U.S. Supreme Court Cases Dealing with Prisoners' Rights

Cooper v. Pate (1964): First successful use of Section 1983 of the Civil Rights Law of 1871 by state or local inmates in federal court to claim federally protected rights, in this case the right to religious equality.

Coleman v. Peyton (1966): Inmates won basic access to courts for lawsuits, thus effectively ending the "hands off" era of the federal courts toward inmates.

Johnson v. Avery (1969): Inmates won the right to assist one another as "jailhouse lawyers" in the preparation of legal cases and materials.

Younger v. Gilmore (1971): Prison inmates won access to adequate law libraries.

Procunier v. Martinez (1974): Inmates gained the assistance of legal interns under certain circumstances.

Wolff v. McDowell, (1974): Inmates' rights to due process in disciplinary hearings were clarified and expanded.

Estelle v. Gamble (1976): The deliberate indifference test, which is often used to determine whether prison health and safety measures fall short of the standard imposed by the Eighth Amendment to the U.S. Constitution, was applied to inmate health, establishing a right to basic care.

Bounds v. Smith (1977): Inmates' rights of access to the courts were clarified and expanded.

Jones v. N.C. Prison Union (1977): Inmates' basic rights of expression and association were affirmed, but at the same time wardens' discretionary authority to limit such rights—for example, if an inmate union is seen to endanger prison discipline and security—was also strongly affirmed.

Bell v. Wolfish (1979): Affirmed that the double-bunking of two jail or prison inmates in a cell designed for one person was constitutionally permissible provided that the institution was relatively clean, modern, and safe and that good faith efforts were underway to relieve overcrowding.

Rhodes v. Chapman (1981): Like *Bell v. Wolfish*, this decision held that double-bunking was constitutionally permissible; in this case the inmate Kelly Chapman sent Ohio governor James A. Rhodes an amputated finger in futile protest against overcrowding and double-bunking.

Smith v. Wade (1983): Inmates won basic safety protection under the deliberate indifference test.

Hudson v. Palmer (1984): The reasonableness test for cell searches was reaffirmed, as was correctional officers' broad discretion to perform searches and shakedowns intended to promote prison security.

Whitley v. Albers (1986): The discretion of officers to use reasonable and at times deadly force in riots and disturbances was reaffirmed.

Hudson v. McMillian (1992): The prohibition against unreasonable force by officers toward inmates in nonemergency situations was reaffirmed.

of the inmates. Racial tensions have long been a problem, but they have increased in the late twentieth century because of the growth of racial and ethnic gangs, some of which have actually originated in jails and prisons. Contraband is a perpetual problem, especially the unauthorized presence of drugs and weapons. With mandatory sentencing there has been an increase in middle-aged and elderly inmates and all the health problems associated with these age groups. Human immunodeficiency virus (HIV), acquired immunodeficiency syndrome (AIDS), and infections among inmates pose serious health problems that typically have been met by leaving ill inmates in the general population, often with cellmates, until their symptoms require intensive treatment. Mental health problems, which also plague inmates, are rarely treated at the personal level, since institutional budgets provide relatively little money for psychotherapy. Many inmates are functionally or even totally illiterate, while an increasing number speak little or no English.

These are just a few of the serious problems that face inmates and the increasingly overburdened correctional personnel who must try to supervise and occasionally help them. At the same time inmate rights, which were expanded and clarified by a number of important Supreme Court decisions in the 1960's and especially in the 1970's, are under serious legal and political attack.

Basic Inmate Rights. The easiest and clearest way to present inmate rights is to relate them to their particular legal foundations, in most cases to the U.S. Bill of Rights. Of special importance in delineating inmates' rights are the Fourteenth Amendment to the U.S. Constitution of 1868 and Section 1983 of the Civil Rights Law of 1871 (usually referred to as #1983), both of which served to bolster the authority to the Bill of Rights after the Civil War of 1861 to 1865 and eventually provided a legal framework for inmate litigation under the Bill of Rights.

Section 1983 stated that any person whose federally protected rights are infringed by a state or local government employee may seek direct redress in the federal courts, bypassing the state or local courts that might be biased in the employee's favor. This provision went virtually unnoticed until the 1950's and 1960's, when it was rediscovered by civil rights attorneys and the American Civil Liberties Union (ACLU). At the same time, the Fourteenth Amendment provisions of due process and equal protection of the laws received increased attention from the federal courts—for example, in the civil rights case of *Brown v. Board of Education* and a variety of police-related criminal justice cases.

It was only a matter of time before inmates' attorneys discovered the new legal strategy. After the 1964 case of *Cooper v. Pate*, the first successful use of #1983 by state or local inmates in federal court to claim federally protected rights, the Supreme Court became increasingly receptive to inmate complaints. By the late 1970's most of the fundamental constitutional issues relating to inmate rights had been addressed and partly resolved. Then in 1980 the backlash against inmate rights began with the federal Civil Rights of Institutionalized Persons Act. Additionally, in the 1990's the former "hands off" policy of the federal courts toward inmates was largely resumed. However, certain of the most basic rights of inmates remain relatively well established and will probably pass the test of time. These rights are rooted in key amendments to the U.S. Constitution.

Constitutional Protections. According to the First Amendment, inmates have the right to choose and pursue their own religious identities within the parameters of institutional safety and security. In this context, inmates' different religions enjoy relative equality under the law. Because of prison security, other First Amendment guarantees are more restricted than inmates' religious freedoms. But limited freedom of speech, press, and assembly do exist, as well as a significant right to seek governmental redress of inmate grievances, both within the institutional governance structure and in the external arena of the state and federal courts.

Inmates do not enjoy the privacy of their persons or living areas to nearly the extent that private citizens do. They may be subjected to searches, shakedowns, or other intrusive measures at almost any time on almost any pretext, provided that institutional security and safety are deemed necessary by prison authorities. However, the reasonableness criterion of the Fourth Amendment, as interpreted within the correctional context, is still considered to apply to these intrusions.

The due process clause of the Fifth Amendment originally applied only to the federal government.

But it has been extended to lower jurisdictional levels by legal absorption within the Fourteenth Amendment, which also contains its own due process clause. Thus, due process is a very significant right of inmates, albeit occasionally limited by their status and the circumstances of incarceration. Inmates' internal grievances and complaints as well as inmate discipline are governed by this sort of due process. For example, while inmates may participate in adversarial hearings, such hearings are not full-blown trials and they rarely involve legal counsel. Once inmates' lawsuits and appeals reach the courts on the outside, they are governed by most of the same due process rights that apply to free citizens. However, inmates rarely appear in court as witnesses in their own behalf and hardly ever serve as their own counsel.

In recent decades inmates have been given greatly expanded access to courts and legal processes, as well as greater access to legal counsel. These rights are guaranteed by the Sixth Amendment to the U.S. Constitution. However, inmates do not always have the financial resources to pay for legal services. In major court cases, such as death penalty appeals, inmates are often assisted by the ACLU. In disciplinary matters and lesser court cases, inmates are permitted to assist one another in the preparation of legal materials and in hearing rooms, but ordinarily they are not permitted to assist one another in the courtroom. Prisons and large jails are required to have adequate legal libraries for inmates, and even small jails are required to provide alternative access to basic legal information—for example, through public defenders and legal interns.

Freedom from cruel and unusual punishment, guaranteed by the Eighth Amendment, does not protect inmates from the death penalty, although it does protect them from unreasonably painful methods of execution. The Eighth Amendment, in applying to the health and safety conditions in jails and prisons, primarily effects the daily lives of inmates. Inmates are legally entitled to basic institutional health care, which is quite comparable to that which many soldiers and students receive from their respective military and educational institutions. The deliberate indifference test is often used to determine whether prison health and safety measures fall short of the standard imposed by the Eighth Amendment. In addition, this amendment protects inmates from excessive or gratuitous brutality.

The Fourteenth Amendment is in many ways the most important amendment for inmate rights. Its due process clause is used to incorporate previous Bill of Rights guarantees into inmates' rights and freedoms on a case-by-case basis, and it applies directly to a number of other procedural matters, such as discipline, grievances, lawsuits, and appeals. As pretrial jail inmates, in the eyes of the law, are not yet undergoing punishment, they must go directly to the Fourteenth Amendment to assert the protections that prison inmates and convicted jail inmates enjoy under the Eighth Amendment. Furthermore, the Fourteenth Amendment's equal protection clause is often used by inmates to assert fundamental equality—for example, the equality of race, gender, or religion—even though the First or other Amendments may also apply. When inmates' attorneys do not know where else in the law to turn, the creative use of the Fourteenth Amendment is often a useful expedient, since it justifies going to federal court under the guidelines of #1983. Without this flexible and powerful aspect of the Fourteenth Amendment, many specific cases that have handled the issue of inmates' rights would not have made it into the federal courts at all, since most of them originated as inmate lawsuits against state or local correctional practitioners.

Suggested Readings. Supreme Court cases dealing with inmates' rights may all be found in the *Supreme Court Reports*, published annually by the U.S. Government Printing Office in Washington, D.C. In using these Reports readers are reminded that most major cases are decided in the spring, while the bound volumes are dated the previous October. Good summaries of most of the important inmates' rights cases may be found in *Briefs of Leading Cases in Corrections*, compiled by R. V. del Carmen et al. (Cincinnati, Ohio: Anderson Publishing, 1993). Further background on the legal and social aspects of inmate life and on the leading problems faced by contemporary corrections may be found in the third edition of *The Dilemmas of Corrections*, edited by K. C. Haas and G. P. Alpert (Prospect Heights, Ill.: Waveland Press, 1995). An ambitious scholarly treatment of the entire American correctional system and its many problems may be found in the seventh edition of *Corrections in*

America by H. E. Allen and C. E. Simonsen (Upper Saddle River, N.J.: Prentice-Hall, 1995). A shorter and more readable treatment of the correctional system, written from a much less critical and political perspective, may be found in the third edition of *Introduction to Corrections* by R. W. Snarr (New York: McGraw-Hill, 1997). There are also many governmental sources of correctional data and information, such as the National Criminal Justice Reference Service (NCJRS), reachable at Box 6000, Rockville, Md. 20850, (800) 851-3420, e-mail askncjrs@ncjrs.org. —*Tom Cook*

See also Constitution, U.S.; Criminal justice system; Cruel and unusual punishment; Death penalty; Due process; Parole; Prison system; Probation, adult.

Privacy rights

The U.S. legal system emphasizes that individuals should have freedom from unwarranted intrusions into their personal affairs.

In contemporary law there are four major categories of privacy rights. First, the Fourth Amendment to the U.S. Constitution places limits on when and how public officials may conduct searches of persons and their homes or property. Second, the U.S. Supreme Court has interpreted the U.S. Constitution so that it includes a generic right to privacy, meaning the freedom to make deeply personal decisions without governmental coercion. Third, the common law generally recognizes the right of persons to lead their lives with reasonable seclusion from public scrutiny. Fourth, a patchwork of federal and state legislation requires respect for privacy in specific ways within both the public and private spheres.

Searches and Seizures. The Fourth Amendment prohibits law-enforcement officials from conducting "unreasonable searches and seizures," and it also suggests that a warrant is usually required when such searches and seizures are conducted. According to the Supreme Court's interpretations, warrantless searches are permitted in several circumstances. The police, for example, do not need a warrant to frisk persons' clothing based on a "reasonable suspicion" that such persons might be carrying a dangerous weapon. Moreover, the police may also search an automobile and its containers when they have probable cause to believe that contraband or criminal evidence is concealed therein.

Historically, state police officers often ignored the requirements of the Fourth Amendment, but the Supreme Court in 1961 forced greater compliance by requiring that criminal trials make use of the exclusionary rule (which excludes evidence acquired illegally). Since 1967 the Supreme Court has recognized that the Fourth Amendment is applicable whenever public officials enter into areas where persons have "a reasonable expectation of privacy." Thus, the amendment strictly regulates any police interceptions of private telephone conversations but authorizes the police to seize contraband objects in "plain view," provided they are lawfully in a position to view such evidence. In 1984 the Court determined that prison inmates have no reasonable expectation of privacy during prison searches.

The Fourth Amendment prohibits unreasonable intrusions into the human body. Public officials are usually not allowed to order surgery or the use of stomach pumps to obtain evidence of a crime. Based on probable cause the police are allowed to conduct less intrusive procedures, such as drawing blood to determine if a driver is intoxicated. In 1989 the Supreme Court gave government agencies a green light to mandate drug testing for those employees who hold sensitive positions, and in 1995 the Court approved of random drug tests for students participating in interscholastic athletics. In 1997, however, Georgia's requirement of drug tests for all political candidates was judged unconstitutional.

The Constitutional Right to Privacy. In the twentieth century the Supreme Court has interpreted the concept of liberty in the due process clauses of the Fifth and Fourteenth Amendments to mean that government may not arbitrarily deprive an individual of personal autonomy or intimate relationships. In the watershed case of *Griswold v. Connecticut* (1965), the Court used this interpretation to overturn a state law that outlawed the selling or use of contraceptives. Emphasizing the liberty of individuals to make free choices about reproduction, the Court based its decision on "a right of privacy older than our Bill of Rights." In 1967 the

Court overturned state laws that prohibited marriage between individuals of different races, thus recognizing that the Constitution protects persons' liberty to choose the marriage partners of their choice.

The most controversial of the "right to privacy" decisions was *Roe v. Wade* (1973), in which the Supreme Court decreed that this constitutional right "was broad enough to encompass a woman's decision whether or not to terminate her pregnancy." Any legal rights of a fetus were judged secondary to a woman's privacy rights, at least until fetuses have attained viability. In later decisions the Supreme Court approved several regulations pertaining to the right to abortion, as long as such regulations did not place an "undue burden" on women's reproductive freedom.

The Supreme Court has gradually extended the right to privacy to other questions of personal autonomy. In 1977, for example, the Court overturned a city's zoning ordinance that had prohibited a grandmother from allowing her grandchildren to live in her single-family home. The Court's official opinion declared that "freedom of personal choice in matters of marriage and family life is one of the liberties protected by the Due Process Clause." In the case of *Cruzan v. Director, Missouri Department of Health* (1990) the Court recognized that competent adults have a constitutional right to refuse medical treatment, even when this refusal will result in death. In 1997, however, the Court allowed states to continue to criminalize doctor-assisted suicides.

At times the Court has upheld laws that in the view of many unnecessarily restrict personal autonomy. Police departments, for example, have been allowed to regulate the hair length of policemen. In the controversial case of *Bowers v. Hardwick* (1986), the Court voted five to four to uphold the authority of states to criminalize all forms of homosexual practices, even within the privacy of an individual's bedroom. The majority of the judges accepted the idea that the Constitution protects only those aspects of privacy sanctioned by American history and moral traditions.

Privacy Torts in Common Law. A tort is a harmful wrong for which a court may award a remedy, usually monetary damages, to a private party. A tort may be set out in a statute or it may be included in the common law (which is judge-made law based on established precedents). The common law of most jurisdictions recognizes four discrete types of privacy torts: invasions into a person's solitude in an unreasonable and highly offensive manner, publicity about highly offensive private information that is not of legitimate concern to the public, publicity about information that places a person in a false light, and the use of persons' names or likenesses without their consent. The four privacy torts frequently overlap with other torts, and some states have codified them into statutes.

It is sometimes possible for persons to win lawsuits against the news media for revealing embarrassing matters of a strictly personal nature. Juries are more likely to award damages, however, when newspeople use fraud or disguise to trespass into private property. Because of the First Amendment's guarantee of freedom of the press, "public persons" cannot win lawsuits for unwanted publicity, but they occasionally win for the reckless presentation of false information. The courts have respected the media's right to report true facts considered "newsworthy," even if such facts are embarrassing to the individuals involved.

Voyeurism is an old way of invading personal privacy. The voyeur, or Peeping Tom, spies on people in private places considered secure, such as hotel bedrooms or bathrooms. The legal cause of action against voyeurs is usually the tort of intrusion, but there are also criminal penalties in some jurisdictions. Since juries tend to sympathize with the victims of such incidents, legal sanctions against voyeurs are the most successful of all claims involving invasions of privacy.

Privacy Statutes. Although privacy legislation is not comprehensive in scope, a host of federal and state statutes define privacy rights in various contexts. The Omnibus Crime Control and Safe Streets Act of 1968 strictly limits the use of electronic surveillance in both the public and private sectors. The federal Credit Reporting Act of 1970 prohibits many unreasonable and careless invasions of consumer privacy. The Privacy Act of 1974 regulates the federal government's use of information about citizens. The Family Education Rights and Privacy Act of 1974 specifies which individuals can gain access to student information in all schools that receive federal funds. The Right to Financial Privacy Act of 1978 provides bank customers with a degree of privacy in their financial records.

Disputes about workers' privacy rights are common in the workplace, and such conflicts are often settled in court. In general, workers have a "legitimate expectation of privacy" in their desks and other spaces reserved for private possessions, and employers are expected to be specific about any limitations on privacy rights. The monitoring of employees, moreover, must usually be justified by good business practices. Civil rights laws place a number of restrictions on the personal questions that may be asked of prospective employees, such as women's marital status. Employers are expected to secure personnel files so that they are not available for public inspection, and files should be restricted to persons who "need to know." Under the Americans with Disabilities Act (ADA) of 1990 employers must be especially careful to protect the confidentiality of personnel records.

With the expansion of computers, individuals have few protections against the unwanted acquisition of private information available in countless data banks. Insurance companies, for example, are allowed to obtain individual health records from sources such as the Medical Information Bureau. Many concerned citizens call for stricter laws at both the federal and state level to protect the confidentiality of such records.

Suggested Readings. For general introductions to the complex topic of privacy rights see Caroline Kennedy and Ellen Alderman's *The Right to Privacy* (New York: Alfred A. Knopf, 1995) and David Elder's *The Law of Privacy* (New York: Clark Boardman, 1991). Two useful guides are Robert Long's *Rights to Privacy* (New York: Wilson, 1997) and Evan Hendricks's *Your Right to Privacy* (Carbondale: Southern Illinois University, 1990). For information on Fourteenth Amendment restraints on government see Darien McWhirter and John Bible's *Privacy as a Constitutional Right* (New York: Quorum Books, 1992). For material on employment law see Kurt Decker's *Employer Privacy Law and Practice* (New York: Wiley, 1987) and Jon Bible and Darien McWhirter's *Privacy in the Workplace* (New York: Quorum Books, 1990). Anne Branscomb examines the difficult field of "information privacy" in *Who Owns Information?* (New York: Basic Books, 1994). Bett Givens explains practical ways to safeguard personal information in *The Privacy Rights Handbook* (New York: Avon Books, 1997).

—*Thomas T. Lewis*

See also Constitution, U.S.; Defamation; Due process; Freedom of press; Internet; Right to die; Search and seizure, illegal.

Private investigators

Private investigators are individuals, partnerships, or corporations, generally licensed by the states, who offer their services for hire to attorneys, insurance companies, government entities, and private individuals.

The services provided by private investigators are similar to those provided by police officers and detectives in that they all investigate the circumstances surrounding certain events. However, private investigators have no police powers. Often private investigators are retired law-enforcement officers, but that is not a requirement for licensure. It is estimated that five thousand private investigations agencies employ 200,000 persons.

Private investigators are often referred to as "private I's" or "private eyes." The origins of this slang term can most likely be traced to the 1850's with the Pinkerton agency, which is still one of the largest private investigations firms in the United States. The Pinkerton agency was the first to use the slogan "We never sleep" and an open eye for its logo.

Private investigators supplement police forces by charging fees for investigative work for defense attorneys (who do not have the resources of the state to conduct investigations for them), insurance companies (when there are suspicions that certain claims may be false), and private individuals (whose concerns may not warrant police intervention, such as marriage or custody disputes). Some private investigations firms provide personal and contract security services, background checks for employment and insurance applications, investigations into workers' compensation claims, and surveillance services to investigate shoplifters, pilferers, and even in-home child-care workers.

Private investigators are licensed in most states, and those states require a criminal background check as well as either experience or training in the specific field of investigations. For example, the state of Florida licenses its private investigators through the State Department and requires either prior police and investigative experience or the service of a two-year term of internship under a currently licensed private investigator.

Even though many private investigators are former law-enforcement officers, their powers are much more limited than those of police officers. Private investigators have no more power than an average citizen to make arrests. They generally limit their activities to gathering information for courts or to reporting to parties requesting their services. Proprietary officers (those working directly for malls, factories, department stores, or government facilities) are often called upon to challenge employees who work in such environments. These officers actually have somewhat more latitude to make searches than police officers, as they are not confined by the search and seizure constraints defined by the U.S. Constitution. Therefore, with proper notification, proprietary officers and investigators may search employees' personal automobiles, purses, and effects.

The numbers of persons involved in private investigations and private security operations have increased at the significant rate of 8 percent per year, as compared to 4 percent for public police officers. This can be attributed to the fact that police resources are limited by local tax bases and that there are more lawsuits filed than ever before. Private suits promising large settlements require investigative services to provide background information and factual data. Also, with the increase in sophisticated surveillance techniques and the perceived need for scrutiny in daily affairs, the demand for the services of private investigators is on the rise.

—C. Randall Eastep

See also Evidence; Law enforcement; Litigation expenses.

Privileged communication

The law protects certain relationships by preventing parties in that relationship from being forced to disclose their communications with one another.

Normally, the objective of a trial is, as reflected in the witness's oath, to obtain "the truth, the whole truth, and nothing but the truth." But trials occur in broader social settings, in which full disclosure of the truth is not always in the best interests of society. Sometimes society benefits more from the protection of certain private and confidential relationships than by fracturing these relationships in the quest for the truth. This proposition is at the heart of evidentiary rules that protect certain confidential communications from forcible disclosure in judicial proceedings. The case of the attorney-client privilege, for example, illustrates how the privilege is expected to further an important social relationship. Communications between attorneys and their clients are often said to be protected, because society benefits when people obtain legal advice, because attorneys need to know the facts in order to render advice, and because clients will not disclose confidential facts unless they are sure that these facts cannot be repeated in court. Thus, to make the benefits of legal advice available to the public at large, the law safeguards the confidentiality of the attorney-client relationship.

The most common forms of privileged communications are those between an attorney and a client, between a husband and a wife, and between a physician and a patient. In addition to these privileges, some jurisdictions recognize others as well, such as privileges for communications between a psychotherapist and a patient and between clergy and communicants. Moreover, confidential communications relating to trade secrets, secrets of state, political votes, and the identities of informers are also privileged. In some jurisdictions statutes or evidentiary rules spell out specific protected privileges. However, the U.S. Congress decided to leave this matter to the courts in federal cases. When it adopted the Federal Rules of Evidence, it did not specify particular protected privileges.

A party whose communications are protected by a privilege has the right to object in court when testimony is sought from a witness that would violate that privilege. Thus, a spouse has the right to object—even if he or she is not a party to a case—when the other spouse is questioned about the substance of husband-wife communications. It is possible, however, to waive the protection normally accorded to particular privileged communications. The most common form of waiver occurs when a party otherwise entitled to a privilege voluntarily discloses the privileged information to a third party. For example, clients who tell friends about the advice they received from their attorneys may be found to have waived the attorney-client privilege. Similarly, the privilege may be waived when the communication it protects has not been made under confidential circumstances. Thus, if a client reveals private information to a lawyer in the presence of the client's friend, it may well be found that the privilege has been waived. In this case, either the client, the lawyer, or the friend might be called upon in court to reveal the substance of the client's communication to the lawyer.   —*Timothy L. Hall*

See also Attorney-client relationship; Attorney confidentiality; Evidence; Objection; Witnesses.

Pro bono legal work

The demand that lawyers perform free legal services for the good of the public—"pro bono publico"—as a requirement for maintaining their licenses to practice law is controversial within the legal profession.

Pro bono work involves the free delivery of legal services to persons of limited means or to charitable, religious, civic, community, governmental, and educational organizations in matters primarily designed to address the needs of poor persons. It also involves providing free legal assistance to individuals, groups, or organizations seeking to obtain or protect civil rights, civil liberties, or public rights. In addition, it means providing free legal services to charitable, governmental, or educational organizations in matters that further their goals and in which payment would significantly deplete their funds. There is no universally accepted definition of pro bono work. The model codes of ethics enacted by bar associations only provide general guidance.

Lawyers who volunteer their time do so for a variety of reasons. They may feel passionate about an issue or type of client. They may want to gain litigation experience or learn a new area of law. According to several studies, approximately 85 percent of the legitimate legal needs of the poor go unmet. The needs of the poor include adequate food, decent shelter, and protection from abuse. Many pro bono programs recruit volunteers to handle public benefits hearings, public housing issues, spousal abuse, and appeals pertaining to Medicaid (a federal health insurance program). Typically, a pro bono program cannot provide legal assistance to every person of limited means who desires assistance. The demand for such services outstrips the supply of lawyers capable of providing them.

Pro bono programs may be established to assist all persons of limited means in a geographical area and to serve special populations such as battered spouses or the homeless. Other programs address a wide range of issues or a particular issue, such as immigration or community economic development. Some programs provide full-case legal representation, while others provide advice only. An example of a pro bono program is that established by the Arizona Asian American Bar Association to assist Americans of Japanese ancestry who suffered a loss of their civil rights during World War II. Another example is the Massachusetts Black Lawyers Association, which created the Macon B. Allen Civil Rights Clinic in Boston. This clinic serves low-income people who wish to pursue claims of employment discrimination on the basis of race, sex, or national origin.

In addition to pro bono lawyers, the poor receive legal aid through alternative dispute resolution programs and nonlawyer legal services. Other providers include judicare programs, in which the government pays private attorneys to aid indigent clients. Governmental support of legal services for the poor is provided through the Legal Services Corporation (LSC), a federally financed nonprofit organization that provides staff attorneys in civil cases for low-income Americans.

Pro Bono Precedents. America's first experience with legal aid was the Freedman's Bureau. Between 1865 and 1868 the bureau retained attorneys in the District of Columbia and some southern states to represent poor African Americans in criminal and civil cases. The first private legal aid society in the United States was the German Legal Aid Society, established in 1876 by German immigrants. The Legal Aid Society of New York was the nation's first legal aid organization to be financed by a combination of funds from bar associations, community chests, individuals, and businesses.

The legal aid movement developed slowly in the twentieth century. In 1963 the U.S. Supreme Court ruled in *Gideon v. Wainwright* that indigent defendants in state felony cases must be provided with counsel. As a result of this ruling, government-sponsored public defender offices opened nationwide to provide legal assistance to felony defendants who could not afford to hire attorneys. Federal funds for legal assistance to the poor were allocated to the Office of Economic Opportunity (OEO), which was part of President Lyndon B. Johnson's "war on Poverty." In 1966 Congress created the OEO Legal Services Program (LSP). This program used the legal system to reform laws and practices perceived as biased against the poor. The LSP's reform initiatives sparked considerable political opposition. In 1974 Congress created the Legal Services Corporation (LSC). The LSC was a quasigovernmental agency governed by a nonpartisan board of directors. It, too, came under attack. In 1987 Tulane Law School in New Orleans, Louisiana, became the first law school to require that its students provide a minimum of twenty hours of legal aid to indigent individuals.

The American Bar Association (ABA) has long recognized the responsibility of lawyers to engage in pro bono work. In 1908 the ABA Canon of Ethics recognized the inherent duty of lawyers to provide legal aid to the indigent in criminal cases. In 1969 the ABA adopted the Model Code of Professional Conduct, which states that every lawyer, regardless of prominence or workload, has the responsibility to find time to serve the disadvantaged. No time requirement was specified. In 1975 the ABA House of Delegates adopted the Montreal Resolution, which states that it is the basic professional responsibility of each lawyer to provide free, public-interest legal services, such as poverty and civil rights law. In 1983 this policy was incorporated into the Model Rules of Professional Conduct.

In December, 1987, the *ABA Journal* and the *American Medical Association Journal* jointly called on lawyers and doctors to contribute fifty hours each year to serving the poor. In 1988 the ABA's House of Delegates adopted the Toronto Resolution, which urges all lawyers to devote no less than fifty hours per year to pro bono and other public-interest services for the needy or to improve the law, the legal system, or the legal profession. The pro bono provision is the only rule in the Model Rules that is not mandatory.

Opposition to Mandatory Pro Bono Service. The proposal that lawyers be required to perform pro bono legal work first surfaced in the late 1970's when the State Bar of California and the Association of the Bar of New York City established an expectation of forty hours of pro bono service annually. The proposals sparked intense opposition and were defeated. Later mandatory pro bono proposals experienced a similar fate. State bar associations are reluctant to adopt mandatory pro bono requirements, because not all lawyers can afford to donate their time.

Lawyers generally agree that access to the courts is a basic right in American society. Courts are a forum in which people can present their grievances and in which wrongs can be corrected. Lawyers also agree that people need legal representation in order to have their disputes resolved relatively quickly, fairly, and as inexpensively as possible. The poor do not have equal access to the law because they have little money. Lack of legal assistance for the poor undermines their right to equal justice under the law and access to the legal system.

Opponents resist mandatory pro bono activities on the basis that it is an unwarranted encroachment on their personal freedom. They generally agree that equal access to the legal system is a serious problem. However, they believe that imposing pro bono work on lawyers is a form of involuntary servitude and an ineffective method for solving the legal problems of the poor. Opponents contend that the courts cannot, and should not, mandate acts of charity. They argue that the shortage of legal services for the poor is a broad social problem. It is undemocratic to require that lawyers be the only professionals to have to solve a problem that must be solved by society as a whole. Opponents are also concerned about the difficulty of documenting and enforcing a mandatory pro bono obligation.

Proponents argue that because pro bono representation is a bedrock professional duty, lawyers simply must do it. By the late twentieth century an overwhelming majority of states had pro bono provisions in their legal ethics codes. These provisions hold that mandatory pro bono is necessary because legal service programs and calls for voluntary help have been insufficient to meet the needs of the poor.

Rules of Conduct. The American Bar Association's Model Rule 6.1 (adopted in 1993) sets forth that lawyers should perform fifty hours of pro bono

service per year. If lawyers cannot provide pro bono services, they should donate the monetary equivalent of fifty hours of service to organizations providing free legal services. This section of the organization's Model Rules of Professional Conduct indicates that a "substantial majority" of this commitment should be spent on behalf of people of limited means or for organizations primarily concerned with the needs of persons of limited means. The law firm Pro Bono Project recommends that lawyers in large law firms perform between fifty and eighty hours of pro bono service per year. The committee that wrote the rule in 1993 said that the private bar alone cannot be expected to fill the gap for service for the poor. It argued that the federal government, by adequately funding the LSC, should bear the responsibility for fixing the problem of unmet legal needs. The government exacerbated the situation by failing adequately to fund the LSC.

A variety of solutions has been offered to resolve the debate over the obligation to provide free legal representation to the poor. For example, mediators have focused on passive enforcement, which is instituted only when practitioners commit ethical violations. This approach is similar to that of mandatory seat belt laws. Under such laws police officers cannot issue citations for violations unless drivers have been stopped for other offenses. Another approach holds that lawyers must pay a user fee or tax in exchange for a license to practice law. Because the license entitles lawyers to use the public asset of client confidentiality or secrecy, they must donate time to pro bono work.

Since the 1970's the organized bar has pressed lawyers to expand their pro bono efforts. At the same time, bar associations have avoided mandating that they do so. Pro bono work is a goal to which lawyers should aspire. Lawyers' responsibility to provide representation to those who cannot afford to pay for it is likely to remain a controversial issue.

Suggested Readings. For an overview of the pro bono debate see *The Law Firm and the Public Good* (Washington, D.C.: The Brookings Institution/The Governance Institute, 1995), edited by Robert A. Katzmann. Jeremy Miller and Vallori Hard trace the history of pro bono service in "Pro Bono: Historical Analysis and a Case Study" in *Western State University Law Review* 21 (Spring, 1994). Consumer activists Ralph Nader and Wesley J. Smith discuss the pro bono activities of large law firms in *No Contest: Corporate Lawyers and the Perversion of Justice in America* (New York: Random House, 1996). Other works on the legal profession may be found in Sol Linowitz's *The Betrayed Profession* (New York: Charles Scribner's Sons, 1994) and Mary Ann Glendon's *A Nation Under Lawyers* (New York: Farrar, Straus & Giroux, 1994). The ABA's Center for Pro Bono is a clearinghouse for information on the private bar associations' involvement in legal services for the poor. The ABA's Center for Professional Responsibility is a source for national and state codes of conduct.   *Fred Buchstein*

See also American Bar Association; Attorney fees; Bar associations; Billable hours; Code of Professional Responsibility; Ethics; Law firm partners and associates; Law firms; Legal clinics; Model Rules of Professional Conduct; Public defenders; Public interest law.

Probable cause

Probable cause is the standard of proof necessary for representatives of the government to make an arrest or to search and seize one's belongings.

The Fourth Amendment to the U.S. Constitution states, "The right of the people to be secure in their persons, houses, papers, and effects, against unreasonable searches and seizures, shall not be violated, and no Warrants shall issue, but upon probable cause, supported by Oath or affirmation, and particularly describing the place to be searched, and the persons or things to be seized." The authors of the Constitution were very concerned about government intrusion into the lives of citizens, and through the Fourth Amendment they sought to ensure that individual privacy would be respected.

The question as to what constitutes probable cause has been considered a number of times by the U.S. Supreme Court. In 1949, in deciding the case of *Brinegar v. United States*, the Court stated, "probable cause is the facts and circumstances within the officers' knowledge and of which they had reasonably trustworthy information and are sufficient in themselves to warrant a man of reasonable caution in the belief that an offense has been or is being committed." This requires that the officer or agent of the government be fairly certain (to have some tangible proof, even if it is not admissible in court) before making an arrest or search or before making application for a warrant.

Probable cause, as a standard of proof, may best be considered as lying on a continuum with mere suspicion at one end and absolute certainty at the other end. Courts have held that reasonable suspicion, a level of proof somewhat lower than probable cause, is needed to stop and frisk suspects. On the scale somewhat higher than probable cause is preponderance of evidence, which is the standard of proof necessary to determine liability in civil cases.

Observational and Informational Probable Cause. There are two basic ways probable cause can be developed: through observation and information. Observational probable cause is formulated by police officers by using their five senses. If they can see, hear, smell, taste, or touch evidence that a crime has been or is being committed, an arrest or a search may be made. When determining the sufficiency of observational probable cause, courts take into consideration police officers' training and experience. Thus, a police officer trained to detect the scent of marijuana is recognized as being able to distinguish that odor to develop probable cause, even if an ordinary citizen may not make that distinction. With observational probable cause the "totality of circumstances" standard is often used by the courts. With this standard, surveillance and other observations over time are compounded to determine whether probable cause exists. Informational probable cause is usually developed through investigations that yield certain facts about suspects. Included here are statements given by witnesses to crimes, victims' statements, and statements given by other police officers and informants. Although probable cause is always required to arrest or search, warrants are not always necessary.

Warrantless Searches. It is clear from the language of the Fourth Amendment that the Founding Fathers intended for agents of the state to produce warrants prior to searching or arresting citizens. However, the courts have recognized the impracticality of that requirement in modern society. As early as 1925 a challenge to the need for officers to actually produce a physical document (warrant) was made by a man named Carroll whose car was searched during Prohibition. After government agents seized illegal liquor from his vehicle, Carroll appealed his conviction, alleging that the search was unconstitutional because the agents had no warrant. The U.S. Supreme Court, in deciding for the government in *Carroll v. United States*, reasoned that automobiles can be moved before a warrant can be obtained and that the police need flexibility when probable cause exists. A lesser standard of proof, reasonable suspicion, is needed by police officers before officers may stop a car. Once the car is stopped, probable cause for a full search may be developed by the circumstances. For example, a police officer may stop a car because it is weaving and, while talking to the driver, may smell marijuana. Although the weaving was not probable cause to search the car (it was reasonable suspicion to stop the car), the smell of marijuana provides the officer with probable cause to search. The U.S. Supreme Court has ruled in *Ross v. United States* (1982) that once probable cause to search a vehicle has been established, the police have the right to search the entire vehicle, including all containers therein. The probable cause requirement for police to conduct a valid search can be waived if the party consents to the search. The consent must be voluntary and intelligently given. Evidence seized without consent or probable cause is subject to exclusion from criminal proceedings pursuant to the exclusionary rule.

Reasonable Expectation of Privacy. Although the Fourth Amendment protects people and not places, not every location is protected by the language of the Fourth Amendment. The U.S. Supreme Court has determined that the requirement for probable cause is restricted to areas in which there is a reasonable expectation of privacy. Evidence or contraband which is in plain view of a police officer is subject to seizure without probable cause. Likewise, if marijuana is grown in an open field behind one's home, no reasonable expectation of privacy exists. The courts have held that persons have a reasonable expectation of privacy in a closed public phone booth but that they do not have a reasonable expectation of privacy while being detained in the rear seat of a police car. Issues related to the expectation of privacy have often generated controversy as increasingly sophisticated surveillance techniques have been developed.

Although police officers are the most likely criminal justice practitioners to develop probable cause, an independent tribunal (a judge or magistrate) must verify probable cause prior to the issuance of a search or arrest warrant. The police officer applying for a search or arrest warrant must outline the probable cause in an affidavit and the judge or magistrate must decide if the evidence is sufficient to support the warrant. As a systemic check, a probable cause hearing is held during the pretrial stage after an arrest so that a judge can ensure that probable cause exists. If it does not exist, the defendant must be released.

Suggested Readings. Thoughts on probable cause are best expressed through legal texts and texts dealing with criminal procedures. Gilbert B. Stuckey's *Procedures in the Justice System* (4th ed. New York: Macmillan, 1991), Harvey Wallace and Cliff Robertson's *Principles of Criminal Law* (White Plains, N.Y.: Longman, 1996), and Neil C. Chamelin and Kenneth R. Evans's *Criminal Law for Police Officers* (4th ed. Englewood Cliffs, N.J.: Prentice-Hall, 1987) are good basic guides. John M. Scheb and John M. Scheb II's *Criminal Law and Procedure* (St. Paul, Minn.: West Publishing, 1994) and Daniel Hall's *Survey of Criminal Law* (2d ed. Albany, N.Y.: Delmar, 1997) are also excellent sources. For an extended discussion on application see Rolando V. del Carmen's *Criminal Procedure: Law and Practice* (3d ed. Belmont, Calif.: Wadsworth, 1995).

—*C. Randall Eastep*

See also Arrest; Attorney fees; Reasonable doubt; Search and seizure, illegal; Search warrant; Stop and frisk; Suspect; Wiretap.

Probate

Probate is a legal process that occurs after people die to ensure that their property is distributed according to their wishes as stated in a last will and testament or, in the absence of such a document, according to the laws of the state in which probate occurs.

Probate law, like all constitutional and common law in the United States, was adopted from English law, being derived from the king's courts, also called common-law courts, in which the procedures were complex and protracted. England replaced the king's courts with ecclesiastical courts charged with handling estate matters in a less complex and faster way. Equity courts were later established in England to transfer the ownership of titled property, such as land, stocks, and bank accounts, with considerably less delay and confusion than was the case in the king's courts. From its beginnings, the United States modeled its probate system on England's complex king's courts.

The Probate Process. The term "probate court" is used in the United States to identify courts that deal with estate matters. In some states such designations as "orphans' courts," "surrogate courts," and "chancery courts" are used to identify courts that attend to probate matters.

If decedents leave a last will and testament, it is the duty of the executor appointed in this document to present the will to the probate court to verify that it meets the legal requirements of the state and that it has been duly dated, signed, and witnessed. When decedents do not leave a will, the court appoints an administrator, whose duties are essentially those of an executor. Usually the family of the deceased has little voice in determining who that administrator shall be.

In most states, two or three people witness the signatures of testators. These witnesses may be called into the probate court to verify their signatures and to affirm that they were present when the will was signed. They may also be asked to attest to the testator's mental state to assure that the testator was capable of understanding its provisions. In most states, if the signed and witnessed will is notarized, the witnesses do not have to appear in court unless the document is being contested. Most states consider handwritten or holographic wills valid as long as they have been dated, signed, and witnessed. The form of the will is not specifically set, but it must clearly state the desired distribution of the testator's property.

A decedent's survivors may avoid probate until such time as they wish to transfer the title of property to their names. If a spouse dies leaving a house or an automobile, the surviving spouse may continue to live in the house or drive the automobile for an indefinite period. However, when the survivor wishes to take title of the house or the automobile, he or she must do so through the probate process.

The probate court is sometimes asked to act prior to the death of persons deemed incapable of handling their own financial affairs because of illness or senility. In such cases, the probate court may appoint a conservator to act on behalf of the disabled person. The court may also appoint guardians to act for minors who own property but have not yet reached legal age.

A decedent's place of residence determines where the estate will be probated, although when people own property and reside for part of the year in more than one state, each state may claim the estate and file a motion to have the will probated in a state other than the one in which the person drew up the will and in which the person died.

The Cost of Probate. Probate is time-consuming and costly. Although an estate's executor may serve in that capacity without meeting any specific requirements, a probate attorney is usually required to attend to matters that must come before the probate court. Besides paying the probate attorney, the estate must pay probate fees and fees for such other matters as the appraisal of the estate.

The executor or administrator may be paid according to a formula, which, in most states, permits payment of two or three percent of the estate's total value. Although probate attorneys in many states can charge whatever they wish, executors usually determine in advance what the attorney's fees will be. They should not exceed the fees that executors are permitted by law.

Most attorneys, if asked about their fees in advance, work within these parameters, although the amount charged for legal help in settling an estate of $10,000 may run as high as 10 percent, whereas the fee for dealing with an estate valued in the millions might be one or two percent. Individual cases vary considerably, but fees negotiated before an attorney is authorized to act for an estate are generally lower than those that are set during the probate process or at its conclusion. The probate court also levies charges against the gross estates with which it deals. These charges vary, but they can run as high as seven percent in some cases or even more if an estate is particularly complicated.

In most cases, it takes between one and two years to settle an estate, although the process may drag on for four or five years, particularly when bequests are made to citizens of foreign countries or when some of the decedent's assets are not liquid. Not all assets are subject to probate. Assets contained in a living trust are available immediately to those named in the trust, although they must pay the appropriate inheritance taxes on them.

Other Probate Issues. In twenty-eight states and the District of Columbia all estates, regardless of size, are subject to probate. In twenty-two states, however, small estates may escape probate. The cut-off point in Minnesota, South Dakota, and Wisconsin, for example, is $5,000, whereas in California no estate with a value under $60,000 need be probated.

Some people mistakenly think that because the federal government exempts the first $625,000 of one's assets from federal inheritance tax, which is in the process of being gradually raised to $1 million), estates under that amount are not subject to probate. This misconception can be costly to those who do not understand that nearly all estates over $10,000 are subject to probate in most states.

Once an estate is probated, all the documents relating to it, including copies of the last will and testament and of the appraisal of the estate, are available to anyone who requests them. This freedom of information robs families of privacy

---

Functions of Probate Courts

- They verify the validity of a last will and testament or, in the absence of a will, appoint an administrator to oversee the probate process and the distribution of the estate

- They ensure that public notice of a decedent's death is printed in newspapers so that creditors and potential heirs can file claims before the estate is distributed

- They receive an inventory of a decedent's estate

- They require the executor or administrator to have the estate appraised

- They ensure that all just claims against the estate are paid

- They verify that all income and inheritance taxes are paid

- They supervise the distribution of the residual estate according to the directions of the will or, lacking a will, in accordance with the laws of the state

in estate matters and, in many cases, subjects them to harassment from unscrupulous sales people trying to entice them into schemes that will, in the end, cost them dearly.

The only way to protect the privacy of the deceased and his or her family is through a living trust, which does not become part of any public record. People who draw up living trusts must remember to transfer their assets into the trust. In most cases, they should also have a will to assure the distribution of any property not included in the trust and to specify final arrangements. Because such wills are considerably less complex than those that distribute all of one's assets, the probate process should be faster and less costly than it would be if all bequests were made through the will. Also, if the bulk of one's estate is contained in a living trust, the remainder may be so small as to escape probate in some of the twenty-two states that exempt small estates from probate.

Living trusts serve another purpose. As real estate prices have increased significantly throughout the United States, the majority of people who die leave estates large enough to require probate. In order to avoid probate, many people establish revocable living trusts that hold their assets for their own use during their lifetimes and are distributed as specified upon their deaths.

The Future of Probate. The probate process has been soundly criticized for many years as unnecessarily expensive, unwieldy, and unfair, particularly as it relates to relatively small estates. The system, however, continues, and it is unlikely to be drastically changed because change must be legislated and many legislators are attorneys who benefit from the process.

In the 1930's New York City reform mayor Fiorello La Guardia declared the probate court to be the most expensive undertaking in the world, yet he was unable to affect any change in it. Lawyers who draw up wills and are generally appointed as the probate attorneys look upon the fees they receive for their services as sinecures that will assure them of a substantial income far into the future.

Because of abuses in the probate process that have come to light in recent years and that have been widely publicized, many people, even those of modest means, have resorted to living trusts as a means of avoiding or minimizing probate.

Assets Exempted from Probate

- Assets held in living trusts
- Proceeds from life insurance policies and certain annuities if left to specific beneficiaries rather than to the estate of the deceased
- Mutual funds, individual retirement accounts (IRAs), and other securities that include a transfer-on-death provision
- Property, including real estate and bank accounts, held in joint tenancy or in tenancy by the entirety
- A spouse's half of community property held in community property states

---

The state legislature of California recently passed a law that permits the trustee of a living trust simply to file an affidavit with the probate court and to publicize a decedent's death in the newspaper so that creditors can file their claims, after which an estate is settled without probate. The state of Washington has approved similar legislation.

It is anticipated that several other states will soon pass legislation to permit estates to be settled without undergoing probate. In all such instances, however, testators must establish living trusts to qualify for exemption from probate.

Suggested Readings. Henry W. Abts III, in *The Living Trust: The Failproof Way to Pass Along Your Estate to Your Heirs Without Lawyers, Courts, or the Probate System* (Chicago: Contemporary Books, 1993) offers valuable comments on the probate system and how to avoid it. Similar in nature is Norman F. Dacey's *How to Avoid Probate!* (New York: Macmillan, 1990). Charles A. DeGrandpre and Kathleen M. Robinson's *Probate Law and Procedure* (Salem, N.H.: Butterworth, 1990) is useful and practical, as is Kay Osberg's slender volume, *Probate: How to Settle an Estate* (New York: McKay, 1990), which is written for the nonprofessional. Jens C. Appel and F. Bruce Gentry's *The Complete Probate Kit* (New York: Wiley, 1991) is directed at the nonprofessional as well. —*R. Baird Shuman*

See also Estates and estate planning; Executors; Future estate; Inheritance tax; Trusts; Wills.

Probation, adult

Probation is a sentencing procedure by which persons convicted of crimes are released by the court and do not go to prison as long as they adhere to certain conditions set by the judge.

In the 1990's probation was the most commonly used punishment in the U.S. criminal justice system. There were about 3,600,000 people on probation in the United States, compared with approximately 1,500,000 persons in prisons and jails. The number of people on probation amounts to one out of every thirty-eight adults and one out of every twenty-one males. Most people on probation have committed relatively minor crimes, such as driving with a suspended license, committing petty theft or larceny, or possessing small amounts of drugs or other controlled substances. The offenders have typically been released to the community under the supervision of a probation officer and are usually required to meet briefly with the officer once a week or perhaps only once a month for counseling.

Probationers must usually meet a series of requirements. Sometimes probationers must stay away from certain persons, such as wives or children they may have harassed or threatened, or from particular places, such as street corners at which drugs are sold. Judges may also order that probationers stay free of drugs or alcohol or that they find and hold a job. Employers generally do not need to be told that a job applicant is on probation. Breaking any of these conditions can lead to imprisonment for violating probation procedures.

The average cost of probation nationwide is about $850 a year per offender, which compares favorably with the average $22,000 a year it costs to keep someone in prison. In many states some of the costs of probation are recovered by requiring probationers to pay part of the cost of their supervision. This cost-effectiveness is one reason that the number of persons on probation has increased dramatically in recent years.

History and Goals of Probation. Probation comes from the Latin *probatus*, which means "tested" or "proved." In the early United States, persons convicted of crimes were eligible for a suspended sentence if they promised to behave well and offered proof that they could observe the laws. The modern system began in Boston in 1841, when John Augustus, a businessman and advocate of rehabilitation, began bailing out convicted offenders, found them jobs, and gave the court monthly reports on their progress toward a better life. Augustus gained the release of more than two thousand prisoners using this method, most of whom were effectively rehabilitated. In 1878 Massachusetts became the first state to allow judges to choose probation as an alternative to a prison sentence. By 1940 all states allowed probation for juvenile offenders and all but six permitted adult probation. Not until the 1980's, however, did all states and the federal government provide for adult probation. The first statistics on probation were collected in 1976, when it was reported that nearly 1,000,000 adults were found to be on probation and 457,528 persons were in prison in the United States.

Probation began as an alternative to imprisonment and was justified as a method of rehabilitation that would save many people, especially nonviolent criminals, from the horrors and potential violence of prison life. Since prisons did not seem to do a very good job of reforming convicts and always seemed to be terribly overcrowded, judges would have an alternative to sending people to the penitentiary. The goal was to reduce crime by allowing offenders an opportunity to prove their goodness in society. The principal goal was rehabilitation, reforming the guilty party, rather than simply punishment, retribution, or revenge.

Central to probation is the notion that persons found to be "good risks" can be placed on probation and that they will not commit more crimes if they are given supervision and counseling. The philosophy of probation is that convicted persons can become law-abiding again. All they need is to be provided with treatment programs, employment, and other services. The focus is not on the harm done by the criminal but on the future reduction of criminal behavior, which can be achieved through proper treatment and supervision.

Violations of probation can be controlled by the ever-present threat that violators will be sent to prison if they break the rules. The idea of probation challenges the "just deserts" school of criminal justice, which proclaims that the purpose of the system is to make those convicted of crimes pay for the damage they have done by undergoing imprisonment. The goal of this method of criminal justice is to punish offenders, not to rehabilitate them.

Probation Decisions. The decision to place a convicted person on probation is one alternative available at a sentencing hearing. The judge is usually informed of the details of the offense in each case and makes the decision to place a person on probation after considering a variety of factors. These include the defendant's prior criminal record, social history, and family and employment record. This information is usually provided by a probation officer assigned to investigate the case. Normally, probation is given only in felony cases, not in misdemeanor cases.

Probation is granted by the judge in most cases if the probation officer recommends it. Two key factors are involved in this decision: the seriousness of the crime and the report on the person's prior criminal record. In most cases the seriousness of the crime is the single most important factor. Generally, persons convicted of having committed nonviolent crimes are much more likely to receive probation than those who have committed violent or drug-related criminal acts. The judge's decision is also influenced by the likelihood of rehabilitation. Persons considered "good risks" are very likely to receive probation, especially if their crimes did not involve violence.

Only a few studies have been done on the revocation of parole. Decisions to end probation and send people to prison follow no particular pattern or set of rules. There seems to be no consistent standard in revocation hearings. Judges are often inconsistent in arriving at these decisions. Generally, however, revocation depends on the nature of the probation violation. Failure to appear at meetings with parole officers is considered particularly grave. Revocation also depends on the probationer's age, prior record, and employment history. For example, the failure to find or retain a job can lead to revocation. However, any decision to revoke probation must be made by a judge, not simply by a probation officer.

Intensive Probation. One alternative to sending a violator to prison for violating probation is to order more intensive probation. This method can also be applied in cases in which a convicted person has committed a serious or violent crime. Intensive probation provides much closer supervision of offenders and is over three times more expensive than regular probation. Offenders in intensive programs are required to contact parole officers very frequently, sometimes as often as once a day or at least once a week.

Georgia, a state with a large investment in intensive probation, requires that serious nonviolent offenders have five face-to-face contact with probation officers every week. The failure rate in this program is about 16 percent, or about one-half the failure rate for regular probationers. Prisoners on either type of probation are extremely unlikely to commit violent crimes, since most have never been convicted of violent crimes. Less than 1 percent of violent crimes in the United States (0.8 percent to be exact) are committed by probationers.

Probation Officers. The major problem with the probation system is the huge caseloads carried by most probation officers. Experts consider thirty cases per officer the best possible situation. However, the average officer in the United States has at least two hundred cases each month. Such huge caseloads prevent many officers from getting actively involved with their clients. Instead, all probationers receive the same treatment, regardless of whether they have been convicted of income tax evasion or armed robbery. Few probationers can get the individual attention they need to remain successfully employed and motivated. The problem seems not to be the idea of probation but the way the system works. There is too little money and too few probation officers to do an effective job.

Another problem since the 1980's has been the fundamental belief on the part of many criminal justice practitioners, from police officers to judges, that probation does not reduce crime. A majority of the U.S. public seems to accept this view. This has led to a major shift in how judges determine sentences. In the 1960's and 1970's probation officers and judges believed that their mission was to reform and rehabilitate persons under their supervision and authority. Probation was supposed to help people convicted of crimes work their way back into society through employment opportunities and counseling. Probation officers saw their job as helping their clients overcome drug or alcohol dependency while meeting their family obligations.

In the 1980's, however, a much harsher form of criminal justice was instituted, with "just deserts"

Average Months of Probation Sentences Imposed by State Courts in 1990

| | | | Probation Sentence in Case of | | |
| | | | | Split Sentence of Probation with: | |
Most Serious Conviction Offense	Total	Straight Probation	Total	Prison	Jail
All offenses	42	42	42	48	40
Violent offenses	48	46	49	58	45
Murder	64	67	63	69	49
Rape	64	61	65	68	63
Robbery	50	50	49	59	44
Aggravated assault	43	43	43	53	40
Other violent offenses	47	45	49	46	50
Property offenses	43	44	42	49	39
Burglary	49	48	47	60	41
Larceny	40	41	37	40	37
Fraud	42	43	41	43	40
Drug offenses	41	42	41	47	38
Possession	38	39	37	38	37
Trafficking	43	44	43	50	40
Weapons offenses	35	34	36	39	35
Other offenses	39	40	39	39	40

Source: U.S. Department of Justice, Bureau of Justice Statistics, *Sourcebook of Criminal Justice Statistics—1993.* Washington, D.C.: U.S. Government Printing Office, 1994.

being the most prominent philosophy. In this view, punishment rather than rehabilitation was the goal, and parole officers responded by focusing their attention on catching probation violators and reporting them to the courts for confinement. New technologies and monitoring devices have made this practice more common. Electronic monitoring devices attached to probationers' legs or ankles enable officers to know where a subject is every minute of the day. House arrest is much more possible with such new devices, many of which have been available only since the mid-1990's. Nevertheless, probation is primarily reserved for people convicted of nonviolent crimes. The costs of normal, nonintensive probation are still about one-twentieth the cost of imprisonment, and a majority of probationers do not commit additional crimes. Probation is a system that works well to reduce future criminal activity by providing rehabilitation for offenders. It has been shown to be the best sentencing alternative to imprisonment.

Suggested Readings. Discussions of the procedures and guidelines used in considering probation can be found in *Probation, Parole, and Community Corrections* (New York: John Wiley & Sons, 1976), edited by Robert M. Carter and Leslie T. Wilkins, and in Frederick A. Hussey and David E. Duffee's *Probation, Parole, and Community Field Services: Policy, Structure, and Process* (New York: Harper & Row, 1980.) An evaluation of the effectiveness of probation versus incarceration is found in Douglas Lipton, Robert Martinson, and Judith Wilks's *The Effectiveness of Correctional Treatment: A Survey of Treatment Evaluation Studies* (New York: Praeger, 1975). A state-by-state description of probation systems is presented in the U.S. Bureau of the Census's *State and Local Probation and Parole Systems* (Washington, D.C.: U.S. Department of Justice, Law Enforcement Assistance Administration, National Criminal Justice Information and Statistics Service, 1978). For an interesting discussion of alternatives to imprisonment see Norval Morris's *The Future of Imprisonment.* (Chicago: University of Chicago Press, 1974.) —Leslie V. Tischauser

See also Criminal justice system; Pardon; Parole officers; Prison system; Probation, juvenile; Sentencing.

Probation, juvenile

As an alternative to or in addition to time spent in correctional institutions, probation is often imposed on persons who have been convicted of crimes, especially juveniles.

Probation is a general term for alternative sentencing, allowing convicted criminals to live outside prison, either in the community or in supervised residential programs. The emphasis is on rehabilitation. By the use of education, training, and counseling, it is hoped that the convict will be able to lead a useful life and not continue criminal activities. Because youthful offenders are often perceived as more likely than older ones to change their outlooks and because prison is often viewed as a "school for criminal activities," juveniles are very often sentenced to probation.

Probation has its roots in the harsh laws of the Middle Ages in Europe, where corporal or even capital punishment was imposed for crimes that would be considered minor by modern standards. Judges sometimes suspended sentences or imposed lesser punishments than those ordinarily called for, especially when children were involved.

The modern American system of probation began in the nineteenth century, especially in Massachusetts, where the first paid probation officer was hired in Boston in 1878. In the latter half of the twentieth century, as Americans became more interested in social problems and the welfare of underprivileged citizens, probation, especially of inner city youth, became widespread.

The Rationale Behind Probation. There have long been a variety of responses to antisocial activities in society. The biblical method of "an eye for an eye," combined with Christian concepts of good and evil, led to a general attitude that those who harm others must suffer pain in retribution. By the nineteenth century and the onset of the Industrial Revolution, this attitude began to change, at least in part thanks to the writings of reformers, notably Charles Dickens, whose novels emphasized the difficult conditions among which members of the working class were forced to live.

In the wake of the Industrial Revolution and the sudden increase of immigration to the United States by people who had few skills, little education, and little knowledge of the English language, an underclass developed, and crime became the only solution for many persons. The problem became more intense in the twentieth century, as American cities became increasingly populated by minority groups, often living in desperate conditions. Reformers became interested in improving the conditions under which such people lived rather than sending them to prison. In more recent times, there has been a great deal of concern that U.S. prisons are overcrowded and that people convicted of relatively minor offenses should be given alternative sentences.

The result of these changes in attitude was a system of alternatives to actual jail sentences, especially for young offenders. Particularly in the latter part of the twentieth century, young criminals began to be viewed as victims of society as much as villains, and new methods were proposed.

The Mechanics and Types of Probation. In modern times the process of sentencing begins with an arraignment, at which time accused persons are brought before a judge and their alleged crimes are stated. At this stage, a probation officer may file a petition with the court if it is felt that an alternative to incarceration is advisable. The decision is based on the seriousness of the crimes, the likelihood of reform, and the environment to which the accused will be returning.

If probation is imposed, it is always conditional. Criminals are assigned probation officers, who monitor their activities. Conditions are generally imposed; persons on probation must refrain from criminal activities, attend school or training programs, and often confine themselves to a particular geographical area. Probationers are kept under regular surveillance, sometimes by electronic means. If they violate the conditions of probation, they may be resentenced to prison. After the probational period has expired, they may be released into society as free citizens.

Juvenile probation is an attempt to give youthful offenders a second chance at leading useful lives in society. There are a great many opinions as to what sort of environment is most likely to allow and encourage youth to take such a course. The first consideration is the environment in which they lived before being arrested. If they came from reasonably sound homes, they would probably be returned to the custody of their parents and be supervised by a probation officer. They would be required to attend school on a regular basis and might also be assigned to community projects. This method was common in the 1960's but was perceived as less desirable in later decades.

Intensive supervised probation, begun in the 1960's for adults and expanded to include juveniles in the 1980's, is a more structured version of community probation. Probationers are often monitored electronically and may be required to pay restitution to their victims. Intensive counseling is also involved.

At the end of the twentieth century, residential programs for juvenile probationers became far more common. Such programs had their origins in the reform schools of the nineteenth and early twentieth centuries, but many varieties were developed. At one extreme is the boot camp system, modeled on military training methods. Probationers are given intensive physical and educational training and their lives are very highly structured. It is hoped that such harsh discipline will be effective in teaching the youths to abide by the rules of society.

Somewhat less restrictive are group homes, in which the juveniles live together in the community, under the supervision of adults, who either live on the premises or work in shifts. The probationers may be entirely restricted to the home, may be taken on supervised outings, or even given limited privileges in the outside environment, depending on their behavior. The rationale behind this system is to allow offenders to gradually work their way back into the community.

Another system, which became increasingly popular in the 1980's, was to involve youths with the natural environment. This might involve something very much like a year-round summer camp, involving sports, swimming, hiking, arts and crafts, and educational programs. It may be an intensive wilderness survival program. In either case, useful work for the Forestry Service or other government agencies may be involved, including the improvement of trails and the cleanup of wilderness areas. The wilderness approach is often considered especially appropriate for juveniles from inner city areas. It is suggested that an extreme change of environment may change youths' outlook and priorities.

If the court has determined that probationers have broken the law primarily because of an unfortunate home environment, the probationers may be placed in foster care. It is hoped that given a more supportive environment, they will change their ways. Parental visitation may or may not be granted. Along with these methods, a tactic called "shock probation" was introduced late in the twentieth century. Youths are taken to prisons, where they are shown the conditions in the hope that they will change their behavior in order to avoid going to prison themselves.

The Effectiveness of Probation. There is a great deal of controversy surrounding the effectiveness of assorted types of juvenile probation and the effectiveness of actual time in prison. Many statistical and individual studies have been conducted, but they have produced mixed results.

It is necessary to balance the welfare of juvenile offenders with the safety of the communities in which they live. At one extreme are those who believe that prisons are a bad influence in themselves. Young people who may be arrested for relatively minor offenses, such as vandalism or petty theft, will associate with hardened criminals and learn to adopt their lifestyle. Also to be considered is that there is a great deal of violence within the prisons, including sexual abuse of young inmates, both male and female.

On the other hand, there are those who cite an apparent increase in crime among youths and stress that lawful members of the community must be protected. These people often point out that a disproportionate number of juvenile offenders come from inner-city environments, in which crime and drug use is rampant, and that if they return to these communities, they are likely to return to crime.

The increasing use of alcohol and illegal drugs among youths confuses the situation further. The use of alcohol by someone under the legal age or the use of relatively benign drugs such as marijuana is a highly significant factor in the statistics involving youthful crime. As opinions on the law involving such offenses vary widely, the statistics are very often biased according to the viewpoints of those doing the studies.

Generally, it has been found that residential programs involving community involvement and useful training has at least some effect, although accurate figures are difficult to come by. Releasing offenders into the community is generally ineffective, especially if the community involved is an area in which both adult and juvenile crime is common.

Conclusions. The prevalence of criminal activities among young people in modern times has led to various attempts to control this problem. Beginning in the late twentieth century there was an increasing call for youths who commit serious crimes, especially violent crimes, to be tried and punished as if they were adults, even including subjecting them to capital punishment. At the same time, there were many attempts to consider alternative punishments in order to prevent young offenders from becoming lifetime criminals.

The problem is not easy to solve. On one hand, there is a natural tendency to want to treat children as gently as possible in the hope that they can overcome unfortunate environmental conditions and become useful members of society. On the other hand, the increasing presence of street gangs and juvenile criminal activity causes great fear among the adult population.

Suggested Readings. Elliott Currie's *Crime and Punishment in America* (New York: Metropolitan Books, 1998) is a general discussion of sentencing alternatives, including probation, based on the premise that traditional prisons are not effective. A general discussion of juvenile crime, with the emphasis on alternatives to actual imprisonment, can be found in Alan R. Coffey's *Juvenile Corrections: Treatment and Rehabilitation* (Englewood Cliffs, N.J.: Prentice-Hall, 1975). Dean L. Champion's *Criminal Justice in the United States* (2d ed. Chicago: Nelson Hall, 1997) is a general summary of the modern legal system of the United States, with an extensive treatment of juvenile crime and alternatives to incarceration. A statistical analysis of assorted probation methods can be found in *Probation, Parole, and Community Corrections* by Robert M. Carter, Daniel Gluer, and Leslie T. Wilkins (3d ed. New York: John Wiley and Sons, 1984). A study of assorted methods of dealing with juvenile crimes is *Beyond Probation* by Charles A. Murray and Louis A. Cox, Jr. (Beverly Hills: Sage Publications, 1979). In *Juvenile Delinquency and Juvenile Justice* (New York: John Wiley and Sons, 1987) Joseph W. Rogers and Larry Mays provide a general discussion on juvenile crime and assorted attempted solutions.

—*Marc Goldstein*

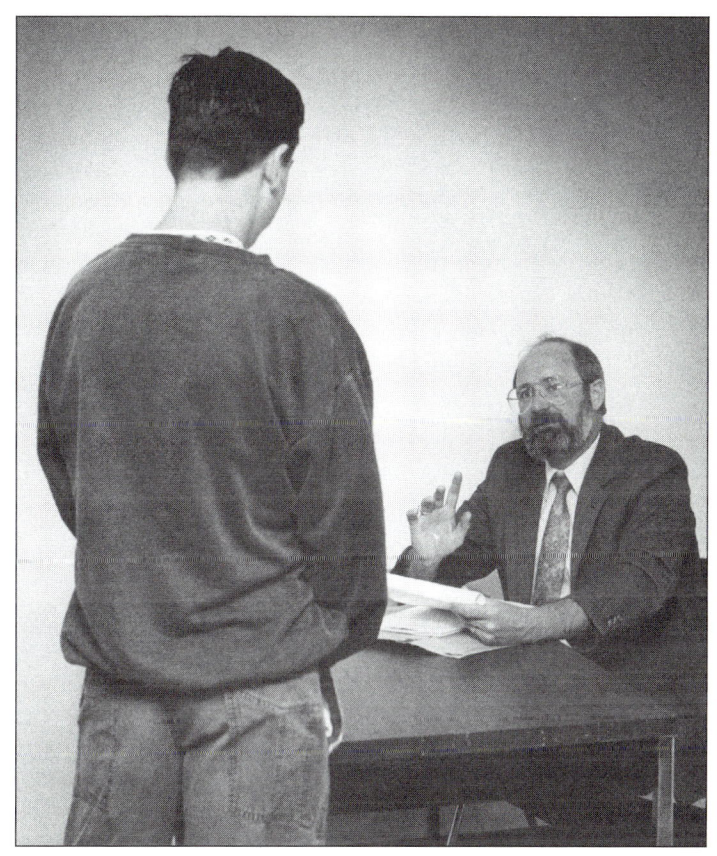

Probation officer talks to youth about alternatives to incarceration. (James L. Shaffer)

See also Age and the law; Juvenile criminal proceedings; Juvenile delinquency; Parole; Probation, adult; Sentencing.

Product liability law

Legislation regulating the liability of manufacturers or sellers of products for personal injury or damage to other property caused by product defects is known as product liability law.

Product liability law has its origin in both tort (a civil wrong by one party against another) and contract law. The public policy giving rise to the doctrine of product liability dictated that consumers needed more protection from dangerous products than is afforded by the law of warranty. The increasing complexity of products has expanded the opportunity for mishap in product design, manufacturing, marketing, or use. This, in turn, has resulted in a significant escalation in the incidence and severity of damage caused by defective products. Product liability law shifted more of the burden of loss from purchasers and users, who historically bore most of the burden, to manufacturers and vendors. The responsibility of manufacturers and vendors was increased in recognition of their ability to prevent most effectively and least expensively damage caused by their own products and in recognition of their superior position to absorb and distribute loss as an expense of production and sale.

Products and Defects. Generally, a product is viewed as any object produced for introduction into trade or commerce possessing intrinsic value, whether it is manufactured as a whole or as only a component part. Most states have enacted statutes expressly excluding from product liability law human tissue, organs, blood, blood products, and approved animal tissue.

To be defective, a product must be either unreasonably dangerous for normal use per se, unreasonably dangerous in construction or composition, unreasonably dangerous due to manufacturers' failure to warn, or unreasonably dangerous in design. The normal use of products includes foreseeable misuse, and manufacturers are obligated to take into account such misuse in designing their products.

A product is defective per se if a reasonable person would conclude that the danger-in-fact of the product or the risks inherent in it, whether foreseeable or not, outweigh its utility or benefit. A product is defective in construction or composition if at the time it leaves the control of its manufacturer it contains an unintended abnormality or condition that makes it more dangerous than it was designed to be. A product is defective if the manufacturer fails to adequately warn about a danger related to the way the product was designed. A manufacturer is required to provide adequate warning of any danger inherent in the normal use of a product which is not within the knowledge of or obvious to the ordinary user. A product is defective by design if, while not unreasonably dangerous per se, alternative products were available to serve the same needs or desires with less risk of harm or if there was a feasible way to design the product with less harmful consequences.

Theories for Recovery. Manufacturers are not absolute insurers that their products' designs will not produce injury. Plaintiffs can sue manufacturers in product liability actions based on one or more of three legal theories for liability that can be cited in most jurisdictions: strict liability, which focuses only on the quality of products; negligence, which focuses on the conduct of defendants; and expressed and implied warranty, which focuses on the performance of the products against the explicit or implicit representations made on their behalf by manufacturers or sellers.

Strict liability in tort is the doctrine most commonly associated with product liability. It had its origin in 1963, when the California Supreme Court held in *Greenman v. Yuba Power Products, Inc.* that "a manufacturer is strictly liable in tort when an article he places on the market, knowing that it is to be used without inspection for defect, proves to have a defect that causes injury to a human being." The liability is "strict" in the sense that plaintiffs need not prove defendants' negligence and because the liability is "in tort." In strict liability cases, defendants may not avail themselves of the usual contract or warranty defenses that may be available in actions for breach of warranty.

To prevail under the strict liability doctrine, a plaintiff must prove that the defendant placed the product on the market, that the product was defective at the time the product left the defendant's possession, that this defect made the product unreasonably dangerous for its intended or a reasonably foreseeable use, and that this defect was a proximate cause of some damage to the plaintiff. The plaintiff must also prove the nature and extent of damage. The conduct of the defendant, no matter how reasonable, is irrelevant here. Further, it is unnecessary for the plaintiff to be the purchaser of the product.

Negligence exists when a manufacturer or vendor has failed to do something that a person of ordinary prudence would have done in the same or similar circumstances. Product liability on the grounds of negligence can be found against a manufacturer, seller, or even a corporation engaged in testing products and affixing a label thereon that indicates its work on such products. The negligence proof requirement of showing that defendants failed to exercise due care makes negligence-based product liability cases significantly more burdensome for plaintiffs than actions in strict tort liability or on breach of an express or implied sales warranty.

In a product liability setting, a warranty is a contractual representation, whether implicit or express, that a product is appropriate for certain specified purposes or uses. It has also been considered an agreement by manufacturers to be responsible for all foreseeable damages that arise from defects in their products. In most jurisdictions a warranty claim is the preferred legal theory for establishing liability for a product-caused injury, because proof of negligence is not required. In some jurisdictions warranty claim has the disadvantage of being available only to products' purchasers. Plaintiffs must only prove their injuries and damages, that the existence of products' defects or condition breached the warranty, and that the breach of warranty was the proximate cause of injury or loss.

Suggested Readings. Perhaps the most comprehensive and detailed discussion of American product liability law, both from a state and federal perspective, is contained in *American Law of Products Liability*, by Robert D. Hursch and Henry J. Bailey (3d ed. Rochester, N.Y.: Lawyers Co-operative Publishing, 1987). As an introduction to this body of law, law students in many major law schools have utilized William L. Prosser and Page Keeton, *Prosser and Keeton on Torts* (5th ed. St. Paul, Minn.: West Publishing, 1984), and *Products Liability: Cases and Materials*, by Dix. W. Noel (St. Paul, Minn.: West Publishing, 1976). Business people have special concerns about how best to avoid liability according to product liability law. Two books offering practical advice are *Products Liability: Are You Vulnerable?*, by Charles O. Smith (Englewood Cliffs, N.J., Prentice-Hall, 1981), and *Products Liability and the Reasonably Safe Product: A Guide for Management, Design and Marketing*, by Alvin S. Weinstein (New York: John Wiley & Sons, 1978).

—*David R. Sobel*

See also Accidents and injuries; Asbestos litigation; Breach of contract; Class-action suits; Consumer protection laws; Damages; Lawsuits; Personal injury law; Torts.

Property liability

The converse of property rights, property liability refers to the responsibility that accompanies the ownership or control of real property.

While the ownership of property confers certain rights, it also involves a measure of responsibility. The nature and extent of a property owner's responsibility varies greatly across governmental jurisdictions and further depends on the type of property, the use to which it is put, the nature of ownership, and other factors. Generally, however, the concept of property liability can be examined in two broad contexts: structures and land.

Structures such as houses, apartments, office buildings, stores, and factories are subject to a host of laws and regulations concerning health and safety. Under most circumstances an owner or operator is responsible for ensuring that a structure meets those requirements. Failure to abide by relevant laws can make an owner criminally liable under certain circumstances. Failure to meet established standards can also cause a property owner to be civilly liable for injuries sustained by tenants, workers, or visitors to the property. Even if no established law or regulation is violated, an owner may be found to be civilly liable for personal injuries, property damage, or theft if these are found to result from the owner's negligence.

The land surrounding a structure (such as a store parking lot or a yard surrounding a private home) can also be subject to property liability decisions. Even undeveloped property, such as a parcel of rangeland, obligates its owner. If there are hazards on the property, such as steep cliffs or deep bodies of water, the owner may be reasonably expected to erect fences, post warning signs, or take other protective actions.

Property liability civil lawsuits regularly arise, sometimes involving large claims for actual and punitive damages. Some of these clash directly with conservative definitions of property rights, and these occasionally capture widespread public attention. For example, on several occasions in the 1980's and 1990's newspapers and talk shows focused on civil lawsuits brought by burglars and vandals who were injured while trespassing.

A growing area of property liability cases in the late twentieth century involved environmental damage. Prior to the development of stricter environmental laws beginning in the 1970's, many lands and bodies of water were degraded by standard business practices, such as dumping untreated toxic wastewater, burying toxic waste, and filling sensitive wetlands. In addition, land has been damaged through accidents and negligence, such as by leaking underground storage tanks and toxic spills. New laws set stricter standards, and many jurisdictions in the late twentieth century began requiring that degraded property be cleaned up and natural habitats restored. The question of who is liable for such actions has been a major source of dispute.

—*Steve D. Boilard*

See also Accidents and injuries; Home ownership; Homeowner insurance; Joint and several liability; Negligence; Neighbor problems; Public nuisance; Real estate law.

Property rights

Rights accompanying the private ownership of real and personal property are central to western economic and social systems.

The concept of private property is central to market-based capitalism and thus is common throughout the Western world. Nevertheless, the specific rights associated with property ownership differ from country to country. Property rights are especially strong in the United States, but even in the U.S. property ownership does not confer absolute rights under all circumstances. Instead, the courts and policymakers are regularly confronted with questions about what kinds of limitations can legally and properly be placed on property owners.

Constitutional Provisions. Property rights in the United States stem from several clauses in the U.S. Constitution. For example, the Second Amendment prohibits the peacetime quartering of soldiers in private homes without the owner's consent—a practice of the British government that the American colonists found particularly odious. It also permits the billeting of soldiers during wartime only "in a manner prescribed by law." The sanctity of one's home is a cherished principle that serves as the bedrock of America's treatment of property rights.

Similarly, the Fourth Amendment states, "The right of the people to be secure in their persons, houses, papers, and effects, against unreasonable searches and seizures, shall not be violated, and no Warrants shall issue, but upon probable cause, supported by Oath or affirmation, and particularly describing the place to be searched, and the persons or things to be seized." This amendment protects citizens from having their homes unreasonably searched and their property unreasonably seized. Searches and seizures are permissible only when there is probable cause, typically supported by a warrant.

The Fifth Amendment contains two clauses relevant to property rights. The first states that "No person shall . . . be deprived of life, liberty, or property, without due process of law." This due process clause guarantees that proper legal proceedings, including such elements as a trial, will be followed before a penalty is imposed. The fact that "property" is included alongside "life" and "liberty" highlights the importance attached to private property by the Constitution's authors.

The second relevant Fifth Amendment clause states, "nor shall private property be taken for public use without just compensation." This is one of the most central and vigorously contested constitutional provisions as regards property rights. It can apply to condemnations of land, by which a public entity such as a state government agency uses its power of eminent domain to force a property owner to turn over land for use by the government. For example, a state department of transportation might need to acquire a piece of privately owned land lying in the path of a proposed new freeway. The just compensation clause requires that the property owner be reimbursed for the land, typically in the form of a payment of the fair market price of the property.

Finally, the Eighth Amendment states, "Excessive bail shall not be required, nor excessive fines imposed." Although bail is typically denominated in dollars, fines can be construed to include various financial assets and other elements of a broader category of property. This clause restricts the imposition of fines and bail to levels that are not out of proportion to the circumstances.

Legal Issues. The just compensation clause of the Fifth Amendment has increasingly been invoked even when no condemnation of property takes place. Instead, property owners claim that governmentally imposed restrictions on the use of their land (such as zoning restrictions) amount to a "regulatory taking." Land use restrictions are a recognized prerogative of local governments, but when new restrictions are imposed after a person has purchased property, a case can be made that use or value of the land was taken. While this argument was initially rejected by most courts, it gradually came to be accepted in the 1980's and 1990's.

A watershed was reached in the case of *Nollan v. California Coastal Commission* (1987), in which the U.S. Supreme Court held that a state agency's demand for an easement on private property amounted to a regulatory taking which required just compensation. Subsequent court decisions clarified the issue of regulatory takings. For example, in *Agins v. City of Tiburon* (1988) the Supreme Court held that a regulatory taking has occurred when at least one of the following conditions is met with respect to a government's regulation of land use: when there is an "impermissible use" of the government's police power or when the regulation denies the property owner "economically viable use" of the property. Additional major cases on the subject have come before the Supreme Court every year or two, creating minor changes in the interpretation of property rights.

The just compensation clause as applied to land use was perhaps the premier property rights issue of the mid- and late twentieth century. Notwithstanding the *Nollan* and *Agins* decisions, there continues to be considerable confusion and controversy surrounding the principle of regulatory takings.

The Eighth Amendment is relevant to cases involving forfeiture. A number of laws at the federal and state level provide for the forfeiture of a person's assets under certain circumstances, including the conviction of specified crimes. For example, federal laws permit the forfeiture of certain assets, including boats and homes, that were purchased with illicit drug proceeds. Such laws have been challenged as running afoul of the Eighth Amendment. In *Bajakajian v. United States* the U.S. Supreme Court established a standard for determining when the excessive fines clause is violated by forfeiture. In that case, which involved a person's failure to report the transportation of a large amount of currency abroad, the Court held that a forfeiture does not violate the Eighth Amendment if two conditions are met: that the property forfeited was an instrumentality of the crime (that is, it was used directly in the perpetration of the crime) and that the value of the property is proportionate to the owner's culpability.

With the vast expansion of computer software in the late twentieth century and the easy accessibility of electronic copying and transmission technology (most notably facilitated by the Internet), intellectual property rights became a major topic for national and international law. Readily available technology made possible the inexpensive copying of intellectual property on such formats as videotapes, compact disks, and computer programs. It is unclear how copyright laws apply in many cases, and in any event modern laws against illegal copying and distribution are difficult to enforce. The issue of intellectual property rights has been at the center of a legal and political debate concerning property rights, antitrust laws, international trade, and freedom of speech.

Suggested Readings. Books providing a theoretical overview of property and property rights include Tom Bethell's *The Noblest Triumph: Property and Prosperity Through the Ages* (New York: St. Martin's Press, 1998) and Itai Sened's *The Political Institution of Private Property* (Cambridge, England: Cambridge University Press, 1997). A collection of essays on the subject of property rights is provided in *Property Rights*, edited by Ellen Frankel Paul et al. (Cambridge, England: Cambridge University Press, 1994). The issue of regulatory takings is discussed in "Takings, Compensation, and Endangered Species Protection on Private Lands," by Robert Innes et al., in *Journal of Economic Perspectives* 12 (Summer, 1998). A somewhat critical assessment of regulatory takings is provided by Gideon Kanner in "Just Compensation Is by No Means Always Just" in *The National Law Journal* 19 (March 24, 1997).

—*Steve D. Boilard*

See also Eminent domain; Home ownership; Leases; Personal property; Property liability; Real property; Trespass.

Property taxes

Taxes on the value of real estate and other forms of property, known as property taxes, are imposed by many state and local governments and are especially important as a source of public school financing.

Perhaps the oldest form of taxes, property taxes constitute an important revenue source for many present-day countries. Although the United States does not impose a property tax at the federal level, state and (especially) local governments impose several such taxes, the most prevalent being taxes on real property that are typically used to finance schools and similar projects. The federal estate tax, although usually described as an inheritance levy, may also be seen as a once-in-a-lifetime property tax that applies to relatively wealthy individuals.

Property taxes are frequently unpopular, because they have a confiscatory flavor and because the valuation of property for tax purposes is often highly subjective. Legions of lawyers are employed in the simple but vital task of attempting to reduce property assessments for taxation purposes. The use of real property tax revenues for public school financing has been especially controversial, because it increases the competitive advantage of wealthy school districts and arguably contributes to social and economic inequality. Property taxes also raise important issues regarding the allocation of the tax burden between homeowners and non-homeowners and between older and younger taxpayers. But even the harshest critics of the existing system usually accept the need for some form of property tax, insisting that the tax be supplemented by other taxes or that revenues from the tax be distributed in a more equitable fashion.

Historical Background. Property taxes are mentioned in the Old and New Testaments, taking the form of a tithe in which one-tenth of agricultural produce was collected for religious or secular purposes. Throughout history, taxes on real and personal property have remained important revenue sources, frequently leading to resentment and even violence when the taxes were perceived as unfair or were put to unpopular uses. For example, taxes imposed to fund the construction of St. Peter's Basilica in Rome contributed to the resentment that led to the Protestant Reformation, and unpopular property and excise taxes were among the causes of the American and French Revolutions. Real property taxes are especially important in increasing the costs associated with real estate and encouraging the breakup of large estates into smaller, individual parcels. Thus, the virtual absence of single-family homes from central New York City has been attributed in part to the exorbitant taxes that would be imposed on such properties.

Many European countries impose some form of property or wealth tax as a supplement to the larger income, excise, and valued-added taxes, as do India and other third-world countries. (A property tax is imposed on specific types of real property or personal assets, while a wealth tax covers all forms of real or personal property.) Although these taxes often raise relatively little revenue, they make a tax system more progressive or redistributive than it would otherwise be and serve a symbolic function by reaching individuals who hold large amounts of property but relatively little taxable income. For example, an individual with $10 million in cash or real estate who does not earn interest or rental income on these assets would escape an income tax entirely but be required to pay at least something under a wealth or property tax. Even if interest or rental income is earned, the income tax on these sources may be lower than that on salaries or other earned income. Countries concerned about the equitable distribution of the tax burden have frequently turned to wealth or property taxes in order to reduce inequities. Property taxation, like antitrust policy, may also have a political purpose in reducing large concentrations of wealth that are sometimes perceived as a threat to democratic institutions.

Property Taxes in the United States. Perhaps because of America's democratic tradition and the reluctance to admit that accumulated wealth as opposed to individual effort plays a role in U.S. society, the United States has never imposed a comprehensive national wealth or property tax. Federal estate and gift taxes accomplish some of the functions of a national property tax, providing a "once-in-a-lifetime" tax on intergenerational property transfers and having the avowed purpose of reducing excessive concentrations of wealth. However, these taxes are imposed only on large estates and are subject to numerous exclusions and planning strategies that make them relatively ineffective in accomplishing their intended results. For example, the estate tax contains special provisions that reduce the tax burden on small businesses and family farms and permit family businesses to be reorganized in a manner that dramatically reduces taxes.

While there is no national property tax, state and local governments impose a variety of taxes on commercial and residential real property, and some states tax other forms of property as well. Real property taxes are typically imposed at the local level, with the state setting minimum standards and providing administrative assistance to the different localities. These taxes are expressed as a percentage of the "assessed value" of the property in question during the taxable year and are used to fund schools and other local government activities such as police, fire, sanitation, and similar services. For

South Dakota governor Bill Janklow points to a chart showing the rise in property taxes in the 1990's. (AP/Wide World Photos)

example, if a house is assessed at a value of $100,000 and the relevant tax rate is 3 percent, the owners of the house are required to pay $3,000 in tax. In some cases, the same property may be subject to two or more taxes by overlapping governmental entities, as when separate taxes are imposed by a local school district and a township or other municipality. For example, a house assessed at a value of $100,000 might be required to pay a school tax rate of 3 percent and an additional 1 or 2 percent for remaining governmental services, so that the combined rate is higher than that under any individual tax.

Real estate taxes are also imposed on commercial property, such as office buildings, stores, and factories. Frequently, however, the tax rate on such properties is higher than that on residential properties and often varies depending on the particular type of facility in question. Although the U.S. Constitution requires that taxpayers receive equal protection under state law and most state constitutions require uniformity in property taxation, these requirements are considered to be met if the same rates are applied to all property in a given category and if the categories themselves have a substantial or reasonable basis. Thus, constitutional principles do not greatly restrict states' abilities to tax different forms of property at differential or varying rates.

In addition to real property taxes, many states and localities impose taxes on other forms of property, including tangible property such as machinery, equipment, automobiles, and jewelry and intangibles such as stocks, bonds, bank accounts, and other types of personal investments. Some jurisdictions also impose property taxes on corporations or public utilities, although these are usually imposed at the state rather than the local level. Governments that impose a tax on tangible or intangible personal property must be careful to comply with federal constitutional provisions that prohibit interference with interstate commerce, although these problems are generally less severe than in the case of state sales or income taxes. A federal court held that taxes on intangibles imposed by Pennsylvania, North Carolina, and other states were unconstitutional because they exempted stock in in-state companies, forcing the states in question to modify their taxes or find alternate revenue sources.

Problems in Levying Property Taxes. Real property tax assessments are necessarily subjective and are often based on complex or unusual formulas, such as a specified percentage of current market value or of market value that existed on a particular date. Reassessments tend to be conducted irregularly and are no less subjective than the original valuation. Thus, it is not surprising that property taxes tend to be unpopular and are a subject of heated political debate. It is also not surprising that taxpayers frequently challenge assessments on both commercial and residential real property and that lawyers skilled in the assessment process are often highly compensated. The issues in assessment cases tend to be arcane and highly factual in nature and involve such questions as whether a swimming pool adds more value to property than a new porch or whether an office building close to a freeway exit is worth more than one a few miles away. A sophisticated legal background is less important to a lawyer in this field than command of the facts and experience in the decision-making process of a particular locality. Thus, most assessment cases are handled by lawyers who specialize in this field, many of whom have no other tax experience or specialized tax training. If taxpayers are unsuccessful at the local level, they may appeal to regional or state courts, including courts of general jurisdiction or specialized tax courts. In the state of New Jersey the New Jersey Tax Court spends virtually all of its time dealing with appeals of property tax cases.

A particular problem with residential property taxes is the conflict between older and younger homeowners. For example, if the homes in a neighborhood sold for an average price of $100,000 in 1980 and an average price of $300,000 in 1998, a recent purchaser will pay three times more tax than an older purchaser on an identical home unless there is a comprehensive reassessment. However, if older purchasers must pay higher taxes, they may be taxed on amounts that exceed what they originally paid for their houses, requiring them to sell other assets or otherwise restrict their lifestyles. In the late 1970's resentment over real property tax increases fueled a voter initiative in California that continues to restrict state spending and is believed to have resulted in a severe decline in the level and quality of state services.

A distinct but related problem arises in commercial property taxes. In order to attract businesses to a state or locality, tax bureaus frequently provide exemptions or abatements from tax for a specified period. For example, a state wishing to attract a new automobile plant may provide for an abatement from state income and property taxes for a three- or five-year period or alternatively allow the tax to be paid at a lower rate than that imposed on other businesses. Such tax abatement is often accompanied by tax-exempt bond financing and other advantages designed to make a state or locality more attractive than others. These arrangements assist in attracting new businesses at the cost of reducing tax revenues and perhaps treating unfairly older companies not receiving similar treatment. Many experts feel that the cost of such arrangements exceeds the advantages to states and localities and undermines the fairness of local tax systems.

Property Taxes and School Financing. Of particular concern to lawyers is the role of property taxes in school financing. For historical reasons property, and especially real property, taxes remain the predominant source of public school financing in most parts of the country. Although there is no necessary connection between the taxing jurisdiction and the nature of the tax—a property tax could in theory be imposed at a statewide or even a national level—in practice most such taxes are imposed at the local level. This in turn provides wealthier school districts with an enormous advantage over those in poorer areas, since the wealthier districts can finance strong educational programs without imposing unacceptably high tax rates. By contrast, poorer districts face a choice of spending less on education or raising taxes so high that they discourage families or businesses from residing in the area.

Since the 1970's numerous lawsuits have been brought on behalf of poorer school districts, arguing that the system of local property tax financing violates the equal protection clause of the Fourteenth Amendment to the U.S. Constitution or equivalent rights under state law. In the 1970's the Supreme Court dealt a severe setback to these efforts, holding in *San Antonio Independent School District v. Rodriguez* (1973) that differential levels of school financing did not necessarily violate the equal protection clause. Attention then turned to individual states, several of which had constitutional provisions requiring equality of educational opportunity or judges who were willing to interpret generic equal protection language in a more liberal manner than the federal courts.

In several states the issue became highly politicized, with the state legislature caught between the courts, which were attempting to force changes in the property tax system, and voters, who were generally skeptical of new taxes or alternate financing arrangements. New Jersey is a good example of this phenomenon. Governor James Florio's attempts to produce an alternate financing system under pressure from the state courts led to his defeat in 1993, while his successor, Christine Whitman, continued to struggle with various formulas for a fair and workable system. California, Texas, and other states have likewise seen a tug-of-war between courts, legislatures, and an electorate indifferent to the school finance issue. At the national level there appears to be a growing consensus against exclusive reliance on property taxes, but there is considerable debate as to what new taxes if any should be imposed and what level of equality should be sought between richer and poorer school districts. This issue is part of a broader debate on educational and welfare policy, and its resolution is likely to depend more on these considerations than on traditional tax policy criteria.

Policy Issues and the Future of Property Taxes. The chief advantages of a property tax are its relative simplicity and its role in maintaining the progressive or redistributive character of the overall tax system. By contrast, its chief disadvantages are valuation problems and the potentially confiscatory nature of the tax—that is, the possibility that too high a property tax level will force people to sell their property in order to pay the tax. These disadvantages make it unlikely that a national wealth or property tax will be enacted in the United States in the immediate future.

Indeed, the present trend appears to be toward reduced reliance on property taxes in the revenue mix. For example, the U.S. Congress significantly weakened the federal estate tax in 1997, and there is sentiment for eliminating the tax altogether. Nevertheless, the longstanding nature of property taxes, together with the sheer demand for revenues, makes it improbable that the tax will disappear. At the local level the most likely outcome appears to be continued imposition of property taxes but supplemented by income tax and other revenues with at least some requirement that tax revenues shall be shared with poorer school districts. While there is unlikely to be a national property tax, there may be increasing efforts at the federal level to reform the income tax system so as to reduce the evasion of tax on income from property transactions, such as interest, rents, and dividends. Changes of this type would increase the level of indirect property taxation and bring the United States more into line with countries that impose direct wealth or property taxes.

Suggested Readings. Because the details of the property tax vary from state to state, much of the material on the tax is of a theoretical or summary nature. A good introduction, including the rationale for property taxation, the allocation of the property tax burden, and related issues is found in Richard A. Musgrave and Peggy B. Musgrave's *Public Finance in Theory and Practice* (5th ed. New York: McGraw-Hill, 1989). *State and Local Taxation: Cases and Materials*, by Jerome R. Hellerstein and Walter Hellerstein (6th ed. St. Paul, Minn.: West Publishing, 1997), is a basic textbook on property tax and other state and local taxes and a useful introduction to the reader unfamiliar with these taxes. More complete information on the various state property tax laws, including rates, exemptions, and procedures for challenging property tax assessments, is found in the American Bar Association (ABA) *Property Tax Deskbook* (Washington: American Bar Association, 1997). Moving from law to policy, a number of books and symposia conduct a lively debate on the future of property tax and its merits compared to income and other taxes. For example, *The Role of the State in Property Taxation*, edited by H. Clyde Reeves (Lexington, Mass.: D. C. Heath, 1983), includes various papers that criticize the property tax for being poorly designed and administered but express hope that new technologies will improve the existing tax system. By contrast, the economist Henry J. Aaron in his book *Who Pays the Property Tax? A New View* (Washington, D.C.: Brookings Institution, 1975), takes a less negative view, concluding that the property tax is not as bad as often imagined but recommending various changes in order to make it less unpopular. In particular, Aaron recommends that states and localities reassess (revalue) property more often and more accurately than in the past and make payments to compensate poor households for the costs of property taxes. *Property Taxation: USA*, edited by Richard W. Lindholm (Madison, Wis.: University of Wisconsin Press, 1967), evaluates the property tax against the background of historical experience.

—*Michael A. Livingston*

See also Estate and gift taxes; Income taxes; Property rights; Tax law.

Property types

Property, which is anything that can be legally possessed, is classified by two general types: real and personal.

Legally, property refers to the aggregate of legal rights of individuals with respect to objects and/or obligations owed to them that are protected and guaranteed by the government. Ownership includes the rights to possess, enjoy, use, and dispose of things that are either tangible or intangible in a manner consistent with the law. The two general types of property are real and personal. Real property is land and anything firmly attached to it, while personal property, or chattels, is movable property not included in real property. Certain items, including the atmosphere and the oceans, are viewed as neither real nor personal property.

Real property, or realty, consists of land, any buildings on the land, trees, any mineral rights under the land, and anything else that is attached to the land or buildings that is intended to remain there permanently. Attachments to buildings are known as fixtures and include heating and plumbing systems and associated appliances, fitted carpets, and built-in cabinets. Mineral rights may or may not be included with the land. In some jurisdictions, landowners may sell or lease mineral and timber rights to outside parties, and the contract continues in effect when the land is sold.

Personal property is classified as tangible or intangible. Tangible personal property, which must be perceptible to the touch and sight, are physical objects with intrinsic value, such as books, furniture, livestock, harvested crops, jewelry, or automobiles. Intangible personal property includes intellectual property—such as copyrights, patents, and computer software—and financial assets—such as stocks, bonds, personal annuities, contract rights, title deeds, and leases.

Property may be acquired or transferred in several ways. It may be bought, found, or received as a gift. Tangible personal property is typically obtained by retail sales transactions, by wills, or by simple oral communication, whereas the transfer of intangible personal property requires the formal reregistration of the property in the new owner's name.

Two basic instruments used in the transfer of real property from one owner to another are deeds and wills. Deeds may contain restrictions, which vary from state to state, on how the purchaser may use the real property. When property is in the names of two or more persons with the right of survivorship or in the names of a husband and wife, the property must pass to the survivor(s). Property may also be distributed by a court order, as in the distribution of a person's estate when a person dies without having left a will. The government may reclaim private land for public use by eminent domain or may cause land to pass from a form of public ownership to private ownership by a grant, such as the federal Homestead Act of 1862.

—Alvin K. Benson

See also Copyright; Deed; Eminent domain; Patents; Personal property; Real property; Wills.

Prosecutors

A government attorney responsible for investigating and pursuing charges against defendants accused of violating criminal laws is known as a prosecutor.

The prosecutor is a central figure in the criminal justice system. By making discretionary decisions about which cases to pursue and which charges to bring, prosecutors play a significant role in determining the fate of people suspected of committing crimes. Prosecutors must work closely with the police in determining how to investigate crimes and which defendants to pursue. After the police make an arrest, the prosecutor takes charge of the case and sees it through to its conclusion, whether charges are dropped or the defendant is convicted and sentenced to prison. Because most American prosecutors are elected officials, they are responsive to the values of their local communities in deciding which charges to apply against criminal defendants.

Types of Prosecutors

U.S. Attorney: Prosecutor for the United States government in each of the ninety-four federal judicial districts nationwide, who is responsible for prosecuting defendants accused of federal crimes

State Attorney General: Chief legal officer in state government, typically elected by the voters, who represents the state in legal matters and prosecutes defendants accused of violating specific state criminal laws

District Attorney or County Prosecutor: Local official, elected by the voters in most cities and counties, who is responsible for prosecuting the majority of criminal defendants accused of violating state criminal laws

---

The Organization of Prosecution. Prosecution in the United States is organized in conjunction with the different levels of government. In particular, the prosecution of federal criminal cases is handled separately from the prosecution of cases alleging violations of state laws and local ordinances.

The attorney general of the United States, an appointed member of the president's cabinet and the head of the U.S. Justice Department, bears overall responsibility for the prosecution of federal crimes. Federal crimes are those acts made punishable by statutes enacted by the U.S. Congress. Examples of federal crimes include smuggling, bank fraud, counterfeiting, drug trafficking, and bank robbery. Many people convicted of federal crimes engaged either in white-collar crimes, such as bank fraud, or in drug trafficking. The prosecution of each federal criminal case occurs in the U.S. district court whose jurisdiction encompasses the city or town where the crime occurred. The federal prosecutor who actually presents the case against the defendant is called a U.S. attorney, and there is one such attorney in each of the ninety-four districts throughout the United States. U.S. attorneys are appointed by the president of the United States and supervised by the U.S. attorney general.

Most crimes, such as burglary, murder, sexual battery, and larceny, are violations of state law. Local prosecutors in each city or county bear primary responsibility for prosecuting state crimes. Depending on the state, these prosecutors are called county prosecutors, district attorneys, or state's attorneys. In most states, local prosecutors are elected officials who must please the public with their performance in order to stay in office. Elected local prosecutors do not answer to any authority other than the voters. There is typically no judge or higher prosecutor who can tell them to pursue or drop particular cases. In only a few states are attorneys general, the chief legal officers of their states, responsible for overseeing the decisions and actions of local prosecutors. State attorneys general, who are usually selected by voters in statewide elections, typically have authority to prosecute only specific categories of cases, such as consumer fraud that occurs statewide. State attorneys general work closely with local prosecutors and share information, but local prosecutors make their own decisions about which defendants to pursue and which charges to file.

The Prosecutor's Duties. The prosecutor's success depends on the police doing a good job in gathering evidence. If the police make mistakes during an investigation, the prosecutor may be deprived of key evidence, either because the police overlooked the evidence or because a judge ruled the evidence inadmissible after it was obtained improperly. Thus, the prosecutor works closely with the police to identify and investigate criminal suspects and thereby helps to ensure that proper evidence is obtained. In many cities the police seek the prosecutor's approval before asking a judge to issue an arrest or search warrant.

After an arrest is made, the prosecutor may make arguments to the court about whether bail should be set and the amount of bail money that suspects must present in order to gain pretrial release. The prosecutor must also present evidence at preliminary hearings in order to persuade a judge that enough evidence exists against a suspect to justify moving the case forward. In order to obtain evidence, the prosecutor interviews witnesses and victims while relying on evidence gathered by the police. Most important, the prosecutor decides which charges to file against the defendant. In a homicide case, for example, the prosecutor must evaluate the suspect's motives and actions in order to decide which charges to pursue. If there is evidence that a killing was premeditated, the charge may be first-degree or aggravated murder. If the killing was intentional but not premeditated or was the result of negligence, the prosecutor may pursue charges of second-degree murder or manslaughter. In some cases the prosecutor decides to drop the charges when there is insufficient evidence, when there are serious doubts about the suspect's guilt, or when the offense is too minor to be worth absorbing the time of staff members in the prosecutor's office.

As cases proceed through various preliminary hearings toward trial, prosecutors decide whether to discuss a plea agreement with the criminal defense attorney representing the defendant. In order to obtain a sure conviction and avoid the time and expense of trial, prosecutors engage in plea bargaining in most cases. In exchange for the defendant's agreement to plead guilty, the prosecutor may offer to reduce charges or to recommend a specific sentence to the judge.

Prosecutors sometimes intentionally overcharge defendants by filing multiple charges, including some for which there is little evidence. By overcharging, prosecutors have more bargaining chips to give away in the plea bargaining process without risking that the defendant will receive a lesser sentence than one that would likely be imposed after conviction at trial. If no plea agreement develops, the prosecutor takes the case to trial.

In addition to their formal duties, local prosecutors often maintain active communications with the news media to keep the public informed of current developments. They also maintain contact with political party leaders in order to enhance their own prospects for reelection. In large cities and counties the prosecutor may not handle any cases directly. Instead, a large staff of assistant prosecutors handles the actual plea bargaining and trials while the prosecutor supervises the assistants, oversees the annual budget, and maintains relations with the news media and governmental offices. Thus, a prosecutor may act as a political figure and government administrator rather than as an actual courtroom attorney. The office of prosecutor is the traditional stepping stone to higher political office, and many judges, legislators, and governors first began their careers as local prosecutors.

The Prosecutor and the Criminal Trial. The prosecutor represents the state in the courtroom by presenting evidence of the defendant's guilt and attempting to persuade the judge or jury to render a guilty verdict.

During jury selection the prosecutor must question prospective jurors in order to exclude those who might be biased. The trial begins when the prosecutor makes an opening statement describing the charges and the evidence that will be presented to prove the defendant's guilt. The prosecutor then bears the burden of presenting sufficient evidence to prove the case, presenting and questioning witnesses, submitting documents and objects into evidence (such as physical evidence), and making arguments about how the evidence demonstrates the defendant's guilt. When the defense presents witnesses and counter-arguments, the prosecutor can ask additional questions about testimony and evidence. The prosecutor can also respond to the arguments made by the defense. The trial concludes when the jury or judge renders a verdict. There can be a guilty verdict only when the prosecutor presents evidence and arguments to persuade the jury or judge that the defendant is guilty beyond a reasonable doubt.

As an officer of the court, the prosecutor is obligated to ensure that the defendant's rights are protected and that a fair trial takes place. However, because local prosecutors are elected officials, critics fear that they feel pressured to please the public by ensuring that someone is convicted for every crime that occurs. Thus, they may become too zealous about their role in stopping criminals and thereby lose sight of their duties to protect defendants' rights and to ensure that the available evidence clearly establishes a defendant's guilt.

When a defendant pleads guilty or is convicted at trial, the prosecutor may recommend a sentence to the judge. In jurisdictions in which judges have discretion to determine sentences, they often place great weight on prosecutors' recommendations. In other jurisdictions, the sentences for specific crimes are mandated by the legislature through sentencing guidelines. Thus, the prosecutor's influence over the ultimate sentence stems from the choice of charges originally pursued rather than from a sentence recommendation after conviction.

Decision Making by Prosecutors. Prosecutors may use different approaches to determine which cases to pursue and how to pursue them. Some prosecutors feel obligated to proceed with any case in which there is evidence that a suspect may be guilty of a crime. In some cases, the prosecutor may be unsure about the defendant's guilt and simply leave it to the jury or judge to decide. In such situations, the prosecutor recognizes that some defendants will ultimately be acquitted at trial because a jury or judge did not believe that the evidence proved guilt beyond a reasonable doubt. Other prosecutors pursue cases only when they themselves are convinced of the defendant's guilt and believe that enough evidence clearly exists to convict them at trial. Such prosecutors are likely to dismiss charges against defendants when the evidence against them is uncertain or weak.

In other jurisdictions prosecutors' decisions about which cases to pursue may be influenced by the available resources in the criminal justice system. If the assistant prosecutors are busy with cases involving serious crimes, defendants charged with minor offenses may have the charges dropped and be set free. Similarly, if the county jail is nearly full, prosecutors may need to take account of available cell space in making bail recommendations or deciding which cases to pursue.

Because local prosecutors are elected officials who frequently want public attention in order to seek higher office, there are risks that prosecutors use political considerations in deciding which cases to prosecute. In some situations, prosecutors have launched investigations against political opponents while ignoring misdeeds committed by political supporters. Other prosecutors have engaged in discriminatory actions against minority religious or racial groups.

Suggested Readings. A discussion of federal prosecutors is presented in James Eisenstein's *Counsel for the United States: U.S. Attorneys in the Political and Legal System* (Baltimore: Johns Hopkins University Press, 1978). The duties and roles of local prosecutors are examined in Lief Carter's *The Limits of Order* (Lexington, Mass.: D.C. Heath, 1974) and David Neubauer's *Criminal Justice in Middle America* (Morristown, N.J.: General Learning Press, 1974). Discussions of decision-making prosecutors are presented in Joan Jacoby's *The American Prosecutor: A Search for Identity* (Lexington, Mass.: D.C.

Heath, 1980) and William McDonald's *The Prosecutor* (Beverly Hills, Calif.: Sage, 1979). For an inside look at prosecution from a prosecutor's perspective see David Heilbroner's *Rough Justice: Days and Nights of a Young D.A.* (New York: Pantheon, 1990) and Judith Rowland's *The Ultimate Violation* (New York: Doubleday, 1985). —*Christopher E. Smith*

See also Attorney types; Criminal justice system; Criminal law; Criminal prosecution; District attorneys; Jury selection; Officers of the court; Trials.

Prostitution

Prostitution is the act of selling sexual services for a fee, a definition which has been expanded in recent years to reflect changes in U.S. society.

A prostitute is a person who engages in sexual activity for a fee. The fee need not be in the form of money. In many states the act of merely offering to perform sexual services for a fee is also defined as prostitution, although this activity is sometimes considered to be a separate offense known as "solicitation" or "soliciting for prostitution." Some jurisdictions also include working in a house of prostitution as within the scope of prostitution statutes. Prostitution is considered a misdemeanor in all of the states in which it is illegal. Penalties range from small fines to imprisonment for up to two years.

Expanded Definition. Although only women historically could be charged with prostitution, in the late twentieth century a prostitute could be either male or female. In most jurisdictions sexual activity includes intercourse; heterosexual and homosexual conduct; and manual, oral, and anal acts of sexual gratification. In response to claims of sex discrimination, many states have expanded their definitions of prostitution to include the conduct of customers by defining prostitution as either purchasing or selling sexual services or offering to purchase or sell sexual services. Some municipalities with high levels of prostitution have responded by enacting ordinances, often known informally as "John laws," which fine the customers of prostitutes. Municipalities with areas in which prostitution is a problem may also publicize the names of customers in the local media in order to discourage them from frequenting such areas.

Although private, consensual sexual activity between adults, even if negotiated for a fee, might seem to fall within the constitutional right to privacy, states have an interest in regulating prostitution. They may wish to prevent venereal disease, sexual exploitation, and other types of criminal misconduct that tend to accompany prostitution, such as pimping, illegal drugs, and police corruption.

Historical Background. The U.S. criminal justice system developed from English common law and from statutes enacted by the state and federal legislatures. Prostitution was not a crime at common law, although the English word dates back to at least the sixteenth century. In the United States prostitution was legal and often regulated in many states until well into the twentieth century. In 1920, for example, the Honolulu military police established a system of prostitution regulation which was taken over by the local police department in 1932. It was not until 1944 that the governor of Hawaii outlawed prostitution.

Even after prostitution was criminalized, some states experimented with lenient penalties. In 1967 New York reduced prostitution from a misdemeanor to a minor violation carrying a maximum fifteen-day sentence. The maximum sentence was increased to ninety days in 1969, when it was felt that prostitution had increased beyond tolerable levels. During the period of Prohibition in the 1920's, when organized crime flourished, prostitution in cities such as Chicago was controlled by powerful gangs. Throughout the 1920's, 1930's, and 1940's it was not uncommon for civic leaders and the police to offer "protection" to houses of prostitution in return for paid bribes.

Prostitution has long been perceived as a problem for the military, primarily because of the spread of venereal disease. The Draft Act of 1917 prohibited prostitution near military training camps. A similar law, the May Act enacted by President Franklin D. Roosevelt in 1941, prohibited "prostitution within such reasonable distance of military and/or naval establishments . . . needful to the efficiency, health and welfare of the army or navy." These laws were directed at the areas surrounding military bases within the United States. During the Vietnam War U.S. military leaders appear to have given tacit approval to servicemen in Vietnam who patronized houses of prostitution by issuing passes to rest and recreation centers in Southeast Asia where prostitution was legal and regulated. The Defense Department at that time, however, was officially opposed to such activity.

Related Offenses. Solicitation is part of the crime of prostitution in some states and a separate offense in others. Solicitation is the active search for customers for the business of sexual gratification. Offering to engage in sexual activity for a fee is an example of such conduct, as is quoting prices for various sex acts. However, a person may not be convicted of this offense if the initial offer is made by an undercover police officer, even if the person soliciting agrees to the offer. In some jurisdictions statutes prohibiting solicitation may be applied to customers of prostitutes. A police officer may testify about statements made by defendants accused of solicitation. Such statements are not inadmissible hearsay, because they are offered only as evidence of verbal acts tending to prove that the defendant solicited. A few states outlaw solicitation by persons who know that they are infected with the human immunodeficiency virus (HIV).

The offense of loitering for the purpose of prostitution or loitering with the intent to solicit for prostitution, sometimes called common nightwalking, seeks to address the public nuisance element of prostitution by criminalizing behavior such as wandering in public places, hailing vehicles, beckoning to passersby, or engaging in conversations with passersby for the purpose of prostitution. Such laws have been frequently challenged as too broad, vague, or violative of the right to free speech and assembly. However, these laws are usually upheld if they list specific overt acts that an experienced police officer would associate with prostitution. If a defendant charged with loitering is a known prostitute, that is, a person with a prior conviction for prostitution, this prior conviction may be used as evidence, as may the fact that a particular area is known to police to be frequented by prostitutes and their customers.

Acts by intermediaries who exploit prostitutes are also prohibited. These laws are directed against persons who act as agents for prostitutes or who derive support from prostitution. Commonly, such persons are called either pimps or madams. Pimps are usually males who obtain customers for prostitutes, who induce others to enter into prostitution, or who receive all or part of the earnings of a prostitute. Madams are usually females who run houses of prostitution. Some statutes prescribe higher penalties for those who compel others to enter into prostitution by force or threat of force, who promote prostitution among minors, or who promote prostitution among spouses, children, or wards. The Model Penal Code makes such offenses felonies as opposed to misdemeanors.

In some jurisdictions it is illegal to transport a person for the purpose of prostitution. In order for state laws of this nature to be valid, they must encompass transportation only within a state. Any state law that presumes to prohibit the interstate transportation of persons for the purpose of pros-

A member of the U.S. Prostitutes Collective pickets outside U.S. immigration offices in San Francisco in 1983 to protest the deportation of a Nevada brothel owner. (AP/Wide World Photos)

titution will be held invalid as in conflict with the federal White Slave Traffic Act (1910), also known as the Mann Act, which prohibits such interstate transportation under the principle that federal legislation regulating any form of interstate commerce always supersedes comparable state legislation.

Maintaining a house of prostitution is also illegal. Laws regarding this offense generally require that prostitution be regularly engaged in on the premises and that the person maintaining or having control of the premises have knowledge of the activity.

Prostitution Law Reform. A well-known example of prostitution law reform occurred in the state of Nevada, where houses of prostitution may be legal and regulated, although the state legislature has given municipalities the power to prohibit, regulate, license, and tax such businesses. Throughout the state, houses of prostitution may not be located on principal business streets or within four hundred yards of schools or churches and may not be conducted in such a way as to create a nuisance. In municipalities in which prostitution is legal, people working in houses of prostitution are generally required to have weekly medical screenings for sexually transmitted diseases.

Although the idea of legalizing prostitution is not new, it generated increased debate with the advent of the acquired immunodeficiency syndrome (AIDS) epidemic in the early 1980's and accompanying public health concerns. Many people feel that laws against prostitution are ineffective because they attempt to legislate morality, while others believe that a legal, regulated system of prostitution is a good defense against the spread of AIDS and other sexually transmitted diseases. The feminist movement has spawned opposing positions on this issue. Some feminists assert that any regulation of adult women's sexual freedom is oppressive, while others argue that prostitution and the sex industry in general reinforce the image of women as sex objects and promote violence against women. Prostitutes themselves have organized in recent years to decriminalize prostitution. They have fought to eliminate all laws relating to prostitution as opposed to fighting for its legalization, which usually entails some form of regulation.

Suggested Readings. Charles Winick and Paul M. Kinsey provide a readable history of prostitution in the United States through the 1960's in *The Lively Commerce: Prostitution in the United States* (Chicago: Quadrangle Books, 1971). A discussion of decriminalization is included in Wendy Chapkis's *Live Sex Acts: Women Performing Erotic Labor* (London: Cassell, 1997), a contemporary study of prostitution in California and Europe that includes interviews with fifty sex industry workers. Another contemporary study of prostitution and sex-oriented business in the United States is Marianne Macy's *Working Sex: An Odyssey Into Our Cultural Underworld* (New York: Carroll & Graff, 1996). For a feminist study of the moral and ethical aspects of prostitution see Kathleen Barry's *The Prostitution of Sexuality* (New York: New York University Press, 1995). The subject of prostitution among minors is covered in Laura J. Smith's *Juveniles in Prostitution: Fact Versus Fiction* (Saratoga, Calif.: R & E Publishers, 1984). Homosexual prostitution is treated in Robin Lloyd's *For Money or Love: Boy Prostitution in America* (New York: Vanguard Press, 1976). *Crossing Over the Line: Legislating Morality and the Mann Act* (Chicago: University of Chicago Press, 1994) by David J. Langum is a history of prostitution in the United States that focuses on the effects of the White Slave Trade Act.

—*Michele Leavitt*

See also Criminal justice system; Criminal law; Criminal prosecution; Criminal record; Entrapment; Loitering; Moral turpitude; Pandering; Privacy rights.

Proximate cause

Proximate cause is a legal requirement for the successful prosecution of negligence cases.

In negligence cases plaintiffs must prove not only that defendants breached a legal duty to them and that the breach was in fact a cause of their injuries but also that the breach of duty was connected closely enough to the injuries to justify requiring the at-fault defendant to pay money damages.

A case of negligence and proximate cause involved a shipping barge that was tied up at a large dock on the Hudson River. The man charged with tying the barge to large concrete pillars on the dock by means of ropes did so carelessly. As a result, chunks of ice floating down the fast-moving river jarred the ship loose and sent it spinning down the river, causing it to strike and damage other barges tied up along the river. It also struck a large bridge that spanned the river, causing it to collapse. Traffic on land was disrupted by the bridge collapse, as a result of which fire engines were unable to get to a burning building on the opposite side of the river from the fire station. The building, which might have been saved by the firemen had the bridge not collapsed, was totally destroyed by the fire. Shipping on the river was also disrupted by the wreckage, and shippers incurred expenses to remove goods from barges and ship them by truck.

The court determined that all these damages were in fact caused by the man who carelessly moored the barge. However, only the damage to the other ships and to the bridge were proximately caused by the man's negligence. All other damages, including the burned building and the additional shipping costs, even though they would not have happened had the man not neglected to carefully tie up the barge, were too remote and unforeseeable to be considered within the scope of proximate cause. —*Michael Scherschligt*

See also Liability, civil and criminal; Negligence; Personal injury law; Torts.

Public accommodations

Businesses providing services as hotels, restaurants, and places of amusement, public accommodations are subject to legal regulations regarding health, safety, and discrimination.

Businesses that provide public accommodations are subject to legal regulations regarding health, safety, discrimination, and other matters. Public accommodations include hotels, motels, restaurants, amusement parks, movie theaters, and other places of public amusement. While specific health and safety laws apply to some public accommodations contexts and not to others, federal and state laws prohibit all public accommodations businesses from engaging in racial and other kinds of discrimination.

Hotels and Motels. Hotels and motels are subject to various legal regulations intended to protect the health and safety of their customers. State and local building codes require that hotels and motels be of sound construction and include fire alarms, fire extinguishers, and automatic fire sprinkler systems. There are also laws governing the number

Roadside motel, an example of public accommodations. (James L. Shaffer)

and location of fire exits, as well as the regular inspection of elevators. Hotels and motels must post notices informing guests about what to do during fires and other emergencies. If these facilities have swimming pools, there are additional rules about keeping safety devices available and posting proper safety notices.

States have "innkeeper laws" that specify the authority and obligations of hotels and motels in charging customers and dealing with guests who leave property behind. Typically, notices must be posted in each room informing guests about the room charge and providing information about what the hotels and motels may do if guests leave property behind. Such laws usually require that hotels and motels hold property for a specified number of days in order to give guests the opportunity to reclaim the property. If guests left unpaid bills at the establishment, provisions may specify that the hotel or motel sell the property and use the proceeds to cover the outstanding bills.

Restaurants and Places of Public Amusement. Restaurants are also subject to laws regarding building construction, fire exits, and fire extinguishers. In addition, restaurants are subject to regular kitchen and dining room inspections by government inspectors to ensure that mandated standards for cleanliness and sanitation are being maintained. Restaurants may be forced to close down and spend time cleaning if such inspections reveal too many violations that might threaten the health of customers and employees. There are often additional health regulations, such as requirements that restaurant employees be tested for tuberculosis. Restaurants and other public accommodations are licensed to serve only a specified number of customers, and they must stop additional customers from entering the establishment if the maximum number of patrons is already present.

Entertainment facilities, such as movie theaters and amusement parks, are subject to safety regulations. These regulations may require regular inspections to ensure that fire safety and other requirements are being met. Amusement parks, in particular, may require additional regulations and inspections, because rides and other activities, if defective, may harm customers.

In addition to health and safety laws enacted by state and local governments, all public accommodations are affected by judicial decisions that establish standards for determining responsibility for injuries that occur at those locations. To ensure that facilities are safe, the law established by such legal cases has created a high standard for such establishments. If facilities permit unsafe conditions to exist, such as broken railings in stairwells or inadequate lighting in parking lots, they may be forced through lawsuits to pay significant financial compensation to persons injured on their premises by such incidents as falling or being assaulted by criminals.

Discrimination. Prior to 1964 widespread racial discrimination in public accommodations made it very difficult for African Americans and members of other minority groups to travel through certain parts of the United States. Hotels, motels, and restaurants often refused to serve them. If movie theaters permitted them to enter, they frequently had to sit in the back of the balcony.

In order to combat this harmful and unfair racial discrimination, the U.S. Congress enacted Title II of the Civil Rights Act of 1964, which prohibited racial discrimination in public accommodations. Business owners in southern states challenged this statute in court by claiming that Congress lacked the power to tell private businesses whom they had to serve as customers. However, in its decisions in *Heart of Atlanta Motel v. United States* (1964) and *Katzenbach v. McClung* (1964) the U.S. Supreme Court supported Congress by declaring that Congress could use its power to regulate interstate commerce as a means to forbid discrimination in those public accommodations businesses that had out-of-state customers or bought food, furniture, and other materials from out-of-state sources. These laws were interpreted so broadly that they effectively covered virtually every public accommodations business, even if there was no proof that the business was frequented by out-of-state customers.

Many states and cities eventually enacted their own antidiscrimination laws, which covered all public accommodations and other businesses. Over time these antidiscrimination laws have been expanded to forbid other forms of discrimination, such as discrimination based on gender or disability. Laws forbidding disability discrimination have often imposed new requirements and costs on public accommodations businesses. For example, businesses must often make their establishments acces-

> **Public Interest Law Firms and Their Objectives**
>
> - **Earthjustice Legal Defense Fund (1997), formerly Sierra Club Legal Defense Fund (1971):** Protects the environment from pollutants and works toward the preservation of species and habitats
> - **Center for Democracy and Technology (1994):** Promotes public policies that advance civil liberties and democratic values in new computer and communications technology
> - **Landmark Legal Foundation (1976):** Promotes individual rights, government accountability, and conservative values
> - **National Right to Work Legal Foundation (1968):** Opposes compulsory union memberships as a condition of employment
> - **NAACP Legal Defense and Education Fund (1940):** Defends African Americans against all forms of racial discrimination and supports affirmative action

sible to people in wheelchairs or persons with disabilities that limit their mobility. These requirements have led to the construction of wheelchair ramps, wheelchair-accessible restrooms, and other modifications to the physical structures of many public accommodations.

If people believe that they have been denied access to public accommodations because of their race, gender, disability, or other characteristics covered under applicable federal, state, and local laws, they may file a complaint with their state or local government agency responsible for investigating civil rights violations. The agency investigates the complaint and attempts to mediate a resolution. There are also opportunities for lawsuits against businesses. Depending on how the antidiscrimination law is written, the lawsuits may be filed by either the victimized individual or the government. Because public accommodations businesses do not want a reputation for discriminating or being hostile to any group of potential customers, civil rights organizations sometimes win apologies for victims and improved customer service by publicizing complaints and applying public pressure without waiting for slow legal processes to move forward.

Suggested Readings. For an overview of legal issues affecting public accommodations, see Jon P. McConnell and Lothar Kreck's *Hospitality Management: Avoiding Legal Pitfalls* (Boston: Cahners Books, 1976). The issue of liability for injuries suffered by customers is part of tort law and is discussed in most books on tort law, such as Marc Franklin and Robert Rabin's *Cases and Materials on Tort Law and Alternatives* (Westbury, N.Y.: Foundation Press, 1992). The Civil Rights Act of 1964, which barred racial discrimination in public accommodations, is discussed in Robert Loevy's *To End All Segregation: The Politics of Passage of the Civil Rights Act of 1964* (Lanham, Md.: University Press of America, 1990) and Christopher E. Smith's *Politics in Constitutional Law* (Chicago: Nelson-Hall, 1992). The impact of the Americans with Disabilities Act (ADA) on public accommodations is examined in Paul Wehman's *The ADA Mandate for Social Change* (Baltimore: P. H. Brookes, 1993) and Maureen Harrison and Steve Gilbert's *The Americans with Disabilities Act Handbook* (Beverly Hills, Calif.: Excellent Books, 1992).

—Christopher E. Smith

See also Civil rights and liberties; Consumer protection laws; Discrimination; Franchise businesses; Personal injury law; Property liability; Race and the law.

Public defenders

> *A government attorney assigned to represent criminal defendants who cannot afford to hire private attorneys.*

Persons charged with a crime in the United States are entitled to have a lawyer represent them. Those who cannot afford to hire their own lawyer are entitled to representation by a lawyer appointed by the court and paid for by the government. In most U.S. cities and many states, this representation is provided by a lawyer or group of lawyers called "public defenders." These attorneys are employed by the government specifically to represent those who cannot afford to hire their own counsel.

The Constitutional Right to Counsel. Before 1963 most persons charged with a crime who could not afford to hire a lawyer to represent them simply represented themselves. Even in very serious cases poor, and sometimes poorly educated, people presented their own cases to juries and judges. There was no nationally recognized right to have a lawyer appointed to represent indigent defendants. The U.S. Supreme Court held in 1942 that criminal defendants were entitled to the appointment of a lawyer at government expense only when special circumstances required a lawyer to make a defendant's trial fair. The Court held that the constitutional guarantee of "due process" required only that defendants have fair trials and that in most cases trials could be fair even though defendant did not have a lawyer.

The Supreme Court recognized two exceptions to this "special circumstances" rule, but these exceptions had limited applicability. First, persons charged with crimes against federal law in federal rather than state courts were entitled under the Sixth Amendment to the U.S. Constitution to have a lawyer appointed to represent them. The assistance of counsel clause of the amendment provides that "in all criminal prosecutions, the accused shall . . . have the assistance of counsel for his defense." Second, persons charged in federal or state courts with capital crimes, for which they could receive the death penalty, were entitled to the appointment of a lawyer. Since the vast majority of criminal charges did not carry a possible death sentence as punishment and most criminal offenses were (and still are) prosecuted in state rather than in federal courts, most people charged with most crimes were represented by a lawyer only if they had the money to hire one. Even persons charged with very serious crimes which could result in long prison terms were routinely tried without counsel.

These rules changed dramatically in 1963, when the U.S. Supreme Court decided in the case of *Gideon v. Wainwright* that having a lawyer represent an accused person was essential to ensuring that every criminal trial was fair. The source of this right was the Sixth Amendment's guarantee of the assistance of counsel. For the first time the Court ruled that the Sixth Amendment's guarantee of the assistance of counsel was fully applicable to the states and required that all indigent persons charged with serious crimes or "felonies" in state courts, as well as those charged in federal courts, had to be provided with a lawyer at government expense.

The Creation of the Public Defender. *Gideon v. Wainwright* resulted in the creation of public defender offices and programs throughout the nation. Some jurisdictions established public defenders to handle most criminal cases against indigent persons while others relied on the appointment of private lawyers to handle these cases. In 1972 the Supreme Court expanded the right to an appointed lawyer to include those persons charged with minor or less serious crimes (misdemeanors) as well as felonies. It later limited this right to those misdemeanor cases in which persons are actually sentenced to imprisonment, excluding cases in which punishment is limited to fines.

The right to have an appointed lawyer can begin at any "critical stage" of a case, even before it comes to trial, such as at an initial or preliminary hearing. This right can begin as soon as a person is arrested, when a person is questioned by police

---

The Sixth Amendment

The office of government public defenders owes its existence to the final phrase of the Sixth Amendment:

In all criminal prosecutions, the accused shall enjoy the right to a speedy and public trial, by an impartial jury of the State and district wherein the crime shall have been committed; which district shall have been previously ascertained by law, and to be informed of the nature and cause of the accusation; to be confronted with the witnesses against him; to have compulsory process for obtaining witnesses in his favor, and to have the assistance of counsel for his defence.

and given the Miranda warnings. These warnings include the right to speak with a lawyer, to have a lawyer appointed if an arrested person cannot afford to hire one, and to remain silent in order to avoid self-incrimination. Often the lawyer appointed is a public defender. Poor persons charged with a crime have a right to the services of a lawyer free of charge during trial, sentencing, and one appeal. The right does not provide for representation for further appeals or for representation in civil cases.

Modern Public Defenders. Although the Supreme Court has held that the U.S. Constitution requires that indigent persons charged with crimes be provided a lawyer at government expense, it has not specified how this must be done. Jurisdictions in the United States use three basic methods to provide such representation: public defenders, assigned counsels, and contract attorneys. Public defenders are lawyers who exclusively represent indigent criminal defendants. They may be organized by city, county, or state into offices, and they are usually employees of one of these units of government. Federal courts have a federal defender system, which provides representation to indigent persons charged with federal crimes. Assigned counsels are private lawyers who makes themselves available for appointment by the court on a case-by-case basis. They may or may not specialize in criminal defense, and they may or may not be screened or specially trained to handle criminal cases. They are paid a fee, which is usually fixed but can vary according to the time they spend on a case or on the type of case they are handling. Contract attorneys are members of organizations, such as law firms or bar associations, which contract with cities, counties, or states to handle a certain number of appointed cases for a set period of time.

Most modern American criminal justice systems and virtually all urban ones rely on some combination of these options to provide representation to a large proportion of criminal defendants. A recent U.S. Department of Justice study found that in 1992 about 80 percent of defendants charged with felonies in the nation's seventy-five largest counties were represented by either a public defender or an assigned counsel. The estimated cost of these services to state and local governments was $1.3 billion in 1990, which was approximately double what these services cost in inflation-adjusted constant dollars in 1979. This rise in expenditures for the representation of poor defendants corresponds to the dramatic increase in incarceration rates in the United States during the 1980's and has led to concerns that increased caseloads and reduced funding may cause poor persons charged with crimes to have less fair trials than wealthy criminal defendants.

Problems of Public Defense. Although public defenders receive their salaries from the government, they are legally and ethically obligated to represent their clients, the accused persons, against the government. This has sometimes made the public, and even some clients, resentful or mistrustful of public defenders. Early studies of the system of public defenders in the late 1960's suggested that public defenders sometimes saw themselves as part of a team, which included the prosecutor and the judge, whose goal was to convince clients to plead guilty. Another strand of critical thinking challenged this critique, noting that effective public defenders could often obtain favorable plea bargains for their clients even if they did so through what appeared to be a less aggressive or less adversarial approach. Whatever their views of themselves, public defenders have become essential components of the criminal justice systems in most densely populated U.S. jurisdictions.

During the 1980's and 1990's many American jurisdictions experienced dramatic increases in the demand for public defender services. Between 1982 and 1986, for example, the U.S. Justice Department found that the caseloads of public defenders in the United States increased by 40 percent. This increase was caused in large part by increased prosecution of drug offenses, often characterized as the "War on Drugs." In some jurisdictions, public defenders were each appointed to handle hundreds of cases a year, which raised questions about their effectiveness as defense lawyers and the quality of representation their clients received.

Some public defenders responded by going to court and refusing to accept additional cases without being provided with additional resources. All lawyers have an ethical obligation to represent clients competently, and some public defenders contended that no one could competently represent hundreds of different clients a year, with each case involving different facts and legal issues. Some courts responded to this demand for the services of public defenders by appointing private lawyers to represent indigent defendants pro bono, without compensation, as part of their obligation to serve the public. Since many of these lawyers had little experience practicing criminal law, this practice raised serious concerns about the quality of the representation they provided.

Standards for Criminal Justice. In an effort to establish uniform standards of practice for criminal defense lawyers, including public defenders, the American Bar Association (ABA), the nation's largest bar association, promulgated *Standards for Criminal Justice*. First published in 1968 and for the third time in 1992, the *Standards* set forth guidelines for effective and ethical conduct by both prosecutors and defense lawyers, as well as benchmarks for effective provision of defense services. They seek to provide to all eligible persons "quality" legal representation, as opposed to just competent counsel. They also stipulate that no public defender or appointed counsel should accept workloads that interfere with providing quality representation and that government must provide adequate funding for these services. While these standards are only recommendations and have no legal weight, they have been influential in defining the role and operation of modern public defender offices.

Suggested Readings. The U.S. Supreme Court case in which the Court recognized the right to appointed counsel for indigent defendants was *Gideon v. Wainright* (1963). An exciting account of the history of this case is Anthony Lewis's *Gideon's Trumpet* (New York: Random House, 1964). Later cases that extended the right of defendants in misdemeanor cases to counsel and later limited this right to those facing misdemeanor charges that could result in a prison sentence were *Argesinger v. Hamlin* (1972) and *Scott v. Illinois* (1979). Statistical information on the use of public defenders nationwide is available in studies by the U.S. Justice Department (*Indigent Defense* by Steven K. Smith and Carol J. DeFrances, Washington, D.C.: Office of Justice Programs, February, 1996) and the National Center for State Courts (*Indigent Defenders: Get the Job Done and Done Well*, Roger A. Hanson and others, Williamsburg, Va.: National Center for State Courts, 1992). A detailed study of the structure and operation of the Cook County, Illinois (Chicago) Public Defender's office, which gives a concise view of a modern, busy public defender's office in a large city, is Lisa J. McIntyre's *The Public Defender: The Practice of Law in the Shadows of Repute* (Chicago: Univ. of Chicago Press, 1987). *How Can You Defend Those People*, by James S. Kunen (New York: Random House, 1983) is an insider's view of being a public defender. Guidelines for effective public defender services are available in the American Bar Association's *Standards for Criminal Justice, Providing Defense Services* (3d ed. Washington, D.C.: American Bar Association, 1992). An assessment of the effects of funding cutbacks on public defenders is Richard Klein and Robert Spangenberg's *The Indigent Defense Crisis* (Washington, D.C.: American Bar Association, 1993). A statistical analysis of this problem is presented in a bulletin by the U.S. Department of Justice, Bureau of Justice Statistics titled *Criminal Defense for the Poor, 1986* (Washington, D.C.: September 1988).   —David M. Siegel

See also Adversary system; American Bar Association; Attorney types; Attorneys, court-appointed; Civil rights and liberties; Criminal justice system; Defendant; Due process; Effective counsel; Felony; Legal clinics; Misdemeanor; Pro bono legal work; Self-representation.

Public domain

Public domain refers to the status of writings and other creative works that are no longer protected by copyright.

Works that have been produced or published without a copyright notice or ones whose copyrights have expired are termed to be in the public domain. The public domain includes products or processes that are no longer protected by copyright or patent. Thus, they are freely available to be copied, printed, published, sold, or used by the public at large.

Whereas patents protect new inventions and improvements to existing mechanical devices, copyrights protect artistic works. Broad categories of copyrighted items not typically in the public domain include literary works, such as books and magazines; musical works, including lyrics; dramatic works, such as plays; sound recordings, such as tapes and compact disks; audiovisual works, including motion pictures and videocassettes; visual art, such as paintings and sculptures; pantomimes and choreographic works; and computer programs and data bases. Copyright owners have the exclusive right to print, publish, copy, and sell their copyrighted work or to prepare derivative works based on the original material, such as an edited film.

Under the terms of the Copyright Act of 1976, any work copyrighted after January 1, 1978, is protected from the public domain from the date of copyright until fifty years after the death of the author. Works that were copyrighted prior to 1978 are protected for twenty-eight years, with an entitlement of forty-seven additional years of protection if the copyright owner applies for a renewal at least one year prior to the expiration date of the copyright. Copyrights that are owned by publishing companies expire seventy-five years after the work was published, or one hundred years from the date that the work was created, whichever is less. Works that were created before January 1, 1978, but remain unpublished will pass into the public domain on December 31, 2002. Anything that was published more than seventy-five years before January 1, 1978, is already in the public domain.

Whether or not an individual must seek a publisher's permission to copy copyrighted materials that are not in the public domain depends on whether the copying complies with the 1976 Copyright Act. This law permits copying parts of copyrighted works for certain purposes, including scholarship, research, criticism, comment, or news reporting. Teachers may also make multiple copies of works for classroom use. However, reprinting copyrighted materials or derivatives of copyrighted materials for commercial purposes is illegal unless written permission has been obtained from the copyright holder. For example, videocassette tapes carry the standard copyright notice and warnings about the legal consequences of copying. Since materials published after March 1, 1984, may be copyrighted if published without copyright notice, the assumption should be that they are not in the public domain and that a request for permission to copy or use them should be obtained from the copyright owner. —*Alvin K. Benson*

See also Common law; Copyright; Patents; Trademarks.

Public interest law

Public interest law involves group legal activity, particularly litigation, that goes beyond the interests of individual clients and strives for legal reform that benefits the larger public; however, groups involved in this activity may have conflicting interpretations of the public interest.

Public interest law came into being because reformers considered the American legal system to be flawed. The legal system in the United States is described as an adversary system in which the parties to a conflict do battle, through their lawyers, in the arena of a courtroom. It was long assumed that this was the best way to arrive at truth, and from truth justice would emerge. In the 1960's and 1970's, however, critics of the adversary system came to believe that it works well only when the two sides have substantially equal resources, such as information and wealth. Often they do not.

Redressing Inequity. Reformers recognize that some groups and interests are unrepresented or underrepresented because they lack economic and political power. Reformers seek to correct this inequity not by radically changing the system but by creating public interest law firms to defend the interests of those who have been harmed by economic or political forces that they, on their own, cannot match. Such law firms seek to promote the public interest by making the legal system, as well as American society, more closely approximate democratic ideals. While private law firms seek to make profits, public interest law firms do not. They promote a cause. Their cause may include environmental protection; consumer protection; the protection of children; equitable treatment of minorities, women, or the disabled; or protection against government restrictions on the use of private property.

To better promote a cause, public interest lawyers and law firms try to attract favorable publicity. Publicity is a means for furthering their cause when it results in increased contributions to the organization. Such contributions increase the firm's ability to promote its vision of the public interest—whatever that may be. Publicity can be beneficial to a cause even when a test case in the courts does not secure the plaintiff's goal, as when Ralph Nader,

Consumer protection advocate Ralph Nader. (Geffen Photos)

perhaps the nation's best known public interest lawyer, was unable to end the airline practice of overselling flights and bumping ticket holders after all seats were filled. The publicity from Nader's case led the Civil Aeronautics Board to regulate the awarding of compensation in the interest of bumped passengers, which it might not have done otherwise.

Public Interest Lawyers. Lawyers who practice public interest law earn less money than attorneys of comparable age and experience who work with private law firms. According to the *National Law Journal*, the median starting salary in small, private law firms (two to ten lawyers) in 1997 was $35,000 per year. The starting salaries for lawyers with public interest law firms varied, but it rarely exceeded $35,000 per year, and most such lawyers earned less than that. Associates hired by top private firms specializing in such fields as intellectual property or securities law receive much higher starting salaries. Because there are large profits to be earned in these fields, private firms can afford to offer high starting salaries to attract some of the most talented recent law-school graduates. Public interest law firms, however, are nonprofit organizations which, therefore, cannot offer competitive salaries.

The low salaries paid by public interest law firms do not, however, result in their being staffed by lawyers of little talent. The characteristics of public interest lawyers are more like those of lawyers in top private law firms than of those hired into small law firms with starting salaries of $35,000. Public interest lawyers are more likely to have graduated from prestigious law schools, to have been in the top 25 percent of their class, and to have been on the law review. Public interest lawyers are more likely to have clerked for a judge, a mark of prestige, than lawyers in small private firms. But if these highly competent people spend their whole careers in public interest law, they will earn far less than partners in major private law firms.

Public interest lawyers are attracted to the practice of public interest law by something other than money. They appear to be motivated by a desire to do good, to make U.S. society better. When asked whether it is worth the loss of income, they say that it is. In addition to the satisfaction derived from the feeling that they are doing good, there are other benefits that may attract them. They sometimes have the opportunity to associate with powerful government officials and other high-profile people. They also have opportunities to handle important cases that sometimes attract much media attention considerably earlier in their careers than they would as young associates in a private, for-profit law firm.

Funding. Since public interest law firms do not receive fees from their clients, they must raise funds from other sources to meet their expenses. In the 1960's and well into the 1970's philanthropic foundations were a major source of such funding. By the mid-1970's, even though these foundations contributed at substantially the same rate, the number of public interest law firms increased.

Thus, the proportion of their funding that came from foundations declined. The late 1970's saw individual foundations, such as the Ford Foundation, actually decreasing their contributions to public interest law firms. The situation was made worse by a weak economy. The decade of the 1980's was a time when those who ran philanthropic foundations were pessimistic about the ability to solve social problems, and they looked with disfavor on litigation, which is the primary tactic of public interest law firms. While foundations in the 1990's were less generous to public interest law firms than they were in the 1960's, they remained a significant source of funding.

With the decline in foundation funding and cuts in federal spending on social programs and environmental protection during the presidency of conservative Republican Ronald Reagan in the 1980's, liberal public interest firms utilized direct mail techniques to raise money and build a base of political support for their efforts. They added many individuals to their membership lists and added corporate donors as well. Besides contributing money, corporate donors sometimes provided access to photocopiers and computers.

Another source of support on which public interest law firms have relied is court-awarded attorney fees. There are several federal statutes that permit the awarding of such fees to successful plaintiffs in matters considered to be in the public interest. In this way, government has itself encouraged public interest litigation. When public interest lawyers are successful and a court awards them fees, the awards are generally at the going rate for private, profit-making lawyers. Since the salaries of public interest lawyers are low, their firms are able to use court-awarded fees to finance other cases.

Public interest law firms have found still other ways to raise funds. Some have participated in workplace fund-raising drives, in which employees may choose to contribute to them. Some have raised funds by publishing attractive magazines, which they send to their dues-paying members. Such magazines can lure sympathetic members of the public into joining the organization. Environmental organizations have successfully used this technique. The National Wildlife Federation produces Ranger Rick, a publication for children.

Some law schools and their alumni organizations have formed public interest law foundations. These foundations offer fellowships to students planning to practice public interest law. They also finance internships at public interest law firms and loan-forgiveness programs for graduates who go into public interest law. In 1993 Ralph Nader's Harvard Law School class of 1958 went beyond this and established the Appleseed Foundation, the aim of which was to establish Appleseed Centers for Law and Justice in communities. The purpose of these Appleseed Centers is to engage in community organizing as well as litigation. A major criticism of liberal public interest law firms has been that they have overemphasized litigation and neglected community organizing.

Ideological Clash. The Appleseed Centers for Law and Justice reflect the goals and values of the left, or liberal, side of the political spectrum. Indeed, most early public interest law firms established in the 1960's and early 1970's reflected the goals and values of political liberals, and Ralph Nader and his supporters were active in the establishment of several of them. By the early 1970's, however, conservatives saw a need to present their own interpretations of the public interest to the courts. They feared that liberal public interest groups had achieved a near monopoly on the legal interpretations being placed before the judiciary and hoped to rectify that situation.

The first conservative public interest law firm, the Pacific Legal Foundation, was established in 1973 in Sacramento, California. In its early years, it had difficulty raising funds, but it presented its conservative view of the public interest through the submission of *amici curiae* (friend of the court) legal briefs in cases in which it took an interest but did not directly represent either party. This is a tactic used by both liberal and conservative public interest groups. It is less costly than actually litigating a case. However, the Pacific Legal Foundation sponsored some cases itself, and, as it began to win and generate some favorable publicity, additional contributions began to flow to the firm, allowing it to grow in size and activity. The Pacific Legal Foundation has been less likely than liberal public interest firms to bring test cases. Instead, it has assisted government agencies being sued by liberal public interest firms. In some civil suits brought by private individuals against businesses, the Pacific Legal Foundation has assisted the businesses in appealing large judgments against them.

Other conservative public interest firms have been created across the United States. Most have remained smaller than the Pacific Legal Foundation. While some conservative organizations have generally supported private property rights and opposed government regulation of business, others have represented conservative positions on social issues. Americans United for Life, for example, has opposed abortion and euthanasia. As ideological clashes take place in other parts of government, they also take place in the courts.

Suggested Readings. Criticism of lawyers for allying themselves with the powerful and neglecting the weak of American society can be found in Ralph Nader and Wesley J. Smith, *No Contest: Corporate Lawyers and the Perversion of Justice in America* (New York: Random House, 1996), and Jerold S. Auerbach, *Unequal Justice: Lawyers and Social Change in Modern America* (New York: Oxford University Press, 1976). A very thorough and objective study of public interest law is Burton Weisbrod, Joel F. Handler, and Neil K. Komesar's *Public Interest Law: An Economic and Institutional Analysis* (Berkeley: University of California Press, 1978). General readers will find a wealth of information in this work. More recent and more accessible to the general reader is Nan Aron, *Liberty and Justice for All: Public Interest Law in the 1980s and Beyond* (Boulder, Colo.: Westview Press, 1989). Most of the information in this book is drawn from liberal groups. For an examination of the conservative public interest movement, see Lee Epstein, *Conservatives in Court* (Knoxville: University of Tennessee Press, 1985).

—*Patricia A. Behlar*

See also Adversary system; *Amicus curiae* brief; Civil action; Court-awarded fees; Law firm partners and associates; Test case.

Public nuisance

An activity that poses a threat to the community is handled in various ways depending on the severity of the risk.

A public nuisance is the use of property by its owner in a way that endangers the community. In some states certain specific activities, such as producing excessive noise, have been defined as public nuisances. To be a public nuisance, an activity must be deliberately engaged in or continued by the owner of the property after the risk of harm is known. It must be shown that the risk to the public is real and substantial and that the owner knew of the risk or should have known about it.

Important considerations in determining how to deal with a public nuisance are the reasonableness of the property owner's behavior and the seriousness of the risk to the public. Factors to be considered include the nature of the harm, the extent and duration of the risk, the value to the public of the activity, and the cost of preventing or reducing the risk.

A court may allow a minor public nuisance to continue if the property owner's behavior is reasonable. Monetary damages may be awarded to those harmed by a more serious public nuisance, and the property owner may face fines and imprisonment. The court may also grant an injunction against a public nuisance, requiring the property owner to stop the activity and pay for its removal.

—*Rose Secrest*

See also Attractive nuisance; Graffiti; Pets; Vagrancy; Vandalism.

Q

Quitclaim deed

A written document intended to transfer ownership of real property from one individual to another, or a quitclaim deed, does not always have to state that the first individual actually owns the property.

A quitclaim deed is a written document in which one individual, known as the grantor, conveys ownership of real property to another individual, known as the grantee, without stating that the grantor actually owns the property. A quitclaim deed is distinguished from a warranty deed, which explicitly states that the grantor owns the property. It is also distinguished from a grant deed, which uses the word "grant" in a way which has been interpreted by many courts as implying that the grantor owns the property. To be valid, a quitclaim deed must be voluntarily signed by the grantor in the presence of witnesses. The grantor must be mentally capable of understanding the consequences of conveying ownership of real property. The grantor must not have been subjected to undue influence, such as threats of violence.

The quitclaim deed must be delivered from the grantor to the grantee either in person or by mail. The grantee must accept the deed voluntarily. The deed must then be recorded in public records, generally by photocopying it and depositing it in its proper place in a record book kept in the office of the clerk or recorder for the county in which the property is located. —*Rose Secrest*

See also Deed; Real estate law; Real property; Title.

R

Race and the law

Despite efforts during the twentieth century to revise U.S. law into an effective tool to combat racial discrimination, many aspects of law continue to be applied and interpreted in ways that perpetuate racial inequality.

Historically, law was used to enforce racial inequality in the United States. Laws defined the status of African American slaves prior to the Civil War. Later, laws enforced rigid racial segregation that severely limited opportunities for African Americans. Laws also adversely affected the treatment of Chinese Americans, Mexican Americans, and members of other ethnic and racial minority groups. In the 1950's the U.S. Supreme Court finally began to interpret the equal protection clause of the U.S. Constitution's Fourteenth Amendment in ways that prohibited discrimination. In the 1960's the U.S. Congress and state legislatures began using their authority to enact laws that barred racial discrimination in education, employment, housing, and other areas. Despite the twentieth century transformation of law into a tool to combat racial discrimination, many laws are interpreted and applied by officials in ways that maintain racial inequality.

Antidiscrimination Law. The Fourteenth Amendment to the U.S. Constitution says that no state may deny to any person the "equal protection" of the law. For nearly a century after the amendment was written in the 1860's, courts did little to ensure that the equal protection clause was used to combat racial discrimination. Until the mid-twentieth century many states had laws that limited opportunities for members of racial minority groups to have equality in employment, housing, and other areas of American life. Beginning in the 1950's the U.S. Supreme Court became active in invalidating laws that promoted racial discrimination. The Supreme Court's most famous case was *Brown v. Board of Education* (1954) which relied on the equal protection clause to forbid racial segregation in public schools. In subsequent years the Supreme Court and other courts made additional decisions against racial discrimination.

In the 1960's the U.S. Congress and state legislatures began to enact antidiscrimination laws. Congress created federal laws against discrimination in employment, voting, and public places such as hotels and restaurants. Congress also created new government agencies responsible for combating discrimination. These agencies included the U.S. Equal Employment Opportunity Commission (EEOC) and the U.S. Civil Rights Commission. Many states and cities also created their own equal employment opportunity commissions and civil rights commissions.

When people believe that they have become victims of discrimination because of their race in employment, housing, or other areas covered by law, they usually file complaints with their state civil rights commission. The commission investigates complaints and attempts to encourage a voluntary resolution of disputes. Employment discrimination claims may also go the federal EEOC. If the complaint remains unresolved, the individual may proceed with a lawsuit or the agency may initiate a lawsuit on behalf of the victimized individual. If a court determines that individuals or companies engaged in improper racial discrimination, they may be ordered to compensate their victims by providing jobs, promotions, or even large sums of money.

Although mechanisms have been created to use law as a means to combat racial discrimination, these mechanisms do not automatically prevent discrimination from occurring. Victims of racial discrimination may have a difficult time gathering the proof necessary to demonstrate to an agency or court that improper discrimination occurred. If an employer declines to hire someone on the grounds that the person is not the most qualified applicant, even if the real reason is racial discrimination, the victim may have great difficulty proving the existence of discrimination. Moreover, it can take years for a victim of discrimination to follow through the slow process of agency investigations and discrimination lawsuits. Thus, many people who honestly believe that they were victims of racial discrimination never pursue claims simply because they cannot afford the time, money, and emotional upheaval involved in fighting a legal battle for several years.

Controversies Involving Antidiscrimination Law. When the U.S. Supreme Court, U.S. Congress, and state legislatures began to act against racial discrimination, the laws and legal decisions they produced attacked widespread, open practices of treating members of racial minority groups as second-class citizens. As the application of law gradually reduced obvious discrimination, new issues arose about how law might address subtle discriminatory practices or remedy the centuries of past discrimination that had operated to trap members of racial minority groups in poverty. Issues also arose concerning how far judges should go in ordering local governments and businesses to change their operations in order to expand opportunities for members of victimized racial groups.

During the 1960's and 1970's, courts moved beyond the Supreme Court's initial prohibition on racial segregation in the schools by ordering school systems to take active steps to undo the results of discrimination. When courts began to order schools to develop significant transportation programs (busing) to mix African American, Hispanic, and Asian American students with white students, many critics argued that court-ordered busing exceeded judges' proper authority to use law to stop discrimination. By the 1990's the composition of the Supreme Court had changed significantly so that the new justices made decisions that limited the authority of lower court judges to order remedies for past discrimination.

Similar controversies arose with respect to discrimination in employment, education, and public contracts. In order to remedy past discrimination, government agencies and universities developed policies granting preferential consideration to members of groups traditionally victimized by discrimination—racial minorities, women, and people with disabilities. While members of these groups did not automatically receive jobs or admission to universities, their group membership counted in their favor in deciding among competing candidates. Governments at all levels—federal, state, and local—developed laws and policies that reserved a portion of public funds spent on roads and other public projects for contracts with businesses owned by members of racial minority groups and women. While this preferential treatment—known as affirmative action—was intended to remedy the effects of past discrimination, critics argued that it constituted reverse discrimination and was in violation of the equal protection clause. During the 1980's and 1990's the new members of the U.S. Supreme Court gradually invalidated or placed significant restrictions on most of these affirmative action programs. As a result, some commentators argue that antidiscrimination laws merely prevent the most obvious kinds of racial discrimination

Average Lengths of Sentences Imposed on Criminal Offenders in Federal Courts in 1995

Average sentence in months for offenders convicted of:

Group	All Offenses	Violent Offenses	Drug Offenses
Whites	48.2	82.6	65.4
African American	85.4	111.2	108.9
Hispanics	50.3	93.4	66.7

Source: U.S. Department of Justice, Bureau of Justice Statistics, *Compendium of Federal Justice Statistics, 1995*, Washington, D.C.: U.S. Department of Justice, 1998.
Note: Statistics were not specifically reported for Native Americans, Asian Americans, and Pacific Islanders.

from occurring but do nothing to alter the established inequalities in society that developed as a result of widespread discriminatory laws during prior decades.

Race and Criminal Law. The equal protection clause forbids racial discrimination by police officers, prosecutors, judges, and corrections officials who work in the criminal justice system. Despite this formal ban on racial discrimination, there are frequent indications that racial discrimination remains a persistent problem in the criminal justice system.

A primary source of potential racial discrimination stems from the discretion possessed by officials to make decisions about what will happen to individuals who come into contact with the criminal justice system. Police officers use discretion to decide which cars to stop and which individuals to arrest. Prosecutors use discretion to decide which individuals to charge and what charges to pursue. Judges make discretionary decisions about sentences, and corrections officials make discretionary decisions about privileges and early release. If these officials use race as a factor in their decisions, they are effectively using the authority of law in order to engage in racial discrimination.

There is evidence that police officers in some places stop African American and Hispanic motorists much more frequently than they stop white motorists. Because many traffic stops are used as a justification to investigate whether drivers are transporting illegal drugs, it appears that racial stereotypes about drug dealers may affect some officers' decisions about whom to stop and search. As a result, many members of racial minority groups have complained about being stopped by the police for no reason, and members of Congress have proposed legislation to require police departments to keep records about the race of motorists who are stopped and arrested. Police discretion may affect other people if officers selectively investigate crimes or employ discrimination in decisions about which people will be arrested and which people will be released with only a warning.

Widespread Discrimination. The risk of racial discrimination exists at each stage of the criminal justice system. There are indications that prosecutors in some places may pursue drug and other cases more frequently and vigorously against members of minority groups. Similarly, there is evidence

Executions in the United States, 1930-1995

Year or Period	Total	White	Black
1930 to 1939	1,667	827	816
1940 to 1949	1,284	490	781
1950 to 1959	717	336	376
1960 to 1967	191	98	93
1968 to 1976	0	0	0
1977 to 1982	6	5	1
1983	5	4	1
1984	21	13	8
1985	18	11	7
1986	18	11	7
1987	25	13	12
1988	11	6	5
1989	16	8	8
1990	23	16	7
1991	14	7	7
1992	31	19	11
1993	38	23	14
1994	31	20	11
1995	56	33	22
All years	**4,172**	**1,940**	**2,187**

Source: U.S. Bureau of the Census, *Statistical Abstract of the United States: 1997.* 117th ed. Washington, D.C.: U.S. Government Printing Office, 1997.

Note: Excludes executions by military authorities. Figures in "Total" column include races other than white and black.

that some white judges may treat members of minority groups more harshly in sentencing. These factors may contribute to the overrepresentation of certain racial minority groups among people imprisoned in many corrections systems.

Another source of racial discrimination emanating from law stems from the design of laws by legislatures. For example, in response to public fears about a "crack epidemic," the U.S. Congress created especially severe punishments for people who sell or carry crack cocaine. Even though crack and powder cocaine are the same chemical substance, one must have one hundred times as much powder cocaine as crack cocaine to receive the same penalty. Crack cocaine is more prevalent among members of minority groups in urban areas while powder cocaine is more prevalent among whites and suburbanites. Thus, the punishments for cocaine crimes tend to fall most severely on members of racial minority groups.

Racial discrimination under the law may also occur when courts do not rigorously enforce the equal protection clause. For example, detailed statistical studies have shown that defendants in murder cases in Georgia were much more likely than other defendants to be sentenced to death if they were African American and their alleged victims were white. Despite this evidence of racial discrimination, the Supreme Court, by a narrow five-to-four vote, decided in *McCleskey v. Kemp* (1987) that statistics may not be used to show the existence of racial discrimination in a state's application of capital punishment.

In another example, the Supreme Court declared in *Batson v. Kentucky* (1986) that prosecutors cannot exclude potential jurors from criminal juries because of their race. However, the Court did not vigorously enforce this principle. When a prosecutor removed African Americans from a jury pool, the Supreme Court said such exclusions were permissible as long as the prosecutor gave nondiscriminatory reasons for doing so, even if the prosecutor's reasons were silly and implausible. Thus, when the Supreme Court permitted the prosecutor in *Purkett v. Elem* (1995) to remove African American jurors because they had curly hair, the nation's highest court effectively signaled to prosecutors that they may use racial discrimination in jury selection as long as they do not actually admit that they are discriminating.

Suggested Readings. A historical picture of U.S. law's support for racial discrimination prior to the mid-twentieth century is presented in Gunnar Myrdal's *An American Dilemma: The Negro Problem and Modern Democracy* (New York: Harper Brothers, 1944). The story of the transformation of law into a tool to combat discrimination is told in Richard Kluger's *Simple Justice* (New York: Random House, 1975). An overview of race and law is provided in Derrick Bell's *Race, Racism, and American Law* (3d ed. Boston: Little, Brown, 1992). Several books focus on the existence of racial discrimination in the criminal justice system. These include Michael Tonry's *Malign Neglect: Race, Crime, and Punishment in America* (New York: Oxford University Press, 1995), Samuel Walker, Cassia Spohn, and Miriam DeLeone's *The Color of Justice: Race, Ethnicity, and Crime in America* (Belmont, Calif.: Wadsworth, 1996), Coramae Richey Mann's *Unequal Justice: A Question of Color* (Bloomington, Ind.: Indiana University Press, 1988), and Randall Kennedy's *Race, Crime, and the Law* (New York: Pantheon, 1997). A book arguing that there is no racial discrimination in the criminal justice system is William Wilbanks's *The Myth of a Racist Criminal Justice System* (Monterey, Calif.: Brooks/Cole, 1987).

—Christopher E. Smith

See also Affirmative action; Civil rights and liberties; Constitution, U.S.; Criminal justice system; Discrimination; Employment discrimination; Equal protection of the law; Supreme Court, U.S.

Rape

The crime of unlawful sexual penetration of a person is the felony of rape.

The most common type of unlawful sexual penetration is that accomplished by force without the consent of the victim, although consensual penetration may also be unlawful when the victim is a minor. In the United States the definition, prosecution, and understanding—in both society and the legal system—of what rape is and how it occurs changed dramatically in the 1970's and 1980's.

Early View of Rape. Before 1970 rape was a crime reported infrequently and often prosecuted unsuccessfully. It was considered a crime of "passion" rather than violence, any report of which required public scrutiny of the victim's "virtue," under the sexist notion that a woman's prior consensual sexual relationships meant that she must have consented despite reporting that she had been raped. The law generally recognized only rape of persons of one sex (women) by persons of the other (men), and under the marital immunity provision, the law did not even recognize as criminal the rape of wives by their husbands. Police departments often collected little or no physical evidence from alleged rape victims and were untrained in the psychological consequences of sexual assault.

By the 1990's many of these practices had been changed by legislation and judicial decision. During the 1970's and 1980's most American jurisdictions restricted or ended the marital immunity rule, made their sexual assault laws "gender neutral" to apply to assaults by persons of either sex on persons of the same or the other sex, and reduced the admissibility of evidence concerning the prior sexual history of alleged rape victims. Courts also changed the meaning of the elements of "force" and "lack of consent," so that "force" could mean a victim's fear of force as well as physical force. Moreover, some courts interpreted "nonconsent" to mean the lack of affirmative consent (actually saying "yes") and explicitly saying "no." Most significantly, perhaps the women's movement altered the public consciousness of rape—through changed concepts of consent, sexual harassment, and sex roles. Notwithstanding the significant legal reforms of the period, systemic problems in the reporting, investigation, and prosecution of sexual offenses and in public attitudes toward rape persist.

Rape Law Before Reform. Eighteenth century English law defined rape as "the carnal knowledge of a woman forcibly and against her will," and until the 1970's most U.S. jurisdictions used a very similar definition. The law applied only to sexual intercourse as "carnal knowledge" and then only when it involved an adult woman. Penetration such as oral or anal sex and sex with minors were punished as other crimes. Force meant actual or threatened violence or physical compulsion—beyond any force inherent in intercourse itself—and usually included physical injury to the woman. Proof of force was difficult without physical injuries to the victim, and "lack of consent" generally was understood as requiring more than simply saying "no." Some jurisdictions required that women "resist to the utmost" to show that force had been used, while most required only reasonable resistance. Choosing to submit rather than suffer physical injury from fighting back, however, was sometimes held to be consent.

Consent—even if given—could be legally insufficient if obtained by fraud or from someone unable to meaningfully consent. A person pretending to be a doctor performing a medical procedure, for example, who actually had intercourse with a victim committed "rape by fraud." Mentally disabled persons or those under the influence of alcohol or other drugs could not validly consent. Children were always viewed as incapable of giving valid consent, so that even consensual sexual intercourse with a minor was rape.

Special rules governed proof of rape. In a case of forcible rape, the defendant could generally present evidence concerning the victim's prior sexual relationships. Jurors who disapproved of sexual relationships generally—or sexual relationships outside of marriage—were thus unsympathetic to unmarried rape victims. Victims were reluctant to report rapes, lest they be forced to disclose private information about their personal lives. Many U.S. jurisdictions also did not permit convictions for rape based only on the victim's testimony; additional proof—called "corroboration"—was required. Corroboration was not required for conviction of other violent felonies, such robbery or arson. Finally, judges in rape cases often instructed juries to be skeptical about rape charges, because it was claimed that such charges were easily made and, once made, difficult to defend against even if the accused person was innocent.

Apart from these rules for trial, rape of a wife by her husband was legally impossible; husbands could not be prosecuted for rape of their wives. This "marital immunity" rule persisted in most U.S. states until the 1980's and continues in some to treat rape of a spouse as a lesser crime than rape of a nonspouse. Several legal theories were offered to justify this rule, which reflected the legal system's reluctance to deal with activities in the home—similar to its traditional unresponsiveness to issues of domestic violence.

A Crime of Violence, Not Passion. Changed attitudes toward rape and sexual offenses in the 1970's and 1980's were principally the result of the women's movement and its efforts to secure for women greater authority over their own lives and greater equality between the sexes. One of the most basic areas of autonomy was that of personal freedom from assault, and feminists sought to increase this by changing the public awareness of choices made in private relationships. By challenging stereotypical beliefs about sexual interaction, they reshaped public attitudes concerning sex.

Many feminists believed that men use force and power to dominate women and keep them subordinate to men. This perspective allowed rape to then be seen more clearly as an act of violence by one person seeking to exercise power over another

Marital Rape Laws in the U.S. and Canada in 1985

- ☐ marital rape always a crime
- ▒ marital rape a crime only after separation or divorce
- ■ marital rape not a crime

rather than as an act of pleasure or love. Along with aspirations that sexual relationships could be based on equality came a view of women's reactions to sex—based on larger perceptions of inequality in their relationships with men—that challenged some of the underlying ideas in rape law. A requirement of physical resistance by the victim to show lack of consent, for example, was challenged by the notion that women feared sexual assaults even if none had been explicitly threatened.

In the 1980's both the terminology and basic meaning of the law of rape changed. The terminology of "rape" changed in three principal ways. First, it became gender neutral and was made applicable to unlawful sexual penetration between persons of either sex or of the same sex. Second, its scope was broadened to apply to any form of unlawful penetration of any part of the victim's body with any part of the offender's body or with any object. Rape itself was often renamed sexual assault or sexual criminal conduct. Unlawful sexual contact without penetration became the lesser included offense of sexual battery. Third, the marital immunity rule was eliminated in some states and restricted in many others. In 1978 two state legislatures removed the marital immunity rule from their laws, and a 1989 review of American rape law concluded that most states had limited the marital immunity rule, although many had preserved it in some form. In several states it still applied unless spouses had separated, while in others persons had to report sexual assaults by their spouses to qualify as rape victims. Finally, some states punished marital rape or spousal rape as a less serious crime than rape of nonspouses.

Apart from these changes in terminology, the meaning of the traditional elements of rape also changed. The concept of "force" was expanded in some jurisdictions to include not just physical force or threatened physical force but also the victim's honest and reasonable fear of such force. At least one jurisdiction defined "force" to mean only the force required to accomplish penetration. A few states expanded the term to include threats of nonphysical force, such as job loss, but most still required that force involve some physical danger or perceived threat of danger. In the late twentieth century a few states still even required resistance by the victim as evidence of force, although this made the criminal liability of the attacker dependent on the reactions of the victim. Many states no longer required the lack of consent, instead allowing defendants to raise it as a defense.

As under the prereform rape law, consent from minors, from persons unable to think clearly because of impairment caused by drugs, alcohol, or a mental disability, or consent obtained by fraud is not legally valid. Modern rape laws generally define these situations as different ways of committing rape or, in some cases, as different offenses. While all jurisdictions hold that unmarried children cannot give consent to engage in sex, the offense of unlawful sexual penetration without force of older teenagers, those who are usually seventeen or eighteen years old, is generally defined as a less serious offense called statutory rape. Any sexual penetration by an adult, with or without force, of an unmarried minor under the age of sixteen is generally considered rape. Similarly, most jurisdictions punish as rape sexual penetration accomplished by drugging or by otherwise preventing a victim from not consenting, whether force is used or not.

Modern Rape Prosecution. The rules governing how a rape charge is proven changed significantly in the 1980's and 1990's. Much of this change was designed to focus trials into cases against accused rapists rather than about the alleged victims. Three important changes occurred during this period. First, the use of evidence concerning the prior sexual conduct of the victim was significantly reduced. The defense strategy of presenting the victim as an immoral or promiscuous woman, or simply a woman who had engaged in prior consensual sexual relationships, was made more difficult through the adoption in most U.S. jurisdictions of rape shield laws. These laws kept out of rape trials most evidence concerning a victim's prior sexual relationships, except evidence concerning a relationship with the defendant or physical evidence. Second, the requirement that proof of a rape be corroborated by evidence other than the victim's testimony has been eliminated or dramatically reduced in most jurisdictions. Third, virtually all states that permitted the use of the cautionary jury instruction that rape is a charge easily made and hard to disprove have ceased to do so, concluding that persons who report that they were raped are as trustworthy as those who report they have been the victims of other crimes.

The effects of these changes on the incidence of rape are unclear. U.S. Justice Department data from police departments around the United States show that the rate of rape between 1970 and 1990 more than doubled—from 18.7 to 41.2 per 100,000 inhabitants. Some of this increase was due to improved reporting of sexual offenses. The years 1990 to 1996 reflected a 10 percent decline in the rate of rape during this period to 36.1 per 100,000 inhabitants, which was roughly the 1980 level.

Most rapes occur between persons who know each other. U.S. Department of Justice figures from 1994 indicate that 69.1 percent of rapes and attempted rapes in the U.S. involve nonstrangers. These data also indicate that nearly two-thirds of all rapes and sexual assaults committed by offenders who know their victims are committed by persons who are either well-known by or related to their victims. The rest of rapes and sexual assaults committed by nonstrangers are committed by casual acquaintances. These data suggest that efforts to affect the way persons interact with those they know may have a much greater impact on the level of rape than efforts to protect persons against attacks by strangers.

Suggested Readings. Annual statistical information on the total number of sexual offenses and the characteristics of victims and offenders is available in the U.S. Department of Justice publication *Sourcebook of Criminal Justice Statistics* (Washington, D.C.: Bureau of Justice Statistics, updated annually). Among the most important books in reshaping public attitudes toward rape is Susan Brownmiller's *Against Our Will: Men, Women, and Rape* (New York: Simon and Schuster, 1975). The inadequacies of the legal system's response to sexual assault and the ways in which it can increase the harm caused by rape are explored in Susan Estrich's *Real Rape* (Cambridge, Mass.: Harvard University Press, 1987). The problem of acquaintance rape is treated in *Dating Violence: Young Women in Danger*, edited by Barrie Levy (Seattle, Wash.: Seal Press, 1998). A review of the effects of rape reform is presented in Stephen Schulhofer's "Unwanted Sex," *Atlantic Monthly* (October, 1998).

—*David M. Siegel*

See also Felony; Lesser included offense; Sexual battery; Sexual harassment.

Real estate law

Real estate law is concerned with all aspects of buying, selling, and renting real estate, including brokerage, appraisal, real estate consulting, and management.

The buying, selling, and management of real property is complex and is, therefore, governed by sets of laws set up within states to regulate realty companies and realtors. Realty companies serve four major functions. They serve as brokers for those who wish to buy or sell property. They serve as appraisers for those who require valuations of their property. They serve as consultants to prospective buyers and sellers, advising them on pricing, market trends, location, and other pertinent matters. Finally, they may serve as managers of rental properties, acting as owners' agents.

Major Functions of Realty Companies

- Brokerage—assisting people in the buying and selling of real property
- Appraisal—establishing the fair value of real property
- Consultation—informing potential buyers and sellers of market conditions
- Management—empowering the realty company to act as the owner's agent in the day-to-day management of real prop-

---

Differences Between Real and Personal Property. Real property is generally construed as consisting of land and its appurtenances, such as the permanent buildings upon it and such items as built-in swimming pools, roads, and other permanent, nonportable improvements. Real property is different from personal property in that it is fixed in a particular location, whereas personal property is usually portable.

Real property, fixed in one place, will presumably remain there permanently. A fountain at the entrance of a dwelling that is used for a special event such as a party or a reception, after which it is removed, is personal property. A fountain that is fixed permanently to the land outside the house becomes part of the real property.

The addition of a permanent fountain or a built-in swimming pool is considered an improvement to the real property because such an improvement is permanent and is not portable. Such an addition will likely result in increased real estate taxes to reflect the amount that it adds to the value of the property but will not result in increased personal property taxes.

The Government and Real Estate. In the United States, as in most other countries, the federal government is the largest owner of property. Its holdings consist of such properties as national parks, military bases, federal buildings, and federal prisons. These vast real estate holdings, except for those under the control of the armed services, are administered by the General Services Administration, which has thousands of employees.

State, county, and local governments also own

considerable real estate, including state, county, and municipal parks, government buildings, schools, prisons, hospitals, and mental institutions. Real estate owned by government agencies at all levels is, like property owned by bona fide religious groups, exempt from property taxes.

State and local governments also exercise considerable control over privately owned property. They are authorized by law to establish building codes, to enforce zoning regulations, and, through community planning, to decide the location of parks, the placement of roads, and the laying of sewer and utility lines.

Governments can also appropriate property for their own use through the right of eminent or public domain. This right permits governments, after due process, to seize property that stands in the way of highway construction, community expansion, or other civic projects. Private property owners in such cases are offered cash settlements for their property. If, after negotiation, they choose not to accept such offers, legal action is brought against them in court, and they may be forced to sell their property at what the court considers fair market value. Often sentiment makes owners reluctant to sell, but if the courts mandate the sale, they must sell. They face forcible eviction if they have not voluntarily vacated the property in question by a stipulated date.

Private property owners who die without leaving wills or trusts to assure the preferred distribution of real property they own may have their property taken by the state following their deaths under a legal procedure called escheat. The government agencies to which such property reverts through escheat must make a legitimate effort to find rightful heirs to the property. If no such heirs are found after a diligent search, however, the property eventually is deeded to the government in whose jurisdiction it lies.

Local governments receive the bulk of their income from real estate taxes. If such taxes are not paid when due, notification of nonpayment is sent to the property owner. If the outstanding taxes remain unpaid, a lien may be placed upon the property on which the taxes are owed. Eventually the property in question can be sold and the outstanding taxes and penalties paid out of the proceeds derived from the sale. Any surplus is returned to the delinquent property owner.

Restrictive Covenants and Easements. Many property deeds contain restrictive covenants, some of which have been ruled unconstitutional and overturned. This is particularly true of previously common restrictions on the transfer of property to buyers of specific nationalities or races.

Common restrictive covenants currently in effect state that the owner of a property does not own the mineral rights to that property. Such covenants may stipulate that no lots under a certain size may be built upon or that no dwelling may occupy more than a given percentage of the land mass on which it stands. Restrictive covenants may specify the uses to which private property may be put, preventing owners from subdividing the property they own or from establishing business enterprises on it if it lies in residential areas.

Often when new electric, water, or telephone service is being installed, the conduits for this service must be laid over private property. In such cases, the company installing the new equipment may request an easement from the property owner on whose land the cable or conduit is to be installed.

Generally owners have little recourse but to grant a legitimate easement that has been requested through proper channels and in accordance with established legal procedures. They have the right

---

Local Government Powers

- Establishing zoning regulations
- Issuing or withholding building permits
- Condemning private property that is not up to code
- Seizing or condemning private property under the law of eminent domain
- Directing private property owners to grant easements
- Taxing real property
- Placing liens on private property whose taxes are in arrears
- Selling private property on which taxes are delinquent
- Seizing private property under the escheat procedure

to voice their objections in court, where they are likely to be denied redress. They may receive remuneration for granting easements, receiving either a lump sum payment or an annual payment for the use of their property.

Brokerage Functions of Realtors. Realtors must be licensed by the state or states within which they work. Perhaps the most common function of realtors is that of helping their clients to buy or sell real property. State laws vary. In some states, realtors are not permitted to make value judgments about the properties they show. They can provide pertinent information about such matters as the kinds of schools, transportation facilities, churches, and shopping facilities within a reasonable radius of the properties, but they often are restrained by law from commenting on whether a property is fairly priced or not.

In some states realtors may provide information about such matters as average utility expenses for a given property, but in some states such information is not publicly accessible. In most jurisdictions realtors can obtain information about the sale prices of other real estate in a specific area, although some states make it difficult to obtain such information, even though it is a matter of public record.

Once a client has decided to buy or make an offer on a specific property, the realtor receives earnest money from the prospective buyer and draws up a contract to purchase, called a binder, that the seller can accept, reject, or modify. After the seller accepts the binder, a final contract is drawn up for signing by buyers and sellers before a notary public. This contract specifies the selling price, the amount of the down payment if any, the closing date, the estimated closing costs, the amount of prorated taxes and, where appropriate, association fees and other pertinent contingencies.

The most common contingency demands that sellers deliver a clear, unencumbered title to the property. Another common contingency may make final settlement dependent on the buyers' selling other property prior to closing. This contingency is generally employed by buyers who occupy a house that they currently have on the market, making them unable or unwilling to commit themselves to the purchase of additional property until they are assured of selling the property they currently own. Another frequent contingency states

---

Major Functions of Real Estate Brokers

- Bringing buyers and sellers together
- Showing available properties to prospective buyers
- Carrying offers from buyers to sellers
- Accepting earnest money
- Drawing up sales contracts for buyers and sellers
- Estimating closing costs
- Establishing closing dates
- Bringing prospective buyers and lenders together
- Arranging for title searches
- Conducting walk-throughs of property before closing
- Attending at closing to make sure that all relevant materials are in order

---

that the closing will be dependent on the ability of the buyers to obtain financing for the purchase they are contemplating. If they cannot qualify for a loan, the seller may be willing to help them with their financing in order to complete the sale.

All realty contracts stipulate that appliances, electrical systems, plumbing, and other accoutrements of the property to be sold must be in working order or that any impediments to their functioning must be revealed in a disclosure statement. If the purchase of a property requires financing, the realtor must help the buyers to obtain an appraisal and must arrange for a title search to verify that the property is unencumbered. Most mortgage companies require that buyers purchase title insurance to assure that any title problems that arise following the sale will be covered by the insurer.

Most realtors receive a commission of between 5 and 7 percent of the purchase price of a residential or commercial property, although in some states commissions are negotiable. Realtors often must share their commissions with the sellers' realtor and usually have to assign part of their commissions to any realty corporation by whom they are employed. Realtors usually receive higher commissions, generally 10 percent of the purchase price, for selling undeveloped land than they receive for selling residential or commercial property. It is customary for commissions to be paid by the sellers of real property.

Appraising Real Property. Licensed real estate appraisers are usually real estate brokers whose experience is sufficient to enable them to make accurate estimates of the value of real property in their areas. If buyers wish to finance real property, they are mandated by law to provide a legitimate appraisal of the property in question. The amount of their loan will be based on that appraisal and is commonly fixed at 90 percent of the appraised valuation or of the purchase price, whichever is less.

Home owners who wish to refinance their mortgages are also required to have the property appraised in order to validate the amount that will be lent on the property, which is used as collateral for the loan. Appraisers in such situations must take into account any increase or decrease in the value of comparable properties. Appraisers are also employed when municipalities seek to gain title to real property under the right of eminent domain or escheat.

Home owners whose real estate taxes seem inordinately high may protest such taxes with an eye toward reducing the amount the taxing agency has given as fair valuation. A simple protest may lead to a reduction in the assessed valuation. In some cases, however, an appraisal will be required to obtain the reduction the home owner seeks.

Real estate appraisers are also employed regularly to determine the value of real property for purposes of inheritance. For example, if the estate of a deceased person contains a house and its surrounding land and the decedent wills a percentage of the property to each of several heirs, one of those heirs may wish to receive the decedent's real property as part of the inheritance. In such cases, an appraiser, under the law, must be employed to determine the fair market value of the property. Such an appraiser might also be employed to determine the fair market value so that estate taxes can be filed accurately.

Consultants and Management. People who buy property for purposes of investment often hire seasoned realtors to act as consultants before they make their investments. Such consultants provide their clients with information about demographic trends in the areas in which they are considering investing. They discuss population growth patterns, trends in community development, taxation trends in given areas, proposed plans for extending public transportation to certain areas, and other information that might affect the value of real estate in specific locales. Such consultants do not necessarily act as brokers. In some jurisdictions, it is considered a conflict of interest for them to do so. Their major function is to provide prospective investors with information that will help them decide where and how to invest their money. Such consultants also ferret out information about financing opportunities for various types of real property. They sometimes arrange for prospective buyers to meet with potential lenders.

Many investors put their money into rental property that they do not wish to manage themselves. Such investors often employ real estate managers to handle the day-to-day details of renting and maintaining their properties. Management fees usually run between 6 and 10 percent of the annual income derived from the rentals in question.

Investors who own many properties usually pay smaller management fees than those who own just one or two properties. Small investors may find it difficult to hire property managers, most of whom prefer handling eight or ten properties owned by a single investor than one or two. Investors who

---

Guidelines That Lenders Consider

- Borrowers' credit history is satisfactory
- The full purchase price of a residence should not exceed three times the purchaser's gross annual income
- Combined family savings at the time of purchase should be at least 20 percent of the purchase price
- Maintenance costs, including mortgage payments, utilities, insurance, and upkeep, should not exceed 25 percent of take-home income
- Down payments should be at least 10 percent of the purchase price

employ realtors to manage their properties often conceal their identities from the people who rent these properties, allowing all dealings to be handled by the management team, which is legally empowered to act for the investor in all matters specified in the management contract.

Most real estate managers have close contact with maintenance people who can make repairs to rental properties as they are needed. In such cases the property owner is responsible for the cost of such repairs but is relieved of the necessity of finding people to do the work.

Financing the Purchase of Real Property. Both developed and undeveloped real property, because it is fixed in a given location, is considered excellent collateral for loans. Most residential and commercial property in the United States is mortgaged. Mortgages on residences are given for various terms, but twenty- and thirty-year mortgages are the most common ones for home purchasers.

Lending institutions specify guidelines for borrowers. Under the terms of a mortgage, home buyers make down payments and agree to repay the remaining balance of the mortgage over a given period of time, usually making anywhere from 240 to 360 payments over the period of the loan. Throughout this period, the lender holds the deed to the property and, if payments are not made, may seize the property after various legal procedures aimed at repayment have been employed.

Down payments are usually fixed at 10 percent of the purchase price, although some programs exist that permit smaller down payments. Monthly mortgage payments for fixed rate mortgages are equal throughout the term of the loan. Adjustable rate mortgages also exist. The initial payments for such mortgages are smaller than those for fixed rate mortgages, but they can be increased throughout the life of the loan. All increases are pegged to the rate of inflation and to the prime rate set periodically by the Federal Reserve Bank.

Suggested Readings. A good starting point for learning about real estate law is William V. Pivar's *Real Estate Ethics* (Chicago: Dearborn Financial Publishing, 1990), which discusses both the legal and ethical aspects of real estate. For an overview of real estate law, readers will find valuable information in Marianne M. Jennings's *Real Estate Law* (3d ed. Boston: PWS Kent, 1992) and in Robert Kratovil and Raymond J. Werner's *Real Estate Law* (10th ed. Englewood Cliffs, N.J.: Prentice-Hall, 1992), both of which are accurate and up to date. For a realistic view of the legal constraints realtors have to take into consideration, Ed Willer's *Real Estate Ready Exam Book* (Raleigh, N.C.: Willer, 1990), which is essentially a cram book, offers valuable specific information. Stuart Saft's *The Real Estate Investor's Survival Guide* (New York: John Wiley and Sons, 1992) is directed at general readers and provides sound information about investing in real estate and the legal aspects of such investment.

—R. Baird Shuman

See also Deed; Earnest money; Eminent domain; Escrow; Foreclosure; Home buying; Home ownership; Home selling; Lien; Mortgages; Property taxes; Real estate listing agreements; Title.

Real estate listing agreements

Contracts between home owners and real estate agents, real estate listing agreements specify binding terms for the sale of property.

A real estate listing agreement is a legally binding contract by which a property owner employs a licensed real estate broker to procure a buyer for a property. The relationship between the broker and the seller is known as an "agency relationship": The broker acts as an agent on behalf of the seller for the purpose of finding a buyer for the property. The agent's duties toward the client include loyalty, diligence, disclosure, and reasonable care.

A real estate listing agreement has several elements. The agreement identifies the owner and the agent; it clearly states the agent's compensation, either as a percentage of the final sales price or a flat fee; and it specifies whether the compensation will be paid in advance or at the time the house sells. It includes a legal description of the property to be sold and states the duration of the contract, typically between thirty days and six months. It includes the price at which the house is being listed, which is generally only a negotiating basis to establish the final price, and spells out any specific terms that the seller requires.

A seller should carefully review all the terms of the agreement. For example, if an agent brings a qualified buyer who is willing to pay the full price listed and meets all the terms of the contract, the seller is required to pay the agent's commission even if the seller refuses the offer. Likewise, if the seller finds a buyer for the home independent of the agent during the period of the listing, the agent is still entitled to the commission. Finally, if the agent shows the property to a potential buyer who buys the house within a specified period after the listing expires, the agent still collects the full commission.

Listing agreements can be of several types. In a multiple listing agreement, any broker who belongs to the multiple listing service can sell the home, and the listing and selling agents share the commission. If the listing agreement calls for a flat fee to the listing agent and another agent procures the buyer, the seller is required to pay the buyer's agent an additional fee. An exclusive right to sell is one in which only the listing agent may sell the house. An open listing is one in which the seller pays a commission to any agent who brings a buyer; if the seller finds a buyer, there is no commission. In net listing arrangements, which are illegal in most states, the seller sets the price he or she wants to realize from the sale and, if the actual selling price is higher, pays the agent a commission based on the difference between the listing price and the selling price.   —*Irene Struthers Rush*

See also Home buying; Home selling; Real estate law; Real property.

Real property

Special procedures are required when land and other rights and objects associated with land use or ownership are transferred from one individual to another.

Real property includes buildings and the land on which they stand. (James L. Shaffer)

Real property, also known as real estate or realty, consists of land and all physical objects erected upon it, growing on it, or affixed to it. Besides the land itself, real property often consists of buildings and fixtures. It may also include items such as crops or trees. Real property may also include items other than physical objects, such as the right to collect profits from the use of the land.

Ownership of real property can only be transferred from one owner to another through a special document known as a deed. A deed is only valid if it is signed by the original owner of the land, known as the grantor, in front of witnesses. The grantor must sign the deed voluntarily and have the mental capacity to understand the consequences of signing it. The deed must then be delivered to the new owner, known as the grantee, who must accept the deed voluntarily. A copy of the deed must then be kept on file in public records.

Use of real property for a limited time in exchange for payments known as rent is transferred from the owner, known as the landlord, to the user, known as the tenant, through arrangements known as rental agreements.

—*Rose Secrest*

See also Deed; Property types; Real estate law; Rental agreements.

Reasonable doubt

Uncertainty that prevents a guilty finding in a criminal trial is known as reasonable doubt.

The standard of proof in criminal cases is "beyond a reasonable doubt." It is the highest level of proof demanded in U.S. courts. A reasonable doubt is generally defined as that based on reason arising from evidence or lack of evidence. For most of U.S. history jurors have been told to equate guilt beyond a reasonable doubt with "moral certainty." In the 1994 case of *Sandoval v. California* the U.S. Supreme Court ruled that such language may be too vague and may tend to confuse juries. It suggested the following definition instead: "It is not a mere possible doubt; because everything relating to human affairs, and depending on moral evidence, is open to some possible or imaginary doubt. It is that state of the case which, after the entire comparison and consideration of all the evidence, leaves the minds of the jurors in that condition that they cannot say they feel an abiding conviction, to a moral certainty, of the truth of the charge."

This standard is much higher than a "preponderance of the evidence," which is used in civil cases. A preponderance of the evidence means that it is more likely than not that the accused is liable. The reasonable doubt standard, along with the presumption of innocence, places the burden of proof heavily on the prosecution, thus serving to protect the rights of the accused.

—*Raymond Frey*

See also Burden of proof; Juries; Jury nullification; Verdict.

Reckless endangerment

Dangerous action recklessly or knowingly undertaken without regard for safety of others is called reckless endangerment.

For conduct to be "reckless," it must indicate disregard for or indifference to consequences under circumstances involving danger to life or safety to others, even though no harm was consciously intended. Most states or jurisdictions have, by statute, defined reckless endangerment as an act or conduct creating a substantial risk of serious injury or death to another individual. The crime of reckless endangerment does not encompass only those situations in which the act is directed at a specific individual. All that is necessary is the creation of a certain degree of risk to another person, regardless of whether the act is directed at that person or not. Reckless conduct can be a lesser included offense of assault and attempted murder.

Two categories of reckless endangerment exist in most jurisdictions: felony and misdemeanor. Misdemeanor reckless endangerment is statutorily defined as "reckless conduct that places another in imminent danger of serious injury." Felony reckless endangerment is that in which the reckless conduct creates a grave risk of death. In Texas, for example, recklessness and a grave risk of death are statutorily presumed if a person knowingly points a firearm at or in the direction of another, whether or not the person believes that the firearm is loaded. Most jurisdictions, however, use general definitions of felony and misdemeanor reckless endangerment and apply them accordingly.

—Dana P. McDermott

See also Assault and battery; Felony; Homicide; Jurisdiction; Lesser included offense; Misdemeanor.

Rehabilitative support

When one spouse needs financial support from the other to become self-supporting after a divorce, he or she may be entitled to rehabilitative support.

Rehabilitative support, or alimony, is a type of financial support paid by one spouse to the other upon the couple's divorce. It is paid for a period of time sufficient to allow the recipient to acquire additional skills or education after the divorce so that he or she is capable of earning higher income in the future.

Rehabilitative support is generally paid in cases in which one spouse has sacrificed his or her earning ability in order to assume more family responsibilities or to allow the other spouse to earn greater income. For instance, when one of the spouses has quit a job in order to take care of the family's children, that spouse may be entitled to rehabilitative alimony should the couple divorce. This is especially so if that spouse has been out of the labor market for a significant period of time and has lost earning capacity.

The amount of rehabilitative support depends upon the parties' needs and abilities during the rehabilitation period. The duration of payments depends on how long it may reasonably take the recipient to improve his or her skills. Rehabilitative alimony is usually paid for a period of one to five years but may be paid for longer periods after a longer marriage or when the recipient is still caring for young children. It is also often coupled with permanent alimony in longer marriages.

—Bernard T. Neuner

See also Age and the law; Alimony and maintenance; Retirement planning.

Release

The settling or giving up of a claim, a cause of action, or a right to be enforced is known as release.

A release is an abandonment of a claim generally in the form of a written settlement agreement. A release means that a party gives up rights. In tort litigation, which involves civil wrongs done by one party against another, more than 95 percent of cases settle prior to a final verdict. The settlement agreement contains a release of a tort cause of action.

Releases of claims exist in other fields of the law as well. For example, a party may agree to release the other party from a contractual duty. A creditor may release a debtor from a debt owed. A guarantor of a promissory note may be released or discharged from the note. A promissory note may be renegotiated. In the field of real property, a quitclaim deed is regarded as a release deed. In the field of bankruptcy, property may be released from the bankruptcy estate for equitable or statutory reasons.

—Michael L. Rustad

See also Consent decree; Quitclaim deed; Real property; Torts.

Religious institutions

Although the U.S. Constitution guarantees the separation of church and state, the business of government and religious institutions nevertheless intersect at numerous points.

The First Amendment to the U.S. Constitution states that "Congress shall make no law respecting an establishment of religion, or prohibiting the free exercise thereof." Not many years after this amendment was ratified, Thomas Jefferson, the third president of the United States, referred to it as erecting a "wall of separation" between church and state. The phrase has since become an important metaphor for interpreting the First Amendment, relied upon regularly by justices of the Supreme Court, politicians, and legal scholars. However, in a practical sense religious institutions and the people who join them find that their activities encounter federal, state, and local laws routinely. These law sometimes burden and sometimes benefit the activities of religious institutions. From federal and state tax laws to local zoning regulations and from laws governing land ownership to those regulating religious displays on public property, government, through its laws, frequently limits how religious institutions may participate in the larger fabric of American society. At the same time, religious institutions sometimes benefit from laws, such as those granting them exemptions from various taxes and those allowing them to receive certain public benefits.

How Religious Institutions Benefit Under the Law. Even though religious rights are said to extend primarily to individuals, it has long been recognized that such individuals associate together in groups and that these group associations, to a certain extent, are a legitimate exercise of individual rights. Thus, religious organizations do derive certain limited benefits under the law. The most obvious and highly prized of these benefits is that religious organizations are normally exempt from corporate income taxes, sales taxes, and most property taxes. These exemptions are extended to various particular forms of religious organizations: churches, denominational headquarters, religious schools, camp and conference centers, church-related seminaries, monasteries and convents, storefront operations, and homeless shelters. In *Walz v. Tax Commission* (1970), the U.S. Supreme Court held that these kinds of tax exemptions received by religious institutions do not offend the establishment clause so long as other charitable and educational institutions receive similar exemptions. When the law singles out religious institutions for favorable treatment, however, the Court has been more inclined to find an establishment clause violation. For example, in *Texas Monthly v. Bullock* (1989) the Court found unconstitutional a sales tax exemption applied only to religious periodicals.

Tax exemption laws are largely applied on a case-by-case basis; many organizations that claim to be religious either never gain or sometimes lose such exemptions. Generally, the burden of proof is placed on the organization, which must prove to an often skeptical court that its activities fit the

Children and teachers at a religious school. Despite the separation of church and state guaranteed by the U.S. Constitution's First Amendment, government and religious institutions nevertheless intersect in numerous ways. (James L. Shaffer)

prescribed guidelines. As a consequence, particular organizations claiming tax-exempt status may be denied that status, even though other organizations pursuing similar activities are granted it. One notable example of this is the exemption of private residential property: Parsonages, manses, rectories, and residential buildings used for religious instruction are normally granted exemptions from property taxes as long as they are owned by a church or other recognized religious organization. On the other hand, residences that are privately owned and used primarily as family dwellings are usually not exempt, even though such activities as religious worship, instruction, or other religious activity may take place within them. Tax courts have regularly denied exemptions to families who claim that their houses are churches on the grounds that the real motive is the avoidance of paying taxes. This has meant that legitimate clergy who own their own homes have normally also been subject to property taxes.

Tax exemptions granted to religious organizations usually do not extend to their workers. Clergy, for example, are subject to personal income and Social Security taxes and are often designated as "self-employed" for tax purposes, even though they work within religious organizations that are themselves tax exempt. Churches are required to withhold federal income and Social Security taxes, state income taxes, and applicable municipal taxes from the salaries of their nonclergy employees in the same way that secular nonprofit and charitable organizations are required to do so.

Religious institutions sometimes receive benefits under the law in the form of a share of generally available public benefits, although the extent to which public benefits may be funneled to religious institutions has been a hotly contested issue under the establishment clause. The burglaries of religious institutions may be investigated by the police and the fires that start in the buildings of religious institutions may be extinguished by public fire departments. In addition, religious institutions may generally gain access to public facilities on terms equal to the access granted to other members of the public. Governments generally may not deny such access on the grounds that it would amount to a breach of the wall of separation between church and state. Nevertheless, current precedents of the U.S. Supreme Court still recognize some limits to the intersection of public benefits and religious institutions. In particular, direct financial aid to a church, synagogue, or other religious institution would almost certainly violate the establishment clause under these precedents.

How Religious Institutions Are Limited by Law. The encounters between religious institutions and the law are not always harmonious. The First Amendment's free exercise clause protects religious institutions from being specifically targeted by government for unfavorable treatment. Nevertheless, in a wide variety of circumstances, laws of general applicability may conflict with the beliefs and practices of religious institutions, and in most cases, religious institutions have been the losers in these conflicts.

The earliest important conflict between religious practice and law to reach the U.S. Supreme Court was *Reynolds v. United States* (1879), in which a member of the Mormon faith (Church of Jesus Christ of Latter-day Saints) was convicted of polygamy, even though he claimed that this practice represented a doctrine of his church. The Supreme Court upheld his conviction, and the Mormon Church was forced to give up its practice of polygamy before the territory of Utah, where the majority of Mormons lived, could finally be granted statehood. Since that time, religious organizations have had limits placed on their activities in a number of ways: Religious buildings must comply with all local building codes and fire safety laws; churches are not normally exempt from local zoning regulations; religious colleges receiving federal and state funding for financial aid are subject to all laws pertaining to discrimination and accessibility for people with disabilities; and, depending on the particular jurisdiction, clergy may not be allowed to claim that their conversations with church members are confidential and therefore privileged.

A relatively recent form of limitation has arisen in cases in which religious and governmental organizations claim an equal interest. In such cases, the courts have decreed that religious organizations have no right to hinder governmental agencies in the normal exercise of their functions. Thus, in *Lyng v. Northwest Indian Cemetery Protective Association* (1988), a Native American tribe was not allowed to prevent construction of a federal highway adjacent to a portion of its property, even though the tribe claimed that the land was "sacred" and

> ### The Establishment Clause and Benefits Enjoyed by Religious Institutions
>
> In *Walz v. Tax Commission* (1970) the U.S. Supreme Court held that corporate income tax, sales tax, and property tax exemptions enjoyed by religious institutions do not offend the establishment clause of the First Amendment to the U.S. Constitution as long as other charitable and educational institutions receive similar exemptions. When the law singles out religious institutions for favorable treatment, however, the Court has been more inclined to find an establishment clause violation. For example, in *Texas Monthly v. Bullock* (1989) the Court found unconstitutional a sales tax exemption applied only to religious periodicals.
>
> Religious institutions sometimes receive benefits under the law in the form of a share of generally available public benefits, although the extent to which public benefits may be funneled to religious institutions has been a hotly contested issue under the establishment clause. The burglaries of religious institutions may be investigated by the police, and the fires that start in the buildings of religious institutions may be extinguished by public fire departments. In addition, religious institutions may generally gain access to public facilities on terms equal to the access granted to other members of the public. Governments generally may not deny such access on the grounds that it would amount to a breach of the wall of separation between church and state. Nevertheless, modern U.S. Supreme Court precedents still recognize some limits to the intersection of public benefits and religious institutions. In particular, direct financial aid to a church, synagogue, or other religious institution would almost certainly violate the establishment clause under these precedents.

used exclusively for religious purposes. In the mid-1980's several churches were denied the status of "sanctuaries" by the Immigration and Naturalization Service (INS) and their leaders were arrested for harboring refugees from Latin America, whom the agency claimed had entered the country illegally.

Clashes Between Religious Institutions and the Law. The history of relations between particular religious groups and governments has often been marked by tension, with religious organizations claiming that the concept of religious freedom has become more theoretical than actual. At the heart of this tension is the law's continued distinction between religious beliefs and religious practice, which most religious groups claim is both arbitrary and false. Also central to this tension is government's use of the establishment clause of the First Amendment, which religious organizations claim advances social secularism at the cost of religious liberty. Issues such as school prayer, the presence of religious groups on public school grounds, religious displays on public property, political lobbying by religious groups, and the use of public school teachers in private religious schools for the purpose of remedial instruction have all been examples of this continuing tension.

A particularly striking example of this tension has been the law's treatment of particular "fringe" groups whose claims to be religious have been denied. The Church of Scientology, established in 1950, fought since 1967 to regain its tax-exempt status as a religion that was revoked by a federal tax court on the grounds that its activities were more commercial than religious. The case was not resolved until 1993, when the original decision was reversed and the church regained its tax-exempt status, thereby opening the door for other such groups to press their own claims as religious organizations.

One outcome of the clash between religious institutions and the law was the passage in 1993 of the Religious Freedom Restoration Act (RFRA). This act was adopted by the U.S. Congress in part after the Supreme Court had upheld the dismissal on drug-related charges of two Oregon state employees who claimed that their use of a hallucinogenic drug was part of a religious ritual (*Employment Division, Department of Human Resources v. Smith*, 1990). Passage of the RFRA was urged by scores of churches and other religious organizations, which claimed that the law interfered too much in purely religious matters and sought to restore what they believed to be the original intent of the First

Amendment's religion clauses. But the RFRA was itself struck down by the Supreme Court in the 1997 case of *Bourne v. Flores*, which stated that Congress had overstepped its authority in attempting to circumvent the Court's previous decision. The end result is that the tension between religious institutions and the law remains very much alive.

Suggested Readings. General treatments of how the law affects religious institutions can be found in Richard Hammar's *Pastor, Church, and Law* (Springfield, Mo.: Gospel Publishing House, 1983) and in Luis Lugo's *Religion, Public Life, and the American Polity* (Knoxville: University of Tennessee, 1994). More specific treatments of the problem of the separation of church and state may be found in Thomas Curry's *The First Freedoms: Church and State in America to the Passage of the First Amendment* (New York: Oxford University Press, 1986), in Leon- ard Levy's *The Establishment Clause: Religion and the First Amendment* (2d ed. Chapel Hill: University of North Carolina Press, 1994), and in Marvin Frankel's *Faith and Freedom: Religious Liberty in America* (New York: Hill and Wang, 1994). Summaries of Supreme Court decisions in cases involving religion can be found in *Religious Liberty and the Supreme Court: Cases That Define the Debate over Church and State*, edited by Terry Eastland (Washington, D.C.: Ethics and Public Policy Center, 1993).

—*Robert C. Davis*

See also Constitution, U.S.; Freedom of religion; Tax law.

Rent control

Rent-control laws permit the establishment of maximum rents and the regulation of evictions in dozens of U.S. municipalities.

Rent control is the government regulation of rental prices of residential housing. The first rent controls in the United States froze rents and restricted evictions during the housing emergency caused by the influx of workers into the defense industries during World War II. With the return to post-War normalcy, such rigid caps were abolished everywhere but New York City, where about seventy thousand rent-controlled apartments remained.

The second generation of rent controls was enacted by more than one hundred U.S. communities during the 1970's and early 1980's. Rent-control laws are in effect in parts of California, Connecticut, Maryland, New Jersey, New York, and the District of Columbia. In controlled municipalities rent stabilization boards determine maximum rents, allowing landlords to pass on to renters some or all of the higher costs resulting from inflation, maintenance, capital improvements, rising utility bills, and tax increases. Most ordinances allow some degree of "vacancy decontrol," permitting rents to be raised significantly when renters move out of their apartments. Evictions are generally curtailed in jurisdictions in which rent control is in force, and the conversion of apartments to other uses, such as condominiums or warehouses, is forbidden in order to maintain rental housing stock. New housing is generally exempted from controls to encourage the expansion of housing construction.

Statutes vary from jurisdiction to jurisdiction as to whether tenants may be evicted in order to provide housing for owners' immediate families or whether rent increases may be limited if rent-control boards determine that owners are making excessive improvements ("gold-plating") in order to gentrify their properties. In Berkeley, California, for example, a base rent has been established for each apartment. The Rent Stabilization Board adjusts this base through annual general adjustments designed to cover citywide increases in maintenance costs and to compensate for inflation. Both tenants and rental property owners may petition for individual adjustments of units' rent ceiling because of special circumstances, such as expensive improvements or health code violations. Evictions may be carried out only if they meet stringent criteria, and illegally evicted tenants may sue landlords for $750 or for three times the amount of actual damages. Tenants may be evicted if their units are to be occupied by immediate family members of owners whose share in their properties is at least 50 percent. Beginning in 1999 landlords are free to set a new base rent when tenants vacate the premises.

Opponents of rent control have enacted several statewide laws to curtail or eliminate the local power to impose rent controls. Massachusetts and Illinois have recently abolished rent control, while California and New York have weakened their statutes. Opponents of controls charge that these laws create costly bureaucracies, produce inefficient utilization of housing space, erode cities' tax base, discourage the proper maintenance of existing rentals, deter the construction of new apartments, and encourage the replacement of rental income with nonregulated forms of payment such as exorbitant finders' fees. Supporters of rent control counter that the vitality, diversity, and stability of neighborhoods must be protected by preventing the displacement of low-income renters. Housing is viewed as a fundamental right rather than as yet another consumer good, because increased rental costs may deprive tenants of a necessity of life.

—*Thomas Koenig*

See also Landlords; Rental agreements; Renters' rights.

Rental agreements

Sometimes known as leases, rental agreements are agreements between landlords and tenants setting forth the terms of tenants' occupancy of landlords' property.

When a landlord rents his or her real estate to a tenant, the landlord and tenant enter into a lease or rental agreement. A rental agreement for real estate provides the tenant with exclusive use of the landlord's property for a certain period of time. The rental agreement may be expressed in either written or verbal terms or may be implied by the parties' conduct. As with all contracts or agreements, whether a rental agreement exists and the terms of the agreement are binding is determined by the intention of the parties.

A rental agreement operates as both a conveyance of an interest in real property, conveying possession from the landlord to the tenant, and a contract between the landlord and tenant setting forth the terms of the tenant's possession of the property. As a conveyance, a lease may be recorded with the appropriate county or state registrar of deeds to give third parties notice of the tenant's interest in the real estate. Recording the lease will memorialize the tenant's priority in the chain of title consistent with the state's title laws.

As a contract, the rental agreement is to be interpreted under the state's rules of law relating to contracts.

Requirements. States have different requirements for the execution of valid rental agreements. In order to standardize those requirements in residential leases, some states have adopted the Uniform Residential Landlord and Tenant Act. In order to be valid a rental agreement must generally contain the identities of the landlord and tenant; a description of the property, whereby it is usually necessary only to describe the street or mailing address of the property; the term or duration of the lease; and the rent to be paid by the tenant, including whether the tenant is also obligated to pay utilities. The parties must agree on all these terms for the agreement to be valid. The rental agreement need not be in writing to be enforceable. The parties may enter into a verbal rental agreement as long as they have agreed on the essential terms. Even when the parties have not expressly considered all the essential terms, if the tenant has taken possession and paid rent that has been accepted by the landlord, the parties' conduct will supply the essential terms.

Although rental agreements need not be in writing to be valid, they must comply with the Statute of Frauds. The Statute of Frauds is a rule of contract law that requires that certain contracts be in writing. The Statute of Frauds requires that any contract taking longer than a certain time to complete, usually one or three years, must be in writing. Thus, depending on the particular state's Statute of Frauds, a rental agreement of longer than one or three years' duration must be in writing. In circumstances in which a written rental agreement is required, it should be signed by both the landlord and the tenant.

The lease must be accepted by the parties. While the tenant's failure to read the lease does not free him or her from carrying out the obligations under the agreement, the tenant must have had full opportunity to review and understand the lease before signing it. For example, if the tenant is illiterate, unable to read English, or unable to understand the terms of the lease for some other reason, the landlord may be obligated to explain it fully to the tenant. The tenant's inability to understand the lease may render the agreement unenforceable.

As contracts, rental agreements are subject to the same laws regarding their interpretation and enforcement as other contracts. Thus, if one of the parties has committed fraud to induce the other party to enter into the rental agreement, the agreement may be unenforceable. Likewise, if both parties have committed a mistake of fact that formed the basis of the agreement or if the agreement contains provisions that are illegal or call for the parties to commit illegal acts, the agreement may be unenforceable and either party may terminate the lease. The tenant may also allege that the rental agreement is unconscionable and therefore unenforceable. To prove that the rental agreement is unconscionable, the tenant must show that its terms are grossly unfair and resulted from the landlord's abuse of his or her superior bargaining power.

Terms of the Rental Agreement. In addition to the basic and necessary terms of rental agreements, rental agreements should also provide a tenancy term. A tenancy for a certain period of one year or more is known as a tenancy for years. A tenancy for years will terminate at the end of the period. A tenancy for an initial period that is automatically renewed is known as a periodic tenancy. The most common example of this is the month-to-month tenancy, but year-to-year tenancies are also common. Either the landlord or the tenant may terminate a periodic tenancy at any time, with appropriate notice to the other party. Under the Residential Landlord and Tenant Act, a month-to-month tenancy may be terminated by giving the other party sixty days' written notice, which is known as a notice to quit. The type of tenancy is important in determining how often a landlord may increase the rent. Under a month-to-month periodic tenancy, the landlord may theoretically increase the rent every month. If the tenancy period is one year, the landlord may impose a rent increase at the end of every one-year period.

The parties may include many other terms in the rental agreement. Generally, the tenant is free to rent the property to another tenant, who is known as a "subtenant," for part of the lease term. The landlord will likely want to include a clause restricting the tenant's right to sublet the property. Although the landlord may seek a provision restricting the tenant's right to sublet, he or she may not unreasonably withhold consent to a sublet of a residential property.

Rental Agreements for Commercial Property

The general principles that apply to residential rental agreements also apply to commercial rental agreements. However, most state laws treat commercial rental agreements and tenancies differently from residential rental agreements. Most state laws offer certain protections to residential tenants because landlords have greater bargaining power in determining the terms of rental agreements. Commercial tenants are, generally, not at such a disadvantage in negotiating with landlords and are not afforded the same protections of law.

Commercial rental agreements often contain terms that differ from those of their residential counterparts. In addition to rent, the tenant is often responsible for paying all utilities and certain other expenses the landlord incurs as a result of owning the building, such as property taxes and insurance. In these cases the rent itself is referred to as "net rent." When those expenses are included, the rent is referred to as "gross rent." The tenant is often responsible to maintain or even make improvements in the property that are compatible with the tenant's use. The landlord's right, and obligation, to enter upon the property to make repairs is far more limited under most commercial leases than under residential leases. Prohibitions or restrictions against assigning or subletting the property are common in commercial rental agreements and are generally enforceable.

The law also supplies a warranty of fitness for a particular purpose in commercial rental agreements, which is similar to a warranty of habitability. The landlord must warrant that the property is suitable for the tenant's purposes. However, unlike a warranty of habitability, a warranty of fitness may be waived by an agreement between the landlord and the tenant.

The rental agreement should also provide the date on which the rent will be paid, a reasonable grace period, and a late charge if the rent is paid after the expiration of the grace period. The rental agreement may also contain a provision allowing the landlord to collect reasonable attorney's fees if he or she has to hire an attorney to collect late rent payment or evict the tenant.

The rental agreement should also contain a provision allowing the landlord access to the property to make repairs or to show the property to other prospective tenants upon or in anticipation of the termination of the lease. The landlord may also reserve the right to enter the property in the event of a tenant's breach of the agreement. However, even in the face of such a provision, the landlord may not use "self-help" to forcibly remove a tenant for breach of the lease without a court's authorization. The rental agreement may also contain provisions terminating the tenancy in the event the property is destroyed or damaged by fire or other disaster.

Finally, landlords commonly include in rental agreements reasonable rules governing tenants' occupancy. For example, the landlord may prohibit the tenant from having pets, hanging signs on the property, altering or damaging the structure, making undue noise, or restricting use of common areas.

Tenants ordinarily have little bargaining power in negotiating any of the terms of rental agreements, especially in urban areas where the supply of apartments is well below the demand. Thus, tenants often accept the terms dictated by landlords without bargaining. With greater bargaining power, commercial tenants often negotiate the terms of rental agreements with landlords.

Terms Implied in the Rental Agreement. In addition to these expressed terms in the contract, certain obligations are implied by law. The landlord is always bound by the implied warranty of habitability. Implied in every residential rental agreement is an implied warranty that the property will be suitable for use as a residence. This implied condition in the rental agreement requires that the landlord deliver the property in habitable condition and maintain it in that condition throughout the lease term. The landlord breaches the warranty of habitability if the property is without heat or sanitary facilities, has roof or plumbing leaks, or contains other defects rendering it uninhabitable. To determine whether the landlord has breached the warranty, a court will consider the seriousness of the problem, the amount of time the problem has remained uncorrected, the nature of the property, and whether the condition of the property violates the jurisdiction's local health or building codes. If the landlord has breached the warranty of habitability, the tenant may withhold rent or repair the condition and deduct the cost of repairs from the rent. The tenant may also terminate the lease and vacate the property. However, the tenant must give the landlord an opportunity to correct the problem before taking advantage of these remedies.

A residential lease also contains an implied warranty of quiet enjoyment of the property. This warranty requires that the landlord provide exclusive possession of the property to the tenant for the lease term. The landlord may not enter the property without notice, except in cases of emergency, or otherwise interfere with the tenant's use of the property. The landlord must also defend the tenant's quiet and peaceful use of the property from interference by third parties. He or she must make a reasonable effort to prevent third parties, especially other tenants, from making too much noise or maintaining hazardous or noxious conditions on the property. If the landlord fails to do so, the tenant may resort to the same remedies as when the landlord has breached the implied warranty of habitability.

Suggested Readings. An excellent and exhaustive discussion of the law of rental agreements in all fifty states is found in volume 49, "Landlord and Tenant," of *American Jurisprudence* (2d ed. Rochester, N.Y.: Lawyers Cooperative, 1995). For information on the negotiation and drafting of rental agreements and leases, see Milton R. Friedman's *Friedman on Leases* (4th ed. New York: Practicing Law Institute, 1997). For a simple and practical treatment of landlords' and tenants' rights, see *Landlord and Tenants: Your Guide to the Law* (Chicago: American Bar Association Press, 1982). In *Legal and Economic Perspectives on the Landlord-Tenant Relationship* (New Brunswick, N.J.: Transaction Books, 1973), Jerome G. Rose provides a social critique of the "maladjustment" in the landlord-tenant relationship. On a similar note see Emily Jane Goodman's *The Tenant Survival Book* (New

York: Bobbs-Merrill, 1972). Tenants' lack of bargaining power is just one symptom of the current housing problem in the United States. In *The Urban Housing Crisis* (New York: Greenwood Press, 1990), Arlene Zarenbka offers an analysis and proposals to help provide more affordable housing in urban areas. Also see Rachel G. Bratt, Chester Hartman, and Ann Myerson's *Critical Perspectives on Housing* (Philadelphia: Temple University Press, 1986) for a comprehensive collection of essays on various aspects of housing and landlord-tenant relations. *Negotiating Commercial Leases: How Owners and Corporate Occupants Can Avoid Costly Errors*, edited by John B. Wood (New York: Practicing Law Institute, 1998), contains several articles on the state of commercial leases. —*Bernard T. Neuner*

See also Contracts; Landlords; Landlord's lien; Leases; Rent control; Renters' rights; Subleases; Unconscionable contracts.

Renters' rights

Renters, or tenants, have broad rights to the peaceful use of a suitable and safe home.

A tenant who rents a home or apartment for use as a residence has broad rights under common law, federal law, and under most state statutes. These include the right to be free from discrimination, the right to require the landlord to maintain the dwelling in a condition that makes it suitable as a residence, or habitable, the right of quiet enjoyment of the dwelling, and the right to reasonable rent. Some states also allow tenants to maintain their leases as long as they pay the rent and abide by the terms of the agreement.

The most important right of tenants is the right not to be discriminated against in housing. Under federal law, a landlord cannot refuse to rent to a person because of the person's race, ethnicity, gender, family status, or disability. Federal law does not protect people from discrimination on the basis of sexual orientation, but many state laws do. Landlords are prohibited not only from rejecting tenants because of their status but also from engaging in more subtle forms of discrimination, such as discouraging people from applying to rent property, delaying in reviewing rental applications, treating one person's application differently from another, and withholding material information about the rental unit. Although landlords may not discriminate in these ways, they still have wide latitude in determining to whom they rent.

Right to a Habitable Home. A tenant is entitled to a home that is habitable, or suitable for use as a dwelling. The landlord must maintain the condition of the home throughout the tenancy. This obligation is known as the landlord's warranty of habitability. The landlord must provide all services and make all repairs necessary to keep the home safe and suitable for living. The landlord's warranty of habitability covers all conditions. The landlord must maintain the premises according to the standards expected by a reasonable person. This includes providing appropriate heat and protection from the elements. The landlord must provide hot water and suitable plumbing facilities. In most states, the landlord must also provide certain appliances, such as a stove and a refrigerator. He or she must also maintain basic cleanliness in the apartment, the building, and its surroundings. The landlord must provide for garbage disposal and must keep the apartment and building reasonably free of pests, vermin, and other unsanitary conditions. He or she must also provide reasonable security to tenants in the building. The landlord must take reasonable action to avoid known security violations and violations of law on the premises.

If the landlord does not maintain the habitability of the premises, the tenant has certain options to remedy the breach. First, the tenant may terminate the lease and vacate the premises. He or she may also demand that the landlord repair the condition within a reasonable time. If the landlord does not make the repair, the tenant may do so and deduct the reasonable cost of the repair from the rent. However, the tenant should be careful only to make a repair appropriate to correct the defect and consistent with the type of property rented. For example, the tenant under most circumstances may not make the repair in the most expensive way possible and deduct the entire cost from the rent. This remedy is of little help to the tenant when the repair is general to the entire apartment complex or building. For example, if the roof of the building leaks, the tenant is unlikely to be able to afford to repair the roof of the entire building.

Another remedy available to the tenant is rent abatement. The tenant may refuse to pay some or all of the rent due as long as the defect remains. If the landlord seeks to evict the tenant for nonpayment of rent, the tenant may assert the landlord's breach of warranty of habitability as a defense to the eviction action. In all such actions, the tenant must act reasonably and must give the landlord reasonable notice to correct the condition. The tenant must also be sure that he or she has not caused the defect by any action other than what would usually be expected of the tenant.

Right to Possession and Quiet Enjoyment. In addition to the tenants' right to habitable living space is the tenants' right to possession and quiet enjoyment of the home. The tenant is entitled to exclusive possession and occupancy of the home. The landlord is obliged to deliver the home to the tenant at the commencement of the lease term. The tenant has the right to the exclusive use of the home, free of interference by the landlord or other tenants. Neither the landlord nor other tenants are entitled to occupy the space in any fashion (unless such terms are part of the lease agreement) or to conduct themselves in such a way as to deprive the tenant of the peaceful and uninterrupted use of the property. The landlord retains the right to enter upon the property in order to conduct repairs and check on the condition of the property. Generally, however, the landlord may not come and go at will. Except in cases of emergency, the landlord must give, or attempt to give, reasonable notice of his or her entry.

The tenant also enjoys the right to the quiet and peaceful use of the home. If other tenants are consistently noisy or unruly and this unreasonably interferes with the tenant's use of the home—for example, if the tenant cannot sleep or conduct day-to-day affairs without interference—the tenant may request that the landlord maintain peace and quiet in the building. If the landlord fails to do so, the tenant may use the same remedies available to him or her for a breach of the landlord's warranty of habitability. A tenant may terminate the tenancy or withhold all or a portion of the rent until the landlord terminates the nuisance.

Tenant's Rights Statutes. Many states have enacted laws that expand upon tenants' rights. For example, some states give tenants the right to maintain and renew their leases for as long as they make timely rent payments and abide by lease terms. These statutes are most prevalent and most favorable to tenants in densely populated states in which rental spaces are relatively scarce. These statutes generally provide that a landlord must continue to renew a tenant's lease, except under certain circumstances. These laws generally prescribe when the landlord may evict a tenant and are sometimes known as "anti-eviction statutes." Even under such laws, the landlord is entitled to remove a tenant at the end of a lease term if the landlord seeks to personally occupy the unit or convert the apartment complex into a condominium.

A landlord may evict a tenant only by filing a lawsuit seeking possession of the premises. He or she may not use "self-help" forcibly to remove a tenant from the premises without a court's authorization. Before commencing an action to evict, the landlord must give the tenant notice that he or she will be filing the action and give the tenant an opportunity to correct the default. If the tenant does not correct the default, the landlord may proceed with the eviction action.

The most common reason for eviction is the tenant's failure to pay the rent due and owing. Tenants may avoid eviction by paying all rent due and owing to date at any time before the tenant is actually removed from the premises. The landlord may also seek to evict the tenant for disorderly conduct that breaches the peace of other tenants. Again, the landlord must give notice to the offending tenant and an opportunity to correct misbehavior. A landlord may also evict a tenant for destruction of the premises or for violating the rules and regulations or terms of the lease. A landlord may also remove a tenant for habitual late payment of rent.

Reasonable Rent and Rent Increases. Generally, the rent terms contained in the written or oral lease will be binding on the parties. At the commencement of a tenancy, the lease terms are generally subject to challenge by a tenant only if they are unconscionable. However, in the landlord-tenant relationship, the landlord generally has significantly more bargaining power than the tenant. If the landlord has used his or her bargaining power to force the tenant to pay a grossly unreasonable rent, the rent term may not be enforceable. A court may then order the tenant to pay a reasonable rent. In some states, once the tenancy has commenced, the landlord is limited to demanding reasonable rent increases. A reasonable rent increase is one that is generally consistent with prevailing rents in the neighborhood.

Rent-control laws are often enacted by cities or towns in which rental space is scarce. Rent-control laws are very controversial. Under such laws rents and rent increases are set by law. The rents are often below the amount of rent that would be charged without rent control. Rent control exists to ensure that a certain level of affordable housing is always available. For that reason, rent-control apartments are very desirable. Rent-control laws usually restrict a tenant's ability to transfer his or her rights to an apartment to another tenant.

Security Deposits. The tenant is entitled to the reasonable return of a security deposit. Generally, a security deposit is a deposit held by the landlord to ensure that the property will be delivered in the same condition as when it was rented, except for reasonable wear and tear. The landlord must return the security deposit and may only apply funds from the security deposit to repair any damage caused by the tenant or other amounts due from the tenant under the terms of the lease, such as unpaid rent. The landlord must usually give the tenant an itemized list of all damage alleged and the amount to be deducted from the security deposit to correct the damage within a short period of time after the tenant vacates the premises. In most states the landlord must keep the security deposit in an interest bearing account and give the tenant annual statements of the interest earned on the deposit.

Suggested Readings. For a simple and practical treatment of landlords' and tenants' rights, see *Landlords and Tenants: Your Guide to the Law* (Chicago: American Bar Association Press, 1982). In his book *Legal and Economic Perspectives on the Landlord-Tenant Relationship* (New Brunswick, N.J.: Transaction Books, 1973), Jerome G. Rose provides a social critique of the "maladjustment" in the landlord-tenant relationship. On a similar note see Emily Jane Goodman's *The Tenant Survival Book* (New York: Bobbs-Merrill, 1972). For a critical view of landlord-tenant relations in New York and in its housing courts, see *Justice Evicted* (New York: American Civil Liberties Union Access to Justice Project, 1987). The housing crisis in the United States has drawn wide critical attention. For an excellent collection of articles on the subject, see Stephen Burghardt's *Tenants and the Urban Housing Crisis* (Dexter, Mich.: New Press, 1972). See also Rachel G. Bratt, Chester Hartman, and Ann Meyerson's *Critical Perspectives on Housing* (Philadelphia: Temple University Press, 1986). In the widely heralded and often cited work *Beyond Brick and Mortar* (Washington, D.C.: Urban Institute Press, 1992), Sandra J. Newman and Ann B. Schnare discuss, in technical terms, the societal importance of housing and housing policy. African Americans and other minority groups have the most difficult time with the current housing situation. For a collection of articles on this topic see Wilehelmina A. Leigh and James B. Stewart's *The Housing Status of Black Americans* (New Brunswick, N.J.: Transaction Publishers, 1992). For a comprehensive discussion of the law of discrimination in housing, see James A. Kushner's *Fair Housing: Discrimination in Real Estate, Community Development, and Revitalization* (New York: McGraw-Hill, 1995). —*Bernard T. Neuner*

See also Fair housing law; Landlords; Rent control; Rental agreements; Subleases.

Repossession

The taking back of property from a debtor is known as repossession.

In most credit transactions in which the repayment of a debt is secured by the right of the creditor to dispose of the personal property of the debtor and use the proceeds to pay the debt, the property remains with or is delivered to the debtor. However, if the debtor defaults by nonpayment of the loan or in some other way, the creditor may get the property back in order to dispose of it. This process is normally known as "repossession."

In the United States, repossession can generally occur in two ways. First, the creditor may go to court and obtain an order requiring a judicial officer to deliver the property from the debtor to the creditor. Such a procedure involves constitutional protections of due process, such as notice before taking the property and the debtor's right to be heard by the court as to why the taking should not occur. This legal proceeding, often called "replevin," decides who has a temporary right to the property in question. If the debtor prevails, repossessed property must be returned.

Second, property may be repossessed by means of "self-help." This method, known at common law and recognized in the Uniform Commercial Code (UCC), involves no judicial action or supervision and no constitutional protections. An example of self-help is the removal of an automobile by the creditor from the debtor's apartment parking lot at night. For the creditor to exercise this right without violation of the debtor's rights, the debtor must be in default, and the repossession can only be performed if there is no breach of the peace. The question of whether the debtor has in fact defaulted can be tricky. First, the creditor may have made a mistake by failing to credit a payment. Without a default the creditor's repossession of the debtor's property violates the law. In addition, in some states consumer legislation may give debtors a second chance to pay prior to repossession.

A breach of the peace is determined for the most part by court decisions. Using force on a debtor clearly is a violation of the law. However, a violation may also occur if a creditor proceeds without force but over the protests of the debtor. In most court decisions, the use of the police or sheriffs to repossess property is also treated as a breach of the peace and is known as "constructive force." Trespass on private property by entering a garage or the debtor's home is treated as a violation. Using trickery may not be a violation, such as obtaining the property by promising to repair it but then not returning it. Other forms of trickery that may lead to violence, such as requesting that the debtor come to the creditor's business to discuss delinquency and then taking the car from the parking lot, have been found to violate the law.

Once property is repossessed, the creditor must act reasonably to dispose of it or accept it in satisfaction of the debt. A debtor can get the property back before its disposition by paying the debt.

—*Fred H. Miller*

See also Automobile purchasing; Consumer protection laws; Credit, consumer; Debt collection; Due process; Home buying; Installment sales contract; Loans, business; Loans, personal; Mortgages; Secured transaction; Usury.

Restraining order, temporary

A temporary command by a court to preserve the status quo pending trial is called a restraining order.

Often the relief sought in a judicial proceeding is monetary: One party seeks money from another for an injury. However, sometimes a party may seek from the court an order requiring another person or entity to do or not do something. One business that believes another business has stolen trade secrets might obtain an order from a court preventing the use of the trade secrets. Court orders of this kind are generally referred to as injunctions. To obtain an injunction a party must file a lawsuit. If the party prevails in the suit, it may obtain the order it seeks, which is referred to more precisely as a permanent injunction.

The law provides temporary orders of two types between the time a party files a lawsuit and the time the party finally obtains a permanent injunction. A court may hold a hearing to decide whether the party seeking an injunction seems likely to prevail in the case. If the court believes that the party is likely to prevail, it may order a preliminary injunction, which is essentially the same as a permanent injunction but merely exists until the trial is over and the court enters a final order granting the permanent injunction. However, because even hearings may take time to schedule and conduct, rules of civil procedure generally permit a party to seek an even more temporary injunction, one designed merely to last until the court has an opportunity to conduct a full hearing of the issue. This kind of temporary injunction is referred to as a temporary restraining order. —*Timothy L. Hall*

See also Civil action; Consent decree; Hearing; Injunction

Retainers

A retainer is a formal agreement between an attorney and a client in which the attorney is hired to take the client's case.

The deposit or advance payment made by a client to an attorney for some of the fees and costs anticipated in a legal case is termed a "retainer," as is the actual agreement between the client and attorney specifying the nature of services to be rendered, costs, and related matters. The retainer fee is held in a trust account that typically pays no interest. In effect, a retainer authorizes an attorney to begin work on a legal case and also assures the attorney that payment will be made. If an attorney were to begin work on a case before actually being hired by a client, the attorney's actions would not be considered legally binding.

There are various types of retainers. When an attorney takes on a specific case, the agreement is called a special retainer. If an attorney agrees to act for a client when needed, it is termed a general retainer. A full payment retainer is payment in full in advance. This is common practice when the client is a credit risk, such as a person involved in a criminal case. This retainer is also used for flat fee matters that can be completed in less than thirty days, such as incorporation or simple wills. With a partial payment retainer an attorney asks for part of the fee in advance (typically half) and the balance on completion of the case. This is appropriate for more expensive flat fee work that will turn around in less than sixty days, such as an estate plan or an immigration hearing. A replenishing retainer is typically used for hourly work. The retainer fee is placed in escrow, and at the end of each month the client is billed to replenish the retainer to its original amount.

An attorney generally asks for a retainer fee in order to have an available fund from which to draw a salary and for any out-of-pocket expenses pertaining to the case. The retainer covers an attorney's knowledge and experience, the time spent working for the client, and any office expenses associated with the client's case. Costs not covered by a retainer but payable by a client are costs for filing a case in court; for copies of official documents; for telephone calls, photocopying, and express mail; and for court reporters who take testimony from witnesses who cannot appear in court and from expert witnesses, such as doctors or scientists. A retained attorney takes money from the retainer fund only as costs or fees are incurred on the client's behalf. If a client changes attorneys or if the attorney concludes the case and has not utilized all of the retainer, the client is refunded the difference.
—*Alvin K. Benson*

See also Attorney fees; Attorney salaries; Attorney trust accounts; Court costs.

Retirement planning

Persons setting up retirement savings plans such as individual retirement accounts (IRAs), Keogh plans, and Roth IRAs often seek legal consultation as they attempt to avoid taxes while generating future retirement income to supplement Social Security, pensions, and other investments.

Retirement planning takes into account estimations of how long persons will work until their anticipated retirement, how long they expect to live after retirement, inflation, the lifestyle they desire, and the beneficiaries of their estates. Retirement income generally comes from Social Security, pensions, investments, and individual savings plans. Most experts recommend that persons save as much as possible, start as early as possible, and take full advantage of tax-deferred accounts.

Many Americans are retiring earlier and living longer. Statistics have shown that once persons reach the age of sixty-five, the average additional life expectancy for men and women is fifteen and nineteen years, respectively. Most Americans work for forty to forty-five years and live in retirement for twenty to twenty-five years, which means that they work approximately two years for each year of retirement or spend one-fifth to one-third of their lives in retirement. Social Security pays benefits to persons who have reached the age of sixty-five, but it was never intended to be the primary source of retirement income. The minimum standards for pension plans in private industry are regulated by the Employee Retirement Income Security Act (ERISA) of 1974, the Retirement Equity Act of 1984, and the Tax Reform Act of 1986.

Many Americans participate in defined contribution plans such as 401(k), profit-sharing, or money purchasing plans, through which employees and/or their employers make annual contributions. Most financial experts suggest that persons plan for a retirement income of approximately 75 percent of their final annual income to maintain their lifestyle, motivating many to set up savings plans such as IRAs, Keogh plans, or Roth IRAs.

These retirement plans, in contrast to savings and other investment accounts, accumulate money tax free, and this tax exempt status substantially enhances retirement finances over several years while creating an excellent tax shelter for middle-class workers.

Laws Regulating Individual Retirement Funds. The U.S. Congress has strongly encouraged workers to plan financially for retirement by enacting laws that motivate both workers and their employers to set aside additional retirement funds. Classic IRAs were made possible by the Employee Retirement Income Security Act of 1974 which enabled the tax-free accumulation of monies put into retirement accounts and the interest they generate until retirement. Withdrawals made from classic IRAs after retirement are subject to ordinary income tax, with the theory being that taxes paid later will be lower since the retiree will probably be in a lower tax bracket than while working. In most cases, contributions to classic IRAs are deductible from personal income tax, thus resulting in a double tax savings, the magnitude of which is dependent on the taxpayer's filing status and total adjusted gross income.

An income tax deduction is allowed for IRA contributions to classic IRAs if the taxpayer is covered by a retirement plan at work. Fully deductible contributions are allowed for couples filing jointly whose adjusted gross income is less than $40,000. Contributions by single persons or heads of households with adjusted gross incomes of less than $25,000 are deductible, and partial tax deductions are allowed if incomes do not exceed $50,000. Established through banks, savings and loan institutions, insurance companies, brokerage firms, and mutual funds, retirement accounts can be purchased by persons earning income as employees or through self-employment. Such income generally stems from personal labor or effort and does not include unearned income, such as dividends, interest, collected rent, or pensions. Since 1985 alimony has been considered earned income for IRA eligibility. Guardians who cosign IRA accounts for their minor children can make a $2,000 annual contribution provided that this amount does not exceed the child's reported earned income from jobs such as paper routes and baby-sitting.

Types of Retirement Accounts. Married persons who both work can each open separate classic IRA accounts and contribute a maximum of $2,000 annually to each of them. If only one spouse works, a joint IRA with a maximal contribution of $2,225 annually is allowed. If funds are withdrawn from an IRA before the purchasers reaches 59.5 years of age, all monies within the plan are subject to income tax and a tax penalty of 10 percent. Some policymakers have pushed to increase this percentage. Persons who continue working past the normal retirement age must stop making contributions to their IRAs and begin withdrawing the money by April 1 of the year after they turn 70.5 years old. The federal tax penalty for not doing so is 50 percent in addition to regular income tax. No IRA tax penalties are imposed if persons die, in which case accumulated finances go to the estate of the deceased, or if persons become disabled.

Keogh plans can be purchased only by self-employed persons for themselves and their employees who have worked full-time for at least three years. Employers give tax deductions for contributions made.

To encourage persons to put aside more retirement money, the Taxpayer Relief Act of 1997 created the Roth IRA, named for Delaware Republican senator William Roth. This type of IRA relaxed many of the legalities of classic IRAs. Contributions to Roth IRAs are not tax-free when made but are not subject to tax upon withdrawal, provided the account is at least five years old and the owner is at least 59.5 years of age. Other advantages of the Roth IRA are that the money does not have to be distributed at age 70.5 or even at death, so that accumulated monies may be passed on to beneficiaries, and that taxpayers with annual incomes up to $160,000 may participate.

Suggested Readings. Fine texts on personal financial planning for retirement with references to laws and ongoing legislation include Carl W. Battle's *Senior Counsel: Legal and Financial Strategies for Age Fifty and Beyond* (New York: Alworth, 1993), Nancy Levitin's *Retirement Rights: The Benefits of Growing Older* (New York: Avon Books, 1994), Joseph L. Matheity's *Medicare and Pensions: Get the Most out of Your Retirement and Medical Benefits* (Thorndike, Maine: Hall, 1996), and Daniel M. Kehrer's *Kiplinger's Twelve Steps to a Worry-Free Retirement* (Washington, D.C.: Kiplinger, 1995). Less technical books dealing with retirement planning include *How to Retire with a Million Dollars* (New

York: Regan, 1998), by Elaine Zimmermann, *Retire Rich: The Baby Boomer's Guide to a Secure Future* (New York: Wiley, 1998), by Bambi Holzer with Elaine Floyd, and *Ready, Set, Retire! How Much Money You Need and the Tax-Smart Way to Get It and Keep It* (Bend, Oreg.: Financial Freedom Press, 1995), by J. William Brimacombe. An excellent article in the March, 1998, issue of *Money Magazine*, by Penelope Wang and Malcolm Fitch, "Win the New Retirement Game: The Tax and Investing Rules Have Changed for All of Us. Here Are the Best Ways to Take Advantage," provides insight into how to maximize retirement benefits within the framework of the tax laws. —*Daniel G. Graetzer*

See also Age and the law; Estates and estate planning; Family law practice; Health and disability insurance; Inheritance tax; Life insurance; Medicare; Nursing homes; Pensions; Rehabilitative support; Retirement plans; Social Security; Tax law.

Retirement plans

For the most part, employee retirement plans are individual savings accounts that have some tax advantages but also some limitations on withdrawals and reinvestment that regular savings accounts do not have.

Retirement plans available to employees and self-employed individuals include Keogh plans, Savings Incentive Match Plan for Employees (SIMPLE), and individual retirement accounts (IRAs). Contributions to these plans are deductible, and the earnings on them remain tax free until the retiree receives distributions. Generally, a 10 percent early withdrawal penalty applies if participants take the money out before they reach the age of fifty-nine and a half.

The two basic kinds of Keogh plans are defined contribution plans and defined benefit plans. A defined contribution plan sets the amount of annual contributions so that the amount of retirement benefits depends on the amount of contributions and the income earned on those contributions. Defined benefit plans fix a specific retirement benefit that is payable regardless of the amount of the contribution or the income earned on the contribution.

The Savings Incentive Match Plan for Employees (SIMPLE) was authorized by the Small Business Job Protection Act of 1996. The SIMPLE plan may be used only by employers with one hundred or fewer employees who received at least $5,000 in compensation from the employer for the preceding year. In 1997 the employee's contribution was not permitted to exceed $6,000 but was indexed for inflation for later years. This plan also requires that the employer match the employee's contribution on a dollar-for-dollar basis up to 3 percent of compensation. Distributions are usually taxed under the rules for IRAs, except an increased early withdrawal penalty of 25 percent applies to distributions within the first two years of participation in the plan.

Both employees and self-employed individuals under the age of seventy and a half can set up and make contributions to an IRA. The maximum contribution to an IRA for any year is the lesser of $2,000 or taxable compensation. Taxable compensation includes any kind of personal service income as well as taxable alimony and separate maintenance payments. There is usually a 10 percent penalty if account holders withdraw any of the funds before they are fifty-nine and a half years old.

While leaving unchanged the annual individual contribution limit of $2,000, the Taxpayer Relief Act of 1997 provided expanded IRA opportunities. The new law provided a waiver of the 10 percent early withdrawal penalty on up to $10,000 of IRA funds for first-time home buyers and on funds used to pay for higher education expenses. Probably the most significant IRA development was the introduction of the Roth IRA (named after Senator William Roth, Chairman of the Senate Finance Committee). The benefit of the Roth IRA is that earnings accumulate tax free and qualified distributions are completely nontaxable. The Roth IRA must exist for five years before any distributions are qualified. Then distributions are qualified if they are made after the account holder is fifty-nine and a half years old, deceased, disabled, or paying expenses up to $10,000 in connection with a first-time home purchase. —*W. Dene Eddings Andrews*

See also Age and the law; Pensions; Retirement planning; Tax law.

Right to die

The right to die refers both to an existing legal protection from unwanted medical treatment even if death results and to attempts to legalize physician-assisted suicide for terminally ill patients.

Beginning in the 1970's the right-to-die movement sought to clarify the legal status of health care providers and family members who allow terminally ill patients to die naturally by withholding the life-extending treatments and procedures afforded by increasingly sophisticated medical technology. The efforts, in courts and in legislatures, led to legal instruments and laws protecting a patient's right to refuse treatment. Allowing a fatal disease to take its natural course without medical intervention is commonly referred to as passive euthanasia (from the Greek meaning "good death").

In the 1980's a parallel effort was initiated to legalize voluntary active euthanasia, or physician-assisted suicide. The practice first captured public attention in 1990, when Dr. Jack Kevorkian began helping people to commit suicide who were terminally ill or had irreversible debilitating conditions, such as Alzheimer's disease. Debated during widely publicized court cases, citizens' referenda, and legislative action, voluntary active euthanasia remained a contentious issue through the 1990's. Most religions held that only God has a right to take a person's life and ethicists warned against the potential abuses of active euthanasia, while patient advocacy groups insisted that an American's constitutional right to autonomy extends to decisions about death. Meanwhile, whether a person has a legal right to commit suicide in order to avoid the pain, dementia, or emotional burden of a lingering terminal illness was not settled completely. In any case, the controversy affects those who, because they help terminally ill patients commit suicide, may be liable to criminal prosecution as much as it concerns the patients themselves.

Passive Euthanasia. Common law and many state statutes recognized a patient's right to refuse medical treatment even before the U.S. Supreme Court ruled that a person has a constitutional right to die derived from the principle of autonomy in the due process clause of the Fourteenth Amendment (*Cruzan v. Director, Missouri Department of Health*, 1990). However, the Supreme Court delimited that right: Only competent people who express their wishes convincingly may refuse life-supporting treatment or terminate ongoing treatment; when a patient's family members and health care providers must act for a demented or unconscious patient, they bear the burden of proof in establishing that the patient, while still competent, had declared the wish to forgo such "heroic measures" as respirators, feeding tubes, and surgery to prolong life.

To help patients and their families meet that burden of proof, all fifty states and the District of Columbia adopted laws recognizing advanced directives that specify how a person wants to be cared for if terminally ill. As of 1997 forty-seven states recognized living wills, a document that describes the conditions under which life-sustaining treatment should be withheld or suspended. The living will may be handwritten, although various model forms exist that can be filled out. Massachusetts, Michigan, and New York allow only agents or proxies empowered by a durable power of attorney to act on behalf of an incompetent patient. The Patient Self-Determination Act, passed by Congress in 1990, requires hospitals to give patients written information explaining their rights under state law to make advanced directives and refuse treatment.

The document or agent usually directs health care providers to make "Do Not Resuscitate" and "No Code" entries in the patient's chart, which forbid intervention during a medical crisis, such as heart failure or respiratory failure. The courts make no legal distinction between withholding treatment and withdrawing treatment after it has been started, although the withdrawal of treatment, according to many theologians and ethicists, is less morally defensible.

Physician-Assisted Suicide. Voluntary active euthanasia can take two forms. In the first, a physician provides the means for a patient to commit suicide and explains its use, but the patient directly administers the means—for instance, by swallowing pills, self-injecting a liquid, or breathing gas through a mask. In the second, on the patient's request the physician administers the lethal agent, a practice that is widely held to violate the Hippocratic oath and to be tantamount to murder.

No state law forbids suicide. However, in thirty-five states statutes make it a crime for one person

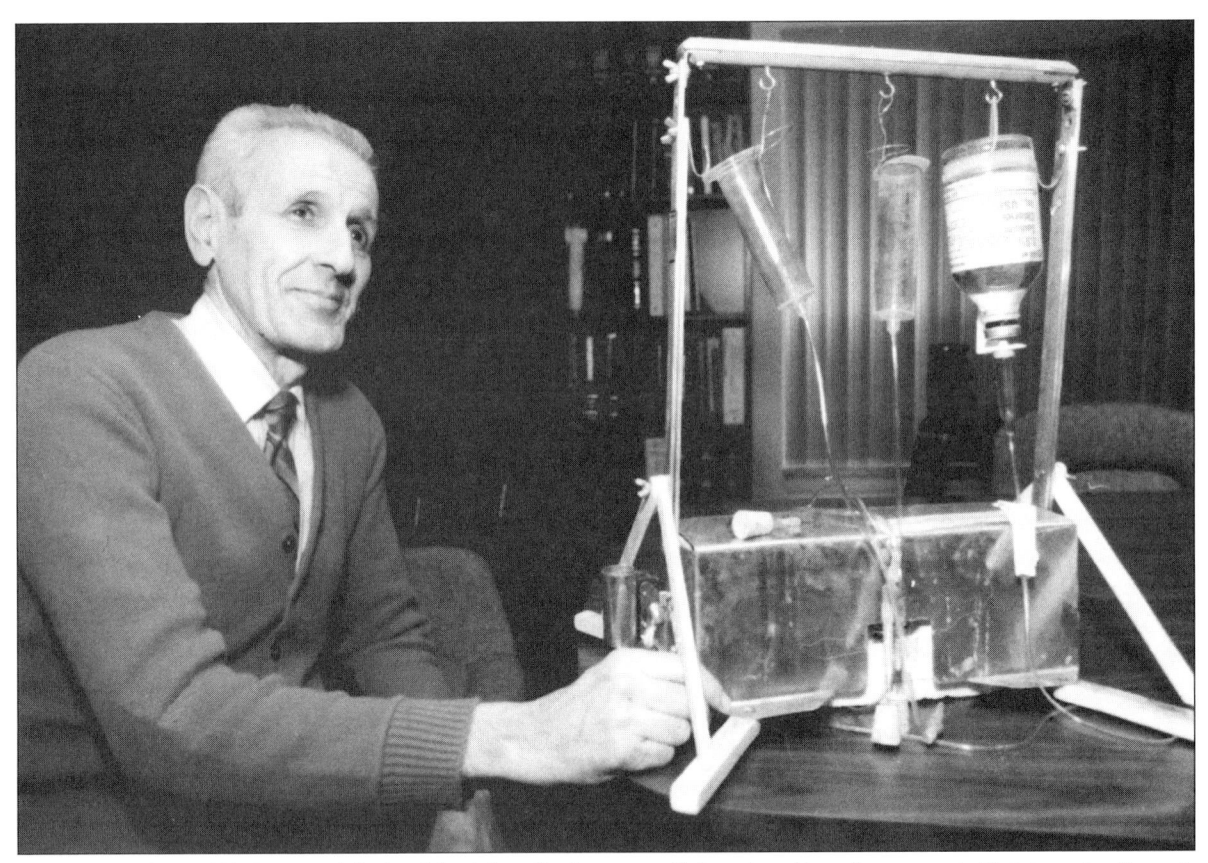

Dr. Jack Kevorkian of Michigan, a defender of the right to die, has repeatedly been the subject of government efforts to curb euthanasia activities by medical professionals. (AP/Wide World Photos)

to assist another to commit suicide by giving advice or providing the means, and another nine cite common law to criminalize assisted suicide. Doctors who help a patient die can be prosecuted for murder or manslaughter. The doctor may be culpable despite the absence of malice, the condition of the patient, or the patient's explicit request for assistance in dying. In 1997 the Supreme Court ruled that state laws forbidding physician-assisted suicide are constitutional (*Vacco v. Quill* and *Washington v. Glucksberg*), and the same year Congress passed an act that denied federal funds to projects in support of physician-assisted suicide.

Nevertheless, the legal status of voluntary active euthanasia remained uncertain after the Supreme Court ruling, because laws legalizing physician-assisted suicide had not been ruled unconstitutional. During the 1990's opinion poles showed that there was considerable support for such laws, not only among the public but also among health care providers. Referenda to legalize physician-assisted suicide failed in Washington in 1991 and in California in 1992, but in 1994 Oregon voters approved the Death with Dignity Act, which authorized physicians to prescribe lethal doses of medication for patients who have fewer than six months to live. The act stipulated, however, that there be a series of interviews to verify that the patient is competent and making an informed decision, that at least one independent medical consultation take place, that next of kin be notified, and that waiting periods totaling seventeen days be upheld. Court challenges blocked implementation of the act until October, 1997, and the next month Oregon voters rejected a referendum to repeal the 1994 act.

In *Vacco v. Quill* and *Washington v. Glucksberg* the Supreme Court implied, according to some analysts, that such laws as Oregon's could be found constitutional. In their written decision, the justices invited further debate.

Suggested Readings. Constance Jones explains the living will, medical power of attorney, and the right-to-die movement in *RIP: The Complete Book of Death and Dying* (New York: HarperCollins, 1997). Melvin I. Urofsky lucidly reviews the legal issues and court cases pertaining to euthanasia in *Letting Go: Death, Dying, and the Law* (New York: Scribner's, 1993). *The Right to Die: Understanding Euthanasia* (New York: Harper & Row, 1986) is an extended historical and legal argument in favor of assisted suicide by Derek Humphry and Ann Wickett, founders of the Hemlock Society. James M. Hoefler's *Deathright: Culture, Medicine, Politics, and the Right to Die* (Boulder, Colo.: Westview Press, 1994) surveys policy issues, judicial decisions, and legislative initiatives related to the right-to-die movement. In *Final Choices: To Live or to Die in an Age of Medical Technology* (New York: Plenum Press, 1993), George M. Burnell, a physician, examines the legal and ethical problems faced by terminally ill patients who refuse life-prolonging medical measures. *Doctor Assisted Suicide and the Euthanasia Movement* (Hudson, Wis.: Gary McCuen Publications, 1994), edited by Gary E. McCuen, contains essays that argue differing viewpoints on the morality of assisted suicide. Lawrence O. Gostin comments on the future of physician-assisted suicide in "Deciding Life and Death in the Courtroom," *The Journal of the American Medical Association* 278 (Nov. 12, 1997). —*Roger Smith*

See also Living wills; Medical malpractice; Medical treatment, consent for; Patients' rights.

Robbery

The illegally taking of another's property using force or the threat of force is known as robbery.

Robbery is one of the most common crimes of violence in the United States. It is one of the most feared, as it involves a face to face confrontation between the victim and the offender. It is also misunderstood, as it is frequently confused with other theft offenses. Robbers, who are arrested for about one of four offenses, generally rely on the swiftness of the crime, the lack of residual evidence of their presence, and the anonymity and randomness of the confrontation. They also rely on the anxiety of their victims.

Elements of the Offense. Robbery is classified by the Federal Bureau of Investigation (FBI) as a violent crime, differentiating it from other theft offenses that are classified as property crimes. Two factors are present in robberies that make them violent crimes: their face to face nature and the threat or use of force.

A key element of robbery is the physical presence of the victim. The victim's presence is crucial to the successful completion of the offense. The victim is frequently required to release or turn over the property demanded by the offender. The offender often seeks property that is more valuable and portable than that sought by persons who commit burglary and other theft offenses. Cash is the most sought after item followed by other negotiable items and jewelry. The presence of the victim also increases the danger that the robbery will escalate to other offenses, such as assault, rape, kidnapping, and murder. The element of force increases the chance that this escalation will occur.

Force or the threat of force involves danger to the victim. There are two categories of robberies that are recognized in most states. The first and most severe is armed robbery. This involves the presence or use of a deadly weapon. A deadly weapon can be a firearm, a knife, a club, or any instrument that can be wielded in a threatening manner. The presence of a deadly weapon implies to the victim that if the victim does not comply with the demands of the robber, the weapon will be used. Some robbers use weapons at the beginning of robberies to soften perceived resistance—for example, some robbers fire a gun into the ceiling or strike their victims in order to stun them. The weapon's presence also facilitates escalation, even if the robber did not plan for it. This includes accidental firearms discharges; victims' unexpected reactions such as fleeing, freezing, or resisting; and interruptions by police or others. Even if a weapon is not used to injure a victim, the crime of armed robbery occurs if the weapon is presented to the victim.

The other category of force is commonly referred to as strong-arm robbery. This is sometimes known by its street name: "mugging." Victims are accosted by stronger individuals who may strike them or knock them down while stealing their property. Offenders do not use weapons in such encounters. Their victims usually sustain minor injuries that do not require hospitalization. Muggers often take property from their victims, as opposed to armed robbers who demand that victims turn over their property. This type of robbery is usually considered a lesser included offense to armed robbery. Occasionally victims of strong-arm robberies are injured severely, in which case a prosecutor may opt for the more serious charge.

The offender must have gained domination or constructive possession over an item for a robbery to be completed. As the victim begins the transfer of the items to the offender, the robbery has been completed. For example, if an offender walks into a store and demands that a clerk empty the cash register into a paper bag but is apprehended before the clerk can respond, this would constitute attempted robbery. However, if the clerk fills the paper bag and hands it to the robber, who is then apprehended, the robbery has been completed because the robber had gained control over the bag of money. Attempted robbery is also a lesser included offense to armed robbery.

Variations on Robbery. Because the main elements of robbery involve confrontation and the use or threat of force, it is not important what the offender is stealing. The crime is the same whether he is stealing a candy bar or $1 million in cash. This distinguishes robbery from other theft offenses, in which the value of the property dictates the level of punishment. Some jurisdictions also require some minimal level of force beyond what is required to steal the items. In these jurisdictions events such as purse-snatching and pickpocketing are not robbery offenses, because the only force used is that which is minimally necessary to remove the property. Other jurisdictions view these offenses as forms of strong-arm robbery because of the personal contact and some use of force.

Another difference among jurisdictions concerns the timing of the use of force. For example, a shoplifter who is detained as he or she exits a store with stolen property and who resists detention would be charged with strong-arm robbery in some jurisdictions. In others such resistance would be viewed as a separate offense, such as resisting arrest or assault.

Some types of robberies have slang names, which might cause persons to regard them as non-robbery offenses. One such offense is the theft of an automobile while the vehicle is in use, which has come to be known as "carjacking." During the early 1990's this type of robbery became more widespread, causing a stir in the press and in the legislatures. Some believed that this was a new offense, but it was was already covered by existing robbery statutes. The U.S. Congress passed a carjacking statute in response to the public outcry, but this type of offense is rarely prosecuted under federal law. Another type of robbery is home invasion. This is a combination of burglary and robbery in which a robber confronts the occupants of the home purposely. As with carjacking, there does not seem to be a logical reason for doing this other than to increase the swiftness with which the event can be completed. This offense carries significantly higher penalties than simple robbery, for the offender is charged with both robbery and burglary.

Punishment. Like most violent crimes, robbery has come to be punished more severely than previously. First offenders of strong-arm robbery are typically sentenced to a minimum of five or more years in prison depending on the state. Robbery inherently involves many factors that increase the sentence in most crime situations. Most states have enacted statutes that enhance a criminal sentence based on aggravating factors. These factors usually include the use of a weapon, the use of a firearm, the level of injury sustained by the victim, and the criminal record of the offender. Robbery offenders often find that many additional years of incarceration are added to their sentences. A first offender who commits a strong-arm robbery may receive a five-year sentence. The same person, upon committing a subsequent armed robbery, may receive life imprisonment.

Suggested Readings. For additional information on the crime of robbery see Phillip E. Johnson's *Criminal Law: Cases, Materials, and Text* (5th ed. St. Paul, Minn.: West Publishing, 1995). Other works dealing with this specific crime include Thomas Gardner and Terry Anderson's *Criminal Law: Principles and Cases* (6th ed. St. Paul, Minn.: West Publishing, 1996) and Sue Titus Reid's *Criminal Law* (4th ed. New York: Macmillan, 1998).

—*Michael L. Barrett*

See also Burglary; Larceny; Lesser included offense; Pickpocketing; Theft.

S

Sales taxes

Taxes imposed on retail sales of goods and services, sales taxes constitute an important source of revenue for state and local governments and are proposed from time to time as a new federal revenue source.

Sales taxes are a form of excise taxes—that is, taxes imposed on a transaction or series of transactions rather than on an individual or business as such. While many excise taxes (notably those on tobacco and alcohol products) are directed at specific categories of goods and services, sales taxes apply to all retail sales within an applicable jurisdiction with the exception of such items as food and medicine, which are specifically exempted. Because of this wide tax base, even a sales tax with a relatively low tax rate can bring in a great deal of revenue, and sales taxes have become an important or even predominant revenue source for many state and local governments. But sales taxes have serious drawbacks: They cause economic distortions and are widely viewed as unfair to poorer taxpayers because of their regressive nature. These limitations, together with political considerations, have thus far prevented the enactment of a national sales tax. State sales taxes also present difficult enforcement problems with respect to mail-order and computer-based purchases, problems which the various state governments are only beginning to cope with successfully.

Rates, Base, Exemptions. Sales taxes are imposed at low rates, typically between three and eight percent of the price of purchased items. The tax is imposed on the seller but is passed on to the buyer when it is added to the amount paid at the time of sale, so that from the buyer's perspective the tax becomes effectively part of the sales price. Thus, the tax is paid in a legal sense by retail merchants but in an economic sense by consumers, whose cost of living is increased by the aggregate amount of sales tax paid on their various purchases.

Unlike a value-added tax (VAT) or other levies, a sales tax is imposed only on retail sales, although the borderline between retail and wholesale purchases is difficult to draw in some cases.

Because a sales tax applies to all and not merely luxury purchases, there is a fear that it will discourage consumers from buying food and other items necessary to maintain a minimum level of health and safety. To deal with this problem, virtually all states provide an exemption or reduced tax rate for food and prescription drugs, while some states extend the exemption to cover clothing, nonprescription medicines, and other categories of items. These exemptions and other administrative matters are determined by state tax bureaus and are appealed to state courts of general jurisdiction or, in some cases, specialized tax courts. The federal courts become involved when the constitutionality of a state sales tax is challenged, as is frequently the case with interstate or mail order sales.

Despite its problems, the sales tax remains an important revenue source. As of January 1, 1988, all but five states imposed sales taxes, as did many localities, most of which rely on state law and simply add an additional percentage tax at the local level. For example, New York State imposes a 4 percent statewide sales tax but permits localities to impose additional rates of up to 4.5 percent for a maximum 8.5 percent rate. Nationwide, sales and income taxes remain the largest sources of state revenue.

Interstate and Mail-Order Sales. The simplicity of the sales tax means that it creates less work for lawyers than income, estate, or other taxes. One area that has attracted interest is the question of interstate and mail-order sales. To prevent persons from evading home state sales taxes, most states impose "use" taxes on purchases of equivalent items in other states. Use taxes are difficult to enforce, and in their place many states have sought to compel out-of-state merchants—notably catalogue sellers such as Land's End or L. L. Bean—to collect taxes on purchases mailed to in-state residents.

Selected State Sales Tax Rates, 1998	
New York*	4.0
Pennsylvania	6.0
Ohio	5.0
Illinois	6.25
Michigan	6.0
North Carolina	4.0
Florida	6.0
Texas	6.25
California	6.0
New Hampshire	No Sales Tax

*New York and several other states allow localities to impose additional taxes.

In *Quill Corporation v. North Dakota* (1992) the U.S. Supreme Court refused to compel an out-of-state retailer to collect use tax but said that the U.S. Congress could require that such a tax be collected if it did so in appropriate legislation. While Congress has yet to act on this matter, the threat of action has induced some mail-order shippers to enter into voluntary withholding agreements with different states, and it is likely that tax evasion by means of mail order sales will eventually be a thing of the past. A related issue concerns the taxation of sales by means of the Internet. Current political sentiment favors a nationwide exemption for such sales, but there is opposition from traditional retailers who fear that they will lose business to Internet sellers.

National Sales Tax and VAT. Even with exemptions for food, clothing, and similar necessities, the sales tax remains a regressive tax, as it tends to cost poorer taxpayers a higher percentage of their income than wealthier individuals. The tax may also distort the economy by discouraging the purchase of some retail items. These and other factors have prevented the sales tax from being enacted at the national as well as the state level. The continuing demand for revenue and the increasing unpopularity of the income tax have served to revive interest in a national sales tax to supplement or replace the existing tax structure. Some observers have suggested a European-style VAT—essentially, a sales tax on retail and wholesale transactions—as an additional alternative. Whether any of these proposals will be enacted remains an open question, but the demand for simple and reliable revenue sources is likely to keep attention focused on the sales tax for some time to come.

Suggested Readings. Because of variations in state sales tax laws, most works on the subject consist of local materials or obscure economic analyses. A basic textbook, providing an introduction to the sales tax and other state taxes is Jerome R. Hellerstein and Walter Hellerstein's *State and Local Taxation: Cases and Materials* (6th ed. St. Paul, Minn.: West Publishing, 1997). More detail on the various state tax laws and the constitutional limitations on the imposition and collection of those taxes is found in Jerome R. Hellerstein and Walter Hellerstein's *State Taxation* (Boston: Warren Gorham Lamont, 1992) and in the American Bar Association (ABA) book *Sales and Use Tax Deskbook* (Washington, D.C.: American Bar Association, 1997). Paul J. Hartman's *Federal Limitations on State and Local Taxation* (Rochester, N.Y.: Lawyers Cooperative Publishing, 1981) is a thoughtful work emphasizing constitutional issues and the resulting limitations on state taxing authority. Perhaps the best introduction to the sales tax is a chapter on sales, use, and other consumption taxes in a good public finance casebook, such as Richard A. Musgrave and Peggy B. Musgrave's *Public Finance in Theory and Practice* (5th ed. New York: McGraw-Hill, 1989), which explains the role of the sales tax in the U.S. tax structure and the practical and policy considerations that are common to the various different state taxes. —*Michael A. Livingston*

See also Business taxes; Income taxes; Property taxes; Tax law.

School law

Laws on attendance, curricula, student behavior, student rights, and the rights of teachers in public schools are some of the issues addressed by school law.

Although the U.S. Constitution does not expressly refer to education, all school rules and regulations are subject to its provisions. Under the Tenth Amendment to the Constitution, which states that

"The powers not delegated to the United States by the Constitution, nor prohibited by it to the States, are reserved to the States respectively, or to the people," public school education is a state function. Therefore, most laws affecting education are to be found in the statutes enacted by state legislatures. Because of the size and complexity of most school systems, the authority to adopt and enforce reasonable rules and regulations is delegated to state and local boards of education, school administrators, and classroom teachers.

Boards of Education. Public education is controlled by the states but is most often a function of cities and towns. All states except Hawaii have created local school boards and granted them broad administrative authority. The local school board reaffirms the deeply-rooted American tradition of local control over education.

The citizens within the school district usually elect school board members. Members are considered public officials, but individual board members have no power to make decisions or set policy on their own; a local board can only act as a body. Board members individually and boards of education as a whole do not run schools. By overseeing the operation of the schools, the board ensures that the schools are well run by the administrators hired for that purpose. As specified in state law the power held by local school boards includes the authority to approve the curriculum, raise revenue to build and maintain schools, select personnel, and enact policies necessary to the efficient operation of the schools in accordance with the law. School board meetings and records must be open to the public. Several states have enacted "open meeting" or "sunshine" laws to ensure that the public is fully informed of the actions of the board.

Attendance and Curriculum. States are not required by federal law to provide a free education to students, but all states do so. Public schools must be accessible to all students, regardless of race, sex, or physical or mental disability. School districts may also set minimum and maximum age requirements of students. Most states require that children between the ages of five and sixteen years of age who are physically and mentally capable attend an approved public or private school. Some states also allow children to be schooled at home, subject to the approval of the local school board or superintendent. Schools must be open a minimum number of days per year (the U.S. average is around 180 days) and state officials are responsible for scheduling make-up days if the schools are closed due to inclement weather or other emergencies.

The states retain the power to determine the public school curriculum, including the selection of appropriate textbooks, as long as there are no constitutional conflicts. All states require instruction in the U.S. Constitution, and most legislatures mandate courses in U.S. history. Other commonly required subjects are English, mathematics, health, and physical education. States also have the power to establish programs of vocational education, bilingual education, and special programs for children with disabilities. Although the states have considerable freedom to determine the best curriculum for their students, some attempts to introduce controversial topics or efforts to impose restrictions on what can be taught have run afoul of the Constitution. The largest number of such cases involve attempts to introduce religious teachings into public schools or to remove certain books from classrooms and school libraries. The U.S. Supreme Court has recognized that local school boards have broad authority to make decisions about the curriculum and that they have a legitimate interest in endorsing programs that reflect the standards of the community and promote respect for authority and traditional values. This power, however, must always be balanced with students' right to have free access to information.

The Rights of Students. The absence of any limitations on student behavior would not permit a school to fulfill its educational mission. School districts have a legitimate interesting in exercising effective discipline, preventing violence, and setting the boundaries of acceptable behavior. The courts have sought to balance the rights of student speech, dress, and behavior against public schools' legitimate interest in maintaining an effective learning atmosphere.

During the first half of the twentieth century courts used the "reasonableness test" to determine if disputed school rules were constitutional. The U.S. Supreme Court ruled in 1915 that it was up to the states to determine whether school regulations promoted discipline among students. If there was any reasonable relationship between a rule and the overall goals of the school, the rule was usually upheld.

This logic was challenged in the landmark Supreme Court decision *Tinker v. Des Moines Independent Community School District* (1969). Mary Beth Tinker and her brother, John Tinker, were suspended in 1965 for wearing black armbands to school to protest U.S. involvement in the Vietnam War. The Court bypassed the "reasonableness test" and ruled that students do not give up their constitutional rights to freedom of expression "at the schoolhouse gate." However, the Court noted, such rights are not absolute. School administrators may curtail student speech or behavior when it "materially disrupts class work or involves substantial disorder or invades the rights of others." For example, a principal has the right to ban T-shirts containing pictures or language deemed to be disruptive to the school environment or contrary to the tastes and traditions of the community.

The same principles apply to student searches. The Fourth Amendment to the U.S. Constitution protects the right of citizens to be secure in their persons, houses, papers, and effects, against unreasonable searches and seizures. The standard for searches in a school setting was set by the case of *New Jersey v. T.L.O.* (1985). The U.S. Supreme Court ruled that to conduct searches of students, teachers or other school officials must have "reasonable grounds for suspecting that the search will turn up evidence that the student has violated or is violating either the law or school rules." In this case, when the assistant principal searched the purse of a student suspected of smoking in the school lavatory and discovered cigarettes and drug paraphernalia, the Court upheld the constitutionality of the search. In addition, student lockers, desks, pockets, or packages may be searched, and blanket, random searches of school lockers are also permitted.

The courts are less clear about the imposition of dress and appearance codes. Such regulations may at times run counter to the First Amendment's protection of freedom of expression. School officials must show that the codes are being imposed for health or safety reasons or to protect students from injury. The enforcement of grooming or dress codes, including the imposition of school uniforms, is a much-disputed area of school law. In Maine a federal district court upheld the right of a vocational school to prohibit the wearing of beards or long hair by students in order to impress potential employers visiting the school. Other courts, however, have concluded that attire and hairstyle preferences are constitutionally protected. Courts

---

Important U.S. School Law Cases

Everson v. Board of Education (1947): Required school districts to provide bus transportation to all students, both public and parochial.

Brown v. Board of Education (1954): Ended legal segregation by abolishing the policy of "separate but equal" in public school education.

Engel v. Vitale (1962): Outlawed Bible reading and prayer in public schools.

Tinker v. Des Moines School District (1969): Struck down a school regulation prohibiting the wearing of black armbands to protest the Vietnam War.

Wisconsin v. Yoder (1972): Held that the free exercise of religion clause of the First Amendment prevented a state from requiring Amish children to attend school beyond the eighth grade.

New Jersey v. T.L.O. (1985): Upheld the right of teachers or other school officials to search students or their lockers if they have reasonable grounds for believing that the law or school rules are being violated.

Hazelwood School District v. Kuhlmeier (1988): Upheld a high-school principal's right to censor a student newspaper.

Lee v. Weisman (1992): Held that prayers delivered at a public high-school graduation violated the establishment clause of the First Amendment to the U.S. Constitution.

have invalidated school rules prohibiting female students from wearing slacks and blue jeans in school. In general, in order for dress or appearance codes to be constitutionally permitted, school officials must show that they have a legitimate educational justification.

Administrators have greater control over school-sponsored student speech, such as speech occurring in the school newspaper, yearbook, or a class play. In the 1988 decision *Hazelwood School District v. Kuhlmeier* the Supreme Court upheld the right of a high school principal to censor the student newspaper because it contained several student-written articles that the principal deemed inappropriate. The Court supported the school official, recognizing that a school district has a legitimate interest in disassociating itself from speech that is vulgar, obscene, or otherwise unsuitable for immature audiences.

Student Discipline. Student misconduct has always been one of the most difficult issues confronting the schools. Problems such as vandalism and drug and alcohol abuse present a real challenge to education officials striving to maintain a safe and secure atmosphere for learning.

All states uphold the right of the schools to enforce reasonable rules of conduct to protect students and ensure a school environment conducive to learning. Schools have been given considerable latitude by the courts in establishing reasonable disciplinary rules and regulations and in imposing punishments or penalties. When children are under the jurisdiction of the school, teachers are said to stand *in loco parentis* (in the place of the parent). Thus, it is necessary for the teacher to have the authority to direct and discipline students, much as a parent would. A school district's rules, however, may be struck down if they are too vague; for example, a rule simply prohibiting "improper conduct" would not be upheld. The most common punishments, which must be in proportion to the seriousness of the offense, are denial of privileges, detention after school, suspension, and expulsion. School rules must be clearly stated and publicized to students and parents and should not impair the constitutionally protected rights of students.

The Rights of Teachers. Until the mid-twentieth century it was common practice to dismiss public school teachers for expressing controversial views. In a landmark 1968 decision, *Pickering v. Board of Education,* the U.S. Supreme Court recognized that teachers have a First Amendment right to express their views on matters of public concern. This case involved a letter by a teacher to the local newspaper criticizing the school board's fiscal policies. The school board dismissed Pickering, claiming that the letter contained false statements that damaged the reputations of the board members and school administrators. The Court held that Pickering's employment by the school district did not mean that he forfeited his right to speak freely on issues of public interest.

The issue of academic freedom—the right to freely teach and engage in research in American colleges and universities—is less clear. While academic freedom is generally accepted, the broad protections granted to the members of college faculties do not extend to public elementary and secondary school teachers. Rather than grant public school teachers the same general protections enjoyed by university professors, the courts have endeavored to deal with questions of academic freedom on a case-by-case basis, weighing the rights of teachers against the interests of the school board in ensuring appropriate classroom instruction. For example, public school teachers are not free to ignore the prescribed curriculum or course content by claiming a right to academic freedom, and the courts have held that teachers who refuse to cover the assigned curriculum are subject to dismissal. Although teachers have some discretion to select appropriate teaching methods that serve a demonstrated educational purpose, the ultimate authority to control the curriculum, including the selection of textbooks and instructional materials, rests with the local school board.

Tenure. Tenure contracts ensure that teachers may be dismissed from their positions only for adequate cause and that the procedures of due process will be followed. After the awarding of tenure, which usually follows a probationary period of approximately three years, a teacher may not be dismissed without clear and abundant evidence of inadequate classroom performance. School boards have the discretionary power to grant tenure, although individual state legislatures determine the basis for tenure and the procedures for attaining tenure status.

A tenure contract provides a teacher with much

job security but does not guarantee permanent employment. Teachers may be reassigned to different schools, grade levels, or subject areas and may be dismissed for cause in accordance with a state's tenure laws. In a number of states, administrative and supervisory personnel, such as principals and superintendents, are not eligible for tenure. In some states, tenured teachers who voluntarily resign their positions in order to become administrators forfeit their tenure rights.

Religion in the Public Schools. Some of the most volatile disputes concerning church-state relations have centered on the public schools. With the exception of school desegregation, more cases involving religion in the schools have been heard than any other school law issue.

The First Amendment, applied to the states through the Fourteenth Amendment, prohibits the governmental establishment of any religion or interference with the free exercise of religious beliefs. In the case of *Everson v. Board of Education* (1947) the U.S. Supreme Court concluded that the government may not pass laws to aid or show preference to any religion. Thus, with the exception of student transportation costs, parochial schools may not receive public funding. The most significant case dealing with the free exercise of religion is *Wisconsin v. Yoder* (1972), in which the Supreme Court exempted Amish children from compulsory school attendance after the eighth grade, holding that the right of the parents to freely practice their religion outweighed the state's interest in mandating that Amish children attend high school.

The establishment clause prohibits organized school prayer, but the free exercise clause allows for individual devotional activities as long as such activities are private and nondisruptive. Religious displays and holiday observances have also presented serious constitutional problems. The Supreme Court struck down a Kentucky law in 1980 that called for the prominent display of the Ten Commandments in public school classrooms. In contrast, the Court has allowed the observance of holidays such as Christmas as long as the overall purpose is educational and does not serve to advance religion. Litigation in this sensitive area remains controversial.

School Desegregation. The 1896 Supreme Court decision *Plessy v. Ferguson* interpreted the equal protection clause of the Fourteenth Amendment to mean that public school students could be legally segregated by race. By the 1950's, however, the Court began to recognize that racial segregation was not equal and deprived African American children equal access to education.

The landmark case of *Brown v. Board of Education* (1954) invalidated the "separate but equal" doctrine, declaring that racially segregated public schools were "inherently unequal." In the decades following this decision the Court struggled to formulate a remedy to allow school districts time to comply while at the same time dealing with states that attempted to ignore or circumvent the decision. One year after *Brown v. Board of Education* the Court attempted to clarify its mandate by saying that segregated school systems must desegregate "with all deliberate speed." This often-quoted phrase was interpreted by the states to mean the Supreme Court recognized that resolving the complex problems involved in desegregating school districts, especially in the South, would take time. Although specific remedies were not suggested by the Court, school districts were informed that they were charged with an "affirmative duty" to take whatever steps necessary to achieve racial balance.

In the decades following *Brown*, school districts, especially urban districts, struggled to comply with the Court's decree. One remedy, school busing, generated tremendous political controversy, as students were moved out of neighborhood schools for purposes of integration. As many cities experienced growing minority populations, meaningful school desegregation could not be accomplished without transferring pupils between urban and suburban districts or, in some cases, merging adjoining districts. These and other controversial remedies illustrate the tremendous difficulty in attempting to achieve racial equality in America's schools.

Suggested Readings. General comprehensive treatments of school law include William D. and Christina M. Valente's *Law in the Schools* (New York: Merrill, 1997), Martha M. McCarthy and Nelda H. Cambron-McCabe's *Public School Law: Teachers' and Students' Rights* (Newton, Mass.: Allyn and Bacon, 1992), and Louis Fischer, David Schimmel, and Cynthia Kelly's *Teachers and the Law* (New York: Longman, 1994). Constitutional issues are discussed in Arval Morris's *The Constitution and American Public Education* (Durham, N.C.: Carolina Academic Press, 1989), Haig A. Bosmajian's *The*

Freedom of Religion (New York: Neal Schuman, 1987), *Race, Law, and Culture: Perspectives on Brown v. Board of Education*, edited by Austin Sarat (New York: Oxford University Press, 1997), Kelly Frels and Merri Schneider-Vogel's *The First Amendment and School Employees: A Practical Management Guide* (Topeka, Kans.: National Organization on Legal Problems of Education, 1986), John W. Johnson's *The Struggle for Student Rights: Tinker v. Des Moines and the 1960's* (Lawrence: University Press of Kansas, 1997), and Robert S. Alley's *School Prayer: The Court, the Congress, and the First Amendment* (New York: Prometheus, 1994). Specialized works on teacher and student rights are Jane R. Price, Alan H. Levine, and Eve Cary's *The Rights of Students* (Carbondale, Ill.: Southern Illinois University Press, 1988), J. Devereux Weeks's *Student Rights Under the Constitution: Selected Federal Decisions Affecting the Public School Community* (Athens: University of Georgia Press, 1992), and David Rubin and Steven Greenhouse's *The Rights of Teachers* (New York: Bantam Books, 1984). Special education issues are discussed in Mitchell L. Yell's *The Law and Special Education* (Englewood Cliffs, N.J.: Prentice-Hall, 1997). —*Raymond Frey*

See also Freedom of religion; Freedom of speech; Home schooling; Truancy; Vandalism.

Search and seizure, illegal

Unauthorized examination and removal of evidence from a person or premises, known as illegal search and seizure, is prohibited by the U.S. Constitution.

Illegal search and seizure is forbidden by the Fourth Amendment to the U.S. Constitution, which states: "The right of the people to be secure in their persons, houses, papers, and effects, against unreasonable searches and seizures, shall not be violated." The right to search and seize is determined only by an appropriate judge. Even in cases of hot pursuit, a judge may review the action to determine whether it was legal. Reasonableness is a judicial question.

Property is seized if it is removed from the premises. Persons are seized if they are not free to walk away; detention or holding for questioning is a seizure. In 1914, in *Weeks v. United States*, the U.S. Supreme Court decided that material seized by federal authorities without a warrant must be returned to the owner and could not be used to convict. That has been called "the exclusionary rule." Before that, the Fourth Amendment was largely ignored. In *Wolf v. Colorado* (1949), illegal searches and seizures by state authorities were declared unconstitutional. States were to decide what, if anything, to exclude. In *Mapp v. Ohio* (1961), the Supreme Court held that evidence illegally obtained could not be used in state court prosecutions. Much litigation followed, as did search warrants, for city police had rarely used them before 1961.

Critics of the U.S. Supreme Court contend that the Court is trying to do away with the exclusionary rule. For example, Supreme Court justice Benjamin Cardozo argued that the exclusionary rule could let the guilty go free. But the opposite choice is unbridled police power and a revocation of the Fourth Amendment. The exclusionary rule has been held not to apply when a warrant is defective because of the judge's action and not police action; when discovery is held to be inevitable, as in the case of an "inventory search"; and when entry was reasonable, although there was no search warrant. Each exception has its opponents: The police can talk magistrates into issuing defective warrants, no discovery is inevitable, and, in general, an open door to evidence destroys the system of restraint.

Fingerprints, handwriting, the voice, the state of sobriety, and the treads of shoes are not private; an officer is therefore entitled to take or measure them without a warrant, although the officer must do so in the least obtrusive way possible. A search of an automobile requires a warrant, but courts have adopted special rules because automobiles are mobile. An order may be imposed on a bank or on a telephone company for its records about a customer in spite of the dissent of the customer. Goods can be seized from a warehouse in spite of the protests of the person who owns the goods but not the warehouse.

Persons may sue in cases of illegal search or seizure, although courts give wide latitude to police officers, whose superiors are not usually considered liable. —*Dwight Jensen*

See also Constitution, U.S.; Police; Privacy rights; Probable cause; Search warrant; Stop and frisk.

Search warrant

A written order by a judge giving law-enforcement officers power to search for evidence is known as a search warrant.

A search warrant is usually an *ex parte* proceeding, meaning that only one side is involved in the hearing. Probably the most common means of obtaining a warrant is for prosecutors or police officers to go before a judge and say, under oath, that if they are allowed to search specific premises, they have reason to believe that they will find specified items. They must make enough of a case to justify the warrant, telling the judge why they thinks that the items may be at that location. The judge may grant the warrant if the grounds are prescribed by a statute. Judicial fiat is not allowed. The judge cannot simply decree that premises be searched; there must be a legal reason for ordering a search warrant. The judge must often balance the interests of individual privacy against the interests the state has to obtain the evidence in question. Telephone requests for warrants are only permitted if time is of the essence. If a search is allowed, the fruits of the search, if there are any that comply with the warrant, may be seized. A judge who determines that items were improperly seized may release them.

History of Search and Seizure. Searches were originally allowed only for stolen goods. They were required apparently because judges or legislatures feared there might be fighting if persons unknown to property owners attempted to enter their property.

During the decade leading up to the American Revolution (1775-1783) writs of assistance became an issue. These writs were orders to a property owner requiring that the person assist officers of the law in searches of the owner's premises to determine if evidence of a crime could be found. In the colonies, James Otis led the fight against the writs of assistance, a fight that led to the Fourth Amendment to the U.S. Constitution, which stated: "The right of the people to be secure in their persons, houses, papers, and effects, against unreasonable searches and seizures, shall not be violated."

Until 1968 search warrants were ordinarily issued only for two purposes: to find the fruits of a crime (such as the money from a robbery or a dead body) and the tools of a crime (such as the pen used in a forgery, the tools used in a burglary, or the knife used in a murder). That had been the law since the English case of *Entick v. Carrington* in 1769, when the Lord Chief Justice of England ruled that a search for "mere evidence," the type of evidence Constable Carrington had conducted against printer Entick and the type contemplated by the writs of assistance, was illegal. The U.S. Supreme Court had chipped away at that restriction over the years, and in 1968, in a Maryland case, it ruled that states could enact laws or prescribe court rules permitting searches for "mere evidence," such as photographs of a crime being committed. California enacted such a rule, under which the police were allowed to search the news offices of the *Stanford Daily* for photographs showing the perpetrators of a crime in 1971. No such photographs were found, and a later act of the U.S. Congress forbade such searches in the future. Some states still prohibit the seizure of personal writings.

Warrants in General. Law-enforcement officers are not the only people who need search warrants. Other government officers—for example, officials of the Occupational Safety and Health Administration (OSHA)—sometimes need warrants to effect inspections that fall under the rubric of searches. The reasonableness of a search is a judicial question that must be decided by a judge, not by a law-enforcement officer. Warrants are required under both state and federal law. States may establish higher standards than those set by the Constitution, but not lower standards. The search must relate to the cause cited in justification of the search warrant, and that cause must be allowed by law.

Aliens may be treated differently from citizens in respect to search warrants, but minors, if they are citizens, may not be treated differently from adults. Renters have privacy on the premises they rent, including motel and hotel rooms. No warrant is required to search trash that has been left in a public place for disposal.

The information on which a search warrant is based may be hearsay and anonymous if the officer has reason to believe it. Police informants must be reliable and present information that can be corroborated. However, the information may not be stale. A search is not considered to have occurred when police officers notice evidence with the naked eye in a place they are allowed to be. A dog sniffing in a public place is not a search. Roadblocks are allowed without warrants if they are erected with reason; discretionary roadblocks are not allowed except when they make minimal intrusions on the public. Airport searches are allowed as long as they are confined to searches for items that endanger aircraft.

A person wronged in a search may sue. However, some immunity is granted to public officials. Persons contemplating a lawsuit for illegal search and seizure should consult an attorney. Search warrants may also be challenged by motions to suppress evidence. Wrongful search and seizure might be a criminal act. Presenting false information in order to obtain a warrant is perjury.

Search warrants must ordinarily be served by officers who first knock and announce themselves. In order to respond and grant entry, reasonable time must be afforded persons whose premises are to be searched. The searching officers need not announce themselves if there is no answer to the knock and are entitled to force entry to the premises if entry is not granted. Under some circumstances officers need not knock or announce themselves. Searches at night are subject to the laws of the state in which they occur.

Suggested Readings. General works that deal with the subject of search warrants include Lewis R. Katz's *Know Your Rights* (Cleveland, Ohio: Banks-Baldwin, 1993), John H. F. Shattuck's *Rights of Privacy* (Skokie, Ill.: National Textbook Company, 1977) and Paula A. Franklin's *The Fourth Amendment* (Morristown, N.J.: Silver Burdett Press 1991). Many search and seizure cases have centered on illegal drugs. One book about this is *Pot Shots* by Michael Stepanian (New York: Dell, 1972). Sometimes the law gives government the power to confiscate property seized in drug cases. Books dealing with that subject include *A License to Steal: The Forfeiture of Property* by Leonard Williams Levy (Chapel Hill: University of North Carolina Press, 1996) and *Forfeiting Our Property Rights: Is Your Property Safe from Seizure?* by Henry J. Hyde (Washington, D.C.: Cato Institute 1995). Search and seizure on school premises has also become an issue and is discussed by Lawrence F. Rossow in *Search and Seizure in the Public Schools* (Topeka, Kans.: National Organization on Legal Problems of Education, 1995).

—Dwight Jensen

See also Constitution, U.S.; District attorneys; Police; Privacy rights; Search and seizure, illegal; Suspect.

Secured transaction

A method of granting specific rights in personal property to secure a debt, secured transactions are carried out so that persons may obtain credit or better terms.

Suppose a person wished to acquire a car on credit. If the party extending the credit (a seller or lender) is not repaid, a long and costly process must occur to obtain a court determination (judgment), followed by legal process to seize and sell enough of the person's property to pay the judgment. Moreover, if the person is insolvent (unable to pay the debt) or the available property is "exempt" from legal process (most states protect persons from the seizure of minimal assets necessary for life), the creditor may never receive full payment. However, if the creditor obtained and perfected a security interest in the car, a claim that allows the car to be taken and sold and the proceeds applied to the debt, the creditor is more likely to receive payment. The ability to obtain this better assurance of ultimate payment is governed by Article 9 of the Uniform Commercial Code (UCC). The same analysis applies if real property, such as a residence, is used as security.

Entering into a Secured Transaction. A seller or lender acquires a security interest when three conditions exist. First, debtors must agree to put up specified property as security (collateral). This agreement is called a security agreement and is normally in writing. Second, debtors must have rights to the collateral. Normally, debtors are the owners of the collateral but may have a lesser interest in it. Finally, the creditor (the secured party) must provide value—that is, make the loan or deliver the property being sold. In more complex transactions, the property may also serve as collateral for later (future) advances or past loans, and other property of the debtor or property the debtor may acquire in the future (after acquired property) may come under the arrangement by its terms. Some of the terms of the security agreement, such as how much the secured party may charge for providing the credit (interest), are governed by laws other than Article 9.

The law generally requires that to prevail over persons other than debtors, secured parties must give public notice of their claim to the property that is serving as collateral, which is called perfecting the security interest. If debtors give secured parties possession of the collateral, as in a pawn transaction, this will suffice to give public notice of the secured parties' claim to the property. If the collateral is a car or similar type of property, normally the notice occurs by indicating the secured party's interest on the certificate of title. There are other methods by which the required notice is given, but the most common is for secured parties to file a form in the public records known as a financing statement. Financing statements are usually filed with the secretary of state in the state where the collateral is kept.

The claim of a secured party to the collateral, once perfected, generally is superior to that of anyone else. For example, the secured party will prevail over a later secured party, over a later purchaser of the property, and over a later creditor who obtains a claim on the property by judicial process. That is, upon the enforcement of the claim the secured party is the person first entitled to the proceeds of sale. However, there are certain important exceptions. For example, a buyer in the ordinary course of business will prevail over even a prior perfected secured party. A buyer from a car dealer will not have to worry about the security interest of the bank that financed the car dealer's inventory of cars if the dealer does not pay the bank.

Enforcement of the Security Interest. If a debtor fails to pay back money owed and such failure is made an event of default in the security agreement, the secured party may repossess, or take back, the collateral. This may be done without judicial process if no breach of the peace occurs. A breach of the peace occurs if there is violence or a serious danger of violence, such as if an altercation with the debtor occurs. It is also a violation of the law for secured parties to use peace officers to assist them, even if the intent is to reduce the chance of a breach of the peace, unless such officers act in an official capacity. Breaking into a house, garage, office, or factory is also not permitted. There are divergent views as to whether trickery is permitted; the line would seem to be that trickery which may trigger violence is not allowed. Thus, telling debtors to come to the bank to discuss late payments with the intent of repossessing their cars from the bank parking lot may lead to possible violence and may not survive scrutiny, while telling them that the collateral must be taken away for repair and then not returning it poses no threat of violence and may not be a violation. Court decisions make secured parties responsible for violations committed by persons hired to repossess collateral. If judicial process is used to repossess, constitutional due process normally requires that debtors be notified of the proceeding and that they have an opportunity to object to the repossession before it occurs.

A debtor whose collateral has been repossessed may redeem it and end the security interest by paying the full debt before the secured party disposes of it. If the debtor does not redeem the collateral, the secured party in some cases may keep it in satisfaction of the debt. However, in most cases a secured party must "realize on the collateral." This generally means that the secured party must dispose of the collateral by sale, lease, or license and apply the proceeds to repayment of the debt. If the proceeds of disposition more than pay off the debt secured by the collateral, the debtor is entitled to the surplus. If the proceeds after application do not cover the debt, the debtor is responsible for the balance and subject to what is called a "deficiency judgment." However, in many states that have special laws protecting consumer debtors, this rule may not be applicable. For example, such a law may grant debtors the right to pay past due amounts and "reinstate" the transaction notwithstanding default or may protect debtors from a "deficiency judgment" for the balance of the debt not satisfied by disposition of the collateral.

Suggested Readings. A number of good discussions of secured transactions are available. Three short and basic treatments are Bradford Stone's *Uniform Commercial Code, Part Four* (4th ed. St. Paul, Minn.: West Publishing, 1988), Henry Bailey III and Richard Hagedorn's *Secured Transactions* (3d ed. St. Paul, Minn.: West Publishing, 1988), and Russell Hakes's *The ABCs of the UCC, Article 9: Secured Transactions* (Chicago: American Bar Association, 1996). More detailed discussions appear in Barkley

Clark's *The Law of Secured Transactions* (2d ed. Warren, Gorham & Lamont, 1988 and supplement), William Lawrence, William Henning, and R. Freyermuth's *Understanding Secured Transactions* (New York: Matthew Bender, 1997), and James White and Robert Summers's *Uniform Commercial Code* (4th ed. St. Paul, Minn.: West Publishing, 1995).

—*Fred H. Miller*

See also Automobile purchasing; Consumer protection laws; Credit, consumer; Debt collection; Home buying; Installment sales contract; Loans, business; Loans, personal; Mortgages; Repossession; Usury.

Self-defense

Self-defense, defined as the protection of oneself and others or of one's property from the threat of an outside force, is used as a legal defense against any charges resulting from self-defensive actions.

The right of self-defense has many historical roots. It was most notably explained by the seventeenth century English philosopher John Locke in his *Second Treatise of Government*: ". . . the law, which was made for my preservation, where it cannot interpose to securing my life from present force, which, if lost, is capable of no reparation, permits me my own defense, and the right of war, a liberty to kill the aggressor, because the aggressor allows not time to appeal to our common judge, nor the decision of the law, for a remedy in a case where the mischief may be irreparable." Locke's ideals are echoed in the basic precepts of the Second Amendment to the U.S. Constitution: "A well regulated Militia, being necessary to the security of a free State, the right of the people to keep and bear Arms, shall not be infringed." This coincides with Locke's argument that a "free state" cannot exist when people are not allowed to protect life and liberty in the event that the law is unable to protect them.

Self-defense can be categorized by the use of two types of force: deadly and nondeadly. Deadly force involves the application, or threat of application, of life-threatening force used in response to a life-threatening attack or a perceived possible attack. This can involve force exercised through the use of a gun or knife or any other type of force that may be lethal to the person against whom it is used. For example, if an unarmed person is assaulted on the street by a healthy young man wielding a knife, the knife constitutes a potentially lethal weapon in comparison to which fists alone are not lethal. However, the use of fists may constitute deadly force when applied against a person in fragile health, for then they are capable of inflicting life-threatening damage.

In the case of an attack with deadly force, a person under attack may be required by law to flee from the attacker if possible without endangering the other's life. Most states, however, do not have this requirement, allowing persons to stand their ground and employ reasonable force to defend themselves from harm. While a few states require that persons flee if possible rather than defend themselves, it is generally accepted that they have the right to remain if they are attacked in their homes or dwellings, if they are victims of dangerous felonies, or if they are trying to arrest an attacker in a lawful way.

The future of the right to self-defense is in a state of flux. The general trend is toward increasing awareness. Results of this trend include increasing gun sales, martial arts education, and a heightened response to incidents of domestic violence. The right to self-defense resides in a gray area of the law, its exercise being subject to personal judgment in the heat of the moment.

—*David Savino and Matthew Lindstrom*

See also Constitution, U.S.; Felony; Gun laws.

Self-employment taxes

Self-employment tax is what self-employed individuals pay to the government to finance their coverage under Social Security.

Persons carrying on a trade or business as sole proprietors, as independent contractors, or as members of partnerships are subject to a variety of tax obligations: federal and state income taxes, franchise taxes, sales taxes, occupational taxes, employment taxes, and self-employment taxes. The self-employment (SE) tax is based on the net earnings from self-employment and the combined rate for Social Security (Old-Age, Survivors, and Disability Insurance) and Medicare (Hospital insurance). Because net earnings from self-employment are determined differently from taxable income, self-employed individuals could have a substantial SE tax liability even though they owe little or no income tax. Moreover, the Internal Revenue Service (IRS) requires that SE tax and income tax on self-employment income be paid in quarterly estimated payments.

Who Must Pay the Self-Employment Tax. Workers who share their Social Security obligations with their employers do not pay SE taxes. However, individuals who have part-time businesses in addition to a regular job are subject to self-employment tax on the net income from their business. Thus, any person carrying on a business or a trade as a sole proprietor, as an independent contractor, or as a member of a partnership is subject to SE taxes, but any wages earned reduces the self-employment tax base. The determination of whether workers are employees or self-employed depends on who has the legal right to control what, when, and how that individual engages in a profitable activity.

Some people are classified as employees for Social Security tax purposes but are self-employed for income tax purposes. Other are treated just the opposite. For example, anyone who performs services as an agent driver or commission driver, as a full-time life insurance sales representative, as a home-worker, or as a traveling or city salesperson is a considered a "statutory employee." Statutory employees are considered employees for Social Security purposes and do not pay SE tax. Conversely, a duly ordained, commissioned, or licensed minister of a church is treated as self-employed for SE tax purposes but as an employee for income tax purposes. Taxpayers who misclassify themselves or persons whom they employ can be held liable for unpaid taxes. This can be avoided by completing and filing IRS Form SS-8, "Determination of Employee Work Status for Purposes of Federal Employment Taxes and Income Tax Withholding."

Computing the Self-Employment Tax. The SE tax is computed on Schedule SE "Self-employment tax" (Form 1040). Because SE tax is to be shown on line 47, Form 1040 must be used to report tax even if no income tax is owed. Individuals filing a joint return must compute their self-employment income and that of their spouses separately. Also, if both taxpayers have self-employment income, they have to file two schedules.

Not all income (or losses) from a business is included in self-employment income. For example, gains and losses from property the taxpayer is not in the business of selling (such as investment property, depreciable property, and fixed assets used for business) are excluded from self-employment income. Rent from real estate and from personal property leased with real estate is not self-employment income unless the taxpayer is doing business as a real estate dealer.

The SE tax is computed on net earnings, which is generally self-employment income reduced by business deductions. Section 162 of the Internal Revenue Code provides the basic foundation of deductibility. In general, each item must meet four conditions to be deductible as a business expense. It must be an expense as opposed to a capital expenditure, it must be ordinary and necessary, it must be paid or incurred, and it must be for carrying on a trade or business. Deductions have been disallowed under the ordinary and necessary standard if they were incurred primarily for personal reasons rather than for business purposes. Also, if self-employed taxpayers use the cash method of accounting, they must actually pay an expense before they may deduct it. Finally, the carrying on standard requires that the taxpayer actually conduct business rather than merely prepare to conduct business. Nevertheless, a separate provision in the Internal Revenue Code (Section 195) allows taxpayers to amortize start-up costs over a sixty-month period.

Estimated Tax Payments. Even though the final annual tax liability cannot be determined until the end of the taxable year, the IRS requires self-employed individuals to pay their taxes (including minimum tax and self-employment tax) in installments throughout the year. This requires that taxpayers estimate the amount of tax they expect to owe for the year after subtracting tax credits and taxes withheld by employers. Taxpayers who do not send enough each quarter by the due date are charged a penalty, even if they are due a refund when they file their tax returns. Taxpayers are not penalized for any year in which the tax liability on their return minus withholding is less than $500. The Tax Relief Act of 1997 increased this threshold to $1,000 for years after 1997.

The due dates for calendar year taxpayers are April 15 for the first quarter, June 15 for the second quarter, September 15 for the third quarter, and January 15 of the following calendar year for the fourth quarter. Calendar-year taxpayers may skip the fourth-quarter payment if they file their returns and pay the tax due by January 31 of the following year. Fiscal year taxpayers (those whose taxable year ends on the last day of any month other than December) use corresponding dates for their taxable year. Due dates are always postponed to the next working day if they fall on a weekend or a holiday. The Internal Revenue Code permits new taxpayers to adopt either accounting period on or before the due date of their first return. However, once an accounting period is adopted, it may not be changed unless approved by the IRS. For these reasons, most individual taxpayers use the calendar year as their accounting period.

Suggested Readings. The primary sources of authority for the rules of federal taxation are the Internal Revenue Code, Treasury Regulations, IRS Rulings, and court decisions. When tax legislation is enacted by the U.S. Congress and signed into law by the U.S. president, it adds or amends the Internal Revenue Code of 1986 (which is Title 26 of the U.S. Code). *The United States Tax Reporter* (New York: Research Institute of America, 1992) is a multivolume reference to the Internal Revenue Code. Each volume provides the law itself, regulations, a plain-language explanation, and references to all court cases and rulings pertaining to specific code sections. *The Standard Federal Tax Reporter* (Chicago: Commerce Clearing House, 1996) is another multivolume reference to the code. It also provides commentary and explanations. Both of these multivolume references are available in the business section of public libraries. Additionally, Gary W. Carter's *Taxes Made Easy for Your Home-Based Business* (New York: Macmillan, 1997) provides a comprehensive overview of the tax obligations of self-employed persons. The IRS publications that address self-employment tax are Publication 533, *Self Employment Tax*; Publication 15A, *Employer's Supplemental Tax Guide*; and Publication 505, *Tax Withholding and Estimated Tax*. To get these and other free IRS Publications, call the IRS at 1-800-TAX-FORM.

—*W. Dene Eddings Andrews*

See also Business taxes; Internal Revenue Service; Sales taxes; Tax law.

Sentencing

A sentence is the response that a society, through some agency of government, makes toward those who are convicted of violating that society's criminal laws.

Sentences are not simply punishments; they may include nonpunitive responses such as psychological treatment. Historically, when a person committed an act of violence, the focus was on making matters whole again, often through restitution to the victim or the victim's family. With the rise in state power and the inability of the peasantry to pay monetary compensation, society increasingly resorted to corporal forms of punishment such as branding, whipping, and execution. It was not until the 1800's that prison was accepted as a reformed method of corporal punishment.

Types of Sentences. There are currently four major types of sentences: fines, whereby the state collects money from the offender; community sentences, whereby a person follows behavioral rules such as restitution or treatment programs; incarceration in jails, prisons, and community treatment facilities; and capital punishment, whereby a person is executed. The specific blend of these sentencing forms may depend on which of five sentencing goals are held most important. Those who believe in deterrence hope that punishment will prevent offenders or potential criminals from committing additional crimes. Those who seek long prison terms hope that they can select and incapacitate future criminals. Those who focus on punishment for its own sake seek retribution for past acts. Those who focus on rehabilitation hope to teach offenders not to commit future bad acts. Those who focus on restitution hope that offenders' future behavior will be altered through their efforts to compensate victims and that victims will regain some sense of wholeness. In addition to these sentencing goals, many argue that sentencing laws and decisions are highly responsive to political pressures and that organizational considerations such as courtroom efficiency and the capacity of the correctional system have a major impact on such decisions.

Prison sentences are either indeterminate or determinate. Indeterminate sentences give offenders both a minimum and a maximum sentence, say from five to fifteen years, whereby the corrections department is given the discretion to release inmates based on appropriate behavior. Determinate sentences set a single period of incarceration, although judges may be given the discretion to pass sentences from a wide range of possibilities. This discretion has increasingly been restricted by mandatory sentencing laws, such as Massachusetts's requirement of a one-year sentence for illegal firearms possession. Similarly, recent sentencing guidelines statutes allow judges to vary sentences only slightly, often by only a few months, in the case of multiple-year sentences. Studies have shown that between indeterminate and determinate sentencing systems there is little overall difference in the time inmates actually serve.

Recent attempts at innovation involve community sentences, such as shock incarceration boot camps, high-tech solutions such as electronic monitoring, and efforts to include offenders in "restoring" victims to their previctimized state.

Sentencing Process. The three branches of government—the legislative, judicial, and administrative—have different levels of responsibility for setting criminal sentences. A legislature takes increasing responsibility if it establishes mandatory sentences or strict sentencing guidelines. Often a judge, the prosecutor, and occasionally a jury make choices within a broad range of options set by the legislature, giving them the primary power in sentencing. Correctional officials may have significant responsibility if the sentences are indeterminate, for they largely decide when an inmate will be released from prison.

The vast majority of defendants plead guilty before trial as a result of a plea bargain with the prosecutor. Such agreements usually include sentence recommendations. Most judges either accept such agreements or must give mandatory or highly restricted sentences. Thus, many argue that prosecutors are now the most powerful sentencing agents in the criminal justice system.

Actual sentences are handed down at sentencing hearings, which, for the majority of defendants, take place either the same day or the day after they are convicted. For the majority of defendants, the only information the judge has in sentencing are

Judge sentences youth in courtroom. (James L. Shaffer)

attorney recommendations and the prior conviction record of the defendant. Some jurisdictions require a presentence report, especially for serious crimes. A probation agent or court official gives the information to the judge for consideration after investigating the crime, its victims, and the defendant.

Legal Rights in Sentencing. Compared to the guilt phase of the criminal process, the U.S. Supreme Court has recognized very few defendants' rights during the sentencing phase of a criminal proceeding. Defendants have the right, under the Sixth Amendment to the Constitution, to have an attorney assist them at the sentencing hearing, but only if an actual jail or prison term is imposed. Defendants do not have the right of allocution—that is, the right to address the court on their own behalf. They also have no right to a presentence report nor do they have the right to see or comment on a presentence report or to call witnesses on their own behalf unless they face the death penalty. Defendants also have no right to cross-examine witnesses or to ask that judges give reasons for their decisions.

Sentencing decisions can easily be biased by unfair information, but the U.S. Supreme Court has said that the quantity of information is very important, saying that a judge may consider almost any information, including alleged prior criminal acts for which the defendant has not been convicted. Some lower courts have even said that judges may consider charges for which defendants have been found not guilty. Also, if judges believe that defendants lied when testifying, they can use this belief to punish defendants at sentencing. If defendants refuse to provide information about another person's criminal activity, they can also be additionally punished at sentencing. Evidence that may not be admitted in criminal trials because it was illegally seized may be admitted during sentencing hearings. Evidence showing the impact of the crime on victims or victims' families is allowed, as are victims' personal characteristics. Only victims' or family members' opinions about how a defendant should be sentenced are not allowed.

While the U.S. Supreme Court has recognized very limited rights for defendants, some state legislatures and courts have recognized that defendants have additional rights during sentencing, and some judges, using their discretion, may also provide defendants with such additional benefits.

Suggested Readings. Michael Tonry's *Sentencing Matters* (New York: Oxford University Press, 1996) provides an excellent history of sentencing and an analysis of current reforms, such as sentencing guidelines, intermediate sanctions, and mandatory penalties. A more specific focus on incapacitation policy is provided by Franklin Zimring and Gordan Hawkins in *Incapacitation: Penal Confinement and the Restraint of Crime* (New York: Oxford University Press, 1995). Similarly, James Byrne, Arthur Lurigio, and Joan Petersilia (eds.) in *Smart Sentencing: The Emergence of Intermediate Sanctions* (Newbury Park, Calif.: Sage Publications, 1992) provide a range of discussions on the issues and controversy surrounding such community sanctions as electronic monitoring and boot camps. Sheldon Krantz and Lynn Branham's *The Law of Sentencing, Corrections, and Prisoners' Rights* (St. Paul, Minn.: West Publishing, 1997) is a good legal text that includes most of the important legal decisions related to sentencing and some examples of state sentencing systems. Lynn Branham and Sheldon Krantz's *Sentencing, Corrections, and Prisoners' Rights* (St. Paul, Minn.: West Publishing, 1994) provides an easy to read summary of federal judicial decisions related to sentencing. —*Peter Gregware*

See also Death penalty; Plea bargain; Probation, adult; Probation, juvenile; Three-strikes laws.

Service contracts

Service contracts include warranties that services will be performed in a skillful and "workmanlike" manner.

The common law of services is based on a standard of workmanship. Dealers are required in service contracts to perform work in a "workmanlike" manner. Contractors agree to furnish supervision, labor, and equipment and perform work this way. The performance standard for repair service contracts is to perform repairs in a workmanlike manner. The existence of an implied warranty in a particular transaction is a question of law for the courts to determine. Good and workmanlike performance depends on the knowledge, training, or experience necessary for the successful practice of a trade or occupation.

Article 2 of the Uniform Commercial Code (UCC) applies to the sale of goods. The law of services is outside Article 2. Many contracts involve sales as well as services. Sales involve the passing of the title of goods from the seller to the buyer in contrast to the rendering of services. If a contract is predominately a sales contract, it is governed by Article 2. In contrast, predominately service contracts are governed by the common-law standard of workmanlike performance.

The rendering of legal or medical services is governed by professional standards of care. Lawyers, engineers, and architects are held to professional standards of care in their respective fields. A doctor is held to the standards of practice followed by the medical profession. The prescription of a drug by a physician is the rendering of medical services and not the sale of goods. Physicians do not promise perfect results but only that they will follow a reasonable standard of care.

The United States economy has shifted from a manufacturing economy to one based on the performance of services. The production of a television program, for example, may involve scores of service contracts. A musical production may involve musical arrangers, composers, conductors, and musicians. The production of a video may involve animation artists, film edit technicians, narrators, mixing technicians, screen writers, and cameramen. Special writers may be hired who perform expert professional services. All of these contracts are governed by the common law, not the Uniform Commercial Code. Agreements for the personal services of actors, narrators and other technical and professional personnel are based chiefly on contract law. Professionals such as doctors, lawyers, and engineers may be subject to a standard of professional negligence.

The parties to service contracts may tailor their contracts according to their individual needs. Lawyers' agreements with clients are subject to bar association and ethical rules. Physicians' agreements with patients are subject to the strictures of informed consent. The principles of good faith and fair dealing apply to all services contracts. This is indicative of the trend in the law, which is to apply warranty concepts by analogy to service contracts.

Automobile dealers sometimes offer service contracts in conjunction with the sale of new cars. These service contracts are sometimes called extended warranty contracts. The ostensible purpose of these contracts is to give buyers added protection beyond ordinary warranties. A growing number of states regulate automobile service contracts. Service contracts statutes vary from state to state. A number of them require companies offering service contracts to register in the state and obtain bonding. There is a discernible trend for automobile service contracts to be placed under state lemon law protection. —*Michael L. Rustad*

See also Automobile purchasing; Contracts; Lemon laws.

Sexual battery

Sexual battery is a form of sexual assault that does not constitute rape.

There are many types of sexual assaults in which the use or threat of force and the issue of consent are not applicable. Many jurisdictions address these forms under a legal provision known as sexual battery. Generally, these are categorized as a lesser-included offense to rape.

Sexual battery occurs when a person of ordinary resolve feels coerced to participate in sex, a condition that is common in encounters that are known as date or acquaintance rape. In date rape, the victim is involved in an intense sexual encounter with the offender but protests having the encounter end in sexual intercourse or other similar sexual conduct. The offender presses the victim using a combination of coercive persuasion and the simple refusal to stop. This type of pressure is one form of sexual battery.

Sexual battery also occurs when the victim is unable to consent to sex because of intoxication or another unconscious or semiconscious state. When persons are in a state of mind in which their ability to assess a sexual situation is impaired, even if it is of their own doing, the person seeking the sex act must refrain from acting. If a woman drinks too much alcohol and falls asleep and a man, wishing to have sex with her but unable to elicit a coherent response, takes her incoherent statement as permission, then sexual battery results.

A third situation involves mistaken identity and arises when persons mistake their sexual partners as their spouses. If a man comes home to find a woman he presumes to be his wife waiting for him in a darkened room and they proceed to have sex, after which the man discovers that the woman is not in fact his wife, then the woman has committed sexual battery.

Another battery situation occurs when the offender is the victim's legal guardian. Even if the two parties consent to having sex, it is not legal for a legal guardian to be sexually involved with a charge. This includes adults who are under probate supervision of persons in their homes or institutions or persons who have voluntarily submitted themselves to treatment at medical or other facilities. Sexual battery also takes place if natural, foster, adoptive, or stepparents have sex with their children who have not reached the age of maturity.

If persons have supervisory or disciplinary authority over others, they should not engage in sexual relations with those persons. This applies even if the encounters are consensual and between adults. An example of this type of authority involves prison guards and inmates. Other examples are police officers and offenders, teachers and their students, and supervisors and their subordinates. Many employers, schools, and universities forbid intimate relationships between persons with different authority levels. —*Michael L. Barrett*

See also Kidnapping; Rape; Sexual harassment.

Sexual harassment

Sexual harassment is a type of sex discrimination involving unwelcome conduct in the workplace or the classroom that adversely affects working conditions.

Conduct that constitutes sexual harassment may include touching, fondling, leering, asking for sex, displaying pornographic posters, and making sexually suggestive comments, particularly if such behavior is persistent or severe. Normal socializing between men and women at work is not illegal. Nor is a single off-color joke. But unwelcome and persistent sexual overtures or a regular pattern of offensive, sex-related jokes might be.

New Legal Area. Sexual harassment is a new and developing area of the law. Lower federal courts began defining sexual harassment as sex discrimination in 1976, a position affirmed in 1980 by the Equal Employment Opportunity Commission (EEOC), the federal agency that oversees workplace compliance with the Civil Rights Act of 1964. The U.S. Supreme Court heard its first workplace sexual harassment case, *Meritor Savings Bank v. Vinson*, in 1986 and its second in 1993. The newness of the subject has contributed to the confusion expressed by some people about what behavior constitutes sexual harassment. Adding to the confusion is the fact that some lower courts have issued contradictory rulings in sexual harassment cases.

Not all harassment is illegal. The Civil Rights Act protects workers only from harassment that is based on sex, race, color, religion, or national origin. To qualify as sexual harassment, behavior must be prompted by a victim's biological sex. In other words, a person would not have been harassed if not for his or her sex. In *Harris v. Forklift Systems, Inc.* (1993) associate U.S. Supreme Court justice Ruth Bader Ginsburg defined sexual harassment as "whether members of one sex are exposed to disadvantageous terms or conditions of employment to which members of the other sex are not exposed." The Court said that judges should consider the circumstances involved, including if the sexual harassment was frequent, severe, physically threatening, or humiliating. Also important is if the sexual harassment interfered with the employee's work performance.

Sexual harassment may be classified as sex discrimination even when the victim of the harassment does not lose a tangible benefit, such as a job, promotion, or course grade. Further, the federal courts have determined that unlawful discrimination covers sexual harassment not only by a person in a superior position (such as a supervisor or teacher) but also by a peer (such as a fellow employee or student). The reasoning is that harassment by coworkers can create a hostile work environment in the same way as racial harassment and that persons subjected to it cannot work effectively.

Relevant Legislation and Case Law. Sexual harassment is considered a violation of Title VII of the Civil Rights Act of 1964 when it occurs in the workplace and of Title IX of the Educational Amendments of 1972 when it occurs in the educational arena. The Civil Rights Act of 1991 expanded the remedies available in cases of workplace sexual

Types of Workplace Sexual Harassment

Harasser	Type	Burden of Proof	Level of Liability
supervisor or other superior	quid pro quo—either an explicit or implicit offer of a benefit in exchange for sex	company	strict liability—company cannot use ignorance as a defense
co-worker or peer	hostile work environment—conduct so severe or pervasive that it alters work conditions	plaintiff—the person bringing the lawsuit	not strict—company can claim it did not and could not know, but must show prompt remedial action

harassment to include compensatory and punitive damages. Many states also have statutes—called fair employment practices laws (FEPs)—that prohibit sexual harassment on the job. In addition, some attorneys have brought legal actions called common-law torts when their clients have suffered serious physical or emotional injury as a result of sexual harassment in the workplace.

Those who initiate civil lawsuits, called plaintiffs, generally bring sexual harassment suits not against their actual harassers but against those who employ the harassers, such as companies or school administrators. If the sexual harassment includes rape or assault, separate criminal charges may be brought against the perpetrator.

The first cases were brought by women who had been sexually harassed by their male bosses. Later cases involved women who faced harassment from coworkers. Since the late 1980's some male employees have brought lawsuits alleging sexual harassment by women. In 1998 the U.S. Supreme Court for the first time considered the issue of same-sex harassment in a case involving heterosexual men. Federal district courts have given conflicting answers when asked if illegal sexual harassment must involve parties of the opposite sex.

Federal courts initially used the perspective of the "reasonable man" to determine if certain conduct is or is not harassment. Then some courts developed the "reasonable woman" standard—that is, would a reasonable woman find the behavior abusive? This was an effort to look at the conduct from the perspective of the victim. The U.S. Supreme Court has applied a "reasonable person" perspective in determining when behavior becomes illegal harassment.

Types of Sexual Harassment. There are two types of sexual harassment, with differing levels of liability for the employer. The first occurs when a person in a position of authority sexually harasses a subordinate, with either a promise of reward if the subordinate complies or threat of punishment if the subordinate refuses. Because the harasser is in a position of power, threats and promises may be implicit rather than explicit. This is called quid pro quo harassment, which means "one thing in exchange for another." It is a type of sexual blackmail.

The second type occurs when a colleague is the source of the harassment. As a coworker, the harasser cannot threaten the victim's job. Nevertheless, such harassment can be so severe or pervasive that it creates a hostile, offensive, or intimidating work environment, making it very difficult for the person who feels harassed to continue working effectively. This is called "hostile work environment" harassment.

Someone who is sexually harassed may suffer various types of job-related injuries, such as loss of a job or other benefit, forced demotion, and retaliation for complaining. Even if a victim of sexual harassment complies with a demand for sex or suffers no economic loss for refusing, the victim may still sue for other costs, such as for psychological stress. For women, sexual harassment can be a degrading reminder that, historically, they have little value outside of their sexual functions. Old attitudes also hurt men because of the assumption that men welcome any and all sexual advances and therefore cannot be sexually harassed.

Because of the personal costs to victims of harassment, a plaintiff may seek damages from the employer, depending on the type of harassment. In quid pro quo harassment the company is held to a strict liability standard. This means that the company is legally responsible for the actions of its agents, even if the company did not know of the behavior and has specific policies against sexual harassment. It is the company that gives the supervisor the authority to hire and fire employees; therefore, the company is responsible for remedying any harm caused by a supervisor's abuse of that authority.

In cases involving hostile work environments, the level of an employer's liability is lower. Guidelines issued in 1980 by the EEOC state that employers are responsible for workplace sexual harassment when they know of such behavior or should have known. They are not legally liable, however, if they take immediate and appropriate action to correct the situation. In this type of lawsuit, the plaintiff must show that the employer knew or should have known of the objectionable behavior and then failed to act.

Sexual Harassment and the Classroom. Sexual harassment of students is also illegal sex discrimination. It interferes with the learning environment. Students can bring legal action under Title IX of the Educational Amendments of 1972 if the school receives any federal funds. However, school employees facing on-the-job harassment, including student workers, bring sexual harassment lawsuits under Title VII.

In 1979 the U.S. Supreme Court found that Title IX entitles students who are victims of sexual harassment and discrimination to sue but not to collect money damages. The Court held that Title IX authorized lawsuits only for back pay or for an injunction to end the harassment. The justices set a new course in 1991, however, in a case called *Franklin v. Gwinnett County Public Schools*. The case involved a high school student whose teacher had continually and severely sexually harassed her. This time the Court said students could sue their schools for monetary damages.

According to studies of sexual harassment in the schools, most of the incidents involve fellow students rather than teachers or professors and fall under the category of a hostile work environment. Some colleges have adopted policy statements that also define consensual sexual relationships between students and professors as sexual harassment because of the unequal power between students and teachers.

Dealing with Sexual Harassment. If persons feel sexually harassed by others, they must first clearly communicate to them that the behavior is unwelcome and that they consider it sexual harassment. If they feel in danger, they should immediately notify their supervisors (or their supervisors' bosses, if the source of the harassment is the supervisor). A written record should be kept, including descriptions of unwelcome behavior, victims' comments, harassers' responses, and the dates of incidences. Persons should be sure to keep performance evaluations in case harassers try to give victims negative job ratings. If the unwelcome conduct occurs again, victims should report it to their supervisors if they have not already done so. If the harassment continues and there has been no prompt, remedial action on the part of the company, persons should file complaints under their companies' grievance procedures, with the Equal Employment Opportunity Commission, or with the state FEP. Persons may not be fired for filing a complaint in a civil rights case.

If these agencies cannot satisfactorily resolve the situation, it may be necessary to take the case to court. Traditional remedies include back pay, reinstatement of employment (if victims have been fired or forced to quit), and attorney's fees. However, litigation is a very time-consuming, expensive, and emotionally draining process. Victims may not win. Furthermore, relationships in the workplace, even with coworkers, may never be the same afterward. For these reasons, persons might choose to pursue mediation through the Equal Employment Opportunity Commission (EEOC) and the creation of an educational program in the workplace. Employers usually agree to the educational approach because it lessens the likelihood that they will be held liable in future lawsuits. Also, given the cost of sexual harassment in terms of employee turnover, absenteeism, and low morale, companies often implement educational programs to improve workplace relations.

Suggested Readings. A number of quality self-help guides for the workplace are available, such as William Petrocelli and Barbara Kate Repa's *Sexual Harassment on the Job* (2d ed. Berkeley, Calif.: Nolo Press, 1995). Resources for the academic community include Judith Berman Brandenburg's *Confronting Sexual Harassment: What Schools and Colleges Can Do* (New York: Teachers College Press, 1997), which covers the legal responsibilities of educational institutions and strategies for addressing sexual harassment, and *Sexual Harassment on College Campuses: Abusing the Ivory Power*, edited by Michele A. Paludi (Albany, N.Y.: SUNY Press, 1996), which includes essays on such topics as consensual relationships with professors, the link between sexual harassment and rape, and the interface of racism and sexism on college campuses. For an interesting history see Kerry Segrave's *The Sexual Harassment of Women in the Workplace, 1600-1993* (Jefferson, N.C.: McFarland, 1994), which chronicles the sexual harassment of female servants, serfs, and slaves; industrial and clerical workers; and women in the military and the professions. A nonlegal exploration of the issue, with case studies, is Celia Morris's *Bearing Witness: Sexual Harassment and Beyond: Everywoman's Story* (Boston: Little, Brown, 1994).

—*Nancy V. Baker*

See also Civil rights and liberties; Discrimination; Employment discrimination; Sexual battery.

Shareholder suit

A shareholder suit is an action brought by stockholders on behalf of the corporations in which they own stock.

When a corporation initiates an action to recover for some injury it has suffered, the board of directors typically sues the party who has wronged the company. In some cases, however, the directors or management of the corporation do not sue and the corporation does not recover for its injuries. In such cases the law allows a stockholder of the corporation to sue on behalf of the corporation in a shareholder suit. This is sometimes called a shareholder's derivative action, since the shareholder is not really the party who is wronged and acts to protect the corporation's interests. The cause of action derives from the corporation. The corporation is a necessary party and is thus made a defendant in the shareholder's derivative action along with the defendant wrongdoers.

Any recovery in a shareholder suit belongs to the corporation, because it is the corporation and not the individual shareholder who has been injured by the actions of wrongdoing defendants. However, a shareholder may recover the reasonable cost from the corporation of bringing the action if he or she is successful in the suit. This recovery may include attorney's fees.

Often shareholder derivative actions are brought to remedy breaches of fiduciary duties of care and loyalty owed to the corporation and its shareholders by its managers and sometimes even directors. These wrongful actions may have benefited a majority of the shareholders, who will not be willing to bring suit to remedy the wrong and thereby give up the benefit they have received. Moreover, it is difficult to get directors to sue themselves or the officers they have selected. In the late twentieth century derivative actions were controlled by statutes or court rules.

State and federal laws have restricted shareholder suits, recognizing that the corporation is governed by the board of directors who normally have the right to decide to bring or not bring lawsuits in the name of the corporation. Typically, laws require that the shareholder be an owner of stock at the time of the wrong and at the time the lawsuit is commenced; that the shareholder demand of the directors (and sometimes the other shareholders) that the corporation bring the lawsuit or give a good reason why this demand should be excused, such as when the wrongdoers are in control of corporate decision making as directors and majority shareholders; and that any settlement of the lawsuit be approved by the court.

Court approval of a shareholder suit is required in order to avoid strike suits, in which a shareholder with a small investment brings the action only for its nuisance value and the corporation pays off the shareholder to go away without any real recovery to the corporation. Otherwise the corporation must spend management time and incur legal expenses as the defendant, since the action is really brought on behalf of the corporation by the shareholder. Some statutes require that a shareholder post a bond to cover the corporation's expenses as a defendant. These are known as a security for expenses statutes and effectively discourage shareholder strike suits.

A shareholder suit is thus one way that the courts and corporation laws have developed to permit shareholder monitoring of those persons who are supposed to act in the corporation's best interests. These suits ensure that if these persons do not protect corporate interests fully, the shareholder may do so derivatively. —*J. Kirkland Grant*

See also Class-action suits; Corporations; Lawsuits; Stockholders.

Sheriffs

The chief law-enforcement administrator in a county, usually an elected person, is known as a sheriff.

Sheriffs, as counties' chief law-enforcement administrators, are responsible for maintaining public order within their jurisdictions. The performance of various other duties may also be required, including the execution of the mandates and judgments of criminal and civil courts, the delivery of writs, the summoning of juries, and the maintenance of county jails. The responsibilities of sheriffs are often so vast that sheriffs' offices are the largest employers of law-enforcement personnel in many areas of the country. In 1987 more than one in five law-enforcement officers (22.4 percent) served in sheriffs' departments. In states that legally require sheriffs, the duties and responsibilities of the office vary widely as do the requirements for holding the office. It is not unusual in many states for individuals to be elected who possess little or no educational training in law enforcement.

The Sheriff in England. The office of sheriff originated in England prior to the Norman conquest of 1066. Each shire, or county, was administered by a representative of the king known as a reeve. The appointed reeve was usually a baron who was an ally of the king. These officials had nearly absolute power within their jurisdictions. Eventually the title "shire reeve" evolved phonetically into "sheriff." The sheriff in the English countryside collected taxes, commanded the militia, delivered writs, and served as judge and jury in all criminal and civil cases. After the reign of William the Conqueror (c. 1028-1087), the sheriff's power and status were dramatically diminished. Under Henry II (1133-1189) the position assumed a law-enforcement role. By the end of the Protestant Reformation in England, specifically during the reign of Elizabeth I (1533-1603), most of the duties and powers once reserved exclusively for the sheriff had been assumed by the newly created offices of constable and justice of the peace.

Early American History. The English settlers of colonial America referred to their first law-enforcement officials as constables, as they had responsibilities very similar to those of their English namesakes. However, the governor of colonial New York appointed sheriffs who functioned in much the same manner as they had in England, exercising considerable power in their county. The sheriff in colonial New York was also responsible for the total oversight of elections, which led to widespread claims of corruption and abuse of power. The office of sheriff was stripped of much of its power following the American Revolution (1775-1783) and sheriffs as the law-enforcement agents of frontier justice did not emerge until after the American Revolution.

American sheriffs prior to the Civil War (1861-1865), who were typically appointed to their position by state, territorial, or city governments, exercised wide-ranging powers. Their many duties included maintaining order, collecting taxes, apprehending criminals, conducting elections, and maintaining local jails. Frontier sheriffs led particularly dangerous lives. They were poorly trained and often ill-equipped to deal with the hardships required of their office. In the Western territories of California, Oregon, Utah, New Mexico, Colorado, Nevada, and Texas they were called upon to travel great distances to apprehend criminals and perform other duties. When granted the authority, sheriffs also appointed deputy sheriffs to assist them in carrying out the duties of their office, especially the apprehension of fleeing criminals. It was not uncommon for sheriffs to "deputize" dozens of volunteers when circumstances required, especially during emergency situations. As the former Western territories achieved U.S. statehood, sheriffs increasingly became elected officeholders.

The Modern Sheriff. By 1900 population shifts in many states from the countryside to the cities required the creation of new law-enforcement agencies, such as city and state police departments. These new agencies assumed much of the work and duties performed by sheriffs' offices. The complexities of organized crime and other developments, especially the automobile and the expanding highway system, necessitated the creation of highly trained and skilled state and federal police agencies capable of dealing with the challenges of modern criminal activity. Most sheriffs, generally popularly elected, did not have the training or professional qualifications to deal with the modern criminal, who could move rapidly from one jurisdiction to another.

Another often-heard complaint was that the sheriffs in many communities were nothing more than servants of the local elites. In 1940 sheriffs around the country who were concerned about the level of professionalism and expertise needed to survive in the ever-changing field of criminal justice began organizing what evolved into the National Sheriffs' Association (NSA). The NSA offers training, information, and other services to sheriffs, deputies, and other personnel throughout the United States, allowing law-enforcement professionals to network and share information about trends in law enforcement and policing. In 1972 the National Sheriff's Institute (NSI) was established by the NSA to provide sheriffs and their administrative staffs with high-quality, low-cost training and programs. Jail administration, liability issues, crime prevention, and public relations are but a few of the many concerns addressed by NSI classes. The NSA also publishes the *Sheriff* magazine, *Community Policing Exchange*, *Sheriff Times*, and several other periodicals.

There are more than 3,000 sheriffs' departments in the United States, which serve as a critical part of today's law-enforcement community. Issues of concern for modern sheriffs as they enter the twenty-first century include funding, community policing, coping with law-enforcement stress, and rising medical costs. In many sparsely populated and unincorporated areas of the United States the locally elected sheriff is still the primary source of law-enforcement protection. Alaska and New Jersey are the only states that do not maintain sheriffs' offices. Sheriffs are elected in forty-six states, and most states require that all law-enforcement personnel, including sheriffs, undergo training before acting in their capacity as law-enforcement officers.

Suggested Readings. The best historical treatments of the role of the sheriff in English and early American colonial government are *The History of Local Government in England*, edited by Bryan Keith-Lucus (New York: Augustus M. Kelly, 1970), and *Town and Country: Essays on the Structure of Local Government in the American Colonies*, edited by Bruce C. Daniels (Middletown, Conn.: Wesleyan University Press, 1978). Those interested in the gunfighting sheriff may refer to Joseph G. Rosa's *The Gunfighter: Man or Myth?* (Norman: University of Oklahoma Press, 1969) and Frank R. Prassel's *The Western Peace Officer: A Legacy of Law and Order* (Norman: University of Oklahoma Press, 1971). For information on the role of the modern American Sheriff, see Paul and Shari Cohn's *Careers in Law Enforcement and Security* (New York: The Rosen Publishing Group, 1990), Lane W. Lancaster's *Government in Rural America* (2d ed. New York: Van Nos-

Sheriffs are the chief law-enforcement officials in counties across the United States. (James L. Shaffer)

trand, 1952), and Herbert Sydney Duncombe's *Modern County Government* (Washington, D.C.: National Association of Counties, 1977).

—*Donald C. Simmons, Jr.*

See also Community-oriented policing; Criminal justice system; Execution of judgment; Law enforcement; Police; State police.

Shoplifting

> *Shoplifting, a form of larceny, occurs when persons intentionally conceal or possess unpurchased merchandise either within or outside the premises of a store with the intent of converting the merchandise to their own use without paying for it.*

Although a form of larceny, shoplifting in most jurisdictions is a separate offense created by statute. Shoplifting statutes have been enacted largely in response to lobbying efforts on behalf of the retail industry. They attempt to negate the difficulty of proving the felonious intent and wrongful taking required under general larceny statutes in the typical shoplifting scenario. Most shoplifting is accomplished by the concealment of goods while the perpetrator is still within the store. Prior to the enactment of shoplifting statutes, which are aimed at this particular circumstance, many defendants argued that such concealment did not satisfy the intent or asportation (removal) elements required by general larceny statutes. When such defenses proved successful, merchants often found themselves defending civil litigation suits brought against them for defamation, false imprisonment, or false arrest. These suits, when the former shoplifting defendant prevails, can be quite costly to merchants, who may be ordered to pay money damages and the litigation expenses of the prevailing party, in addition to their own litigation expenses.

Shoplifting Statutes. Shoplifting statutes vary from state to state. Typically, however, they prohibit the intentional concealment of goods for the purpose of depriving the merchant of the proceeds, benefit, or use of the merchandise; the willful taking of goods with the intent to convert them to one's own use without paying for them; and the switching of price tags in order to pay less than the actual price for goods.

Many statutes establish a presumption of intent from the act of concealment. The term concealment is defined in terms of its common usage—that is, to cover or hide an object in order to prevent observation and discovery. Under these statutes, people who conceal goods on their person or elsewhere are presumed to do so with the intention of converting the goods to their own use. In such situations, the concealment creates a prima facie inference of shoplifting (an inference that is true or valid on first view). Conversely, the placing of an object in such a position so that it is still visible, such as in an open purse or a transparent bag, may not be considered sufficient concealment.

Shoplifting in many jurisdictions is a misdemeanor and is punishable by fines and short jail terms. First offenders are usually given a suspended sentence, a period of probation, or they are fined. If the merchandise is damaged or not recoverable, the convicted defendant may also be ordered to pay restitution to the merchant. As a condition of their probation, defendants who are placed on probation may also be barred from entering the store where they were arrested.

Although shoplifting is popularly considered to be a minor offense, the statutory scheme in some states creates different degrees of shoplifting, the most serious of which may be treated as felonies. For example, if the merchandise in question is valued at over a certain amount of money, usually in the $200 to $500 range, the statutory penalties may be increased. Similarly, persons with prior convictions for shoplifting may be subjected to more severe penalties or even mandatory jail terms.

Types of Shoplifters. Shoplifting is quite common among juveniles. The motives of juvenile offenders vary to some degree from the motives of more mature shoplifters, who generally steal simply to gain economic benefit. Young offenders typically steal for the thrill of the forbidden experience, in response to peer pressure, or because they believe that the store will not miss what they take. Often, they take small items such as makeup, compact disks, and accessories, although clothing is also a common object of young shoplifters.

Employees are another group of shoplifters. They are in a position to know the location and value of merchandise, as well as the security measures that their employers use. Employee shoplifting, which involves the taking of actual merchandise, is generally different from embezzlement, in which an employee or agent steals funds and attempts to conceal the theft, usually by the manipulation of account books or other records.

Still another group of shoplifters are professionals, sometimes called "boosters," who study stores, use elaborate concealment devices such as false bottom packaging, and sell their stolen merchandise on the street. Even though these people comprise a small percentage of shoplifters, they may account for a significant percentage of shoplifting losses. Although kleptomania, a compulsive psychological disorder, is sometimes raised as a defense to shoplifting, very few shoplifters are actually kleptomaniacs.

Loss Prevention. In addition to lobbying for more stringent shoplifting laws and for harsher sentencing, the retail industry has also taken a proactive approach to the shoplifting problem by installing electronic article surveillance systems. These systems feature tags with small electronic sensors that set off sound and light alarms. Some types of tags are attached to goods by the merchants while others are embedded in the packaging or the product itself by manufacturers. The benefit of this type of loss approach is twofold. First, potential shoplifters are deterred from theft by the presence of the tags; and second, merchants can avoid the necessity of prosecution and the attendant risks and costs of prosecution by stopping theft before it occurs.

Suggested Readings. There are many books available on the subject of loss prevention and the detection and prosecution of shoplifters. These include *Retail Security Versus the Shoplifter: Confronting the Shoplifter While Protecting the Merchant*, by George L. Keckeisen (Springfield, Ill.: Charles C. Thomas, 1993), and *Every Retailer's Guide to Loss Prevention: Keep Your Profits! Stop Theft!*, by Michael Brough and Derek Brown (Bellingham, Wash.: Self-Counsel Press, 1989). For a sociological analysis of the shoplifting phenomenon see *The Sociology of Shoplifting: Boosters and Snitches Today*, by Lloyd W. Klemke (Westport, Conn.: Praeger, 1992). Two books aimed at young adult readers that discuss shoplifting and the consequences to young offenders are *The Law and You: A Handbook for Young People*, by Elinor Porter Swiger (Indianapolis, Ind.: Bobbs-Merrill, 1973), and *Shoplifting*, by L. B. Taylor (New York: F. Watts, 1979).
—*Michele Leavitt*

See also Criminal justice system; Criminal prosecution; Criminal record; Defendant; Embezzlement; Juvenile criminal proceedings; Juvenile delinquency; Larceny; Theft.

Slander

A spoken statement by one person which is false and injures another person's reputation is slander.

Slander is an oral statement that wrongfully injures another individual's reputation. Written statements that injure another person's reputation are referred to as libels. Slander and libel, collectively, are known as defamations. In general, the law treats libels as greater wrongs than slanders, since a libel—written and therefore enduring as it is—is thought to pose a more serious threat to a person's reputation than the spoken slander that has no permanent existence.

A person slandered is in most cases entitled to sue the slanderer for damages in court. To prove a case of slander, the allegedly slandered person must prove several key facts. First, to be slanderous, an oral statement must be made to someone other than the person slandered. The law generally does not protect against the humiliation of having someone say something derogatory to one's face. It protects, instead, the injury to reputation caused when such a statement is made public. Second, the slanderous statement must be false. One can always defend against a charge of slander by demonstrating that the offensive statement was true. Third, the slanderous statement must have caused injury to the slandered person's reputation.

—*Timothy L. Hall*

See also Defamation; Freedom of speech; Libel.

Small businesses

Businesses involving a limited number of persons and products and organized as corporations, partnerships, or limited liability companies, small businesses provide legal and practical challenges for lawyers in the fields of business, tax, and regulatory law.

In discussing small businesses, certain distinctions must be made. In absolute terms the great majority of companies in the United States are small businesses, which are the backbone of the U.S. or any economy. Nevertheless, a high percentage of employment and productivity is concentrated in large corporations, and it is these corporations that have generally set the tone for developments in corporate, tax, and other legal specialties in the past century. There is thus a tendency for laws to be drafted with large companies in mind and only later adjusted to take into account small business concerns. This is compensated to some extent by a romantic view of small businesses and a sense that they need or deserve special help in competing with larger companies. Smallness is frequently defined by numbers of owners and ownership structure—for example, whether or not a company sells shares on a public stock exchange. Many "small" companies are thus actually rather large and even dominant in particular industries.

Choice of Entity and Capital Structure. Lawyers are involved at various phases of small business life but particularly at the formation stage. The first major decision for a small business lawyer is the form of legal entity that the business should take. Small businesses may choose to become corporations, general or limited partnerships, or limited liability corporations (LLCs), which are similar to partnerships but allow all the participants to restrict their individual liability for business debts. Businesses choosing to incorporate must also decide whether to file an election under Subchapter S of the Internal Revenue Code, which provides more favorable tax rules but at the cost of various restrictions on financing and operations.

The choice of entity is complex and involves a mixture of tax, liability, and practical concerns. Traditionally the choice was between a corporation, which had the advantage of limited liability and access to public investors, and a partnership, which had significant tax advantages but raised liability and financing concerns. In the 1990's the LLC became increasingly attractive, because it combines limited liability with favorable tax treatment and is also highly flexible in its operation. For example, an LLC may have various classes of members, receiving different allocations of income and

Family-owned corner markets represent the quintessential small business in America. (James L. Shaffer)

participating in varying degrees in management, but all having limited liability under applicable state laws. The LLC became especially attractive after implementation of the so-called "check a box" rules by the Internal Revenue Service (IRS), which allow an LLC to avoid corporate income tax even if it has many corporate-like characteristics. For these reasons the LLC has increasingly become the entity of choice for new, small businesses, although lawyers in some states remain concerned about state and local taxes and investor response to the LLC concept.

Most older businesses continue to operate as corporations or partnerships, although some have converted to LLCs or to limited liability partnerships (LLPs), which are largely identical to partnerships except for the treatment of tort liabilities. Large businesses operate primarily as corporations in order to ensure access to financial markets and because of the difficulty of operating a large business in the partnership or LLC format.

In addition to choice of entity, a lawyer for a small business must consider how the business should be capitalized—that is, who should be allocated what share of stock, bonds, or partnership/LLC interests. Together with this the allocation of decision-making power must also be considered, including voting agreements, unanimity or "supermajority" requirements for specified categories of business decisions, and restrictions on the transfer of business interests. Most, although not all, of these decisions are required regardless of the form of entity chosen. Lawyers must strike a delicate balance in providing advice: Often it is their role to raise unpleasant subjects such as the possible death of business participants or disagreement among them while trying to derive a common allocation and management scheme from the divergent interests of the various actors. The lawyer is frequently the only outside advisor to the business, and it is usually better to resolve issues in the early, optimistic phase than to postpone solutions until the future.

The Revised Model Business Corporation Act (RMBCA) of 1984, together with many state corporate laws, includes a special set of rules that may be adopted by small or "closely held" corporations. These rules permit more flexibility than the usual statutes and somewhat reduce the administrative burden associated with incorporation. Most state LLC statutes were similarly designed to provide a high degree of flexibility without sacrificing tax or other economic advantages.

Tax, Employment, and other Regulatory Law. In addition to business formation issues, lawyers counsel small businesses on adherence to a range of state and federal laws, including tax, environmental, labor and employment, and other regulatory statutes. To a large extent this parallels the work of corporate lawyers. However, some laws present special challenges or have a disproportionate impact on small businesses. For example, emerging sexual harassment laws pose a dilemma for small businesses that wish to avoid liability but may not have the facilities to provide a full-scale counseling and grievance system in the manner of a large corporation. Environmental laws have similarly been criticized for imposing a disproportionate burden on smaller companies. Even if these laws apply equally to small and large companies, they may appear unfair to small businesses, which lack the sophisticated administrative structures necessary to comply with these rules.

Whether these criticisms are fair nor not, it is certainly the case that small businesses have fewer resources than their larger competitors, and lawyers working for them face strong pressure to reduce costs while providing accurate and useful legal advice. Many small (and some large) businesses have attempted to control costs by relying on in-house counsel for most matters and using outside lawyers only when absolutely necessary. For example, a business may use its in-house lawyers to handle employee complaints and other routine litigation, calling on outside counsel only for cases involving sophisticated or novel issues.

To compensate for the risks and burdens of small business, the federal government operates various business assistance programs, many of them through the Small Business Administration (SBA), which administers loan and grant programs and assists businesses in assorted legal and financial matters. States and localities operate similar programs and offer tax abatements and other concessions in order to lure businesses from other locations. The federal antitrust laws also protect small businesses by preventing excessive concentration of economic power within any individual industry.

Federal tax laws include many provisions, notably the Subchapter S rules that benefit small business by providing lower tax rates or more generous deductions, credits, and other tax benefits. Other tax provisions, including fringe benefit and pension rules, may be more advantageous to large companies, because small businesses are less able to utilize the benefits these provisions offer.

Professional Responsibility Issues. Small business practice presents a number of ethical issues that are less common among large clients. An immediate question is whether one lawyer can represent all the business participants, who have a shared interest in the business's success but adverse interests in dividing profits and assigning management roles. Usually this question is resolved in the affirmative, but the lawyer must be sure that the parties understand their potential conflict of interest. If the participants begin to argue too heavily, the lawyer should make clear that he or she can no longer represent all of them at once.

A further question arises when clients ask lawyers to be partners in business ventures or offer to compensate them with stocks and partnership interests rather than cash. Ethical rules vary on this issue, but lawyers are generally advised to be wary of such arrangements, which may reduce the distance between themselves and their clients and interfere with their professional judgment. Lawyers must also be careful to avoid commingling personal and business funds and not engage in other activities that may compromise their professional integrity

Policy Issues and Changes. Underlying the entire issue of small businesses is the question of whether they are necessarily better than big businesses. A certain mystique surrounds small businesses, which are thought to be centers of individualism and creativity as opposed to the more conservative world of large corporations. This belief lies behind tax and other subsidies for small business as well as SBA and similar assistance programs. Nevertheless, much research and development is done by large companies, and the romantic view of small businesses may be a distortion to some extent.

The consensus among legal experts is that small businesses deserve help with specific regulatory or administrative requirements that impose an undue burden upon them but should not automatically be favored over large companies in all policy areas. This view is reflected in the current legal regime, which includes special provisions for small businesses in some areas, such as the LLC rules and close corporation statutes, but otherwise subjects them to the same rules as large corporations.

Suggested Readings. A large number of books consider the legal problems of small businesses from a planning perspective. These include Marc J. Lane's *Legal Handbook for Small Business* (New York: American Management Associations, 1972), a compendium of legal and practical tips for the owners of new businesses, and Leonard D. DuBoff's *The Law (in Plain English) for Small Business* (2d ed. New York: John Wiley & Sons, 1991), a somewhat more detailed work that includes information on contracts, patents, insurance, and tax and estate law. More extensive works focusing on particular types of small businesses include Robert A. Cooke's *How to Start Your Own (Subchapter) S Corporation* (New York: John Wiley & Sons, 1995) and Jerome P. Friedlander's *The Limited Liability Company* (Charlottesville, Va.: The Michie Company, 1994), a useful and not overly technical introduction to the LLC concept. Louis A. Mezzullo's *An Estate Planner's Guide to Family Business Entities* (Chicago: American Bar Association, 1998) considers similar topics, with an emphasis on estate planning concerns, and includes sample forms designed to accomplish business goals while reducing payments of estate and income tax. On a somewhat more technical level, F. Hodge O'Neal and Robert B. Thompson's *O'Neal's Close Corporations: Law and Practice* (3d ed. Deerfield, Ill.: Clark Boardman Callaghan, 1996) is the preeminent source on the law of small corporations, while Richard D. Harroch's *Start-Up Companies: Planning, Financing, and Operating the Successful Business* (New York: Law Journal Seminars-Press, 1988) provides a comprehensive, step-by-step guide to numerous small business transactions. The effect of government regulation is considered by Roland J. Cole and Philip D. Tegeler in *Government Requirements of Small Business* (Lexington, Mass.: Lexington Books, 1980). A critical view of antitrust policy, and thus implicitly of the view that "bigness" is inherently bad, is contained in Robert H. Bork's *The Antitrust Paradox: A Policy at War with Itself* (New York: Basic Books, 1978). For a contrasting view, the reader may enjoy E. F. Schumacher's *Small Is Beautiful: Economics as if People Mattered* (New York: Harper & Row, 1973). Although not a legal work, Schumacher's book captures some of the romanticization of smallness and the corresponding demonization of large organizations. —*Michael A. Livingston*

See also Business taxes; Corporations; Loans, business; Partnerships; Stockholders.

Small claims court

Small claims courts are courts that have jurisdiction in cases in which the money being sued for is not above a certain amount.

State court systems are composed of numerous specialized courts that have been created to handle specific types of civil cases, such as courts of domestic relations, which handle matters of divorce, child custody, and child support; probate courts, which handle the settlement of estates and wills; and small claims courts, which handle cases involving small amounts of money.

Historical Development. The label small claims court generally does not refer to an autonomous court; rather, it is a special procedure carried out in a special part of the jurisdiction of an existing trial court. These small claims courts have evolved as a result of the need to resolve disputes in which it is not financially feasible to retain an attorney because the amounts of claims may be less than the cost of legal assistance.

The first small claims court was established in Cleveland, Ohio, in the early part of the twentieth century. By the 1920's other major cities, including Chicago, Minneapolis, New York, and Philadelphia, had established such courts. In addition, the state of Massachusetts created a small claims court based on the Cleveland model, which instituted a simplified filing process, a nominal filing fee, and no requirement that the parties be represented by lawyers. In the late twentieth century there were small claims courts in all fifty states, either as separate entities or as a part of a magistrate or justice of the peace system.

Small claims courts perform an important function for states' judicial systems and the parties involved in lawsuits. For the state small claims courts remove relatively minor civil cases from major courts and allow such courts to focus on larger, more complex civil suits. For the principals in lawsuits allow small claims courts civil disputes to be settled legally at a relatively low cost. This is important because attorney fees may be much greater than the monetary settlements in such minor cases. The dollar limit for cases brought before small claims courts ranges from $1,500 to $15,000. In most states the limit is $5,000 or less. In a few states small claims courts may also have jurisdiction over minor legal disputes such as evictions from rental property and restitution for items not returned to their proper owners.

Suits against the federal government, a federal agency, or a federal employee cannot be brought in a small claims court. Rather, such suits must be filed in a federal district court, tax court, or the court of claims. Civil suits involving federal law may also be heard by federal magistrates.

Small Claims Court Procedure. The procedure followed in small claims courts is relatively uniform within the system. A plaintiff must first file a form and pay a filing fee in the court which has jurisdiction in the case. Some states waive filing fees if the plaintiff is unable to afford it. The form gives the defendant's name and address, the reason for the suit, where the dispute took place, and the amount sought. The claim is then sent to the defendant by registered mail or served directly by the proper authority. This could be a representative from the sheriff's office, a constable's office, or a process server. Once there is proof that the defendant received the claim, he or she has a set period of time, usually fifteen to thirty days, to respond to it. If the defendant fails to respond or to show up on the assigned date of the hearing, a default judgment is issued. This is a relatively frequent occurrence in small claims court.

The courtroom procedure for small claims court is fairly informal. In some states the plaintiff and defendant present their claim and defense to a judge. Some states provide the option of a jury trial if the disputants request it. In most states attorneys may represent clients. In a few states, such as California, attorneys are not allowed to represent clients in court, although attorneys may be consulted before or after trial. During the hearing itself rules of evidence are not strictly followed. Objections to testimony may not be allowed. The plaintiff orally presents the case and submits documentation such as photos, bills, receipts, or contracts, if available. Witnesses may be subpoenaed to appear in court on behalf of either party. Notarized statements may also be allowed. In general, the entire case is heard in fifteen to thirty minutes. The judge may issue an immediate verdict or the decision may be handed down several days after the hearing. The judge's decision can be appealed to the next higher court; however, this is seldom done because the costs involved may be higher than the amount of the claim. If the plaintiff wins the suit, the responsibility for collection of the claim is left to the plaintiff. Frequently this is done through garnishment of wages or through the attachment of property through a writ of execution. In many cases, however, a defendant may lack the necessary resources to pay the claim, and the judgment is never collected.

Assessment of Small Claims Courts. Small claims courts have been criticized for their failure to fulfill the goals of their founders. In particular, critics have argued that these courts have become collection agencies for businesses, that there is a high rate of default by low income defendants, that unrepresented litigants encounter problems, that there are problems with collecting judgments, and that there are too many cases for judges to handle. Studies of small claims courts support some of these criticisms. First, a high percentage of plaintiffs are businesses, while a high percentage of defendants are individuals. Second, over 90 percent of all cases that reach a judgment are decided in favor of the plaintiff, more than half of which are by default. One explanation for this is that defendants in small claims courts rarely present a valid legal response to claims. Finally, in those states that allow attorney representation, such representation has little impact on the plaintiff's ability to win a case. Nevertheless, it tends to increase the defendant's chances. Judges in small claims courts emphasize that these courts have a therapeutic function, because they allow persons to vent their frustrations. Thus, while the results of small claims courts do not match the ideal, they provide persons with a forum through which disputes can be settled at minimal cost.

Suggested Readings. There are several practical guides by attorneys on the proceedings of small claims court. They include Paul Bergman and Sara Berman-Barrett's *Represent Yourself in Court: How to Prepare and Try a Winning Case* (2d ed. Berkeley, Calif.: Nolo Press, 1998) and Ralph Warner's *Everybody's Guide to Small Claims Court* (7th ed. Berkeley, Calif.: Nolo Press, 1997). In addition, there are two studies of small claims courts. One is *Small Claims Court: A Comparative Study*, edited by Christopher J. Whelan (Oxford, England: Clarendon Press, 1991), and *Small Claims Court: A National Examination*, by John C. Ruhnka, Steven Weller, and John Martin (Williamsburg, Va.: National Center for State Courts, 1975).   —William V. Moore

See also Court types; Defendant self-representation; Garnishment; Litigation expenses; Subpoena.

Smoking and tobacco use

Tobacco, especially in the form of cigarettes, is one of the most popular and controversial habits in the United States and the subject of various types of laws and statutes.

Tobacco was first grown in the Americas, especially the southern part of what is now the United States, Mexico, and the Caribbean islands. Native American tribes used to smoke this leaf in various ways long before European explorers arrived in the area, often using it in religious ceremonies. The earliest European settlers discovered this plant early on and began growing it as a commercial crop, first in the West Indies and later in Southern Europe and the Middle East.

Early European reactions were mixed. Sir Walter Raleigh (1552-1618), one of the earliest European growers of the crop, extolled its virtues. His monarch, King James I of England (1566-1625), called tobacco a "noxious weed" and opposed its proliferation.

Tobacco was a major cash crop even in colonial times. Many well-known Americans, including President George Washington, made their fortunes growing and selling tobacco. Despite some early opposition to its use, no serious attempts to regulate it were made before the late nineteenth century. At that time opposition to tobacco use had grown considerably, although legislative efforts were largely confined to cigarettes, which were first mass produced in 1884. In 1897 the federal government banned the use of coupons for special deals, and in 1901 the state of New Hampshire banned cigarettes entirely. In 1907 Illinois followed suit, and by 1909, twelve states and many cities had done the same. This situation did not last very long. By 1927 all state laws banning or regulating cigarettes had been repealed. It was not until the 1960's, in the wake of strong scientific evidence that cigarettes were a major health hazard, that such legislation was again attempted on a large scale.

Taxation. The first time tobacco was taxed in the United States was during the Civil War, when the Union government imposed such taxes in an attempt to raise funds to further the war effort. The effectiveness of such taxes was probably questionable at best, since most of the states that grew tobacco had seceded from the Union and did not pay federal taxes. After the war, tobacco taxes were lowered but remained in place. State governments and some cities quickly imposed taxes on tobacco. Along the way, various governmental bodies decided that cigarettes were liable to sales taxes in addition to the other taxes already imposed. An interesting, if unforeseen, problem resulted from the variety of local taxes.

Cigarettes have always been subjected to higher taxes in northern states, where tobacco is not a significant crop, than in southern states, where it is a major source of business. By the 1960's the cost of a pack of cigarettes in New York was considerably higher than in Virginia or North Carolina, and it became common for people traveling north to smuggle cigarettes from the South and sell them at a considerable profit while still charging less than retail outlets.

At this time, taxes accounted for fully half the price of cigarettes in some areas, making them, along with alcoholic beverages, the most highly taxed items on the market. Nevertheless, there was little public protest, at least until the 1980's, against such taxation and no clear evidence that rising costs were preventing people from smoking.

This fact has been used as an argument illustrating the addictive nature of nicotine, the most commonly studied drug found in tobacco. Just as heroin addicts continue to use the drug even if they must commit violent crimes to support their habits, cigarette addicts continue to smoke regardless of how much cigarettes cost. At the same time, the same facts have been used by the opposing side to insist that high taxation is not a deterrent to smoking but merely a drain on the funds of smokers.

Restrictions and Warnings. On January 11, 1964, Luther L. Terry, surgeon general of the United States, issued a report linking cigarette smoking to several diseases, especially lung cancer, heart failure, and assorted respiratory problems. This gave smoking opponents a rallying cry, and a new round of legislation began. The first direct result of the surgeon general's report was the requirement that cigarette packs, and later advertisements, carry warning labels. The first label requirement was passed in 1964 and became effective in January, 1965. Later, these warning were strengthened.

Some controversy has always surrounded these warnings. Proponents point to the fact that many dangerous products, especially drugs, carry warnings. Whether the presence of written warnings, in addition to campaigns by public and private health agencies, actually have any affect on people's smoking habits has never been positively determined. Ironically, the tobacco industry itself made little protest against having to print warning labels on cigarette packages, and subsequent lawsuits showed why. Once the labels were in place, tobacco companies sued by consumers who developed diseases directly related to cigarette smoking had a ready-made defense. They had warned consumers about the risks of tobacco smoking, who chose to ignore the warnings.

The second major attack was on cigarette advertising. It was argued that much advertising either depicted cigarette smoking as a manly, heroic habit or showed pictures of people enjoying the pleasures of tobacco in beautiful natural settings. Particular concern was expressed that many such advertisements appealed to children. In 1969 the federal Public Health Cigarette Smoking Act banned all advertising on television and radio. The rationale behind this act was that children had ready access to these media and were greatly influenced by ads, especially on television. At the same time, television messages warning of the dangers of cigarettes proliferated on television.

With the unfortunate example of Prohibition (the alcoholic beverage ban of the 1920's) behind them, government agencies made no serious attempts to ban cigarette smoking entirely. However, attempts based on the example of liquor laws were made by the federal government and state governments to restrict sales of cigarettes to minors. Later, there was some argument as to whether the federal government had any such power, but this soon became irrelevant. By 1995 forty-six states had banned cigarette sales to people under eighteen years of age. Once again, the effectiveness of such laws was questionable. Only a few states passed laws against cigarette machines outside taverns and other businesses that only allowed adults to enter, and enforcement was often lax.

The argument in favor of restriction of sales of tobacco products to minors is based on the statistically evident fact that most people who become life-long cigarette smokers start in their teens, and that older people have had more of a chance to realize the dangers of smoking.

Environmental Smoke Hazards. The greatest area of controversy in the late twentieth century involved the hazards of cigarette smoking faced by nonsmokers. While pro-tobacco arguments about the right of individual adults to risk their own health might be convincing, endangering people by exposing them to second-hand smoke was a clear justification for banning smoking in specific areas. On the private level, some institutions had regulated smoking for many decades, but this practice became common following the 1964 Surgeon General's report and accelerated in ensuing decades. By the 1990's many states and localities had banned smoking in most public buildings, often with the exception of restaurants and bars. These establishments were usually required to have smoking and nonsmoking sections, and in many areas small establishments were required to ban smoking completely.

This solution generally pleased neither smokers nor nonsmokers. As smoking sections in small restaurants were often close to smoke-free areas, smoke contamination was feared. On the other hand, those who opposed smoking regulations insisted that environmental smoke hazards were unproven and that the rights of smokers were being infringed.

Future Prospects. In 1994 the commissioner of the Federal Drug Administration (FDA), David A. Kessler, testified before the U.S. Congress that the FDA was considering regulating tobacco as a drug. Before long a new round of legal suits was underway. Supporters suggested that this was quite reasonable, as nicotine, an active ingredient in tobacco, was proven to be addictive. Opponents insisted that tobacco was not a dangerous drug in the sense that alcohol and heroin were, that it did not seriously inhibit coordination or judgment, and that it was a matter of free choice. In 1998 a federal appeals court ruled that the FDA had such power to classify tobacco as a drug. The question may never be resolved to all sides' satisfaction.

The administration of President Bill Clinton made some attempts to regulate tobacco further and to greatly increase federal taxes. Once again, arguments on both sides were strong. If tobacco is a public health menace, it is the duty of government to regulate its use. If it is a matter of free choice by individuals, the federal government has no such power, and state and local governments are highly limited in their authority. The controversy, as always, is between the responsibility of government to protect people against dangerous substances and the right of individuals to decide their own fate. This question also pertains to drug use, prostitution, and many other so-called "crimes without victims."

The health hazards to smokers are beyond doubt. The health hazards to those exposed to

Increased public awareness of the health hazards posed by tobacco use have led to a growing number of laws restricting smoking. (James L. Shaffer)

other people's smoke is unsettled. The right of people to endanger their own health is one of the most pervasive questions in a democratic society.

There have been arguments that cigarette smokers are more likely to lose work time due to health problems and that they are less productive. There have been arguments that smokers raise the insurance rates of the general public by increasing their own health costs. Once again, these arguments are countered by the proposition that this sort of question is the province of insurers and employers, not governmental agencies.

As the twentieth century drew to a close, cigarette billboards carried warning labels and were still opposed by those wanting to ban advertising entirely. Cigarette taxes, already high, were rising. More and more places of business were banning smoking entirely, while the big tobacco companies were sending out mailings to admitted smokers extolling "smokers' rights." The question remains a difficult one. The greatest problem in a democratic society has always been the question of balancing individual rights against the public good.

Suggested Readings. An obviously biased attack on the tobacco industry can be found in *The Smoking Gun: How the Tobacco Company Gets Away with Murder* (Philadelphia: George P. Sheckly, 1984.) Susan Wagner's *Cigarette Country: Tobacco in American History* (New York: Praeger, 1971) is a history of tobacco use in the United States, with an emphasis on the various legal and legislative actions intended to curb tobacco use. The *Cigarette Papers*, by Stanton A. Glantz et al. (Berkeley: University of California Press, 1996), is an extensive study of the health effects of cigarette smoke and of various legislative attempts to regulate cigarette smoking. It also discusses the tobacco industry's opposition to such moves. Philip J. Hilts's *Smoke Screen* (Reading, Mass.: Addison Wesley, 1996) is a discussion of the resistance of the tobacco companies to the attack on tobacco. *Clearing the Air* (Lexington, Mass.: Lexington Books, 1988), edited by Robert D. Tollison, is a report on the opinions of eighty-eight scientists from the 1987 International Study on Environmental Smoke, which investigated the effects of tobacco on nonsmokers and recommended legal action. —*Marc Goldstein*

See also Age and the law; Commercial litigation; Environmental legislation; Public interest law.

Smuggling

Smuggling is the illegal importation of goods or controlled substances from outside a country.

Smuggling is the illegal movement of people, products, money, information, ideas, technology, industrial secrets, and national treasures across international borders. It thrives where avoiding the payment of duties is profitable and where the buying and selling of illegal goods are financially rewarding.

Laws against smuggling are designed to protect the wealth of a country and to protect the public from the dangers of disease, narcotics, and, sometimes, immoral ideas, books, and videos. Smugglers do not pay customs duties, or taxes, on certain goods, which are a significant source of federal revenues. Before the United States began to levy income tax in 1913, customs duties provided most of the federal government's revenues. Most laws against smuggling and law-enforcement efforts are directed not toward keeping goods out of the country, but toward collecting a duty on their import. Laws against smuggling illegal drugs is a notable exception.

Long History. Smuggling is perhaps the second oldest profession. It is a form of transnational commerce. The growth of smuggling has coincided with the expansion of international business opportunities. Smuggling occurs all over the world, despite the efforts of customs officers at international airports, seaports, and national border crossings. What is considered illegal has changed over time. For instance, money laundering was not a crime until at least 1970, when the U.S. Congress made it illegal to take $5,000 or more out of the United States without first reporting it. Most crime-fighting efforts in the last decades of the twentieth century have been concerned with the enforcement of criminal laws that did not exist even decades ago, including laws prohibiting drugs, insider trading, money laundering, and the smuggling of sophisticated weaponry and computer software. Law-enforcement concerns have changed over time. For example, suppressing the African slave trade was a major focus of U.S. law enforcement between independence in 1776 and the Civil War from 1861 to 1865. Between 1920 and

1933 investigators concentrated on stopping illicit traffic in alcoholic beverages.

Law-enforcement efforts to stop smuggling focus on arresting and convicting criminals and seizing their money and contraband, including illegal drugs, explosives, firearms, and livestock that may carry diseases. U.S. Customs Service agents, treasury agents, drug-enforcement agents, and other law-enforcement officers are interested in both apprehending criminals, deterring crime, and maximizing the collection of revenues. Interpol, the international police commission, helps regional and national police forces in fighting crime.

Beyond National Borders. The fundamental problem of international law enforcement is that governments have jurisdiction only within their borders or embassies. Other problems arise from differences in laws and legal systems, especially in capital punishment and political offense cases. Violations of U.S. laws may not be violations of laws in other countries. A country may even profit from being the source of goods that are legally purchased or grown but illegally smuggled into other countries, such as drugs. Foreign law-enforcement agencies are often reluctant to devote resources to enforcing the customs laws of other governments. Many smuggling cases depend on extraditing smugglers from one country to another. To overcome this limitation, governments sign extradition and mutual legal assistance treaties to stop smuggling and other international crimes. Countries also send law-enforcement officers to other countries, sometimes covertly, to stop criminals and seize their contraband.

Obtaining evidence from other countries in a form that is admissible in U.S. courts is essential to the success of prosecuting crimes. The principal means of obtaining evidence from another country is by letters rogatory. These documents are written requests from a court in one country to a foreign court requesting evidence or other legal assistance that is needed in a hearing or trial. Investigators resort to letters rogatory when Interpol and other international police agencies are unable to produce evidence, typically because a court must authorize obtaining evidence. A complicating factor is that foreign courts may be unfamiliar with the constitutional safeguards and evidentiary rules of U.S. law. U.S. courts also sometimes regard foreign legal processes as equally confusing.

A major difficulty hampering efforts to stop smuggling and other types of international crime is government corruption. Institutionalized corruption is found in virtually every country. For example, drug barons have bribed police and customs officials. Countries sometimes agree to ban trade with other countries they suspect of smuggling in order to put pressure on them. They may refuse to sell countries arms, oil, or other vital supplies, hoping to force a change in policy. Citizens or countries that try to avoid an embargo by smuggling are breaking the law.

Extradition. U.S. law-enforcement officers have many options to deal with criminals who have fled to another country or who live abroad and refuse to come to the United States to face trial. Law-enforcement agencies can request that foreign governments formally surrender fugitives under extradition laws or treaties. Unlike most other governments, the U.S. government lacks the legal authority either to extradite persons without an extradition treaty or to prosecute them for acts committed abroad that violate foreign but not U.S. laws. They can ask other governments to deport alleged criminals or otherwise force them to leave. The authorities can ask foreign governments to prosecute alleged criminals in their own courts. Law-enforcement officers can resort to other methods, including abduction and trickery, methods which have long been used by U.S. government.

Investigators employ many tools and techniques to fight smuggling rings. Their arsenal includes undercover operations, wiretapping and other forms of electronic surveillance, informants, offers of immunity from prosecution, freezing smugglers' assets, and financial incentives to induce smugglers to cooperate with law-enforcement officials. Investigators have also employed the technique of controlled delivery, especially in drug cases, by which agents allow a consignment of illegal drugs to continue on its way under their control and surveillance in order to secure evidence against drug cartels. U.S. law-enforcement agencies have also increased the number of investigative personnel stationed in other countries and their participation in joint investigations with foreign police agencies. Antidrug smuggling initiatives include destroying drugs or drug crops, including coca and opium, in their countries of origin and arresting persons and cartels who allegedly process and smuggle drugs.

Customs officers have tried to close the borders and coasts of the United States to drug smugglers. Smugglers' advantage has narrowed with the increase in cooperation between countries and law-enforcement officers. Investigators have concentrated their efforts on putting smugglers and other international criminals in jail and seizing their contraband and financial assets.

Suggested Readings. Philip Steele examines the history of smuggling and explores the operations and motivations of smugglers and their contraband in *Smuggling* (New York: New Discovery Books, 1993). Other general works on smuggling include M. C. Finn's *The Complete Book of International Smuggling* (Boulder, Colo.: Paladin Press, 1983). Ethan A. Nadelmann provides an excellent overview of international law enforcement and transnational crime in *Cops Across Borders: The Internationalization of U.S. Criminal Law Enforcement* (University Park: Pennsylvania State University Press, 1993). For insight into the agencies leading the fight against smuggling, see *The U.S. Customs Service: A Bicentennial History* (Washington, D.C.: Government Printing Office, 1989) and Malcolm Anderson's *Policing the World: Interpol and the Politics of International Police Co-operation* (New York: Oxford University Press, 1989). —*Fred Buchstein*

See also Coast Guard, U.S.; Counterfeiting; Criminal justice system; Criminal law; Drugs, illegal; Import permits; International law; Interpol.

Social Security

In the United States the term Social Security refers specifically to the programs established under the Social Security Act, originally enacted in 1935.

The Social Security Act is a comprehensive law consisting of twenty titles or subjects, several of which are no longer operative. As of December 31, 1984, the main titles were Old-Age, Survivors', and Disability Insurance (OASDI); Medicare, including hospital insurance and supplementary medical insurance covering other medical costs; Supplemental Security Income (SSI); Unemployment Compensation; Aid to Families with Dependent Children (AFDC); Medicaid; Social Services for Adults and Children; and Maternal and Child Health and Crippled Children's Services. The taxing provisions for financing Old-Age, Survivors', and Disability Insurance, hospital insurance, and unemployment compensation are part of the Internal Revenue Code and are administered by the Internal Revenue Service (IRS).

From its inception the Social Security Act of 1935 has been the centerpiece of social legislation in the United States. The original act included a federal old-age benefits program and various federal-state programs covering the elderly, blind, and unemployed and children with disabilities. The Social Security Act included both contributory (social insurance) and noncontributory (public assistance) programs.

The original Social Security Act of 1935 has been modified by major amendments more than twenty times. Survivors' insurance benefits were added in 1939. The original act did not include any programs for benefits to persons with disabilities. Disability benefits were made a part of the act in 1956. Medicare benefits were added in 1965. The Medicare program, which went into effect in 1966, was first administered by the Social Security Administration (SSA); in 1977 the Medicare program was transferred to the newly created Health Care Financing Administration (HCFA).

Retirement, Disability, Death, and Medicare Benefits. Old-Age, Survivors', and Disability Insurance, Medicare hospital insurance, and Medicare Supplementary Medical Insurance (SMI) are separately financed segments of the Social Security program. The OASDI program provides benefits for older persons, for persons with disabilities, and for survivors of deceased workers. The cash benefits for OASDI are financed by payroll taxes levied on employees, their employers, and the self-employed. The rate of these contributions is based on the employee's taxable earnings up to a maximum taxable amount, with the employer contributing an equal amount; self-employed persons contribute twice the amount levied on employees.

Medicare benefits are divided into two parts: a basic hospital-insurance plan covering hospital care, extended care, home health services, and hospice care for terminally ill patients; and a voluntary medical insurance program covering physicians' fees, outpatient services, and other medical services. Medicare costs are met by Social Security contributions, monthly premiums from participants, and general revenues.

The maximum amount of income subject to taxation for OASDI and Medicare hospital insurance, originally $3,000, had increased to $68,400 by 1998. The total Federal Insurance Contributions Act (FICA) tax is 15.3 percent, half of which is paid by the employer and half by the employee, of which 12.4 percent is for OASDI. Only this portion of the tax is subject to the above limits. There is no maximum for earnings subject to the hospital insurance (Medicare) portion of the FICA tax, which is 2.9 percent, half of which is payable by the employer and half by the employee.

In 1996 some 124 million persons contributed to Social Security funds. During an average month 43 million people drew Social Security cash benefits. The amount of a person's cash benefits is determined by the combined wages, salaries, and self-employment income of the primary earner or earners in a family. Dependent children and noncontributing spouses receive additional amounts. The law specifies certain minimum and maximum monthly benefits. In order to keep the cash benefits in line with inflation, they are annually indexed to the increase in the cost of living as it is gauged in the consumer price index.

The 1986 amendments to the Age Discrimination in Employment Act (ADEA) state that, with some exceptions (such as for firefighters, police officers, and tenured university faculty), an individual cannot be compelled to retire because of age. Since 1983 individuals aged seventy and older have been entitled to receive full Social Security benefits even if they continue working. For other eligible workers the amount of benefits is based on age and earnings. The first step in figuring benefits is to determine the primary insurance amount (PIA). All benefits are based on it. One basic formula is used to compute most PIAs, but the PIA is extremely complicated and is almost always calculated by the Social Security Administration's computers.

Social Security benefits are based on a percentage of earned income. The primary insurance amount is a certain percentage of average indexed monthly earnings. PIAs will be different for workers earning at the maximum, high, average, or low levels. The maximum level is defined by statute. High earnings are defined as those equal to 160 percent of the national average wage index, average earnings are defined as those equal to the national average wage index, and low earnings are defined as earnings equal to 45 percent of the national average wage index.

A spouse first claiming benefits at the age of sixty-five or older may receive 50 percent of the amount paid to the worker. Benefits are reduced if entitlement to the spouse's benefits begins before the month in which the spouse turns sixty-five. Similar percentages are payable to disabled individuals and their spouses. Surviving spouses and children receive a percentage of the retirement benefit computed from the earnings of the deceased earner.

Ida M. Fuller of Ludlow, Vermont, the first person to receive a Social Security increase under a Social Security law enacted in 1950. (AP/Wide World Photos)

Unemployment Compensation. The U.S. unemployment compensation program, established by the Social Security Act of 1935, and the employment service programs, established in 1933, form a federal-state cooperative system. The Federal Unemployment Tax Act of 1954 levies on employers an excise tax on their taxable payroll. Most of the federal tax can be offset by employer contributions to state funds under an approved state unemployment compensation law. A small portion of the tax is retained by the federal government to pay for the administrative costs of unemployment compensation, employment service programs, and loans to states whose funds run low.

State financing and benefits laws vary widely. In general, unemployment compensation benefits under state laws are intended to replace about 50 percent of an average worker's previous wages. Maximum weekly benefits provisions, however, result in benefits of less than 50 percent for most higher-earning workers. All states pay benefits to some unemployed persons for twenty-six weeks. In some states the duration of benefits depends on the amount a worker earned and the number of weeks he or she worked in a previous year, while in others all recipients are entitled to benefits for the same length of time. During periods of heavy unemployment federal law authorizes extended benefits, in some cases up to thirty-nine weeks. In 1975 extended benefits were payable for up to sixty-five weeks. Extended benefits are financed in part by federal employer taxes.

Other Programs. The Social Security Act provides for money grants to states to pay part of the costs of Aid to Families with Dependent Children and Medicaid (Medical assistance) to needy persons who cannot afford the costs of medical care. AFDC and Medicaid programs are administered by the states; the federal government, besides contributing a share of the costs of benefits, pays for part of the administration of the programs. Under the Supplemental Security Income program the federal government provides payments to needy, older, and blind persons and to persons with disabilities. In determining the amount of aid given, the programs take into consideration the income and resources of the individual and the family. Under the Social Security Act, the federal government also provides financial grants for maternal and child health, for services for children with disabilities, for child welfare services, and for social services such as day care for the children of working mothers.

Medicaid, a federal-state program, is usually operated by state welfare or health departments within the guidelines issued by the Health Care Financing Administration. Medicaid furnishes at least five basic services to needy persons: inpatient hospital care, outpatient hospital care, physicians' services, skilled nursing-home services for adults, and laboratory and X-ray services. Those who are eligible include families and certain children who qualify for public assistance and may include older and blind adults and adults with disabilities who are eligible for the Supplemental Security Income program of the Social Security Administration. States may also include persons and families termed "medically needy" who meet eligibility requirements except those for financial assistance. Each state decides who is eligible for Medicaid benefits and what services shall be included. Some benefits frequently provided are dental care; ambulance services; and the costs of drugs, eyeglasses, and hearing aids. All the states, the District of Columbia, Guam, Puerto Rico, and the Virgin Islands operate Medicaid plans.

Application Process. Persons may apply for Social Security benefits by calling the Social Security information service, the job of which also includes making appointments so that persons may apply for benefits. The Social Security Administration employee who takes the phone call advises potential applicants of the location of the nearest SSA regional office and gives persons a time and date when a regional office staff member will call to complete the application. After the call, applications will be sent to applicants for signing, who will be directed to send them back with several original documents (such as birth, death, and employment records). Social Security regional offices also send out traveling representatives to some locations in their service area on a scheduled basis, and those representatives meet with people seeking information or wishing to apply for benefits. For retirement or survivor's benefits, obtaining the necessary information is usually straightforward and the application can be processed relatively quickly (within sixty days). Those seeking retirement benefits may do so immediately upon retirement if they have applied prior to retirement.

For those seeking disability benefits the process may be more complicated, since in addition to proving that the disabled party is "insured" by having paid Social Security taxes during twenty of the most recent forty quarters, the person must also prove the existence of a permanent and total disability from either a medical or vocational standpoint. As a result, attorneys and other representatives work much more frequently with clients seeking disability benefits. The disability approval process may take much longer than the process of applying for and receiving either retirement or survivor's benefits.

Every step in the Social Security Administration approval process may be appealed, and the appeals process is described in each notice a person receives. Applications for unemployment compensation and the other state and federal programs must be made with the state agency in charge of the benefits. Each state may have a slightly different administrative structure.

Suggested Readings. *Social Security in the Twenty-First Century*, edited by Eric Kingson and James H. Schulz (New York: Oxford University Press, 1997), discusses new policy-oriented work and advances views on the issues confronting the Social Security system at the dawn of the twenty-first century. Robert J. Myers's *Social Security* (Philadelphia: University of Pennsylvania Press, 1993) is a lengthy textbook written by an acknowledged authority on social insurance and designed to be a factual description of the various social insurance and allied programs operating in the United States. William Thomas's *Social Security Manual* (Cincinnati, Ohio: National Underwriter, 1990) presents an overview of Social Security and Medicare in question-and-answer format and also contains a good index. It includes Social Security tables, including primary benefit amounts for retirement, survivors', and disability benefits. Faustin F. Jehle's *The Complete and Easy Guide to Social Security and Medicare* (Peterborough, N.H.: Fraser-Vann, 1993) is a reader-friendly reference book that includes a brief history of Social Security programs. Individual chapters include questions and answers and sources of additional information. The book has two appendices: definitions of government terms and forms. The latter appendix includes appeal forms, for use in processing all the various benefits. —*Diane S. Griffin*

See also Age and the law; Medicaid; Medicare; Nursing homes; Pensions; Retirement planning; Unemployment insurance.

Solicitation of legal clients

Lawyers may generally solicit clients through the mails but not through direct telephone soliciting or person contact.

Among the most noxious images of lawyers is that of the "ambulance chaser," the lawyer who races to the scene of an accident in the hope of finding a client among twisted metal and bloody pavement. In fact, legal ethics rules almost invariably prohibit lawyers from approaching potential clients in person for the purpose of obtaining legal fees. Generally, potential clients are viewed as all too susceptible to the beguiling wiles of lawyers and too likely to be unduly influenced when encountering them directly over the telephone or in person.

The prohibition against ambulance chasing does not apply to all forms of solicitation. The speech of lawyers seeking clients receives some protection from the U.S. Constitution's First Amendment guarantee of free speech. As a consequence, the U.S. Supreme Court has held that legal ethics rules cannot categorically ban all forms of solicitation, especially those that do not involve in-person or live telephone contact between lawyers and potential clients. Thus, lawyers may, with limited exceptions, solicit clients through the mails either by sending anonymous announcements or by targeting individuals whom they believe might have need of particular legal services. For example, a lawyer might find from the local courthouse a list of those persons against whom real estate foreclosure proceedings have been inaugurated and send a letter to those persons offering to provide legal assistance. Furthermore, the Supreme Court has held that even the rules against in-person solicitation do not apply to lawyers who do not solicit clients for the purpose of earning fees. Thus, public interest lawyers may generally solicit clients—even in person—when they do not plan to charge the clients a fee.

Just because lawyers use the mails to solicit clients does not mean that legal and ethical scrutiny of solicitation ends. First, some states have imposed waiting periods before lawyers may attempt to contact accident victims, even through the mails. The Supreme Court has upheld this kind of restriction. Moreover, even when a form of solicitation is permissible in principle, lawyers may not make misrepresentations to potential clients or exert undue influence or badger them after having been told to stop soliciting.

Persons who believe themselves to have been improperly solicited by lawyers may register complaints with the state or local bar association. A lawyer who engages in an improper solicitation may be found guilty of an ethical violation. In such a case, the bar may sanction the guilty lawyer in a variety of ways, including through reprimanding, suspending, or disbarring the lawyer.

—*Timothy L. Hall*

See also Advertising, legal; Champerty and maintenance; Ethics; Model Rules of Professional Conduct; Personal injury attorneys.

Space law

A series of five international agreements as well as federal laws and regulations govern all activities in space.

Historically, most nations have claimed sovereignty over the airspace above their territories and have regulated the flight of aircraft in their airspace. The 1957 launching of the world's first earth-orbiting satellite, *Sputnik* I, by the Soviet Union required the development of new principles of international law, since *Sputnik* I passed over many nations, including the United States.

Space activities are regulated by five international agreements. The Outer Space Treaty, signed in 1967, established four legal principles: Outer space is to be used for peaceful purposes, the deployment of weapons of mass destruction in space is prohibited, the moon and other celestial bodies may be used freely by all nations, and no nation can establish a claim of sovereignty to any of these bodies. The treaty established that a satellite orbiting Earth is in outer space, thus allowing any nation to place in orbit a satellite whose path carries it over the territory of any other nation.

The Rescue Agreement was signed by the major spacefaring nations in 1968. This agreement established the principle that the emergency landing of a spacecraft on the territory of another nation is permissible and required that the other nation assist in the rescue and speedy return of the astronauts and their spacecraft to the home nation.

The Liability Convention, signed in 1972, makes each country liable for damage or injury caused to persons or property in another country by space objects launched from their territory. When the Soviet Union's *Cosmos* 954 spy satellite crashed in Canada in January, 1978, the Soviet Union paid the Canadian government about $6 million for the cost of cleaning up radioactive debris from the satellite's uranium-fueled power supply. The Liability Convention specifically makes the nation from which a space vehicle was launched liable for damage even if an individual or private enterprise within that nation, rather than the government, conducted the launching. Thus, to ensure compliance with safety regulations the U.S. government regulates private space launchings from its territory, requiring permits for this activity.

The Registration Convention, adopted by the General Assembly of the United Nations in 1974, requires that each nation maintain a registry listing all objects launched from its territory into Earth orbit or beyond. Each nation is required to provide to the Secretary-General of the United Nations the date and place of launching, the registration number, the orbital parameters, and the general function of each object launched into space. Information on all satellites, including military spy satellites, is generally provided to the United Nations in compliance with this agreement.

The Moon Treaty (July 3, 1979) generally restates the principles of the Outer Space Treaty, requiring that the Moon be used for peaceful purposes and establishing that no nation shall claim any part of the Moon as its territory. One controversial aspect of the Moon Treaty establishes the natural resources of the Moon as "the common heritage of mankind." The treaty requires that benefits from those natural resources be equitably shared by all nations. The extent to which this provision might hamper the economic development of the Moon has resulted in the refusal of the United States to sign this treaty. —*George J. Flynn*

See also Freedom of Information Act.

Speedy-trial requirement

The guarantee that an accused person has the right to a speedy trial is one of the fundamental features of U.S. constitutional law.

The Sixth Amendment to the U.S. Constitution provides that in all criminal prosecutions the accused shall enjoy the right to a speedy trial. Applying the due process clause of the Fourteenth Amendment, the U.S. Supreme Court ruled in *Klopfer v. North Carolina* (1967) that this right applies to state trials as well. Chief Justice Earl Warren wrote that "the right to a speedy trial is as fundamental as any of the rights secured by the Sixth Amendment," and like the right to counsel, he reasoned, it should also be applied to the states.

Not only do trial delays create an enormous backlog of cases that clog the judicial system, but they also make it difficult for the accused to present an adequate defense. Even if the accused person is free on bail, employment may be disrupted, reputations harmed, and financial resources depleted.

Delay is a common defense tactic, because there are many instances in which delay favors the accused. Most often it puts pressure on the prosecution to make concessions. To avoid a lengthy trial a prosecutor may offer to reduce the charges against a defendant in return for a guilty plea. There is also the danger that a person on bail awaiting trial may commit other crimes or forfeit bail.

The term "speedy trial" is vague at best, and over the years the U.S. Supreme Court has attempted to clarify its meaning. In *Barker v. Wingo* (1972) the Court stated that the factors to be considered in determining whether a delay is justified are, generally, the length of the delay, the reason for the delay, the defendant's claim to the right to a speedy trial, and prejudice toward the defendant. In *Barker* a delay of five and a half years caused by sixteen state requested continuances was allowed because of the need to convict a codefendant before proceeding against the accused and because of the illness of the chief investigating officer. When Willie Barker was eventually brought to trial, he was convicted and given a life sentence. The Court held that since the defendant did not ask for a speedy trial and did not assert that his right had been violated until three years after his arrest, he had not been deprived of his due process right to a speedy trial.

Most states have statutes that fix the period of time during which an accused must be brought to trial. In addition, to ensure that a person's trial in a federal court not be unduly delayed or that a suspect not be held in custody indefinitely, the U.S. Congress passed the Speedy Trial Act of 1974. According to this act, which was supposed to go into effect by 1979, federal cases had to be brought to trial within one hundred days of a person's arrest. If cases were not tried within this period, federal prosecutors faced the possibility that their charges against defendants would be dismissed. Despite the planned five-year delay in the implementation of the Speedy Trial Act, the federal courts were backlogged with cases to such an extent that Congress was forced to postpone its implementation indefinitely. —*Raymond Frey*

See also Bail; Criminal prosecution; Indictment; Plea bargain; Trials.

Spousal abuse

Persons commit criminal acts when they emotionally, physically, mentally, or sexually abuse their spouses.

Although once largely neglected as an area of appropriate social concern, domestic violence had become by the late twentieth century a serious issue of legal reform. Prior to the twentieth century, victims of domestic violence could anticipate little recourse from the law. General laws against physical assault frequently made exceptions when those assaults were perpetrated by one spouse upon another. In fact, older cases sometimes adopted the rule that a husband could not be punished at all for beating his wife as long as the instrument used was a stick that might pass through a wedding ring. In addition, although a person injured by another is normally entitled to sue for damages, the laws of most jurisdictions prevented spouses from suing one another for injuries of this sort. However, modern attitudes have recognized domestic violence as a serious legal problem with substantial social consequences. As a result, most jurisdictions have adopted more vigorous punishments for domestic violence and have explored techniques for investigating and prosecuting instances of this kind of violence.

The Range of Spousal Abuse. Although people who abuse their spouses may be male or female, abusers are overwhelmingly male. In the late 1990's, 97 percent of reported cases of spousal abuse involved male violence toward women. In fact, according to U.S. Justice Department statistics, domestic violence was the leading cause of injury to women between the ages of nineteen and forty-four. Domestic violence caused more injuries to these women than did all car accidents, muggings, and rapes involving women in this age group. Statistics also showed that 25 to 30 percent of women who visited hospital emergency rooms did so because of domestic violence and that 50 percent of the women and children who were homeless were victims of this type of abuse. Moreover, according to the Federal Bureau of Investigation (FBI), 63 percent of the young men ages eleven to twenty who were in jail for homicide in 1995 were there because they had murdered their mothers' abusive husbands, boyfriends, or domestic partners.

Usually women have to make seven or eight attempts before they can actually succeed in leaving an abusive husband or partner. However, when they finally decide to leave, women put themselves at the greatest risk of violence from men. Seventy-five percent of women who are murdered by their husbands or boyfriends are killed after they leave the relationship. Nationally about fourteen hundred women are killed by their mates each year.

Spousal abuse does not necessarily take the form of physical acts of violence. It can also be emotional disparagement, mental torture, and sexual violence. Making angry or threatening gestures or using physical size to intimidate can be construed to be spousal abuse, as can destruction of a spouse's personal property, punching walls, throwing and breaking things, and making verbal threats. Degrading behavior toward persons based on gender or sexual orientation can also be spousal abuse, as can forcing a spouse to engage in sexual activity. Using weapons against a spouse, threatening a spouse with a weapon, or keeping weapons to intimidate a spouse are acts of spousal abuse. The mate who threatens to kill a partner's pets or loved ones is guilty of spousal abuse.

Punishment of Spousal Abuse. Since the mid-1980's most jurisdictions have seen domestic violence as not just a family matter but as criminal activity. However, the penalties that have been levied against abusers have varied from state to state. In general, however, the sort of assault that would be classified as a felony if it occurred between strangers is often classified as a misdemeanor when it involves domestic partners. Thus, domestic violence convictions have often received less severe penalties than have convictions for similar offenses that involved violence against persons with whom the perpetrator did not have a domestic relationship.

In spousal abuse cases law-enforcement officers make no attempt to investigate besides taking a statement from the abused party. In such a situation, if the person who was abused does not want to testify against the abuser, there will be no conviction. Of course, people who are abused are often unwilling to testify against their abusers for fear that the abuse will intensify. Often, when victims file complaints against abusers, they want to rescind them after the immediate danger has passed, because they think that their abusers will make their lives even more difficult. In some states, such as West Virginia, law-enforcement officials are not allowed to rescind warrants against abusers if there is other evidence, besides victims' testimony, that abuse has taken place.

In many jurisdictions the prosecution of spousal abuse cases has not had a high priority among prosecutors. This is because such cases have traditionally been seen as private matters between family members. There has also been the general, as well as traditional, perception that abuse victims bring abuse upon themselves through their behavior. A general perception is that if abuse victims remain in the abusive situation, the abuse somehow satisfies the victim's emotional needs. Such perceptions turn victims into perpetrators. Victims of spousal abuse have difficulty leaving their abusers because they are often financially dependent on them. Abusers and abused also have joint children.

Prosecutors are likely to prosecute domestic violence cases when they involve severe physical injury or death. They are less likely to prosecute cases that involve intimidation, verbal threats, and rape. Cases involving physical injury or death may be

Although once largely neglected as an area of social concern, domestic violence has become a serious issue calling for legal reform. (James L. Shaffer)

easier to build and to prove than other types of cases. Prosecutors may be better able to build public support for the prosecution of these sorts of cases, because they are analogous to cases that involve what are traditionally believed to be criminal acts.

Federal Law. In 1994 President Bill Clinton signed into law the Violence Against Women Act. This law, which was part of the Violent Crime Control and Law Enforcement Act, provided for federal sentences for people who traveled among states with the intent to harass, injure, or intimidate a spouse or domestic partner. It also provided that states had to recognize protection orders issued by other jurisdictions. Grant money was provided so that states could set up registries to track protection orders for victims of domestic violence and warrants from one jurisdiction to another. This law made clear that victims of domestic violence have the civil right to ask for restitution from abusers and the right to speak to a court prior to the sentencing of an abuser. In 1995 the U.S. Justice Department established the Office of Violence Against Women to prosecute crimes in violation of this act and to educate the public on the idea that spousal abuse is not just a domestic matter but a crime.

The Violence Against Women Act included an appropriation of $1.8 billion for research on spousal abuse and for programs to help victims of domestic violence; $800 million of this money was given to states as grant money to hire more prosecutors and counselors and to set up programs to aid victims. In 1996 the Domestic Violence Hotline, a nationwide crisis intervention hotline, was established, which victims of spousal abuse can call to report abuse, ask for advice, and seek the location of women's and children's shelters.

Suggested Readings. Discussion of women as victims of spousal abuse can be found in "The National Women's Study," a 1992 study by the Crime Victims' Research and Treatment Center of the Medical University of South Carolina in Charleston. Its editors, Pauline Bart and Eileen Moran, support the thesis that violence against women permeates every societal level in *Violence*

Against Women: The Bloody Footprints (Thousand Oaks, Calif.: Sage, 1993). Ann Jones presents statistics on domestic battering in *Next Time She'll Be Dead* (Boston: Beacon Press, 1993). Statistics on spousal abuse can also be found in "Violence Against Women: A National Crime Victimization Survey Report" (Washington, D.C.: U.S. Department of Justice, 1994). Martha Albertson and Roxanne Mykituik explore diverse legal and feminist responses to domestic abuse in *The Public Nature of Private Violence: Women and the Discovery of Abuse* (New York: Routledge, 1994).

—*Annita Marie Ward*

See also Divorce; Marriage; Rape; Restraining order, temporary; Stalking.

Stakeout

The observation of a building or an area by police officers in order to arrest suspects during the commission of a crime, known as a "stakeout," generally does not require special legal permission but may be less effective than other forms of surveillance.

A stakeout is a form of surveillance in which police officers, usually plainclothes detectives, watch a building or an area where suspects are expected to commit a crime. Generally, suspects' identity is unknown, but their methods of operation are known. This allows police to predict where they are likely to commit a crime. If a number of gas stations have been robbed in a particular area, for example, police are likely to watch other gas stations in that area. Because officers involved in a stakeout watch areas in public view or the interiors of buildings with the permission of their owners, no special legal permission is needed. Other forms of surveillance that violate privacy, such as wiretaps, require specific permission from a court.

A stakeout is often effective in leading to the arrest of suspects during the commission of a crime, but it has disadvantages. Police officers must be willing to spend much time watching an area. They must also take care not to be observed by the suspects or the suspects will simply avoid the area.

—*Rose Secrest*

See also Arrest; Police; Police detectives; Search warrant; Suspect; Wiretap.

Stalking

Stalking is generally defined by state statutes as the malicious, intentional, and repeated following and harassing of another person.

After the murder of television actress Rebecca Schaeffer, California in 1990 adopted the first stalking law in the United States. All states and the District of Columbia now have such statutes, giving police the power to arrest for behavior which was formerly legal but which typically escalates from annoying to obsessive, violent, and potentially fatal.

The National Violence Against Women Survey, which canvassed 8,000 women and 8,000 men in 1995-1996, placed the prevalence of stalking at 1.4 million victims per year. A strong link between stalking and domestic violence was demonstrated by the survey's finding that of women stalked by a current or former intimate, 80 percent were physically assaulted at some time in the relationship. Most stalking involves current or former intimates. The few incidents involving strangers usually affect celebrities or other public figures.

To be arrested, a stalker must exhibit a course of conduct, which is a series of acts over a period of time showing a consistent purpose. These acts must cause a reasonable person to fear bodily injury or—in some states—sexual assault. The acts could include nonconsensual communication, maintaining physical or visual contact, and conveying written or verbal threats. In at least forty states, the fear need not be provoked by an explicit threat. The National Institute of Justice developed a model antistalking code in 1993, and many states have since modified their statutes to conform to this code and to avoid difficulties in implementation and constitutional challenges because of vagueness or overbreadth.

In many states, stalking can be either a misdemeanor (with a jail sentence of up to one year) or a felony (with a sentence usually from three to five years). Collecting civil damages from stalkers is also an option. The Violence Against Women Act (1994) permits victims of gender-motivated offenses to recover civil damages, but the act is limited to incidents in which state lines are crossed. The stalking statutes of at least four states also allow recovery of civil damages. A disadvantage to bringing civil charges is that the jury cannot send a stalker to prison. A criminal court, however, must prove its case against the stalker beyond a reasonable doubt. This is much more difficult than the civil burden of proof, which is based on the preponderance of evidence.

Other federal laws involving stalking include the Interstate Stalking Punishment Act (1996), making it a federal crime to cross state lines to stalk a victim, whether or not a restraining order is in effect. The Freedom of Access to Clinic Entrances Act (FACE) (1993) allows federal civil and criminal penalties against persons who interfere with the provision of reproductive health services, whether or not the incidents happen at or near a clinic. Prolife activists have included stalking in their tactics against abortion clinic staff and patients. The Driver's Privacy Protection Act (1994), which took effect on September 13, 1997, made illegal the disclosure of personal information (such as addresses and telephone numbers) by departments of motor vehicles (DMVs). Stalkers and abortion opponents have used DMV databases to obtain information about the people they harass. —*Glenn Ellen Starr*

See also Restraining order, temporary; Spousal abuse.

State judicial systems

As each state possesses the authority to design and operate its own judicial system, there are differences among states in the organization and number of courts.

Every state needs a judicial system to handle the prosecution of criminal offenses and civil lawsuits over contracts, personal injuries, and other legal matters. In the U.S. system of governance, each state possesses the authority to design and operate its own judicial system in order to handle matters that arise under its own state laws. Although the judicial system in each state contains two basic kinds of courts, trial and appellate, there are notable differences in the organization and number of courts within the various states.

Trial Courts. The first level of state judicial systems consists of trial courts. Trial courts are the settings in which civil and criminal cases begin. Typically, a single judge presides over a trial court and is responsible for making all decisions except for verdicts in jury trials, which are issued by juries. In jury trials, a judge makes sure that court procedures are followed properly and gives juries instructions about what to consider in arriving at verdicts. Trial courts handle preliminary matters, such as bail hearings, arraignments, and preliminary hearings. They also have responsibility for plea bargains in criminal cases, settlements in civil cases, and trials in both kinds of cases. In criminal cases offenders' sentences are determined by trial court judges.

All states have trial courts of general jurisdiction. These are basic trial courts with authority over all kinds of legal matters. States use different names for these courts. They are most commonly called circuit courts (Michigan), superior courts (California), district courts (Idaho), or courts of common pleas (Ohio). These are the settings for jury trials in civil and criminal cases. They also may hear appeals from decisions made in any lower level trial courts within the state.

Many states have lower level trial courts, known as trial courts of limited jurisdiction. Usually these courts have specialized, limited authority. These courts also operate under various names, such as district courts (Kentucky), justice courts (Mississippi), municipal courts (Missouri), magistrate court (South Carolina), probate court (Rhode Island), and juvenile court (Georgia). Some of these courts handle only specific matters, such as traffic tickets, wills, juvenile offenders, or small claims. Others may handle only lesser criminal offenses, such as misdemeanors or petty offenses, and civil cases that concern modest amounts of money, usually with a maximum of $1,000 to $10,000 depending on the state's law. Any lawsuits involving larger amounts of money or criminal cases involving felonies must be heard in a trial court of general jurisdiction.

Appellate Courts. Appellate courts are authorized to hear appeals, which are based on claims that a trial court made specific mistakes in processing or deciding a case. In criminal cases the appellate court does not listen to evidence and second-guess the trial judge's or jury's verdict about a defendant's guilt. Instead, the appellate court simply examines whether there were any mistakes in following court procedures or applying relevant law.

People who win appeals do not necessarily win their cases. They often merely gain a new trial in the trial court. Similarly, in civil cases the appellate court does not listen to evidence in order to issue its own verdict about who should win a lawsuit. The appellate court looks for errors made by the trial court in following the law.

Appellate courts operate differently from trial courts. Instead of a single judge acting as the decision maker, small groups of judges make decisions together in appellate courts. These groups typically range in size from three to nine judges depending on state law.

Most states have two levels of appellate courts. Intermediate appellate courts, typically called courts of appeals, handle the initial appeals from trial court decisions. Such courts usually sit in panels of three judges and handle a heavy caseload of appeals with the assistance of staff attorneys and law clerks. At the top of the judicial system is the court of last resort, typically called the state's supreme court. These courts handle a smaller caseload because most have the power to carefully select which cases they wish to hear and which cases will remain bound by the decision of the court of appeals. Most state supreme courts are composed of five or seven judges, although a few emulate the U.S. Supreme Court by having nine judges, who are usually called justices. For most cases involving the interpretation of state statutes or provisions of state constitutions, the state supreme court is the final authority.

Debates About State Judicial Systems. There are continual debates about the effectiveness and quality of decision making in state judicial systems. Because each state can design its own system, states periodically experiment with new ideas intended to improve the efficiency or effectiveness of their courts.

One major controversy concerns the best method for selecting the judges who will serve as decision makers in state judicial systems. In some states judges are elected, either through partisan or nonpartisan elections. In other states judges are selected through a merit selection process in which committees review applications and make recommendations to the governor about whom to appoint. A few states permit the governor or the legislature to appoint judges directly. There have long been claims that elected judges lack the independence necessary to make courageous decisions, because they will fear being voted out of office in the next election.

A second controversy concerns the centralization of state judicial systems. Streamlined court systems with few courts of limited jurisdiction may be easier to administer and run, especially if courts are funded by the state and not by individual counties and cities. Centralized court systems often have professional court administrators in a state capital who make decisions about how to allocate funds, computerize case records, and take other steps to run courts effectively. In contrast, states that have multiple courts of limited jurisdiction may find their courts heavily affected by local political parties that compete vigorously to have their own loyal partisans gain judgeships and jobs as clerks and bailiffs. In such systems the funding, efficiency, and professionalism of courts may vary significantly from county to county within a single state.

Suggested Readings. A general description of state judicial systems, their organization, operations, and problems is contained in Christopher E. Smith's *Courts, Politics, and the Judicial Process* (2d ed. Chicago: Nelson-Hall, 1997). A specific examination of issues affecting state courts is presented in *The Politics of State Courts* (New York: Longman, 1992) by Harry P. Stumpf and John H. Culver. Specific details about the structure of judicial systems in each of the fifty states are presented by David B. Rottman, Carol R. Flango, and R. Shedine Lockley in *State Court Organization 1993* (Washington, D.C.: U.S. Bureau of Justice Statistics, 1995).

—*Christopher E. Smith*

See also Annotated codes; Appeal; Appellate practice; Court types; Federal judicial system; Judicial appointments and elections; Jurisdiction; Small claims court; Traffic court; Trials.

State police

Law-enforcement organizations that operate directly under the authority of state governments, state police carry out certain specific functions, principally highway safety and criminal investigations.

The U.S. Constitution assigned to the states the responsibility for maintaining law and order. Until

1900, however, the states entrusted policing mainly to local communities. In case of riots or other serious disorders, governors called out the militia. In Texas the Rangers, a mounted militia, kept the peace in isolated areas in addition to fighting Native Americans and patrolling the Mexican border. Between 1865 and 1875 Massachusetts experimented with a state constabulary. In the late nineteenth century public sentiment remained hostile toward the idea of professional state police forces.

Early State Police Forces. In the 1890's the United States underwent rapid industrialization and grew more interdependent, its parts connected by a vast network of railroads. Crime became more mobile and complex, challenging the resources of local police. At the dawn of the twentieth century there was a pressing need for more specialized, better-trained police at the state level.

The first state to meet that need was Pennsylvania. Like many other newly industrialized areas of the Northeast and Midwest since the Civil War (1861-1865), Pennsylvania suffered chronically from severe social unrest, especially among workers in its coal mines and factories. A fierce, lengthy strike in the anthracite mines in 1902 aroused public opinion to demand that other, more civilized means be found of calming industrial disputes than the indiscriminate clubbing of mine workers by private police. This outcry set in motion a reform movement led by Governor Samuel W. Pennypacker to create a state police. The governor sent John C. Groome, a former officer in the Philippine Constabulary, to Ireland, where he studied the Royal Irish Constabulary (RIC). In 1905 Groome organized the Pennsylvania State Police, recruiting 228 men with military backgrounds, some of whom had also been officers in the Philippine Constabulary. They were given rigorous training and then deployed in four units in western Pennsylvania, where they proved to be impartial and effective at quelling disorder.

Fourteen states established police forces during the next twenty years, the eastern states generally following Pennsylvania's example. Western states, such as Nevada and Colorado, created forces that were extremely brutal and partial to the interests of wealthy absentee employers, especially in the mining industry. In the 1920's modern highways spread out across the United States, creating a new task for state police: traffic control. This required a new approach to policing. Persons wealthy enough to own or drive automobiles were likely to be prosperous merchants and professionals rather than foreign-born coal miners. Police had to be recruited and trained who could deal civilly with middle-class taxpayers, offering traffic safety programs and mildly enforcing traffic regulations.

At the same time, the expense of installing the technology to fight crime led many states to establish bureaus of criminal identification. By 1940 highway patrols or state police were at work in more than 80 percent of the states. They had earned reputations as "elite lawmen." Since World War II state police have continued to be concerned mainly with traffic control, while assuming a more significant role in criminal investigation. State police agencies are characterized by their narrow, specific mandates, reflecting public distrust of centralized policing in the European tradition.

Organization of State Police. The term "state police" is broadly understood to refer to the various agencies of law enforcement that function directly under the authority of the governments of the states, in contrast to county and local police agencies and federal police agencies. This broad definition of state police includes highway patrols, state police forces, and a variety of state investigative agencies. In 1993 there were 87,000 state police in the widest sense of the term, which amounted to 9.7 percent of all sworn law enforcement personnel in the United States. In contrast, there were 110,000 federal, 173,000 county, and 465,000 municipal police. All U.S. states except Hawaii have state policing agencies. Twenty-six states have highway patrols and twenty-three have state police agencies. Thirty-five states have investigative agencies that are separate from highway patrols or state police. There are, in addition, a great number of specialized investigative bodies, such as fire marshals and fish and wildlife agents. All state law-enforcement entities derive their authority to investigate wrongdoing or enforce the law from the state legislatures, from which they receive most of their funds.

State law enforcement is organized differently from state to state. In some states several agencies are centralized in one department. The Iowa Department of Public Safety, which is headed by a commissioner who reports to the governor, oversees the divisions of state patrol, criminal investiga-

State Police Forces

Highway Patrols	State Police Agencies
Alabama	Alaska
Arizona	Arkansas
California	Connecticut
Colorado	Delaware
Florida	Idaho
Georgia	Illinois
Iowa	Indiana
Kansas	Kentucky
Minnesota	Louisiana
Mississippi	Maine
Missouri	Maryland
Montana	Massachusetts
Nebraska	Michigan
Nevada	New Hampshire
North Carolina	New Jersey
North Dakota	New Mexico
Ohio	New York
Oklahoma	Oregon
South Carolina	Pennsylvania
South Dakota	Rhode Island
Tennessee	Vermont
Texas	Virginia
Utah	West Virginia
Washington	
Wisconsin	
Wyoming	

tion, fire marshal, capitol security, communications, and administrative services. In other states, law-enforcement agencies are organized in various departments. The California Highway Patrol, for example, is organized in the Business, Transportation, and Housing Agency while the state's investigative agencies are grouped together in the Division of Law Enforcement under a director appointed by the state attorney general. Some state police agencies are controlled by commissions and others by state governors.

State Police Powers. State police in the narrow sense, in contrast to highway patrols, have statewide powers to arrest persons suspected of both criminal and traffic offenses. Most state police agencies have plainclothes and uniformed agents. They provide the auxiliary services of record-keeping, training, communications, and forensics. Pennsylvania has the largest state police agency and Idaho the smallest.

State highway patrols are usually limited to enforcing traffic regulations, but they are empowered to assist any law-enforcement officer upon request. The investigation of crime is generally left to separate state investigative agencies. California has the largest highway patrol and Wyoming the smallest.

Investigative agencies with statewide authority to arrest have primary jurisdiction in certain crimes. Criminal investigative personnel are plainclothes officers who provide a variety of auxiliary services. They are distinguished from other state investigative agents, such as fish and game inspectors, whose powers are limited to a particular area of enforcement. Florida has the largest state bureau of investigation and North Dakota and South Dakota the smallest.

Role of State Police Broadly Considered. All state law-enforcement agencies require that applicants be U.S. citizens and state residents. Most state police agencies provide a basic course of instruction and training, usually at police academies, and in-service training. The minimum educational requirement is usually a high-school diploma or equivalent. The investigative agencies of California and several other states require that applicants must have completed two or more years of college, concentrating on police sciences.

Regardless of how differently state police systems are organized, they share common functions within law enforcement. They investigate certain crimes as prescribed by state law and provide forensic and other technical services to local police. They also provide specialized investigators, such as narcotics squads, to assist investigations by local agencies. State police enforce, with the power of arrest, state traffic laws and laws pertaining to certain criminal offenses. Usually state constitutions assign to county and municipal police the general responsibility for enforcing state laws and keeping the peace. If rural or unincorporated areas are unwilling or unable to perform these functions, they may contract or arrange for service by state police, as is the case in Alaska, Rhode Island, and Connecticut.

On rare occasions state governments may call upon their police to temporarily assume law-enforcement duties in municipalities, as in New York City in 1935 and Trenton, New Jersey, in 1983. With a few exceptions, the state police's authority to carry arms and to arrest is limited to the areas within state borders. States may enter into mutual agreements with one another that allow their respective police to cross borders in pursuit of fugitives.

State police forces provide information to themselves, to local police within their states, and to other state and federal agencies. Every state has access to the National Crime Information Center of the Federal Bureau of Investigation (FBI). They all have computer information systems for processing criminal records. The effectiveness of communication is improved by regional cooperation, as in the New England State Police Compact, under which police forces share resources in the investigation of organized crime. In most cases state law-enforcement agencies are responsible for collecting, transmitting, and publishing states' crime statistics. State law-enforcement agencies also supply forensic services to their own personnel and to other criminal justice agencies. For the most part, the employees of states' forensic institutions are civilians.

Examples of State Police Forces. Established in May 1905, the Pennsylvania state police was the first state police force in the United States. It is also the largest. Its organization is centralized under a commissioner, who is appointed by the governor and has the rank of colonel. Reporting directly to the commissioner is the Bureau of Professional Responsibility, the Office of General Counsel, the Office of the Budget, and Public Information. A chief of staff responsible for several bureaus of technical and administrative services also reports to the commissioner. A deputy commissioner responsible for a bureau of highway patrol, a bureau of criminal investigation, and five area commands also reports to the commissioner. In addition to the main forensic laboratory in Harrisburg, there are four regional crime laboratories serving local police. The Bureau of Criminal Investigation includes divisions of general investigation, organized crime, fire marshal, and drug-law enforcement.

Recruits to the Pennsylvania state police must be U.S. citizens, state residents, and high-school graduates, and they must meet certain physical requirements. Cadets undergo a twenty-week trooper course at the training academy in Hershey followed by field training and periodic in-service instruction.

Founded in 1929, the California Highway Patrol has grown to be the largest agency of its kind in the United States that focuses on traffic control. Situated in the Business, Transportation, and Housing Agency, it is led by a commissioner, who is appointed by the governor. It is one of two primary state law-enforcement agencies, the other being the California Division of Law Enforcement, which is responsible for criminal identification and investigation and forensic and other technical investigative services. The California Highway Patrol requires its recruits to be U.S. citizens, holders of valid California driver's licenses and high-school graduates. Moreover, they must meet certain physical and legal requirements. Recruits undergo a basic training course of twenty-two weeks at the academy in Yolo County.

Suggested Readings. Kenneth H. Bechtel's *State Police in the United States: a Socio-Historical Analysis* (New York: Greenwood Press, 1995) is a thorough, well-balanced study that examines the evolution of state policing in the political, economic, and social context of the early twentieth century. Donald A. Torres's *Handbook of State Police, Highway Patrols, and Investigative Agencies* (New York: Greenwood Press, 1987) thoroughly treats the organization and administration of state police forces. This book is enhanced by many tables illustrating state police organization, illustrations of state uniforms and badges, and a detailed catalog of state police agencies. David R. Johnson's *American Law Enforcement: A History* (St. Louis, Mo.: Forum Press, 1981) provides a chapter on the history of the state police. Bruce Smith's *The State Police: Organization and Administration* (Montclair, N.J.: Patterson Smith, 1969) is an early, influential study favorable to the concept of a centralized, professional state police force. Individual state police forces are described in Phillip M. Conti's *The Pennsylvania State Police. A History of Service to the Commonwealth, 1905 to the Present* (Harrisburg, Pa.: Stackpole Books, 1977) and Scott M. Fisher's *Courtesy, Service, Protection: The Iowa State Patrol* (Dubuque, Iowa: Kendall-Hunt, 1993). John Stark's *Troopers: Behind the Badge* (West Trenton: New Jersey State Police Memorial Association, 1993) is a journalist's lively, anecdotal account of the men and women in one of the larger state police agencies. John P. Kenney's *The California Police* (Springfield, Ill.: Thomas, 1964) is a brief overview of the largest state law-enforcement system. Frank R. Prassel's *The Western Peace Officer: A Legacy of Law and Order* (Norman: University of Oklahoma Press, 1972) offers useful information on policing in the Western states.

—*Charles H. O'Brien*

See also Criminal justice system; Law enforcement; Police; Traffic law.

Statute

A law enacted by a legislative body such as the U.S. Congress or state legislatures and interpreted by courts, administrative agencies, and practicing lawyers of the appropriate jurisdiction is known as a statute.

Statutes, or laws written by legislatures, are often contrasted with common law—that is, law arising primarily from judicial decisions and only later, if ever, codified in statutory or similar form. In the United States, Great Britain, and other English-speaking countries most law was traditionally of the common-law variety, the decision of legal questions being based on results in prior cases (precedent) and judges' own sense of equity or fairness in the case at hand. In the twentieth century the vastly increased pace of regulatory legislation, including antitrust, securities, environmental, labor, and various antidiscrimination laws, together with tax and commercial law statutes, meant that statutory law had become as important or more important than common law, especially at the federal level. Indeed, courts and practicing attorneys still spend much of their time dealing with the interpretation and application of federal and state statutes. In this sense, the difference between the English-speaking countries and the so-called civil law jurisdictions, such as France and Italy, which do not have a common-law tradition and have always relied primarily on statutory law, has been reduced in recent times.

Statutes create work for lawyers at all levels of the legislation and interpretation process. Many senators, congressmen, and state legislators are themselves practicing attorneys, and legislative committees employ staff attorneys to provide technical assistance in drafting various bills. At the administrative level—for example, the Internal Revenue Service (IRS) for tax laws and the Justice Department for antitrust or antidiscrimination statutes—still more lawyers are required to write regulations and supervise enforcement efforts. Finally, many private attorneys emphasize statutory law in their day-to-day practice, especially in specialty areas that are largely statutory in nature. This type of practice is highly challenging, because it requires familiarity with legislative and administrative sources together with more widely known judicial or court decisions. Thus, a tax lawyer must remain up to date about new and proposed tax legislation, IRS regulations and rulings, and judicial decisions in tax-related cases.

A major debate has focused on the interpretation of statutes. While U.S. Supreme Court Justice Antonin Scalia and others have argued that statutes should be interpreted according to their literal language, their opponents have argued that legislative history, including committee reports and floor debates, should be accorded greater and at times decisive weight. A parallel debate has focused on the degree of deference that courts should accord to administrative agency decisions that delineate the scope or breadth of particular statutes. How these debates will turn out is uncertain, but the vehemence with which they have been conducted highlights the increasing importance of statutory law throughout the American legal system.

—*Michael A. Livingston*

See also Administrative practice; Civil law; Common law; Judges; Legislative counsel.

Statute of limitations

A statute of limitations is a law defining the time period within which a civil lawsuit or criminal prosecution must be commenced.

All state governments and the federal government have enacted statutes of limitations requiring that legal actions be commenced within specified time periods. If a legal action is commenced after the applicable time period has expired, the court will dismiss the action without considering its merits.

Statutes of limitations help ensure that legal actions are resolved before evidence is lost or destroyed and help relieve persons of the fear of prosecution for misdeeds committed in the distant past.

In general, five steps must be taken in order to determine whether a particular action is timely. First, the court must choose the governing law. The court must determine whether federal or state law applies, and if state law applies, it must choose the applicable state law.

Second, the court must decide which time periods to apply to the particular action. Statutes of limitations typically provide different time periods for different categories of claims or charges. The process of selecting the proper category for each claim or charge is called classification.

Third, the court must determine when the time period begins. The traditional rule is that the statute of limitations begins when a legal claim first accrues, or comes into existence. Under the traditional rule, the statute of limitation begins either on the day the allegedly wrongful conduct occurs or on the day someone is injured as a result of wrongful conduct. In some cases, however, the injured person could not reasonably be expected to discover the wrongful conduct or injury until many months after it occurs. For example, a business may not discover that an employee has embezzled funds until an audit has been completed. In such cases, the law applies the discovery rule. Under the discovery rule, the statute of limitations does not begin until the injured person knows, or reasonably should have discovered, all of the facts necessary to support a legal claim.

Fourth, the court must decide if the time period should be extended, or tolled. For example, if the injured person is a minor, in most states the statute of limitations is tolled until the injured person reaches eighteen years of age. In addition, the parties to a legal action may agree to toll the statute of limitations while they are attempting to negotiate a settlement.

Fifth, the court must determine whether the action was commenced within the time period allowed, without counting any days during which the time period was tolled. In federal court and in most state courts a civil lawsuit is commenced the day the complaint is filed. In some states, however, a lawsuit is not commenced until the defendant has been served with legal papers. A criminal prosecution is commenced when the charging document—either a complaint, an indictment, or an information—is filed. —*Tyler Trent Ochoa*

See also Adverse possession; Cause of action; Civil action; Criminal prosecution; Indictment; Lawsuits; Statute.

Statutory fee ceilings

Laws limiting the amounts of attorneys fees, otherwise known as statutory fee ceilings, stipulate that fees may be recovered in particular kinds of cases.

In the late twentieth century insurance companies and physicians, who were often forced to pay large settlements, or judgments, in personal injury cases, complained that lawyers encouraged such cases through the use of contingency fees. A contingency fee is a legal fee arrangement that allows an attorney to take as a fee a percentage of the recovery in a case—traditionally 30 to 40 percent. Although lawyers receive no payment under this kind of arrangement unless they obtain some recovery, the arrangement also allows for spectacular fees in at least some cases. Opponents of contingency fees argue that they encourage lawyers to pursue dubious claims and—even in meritorious cases—siphon off too much money from injured parties into the pockets of lawyers. A few jurisdictions have agreed with these criticisms and have enacted laws that place limits on the amounts lawyers can recover under a contingency fee agreement.

Statutory limits on attorneys fees typically take one of two forms. First, they may impose a sliding scale on fees, which allows lawyers to take a greater percentage of the overall recovery when the recovery is small and then gradually decreases this percentage as the recover increases. Second, statutory fee ceilings sometimes impose an absolute limit—such as one-third of the recovery—on the fee that a lawyer may obtain from a case. To encourage lawyers to accept such cases, this kind of law sometimes allows a greater percentage in smaller cases.

—*Timothy L. Hall*

See also Attorney fees; Attorney salaries; Billable hours; Contingency fees; Personal injury attorneys.

Stepparents

Although many children in the United States are raised in stepfamilies, stepparents who do not adopt their stepchildren have very few legal rights and responsibilities toward them.

A stepfamily is formed whenever a parent who has the custody of minor children marries someone who is not the children's other parent. In the United States many children become members of stepfamilies after their parents divorce and their custodial parent later remarries. Stepfamilies are also formed when a parent raising children alone following the death of the other parent marries or when a single parent marries a person who is not the children's other parent. Many questions arise about the legal rights and responsibilities of the stepparent toward the stepchildren in these circumstances.

Child Support and Inheritance. Both the mother and father are legally required to support their minor children, even if they do not reside together as a family. This obligation does not change when a stepfamily is formed by the custodial parent's marriage to another adult. However, the question may arise as to whether the stepparent, who resides with the custodial parent and the children, must also contribute to the children's support.

As a practical matter, the stepparent who pays for household expenses, such as food and rent or the mortgage, helps to support everyone in the household, including the stepchildren. Most stepparents willingly contribute to the support of their stepchildren in this manner. However, the laws in most states do not require that stepparents support their stepchildren. Child support is regarded as the sole responsibility of the two parents.

Besides child support, another economic benefit conferred by law upon children is the right to inherit property when their parents die, if the parents do not leave their property by will to someone else. In other words, children (whether minors or adults) who survive their parents are the parents' legal heirs. Stepchildren are not considered "children" of a deceased stepparent for this purpose. Thus, stepchildren are not the heirs of their stepparent.

Of course, every person can make a will that gives property at death to named beneficiaries other than heirs. Therefore, a stepparent who wishes to pass property at death to stepchildren (whether minors or adults) must make a will that names the stepchildren as beneficiaries.

Custody Rights. An important legal right and responsibility of parents is their authority to make important child-rearing decisions for their minor children. For example, parents have a great deal of discretion about how to educate their children and about the types of medical care they shall receive. This aspect of parental authority is called "legal custody."

In the stepfamily the custodial parent is generally the sole legal custodian of the stepchildren. As a practical matter, therefore, schools and hospitals require the signature or consent of the custodial parent before they take any action involving the children. In some states, however, the stepparent may also be recognized as a "legal custodian" for these purposes under a legal doctrine called *in loco parentis*, which is Latin for "in the place of a parent." This doctrine provides that the stepparent who stands in the place of a parent by assuming an active role in raising the children may be regarded as a parent by schools and medical care providers.

Divorce in the Stepfamily. In an age of high divorce rates, many stepfamilies are terminated when the marriage between the custodial parent and the stepparent ends in divorce. In most cases, the stepparent following a divorce no longer lives with the stepchildren, who remain in the custody of their custodial parent. A number of legal issues involving the rights and responsibilities of the stepparent may arise at this time.

First, in terms of child support, stepparents are generally relieved of all financial responsibility at the time of divorce. Second, stepparents sometimes seek visitation rights with their stepchildren who remain in the custody of the custodial parent. Divorce courts in a growing number of states have become willing to entertain such requests. A visitation order, which requires that the custodial parent permit the stepparent to spend time with the children in the future, is granted only if the judge believes that this is good for the children.

Stepparent Adoption and Surnames. The legal process of adoption involves the creation of a legal parent-child relationship between adopting adults and their nonbiological children. In the stepfamily a full legal parent-child relationship already exists between the custodial parent and the children. A legal parent-child relationship may also be created between the stepparent and the children when the stepparent adopts the stepchildren, but only if the children's legal relationship with their other, noncustodial parent has been terminated by death or by a court order.

When many stepfamilies first form, the stepchildren do not share the stepparent's last name. Often, the children assume the stepparent's last name at the time of adoption. It may be possible for stepchildren to use the stepparent's last name even if no adoption occurs, but the noncustodial parent may object to this. Following a stepparent adoption, the noncustodial parent no longer has any right to object to a name change by the children.

Following adoption the stepparent has the same rights and duties as any other parent, including the responsibility for the support of the adopted stepchildren. The adoptive stepparent must support the minor stepchildren, even if the marriage to the custodial parent ends in divorce. Furthermore, the adoptive stepparent has the same rights as the custodial parent to make child-rearing decisions. In the event of divorce, the adoptive stepparent has equal rights to custody and visitation. In other words, in the adoption proceeding the stepparent becomes, in the eyes of the law, the second parent of the children for all purposes.

Suggested Readings. Readers who are interested in stepfamilies will find numerous treatises dealing with the social science aspects of the stepparent-stepchild relationship but very few books about the legal rights and responsibilities of stepparents. One treatise on the subject is *Stepfamilies and the Law* by Margaret M. Mahoney (Ann Arbor: University of Michigan Press, 1994). Two volumes containing information on the legal issues and other aspects of the stepfamily are *Stepfamilies: History, Research, and Policy*, edited by Irene Levin and Marvin B. Sussman (New York: The Haworth Press, 1997) and *Stepfamilies: Who Benefits? Who Does Not?*, edited by Alan Booth (Hillsdale, N.J.: Lawrence Erlbaum, 1994). —*Margaret M. Mahoney*

See also Adoption; Child custody and support; Divorce; Family law practice; Parental responsibility for children.

Stock certificate

A stock certificate is evidence of ownership of shares of capital stock in a corporation and a convenient instrument for transfer of ownership.

A share of stock is a unit of ownership interest in a corporation. A stock certificate is issued when an investor pays for the shares and becomes one of the owners of the company, or a stockholder. The stockholder pays for the shares in cash, property, or services. Unlike corporate debt, which is incurred when an investor loans money to a corporation and expects repayment in a certain period of time, the investor's stock interest in a corporation is known as equity and normally is not repaid by the company. The investor's interest is an intangible one, since the funds provided by the investor are used to acquire assets owned by the corporation. It is not represented by any physical thing but only by the stock certificate, which is the only tangible evidence of the stockholder's interest in the corporation and its assets.

Typically, the stock certificate is printed and identifies the company issuing the shares, the state in which the business is incorporated, the total number of shares the corporation is authorized to issue, the shareholder's name and address, the number of shares owned by the certificateholder, and sometimes any special rights attributable to the shares. In some cases the certificate may be engraved; it is always signed by corporate officers and sometimes by a bank or trust company acting as the corporation's agent. The content and type of certificate are governed by the law in which the corporation is organized.

One of the attributes of the corporate form of business is the free transferability of ownership interests. This is accomplished by the sale of the owner's interest through transferring the physical evidence of the stockholder's ownership—the stock certificate. The reverse side of the stock certificate provides transfer instructions. After an initial investor sells stock in a corporation, the corporation issues new certificates to investors who acquire this stock upon surrender of the old certificate with transfer instructions. The most familiar exchanges of stock certificates take place by sales of shares through stockbrokers on securities exchanges such as the New York or American Stock Exchanges. Sales of stock are reported in the newspapers.

In the 1990's state corporation laws permitted the buying and selling of uncertificated shares—that is, stock for which no certificate is issued. Sales of both certificated and uncertificated shares are governed by Article 8 of the Uniform Commercial Code (UCC). —*J. Kirkland Grant*

See also Bond; Brokerage account; Corporations; Intangible asset; Stockholders.

Stockholders

The owners of stocks or shares in a corporation delegate the day-to-day management of the firm to directors and officers but retain ultimate power over corporate decisions and may be parties to suits against or on behalf of the corporation if their expectations are not met.

Corporations differ from other forms of business organizations because the ownership of the business is separate from its management or control. The stockholders (sometimes called shareholders) own the company and elect the board of directors, which is the supreme managerial body. But the directors and the officers chosen by the directors, such as the president and the treasurer, run the company on a day-to-day basis, usually without consulting the stockholders on most matters.

Stockholder Veto. Stockholders have veto power over some extraordinary corporate decisions, including mergers, consolidations, and the sale of substantially all corporate assets, and have ordinary decision-making powers as specified in the corporate charter. However, even when approval is required, it is difficult to muster opposition to corporate management, since most stockholders are uninformed about corporate affairs and are unable to attend stockholder meetings. Management also has an advantage in soliciting proxies (effectively, absentee ballots) from individual stockholders in advance of stockholder meetings. For these reasons the power of stockholders is often illusory, especially in large corporations, and the stockholders may have an effective status more akin to passive investors than active participants in the corporation.

Given the difficulty of stockholder action, the most effective remedy for dissatisfied stockholders

Stockholders meeting of the American Telephone and Telegraph Company (AT&T), 1996. (AP/Wide World Photos)

is often to sell their shares and reinvest the money in other business ventures. Some scholars believe that the implicit threat of unhappy stockholders unloading their stock and thus depressing the price of the company's stock is sufficient to exercise a measure of stockholder control on corporate management. Others believe that this is unlikely, given the difficulty stockholders may have in gathering information on management decisions and on the variety of other factors that may affect the performance of corporate stock.

The influence of stockholders—especially large stockholders—becomes greater when there is a takeover bid or similar contest for control of the corporation. In such cases there may be aggressive competition for the support of the stockholders, who may be in a position to demand higher stock prices or other concessions in return for approving the relevant transaction. Lawyers play an important role in these clashes, creating various roadblocks to unfriendly acquisitions and, not coincidentally, driving up the price that must be paid to existing stockholders in order to effect an ownership change.

The Special Case of Close Corporations. The separation of ownership from management is characteristic primarily of large corporations, such as those that trade on major stock exchanges. Small, family-owned corporations differ from those types of corporations in that the stockholders—that is, the owners—are frequently the same people who wish to serve as directors or officers of the corporation. These "close" corporations often adopt devices that give the stockholders the right to serve on the board of directors for a short or indefinite period of time or to decide who else may serve on the board in their stead.

Small corporations frequently give stockholders the right to participate in corporate decision making on a variety of large and small issues. For example, many small corporations require that a supermajority (80 percent or more) of both the shareholders and directors approve such matters as paying dividends, entering into employment agreements, or making other significant decisions. The role of stockholders in small corporations thus tends to be more active than in larger businesses, and the line between ownership and control is fuzzier in such cases. To prevent this increased power from falling into the wrong hands, lawyers frequently advise small corporations to adopt share transfer restrictions, which require approval by one or all of the remaining stockholders before stock may be sold to an outside investor.

Securities Laws and Shareholder Suits. The difficulty of stockholder oversight in large corporations may tempt directors and officers to engage in self-interested or incompetent behavior, which reduces the value of the corporation and its stock. Stockholders who believe this has happened may file shareholder or derivative suits against the directors or officers for breach of either their duty of care or duty of loyalty to the corporation. Although brought in the name of the corporation, these suits frequently originate with corporate lawyers who receive a large portion of the settlement or other award to the stockholders in the case. For their part the corporation's lawyers devote substantial energy to counseling the business as to how to avoid derivative suits or how to settle them on favorable terms once they are brought.

Disgruntled stockholders may also bring suits under federal securities laws, arguing that management's behavior has caused them to pay too much or receive too little for their shares. Recent legislation has reduced the scope of these lawsuits, but they remain an important tool for dissatisfied stockholders who seek an alternative to accepting management behavior or simply selling their shares in the corporation.

Stockholders and "Stakeholders." The term "stockholder" refers to holders of both common and preferred stock. Common stock includes most corporate stock and is usually purchased with an eye toward capital appreciation (that is, increasing share values), although it may also pay dividends on annual or quarterly earnings. Preferred stock receives preferential dividend treatment but usually has less voting power than common stock and less opportunity to share in a company's growth. Holders of bonds, notes, and other debt instruments are not generally treated as stockholders, although they may have important influence on corporate affairs, particularly in the case of small businesses.

In the late twentieth century it was suggested that corporate "stakeholders" such as employees, customers, and the general public should be given a role in corporate affairs, despite their lack of formal ownership status. This argument has had only limited influence, but corporations regularly include representatives of these groups on their boards of directors, recognizing the need to respond to groups and constituencies outside their own stockholders.

Suggested Readings. The issue of stockholders and their rights tends to be considered as part of the broader corporate law area rather than as an independent subject. Lewis D. Solomon and Alan R. Palmiter's *Corporations: Examples and Explanations* (2d ed. Boston: Little, Brown & Co., 1994) is a student-friendly summary of various corporate law issues and includes chapters on corporate governance, shareholder litigation, and the general role of shareholders in a public corporation. Alan R. Palmiter's *Securities Regulation: Examples and Explanations* (New York: Aspen Law and Business, 1998) performs a similar function for securities law and litigation. An interesting perspective on stockholders' role in corporate governance is provided by Fred D. Baldwin in *Conflicting Interests* (Lexington, Mass.: Lexington Books, 1984). A former commissioner of the Securities and Exchange Commission (SEC), Baldwin argues that shareholder rights are impeded by the lack of a national political movement to compete with corporate management, on one hand, and environmental and similar lobbying groups, on the other. —*Michael A. Livingston*

See also Brokerage account; Commercial litigation; Corporations; Shareholder suit; Stock certificate.

Stop and frisk

In order to protect the police from potentially armed suspicious persons during initial street encounters, police officers are permitted to conduct limited detentions and conduct limited searches for weapons.

Under the Fourth Amendment to the U.S. Constitution police officers are permitted to conduct warrantless searches incidental to a lawful arrest provided that the arrest and subsequent search is reasonable and is based on probable cause. Probable cause has been defined by the courts as

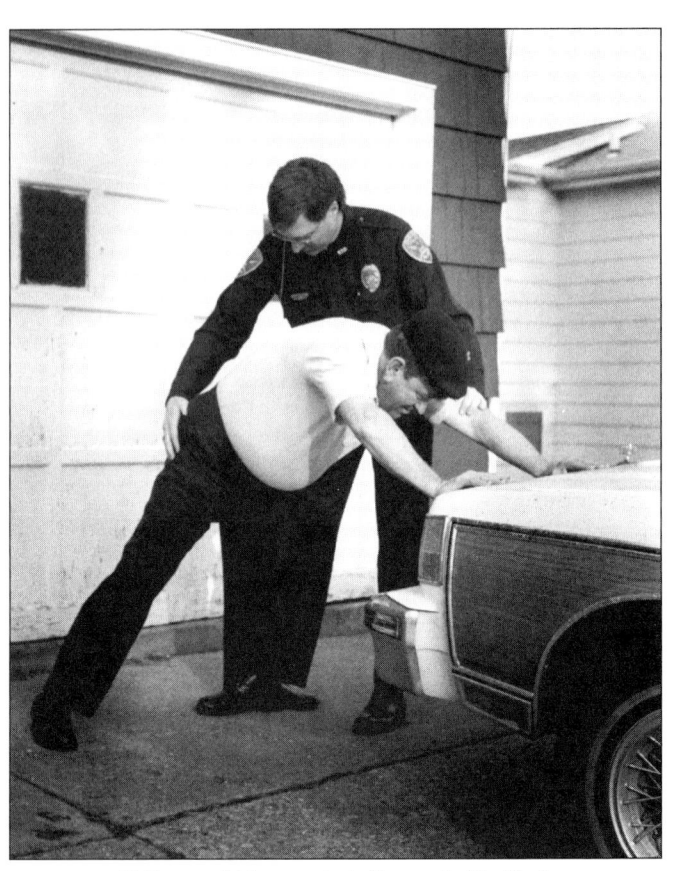

Policeman frisks a suspect. (James L. Shaffer)

enough information to make a police officer believe that a crime has been, is being, or is about to be committed and that the person arrested is the suspect in the crime.

Most suspicious activities observed by the police during routine patrols, however, do not present enough elements of suspicion to reach the probable cause requirements for arrests. Therefore, the justification for a search incidental to an arrest does not exist. This situation presents a serious constitutional dilemma for police officers who are concerned for their safety while initially investigating suspicious persons in a patrol environment.

The police are sworn to respond to suspicious activities within their jurisdictions, all of which present potential dangers, yet many do not result in arrests upon initial investigation. To alleviate all doubts as to the nature of suspicious activities, however, the police must make an initial contact with the suspicious person. Such encounters may be viewed by suspicious persons as illegal invasions of their privacy and therefore an abuse of police power. To balance the people's right to investigate suspicious activities with less than probable cause while protecting the suspicious person's rights against police abuse, the U.S. Supreme Court established a legal doctrine that clarified and balanced these competing interests. This doctrine has come to be known as the "stop and frisk" doctrine.

In *Terry v. Ohio* (1968) the U.S. Supreme Court established a number of procedural rules that apply to initial police investigatory contacts on the street when the police have less than probable cause to arrest. The Court, in defining the parameters of constitutionally permitted police contacts, established that contacts based on reasonable suspicion rather than probable cause are permissible under certain limited circumstances. Reasonable suspicion is defined as information based on more than a mere hunch or intuition that criminal activity is afoot but less than the information needed to make a probable cause arrest. Reasonable suspicion contacts are commonly referred to as "stops" and are generally short-term in duration. Particularly concerned with the safety of police officers engaged in reasonable suspicion stops, the courts have allowed the police to conduct limited, nonintrusive, outer garment searches of suspicious persons for potential weapons that could be used against the police. Such limited searches are known as "frisk" or "pat down" searches. If the "frisk" reveals that the suspicious person is carrying an illegal weapon, probable cause to arrest is then established and a full search incidental to a lawful arrest allowed.
—*Frank Andritzky*

See also Arrest; Loitering; Police; Probable cause; Search and seizure, illegal; Stakeout; Suspect.

Study-abroad programs

Programs by law schools exist that offer students the opportunity to study law in an international setting.

Study abroad programs are offered by more than sixty law schools in over forty countries. The majority of these are summer programs, but eight schools offer semester-length programs. Most semester-length programs are based in London, England. A listing of study abroad programs, course descriptions, dates, and tuition can be found on the American Bar Association's website: www.abanet.org/legaled.

Study abroad programs generally focus on international law courses that examine subjects such as tax, business, human rights, and environmental law from an international perspective. There is often an emphasis on comparing the legal system of the host country with that in the United States. Most programs include cultural excursions and visits to the host country's legal and political institutions.

In addition to giving students the opportunity to live and travel abroad, overseas programs enhance students' marketability once they graduate from law school. The integrated global marketplace has resulted in the establishment of international law firms that offer international expertise. Lawyers who are acquainted with international law and foreign legal systems and institutions are therefore valuable to law firms.

Law schools generally allow their students to attend other law schools as part of study abroad programs, but approval must be obtained beforehand.
—*Colleen P. Graffy*

See also Association of American Law Schools; Legal education.

Subleases

Leases by tenants of part of their interest in rented property are known as subleases.

A tenant holding a written or oral lease in rented property may rent the property to another tenant. The lease between the original tenant and the new tenant is known as a sublease. The new tenant is known as a subtenant. A tenant is generally free to sublease the property unless it is expressly prohibited by a written provision in the original lease. Although the landlord may prohibit subleases by the express terms of the lease, courts generally disfavor such restrictions and interpret them narrowly and strictly against the landlord. When the original lease prohibits subleasing without the landlord's consent, the landlord may not unreasonably withhold consent. Consent may be implied from the landlord's conduct or failure to object to the sublease after he or she has been notified of intent to sublet.

If not prohibited by the original lease, the tenant is free to enter into any sublease terms with a subtenant that may be agreeable to both. For instance, the tenant may charge a rent that is higher than the rent set forth in the original lease. However, the subtenant must abide by all of the original tenant's obligations under the lease. For instance, if the original lease prohibited the tenant from having pets, the subtenant will also be prohibited from having pets. The tenant may not grant the subtenant any greater rights than he or she enjoyed under the original lease. The tenant may also rent all or part of the property for all or part of the original lease term. However, the tenant must retain some of his or her interest under the lease or the transaction.

A sublease differs from an assignment of the original lease. When the tenant transfers all of his or her interest under the lease to another tenant, the tenant has assigned his or her interest in the lease. The new tenant then stands in the shoes of the original tenant and is obligated to pay rent directly to the landlord and abide by all other lease terms. However, unless the landlord releases the original tenant from the obligations under the lease, the original tenant remains obligated to the extent that the new tenant fails to abide by the lease terms.

Under a sublease only part of the tenant's rights under the lease are transferred to the subtenant. The tenant retains a reversionary interest in the lease. The subtenant is obligated to the original tenant and not to the landlord. The original tenant remains obligated to discharge to the landlord all of the obligations under the original lease. This presents potential problems for the subtenant. For example, if the subtenant pays his or her rent to the original tenant but the original tenant fails to pay the rent to the landlord, the landlord may nonetheless evict the subtenant.

—*Bernard T. Neuner*

See also Eviction; Landlords; Landlord's lien; Leases; Rent control; Rental agreements; Renters' rights.

Subpoena

A subpoena is a court order directing a person either to appear in court to testify or to produce documents that are relevant to a case.

Subpoena is a word derived from Latin that literally means "under penalty." A subpoena carries considerably more weight than a summons. Since a summons only states that legal action is being taken against an individual, that individual would not be breaking the law by not appearing in court. However, a subpoenaed witness is ordered to appear to give testimony at a specified time and place and is subject to penalty if the order is disobeyed. An individual receiving a subpoena to appear as a witness may be ordered to testify in court, before an administrative or other body, or to a court reporter. The Sixth Amendment to the U.S. Constitution guarantees that criminal defendants have the right to have witnesses subpoenaed in their favor, and it is typically wise to do so in order to guarantee that the witnesses will appear at the legal proceedings.

Subpoenas are issued for a variety of reasons by a variety of legal authorities, including a lawyer for the parties involved in a suit, a grand jury for witnesses to a crime, a prosecutor, a court clerk, a coroner, legislative committees, and administrative agencies. There are two basic types of subpoenas. The type referred to simply as a subpoena requires that an individual testify as a witness. The other type, a *subpoena duces tecum*, requires that witnesses must bring with them any documents or papers in their possession that may be relevant to the case under investigation. Before formal charges have been filed in a case, investigatory subpoenas may be issued requiring witnesses to appear at a hearing and to bring with them any pertinent documents or papers. Likewise, after formal charges are filed in a case, subpoenas can again be issued requiring witnesses to appear at a hearing or in court to give depositions or produce relevant documents or papers.

A valid subpoena must be issued by an officer authorized by the court, and it must typically be delivered personally within the proper time and to the proper place. It is very important that a person who has been subpoenaed appear at the specified time and place stated in the subpoena. An individual failing to do so can be held in contempt of court, fined, or imprisoned and may also be liable for damages sustained by the aggrieved party. For legitimate reasons, such as illness or a family death, a subpoenaed individual may postpone the appearance date.

It is wise for individuals to consult a lawyer if they object to a subpoena. A lawyer may raise objections to a subpoena prior to the appearance date by making a motion to quash the subpoena or a formal objection in writing. In either case, a hearing will be held to consider the lawyer's request, and a decision will be rendered as to whether the subpoena will be enforced or not.

—*Alvin K. Benson*

See also Discovery; Lawsuits; Summons; Testimony; Witnesses; Witnesses, expert.

Subrogation

An equitable doctrine in which one party obtains all the rights to pursue legal remedies that another party had is known as subrogation.

Subrogation is the substitution of one person for another as a creditor. The subrogation remedy permits one party to exercise all the rights of another party. The party exercising the rights of subrogation "steps into the shoes" of another party. The party that steps into the other's shoes succeeds to the first person's rights in law and equity.

Subrogation is a doctrine frequently used by insurers. A health plan may provide that the insurer shall be subrogated to all rights of recovery which a person or a person's dependents may have against any person or recovery. This means that if the insured receives an insurance settlement, the insurer has rights to "step into the shoes" of the insured. The insurer has a lien for the amount of benefits paid if the insured recovers a tort or settlement. If the insured does not sue, the insurer can bring suit against the liable party to recover insurance benefits paid. If an insurer is required to pay for an automobile damaged in an accident, the insurer is subrogated to the rights of the insured for any value remaining in the automobile. If the insured has a cause of action against a negligent driver, the insurer may assume the rights to the extent of its claim.

The Federal Deposit Insurance Corporation (FDIC) used subrogation as a tool to recover funds in the wake of the savings and loan crisis in the late 1980's and early 1990's. The FDIC was subrogated to the rights of depositors for accounts that were insured.

Guarantors or accommodation parties may be asked to pay a promissory note because a borrower is unable to pay. A guarantor or other accommodation party who pays the instrument has a right to enforce rights against the accommodated party. This is a codification of the common-law right of subrogation. The accommodation party who pays the instrument has a right to enforce it against the accommodated party. In other words, the guarantor has a right of subrogation against the borrower.

—*Michael L. Rustad*

See also Banking law; Health and disability insurance; Insurance law; Negotiable instrument.

Substantive law

Rights and duties that give rise to a cause of action are known as substantive law, as opposed to procedural law, which refers to the machinery for enforcing substantive rights and carrying on lawsuits.

Legal philosophers traditionally divide law into substantive and procedural law. The difference between substantive and procedure law is that substantive law creates rights, duties, and obligations. Procedural law is the method for enforcing rights. For example, a statute that instructs courts to presume negligence in certain circumstances is substantive. State courts frequently observe that a procedural law helps to secure and enforce substantive rights.

Courts distinguish between substantive criminal law and substantive civil law. Criminal procedure, for example, provides the rules for enforcing the rights of criminal defendants. In the field of tort law, the procedural device of the class action permits plaintiffs to vindicate substantive rights. The ban on retroactive operation of law extends to laws that are substantive. Laws that are merely procedural may be retroactively enforced if they are so designed by the legislature. Substantive provisions may not be retroactively enforced. The distinction between procedural and substantive law is also important in the choice of law. A party's choice of law only controls the source of substantive law.

In cases involving litigants from different states, procedural issues are controlled by the forum state—that is, the state in which the case is litigated. Procedural matters, such as the appropriate statute of limitations, are typically governed by the laws of the forum. The dividing line between substantive and procedural law is increasingly difficult to draw in many fields of law. Procedural rules have substantive consequences and substantive law has procedural consequences. —*Michael L. Rustad*

See also Civil law; Common law; Criminal law; Statute of limitations; Torts.

Summary judgment

A decision on a lawsuit without a trial can only be issued by a court if the facts of the case are not in question.

A summary judgment is a decision made by a court at the request of a party involved in a lawsuit without the need for a trial. The decision can be made without hearing evidence only if the two sides do not dispute the facts involved in the case. The judgment is made strictly on the court's interpretation of the laws that apply to the situation.

Summary judgments can only be made in civil actions. They are not allowed in criminal cases. Either party involved in a lawsuit can make a request for a summary judgment by claiming that the facts of the case are not in doubt. If the other side disagrees, it can submit a list of specific facts in dispute.

State and federal regulations determine how a request for summary judgment can be made. For example, it may be necessary for a party involved in a lawsuit to make a request for summary judgment at least twenty days after the lawsuit was first initiated. It may also be necessary to make the request at least ten days before the date set to hear such requests. In general, one side involved in a lawsuit is allowed to make a request for summary judgment immediately after the opposing side has made its own request. —*Rose Secrest*

See also Civil action; Dismissal.

Summer clerkships

The period of time that a law student spends in the office of a practicing attorney or law firm before being admitted to a state bar is known as a summer clerkship.

Summer clerkship programs are designed so that the law student serves as an apprentice to the profession. Each year law firms recruit law students to participate in summer training programs. These programs are usually for an eight- to twelve-week period. Students are provided an opportunity to expand their academic knowledge through actual experience within a law office. Summer clerks are usually in their first or second year of law school and assist the various categories of attorneys with research and writing projects. Mentoring review and specific feedback assures summer clerks exposure to a variety of legal experiences and development skills.

The objectives of summer clerkship training are generally twofold. One is to introduce law students to the practical issues of legal work through numerous well-planned and proctored assignments; another is to evaluate a clerk's progress through various stages and provide appropriate feedback through training efforts.

The trend by law firms and corporations is to focus their summer clerkship hiring efforts on second-year students in the hope that offers for associate positions following graduation will be based on clerks' job performance during the previous summer clerkship.

Career service offices at law schools provide summer clerkship counseling services for law students. Second-year students who wish to apply for summer clerkships should do so by October or November. First-year students usually apply in December and January. —*Earl R. Andresen*

See also Commercial litigation; Judicial clerks; Law-student clerks; Legal education; Liability, civil and criminal; Product liability law.

Summons

A summons is a legal document notifying a person to appear in court and answer a complaint or charge.

When legal action is initiated against persons, those persons receive a summons stating that they are defendants and must file an answer with the court by a specified date. Attached to the summons is a complaint, typically involving a lawsuit, with details of the charges. A summons is usually prepared by an officer of the court or, in some cases, by the plaintiff's attorney. In contrast to a subpoena, a person receiving a summons does not break the law by not appearing in court, but if the defendant is absent, the plaintiff will most likely win the case.

In general, a summons must be handed directly to the defendant. However, if the defendant is a nonresident of a state, most states allow the publication of a summons as a notice in a newspaper. If a defendant is a state resident and leaves the state for the purpose of concealment, then most state statutes allow mailing a copy of the summons to the last known address, leaving the summons with a person of suitable age and discretion at the defendant's residence, or, if such a responsible person cannot be found, attaching the summons to the door of the residence. Even if the defendant never receives a copy of the official summons, a plaintiff can pursue the case as long as the summons was delivered by the specified time according to a method described in the state's laws.

—*Alvin K. Benson*

See also Defendant; Lawsuits; Subpoena.

Superfund litigation

Litigation that requires industries to disclose knowledge about their abandoned hazardous waste sites and to be responsible for cleaning them up.

Unlike other environmental litigation focusing on the current activities of operating industries, such as litigation stemming from the Clean Air Act (1963) and the Clean Water Act (1972), Superfund litigation focuses on toxic waste sites that have been abandoned. Enacted in 1980 by the federal Comprehensive Environmental Response, Compensation, and Liability Act (CERCLA), the Superfund statute responded to public concerns when environmental contamination was discovered at Love Canal in New York state.

Superfund litigation is based on two significant principles: the quick cleanup of sites that cannot await the conclusion of litigation over who caused the contamination or how best to remedy the problem and the belief that the parties who caused the contamination, not the American taxpayer, should pay for the cleanup. Four categories of parties may be liable for Superfund cleanup costs: the current owners and operators of an industrial facility, the owners and operators at the time hazardous substances were disposed of at the site, the transporters that hauled hazardous substances to a disposal site that they selected, and the persons who arranged for the disposal or treatment of hazardous substances. Liability is strict and retroactive; for example, parties may be liable even if their actions were legal and nonnegligent and even if their actions occurred before the passage of CERCLA. Liability is also joint, which means that all responsible parties may be held liable for the entire cost of cleanup. For the government to establish liability against one of the four categories of parties, it must prove that a facility released hazardous substances into the environment.

During the 1980's Superfund litigation was forcefully enacted by the Environmental Protection Agency (EPA) and the Justice Department despite the criticisms they received, primarily from parties that would be most hurt by the implementation of the litigation. Since the early 1990's both agencies have admitted that some of the liability laws are heavy handed and should be implemented more fairly. These agencies' goals are not to put industries out of business but to protect the environment and to make all responsible parties pay for their fair share when a contaminated site is cleaned up. Although both agencies support administrative reforms and changes in CERCLA itself to address the unintended effects that some liability provisions have had, they both stress that the strict, retroactive, and joint liability scheme inherent in Superfund litigation is crucial.

Without a doubt, Superfund litigation leading

to pollution prevention, waste minimization, and proper waste disposal has had a positive effect on the environment. A second more important benefit of this litigation is that it has caused a revolution in industry's approach to hazardous waste handling and in America's attitude toward hazardous waste. —*Cassandra Kircher*

See also Asbestos litigation; Environmental legislation; Environmental practice.

Supreme Court, U.S.

The Supreme Court, the highest court in the United States, is the final interpreter of whether the laws and actions of the United States government, states, cities, and its citizens are permissible under the U.S. Constitution.

The Supreme Court defines the authority and powers of the national government, states, and cities and the nature of individual rights. Individual rights, such as the freedom of speech and the right to privacy, protect citizens from the abuses of government authority. The present size of the Supreme Court, nine, was last set by the U.S. Congress in 1869. The most important power of the Supreme Court is its power of judicial review, through which its justices determine whether national, state, or city laws violate the Constitution. Judicial review is also its most controversial power, because in exercising it nine justices can nullify the decisions of government bodies that are democratically elected. Some of the Supreme Court's most controversial decisions have been *Roe v. Wade* (1973), which protected women's right to abortion as part of the right to privacy and thus declared state criminal abortion laws to be unconstitutional, and *Brown v. Board of Education* (1954) which outlawed racial segregation in the schools, thus overturning decades of segregation in the U.S. South. Supreme Court power is also very substantial when it interprets what a law passed by Congress means.

Appointment and Jurisdiction. Supreme Court justices are chosen by the president of the United States with the advice and consent of the U.S. Senate. It is not unusual for presidential nominees to withdraw their names from consideration when negative information about them comes to light, nor is it unusual for nominees to be turned down by the Senate for many reasons, including Senate opposition to a nominee's views on legal questions. Appointment to the Supreme Court is for life or good behavior. Only through resignation, death, or impeachment by the U.S. House of Representatives and trial by the Senate do justices leave the Supreme Court. Only one justice has been formally impeached.

Article III of the Constitution specifies that the Supreme Court has both original and appellate jurisdiction. It has original and exclusive jurisdiction—that is, it is the court of first resort—in controversies between two or more states. It has original but not exclusive jurisdiction in cases involving public ministers and consuls and in all actions by a state against citizens of another state or against aliens. However, late twentieth century practice was for the Court to take most cases on appeal from federal district and circuit courts or the highest level state appellate courts. Parties seeking Supreme Court action request the Court to reply positively to writs of *certiorari*, writs to direct lower courts to supply the Supreme Court with the records in a case. The Supreme Court has complete discretion as to whether it hears cases.

The Rule of Four. For the Court to agree to hear a case, four justices must agree to take it. This is known as the rule of four. In the 1990's most justices allowed their law clerks, individually or in pools, to review the appeals to the Court for action. Clerks make summaries of legal issues, on the basis of which the justices decide whether to hear a case. Losing parties in federal district and circuit courts, in specialized courts that have been set up by Congress such as the tax Court, and in state supreme courts appeal to the U.S. Supreme Court to reverse the actions of these lower courts. For a case to be taken on appeal from a state court it must present a substantial federal question—for example, a state law's violation of the U.S. Constitution. In many instances the Supreme Court takes cases when the federal circuit and district courts have conflicting interpretations of constitutional rights and federal laws, especially when the issues in conflict are important to the nation. A good example of this is the Court's 1992 decision to reaffirm the central holdings of *Roe v. Wade*. By so doing, the Supreme Court ensures that the Constitution, the laws of the United States, and its treaties continue to be the "supreme law of the land" and binding on all courts and individuals in the United States.

In the 1990's more than 4,500 cases were brought to the Supreme Court. However, in fewer than 130 of these cases did the Supreme Court hear oral arguments and write full opinions. Another 75 to 125 cases each year were reviewed by the Court through brief decisions without oral arguments.

Briefs. All cases require that there be real controversies between two parties, such as individuals, states, cities, or corporations. The opposing parties must present detailed legal briefs. These documents must marshal all possible relevant legal principles and precedents. Although the crux of each brief usually focuses on the interpretation of the specific statute or legal principle at issue in the case, some influential briefs in the Court's history have used social science data in support of their positions. For example, in *Brown v. Board of Education* the lawyers representing the children seeking to end racial segregation supplemented their legal brief with psychological studies showing the adverse effects of school segregation on the development of African American children. Whether social science data should be used in determining individual rights is controversial, because it is feared that any change in this data might undermine the individual rights defined by the Supreme Court.

At the Court's invitation or at the mutual request of both parties to a case, advocacy groups may file *amicus* briefs on a party's behalf. These briefs, however, differ significantly from the primary briefs of the two parties. They are usually filed by groups that are interested in preserving or extending certain legal principles rather than in the outcomes of the specific cases they are addressing. A group such as the National Association for the Advancement of Colored People (NAACP) might file a brief in a school desegregation case in order to further its larger goal of African American equality. A group such as the American Civil Liberties Union (ACLU) might file a brief in a flag burning case because it wishes to see the First Amendment's freedom of speech and assembly preserved. In approximately half of the cases during each Court term, the Justice Department files a brief on behalf of the U.S. government.

Oral Argument and Voting. After the justices have read the briefs filed by the opposing sides in a case, they set a date to hear oral argument. In their oral arguments, the attorneys for each party present their side of the case for an allotted period of time, usually thirty minutes. The justices often interrupt the attorneys with questions and discuss legal issues among themselves. In most cases oral argument plays a minor role in the final decision. However, in some cases oral argument is crucial. For example, in landmark decisions, such as *Brown v. Board of Education*, the Supreme Court asks that important constitutional questions be reargued in a later round of oral arguments.

A few days after hearing oral argument the justices confer to discuss and vote on cases. Conferences are secret. At times the notes of justices offer a clue to conference proceedings. Chief Justice William Rehnquist has introduced the practice of first allowing the justices to state their views on a case before permitting debate. Workload constraints limit the time the justices spend discussing cases in conference. Only occasionally do these conferences win over an undecided justice to a particular position.

Chief Justices of the United States

Chief Justice	Years Served	Appointed by
John Jay	1789-1795	George Washington
Oliver Ellsworth	1796-1800	George Washington
John Marshall	1801-1835	John Adams
Roger B. Taney	1836-1864	Andrew Jackson
Salmon P. Chase	1864-1873	Abraham Lincoln
Morrison R. Waite	1874-1888	Ulysses S. Grant
Melville W. Fuller	1888-1910	Grover Cleveland
Edward D. White	1910-1921	William Howard Taft
William Howard Taft	1921-1930	Warren G. Harding
Charles Evans Hughes	1930-1941	Herbert Hoover
Harlan Fiske Stone	1941-1946	Franklin D. Roosevelt
Fred M. Vinson	1946-1953	Harry S Truman
Earl Warren	1953-1969	Dwight D. Eisenhower
Warren E. Burger	1969-1986	Richard M. Nixon
William Rehnquist	1986-	Ronald Reagan

Members of the U.S. Supreme Court in 1993. Standing from left are Clarence Thomas, Anthony Kennedy, David Souter, and Ruth Bader Ginsburg. Seated from left are Sandra Day O'Connor, Harry Blackmun, William Rehnquist, John Paul Stevens, and Antonin Scalia. (AP/Wide World Photos)

Opinion Writing. After the justices vote on a case in conference, they must decide who writes the majority opinion stating the legal findings of the Court. If the chief justice votes with the majority, he either writes the opinion himself or assigns it to another justice who has voted with the majority. If the chief justice dissents in a case, the senior justice who voted with the majority either writes the opinion or assigns it. The majority opinion is the most important written opinion in each case and is always printed first. Any justice may decide to affirm the majority decision or dissent. Members of the Court who agree entirely or to some degree with the majority decision may choose to write a concurring opinion. They usually do so for a number of reasons. First, they may agree with the majority decision but disagree with the legal principles that were used to support it. A concurring opinion allows them to offer an alternative justification for a decision. Second, justices might agree with both the majority decision and its reasoning but wish to clarify their own views on the case or respond to one or more issues raised by a dissenting opinion. Finally, in some cases justices may write both a concurring opinion and a dissenting opinion on some aspect of the majority opinion with which they disagree. Concurring opinions were rare for most of the Court's history. They became more common in the mid-twentieth century and especially prevalent in the 1960's and 1970's. In the late twentieth century each member of the Court usually wrote from four to twelve concurrent opinions each term.

Conference voting is only an initial show of justices' positions. During the drafting of written opinions justices circulate drafts of written opinions for comment. Any justice might contribute to the draft of a colleague's opinion, make suggestions for revisions, or, in rare cases, even switch sides. Compromises over the language in opinions is common. They result from justices' efforts to win support for their views. For example, a justice writing an opinion may tone down language or add or subtract a principle to win over another justice. Despite the role that such compromise can play in Supreme Court decision making, justices change their initial conference votes in less than 10 percent of the cases they hear. Furthermore, changes in voting alignment usually serve only to increase the size of the majority.

Usually, dissenting opinions are not as legally significant as the majority opinion, for they do not form a precedent that justices feel obliged to follow in later cases. However, dissenting opinions can prove to be more important than even some majority opinions. Such opinions might be unusually forceful or eloquent, as was Justice Oliver Wendell Holmes's dissent in *Gitlow v. New York* (1925), or might advance a novel or influential method of interpretation, as did Justice Thurgood Marshall's unique "sliding-scale" principle in *San Antonio Independent School District v. Rodriguez* (1973). A dissenting opinion might subsequently prove so influential that it informs the majority opinion in later cases, giving justices who are not in the majority a chance to have great influence on future Court decision making.

Suggested Readings. Two of the best treatments of the Supreme Court as a decision-making institution include David M. O'Brien's *Storm Center* (3d ed. New York: W. W. Norton, 1993) and Henry J. Abraham's *The Judicial Process* (6th ed. New York: Oxford University Press, 1993). An important book on how the Supreme Court decides what to place on its agenda is *Deciding to Decide: Agenda Setting in the United States Supreme Court* (Cambridge, Mass.: Harvard University Press, 1991) by H. W. Perry, Jr. A book that describes how Supreme Court justices apply legal principles in writing opinions is Ronald Kahn's *The Supreme Court and Constitutional Theory, 1953-1993* (Lawrence: The University Press of Kansas, 1994). See Gerald N. Rosenberg's *The Hollow Hope: Can Courts Bring About Social Change?* (Chicago: University of Chicago Press, 1991) for the view that elected American political institutions, not the Supreme Court, are the major causes of social change. For a contrasting view see Lee Epstein and Joseph F. Kobylka's *The Supreme Court and Legal Change: Abortion and the Death Penalty* (Chapel Hill: The University of North Carolina Press, 1992), which analyzes how legal advocacy groups influence social change by bringing cases to the Supreme Court.

—*Ronald Kahn*

See also Appellate practice; Case law; *Certiorari*, writ of; Constitution, U.S.; Federal judicial system.

Surrogate parenting

Surrogate parenting occurs when a woman, after signing a legal agreement covering aspects of her pregnancy and delivery, becomes pregnant in order to give birth to a child who will be legally parented by someone else.

Surrogate parenting, or surrogate mothering, is not acceptable in many parts of the United States, but it is legal in states such as California and Texas, where a number of private agencies are available to handle arrangements for women who want to be surrogates or for individuals or couples who want to engage the services of surrogates. Surrogate parenting exists for people who wish to parent children from birth but are unable to bear them. Traditionally, such people have been able to parent only if they could adopt a child.

Surrogate parenting is a product of modern science wedded to the legal profession, but it is a controversial product. To initiate the process, an individual or couple usually finds a woman who agrees to be a surrogate. Often this woman must have certain specified characteristics; for example, she must be of a certain age and race and have a certain educational background. Such characteristics are more likely to be specified if the woman is to be the biological (genetic) mother of the baby. A legal agreement is then drawn up and signed by all the parties. This agreement specifies when the parents will take custody of the child and details how and when the parents will pay for the surrogate's living and medical expenses during pregnancy. Often a trust fund is established to cover these expenses. As part of the agreement, the surrogate may be required to refrain from certain practices during pregnancy, such as smoking and drinking alcohol. The surrogate agrees to give up all parental rights to the child and may agree to live in a certain place during pregnancy.

Surrogacy can be achieved in several ways. When possible, the surrogate may be artificially inseminated with sperm from the man who will be the legal father of the child. In such a case the baby will be the biological (genetic) child of this man and the surrogate mother. Through in vitro fertilization it is also possible for an embryo formed from the egg of the woman who will be the baby's mother and the sperm of the man who will be the baby's father to be implanted in the surrogate mother. In this case, the baby's legal parents will also be its biological (genetic) parents. It is also possible to implant an embryo in the surrogate mother that is the product of neither the egg nor the sperm of the legal parents-to-be.

Surrogate parenting is a controversial issue about which there are many questions. Many people view with abhorrence the idea that women might want to give birth for compensation. However, as baby selling is illegal in all parts of the United States, strictly speaking no one can be a surrogate mother for money. The majority of surrogates claim they do it to provide babies for people who could not otherwise have them. People who make agreements with surrogates often fear that the surrogate will claim parental rights when the baby is born. This is one of the reasons that many agencies require surrogate mothers to have children of their own, thinking that surrogate mothers with children will be less likely to want to keep the children to whom they have given birth.

—*Annita Marie Ward*

See also Adopted children's rights; Adoption; Parental responsibility for children.

Suspect

Individuals who are believed to be involved in a crime may be briefly questioned and quickly searched for weapons, but they may not be arrested or undergo a full search without probable cause.

Suspect detained and handcuffed by police officers. (James L. Shaffer)

Suspects are individuals whom police officers believe may have committed a crime or are about to commit a crime. Police officers are allowed to subject suspects to a procedure known as a stop and frisk. This procedure involves briefly questioning the suspects and patting the outside of their clothing to determine if they are carrying weapons. If the stop and frisk reveals no weapons and no other evidence of illegal activity, the police must release the suspects.

In order to arrest suspects or to conduct a more thorough search, police officers must have probable cause. Probable cause requires evidence that a particular crime has been committed or is about to be committed and that specific suspects are responsible.

In public places or in emergency situations, the police may arrest suspects or conduct searches without warrants. A hearing is then held to determine if the police had probable cause to make the arrests or conduct the searches. In order to arrest suspects or conduct searches in private places when no urgency exists, a hearing is first held to determine probable cause, and then an arrest warrant or a search warrant is issued.   —*Rose Secrest*

See also Arrest; Miranda rights; Police; Probable cause; Search warrant; Stop and frisk.

T

Tax law

A specialized field of law, tax law deals with federal income taxes and other state, federal, and foreign tax systems.

Tax lawyers are often perceived as technical specialists, but their most important function is to combine their legal knowledge with a knowledge of their clients' practical and business needs and thus to enable them to reduce taxes without sacrificing other important goals. To accomplish this, tax lawyers must have both extensive knowledge of the Internal Revenue Code and related tax statutes and a high degree of intellectual and business skills. Tax law is historically an elite field, and the best tax lawyers have historically commanded large salaries as well as considerable esteem within the legal profession. Tax lawyers have faced a stagnant market and an increasingly sophisticated challenge from accounting firms, which have taken on many of the functions traditionally performed by tax attorneys. However, the perennial nature of taxation means that tax law is likely to remain an important and lucrative specialty for many years to come.

Tax Lawyers as Advisors. Tax lawyers' first responsibility is to advise their clients about the tax consequences of business and personal transactions. For U.S. taxpayers, this advice most frequently concerns federal and state income taxes, which are important and widespread enough to affect the outcome of any significant financial activity. Wealthy persons often consult tax lawyers about federal estate and gift taxes and their effects on long-range financial planning. With the rise of an expanding global economy, tax lawyers are increasingly called upon to provide advice on international taxation, requiring them to become experts on foreign as well as U.S. tax law. For example, a U.S. company opening an overseas office or a foreign company opening a plant in the United States must be aware of the tax consequences in both countries and how the two tax systems interact through treaties and other legal arrangements.

The work of tax lawyers is divided into two essential categories. The first—lawyers' advisory capacity—involves providing advice to taxpayers before they enter into transactions, with the goal of structuring such transactions so that they result in the payment of the lowest possible taxes. For example, a group of people commencing a small business might consult a tax lawyer for advice as to whether to conduct their business as a corporation, a partnership, or a limited liability company (LLC), since under the right conditions the choice of one or more of these entities might result in a considerable tax savings. In providing this advice, lawyers must consider the appropriate tax consequences and other issues associated with each of these business forms, such as limited liability and the company's ability to market shares. At the opposite end of the spectrum, large corporations may consult tax lawyers about the structuring or restructuring of vast multinational enterprises with an eye toward reducing the aggregate of U.S. and foreign taxes on these operations.

Individuals and businesses consult tax attorneys for advice on various tax matters—such as estate taxes, capital gains provisions, or fringe benefit and pension tax rules—that affect the value of compensation packages and the return on personal investments or retirement plans. Because good tax advice must promote clients' business or personal goals while reducing their taxes, tax lawyers frequently work together with corporate, estate, or other nontax lawyers in performing advisory functions. The advisory function is probably the most exciting aspect of tax practice and perhaps the most lucrative: A relatively small amount of advice can frequently save persons large amounts in taxes, and clients are rarely sorry to pay attorney fees when they result in substantial tax savings.

Adversarial Role. Tax lawyers' second, or adversarial, function occurs after a transaction has taken place and its tax treatment is challenged by the IRS or the equivalent state or foreign agency, leading to a higher tax assessment. Although only occasionally called upon to complete individual or business tax returns, a function that is more typically left to accountants or taxpayers themselves, tax lawyers are often called upon to assist taxpayers in controversies resulting from items included on, or missing from, their returns. The first stage of this work involves representation before the Internal Revenue Service (IRS) or equivalent agency, during which lawyers present taxpayers' side of the controversy and typically seek to resolve the issue by settling for an amount between what the IRS demands and what the taxpayers believe they owe.

If the matter cannot be resolved at this stage, lawyers may represent their clients before the regular federal or state courts or, alternatively, the U.S. Tax Court, a special court established specifically to hear federal tax cases. The decisions rendered by these courts, in turn, are appealable to the courts of appeals or eventually to the state supreme courts or the U.S. Supreme Court. For example, several famous cases dealing with tax shelter deductions and charitable contributions reached the Supreme Court in the 1970's and 1980's, although the former were largely mooted by subsequent legislation aimed at restricting tax shelter abuses. The Court has also decided many state tax cases, including those dealing with the responsibility of mail-

State Rankings in Per Capita State Tax Revenue in 1995

Source: U.S. Bureau of the Census, *Statistical Abstract of the United States: 1997.* 117th ed. Washington, D.C.: U.S. Government Printing Office, 1997.

order companies to collect sales taxes on purchases mailed to out-of state customers.

Unlike corporate lawyers, who generally hand over their courtroom work to litigation specialists, tax lawyers usually handle their own litigation matters, although they may be assisted by experts in judicial procedure or by lawyers with particular knowledge of the courts or judges in question. Thus, in addition to their intellectual and business acumen, tax lawyers must possess at least some courtroom skills and the strategic sense to know which cases are worth pursuing in the various judicial fora.

Training and Specialization. No specialized training is required to practice tax law, and the majority of tax lawyers possess only a regular juris doctor degree (JD), which they supplement with refresher courses and extensive "on-the-job" training at their law firms. An increasing number of lawyers have completed legum magister (LLM) degrees in taxation, either on a full-time basis immediately following law school or on a part-time basis while working at law firms or other offices. The LLM program usually involves a rigorous sequence of ten or more individual and business tax courses covering various specialized areas such as pension and international taxation as well as corporate and individual taxes. These courses go into greater detail than those offered under typical JD programs.

The value of the LLM is debated: Some tax lawyers regard it is a necessity for high-level practice while others believe that the distraction from law firm activities, especially if it affects part-time students, outweighs any benefit gained from completing the program. Law students who are interested in practicing tax law and who do not plan to complete an LLM are usually advised to take at least the basic courses on income tax, estate tax, and corporate or partnership tax that are offered at their law schools in order to acquire general background knowledge and to determine if tax practice is indeed to their liking. It should be noted that a mathematics background is not, generally speaking, a prerequisite for being a tax lawyer. While there is certainly a quantitative aspect to taxation, calculations are most frequently left to accountants and business persons. Tax law involves the application of legal reasoning and precedent in a manner that is not very different from other areas of legal practice.

Tax lawyers' level of specialization also varies in different contexts. At large, corporate-style law firms, tax departments tend to be rigorously separated, although tax and nontax lawyers work together on various business transactions. At smaller firms, specialties more frequently overlap, so that the same lawyer may be called upon to be an expert in taxation and corporate law or taxation and estate planning. There are also tax specialty or "boutique" law firms, especially in major cities, although several of these have merged into larger, general-purpose law firms. Because tax practice has not grown as rapidly as other areas of law, cross-specialization appears likely to increase, and prospective tax specialists are frequently advised to combine a tax speciality with expertise in one or more other areas of law. For example, many lawyers advertise themselves as specialists in taxation and business law or taxation and estate planning, specialties that provide them with a broader client base and insulate them, at least partially, from market decline.

In addition to working for private law firms, many tax lawyers work for the federal or for state governments as IRS field attorneys or in the drafting of federal or state tax laws and regulations. IRS and Justice Department attorneys frequently work together on the litigation of federal tax cases, seeking both to win their cases and to set precedents that protect the overall revenue stream. Treasury Department lawyers and economists worked together to produce the proposals that became the Tax Reform Act of 1986.

If the specialized nature of tax law is at times the cause of some derision—witness the treatment of tax attorneys in the television show *L.A. Law* and in other fields of popular culture—it also brings many tax practitioners a high degree of satisfaction. The sense of belonging to a small, intellectually elite fraternity remains strong among tax lawyers, a sense of community strengthened by the proliferation of tax specialty journals (*Tax Notes*, *Tax Lawyer*, the *Tax Law Review*), on-line services, and a vast array of conferences, workshops, and other activities. Many of the leading minds in the tax field, from Randolph Paul to Stanley Surrey to Martin Ginsburg, have devoted substantial portions of their careers to teaching and government service, and among private tax attorneys it is quite common to have spent two or three years in public service, to have taught adjunct tax courses, or to have participated in the growth and maintenance of the broader, ongoing tax community.

Lawyers, Accountants, and the Future of Tax Law. In the 1990's tax law witnessed three challenges that, while not wholly unprecedented, raise serious questions about the future vitality and character of the field. The first is simply a matter of numbers. While many tax lawyers remain—the American Bar Association (ABA) tax section reports more than twenty-thousand current members—tax practice has not grown as rapidly as other specialties, notably employment law, intellectual property law, and health-related law and legal practice. The result is that the proportion of tax lawyers has declined markedly. In a recent ranking of legal specialties, tax law was outside the top five for the first time in memory. Much of this shrinkage has resulted from the decline of tax shelters and may, in the long run, prove beneficial to the tax field. However, this phenomenon means that the existing network of tax institutions, in particular the LLM programs that have grown rapidly, may prove difficult to maintain in the future and that at least some students may be discouraged from specializing in tax law.

A second development concerns the relationship between tax law and accounting firms. Historically the "Big Six" accounting firms have dominated the preparation of tax returns and related work but have left the most sophisticated transactional work, together with nearly all tax litigation, to tax or general purpose law firms. With more and more tax work becoming international in nature and with clients increasingly anxious to consolidate costs, this situation changed significantly in the 1990's. Big Six firms have increasingly begun to hire top law school graduates and to lure experienced tax lawyers away from elite law firms so that high-level (and especially international) tax practice threatens to become concentrated in the accounting field. While lawyers have traditionally resisted domination by nonlegal experts and nonlawyers are still prohibited from representing tax clients in most of the federal courts, it is likely that the increasing presence of lawyers will change the culture of accounting firms, making them more reflective of lawyer's points of view. The increasing assertiveness of accounting firms may, in turn, reduce much of the independence and elitism that tax lawyers have traditionally considered their right.

Finally, tax lawyers face the continuing possibility of a major overhaul of federal tax law that would render at least some of their existing expertise obsolete. In the short run, systematic tax reform may actually create more work for tax lawyers, especially those engaged in legislation-oriented practices, as those involved in taxation strive to understand the new system and seek appropriate transitional relief. The long-run effect is harder to predict, and a simplified flat tax or sales tax structure might well reduce the demand for tax lawyers and their usual services.

Suggested Readings. The technical nature of tax law means that many tax sources are beyond the grasp of the general reader, but a few selections may suffice to give some taste of the challenges that shape the field. A good historical overview of the tax system, designed with the nonlawyer in mind, is W. Elliot Brownlee's *Federal Taxation in America* (New York: Cambridge University Press, 1991). The classic work on the tax legislative process and hence on the origins of tax law is Jeffrey H. Birnbaum and Alan S. Murray's *Showdown at Gucci Gulch: Lawyers, Lobbyists, and the Unlikely Triumph of Tax Reform* (New York: Random House, 1987). Birnbaum and Murray offer a highly readable, nontechnical account of the passage of the Tax Reform Act of 1986, a case study in the idealism and cynicism that characterize modern tax law. Louis Eisenstein's *The Ideologies of Taxation* (New York: Ronald Press, 1961) is somewhat more reflective in nature, providing a sensitive treatment of the ideals of tax law and how they clash with political reality in the lawmaking process. A longtime Washington tax lawyer, Eisenstein captures what may be the essential point about tax law: that the complexity of the law results from a clash of irreconcilable goals, such as fairness versus efficiency. Moving from ideals to reality, Edwin S. Cohen, *A Lawyer's Life: Deep in the Heart of Taxes* (Arlington, Va.: Tax Analysts Press, 1994), describes tax law from the perspective of a practicing attorney, emphasizing the day-to-day challenges facing tax lawyers and the frustrations they encounter in trying to achieve their client's goals without abandoning their own principles or family life. Those more interested in entertainment or wishing to comprehend the popular image of the tax lawyer may be fascinated by the portrayals contained in John Grisham's *The Firm* (New York: Dell Publishing, 1991), in which a tax lawyer is the swashbuckling hero. The Grisham portrayals, together with other examples of the image and reality of tax lawyers, are discussed in "Mamas, Don't Let Your Babies Grow Up to Be Tax Lawyers," an irreverent but creative article by Paul Caron in the *Virginia Tax Review* 13 (1994), which also discusses some of the more substantive differences between tax lawyers and their nontax legal colleagues. The reader may wish to browse through the Internal Revenue Code of 1986 to get a feel for what tax lawyers must deal with on a day-to-day basis.

—Michael A. Livingston

See also Business taxes; Income taxes; Internal Revenue Service; Property taxes; Sales taxes.

Telephone law

Since its beginnings as an important medium of communication in the early twentieth century, the telephone system has been a target of governmental regulations while it has become both a medium and a target of a wide variety of criminal activities.

The telephone was invented by Alexander Graham Bell in 1876. Bell was a shrewd businessman as well as an inventor, who began the huge communications network that would eventually be known as the Bell System. For most of the next century, despite improvements, the system remained directly under the control of people, from business executives to a growing number of switchboard operators. As such, it was treated by the legal system as a "common carrier," a term defined as a medium that could be accessed voluntarily by anyone who chose to pay for it, and was used only for direct communications between individuals.

Electronic advances of the late twentieth century changed this situation drastically. Except in a few rural areas, where more primitive systems long remained in place, almost all local and long distance calling was done electronically, and operators were only encountered when special problems occurred. As phone lines were used to link computers, fax machines, and other technological devices and as more and more business was conducted electronically, a new type of crime developed. Money could be stolen electronically, secret information could be accessed from home computers, and telephone service itself could be stolen by anyone who figured out how to get computer access codes.

The Bell System and Antitrust Action. Although a few independent companies existed to handle local and long distance services before the 1982 divestiture of the American Telephone and Telegraph Company (AT&T), the Bell System was an almost complete monopoly. AT&T was the holding company, or general coordinator of the system. Subsidiaries included twenty-two local calling systems, called Baby Bells, which handled approximately 80 percent of local calls. Western Electric was a subsidiary that produced all the electronic equipment used in the system. Long Lines Division handled over 90 percent of long distance calls. The Bell Telephone Laboratory engaged in telephone research. The 1982 Divestiture Act forced AT&T to sell off its local carriers, which became independent companies. In return, the company was no longer obligated to adhere to a 1956 agreement with the U.S. Justice Department that forbade it from engaging in businesses other than telephone service. AT&T quickly became involved in computer technology and in selling electronic equipment.

An important result of the AT&T breakup was that other long-distance services, which previously had to deal directly with AT&T, now dealt with individual consumers and smaller telephone companies and began to claim a greater share of the market. Another result, however, was that the federal government lost a great deal of its power to control phone services. Local services were under the jurisdiction of state and local governments, and since there was now open competition in the long distance system, the federal government had less excuse to control rates.

A looming problem of the 1990's had to do with the old antitrust problem. Even after the divestiture of AT&T, local companies still had absolute control over local calls, which meant that the breakup of the parent company did not allow competition for local service. There have been a few attempts in some areas to break up these local monopolies, but by and large these attempts have been futile.

Phone Phreaks and Computer Hackers. While Americans have generally been supportive of business concerns, there has always been some mistrust of very large businesses, just as there has always been distrust of big government. The powers of AT&T were formidable, and the huge conglomerate was usually referred to by the general public as the phone company. Thus, it was not surprising that in the general rebellion of the 1960's, AT&T became a prime target.

The term "phone phreaks" was applied to those who considered it a revolutionary act to interfere with phone services and to defraud the phone company whenever possible. In the 1960's this was relatively easy to do.

Telephones at that time responded to auditory signals. By inserting appropriately weighted and sized slugs into pay phones, the proper signals were generated. In addition, a "blue box" was developed, which mimicked the sounds to which the system responded. Free local and long distance calls could be gotten by the use of this device. The blue box became obsolete as telephones began to respond to electronic messages rather than sound. At the same time, however, the rewards for telephone crime became greater. In the 1980's and 1990's banking and credit card systems became controlled by computer networks, and those networks were linked by telephone lines. Confidential information was also stored and transmitted by the same interlocked systems.

Computer hackers were the next generation of phone phreaks. In some cases, these hackers were merely young people trying to find a new source of fun. It was an intellectual challenge to find a way into a computer network. School records could be altered, grades changed, phony letters sent. Serious crimes could also be committed. All that is needed to access a computer file is the proper access codes and passwords. Since many computer systems are linked through an almost universal international phone system, only the strictest security systems will prevent abuse. There is a constant race between hackers and authorities to control the system.

It is relatively easy for hackers to obtain access codes. They simply program their computers to scan through possible codes, hook the machine into the computer system, and program it to record any codes it finds useful. Passwords may be more personally transmitted, however, requiring direct telephone use. However, a call from a pay phone, with or without an electronically disguised voice, is almost impossible to trace to the caller, and a convincing caller can sometimes persuade persons at organizations to provide passwords.

Computers are used by large businesses to develop mailing lists. Such lists are generally specialized and include all sorts of information about consumers. These lists may be keyed to names and addresses, Social Security numbers, or telephone numbers. Since Social Security numbers are printed on phone bills and phone numbers are listed in telephone directories by name, all these identifying factors are linked by computer and phone lines. A sufficiently competent hacker has access to a tremendous amount of information.

Regulation of Private Communications. Apart from antitrust actions and the regulation of interstate telephone rates, the federal government has little power over telephone communications. Specifically, government attempts to regulate the content of what may be said or recorded on telephone lines have largely been futile.

Legislation involving mass communication has a long and complex history. According to the First Amendment to the U.S. Constitution, free speech is protected, but public means of communication have always been regulated when individual rights may be infringed. As a common carrier, the telephone system is considered to be under the protection of the First Amendment to the U.S. Constitution and as private as mail service. This means that although obscene calls are theoretically illegal, as public obscenity is not considered protected free speech, no governmental agency may monitor telephone communications without proving due cause and obtaining a warrant. It also means that the federal government may not intervene in telephone communications unless calls are made between states.

Prank calls, fraudulent business propositions, and other misuses of the telephone system have long been common, but there is little any governmental agency can do about these problems apart from warning consumers not to give out personal information too casually. Modern electronic devices have greatly reduced the effectiveness of such crimes. People can avoid unpleasant calls by using answering machines to record conversations. If a caller acknowledges on a recording that the call is being recorded, the recording can be used as evidence in court. Some devices inform recipients of the numbers of calling parties.

Future Developments. As the electronic age of the late twentieth century dawned, the situation of telephone crime became much more complicated. By the 1990's the system known by a variety of names such as the Web and the Net had begun the process of linking virtually all mass media forms, and telephone lines were very often the linking device. By the 1990's the line between telephone service and computer networks had become blurred. Written messages, even contracts, could be transmitted by fax machines, which ran over telephone lines with or without connection to computers. Electronic mail, or e-mail, which required a computer, was linked through telephone lines, allowing users to communicate across the globe. Telephone laws and computer laws became intertwined.

Suggested Readings. *Essential Principles of Communications Law* by Donald E. Lively (New York: Praeger, 1992) is a lengthy and comprehensive description of American laws affecting the mass media and their historical background. Included is a lengthy report on government regulation of common carriers, including telephone service. Paul W. MacAvoy's *Regulation and the Performance of the American Economy* (New York: W. W. Norton, 1992) is a largely statistical study of government regulation of businesses and the effects of this regulation on the economy. Included is a discussion of the 1992 AT&T divestiture. A more specific discussion of the divestiture is Steve Coll's *The Deal of the Century: The Breakup of AT&T* (New York: Atheneum, 1986). This is a highly personalized story of the 1982 federal act and a discussion of its causes and aftermath. *Telecommunications and America: Markets Without Boundaries* (Westport, Conn.: Quorum Books, 1984) is a survey of the history of the Bell System, including discussions of business practices, federal and state regulations, and the ultimate breakup of the company in 1982. Bruce Sterling's *The Hacker Crackdown: Law and Disorder on the Electronic Frontier* (New York: Bantam Books, 1992) is an extensive report on assorted attempts to sabotage the telephone system and the computer network and a discussion of efforts by telephone companies and civil authorities to counter these efforts. —*Marc Goldstein*

See also Antitrust law; Privacy rights; Public interest law; White-collar crime; Wiretap.

Television courtroom programs

Reality-based programs depicting trials, popular since the early days of television, have spawned a television channel devoted entirely to real-life trials, in which the drama and conflict of the courtroom can be viewed by millions.

The courtroom is an arena in which the very essence of human drama occurs. Emotions normally run high, and the adversarial nature of the proceedings ensure that conflict is usually rife. Given this fact, there has been controversy for at least two generations about the effects of live media coverage of trials. Movie cameras have been permitted to record at least portions of some major trials, such as the 1935 trial involving the kidnapping of Charles Lindbergh's baby. The grandstanding for the media by the participants in that trial led to a general ban on motion picture cameras in courtrooms.

In 1963 the American Bar Association (ABA) recommended that television cameras be banned from courtrooms as well, although most states had already done so in the 1950's. This was strengthened by the U.S. Supreme Court in *Estes v. Texas* (1965), which held that the right to a fair trial guaranteed by the Sixth Amendment to the U.S. Constitution took precedence over the media's right to cover trials. If television could not have access to real courtrooms, it did the next best thing by re-creating them in so-called reality-based programs.

The Early Days of Courtroom Programs. As early as 1948 the short-lived Dumont Network presented *They Stand Accused*, which ran on the Columbia Broadcasting System (CBS) for several years. Such shows were dramatic and usually required only a single set, so that they were inexpensive to produce. Also, the public image of lawyers in those years was generally positive. They were primarily seen as being on the side of right and justice.

Dumont then presented *Famous Jury Trials* in 1949, which re-created actual murder cases enacted in flashbacks. Courtroom programs that had their genesis in the 1950's included *The Verdict Is Yours*, which was a remake of *They Stand Accused*; *Divorce Court*, which was syndicated; and *Accused*, which ran in the evenings and had two daytime versions, *Day in Court* and *Morning Court*. Other programs in that period were *The People's Court of Small Claims, Traffic Court, The Court of Last Resort,* and *Night Court USA*. *Night Court USA* was probably the only courtroom series that used actors exclusively, perhaps because it presented as much titillation as television could get away with in those days.

Most reality-based courtroom programs were similar in that they incorporated a mix of real people, such as lawyers and judges, with actors. The overall level of acting was considered to be quite low, if not wretched. However, the shows differed from one another. For example, some were fully scripted, some were not. On one program the studio audience acted as the jury. The most successful series that began in the 1950's was *Divorce Court*, which initially was on the air for eleven years and returned for seven more years in the mid-1980's. The later series highlighted the more lurid aspects of divorce. A retired justice of the peace served as the judge, and during its entire run over 5,500 actors were used. A 1990's version called *The New Divorce Court* was not successful.

The Return of Courtroom Programs. By the 1960's interest in these kinds of pseudotrial recreations had diminished in favor of totally dramatized courtroom dramas such as *Perry Mason*. However, in the 1980's the pendulum began to swing back. The U.S. Supreme Court in *Chandler v. Florida* (1981) ruled that individual states could decide on the televising of trials. The attempted murder case of Claus von Bulow was the first of the notorious trials to be covered live. Soon, more than twenty states had begun allowing television coverage of live trials; by 1993 all but three states and the District of Columbia had done so. In 1996 federal appeals courts opened their doors as well.

On television the advent of the phenomenally successful syndicated show *The People's Court* with

Popular Television Legal Dramas

Years	Stars	Title
1957-1966	Raymond Burr	*Perry Mason*
1961-1965	E.G. Marshall Robert Reed	*The Defenders*
1963-1964	Ben Gazzara Chuck Connors	*Arrest & Trial*
1967-1969	Carl Betz	*Judd, for the Defense*
1969-1972	Burl Ives Joseph Campanella James Farentino	*The Lawyers (The Bold Ones)*
1970-1971	Lee J. Cobb Zalman King	*Young Lawyers*
1970-1971	Robert Foxworth	*Storefront Lawyers*
1971-1974	Arthur Hill Lee Majors	*Owen Marshall, Counselor at Law*
1973-1974	Monte Markham	*The New Adventures of Perry Mason*
1986-1994	Richard Dysart	*L.A. Law*
1986-	Andy Griffith	*Matlock*
1990-	Ensemble	*Law & Order*
1996-	Ensemble	*The Practice*

Judge Joseph Wapner brought the reality-based courtroom genre back to life in 1981. It was the progenitor of other series, including *The Judge* (syndicated), *Superior Court*, and *Guilty or Innocent*, an odd combination of courtroom drama and game show. *The People's Court* seemed to strike the most responsive chord with viewers.

Its cases came from actual filings in Southern California small claims courts, and claimants waived their rights to appear in an actual court, agreeing to abide by Wapner's decisions. The retired Superior Court judge became a symbol (some said a sex symbol) of kindly but firm authority, a 1950's father figure of the type not much seen on television in the late twentieth century. It was even rumored, perhaps only half-seriously, that he was being considered for a seat on the U.S. Supreme Court.

In the 1980's the Cable News Network (CNN) pioneered high-intensity coverage of real-life trials. Inevitably, in 1991 Time-Warner and Cablevision launched an entire channel devoted to the coverage of real trials, either live or via replay. With commentary and analysis by legal journalists, the Courtroom Television Network, known popularly as Court TV, proved to be a success. Its coverage of high-profile cases, such as that of O. J. Simpson, ensured a devoted following.

Legal Opinion. Jurists and lawyers are by no means all convinced of the benefits of a camera in the courtroom. Some opine that television is the primary means of education for much of the public and therefore a necessary tool in demonstrating how the justice system works. Others believe that meaningful education may not be possible because coverage can be incomplete and limited to the sensational parts of a trial. Such coverage can contribute to misperception of the process, in extreme cases causing violent public reaction, even rioting.

As for reality-based courtroom drama, the reaction among legal professionals has been mixed. Due to the constraints of time and the audience's attention span, some of the shows have been more akin to soap operas than real trials. Sensationalism and histrionics are often the order of the day. Even in those series that appear to be a bit more realistic, critics complain about the unrealistic bullying of litigants and the compression of events to fit the program's schedule. If skewed coverage of actual trials can mislead the viewer, dramatized trials are even guiltier of this. But controversial or not, it is probable that reality-based television courtroom programs will continue to be seen in one form or another. Their influence obviously has been considerable; litigants in real small claims courts actually have cited precedents from *The People's Court*.

In recent years the television courtroom genre has been revitalized by the acerbic *Judge Judy* (Judy Sheindlin) and such syndicated series as *Judge Mills Lane* and *Judge Joe Brown*. In 1998 Wapner returned in something called *Judge Wapner's Animal Planet* (Animal Planet TV Channel). Even the Playboy Channel is rumored to be contemplating *Sex Court*, in which litigants will air their sex grievances.

Suggested Readings. Among the general reference books that contain descriptions of courtroom television programs are Les Brown's *Encyclopedia of Television* (3d ed. Detroit: Gale Research, 1992) and Wesley Hyatt's *The Encyclopedia of Daytime Television* (New York: Billboard Books, 1997). An article that discusses some of the series is Michael Pollan's "Reality Shows: The Syndicated Bench" in *Channels* 7 (1987). "Enter the People's Court," by J. Dipenza in *Emmy Magazine* 9 (1987), looks at the most popular of the shows. An overview of legal professionals' opinions about the effects of such programming is found in Richard Mahler's "Television on Trial" in *Emmy Magazine* 5 (1983). —*Roy Liebman*

See also Films about the legal professions; Literature about the legal professions; Television dramas about the legal profession; Filmography.

Television dramas about the legal profession

Portrayals of the law and the legal profession in television dramas have both reflected and distorted these American institutions.

Television has exposed millions of viewers to the details of criminal and civil law, but it has often done so at the risk of fostering oversimplification and in some instances misinformation. On occasion, television legal dramas have served as a vital public forum to explore some of the most important social and political issues of the day.

Early Television Legal Dramas. Despite the appearance of pioneering (but long-forgotten) shows in the 1950's such as *The Verdict Is Yours* and *Famous*

Jury Trials, the birth of this genre came in 1957 with *Perry Mason*, which ran for nine seasons on the Columbia Broadcasting System (CBS) until 1966. Starring Raymond Burr, *Perry Mason* introduced the standard framework of the legal drama which persists, with variations, to this day. A single case (usually criminal and usually murder) is first investigated and then goes to trial, resulting in a verdict. *Perry Mason* remains the most successful and longest-running lawyer series.

Perry Mason is legendary for having hardly ever lost a case. In the trial he lost in 1963, he still exonerated his client before the show ended. Based on the radio drama created by Erle Stanley Gardner, which was broadcast from 1943 to 1955, *Perry Mason* became famous for the inevitable moment at the climax of almost every episode when the "real" murderer would break down on the witness stand under Mason's relentless cross-examination and confess his or her guilt.

Midway through *Perry Mason*'s television run, in 1961, one of the most highly respected television legal dramas, "The Defenders," premiered. Starring E. G. Marshall and Robert Reed as father and son law partners in the firm of Preston & Preston, the series, which ran until 1965, tackled controversial issues such as abortion, the right to travel, and mercy killing. In 1964 *The Defenders* won several Emmy Awards as the first dramatic television show to address blacklisting, the witch-hunting method by which suspected Communists were driven out of the entertainment industry in the 1950's. To this day *The Defenders* symbolizes the potential for the television legal drama to confront serious contemporary political and social issues in the context of a dramatic prime-time series.

Ahead of its time, *Arrest & Trial* ran only one year, from 1963 to 1964. Starring Ben Gazzara as a police detective and Chuck Connors as a defense attorney, the program lasted ninety minutes, the first half of which was devoted to a criminal investigation and the second to the trial.

Judd, for the Defense, which ran from 1967 to 1969, continued the tradition of *The Defenders* by exploring topical issues such as draft evasion, labor activism, and the murder of civil rights activists. Carl Betz starred as Judd, a high-priced Houston lawyer, not unlike F. Lee Bailey, who traveled across the country fighting major legal battles.

In the early 1970's there were several forgettable legal series including *The Lawyers* (a segment of the series called *The Bold Ones*), *Young Lawyers* (portraying a group of idealistic law students helping indigent clients), and *Storefront Lawyers* (which began as a series about pro bono lawyers working in the inner city and later was recast as a story about a blue chip law firm representing the rich and poor alike).

A more realistic portrayal of the practice of law returned to television in *Owen Marshall, Counselor at Law*, which ran from 1971 to 1974. Starring the highly accomplished actor Arthur Hill, *Owen Marshall* depicted the human side of a small town law practice. Marshall handled civil and criminal matters alike with warmth and sensitivity; he was to law what Dr. Marcus Welby (from another television series of the same era) was to medicine. Indeed, Marshall and Welby appeared together in several joint episodes. The series, coproduced by a University of Wisconsin law professor, won several public service awards.

Return of Television Legal Dramas. For over a decade television was bereft of any dramatic legal series. Then in 1986 producer Steven Bochco introduced the innovative series *L.A. Law*. With an ensemble cast, the show brought to television a new, more cynical view of what lawyers actually do. *L.A. Law* was built around the workings of a medium-sized Los Angeles law firm whose partners handled a wide range of civil and criminal cases. The show also served up equal doses of office politics and romance, which had been rare in earlier dramas. While the series did address controversial issues such as the outing of prominent homosexuals and the refusal of insurance companies to cover medication for acquired immunodeficiency syndrome (AIDS), it did not display the seriousness of *The Defenders* or *Arrest & Trial*. The series reflected an increasingly negative attitude toward lawyers and greater frustration with the judicial system in general. The lawyers in *L.A. Law* were hardly pillars of the community. The show ran from 1986 until 1994, aptly serving as a symbol of the 1990's.

The same year *L.A. Law* debuted, a more traditional series, *Matlock* starring Mayberry's own Andy Griffith, also premiered. Ben Matlock was a Harvard educated lawyer practicing with his daughter and a devoted assistant in Atlanta, Georgia. A sly and folksy, but highly experienced lawyer, Matlock always solved the mysteries in which his clients found themselves caught up. The show broke little ground and rarely dealt with controversial topics, but its huge popularity was evidence that the viewing public still liked the comfort of a good old country lawyer.

In 1990 a format that had failed in *Arrest & Trial* succeeded brilliantly on *Law and Order*, created by producer Dick Wolf. With an ensemble cast, the first half of each episode was devoted to a police investigation and the second to prosecution and trial. Not since *The Defenders* had a television legal drama presented as realistic, serious, and topical a treatment of the legal system. The program, set in New York City, addressed important substantive issues, often dramatizing contemporary controversies such as the Mike Tyson rape trial and the sexual harassment allegations that Anita Hill raised against Supreme Court justice nominee Clarence Thomas. The series also illuminated complex procedural issues, such as illegally obtained evidence, the right to self-defense, and the right against self-incrimination. *Law and Order* set a high standard against which all future legal dramas will be judged.

In 1996 the American Broadcasting Company (ABC) introduced *The Practice*, which portrayed a group of young lawyers trying to keep their fledgling Boston law firm afloat. The show combined difficult legal issues, such as toxic waste, the death penalty, and corrupt doctors, with the personal lives of the lawyers, including a torrid (and ethically questionable) love affair between the firm's star criminal lawyer and the local prosecutor.

Myths and Distortions. Confined to a one-hour format, most legal series conflate the events that occur in normal legal matters. Cases begin and end in the span of a single episode. Legal proceedings move with a swiftness unknown in all but a few courtrooms. Suspects are arrested, evidence is gathered, witnesses are interviewed, and cases are tried in record time. For television writers and producers, justice delayed is truly justice denied. The real concern is the impact of this format on audiences. Exposed to such unrealistically speedy trials, many viewers are appalled when they experience the delays in real civil and criminal cases.

Another staple of legal dramas is the emphasis on oral proceedings in open court to the virtual exclusion of written briefs and legal memoranda. Given the limited dramatic possibilities presented by a lawyer quietly studying detailed legal papers, it is no wonder that television has all but ignored this critical aspect of criminal and civil litigation. Few legal dramas adequately capture the role played by written arguments, which inevitably precede and influence a judge's analysis of pending legal issues. Most legal dramas perpetuate the misleading impression that judges hear cases for the first time and base their decisions on what the lawyers have just said in open court. In fact, the opposite is closer to the truth. Most legal arguments are decided by the written briefs. Some judges don't even entertain oral arguments, and when they do they often admonish the lawyers not to repeat what they already stated in writing and chastise attorneys who bring up new points not briefed in writing.

This exposes yet another myth of television legal dramas. It is the rare series that reveals that judges decide most issues by applying established legal precedents, using prior court decisions in closely analogous factual situations. On television, with a few exceptions, the body of case law decided by state appellate courts or the U.S. Supreme Court, to which most trial lawyers consistently refer, plays little or any role.

Most legal dramas on television depict the courtroom side of the law, whether it be criminal or civil. The vast range of business and transactional law, such as negotiating contracts, writing wills, or forming businesses, is almost never portrayed on television. Since this type of work is rarely as dramatic as a good courtroom battle, television has shied away from it, unable or unwilling to communicate the true drama of these transactions in the lives of the real people and businesses involved. It is easier to write a murder trial than tell the story of a complex corporate takeover.

Few television legal dramas dwell on the difficult matter of legal fees. Typically, new clients simply meet the lawyer and explain their predicament and the lawyer sallies forth to do everything necessary, without a moment spent talking about what it will cost in legal fees and expenses. Here again the television audience gets a distorted image of the critical financial component of the attorney-client relationship. Most lawyers don't work for free; they receive either hourly fees, set fees for specific projects, or a percentage of any recovery. However it is calculated, the fee a lawyer charges must be discussed and agreed to at the outset of a lawyer's engagement, yet television legal dramas regularly skip this important step. Consequently viewers are denied the opportunity to see the dynamics of this process and to learn more about their rights and responsibilities as clients.

Serving the Public Interest. For all their drawbacks, TV legal dramas have exposed millions of Americans to many aspects of the legal profession. More lawyers than will admit it got their first taste of what it is like to be a lawyer from *Perry Mason* and other lawyer series. Scores of young men, and later young women, without any other exposure to the legal profession could see various versions of what lawyers, judges, prosecutors, and investigators do, even taking dramatic license into account. Surely television legal dramas cut corners and overlook details, but on the wide canvas that television, film, and the stage use to portray any aspect of reality, these programs paint pictures of one of the most vital professions in U.S. society. The very fact that legal dramas consistently sustain prime time television series communicates the central role that the law and lawyers play in the lives of Americans.

In the end these programs must be kept in perspective. They are fictional television entertainment and nothing more. Some have been inspiring, some embarrassing, and most just average television fare. None are a substitute for law school, a summer job in a law firm, or frequent visits to the local courthouse. But given the fact that the law sits at the center of so many of life's important events and vital issues, it is no wonder that it has provided grist for the television mill.

Suggested Readings. The most comprehensive compendium of television legal dramas can be found in *The Complete Directory to Prime Time Network TV Shows, 1946-Present*, edited by Tim Brooks and Earle Marsh (5th ed. New York: Ballantine Books, 1995). An entire issue of the widely available *University of San Francisco Law Review* 4 (Summer, 1996) is devoted to a symposium entitled "Picturing Justice: Images of Law and Lawyers in the Visual Media." Numerous scholarly pieces discuss all aspects of the depiction of the legal profession in the media. A book dealing with a specific television series is *L.A. Law Handbook* (Las Vegas, Nev.: Movie Publications Services, 1991). Another such book is David Martindale's *Perry Mason Casebook* (Las Vegas, Nev.: Movie Publications Services, 1991).
—*Stephen F. Rohde*

See also Films about the legal professions; Literature about the legal professions; Television courtroom programs.

Tenancy in common

An arrangement by which two or more individuals share divided ownership of property, tenancy in common, allows the owners to transfer ownership freely but does not allow surviving owners to automatically obtain ownership from deceased owners.

Tenancy in common is one of the forms of concurrent estate. Concurrent estate exists whenever property is owned by more than one person. Tenancy in common is distinguished by the fact that each owner has ownership of a specific part of property that has been divided into shares. The shares need not be equal in size.

Unlike joint tenancy, a form of concurrent estate in which each owner has full ownership of undivided property, tenancy in common allows each owner to freely sell or otherwise transfer ownership of a share to a new owner. Tenancy in common is also distinguished from joint tenancy by the fact that there is no right of survivorship. That is, ownership of a share is not automatically transferred to the other owners of the property when one owner dies. Instead, ownership of the share is transferred to the deceased owner's heirs.

Tenancy in common may be created by deed, will, or law. It also comes into being when an owner involved in a joint tenancy transfers ownership to a new owner. Tenancy in common is also created when a married couple involved in a joint tenancy, which is known as tenancy by the entirety, is divorced.
—*Rose Secrest*

See also Community property; Joint tenancy; Property rights.

Test case

A legal case undertaken to test a point of law is known as a test case.

All state and federal laws must comport with the Constitution of the United States. The adversarial system of trial, which underlies the U.S. judicial system, permits judges to declare laws unconstitutional only in the context of deciding actual legal disputes. Thus, individuals and organizations opposed to a particular law who wish the courts to invalidate it must resort to litigation. The purpose of such litigation is to test in the courts the constitutionality or a particular interpretation of a law.

Test cases are a regular feature of American politics, because the stakes in many constitutional disputes are high. Groups have an incentive to initiate such cases when the rewards of success or costs of failure are substantial. Examples of famous test cases are *Scott v. Sandford* (1857), in which the Court decided that a slave could not be considered a citizen; *Tennessee v. Scopes* (1925), also known as the Scopes "monkey" trial, which dealt with the teaching of evolution in the schools; and *Griswold v. Connecticut* (1965), in which the Court recognized a constitutional right to privacy.

In the 1850's the country was divided over the question of the extension of slavery to the western territories. Abolitionists believed the Missouri Compromise of 1820 was unconstitutional because it permitted slavery in the territories southwest of Missouri. In order to force the Supreme Court to resolve this divisive issue, a group of abolitionists arranged for a slave, Dred Scott, to sue his master in a U.S. district court. The Supreme Court accepted the case on appeal and struck down the 1820 act of the U.S. Congress but for reasons favorable to the South. The law was unconstitutional, said Chief Justice Roger Taney, because it closed the territories west and north of Missouri to slaveholders. The decision helped precipitate the Civil War.

Test cases often begin with an act of civil disobedience. Those who believed in the strict separation of church and state opposed laws supporting Christianity in public institutions and looked for an opportunity to bring the question before the courts. In 1925 John Scopes, a biology teacher in Dayton, Tennessee, was persuaded to defy a state law prohibiting the teaching of Charles Darwin's theory of evolution. The state's prosecution of the teacher provided an opportunity to test the constitutional validity of such laws.

Liberal interest groups were appalled at a Connecticut statute proscribing the use of birth control devices and the dissemination of information on their use. Because it was a criminal statute, Planned Parenthood was unable to launch a successful test case in the absence of a prosecution. The U.S. Supreme Court dismissed cases in 1943 and 1961 on the grounds that the appellants had suffered no harm. Prosecutors finally charged Estelle Griswold, the executive director of Planned Parenthood, with a misdemeanor after she openly defied the law. On appeal, the U.S. Supreme Court found the statute in violation of the Constitution's implied right of privacy.

Organizations that have financed large numbers of test cases include Jehovah's Witnesses, the American Civil Liberties Union (ACLU), and the National Association for the Advancement of Colored People (NAACP). Because of changes in the Supreme Court's rules governing lawsuits, it is much easier for controversial laws to be tested in the courts than in the 1960's.

—*Kenneth M. Holland*

See also Appellate practice; Constitution, U.S.; Public interest law; Supreme Court, U.S..

Testimony

Evidence provided by a witness in a legal case, testimony is given under oath either orally or in the form of affidavits or depositions.

Testimony is critical because it provides support for arguments and positions advocated by either side in a legal proceeding. Although testimony can loosely be defined as evidence, it is distinguishable from evidence derived from writings or other sources. For evidence to be testimony, a witness must speak under oath to a judge or tribunal.

Testimony is a component in three aspects of the legal process: grand jury hearings, preliminary hearings, and trials. A grand jury consists of a body of citizens who determine whether probable cause exists that a crime has been committed. In order to make that determination, they hear testimony from witnesses presented by the state, or prosecution. If they determine that probable cause exists, they return an indictment against the defendant.

Young girl is questioned by judge while testifying in court. (James L. Shaffer)

In a preliminary hearing, a judge hears testimony from prosecution witnesses and makes a decision as to whether or not an individual should be held for trial. In a criminal or civil trial, witnesses are questioned through direct and cross-examination and a judge or jury listens to the testimony in order to reach a verdict. In all three instances, witnesses take oaths in which they swear or affirm to tell the truth.

Testimony in a grand jury is usually secret and is not used in later trials. However, testimony in a preliminary hearing is preserved for later use, either by a court reporter or tape recorder. The testimony provided in a preliminary hearing might be used in a trial to refresh a witness's memory or to demonstrate inconsistencies in the testimony. The testimony in a preliminary hearing may also be used at trial if a witness dies or becomes unavailable to testify.

The prosecution in a criminal case and the plaintiff in a civil case present their testimony first because they have the burden of proof. Testimony is provided in brief question-answer format; witnesses usually do not tell their stories in a continuous narrative. In direct examination, the attorneys question the witnesses that support their side of a case. Typically, the questions are open-ended in order for the witnesses to elaborate on their testimony, thus presenting a strong case. In cross-examination, the attorneys question the witnesses on the opposing side. The attorney may attempt to obtain testimony by using closed-ended or leading questions so that the witness does not have a chance to elaborate on answers. During closing arguments, attorneys make convincing arguments and provide reasons for the jurors or judge to return a verdict in their favor. They draw on the testimony of witnesses to help support their arguments.

Ann Burnett

See also Cross-examination; Evidence; Grand juries; Preliminary hearing; Witnesses.

Theft

The taking and carrying away of the property of another person with the intent to misappropriate or deprive that person of the property is known as theft.

Theft offenses involve the misappropriation of the property of other persons. The common-law crime of larceny was the taking and carrying away of the personal property of another with an intent to misappropriate. At common law, there were a number of theft offenses that varied depending on whether force was used. A growing number of states have enacted crimes to punish the theft of services. States typically classify degrees of theft crimes. In Alaska, for example, persons commit the crime of theft in the first degree if they commit theft of property or services worth $25,000 or more. Second-degree theft applies if the value of property or services is $500 or more but less than $25,000. Third-degree theft is charged if the value of the property or services is $50 or more but less than $500. The fourth-degree theft offense applies if the value of the property or services is less than $50. Many states calibrate the degree of theft crimes based on the value of the stolen property or services.

The federal government has enacted a number of statutes punishing the theft of services. The Cable Communications Act of 1984, for example, prohibits the unauthorized reception of communications services over a cable system. The Economic Espionage Act of 1996 creates federal criminal liability for the theft of trade secrets. Many states have specialized theft statutes dealing with the issuance of bad checks, unlawful possession of stolen property, or obtaining a credit card by fraudulent means. Larceny by trick was a common-law form of larceny in which a defendant gained property by means of a false representation.

Theft offenses also include robbery, burglary, larceny, and the handling of stolen goods. Robbery is the commission of theft by threatening to use physical force. Many states define aggravated robbery as the theft of property using deadly weapons. In contrast, larceny is the taking and carrying away of the personal property of another by fraud or stealth. Many states provide greater penalties when the crime of grand larceny is committed at night by one person against another. Embezzlement is the fraudulent conversion of property of another that is already in lawful possession. All jurisdictions have enacted bad check statutes to deal with those who issue checks with a fraudulent intent.

—*Michael L. Rustad*

See also Burglary; Criminal intent; Criminal law; Larceny; Lesser included offense; Pickpocketing; Shoplifting; Small businesses.

Auto theft is one of the most frequently committed felonies in American cities. (James L. Shaffer)

Three-strikes laws

Laws mandating more severe prison sentences for three-time offenders are known as three strikes laws.

Sometimes referred to as recidivist statutes, three strikes laws impose more severe penalties on offenders who have multiple felony convictions than on those without multiple convictions. Life imprisonment is often the more severe penalty. The idea behind this type of legislation is to remove three-time offenders from society, as prior rehabilitative efforts evidently have not succeeded. New York was the first jurisdiction in the country to have such legislation. At the present time, virtually all jurisdictions have some provision that either requires or permits increased sentences for persons with a prior conviction or convictions.

Approximately half of all jurisdictions authorize life sentences for persons convicted of a felony for the third or fourth time. In the event of third felony convictions, Illinois classifies persons as "habitual criminals" and authorizes a life sentence if all three felonies involved force or the threat of force. In Texas a first-degree felony conviction subsequent to a prior felony conviction is punished by a sentence of life imprisonment or fifteen to ninety-nine years. A third felony conviction receives a sentence of life imprisonment or twenty five to ninety-nine years. Texas also has a recidivist statute for misdemeanors. If an individual has a prior misdemeanor or felony conviction, a subsequent misdemeanor conviction could result in a sentence of as much as one year. Massachusetts has a more general and somewhat less severe statute for habitual criminals. Anyone who has been twice convicted of crime and sentenced to prison shall, upon conviction of a felony, be punished for that felony by imprisonment for the maximum term provided by law. That is, a habitual criminal in Massachusetts receives the maximum penalty for a felony, such as five, ten, or twenty years, rather than life imprisonment, as is common in approximately half of all jurisdictions. Jurisdictions generally include in their counting of felonies those for which convictions occurred in other jurisdictions (including at the federal level). New York and other jurisdictions include in the count convictions for misdemeanors in other jurisdictions that would have been felonies in their own jurisdictions. Notably, the crime of escape from prison is usually excluded from the count.

Questions have arisen as to whether three strikes laws violate due process, the protection offered by the Eighth Amendment to the U.S. Constitution against cruel and unusual punishment, and double jeopardy provisions. The laws do not grant prosecutors unbridled discretion in determining who should be sentenced to life imprisonment and do not require imposition of life imprisonment while foreclosing consideration of mitigating factors. Thus, it has been concluded that three strikes laws violate no constitutional rights, because they do no more than describe circumstances under which increased punishment may be imposed.

—*Dana P. McDermott*

See also Conviction; Criminal record; Cruel and unusual punishment; Double jeopardy; Due process; Felony; Sentencing.

Title

A title is a legal document showing that the owner of property has just and legal possession of that property.

The term "title" describes the way that an owner obtains lawful possession of valuable property. Typically it is a legal document that describes the interest of the owner. Deeds to real property, ownership of automobiles, patents for inventions, or copyrights held by an author are all examples of titles.

Titles can be acquired by purchase or inheritance, and different types of titles to a property can be held. For example, a mortgage that is held by a financial institution on property owned by an individual with a legal title to that property is an equitable title that expires on final payment. A deed to a title is legal evidence of that title and of the holder's rights to possess that property. It must be signed by the persons directly involved in the agreement, must be delivered, and must give an adequate description of the property. A trust deed conveys property in trust and usually evidences a mortgage, while a warranty deed guarantees the buyer that no claims exist against the title to the property.

A clear title to property is one for which the property is free of any encumbrances, such as an easement that could allow a neighbor the right to cross a property to gain access to a highway. A clear title ensures that the holder is the only legitimate possessor of the stated property and has no fear of a challenge being made to ownership. Thus, a clear title is unflawed by liens (debt claims) or by competing titles and reveals no breaks in the chain of legal ownership. A prospective buyer is much more likely to buy property that has no encumbrances of any kind that could weaken clear title to the property. The possibility that a title to a property could be challenged has led to the development of title insurance, which protects the owner against defects in the deed or title. Title companies examine real estate titles and, commonly, issue title insurance.

Before buying property, the buyer should have a title search performed, obtain an abstract of title from the seller, and hire a lawyer to examine it. An abstract gives a brief history of the title (chain of title) to the property, listing the individuals who have owned the property before it came into the possession of the present owner. The abstract also records all deeds, wills, mortgages, and other documents that would affect the ownership of the property. After the property records have been traced and the title has been found to be clear, the title is sometimes guaranteed, or insured. In some states, a more efficient system of insuring title to real property provides for registration of a clear title with public authorities. Once this is accomplished, an abstract of title is no longer necessary.

—*Alvin K. Benson*

See also Deed; Easement; Lien; Title companies; Title search.

Title companies

Companies that assist in the purchase or sale of homes, title companies verify a proper title to property, issue title insurance against any undisclosed problems that may arise and, in some cases, provide other services in respect to home sales.

A title is a legal document that identifies a person's right to own property. Title companies are, perhaps, best equipped to verify the legal assurance that ownership is valid. Title agents and companies offer a variety of services. They may limit themselves to conducting title searches or offer title insurance. A more comprehensive company may offer a more complete range of services, including entire packages for home purchase needs.

The purchase of a dwelling, house, and land is probably the single most significant expense incurred by the majority of people. The failure to adhere to the laws and regulations pertaining to this purchase can have devastating and long-lasting effects on buyers and sellers. Although some persons choose to handle the sale or purchase of a home themselves, it is prudent to seek out the assistance of professionals to oversee the many details associated with such a purchase or sale. Professionals include real estate agents, attorneys, mortgage lenders, banks, savings and loan organizations, and title companies. Pertinent to real estate transactions is the assurance that all pending and future irregularities that could hamper or nullify a sale be identified and, if necessary, corrected.

A title search entails the examination of public records to verify that the present owner of a property is, in fact, the proper owner and that no prior liens of any kind are pending against the property. Title insurance is a policy offered by a title company and purchased by the buyer that compensates the buyer against any irregularities discovered after a title has been deemed valid. Title insurance can extend beyond this coverage to identify problems relating to the property prior to clearing the title. It then becomes the seller's responsibility to correct these problems before a sale is finalized. Identifiable problems can include existing mortgages, outstanding taxes, and other liens. Should undiscovered irregularities against a property be found after title clearance has been issued, it becomes the responsibility of the title company issuing the policy to defend the new owner or assume any outstanding debts. Legal fees, court costs, and judgment settlements are covered by title insurance. Title insurance can also be purchased by the seller of properties to protect against previously undiscovered liens. Mortgage lenders may also purchase title insurance to protect their investments should borrowers default on their payments.

Title companies often assume other responsibilities relating to the sale and purchase of homes. They work with banks and other mortgage lenders to arrange financing. They may themselves provide mortgage credit. Other services include home appraisals, home inspections, home insurance, legal assistance, record handling, and closing details. A title company may be part of a multifaceted organization that includes mortgage lenders, lawyers, and credit reporting services.

The American Land Title Association is the trade group representing title companies in the United States. It serves both as a source of information and educational training for its member companies. It also represents their interests in developing and improving state and federal laws pertaining to the regulation of title companies and the requirements involved in buying and selling property. —*Gordon A. Parker*

See also Home buying; Home ownership; Home selling; Homeowner insurance; Mortgages; Property liability; Property rights; Real estate law; Title; Title search.

Title search

A search of public records, a title search is undertaken to confirm the status of title to real property.

The purpose of a title search is to determine and, in many cases, to give an opinion as to the status of title for particular real property. Title searches are often conducted when real property is to be sold or mortgaged. In such a case, a title examiner, who may also be referred to as an "abstractor," obtains the information necessary for the issuance of a policy of title insurance or for an attorney or title insurance company to give an opinion or report on title to a prospective purchaser or lender.

In order to obtain this information, a title examiner must search the public records of the county or municipality in which the real property is located. The title examiner requires certain basic information in order to begin a title search, including a description of the property and the names of the prospective transferors. The deed or instrument of conveyance through which the current transferors obtained the property, tax records, and recorded maps are also helpful in beginning a title search. Once title examiners obtain the necessary background information to begin a search, they establish the chain of title for the subject property, which consists of all the owners of the property and the instruments through which the property was conveyed within the search period. Beginning with the prospective transferor, the title examiner inspects the public records for each owner. A title examiner may perform this search by owner name, although it may also be possible to perform the search by property address, description, or location. Indexes of property conveyances maintained by public records offices may be utilized in the search. The length of the search period may vary depending upon the laws of the state in which the search is performed and on previous title insurance policies and title work files to which the title examiner has access. Generally, the search period should be long enough to uncover any instrument or conveyance that affects title to the property.

As title examiners review instruments conveying or affecting title, they may make photocopies or create abstracts of the instruments. These copies and abstracts serve as references for the attorney or title insurance company issuing title insurance. Examples of instruments affecting title include mortgages in which the property is conveyed to a lender as collateral, easements and rights of way affecting the property, instruments that create restrictions for use of the property, leases, and options to purchase. In addition, a title examiner should check for unpaid and overdue property taxes, county or municipal assessments levied against the property, zoning restrictions, judgments, current court proceedings, and any other instrument or circumstance regarding a current or previous owner which could affect title to the property. —*Erin Gwen Palmer*

See also Home buying; Real estate law; Real property; Title; Title companies.

Torts

Civil wrongs done by one party against another, excluding breaches of contract, are known as torts.

Tort law primarily redresses personal injuries—both physical and emotional—and to a lesser extent certain property harms. Traditionally, tort law has been primarily a creature of the common law.

In other words, torts have been recognized, applied, and refined by the courts through individual case decisions. With the development of the law, legislative enactments, such as so-called tort reform statutes, have begun to play a significant role in shaping tort law.

Tort law is distinguished from contract law and property law in that it primarily protects personal physical and emotional interests, generally on the basis of legal duties that the courts have imposed through case decisions. Moreover, unlike contract liability, tort liability generally is not governed by written documents or oral agreements. Although some aspects of tort law date back hundreds of years, tort law is constantly evolving to address the changing circumstances of society, and new torts are recognized as the need arises.

Tort claims fall into several broad categories: intentional torts, negligence, and strict liability. These categories vary in the degree of fault or culpability required on defendants' part in order to impose liability for damages. Within each category, there are common factors to consider, such as the elements of a claim, the defenses to a claim, and the damages recoverable for a claim.

Intentional Torts. Intentional torts generally have well-settled elements that plaintiffs must prove in order to establish a *prima facie* ("on its face") claim—in other words, a claim that is sufficient on first appearance without the need for investigation or evaluation. Among the oldest intentional torts are battery, assault, false imprisonment, and trespassing. Other intentional torts include the intentional infliction of emotional distress, conversion (the illegal taking of another's property without permission), fraud, defamation, invasion of privacy, misuse of legal procedure, and interference with certain family and economic relationships. The element common to all of these torts is the requirement that perpetrators have acted intentionally or recklessly. Merely careless conduct will not give rise to liability for these torts.

The primary purpose of the intentional torts is to protect persons against intentional invasions of bodily and mental integrity. Thus, the tort of battery protects against improper physical contacts, the tort of assault against the imminent threat of such contacts, and the tort of false imprisonment against improper confinement. Other intentional torts protect against improper harm to reputation, privacy, intimate relationships, or peace of mind. Some intentional torts, such as the trespass torts, and certain economic torts essentially protect property interests from improper interference or intrusion.

Typical defenses against intentional tort claims such as battery, assault, false imprisonment, and trespass include that the plaintiff consented to the defendant's conduct; that the defendant was acting in self-defense, in defense of others, or in defense of property; or that the defendant was acting to protect the public's interests. All of these defenses have well-settled rules that limit their application. For example, the use of deadly force in self-defense generally is not permitted unless persons are threatened with deadly force and have first attempted to withdraw from the situation. Because the courts have decided that certain torts might improperly restrict free speech rights, there also are constitutional defenses available to some intentional tort claims, such as defamation.

Damages recoverable for intentional tort claims include nominal damages, compensatory damages, and punitive damages. Nominal damages are awards of one dollar, signifying that the plaintiff has established that the defendant violated the plaintiff's rights while not proving any actual harm (for example, trespassing across plaintiff's land without causing damage). Compensatory damages may consist of reimbursement for medical expenses, lost wages, physical pain and suffering, and emotional harm. Punitive damages are awarded above and beyond compensatory damages in order to punish defendants for serious misconduct and to deter them and others from engaging in such conduct in the future. Typically, all three forms of damages may be available for intentional torts such as battery, assault, false imprisonment, intentional infliction of emotional distress, and trespassing.

Negligence. Negligence differs from the intentional torts in that the law may impose liability on a defendant for acting with a certain degree of carelessness. Intent or recklessness is not required to establish negligence. The classic formulation of the negligence standard is that each person must exercise the care that a reasonable and prudent person would exercise in the circumstances presented by a particular situation. Failure to exercise that level of care may result in liability for damages for harm caused. Negligence is sometimes described as consisting of five elements: a legal duty

Elements of Common Torts

Traditional Intentional Torts

Tort	Elements
Assault	Intentional creation of a situation giving plaintiff reason to fear imminent battery
Conversion	Intentional exercise of dominion or control over personal property sufficiently serious to amount to permanent deprivation or destruction of property
False imprisonment	Intentional confinement that is unlawful and of which the plaintiff is aware
Intentional infliction of emotional distress	Intentional or reckless conduct that is extreme and outrageous and that causes severe emotional distress
Trespass to chattels	Intentional harm to, interference with, or use or possession of another's personal property
Trespass to land	Intentional entry into, or physical invasion of, land of another

Other Intentional Torts

Tort	Elements
Abuse of process	Defendant makes otherwise legitimate use of legal process for an improper purpose or to accomplish an objective not authorized by the process
Defamation	Defendant made defamatory statement of and concerning the plaintiff, published the statement to others, and damaged plaintiff. In order to satisfy First Amendment free speech concerns, in cases involving matters of public concern and public officials or figures, plaintiffs also must prove that the statement is actually false and that the defendant made the statement with knowledge of its falsity or in reckless disregard of the truth (actual malice)
Fraud	Misrepresentation of a material fact by defendant; knowledge by defendant that the representation is false; defendant intended to induce plaintiff to act or refrain from acting in reliance on misrepresentation; plaintiff actually relied on the misrepresentation; plaintiff's reliance was reasonable; there was actual damage to plaintiff
Malicious prosecution	Defendant initiated prior legal proceeding against plaintiff; prior proceeding terminated in plaintiff's favor; there was absence of probable cause for prior proceeding; defendant acted with malice or improper purpose in initiating prior proceeding; there were damages to plaintiff

(continued)

Elements of Common Torts (continued)

Negligence

Tort	Elements
Negligence	Existence of a legal duty; defendant breached legal duty; defendant's breach was the cause of plaintiff's injuries; there are no policy reasons to preclude liability (proximate cause); plaintiff suffered actual damages

Strict Liability

Tort	Elements
Animals	Liability for trespass by livestock; harm results from a wild animal's dangerous propensity that is characteristic of the animal or known to the owner; harm results from a domestic animal's dangerous propensity that is abnormal to that class of animal and of which owner had knowledge
Abnormally dangerous activities	Activity that involves a high degree of risk; resulting harm is likely to be great; defendant cannot avoid the harm by exercising care; the activity is not a matter of common usage; the activity is not appropriate to the location; the activity's value to the community is outweighed by the risks

Product Liability

Tort	Elements
Defectiveness	Negligence; implied warranty of merchantability; strict liability in tort
Representations	Intentional misrepresentation; negligent misrepresentation; strict liability for public misrepresentation; express warranty; implied warranty of fitness for a particular purpose

on the defendant's part, breach of that duty, a causal link between the defendant's breach and the plaintiff's harm, the lack of policy or other reasons for limiting the defendant's liability ("proximate cause"), and actual harm to the plaintiff.

In virtually all circumstances, every person has the legal duty to behave as would a reasonable and prudent person, but the courts also have adopted some specific legal duties tailored to certain recurring situations. For instance, the courts traditionally have held that persons have no legal duty to come to the aid of or protect others from harm. This doctrine, sometimes referred to as the "failure to act" or "nonfeasance" principle, is riddled with exceptions, such as when a "special relationship" exists either between the plaintiff and the defendant (for example, an innkeeper and the guests whom he has a duty to protect) or between the defendant and a third party who caused the plaintiff's injuries (for example, a jailer and the public which he has a duty to protect from escaping prisoners). The courts have also created special or limited duties for situations such as the negligent infliction of emotional distress, harm to the unborn, and the liability of owners and occupiers of land for harm that occurs on their premises.

Typical defenses to negligence claims include that the plaintiff also was at fault in causing the harm or that the plaintiff assumed the risk of harm. Under the old rule of contributory negligence, if a plaintiff was even 1 percent at fault in causing an accident, the defendant had no liability to the plaintiff. Because that rule often imposed unnecessary and unfair hardships on plaintiffs, most states have changed their laws to adopt a system of comparative negligence. Under comparative negligence, a plaintiff's fault will not generally bar recovery unless the plaintiff is at least as much at fault as the defendant (50 percent or greater), and in some states even then the plaintiff may still recover damages for the portion of fault that is assigned to the defendant.

Most states also recognize a defense of assumption of the risk, at least in some situations. For example, if a plaintiff signs a written document absolving a defendant of any liability in the event an accident occurs, such an express assumption of the risk generally would be enforceable. Some states also recognize an implied assumption of the risk defense in situations in which, based on the circumstances, a court concludes that the plaintiff knew, understood, and voluntarily encountered the risks that resulted in harm.

Damages recoverable for negligence claims are primarily compensatory damages. Nominal damages (the one dollar award) are not available, nor are punitive damages generally recoverable. Mere negligence does not rise to the level of intentional or reckless misconduct typically required to award punitive damages.

Strict Liability. The essence of strict liability is that some activities are sufficiently dangerous that defendants engaging in them should bear legal responsibility for any harm caused, even if the defendant was not negligent or did not act to cause harm intentionally or recklessly. Because strict liability is a potent legal remedy and is sometimes referred to as imposing "liability without fault," the courts generally are reluctant to impose it. There are three categories of cases in which strict liability may apply: liability for domestic and wild animals, liability for conducting abnormally dangerous activities, and products liability.

Historically, strict liability was applied to harm caused by trespassing livestock and to harm caused by defendants' wild and domestic animals. Some states still apply strict liability for trespassing livestock, although many do not. Most still apply some form of strict liability for harm caused by defendants' wild animals, such as pet lions, tigers, or bears, and for harm caused by domestic animals, such as dogs.

Most states also impose strict liability for activities that are considered "abnormally dangerous." The theory behind this form of strict liability is that because some activities simply cannot be conducted with absolute safety, defendants should be encouraged to move such activities to safer locations, such as rural areas instead of near or within large cities. Although what constitutes an abnormally dangerous activity is decided on a case-by-case basis by examining several factors, courts have at times held such activities as blasting with explosives, storage of explosives, building and maintaining reservoirs, the operation of nuclear power plants, and the disposal of hazardous wastes to be abnormally dangerous activities giving rise to strict liability.

The final major category of strict liability is products liability. Some states have applied strict liability to the manufacturers, distributors, wholesalers, and even retailers of products that cause harm to consumers. Typically, the application of strict liability depends on whether a product is "defective." Some states, however, have rejected strict liability for products and others have limited or altered it by statute.

Although liability may be considered strict, there are defenses against strict liability claims. Typical defenses against claims involving animals and abnormally dangerous activities include that the plaintiff was a trespasser at the time of the injury, that the plaintiff acted recklessly in encountering the danger, that the injury was the result of unforeseeable acts of nature, that the plaintiff was unusually susceptible to being harmed by the defendant's activity (that is, the average person would not have been harmed), and that the defendant's activity has the approval of the government, such as when a zoo is operated by a city. One defense against strict products liability is that given the level of knowledge ("state of the art") at the time of manufacture, the defendant did not know about and could not have discovered the defect. Generally, only compensatory damages are recoverable in strict liability cases.

Immunities and Tort Claims Acts. Historically, the courts recognized certain immunities from tort liability. For example, at one time many states recognized immunity for charitable organizations and immunity among family members, such as spouses, or among parents and children. Generally, such immunities have been abolished.

Only one significant tort immunity remains: the sovereign immunity of government entities. The states and the federal government all have tort claims acts, statutes that waive the sovereign immunity of the government in certain circumstances and make governments liable for the torts of their employees. Tort claims acts do not define torts; they simply remove sovereign immunity as a defense to ordinary tort claims against the government. Tort claims acts, however, generally retain sovereign immunity for some types of governmental activities, including the government's performance of discretionary functions or law-enforcement activities. Tort claims acts also often place restrictions on the procedures for determining such claims (for example, the federal statute does not permit jury trials), they limit the damages recoverable from the government (for example, by prohibiting punitive damage awards), and they may limit liability to a certain monetary amount per occurrence.

Suggested Readings. For a general explanation of the torts, defenses, immunities, damages, and various other tort-related topics, the classic treatment is William L. Prosser and Page Keeton, *Prosser and Keeton on Torts* (5th ed. St. Paul, Minn.: West Publishing, 1984). General discussions of tort law principles with greater emphasis on the application of tort law and examples include J. Diamond, L. Levine, and M. Madden, *Understanding Torts* (New York: Matthew Bender, 1996), and Joseph L. Glannon, *The Law of Torts: Examples and Explanations* (Boston: Little, Brown, 1995). An important reference in the tort law area is *Restatement of the Law Second of Torts* (Philadelphia: American Law Institute, 1965-79), a collective effort by lawyers, judges, and legal scholars to both declare what the rules of tort law are and, sometimes, what they should be. The *Restatement* includes comments and illustrations in addition to black letter law. For those interested in the intellectual and more theoretical aspects of tort law, there are several works of interest, including G. Edward White, *Tort Law in America: An Intellectual History* (New York: Oxford University Press, 1980), Robert L. Rabin, *Perspectives on Tort Law* (4th ed. Boston: Little, Brown, 1995), *Foundations of Tort Law*, edited by S. Levmore (New York: Oxford University Press, 1994), and *A Torts Anthology*, edited by Lawrence C. Levine, Julie S. Davies, and Edward S. Kionka (Cincinnati, Ohio: Anderson, 1993). —*Stephen R. McAllister*

See also Damages; Liability, civil and criminal; Negligence; Product liability law; Trespass.

Trade secret

Trade secret laws that protect from disclosure products, information, formulas, patterns, techniques, or processes because they are sources of economic value for a person or company.

Trade secret protection evolved from common law grounded in the core substantive areas of property, torts, criminal law, and contracts. Although one might initially believe that a close relationship exists between trade secret law and trademark law because of the similarity in names, trade secret law actually draws on none of the traditional intellectual property areas involved in trademark law.

In 1939 the Restatement of Torts formalized a definition for trade secrets and commented that the prevailing view of liability rested on a general duty of good faith. While the Restatement was persuasive, it did not have the force of law. However, since its inception it has been referenced by most cases dealing with trade secret issues. All references to trade secrets were dropped from later editions of the Restatement.

In 1979 the Uniform Trade Secrets Act (UTSA) was promulgated by the National Conference of Commissioners on Uniform State Laws and has since been adopted by approximately forty states. UTSA defines a trade secret as information, including a formula, pattern, compilation program device, method, technique, or process, that derives independent economic value, actual or potential, from not being generally known to and not being readily ascertainable by proper means by other persons who can obtain economic value from its disclosure or use and is the subject of efforts that are reasonable under the circumstances to maintain its secrecy.

The initial hurdle in proceeding with a trade secret case involves defining the protected material. For tangible products this is easy, but if the claimed subject matter is a process or information, difficulties may arise. After characterizing the subject matter, one must show that it has commercial value. This does not mean that one must show that the subject matter was directly responsible for the generation of profits, nor does it mean that only for-profit ventures can bring suit.

To be successful in a lawsuit against persons accused of violating trade secrets, one must show that reasonable means were undertaken to maintain secrecy. Trade secret cases arise as a result of conditions of employment. In the workplace many individuals may have access to "secret" information. An employer must therefore be sure to have specific procedures in place that indicate that some attention to secrecy is addressed. In addition to the procedures, written contracts should be maintained that specifically set forth subject matter, protocol, and penalties.

A violator of trade secrecy rules is only liable for civil penalties under the UTSA. However, the UTSA expressly states that it does not affect a plaintiff's ability to secure contractual relief, additional civil relief, or criminal remedies. Furthermore, one may secure relief from the International Trade Commission. Common defenses to trade secret actions are innocent use, calculated or inadvertent public dedication of the subject matter, and statute of limitations expiration. The UTSA has a three-year statute of limitations.

As long as a work fits within the broad definition of trade secrets and secrecy is in fact maintained, protection under trade secret law may last into perpetuity. —*Darryl C. Wilson*

See also Civil law; Patents; Torts; Trademarks; Uniform laws.

Trademarks

Based on the concept of unfair trade, trademarks are any words, names, symbols, or devises—or any combination thereof—used by manufacturers to identify their goods and distinguish them from those of their competitors.

The concept of trademark originated in the Middle Ages, when marks were used by guilds to designate the origin of goods. Quickly, however, trademarks became marketing tools, signifying not just the identity of producers but also the distinctive qualities of their products. The Anglo-Saxon common law of trademarks was intended to prevent unscrupulous producers from "palming off" their goods as those of other persons—in effect, taking advantage of the reputation of better-known or more well-respected competitors. In the United States trademark law developed not only to protect producers but also to afford them a method of promoting their wares and making their wares easily recognizable to potential customers.

Trademark Law in the United States. Because trademarks are an outgrowth of the law governing unfair competition and because they have no express constitutional protection, unlike patents and copyrights, they were traditionally governed by state rather than federal law. However, in 1946 Congress passed the Lanham Act, permitting trademarks to be enforced at the federal level. The Lanham Act, grounded in the federal government's power to regulate interstate commerce, did not change existing state laws. Instead, it provided for federal registration and protection against infringement.

The traditional or common law governing trademarks has expanded in the modern era to include not just protection of producers' rights in their products but also the protection of the goodwill associated with these products. Because they are meant to forestall confusion in the marketplace, trademarks also serve as a form of quality assurance, protecting the public against inferior goods masquerading as known quantities.

Outside the marketplace, trademarks really have no purpose—or existence. Trademarks can only be acquired in the United States through use and only when there is the possibility that consumers might confuse products, either because they are similar or because they are sold in the same geographical areas. The Lanham Act does not itself create trademarks; rather, it provides for the registration of existing trademarks that have already been used in interstate commerce.

Trademarks vs. Patents and Copyrights. Trademarks are often grouped with patents and copyrights under the rubric of "intellectual property."

Article 1, section 8 of the Constitution authorizes Congress to secure "for limited Time to Authors and Inventors the exclusive Right to their respective Writings and Discoveries." Accordingly, the U.S. Patent and Trademark Office grants patents for time-limited monopoly rights to new, useful, and nonobvious inventions. Under United States copyright law, copyrights subsist in original "writings" (meaning any tangible expression fixed in any medium) from the moment they are set down, and they last for a defined period. Like patents and unlike trademarks, copyrights are governed by federal law. Unlike patents but like trademarks, copyrights are not granted by a federal agency, although they can be registered with the U.S. Copyright Office. Patents, copyrights, and trademarks are independent rights, all of which can apply to a single product. Components of a personal computer's hardware may be protected by patents, while at the same time its software is protected by copyright and its name is protected as a trademark. But while patent and copyright monopolies eventually expire, trademark protection is eternal: As long as it is used and enforced by its maker, a trademark can confer a perpetual monopoly. A mark that is protected as a trademark can also be protected by patent and copyright laws. For example, the shape of a personal computer—if it is novel, ornamental, and nonobvious—can be protected by a design patent at the same time that it is registered as a trademark. If such a computer has a highly designed logo, the logo might be protected from copying by copyright law as well as by its registration as a trademark.

Securing, Registering, and Protecting Trademarks. In order to be useful and enforceable, a trademark must above all be distinctive. If a producer attempts to register a trademark that too closely resembles an existing, recognized product mark or one that is too common or descriptive, the U.S. Trademark Office will deny registration. The generic name of a product—for example, dog food or automobile tires—can never be a trademark. A term describing some aspect of the product, such as honey-baked ham, can only become a trademark after it has been used for some time in connection with the product, thus acquiring secondary meaning. Similarly, surnames and geographical designations cannot be registered as trademarks unless they have acquired secondary meaning in the minds of consumers. The same holds true for the trade names of businesses: While International Business Machines (IBM) was originally only the name of a company, eventually it was also used as a trademark for that company's products. Arbitrary or fanciful marks—such as Camels for cigarettes or Exxon for gasoline—are least likely to cause consumer confusion and easiest to register.

While color alone is not usually regarded as a valid identifying product mark, the combination of certain colors and a singular design, called "trade dress," is protected under the Lanham Act. Federal courts can thus consider infringement actions under the act even when the plaintiff's packaging has not been registered as a trademark. The Lanham Act does provide, however, for the registration of identifiers other than trademarks. Service marks, such as the names of banks and restaurants, perform the same function with regard to services as trademarks do to goods. Certification marks, such as the Good Housekeeping Seal of Approval, allow companies to indicate that their goods or services have passed certain standards of quality or to certify regional origin. Collective marks, such as a 4H Club symbol, indicate that goods or services are produced by members of a certain group. In the case of both certification and collective marks, however, the owners of such marks may not necessarily be the producers of the goods and services bearing the marks.

To be eligible for registration, a mark must currently be used in connection with goods or services in interstate commerce. After a trademark application has been approved, it can be placed on one of two registers: The Principle Register is reserved for arbitrary or fanciful marks or for descriptive marks that have acquired secondary meaning, while those descriptive marks that are capable of acquiring secondary meaning are placed on the Secondary Register.

In order to maintain their monopoly rights, trademark holders must use their marks, and they must file affidavits of use with the Patent and Trademark Office. Owners must also constantly police their marks; unchecked infringement can result in consumer confusion, counterfeiting, or, ultimately, the dilution of the strength of a trade or service mark. Sometimes even the best efforts are not enough: Aspirin and cellophane proved to be such successful products that what were once trademarks worked their way into the culture, becoming generic terms that anyone could freely use.

Suggested Readings. A good overview of trademark law can be found in the widely available Nutshell Series volume by Arthur R. Miller and Michael H. Davis, *Intellectual Property: Patents, Trademarks, and Copyright* (2d ed. St. Paul, Minn.: West Publishing, 1990). Siegrun D. Kane's *Trademark Law: A Practitioner's Guide* (3d ed. New York: Practicing Law Institute, 1997) provides a more in-depth look at the subject. Those who are more interested in practical applications can profitably consult Robert E. Lee's *A Trademark Guide for Entrepreneurs* (Stamford, Conn: Kent Press, 1996). Both Kate McGrath's *Trademark: Legal Care for Your Business and Product Name* (3d ed. Berkeley, Calif: Nolo Press, 1997) and Mark Warda's *How to Register Your Own Trademark: With Forms* (2d ed., Naperville, Ill: Sourcebooks, 1997) provide detailed information on securing, registering, and maintaining trademarks.
—Lisa Paddock

See also Copyright; Counterfeiting; Intangible asset; Patents; Public domain; Trade secret.

Traffic court

Courts that deal with infractions of driving laws that are not as serious as felonies or misdemeanors are known as traffic courts.

Traffic courts were established to handle routine traffic violations, such as speed law violations, driver and vehicle safety code infractions, parking tickets, and offenses against other rules of the road. Traffic crimes did not fit well into traditional state criminal court systems. If traffic violations resulted in full criminal trials, the system would be overwhelmed with juries, lawyers, and convictions. Costs would be enormous and many persons would be upset with the police and justice system for the vigorous enforcement of what seem to be insignificant crimes.

There are more than 150 million licensed drivers in the United States and a total of more than 25 million automobile accidents every year, more than 50,000 of which involve fatalities. The costs of these accidents reach more than $30 billion a year. The purpose of traffic law enforcement and traffic courts is to reduce the number of accidents and deaths. One result is that more than 20,000 traffic citations are filed every day in the United States.

Routine traffic violations are handled differently from more serious offenses such as driving under the influence of alcohol or drugs (DUI). For crimes such as speeding or running through a traffic sign there is no need to prove criminal intent, as is true with other types of crimes. Simply committing the act is proof of guilt. Traffic courts were established specifically to handle proceedings involving what are legally called "traffic infractions." Most U.S. states have three types of criminal acts: misdemeanors, felonies, and infractions. Infractions are dealt with by civil rather than criminal procedures. The right to an attorney, or trial by jury, may not apply in cases involving infractions. Convictions do not result in prison or probation and fines are often held to $50 or less. More serious traffic crimes, such as driving under the influence, are handled in more traditional court proceedings, in which defendants have the right to an attorney and a trial by jury.

Highways can be very dangerous. Traffic laws have done a good job in creating order out of potential chaos. Drivers generally respect speed laws, traffic signs, and traffic lights, even when no police cars are visible. The success of the system is illustrated by the fact that the long-term trend has shown a decrease in traffic fatalities. The National Safety Council reports that there is only one serious traffic accident for every 60,000 miles driven, and Americans drive more than 2 trillion miles a year. The effect of traffic law enforcement by police and courts is demonstrated by the success of state laws requiring cyclists to wear helmets. Prior to passage of laws requiring helmets, only 50 percent of cyclists wore helmets, but after vigorous enforcement by the police and judges, that number grew to almost 100 percent, and the number of deaths in motorcycle accidents dropped dramatically. In the three states that refused to pass such laws, the number of fatalities remained at a very high level.

The strict enforcement of laws and efficient procedures in traffic courts have, according to many studies, led to fewer accidents and better driving habits. Studies of speed-law enforcement have shown that it is not so much the severity of the penalty as the likelihood of being caught and convicted that reduces violations. On the other hand, studies have not indicated that there is any real benefit to sending traffic law violators to traffic school. —*Leslie V. Tischauser*

See also Drunk driving; Felony; Misdemeanor; Traffic law; Traffic schools.

Traffic law

Traffic law consists of those prescribed rules for the orderly and safe flow of traffic which have been enacted into statutes or ordinances.

A violation of a traffic law is usually a minor criminal offense, although in some jurisdictions less serious traffic offenses have been decriminalized and are called infractions. While there may be separate rules of procedure in traffic cases, the basic procedure, especially in serious offenses, is the same as in criminal cases. The state or municipality is the party that brings the charge. The burden of proof is beyond a reasonable doubt, and the same constitutional protections are afforded as apply in criminal cases.

The penalty meted out for minor traffic violations is a fine. In addition, most states have established point systems in which points are assessed on one's driving record for each moving traffic violation. The number of points assessed varies according to the seriousness of the violation. When persons accumulate a certain number of points within a period of time, their driver's licenses may be suspended. In some states persons can remove points or even avoid conviction for minor traffic offenses by attending traffic school. An indirect consequence of traffic conviction may be an increase in insurance premiums through loss of a safe driver discount or because a bad driving record places a driver in a higher-risk category. Professional drivers must also consider the effects of traffic violations on their employment records.

As a general rule a traffic law applies only if a violation occurs on a public street, highway, or public way. There are important exceptions, however. In many jurisdictions the offense of drunk driving can occur anywhere, even on private property. The definition section and the cited section of the traffic code should always be carefully reviewed to determine under what circumstances a violation can occur.

In almost all traffic offenses a specific intent to violate the law is not necessary. Accordingly, persons cannot use as a defense that they did not see a stop sign or did not know that they had exceeded the speed limit. These matters, however, may be raised in mitigation.

Traffic Ticket. The usual procedure that is followed when a motorist appears to have violated a minor traffic law is for the officer to stop the vehicle and issue the driver a citation or ticket. This advises the person of the date, time, and place for the court appearance and of the particular offense for which the motorist is charged. The U.S. Supreme Court has ruled that the mere stop and issuance of a ticket is not an arrest. It is therefore not necessary for an officer to read a motorist the Miranda rights, which are warnings to suspects that they enjoy certain constitutional safeguards during questioning by law-enforcement officials. Any statements or admissions made at the time of the stop can be used in court against the driver without showing that the Miranda rights were read. It is most important at the time of a stop for the driver to give only essential information to the officer. Many persons have lost cases in court by telling police officers that they were going too fast to stop at a red light or by saying that they were driving only sixty-five miles per hour when an officer accused them of driving seventy miles per hour in a fifty-five mile per hour zone.

After the issuance of the ticket the officer usually provides information as to how to avoid a court appearance by merely paying a fine in person or by mail. It should be noted that before alleged offenders are allowed to leave, a computer check is made to determine whether they have valid driver's licenses and whether there are any warrants outstanding against them. In the past nonresident drivers were required to post a bond with cash, a credit card, or an automobile club card. If they failed to make court appearances, which was often the case, the bond was forfeited and the case closed. Since almost all states have become signatories to the Non-Resident Violator Compact, the bond requirement may be waived for minor violations and nonresident drivers treated the same as local residents by being given the option of mailing in the fine or appearing in court at a later date.

Failure to appear in court or pay the fine has serious consequences. A local resident who ignores a citation will ultimately discover that a warrant has been issued, and the next encounter with a police officer will trigger an arrest. Out-of-state residents who ignore traffic tickets may find that the motor vehicle authority in their states have suspended their driving privileges under the Non-Resident Violator Compact.

Speeding Offense. Speeding is the most common type of traffic violation, followed by stop sign and red light violations. Speed laws may be absolute in that the mere fact that a driver has exceeded the speed limit constitutes a violation. The 55 mile per hour speed limit imposed by the federal government in the 1970's as an energy conservation measure but since repealed was such a law.

More commonly, speeding laws are drafted so that a violation occurs only if the speed is unreasonable and improper. To make enforcement easier the law establishes speed limits and provides that they be posted. Drivers who exceed the posted speed limit are then considered to be in violation unless they show that the speed they were driving was reasonable and proper under the circumstances. Thus, if someone is charged with exceeding the posted 25 mile per hour speed limit in a business district in the early hours of the morning, a good argument could be made that a faster speed was not unreasonable or improper, since there was little or no vehicular or pedestrian traffic at that time.

The assured clear distance law regulates another type of speeding violation. Rear-end collisions are usually the result of violating this law. The basic rule of the road is that a motorist who is traveling behind another vehicle must be able to stop without colliding with the vehicle in front or any discernible object ahead in the path of travel.

With any traffic offense it is most important to carefully read the section of the traffic code under which a citation is issued. Each and every element of the offense must be present and proven by the arresting authority. It is not enough, for example, to be merely exceeding the posted speed limit in a school zone. A careful reading of the code section would probably disclose that children must actually be coming to or leaving school during opening or closing hours or at recess. This would be true even though flashers were operating warning of the school zone.

Testing devices require careful scrutiny. If a radar device is used, the traffic code, administrative rules, and case law should be researched to determine compliance. There are always very specific and definite rules as to calibration—that is, the check that has to be made to determine if the device is in good working order. The officer operating the radar device must also be trained and qualified in its use. Evidence that these requirements have been met must be introduced before any radar reading may be used as evidence against an allegedly errant drive.

Serious Traffic Offenses. Not all traffic violations are of such a minor nature that they are handled by a traffic ticket and a fine. Vehicular homicide and drunk driving are most serious crimes punishable by possible jail or even prison terms. Driving under suspension, hit-and-run accidents, drag racing, and fleeing from police officers

Police officer cites a driver for violating a traffic law. (James L. Shaffer)

are likewise classified as serious traffic offenses in most states. In a drunk driving case an arrest is made at the scene and the driver is transported to a lockup facility or patrol post. The Miranda rights are read to the driver as soon as practicable after the arrest so that any statements made by the driver may be used in court. In the other serious traffic offenses the driver may just be given a traffic citation to appear in court. In the case of nonresidents, a cash or surety bond is usually required. A court appearance in these serious cases is required, however, and cannot be avoided by the mere payment of a fine. If a jail or prison sentence is to be imposed, accused persons are entitled to a court-appointed attorney if they are unable to pay for one. As to the right to a jury trial, the law varies from state to state. Under the U.S. Constitution as interpreted by court decisions, a defendant has the right to a jury trial when the offense charged carries with it a term of imprisonment of more than six months.

Civil Liability. A violation of a traffic law may cause an accident that results in property damage or personal injury. The issue then arises as to who is liable for the damages. In states that have a no-fault insurance law, it may be that the parties can only recover their losses from their own insurance companies. In states without a no-fault law, the loss can be recovered from the other party provided the other party was at fault. Fault in a motor vehicle accident is usually determined by a violation of a traffic law if the violation caused the accident. Accordingly, if one driver ran a red light which resulted in an accident, the driver in legal terms would be negligent per se and the proximate cause of the accident. The driver or the driver's insurance company would be liable for the damages to the driver and owner of the other vehicle. If both drivers violated the law, the issue of contributory negligence would apply, which would prevent or limit recovery by either driver.

Persons involved in traffic accidents should not admit fault at the scene or enter a guilty plea in traffic court, as these acts would be admissions that could be used at a civil trial to recover for damages. A driver cited for a violation of a traffic law under such circumstance who seeks to avoid the inconvenience and expense of contesting a traffic charge should enter a no-contest plea. Such a plea would not be admissible at a civil trial.

Suggested Readings. The primary and most important source of traffic laws are the statutory laws of the states. One section or title will generally contain all or most of the traffic laws. Municipalities in some jurisdictions reenact the state code so that offenders are charged with violating a municipal ordinance. An excellent research tool for obtaining basic information on traffic laws and licensing, together with addresses for motor vehicle bureaus or their equivalent in each of the fifty states and the District of Columbia, is Michael Shankey's *The MVR Book: A Motor Services Guide* (Tempe, Ariz.: BRB Publications, 1996). Other readily available books on traffic law are guides to contesting traffic tickets. Typical of such guides are Phil Bello's *How to Win in Traffic Court: The Non-Lawyers Guide to Successfully Defending Traffic Violations* (Gibbsbora, N.J.: Major Market Books, 1989), Alex Carroll's *Beat the Cops: The Guide to Fighting Your Traffic Ticket and Winning* (Santa Barbara, Calif.: Ace, 1995), James A. Glass's *Traffic Court: How to Win* (Arcadia, Calif.: Allenby Press, 1988), and Tim Matheson's *Traffic Tickets, Fines, and Other Annoying Things* (Secaucus, N.J.: Citadel Press, 1984). All of these guides contain easily understood explanations of traffic laws and what elements must be present before a violation can occur. As some of the terms and procedures are keyed to particular states, care must exercised in their use. —*Gilbert T. Cave*

See also Alcohol; Arrest; Automobile accidents; Driving licenses; Drunk driving; Exclusionary rule; Hit-and-run accident; Night court; No-fault insurance; Traffic court; Traffic schools.

Traffic schools

Traffic schools, private and public, provide rehabilitation for drivers convicted of driving offenses, instruction for new and inexperienced drivers, and specialized instruction for drivers with special needs.

In 1995 over 41,000 people were killed in traffic accidents and the cost of motor vehicle crashes was estimated at $4,000 per second. These statistics point to the need for safer driving, and the task of producing safer drivers falls mainly to traffic schools and driver education. It is projected that approximately one in every five Americans will be

Traffic Statistics

- Motor vehicle crashes cost American society an estimated $4,400 per second—that is, approximately $26,400 in the time it took to read this sentence.

- Male drivers ages fifteen to twenty years old in 1994 were involved in 40 percent of fatal crashes while speeding.

- The chances for death or serious injury double every 10 miles per hour over 50 miles per hour that a vehicle travels.

- It costs a car that travels one hundred miles at 55 miles per hour $4.36 for gas, while it costs a car that travels one hundred miles at 75 miles per hour $6.64 for gas.

- In 1995, 41,798 people were killed in traffic crashes and 3,386,000 people were injured.

- The leading cause of death for people between the ages of five and twenty-seven years old is motor vehicle crashes.

- In 1995 an estimated 115 people died each day in motor vehicle crashes—one every thirteen minutes.

- It is estimated that 9,797 lives were saved in 1995 by the use of seat belts.

- It is estimated that 475 lives were saved in 1995 by air bags.

- It is estimated that 1 in every 127 drivers in 1994 was arrested for driving under the influence of alcohol or drugs.

- It is estimated that 1 in every 5 Americans will be involved in an alcohol-related crash at some point in his or her life.

- In 1995 almost two-thirds of all passenger vehicle occupants killed in traffic crashes were not wearing seat belts.

- Men accounted for about 67 percent of all traffic fatalities in the late 1990's.

- Of all age groups, drivers under the age of twenty five had the highest rate of involvement in fatal crashes.

- Young drivers between the ages of fifteen and twenty years old account for 6.7 percent of all licensed drivers in the United States.

- The days in which motor vehicle deaths of teenagers occur most are Saturday, which accounts for 21 percent of all teenage motor vehicle deaths, and Sunday, which accounts for 18 percent of all teenage motor vehicle deaths.

- The months in which motor vehicle deaths of teenagers occur most are June, July, and August, with each accounting for 10 percent of all teenage motor vehicle deaths.

- Young drinking drivers are involved in fatal crashes at more than twice the rate of drivers aged twenty-one and older.

Sources: National Highway Traffic Safety Administration (NHTSA), Insurance Institute for Highway Safety, and the U.S. Department of Transportation.

involved in an alcohol-related crash at some time during their driving lives. The court system must deal with persons driving under the influence of alcohol or drugs (DUI).

One approach to the problem of driving under the influence and to other traffic violations is the mandatory enrollment of convicted drivers in traffic school programs. Many states use the successful completion of a traffic school program to reduce or remove DUI and other traffic violations. To rehabilitate traffic offenders, private traffic schools offer a variety of programs. Many states employ a point system for various traffic offenses. The more serious the offence, the greater the points assigned, until a specific total number of points is reached and a person's driver's license is suspended. In some cases the successful completion of an approved traffic school course is sufficient for removing points from one's driving record. In some instances, driver education courses in public and private schools, as recognized by the courts, also serve to provide the appropriate training so that court-imposed penalties may be reduced.

Rehabilitation is not the only purpose of traffic schools. New and inexperienced drivers enroll in traffic schools to acquire skills and experience in driving. In most states young, teenage drivers who have reached the legal driving age must undergo some form of driver training in order to obtain a permanent license. This training is often conducted in schools, in which driver education is an established part of the curriculum. Teachers who give driver education classes are licensed upon completion of specially designed programs as part of their college or university training. The Driving School Association of America (DSAA), representing 350 driving schools in the United States and Canada, serves as a medium of exchange for ideas and policies relating to driver training at all levels. It is also possible to enroll and complete traffic school courses at home through videotaped programs and on-line Internet courses.

A number of specialized traffic schools meet the specialized needs of certain programs. Commercial truck, bus, and cab drivers receive special training in the operation and handling of their vehicles. There are schools for race car drivers, airplane pilots, school-bus drivers, motorcyclists, persons with disabilities, and off-highway vehicle operators. Law-enforcement officers require specialized training. Business executives and others who may face dangers such as kidnappings and terrorist attacks can receive specialized defensive driver training.

Traffic school training involves more than just learning to handle an automobile. Traffic laws, safe driving procedures, vehicle operation, emergency repairs, emergency driving measures (such as swerving and panic stops), accident avoidance, and accident reporting are also covered.

—*Gordon A. Parker*

See also Alcohol; Automobile accidents; Driving licenses; Traffic court; Traffic law.

Treason

A serious crime, treason involves a person's betrayal of the government to which he or she owes allegiance by waging war against it or by giving aid and comfort to its enemies.

In Article III, section 3, of the U.S. Constitution the definition of treason is clearly stated. According to the Constitution a person who levies war against the United States or gives its enemies aid and comfort is guilty of treason. Treason is the only crime that the Constitution defines. Since subversive acts committed during peacetime are not considered treasonous, someone must commit these acts when the United States is at war. In a controversial case in 1951, Julius and Ethel Rosenberg were convicted of espionage after they were accused of stealing U.S. atomic secrets during World War II and passing them on to the Soviet Union. They were not charged with treason against the United States because the Soviet Union had been a U.S. ally during the war.

One of the crucial elements of the crime of treason concerns intent. A person must intend to wage war or give aid and comfort to an enemy of the United States for there to be treason. Since treason does not happen by mistake, if aid and comfort is given to an enemy without intent, no one can be charged with treason. In addition to intent, there must be an overt act stemming from the traitorous intent for there to be treason. Someone who expresses a point of view that is contrary to government policy during wartime cannot be charged with treason. If that same person provides an enemy with weapons, information, shelter, or troops, that person has committed treason against the United States. Since treason involves a breach of allegiance, only citizens and particular aliens who owe temporary allegiance to the United States can commit treason. While aliens who live in the United States can commit treason, a traitorous act does not have to take place on U.S. soil. During World War II Mildred Gillars, a U.S. citizen, broadcast Nazi propaganda to Allied troops from a German radio station. In 1949 she was convicted of treason and sentenced to a prison term of ten to thirty years. While treason can be punishable by death, the minimum penalty is five years in prison and a fine of $10,000. No person who has been coerced into committing a treasonous act, however, can be found guilty of treason. If a defendant who stands accused of treason does not confess voluntarily in open court, a conviction can be handed down only if at least two witnesses are willing to testify in open court that the defendant committed an overt act of treason. Since treason is such a serious crime, the United States employs these very stringent direct evidence rules in order to protect individuals from government abuse. —*Jeffry Jensen*

See also Conspiracy; Criminal intent; Death penalty.

Trespass

Illegal entry into another party's property or land is known as trespass.

The law of trespass varies from state to state and depends on state statutes and court precedents. In general, trespass is defined as an unlawful interference or invasion of a property right. One may not enter through a door uninvited. If a gate is in a fence and the door is just beyond it, one may go to the door. If the land is fenced or properly posted, one may not cross the fence or the posting line. If the land is open to a place where persons are entitled to be, such as a public road, they may enter the premises as long as they do nothing unlawful or damaging and as long as they have not been told to leave or stay out. If they are told by the owner or an agent of the owner to leave or stay out, persons must comply. These are general rules and should be considered in light of the law.

Trespass may be civil, in which case the redress in court depends on the outcome of a civil suit, or it may be criminal, in which case the redress in court is based on a criminal charge. Intent is not an element of civil trespass but is an element in criminal trespass, although ill will is not required. A person might have trespassed with no ill will but still have done so willfully. In most states trespass becomes criminal only if it is accompanied by or tends to create a breach of the peace.

Taking goods that one is not authorized to take can constitute a trespass. If a person has been invited onto property but thereupon picks up an axe without authorization and carries it home, trespass has occurred provided the action is brought by the owner of the axe.

A person may enter private property in order to recover property to which one is entitled, although a court order is often required before such entry is permitted. Persons may enter another's property legally for other reasons as well. It is legal to enter someone else's property if it is necessary to defend one's own property or to prevent injury. Police and firemen may trespass in order to carry out reasonable duties. Officers who have entered premises legally may invite others in if they are needed, but anyone invited in must leave as soon as the required duties are performed and without taking advantage of entering.

If trespass is proved in civil cases, at least nominal damages are allowed, and the damages allowed might be more than nominal if they are justified. Damages for pain and suffering are allowed. Exemplary damages are governed by state law but are generally not permitted if the civil case also results in a criminal case. —*Dwight Jensen*

See also Civil law; Property rights; Real property; Torts.

Trial publicity

Trial publicity is information about a trial disseminated through the print or broadcast media.

Issues regarding trial publicity emerge from two opposing principles: the right of the accused to a fair trial and the constitutional imperative that court proceedings be public. The two concerns conflict when trial publicity threatens to bias the outcome of a trial.

Traditionally, tacit professional limitations were imposed on attorneys, restricting the information they could reveal to the news media. By the late twentieth century the potential for instantaneous, in-depth trial coverage by electronic media made trial publicity a broader social issue involving the whole judicial system, the public's right to know, and the professional conduct of journalists. The result is freer movement of information to the public and less accountability for any one party or institution.

The principle of publicity was key to the development of modern mass democracies in Europe and America. It was through the publicizing of the private affairs of kings and other ruling authorities that a public sphere of discourse developed. Consequently, most modern constitutions call for conducting the affairs of state in public. The Sixth Amendment to the U.S. Constitution states that "the accused shall enjoy the right to a speedy and public trial." This ensures that justice will be carried out under the watchful eye of other private citizens.

In the eighteenth and nineteenth centuries the right to a public trial meant that private citizens and print journalists could attend court proceedings. In the twentieth century access was sometimes extended to radio and television broadcasters as well. However, the U.S. Supreme Court has been reluctant to grant to broadcast journalists the access given to citizens and print journalists. The Supreme Court takes the position that broadcast technology adversely affects court proceedings.

In some cases the individual's right to privacy takes precedence over the public's right to know. In certain states an attorney can move to close the courtroom. If the attorney shows good cause the judge may remove spectators from the courtroom for part or all of the proceedings. This is most often done in cases involving juveniles, adoptions, or rape. Judges may also clear the courtroom if witnesses must provide embarrassing evidence, usually in cases involving sexual assault.

Typically, trial publicity is limited to coverage of a crime, the police investigation, and regular reports on courtroom testimony. In the majority of trials, publicity is not a problem. If a judge believes that trial publicity may bias the proceedings, a gag order can be issued restricting what parties in the trial may say to journalists. A judge may also sequester a jury by cutting off their access to news broadcasts and newspapers and by restricting them to their hotel rooms and court facilities. However, it is rare for gag orders to be enforced or for a jury to be sequestered.

If excessive local publicity presents a problem, a judge may also call for a change of venue by moving the trial to an area in which the pool of potential jurors is less exposed to news coverage of the case in question. —*Thomas J. Roach*

See also Constitution, U.S.; Gag order; Juries; Jury sequestration.

Trial transcript

The official record of trial proceedings, a trial transcript is used chiefly by an appellate court in evaluating whether any errors occurred in the trial court.

A trial consists in the main of statements made by lawyers and the judge and of the questions asked of witnesses and the answers given by them. A court reporter normally records these matters as they are spoken and produces a formal trial transcript. With the benefit of special training and equipment, court reporters can produce a verbatim record of the words spoken in a proceeding.

Sometimes the transcript of the trial is used during the trial itself. For example, a lawyer cross-examining a witness might wish to confront the witness with statements made during direct examination. In these cases, the lawyer requests that the court reporter produce a transcript of the witness's testimony so that the lawyer can present it to the witness and question the witness about it.

More commonly, however, the trial transcript is a key portion of the material considered by an appellate court when a case is appealed. On appeal, the appellate court does not conduct a trial again and hear the testimony of witnesses and the arguments of lawyers. Instead, the appellate court reviews what happened in the trial court to determine whether legal errors were made. The appellate court reviews the record of the trial, which includes the trial transcript, the evidence offered by the parties, and any official court documents filed with the trial court. Of these items, the trial transcript is normally the most important source for the appellate court to determine what happened during the trial.

Although the court reporter does not charge the parties in the case for transcribing the proceedings, the reporter does charge for making a formal transcript. This charge can be quite substantial, especially in cases that last for extended periods of time. The party wishing to appeal a case must normally shoulder the cost of having a transcript prepared, because the appellate court generally does not consider an appeal without a record (including the transcript) of the trial.

In at least some cases the U.S. Supreme Court has found that due process of law requires that indigent persons not be denied access to courts simply because they lack the financial resources to pay for a trial transcript. In *Griffin v. Illinois* (1956), for example, the Supreme Court determined that a state must furnish a free trial transcript for indigent criminal defendants if the transcript is necessary for appellate review. Similarly, in *M.L.B. v. S.L.J.* (1996) the Court ruled as unconstitutional a state law that prevented a parent from appealing the termination of parental rights to a child unless the parent paid for a record of the termination proceedings. In *M.L.B.* these costs amounted to $2,352.36. —Timothy L. Hall

See also Appeal; Court reporters; Evidence; Testimony; Trials; Witnesses.

Trials

Courtroom proceedings involving presentation of evidence and arguments by lawyers to a judge or jury, trials are used to seek the truth and arrive at verdicts in civil and criminal cases.

The outcomes of civil and criminal cases in the American legal system are determined by the actions of lawyers representing opposing sides. When opposing attorneys cannot negotiate agreements to end legal cases, called "settlements" in civil cases and "plea bargains" in criminal cases, the legal system provides a procedure for a judge or jury to decide the relevant facts, apply the appropriate laws, and issue a decision. This truth-seeking procedure is called a trial.

Origins and Modern Forms. U.S. trials have their origins in English traditions. Prior to the thirteenth century the guilt of criminal suspects in England was determined by making them undergo physical ordeals. For example, they were forced to lift red-hot irons, were placed into boiling water, or thrown into ponds with their hands and feet tied. People assumed that if persons were killed or injured during such physical trials, God was showing that they were guilty. When Pope Innocent III (1160-1216) forbade the clergy in 1215 to endorse the results of such ordeals, legalistic trials began to develop as a means of discovering facts and determining guilt. Groups of citizens were called upon to serve on juries that decided whether accused persons were guilty of crimes.

Trials are very time-consuming. Lawyers frequently spend weeks or months preparing for trial. They must interview potential witnesses, examine relevant documents and physical evidence, and plan a strategy for presenting evidence and arguments. Trials are also very expensive because they absorb so much of a lawyer's time and may involve the hiring of investigators and expert witnesses.

After both sides have prepared their cases, a trial takes place in a courtroom. A trial constitutes the ultimate truth-seeking process in an adversarial legal system. Lawyers for each side attempt to persuade the decision maker, whether the judge or jury, that their clients should prevail. Opposing lawyers must follow detailed rules about the kinds of evidence and arguments they may present in court. Each side's opening arguments present an overview of the case. Then each side presents its evidence and attempts to point out the weaknesses in the other side's evidence. Witnesses are questioned by the opposing attorneys. Each side may also present physical evidence, such as weapons or documents relevant to the case. Expert witnesses may also be called to the stand, such as psychiatrists or scientists who have special knowledge relevant to the case. Presentation of evidence is followed by closing arguments in which the opposing attorneys attempt to persuade the judge or jury to issue a verdict favorable to their side.

Judge and Jury. The judge supervises the trial to make sure that the rules of evidence and procedure are followed. In a jury trial the judge also supervises

Trials, a central pillar of the adversary system in the United States, involve judges, defense attorneys, prosecutors, witnesses, jurors, and court reporters. (James L. Shaffer)

the selection of jurors, instructs the jurors on what information they may consider in reaching a decision, or verdict, and informs them about the relevant law that they must apply in their deliberations.

In reaching a verdict, jurors are sent to a private room to discuss the facts and the law involved in the case. No one else is allowed in the room and no one is allowed to listen to jurors' deliberations. Jurors elect their own foreperson to guide their discussions. They must continue to meet, sometimes for days, until they either reach a verdict or convince the judge to declare a mistrial when they are hopelessly deadlocked. When a mistrial is declared, either because the jury is deadlocked or because one of the opposing sides in the case violated a procedural rule, a new trial takes place in front of a new jury, unless the prosecutor drops the charges in a criminal case or the plaintiff decides to drop a civil lawsuit.

Trial verdicts may be appealed to a higher court only when one side claims that the trial judge made an error in enforcing rules of evidence and court procedure. Appellate courts are not permitted to disagree with a trial verdict or with the trial judge and jury's determination of the facts. Appellate courts can merely order a new trial if a significant error by a trial judge violated court procedures or led to a misapplication of the appropriate law. Because appellate courts have only limited authority to reverse the decisions of trial judges and jurors, trials are especially important procedures for determining the outcomes of legal cases.

Trials are relatively infrequent in both criminal and civil cases. In most jurisdictions, typically only 10 percent of cases are resolved through trials. Most cases end prior to trial through a settlement agreement in civil cases and plea bargaining in criminal cases. Although trials are unusual, they are extremely important. Trials often occur in the most difficult or serious cases when the two sides cannot reach an agreement. Thus, most cases concerning the death penalty are decided through trials rather than plea bargains. Trials also have an impact on cases resolved through settlements and plea bargains. When the attorneys for each side meet to discuss a settlement or plea bargain, their discussions are based on their predictions about how the case is likely to turn out if it goes to trial. If a criminal defense attorney believes that a jury will convict a defendant at trial because the prosecution's evidence is strong, the defense attorney may seek a plea bargain to avoid the maximum possible punishment. Similarly, if attorneys in a civil case believe that the evidence favors the opposition, they will likely cooperate in reaching settlement agreements that avoid the worst possible outcomes for their clients. The anticipated expense of carrying cases to trial may also lead to settlements in civil cases. Thus, trials or the perspective of trials guides or determines the outcomes of most legal cases.

Jury Trials. In criminal cases the Sixth Amendment to the U.S. Constitution guarantees the right to trial by jury, but this right only applies when a defendant faces "serious" charges, which are defined as those for which the possible punishment is more than six months in jail or prison. In reality, people may face the possibility of serving years in prison without having a jury trial, because the U.S. Supreme Court ruled in *Lewis v. United States* (1996) that there is no right to a jury trial for people charged with multiple nonserious offenses, even when they face the possibility of several separate six-month sentences consecutively. The right to a jury in criminal cases does not depend on the total possible sentence. Rather, it depends on whether a defendant is charged with a crime which by itself can incur a sentence longer than six months' imprisonment.

There is no general constitutional right to jury trials in civil cases, which are lawsuits involving disputes among individuals, corporations, government agencies, and other entities not involved in the prosecution of crimes. The Seventh Amendment to the U.S. Constitution entitles persons to civil jury trials in certain cases in federal court, but the vast majority of civil cases concern contracts, torts, real estate, and other matters handled by state courts. Thus, the opportunity to have a jury trial in a civil case depends on the state or federal statute under which lawsuits are initiated. For some types of civil cases, statutes specify that trials shall be held before a judge without a jury.

Jury trials provide citizens with the opportunity to serve as decision makers in the legal process. Jury service is an important civic responsibility. When called upon to serve on a jury, a citizen is asked to make important decisions about how laws should be applied and about when criminal punishment should be imposed, depriving persons of life and liberty. Potential jurors are usually called to court from voter registration lists, driver's license roles, and other records available to the government. The attorneys for both sides in a case are permitted to request that specific individuals be excluded from the jury if there is reason to believe that they may be unable to be objective in deciding the case. Each side is also permitted to exclude a limited number of potential jurors for strategic reasons without providing a reason for these exclusions.

Some critics believe that citizen jurors are not capable of understanding complex legal issues. Others believe that jurors often decide cases based on their own emotions and prejudices rather than on the facts. As a result, some have proposed that jury trials be reformed, so that jurors are given clearer instructions and permitted to take notes and ask questions during trial. These suggestions are intended to help jurors collect and understand information more effectively before they are called upon to issue a verdict.

Bench Trials. Only about half of all trials are jury trials. The rest are trials before a judge, which are called bench trials. In some civil cases, state and federal statutes permit only bench trials. Attorneys make strategic decisions to request bench trials. They may seek a bench trial if a case is so controversial, such as a notorious sex crime case, that they fear jurors will be unduly influenced by their emotions. Attorneys may also seek a bench trial if they believe that a particular judge will understand or sympathize with their arguments. Attorneys may also seek a bench trial if they believe juries' decisions are so unpredictable that it is not worth putting their client's fate in the hands of citizens randomly drawn from the community.

In a bench trial, the judge may be less concerned about strictly enforcing rules of evidence. If a jury hears or sees improper evidence, its decision may be affected. If a judge hears improper evidence, the judge recognizes the need to exclude it from consideration in reaching a verdict.

Civil and Criminal Trials. The constitutional right to jury trials in serious criminal cases distinguishes such cases from civil cases in which no such right exists. The standard of proof required for verdicts also differs in civil and criminal cases. In civil cases, verdicts typically must be supported by only "a preponderance of evidence"—in other words, by the doctrine that it is more likely than not that the plaintiff should prevail. By contrast, in criminal cases guilt must be proven "beyond a reasonable doubt." Depending on the applicable state or federal law, civil trial juries may be smaller than criminal trial juries. For example, federal courts use six-member juries for civil cases and twelve-member juries for criminal cases. Additionally, the relevant rules of evidence and procedure often differ in criminal and civil cases, with stricter rules typically applying in criminal cases because criminal defendants enjoy various constitutional rights that are not applicable to litigants in civil cases.

Suggested Readings. The details of trials and pretrial processes are presented in Frank Miller, Robert Dawson, George Dix, and Raymond Parnas, *Prosecution and Adjudication* (4th ed. Westbury, N.Y.: Foundation Press, 1991). A comparison of civil and criminal trials in different jurisdictions is presented in a report entitled *On Trial: The Length of Civil and Criminal Trials* (Williamsburg, Va.: National Center for State Courts, 1988). Several of the most famous trials in U.S. history are described in books about the legendary trial lawyer Clarence Darrow. Such books include Irving Stone's *Clarence Darrow for the Defense* (New York: Doubleday, 1941) and Arthur Weinberg's *Attorney for the Damned* (New York: Simon & Schuster, 1957). Other books examine individual cases, such as Seymour Wishman's *Anatomy of a Jury* (New York: Penguin, 1986), which concerns a murder trial. The details of attorneys' preparations for a civil trial are presented in Gerald Stern's *Buffalo Creek Disaster* (New York: Random House, 1976). —*Christopher E. Smith*

See also Acquittal; Adversary system; Conviction; Evidence; Juries; Mistrial; Plea; Plea bargain; Reasonable doubt; Sentencing; Speedy trial requirement; Trial publicity; Trial transcript; Verdict.

Truancy

The failure of a minor to attend school is not a crime in and of itself but may be used as probable cause to investigate the minor on suspicion of more serious infractions.

Everywhere in the United States school attendance is legally required of children. This requirement usually affects children between the ages of seven and sixteen, although in a few states the age of compulsory education extends to adolescents as old as eighteen years of age.

Truancy, the failure of a child between these ages to attend school, is not generally regarded as a crime in itself but may have consequences of two kinds. If a person who appears to be within the relevant age range is discovered by police outside of school grounds during school hours, the police may question, detain, and even search the youth on suspicion of criminal activity. Truancy is considered reasonable evidence of delinquency.

In addition, compulsory education laws require parents to ensure their children's attendance in school. Sufficient unwarranted absences from school by children may lead to prosecution of their parents for neglect or for endangerment of their children's welfare.

Such laws have been challenged many times and in many different ways. Parents or community groups may object to the curriculum on various grounds and refuse to let their children attend school. Since state laws generally include language involving "alternate institutions" and "home instruction," such challenges have been treated in differing ways. The greatest number of challenges have been on religious grounds and have usually been lodged, in modern times, by fundamentalists who object to certain secular teachings in science.

Such challenges and forms of alternative education greatly complicate attempts to compile statistics on the prevalence of truancy. School attendance records do not generally state whether children were absent because their parents kept them home in protest or because the children chose not to attend. They also do not consider alternative educational methods that are not approved by the state.

In general, truancy is considered a minor offense, and unless there is evidence of criminal activity the first step is to contact parents. If truant behavior becomes regular or if the truant engages in more serious antisocial activity, the parents may be investigated, which in some cases may lead to criminal prosecution. Serious repercussions for truancy alone, however, are rare.

Of more interest to educators and others is the fact that truant children do not receive a proper education, and a variety of approaches have been attempted to encourage children to attend school willingly, including alternative teaching methods and multicultural instruction. There is also a prevalent feeling that children who do not attend school by their own choice are not under proper supervision and may become involved in dangerous or illegal activity. Once again, the statistics are unreliable. In addition, since truancy is likely to be most prevalent among children who are already not properly supervised by their parents, a direct cause-and-effect relationship is difficult to ascertain.

—*Marc Goldstein*

See also Home schooling; Juvenile delinquency; School law.

Trustees

A trustee is a person or group holding property or money for the benefit of another party.

A trust is a form of property ownership in which one person agrees to hold money or property for the benefit of another. Most trust funds involve three parties: a settlor, a trustee, and a beneficiary. The settlor, also called the trustor or donor, creates a trust by giving property or money to the trustee. The trustee has both the right and the fiduciary duty to hold or invest the property or money in accordance with the terms of the trust and to do so solely for the interest of the beneficiary. Thus, according to the law, the trustee is regarded as the legal owner of the property or money and the beneficiary as the equitable owner. The beneficiary has no right or power to instruct the trustee how to manage the trust.

If one agrees to be a trustee, that person cannot resign from the position unless it is stipulated in the terms of the trust or approved by a court. Because of the powers invested in a trustee, careful consideration should be given to selecting one. The size of the trust generally dictates whether the trustee should be an individual or a commercial institution. Trust companies or trust departments of banks have been formed to act as trustees, and their services are paid out of the income of the trust.

—*Alvin K. Benson*

See also Attorney trust accounts; Fiduciaries; Trusts; Trusts, charitable.

Trusts

Trusts are legal devices designed to hold property for the benefit of others as designated by the person who owns that property and has put it into a living trust.

Trusts originated in England shortly after the Norman Conquest in 1066. They are judicial devices unique to the legal systems of Great Britain and the United States. During the medieval era, when they came into being, women in Great Britain were prohibited by law from owning property in their own right and, under the so-called mortmain acts, churches could not own land.

Medieval lawyers contrived means of overcoming both of these obstacles by inventing trusts, which originally were simply designated "use." At that time, the legal system honored only legal title to property, which for most people consisted mainly of land. By using a trust instrument, property owners were able, quite within the law, to specify that their holdings should be administered by a trustee for the benefit of one or more designated persons, often female relatives, during the lifetimes of such persons or for the benefit of one or more organizations, such as churches.

Persons Involved in Trusts. Four categories of people may be involved directly in living trusts: the trustor, the settlor, the trustee or trustees, and the beneficiary or beneficiaries.

The trustor is the person who establishes the living trust. In most cases this person is the same as the settlor, although in situations in which settlors are mentally or physically incapacitated, a person close to the settlor may set up the trust in that person's behalf.

The settlor is the person who owns the property that is to be put into a trust. This person, if physically and mentally competent, expresses, usually in writing, a desire to place the legal title to some or all of his or her property in a trust that may benefit the settlor during his or her lifetime but the benefits of which will pass on after the settlor's death to one or more beneficiaries, either individuals or organizations. Settlors may establish revocable living trusts, which they can alter or dissolve at any time simply by expressing in writing their desire to make changes or to dissolve the trust.

Settlors have absolute power over the assets in a

> **Steps in Establishing Living Trusts**
>
> - Trustors or settlors must take the initiative in having a trust document drawn up by attorneys who specialize in estate matters
> - Trustors or settlors must appoint one or more trustees, but settlors themselves may act as sole trustees
> - Trustors or settlors must name one or more successor trustees to administer the trust upon the settlor's death or incapacity
> - Settlors or trustors in collaboration with settlors must name one or more beneficiaries; settlors have the right to name themselves as sole beneficiaries during their lifetimes but must name a beneficiary or beneficiaries who will benefit from the trust upon the settlor's death
> - Trustors or settlors must transfer into the trust all assets they wish to be held in trust, including such items as bank accounts, securities, and real estate and such personal property as works of art, jewelry, automobiles, boats, and airplanes

revocable trust until their deaths, at which time the provisions in most trusts become irrevocable. Irrevocable trusts, whether they are originally drawn up as such or become irrevocable through the death of the settlor, are not subject to alteration. Most people who establish trusts prefer the flexibility of the revocable living trust, although a person of advanced age who faces the possibility of becoming senile or severely physically debilitated may view the irrevocable trust as insurance against future injudicious actions. Trustors who act on behalf of disabled settlors frequently establish irrevocable trusts.

Another party involved in living trusts is the trustee. The settlor often serves as trustee, although the trustee may be one or more persons appointed because of their loyalty to the settlor or because of their special competencies. The trustee may also be an organization, such as the trust department of a bank, that assumes responsibility for administering the trust according to the dictates of the settlor as expressed in the trust document.

If the settlor is the trustee, then one or more successor trustees must also be named to serve if the settlor dies or is incapacitated. Because banks and other financial organizations are often reluctant to administer small trusts, a settlor may be forced to appoint as trustee or successor trustee one or more individuals who are willing to act in that capacity.

The beneficiary or beneficiaries are also parties in living trusts. Settlors may be the beneficiaries during their lifetimes, but living trusts contain directions for the distribution of the property held in trust upon their deaths. Unless the settlor has specifically directed that the beneficiary or beneficiaries shall receive only the interest earned by the trust or only a portion of the principal, the proceeds held in the living trust will, immediately upon the death of the settlor, be passed on *in toto* to those named as beneficiaries.

The greatest benefit of the living trust is that it keeps all of the trust's assets from having to pass through probate and that its provisions are not available for public scrutiny. Those benefiting from the trust, however, are still subject to inheritance and other taxes owed by the estate of the settlor.

The Settlor's Rights. The settlor has no rights to the assets in a living trust unless such rights have been specified at the time the trust is established and validated. If a revocable living trust is established, that trust must specifically detail the rights of the settlor to alter, amend, or dissolve the trust. Settlors, in establishing trusts, revoke their ownership of all the assets they put into the trust, giving the trustee or trustees full discretionary power to use those assets as they see fit.

Trustees, of course, serve under a fiduciary mandate to act responsibly and judiciously in handling the assets in the trust. When the settlor and the trustee are the same person, the settlor has, in essence, retained control of the property that has been transferred into the trust. On the other hand, if the two positions are not held by the same person, it is the trustee who determines how the assets in the trust shall be managed.

It is the chief responsibility of the trustee or trustees to carry out the provisions of the trust and to protect the property held in it for the benefit of those named as beneficiaries. Trustees and successor trustees are held personally responsible if they act imprudently or if they do not follow the settlor's instructions as stated in the trust agreement.

Termination of a Living Trust. If a living trust is revocable, it can be terminated any time the settlor wishes to dissolve it. However, if such a trust is in effect at the time of the settlor's death, it can be terminated as soon as the property contained in it has been distributed to the beneficiary or beneficiaries. When the assets in the trust consist of bank accounts, stocks, bonds, and other liquid assets, this often can be accomplished in a matter of days. On the other hand, termination of the trust may be delayed if real estate and personal property need to be sold, if beneficiaries cannot be readily located, or if the settlor has made stipulations that necessitate the trust's being continued following his or her death.

Some trusts hold their assets following the settlor's death until specific conditions are met. For example, some trusts may be held open to provide for the education of a minor. Upon the beneficiary's completion of the education as specified, assuming that all the other conditions of the trust have been met, the trust may be terminated.

Settlors may decree that their beneficiaries, perhaps a spouse or a child or children, be permitted to draw from the principal held in the trust only in cases of bona fide emergencies or that only the interest that the trust's assets generate may be distributed to the beneficiaries. Upon the death of the last beneficiary upon whom this limitation is imposed, the assets may be passed in full or in part to members of a succeeding generation, such as grandchildren or to a designated charitable organization.

Setting up the trust in this way is attractive to some affluent settlors, because it avoids double taxation, inheritance tax being paid only by the recipients of the principal, while only income tax must be paid on the income derived from the trust's assets. A trust may also specify that part of the principal be available immediately to a specified beneficiary or beneficiaries but that the remainder of the principal be left to earn interest that may or may not be distributed to such beneficiaries.

Some living trusts are not terminated until many years after a settlor's death. This is especially true in the case of trusts that contain large assets, portions of which are to be used for the benefit of one or two succeeding generations but the remainder of which is to be passed on to charitable organiza-

---

Advantages of Living Trusts

- Assets held in trust are exempted from the probate process
- Settlors may avoid personal liability in certain legal actions
- Privacy is assured because trust documents are not available to the public as are wills, appraisals, and other documents associated with probate
- Distribution and disposition of assets held in trust can be almost immediate upon the settlor's death
- Provision for the distribution of assets held in trust cannot be contested
- An estate held in trust, although still subject to inheritance taxes, avoids many expenses associated with probate
- Whereas states may mandate that a surviving spouse receive one-third to one-half of the decedent's assets, the assets held in trust cannot be distributed except as directed by the settlor

tions or foundations. In such instances, a bank or other financial institution, often working jointly with a successor trustee, usually administers the trust, which may continue in effect for an indefinite period.

Types of Living Trusts. For many people, especially married couples, the A-B type of trust is desirable. This kind of trust provides survivors protection from substantial estate taxes, because estate taxes up to the prescribed limit, which was $625,000 in the late 1990's and expected gradually to increase to $1 million dollars over several years, are deferred until the death of the second member of the trust, when they are levied against the trust. The A type of trust, which should be considered only by single people with assets under the amount of the federal exemption, has no such provision and requires settlement of estate taxes upon the death of the settlor even if there is a surviving spouse.

A-B Trusts involving two people are not separate trusts. Rather, they are divisions of a single trust. The assets of the trust are equally divided between two people, often married couples. On the death of one of these people, half the proceeds flow into the A Trust. The remaining half goes into the B Trust, on which inheritance tax is paid on any amount in excess of the federal tax exemption in effect at that time. The assets of the B Trust, which becomes an irrevocable trust, are held for the benefit of the survivor and, upon the death of the survivor, are subject to no additional taxation.

For married couples whose assets amount to twice the estate exemption permitted by the federal government, at present $1.3 million and increasing in gradual increments, an A-B-C Trust, also designated a Qualified Terminal Interest Property Trust (Q-TIP), is generally desirable. The provisions of such a trust allow assets up to the amount of the federal exemption to be placed in the decedent's B Trust, with the surplus flowing into the C Trust.

Although the excess could pass into a spouse's A Trust and be tax-exempt under the unlimited marital deduction law, by putting the proceeds into the C Trust the surviving spouse may claim all the income from those assets during his or her lifetime, but the decedent names the ultimate beneficiaries of the trust. The surviving spouse cannot change the beneficiaries or any of the provisions of the C Trust. Such a trust may allow but is not obligated to allow the surviving spouse access to the principal in it.

The Qualified Domestic Trust (Q-DOT) is used along with the Q-TIP Trust by married couples if one of the spouses is not a citizen of the United States. Under legislation passed by the U.S. Congress in 1988, the trustee of a Q-DOT must be a U.S. citizen if the Q-TIP Trust is to qualify for the deferral of estate taxes. The trustee could be the member of such a marriage who has U.S. citizenship, but provision would have to be made for a successor trustee who has citizenship to assume responsibility if the trustee who has citizenship dies before the noncitizen.

Although a living trust, if properly executed, will contain all of one's assets, it is desirable for a settlor to execute a "pour-over" will as well as a trust. Such a will transfers into an existing trust any assets that have inadvertently been excluded from it previously. This document names the settlor and his or her marital status, revokes prior wills, and puts into the living trust all personal assets and household effects that are not already a part of the trust. This can be done quite simply. However, if real property that has been inadvertently excluded from the trust is to be entered into it, such property must pass through probate and an executor must be appointed to see to its proper disposition, which can delay substantially the settling of a trust that could otherwise be quickly terminated.

Inasmuch as a major purpose of a living trust is to avoid probate, one might question the necessity for a pour-over will, which may necessitate probate. It must be remembered, however, that some assets come into an estate following the death of a settlor. For example, if a settlor has a legal action pending and it is finally decided posthumously in his or her favor, a cash settlement might be realized. Such a settlement would not automatically become a part of any existing trust but might be paid to the estate of the decedent, as might proceeds from an estate that names the decedent as an heir but has not been settled prior to that person's death. The pour-over will would, therefore, be a necessary device for assuring that such proceeds become a part of the decedent's trust.

Individual and Corporate Trustees. In establishing a living trust, one must decide whether it is best to name individuals as trustees or successor trustees or to assign this task to a financial institution with a strong trust department. Settlors usually will be their own trustees until they die or are incapacitated, although personal circumstances, such as frequent and extensive travel or the assumption of a major political office, might make them feel more comfortable or even legally necessitate their naming a trustee to manage their affairs. In the case of politicians and other high government officials, blind trusts are set up so that the settlor will avoid being accused of conflicts of interest.

Often estates valued at under a million dollars are administered by individual trustees or successor trustees appointed by the settlor. Many banks do not wish to be the sole trustees for estates smaller than this. Most banks, however, are willing and able for a fee to assist successor trustees if they are called upon to do so. They usually handle the paper work for the trust, keeping records and making sure that all the conditions of the trust are met, thereby protecting the trustee from charges of impropriety. A financial institution should certainly be named successor trustee when a settlor has no family or close friends to oversee the disposition of his or her assets or when the settlor has a handicapped or disabled child who must be cared for after the parent's death.

Suggested Readings. Among the most useful and practical sources for the nonspecialist is *The Living Trust: The Failproof Way to Pass Along Your Estate to Your Heirs Without Lawyers, Courts, or the Probate System* (Chicago: Contemporary Books, 1993) by Henry W. Abts, III, which deals with the specifics of setting up various kinds of trusts. Eminently useful as well is Norman F. Dacey's *How to Avoid Probate!* (New York: Macmillan, 1990), which discusses fully and accurately the use of living trusts as a way of simplifying the settlement of estates. Nan L. Goddart's *The Truth About Living Trusts* (Chicago: Dearborn Financial Publishing, 1995) is about as user friendly as a book in this field can be, presenting its case for living trusts persuasively. Mark L. Ascher's *Federal Income Taxation of Trusts and Estates* (Durham: North Carolina Academic Press, 1988), while quite specialized, offers essential information about the tax implications of various kinds of trusts, as does Jonathan G. Blattmachr's *Income Taxation of Estates and Trusts* (13th ed., New York: Practicing Law Institute, 1989). Directed primarily to lay readers, Eugene J. Daly's *Thy Will Be Done: A Guide to Wills, Taxation, and Estate Planning for Older Persons* (Buffalo, N.Y.: Prometheus Books, 1990) is lively and easily accessible to those with little experience in the field. Dennis Hower's *Wills, Trusts, and Estate Administration for the Paralegal* (3d ed. St. Paul, Minn.: West Publishing, 1990), although written for a somewhat specialized audience, is accessible. Kenneth J. Namjestnik in *Trust Risk Management: Assessing and Controlling Fiduciary Risk* (Chicago: Probus, 1992) focuses on trustee responsibilities, highlighting vulnerabilities and ways to minimize fiduciary risk.

—*R. Baird Shuman*

See also Estate and gift taxes; Estates and estate planning; Executors; Future estate; Inheritance tax; Probate; Trusts, charitable; Wills.

Trusts, charitable

Arrangements by which one person gives property to another to be used for the benefit of the public.

The person who establishes a trust is known as the settlor and the person who administers the trust is known as the trustee. Unlike other trusts, charitable trusts are allowed to exist for an unlimited period of time. Charitable trusts are generally exempt from taxes if they meet certain requirements.

A charitable trust must have a specific purpose intended to benefit human beings. The benefit may be direct, as in a trust that educates the illiterate, or indirect, as in a trust that shelters stray animals. If the trust produces profits—for example, a trust that operates a successful hospital—the profits must be used to continue the charitable services of the trust.

A charitable trust must benefit a specific segment of the public. This segment must be large enough so that the entire community has an interest in enforcing the trust. The exact individuals who will benefit from the trust must not be named in the trust. A trust to benefit the homeless in a particular city, for example, is acceptable, but a trust to benefit a list of specific homeless persons is not.

—*Rose Secrest*

See also Charitable contributions; Trustees; Trusts.

U

Unauthorized practice of law

The practice of law by a person lacking a law license in the relevant jurisdiction is unauthorized, as is the filing or preparation of court pleadings or other activities on behalf of a client by an unlicensed person.

The practice of law is a profession consisting of attorneys licensed by state authorities. A person is licensed by law in the jurisdiction in which he or she practices. Most states permit a lawyer licensed in one jurisdiction to make a special appearance in another state's court. However, a license must be obtained if that person is to hold himself or herself out as a lawyer in that state. As the practice of law has become nationalized, many attorneys hold memberships in several state bars.

A few states have reciprocity agreements that permit members of another state's bar to receive membership upon application. Vermont requires licensed lawyers of another state to complete a six-month internship with a Vermont attorney or pass the Vermont bar examination to qualify for membership in that state. Most states require that applicants to the bar pass a written bar examination, meet a moral character requirement, and have graduated from an accredited law school.

Law is a regulated profession to protect the public against persons who hold themselves out to the public as lawyers but who lack the training to competently perform legal work. The public interest requires that those persons rendering legal advice have competence. To protect this public interest, it is necessary to investigate complaints of the unauthorized practice of law. The highest court in most states appoints committees to investigate and punish the unauthorized practice of law. Unlicensed persons who hold themselves out to the public as lawyers may be punished by criminal and civil sanctions depending on the activities in which they have engaged.

Lawyers may employ the services of paraprofessionals and delegate functions to them as long as the work they perform is supervised by a licensed member of the bar. Lawyers may provide professional advice and instructions to nonlawyers whose work requires knowledge of the law, such as claims adjusters or employees of financial institutions. Licensed lawyers may not assist a person who is not a member of the bar in the performance of activity that constitutes the unauthorized practice of law. A lawyer aids in the unauthorized practice of law by delegating key duties to such persons as real estate brokers. An attorney, for example, may not knowingly delegate to a broker the legal responsibility of answering legal questions. Similarly, a lawyer may not allow any person who has been suspended from the practice of law to have a presence in an office in which the practice of law is conducted by the lawyer. Solicitation by a lawyer not admitted to practice law is a form of unauthorized practice of law. —*Michael L. Rustad*

See also American Bar Association; Attorney-client relationship; Attorney types.

Unconscionable contracts

Contracts in which one of the parties has no meaningful choice and in which contract terms are unreasonably favorable to the other party are characterized as unconscionable contracts.

Courts have the power to refuse to enforce contractual terms that are unreasonably unfavorable to the stronger party. Unconscionability is marked by gross inequality of bargaining power as well as unfair terms. Courts have found contracts to be unconscionable when the consumer did not have a reasonable opportunity to understand the terms of the contract or the terms were hidden in a deceptive manner. Courts refuse to enforce unconscionable sales of goods, consumer credit sales, leases, and loans and have the discretion to deny enforcement of an unconscionable term or an entire contract under Article 2 of the Uniform Commercial Code (UCC). Courts may enforce the remainder of an agreement without the unconscionable provision or limit application to avoid an unconscionable result.

Unconscionability is chiefly a doctrine applied to consumer transactions. If both parties are commercial entities, they are expected to understand the meaning of a contract or a clause. Whether a contract is unconscionable is a matter of law that the court must determine. The stronger party is given a reasonable opportunity to present evidence as to the setting, purposes, and effects of a contract. The court determines whether a contract is unconscionable by the circumstances surrounding the agreement. Unconscionability is determined at the time of the contract.

Unconscionability is principally a consumer remedy applied to warranty disclaimers or other limitations of consumers' legal remedies. If a consumer purchases four new car tires from a seller and is injured along with his or her family when a tire blow-out causes the car to veer off the road, flip over, and burn, the consumer may file a breach of warranty lawsuit. If the manufacturer produces a sales agreement with a clause limiting the buyer's remedy to replacement of the defective tire, the consumer's attorney may argue that the purported disclaimer of limitation of consequential damages such as the personal injury of the family was unconscionable.

Courts may find a disclaimer or limitation of remedy unconscionable even though it contains conspicuous and specific disclaimers. The federal Magnuson-Moss Warranty Act of 1975 specifically invalidates warranty disclaimers that are unreasonable or unconscionable. The courts recognize two types of unconscionability: procedural and substantive. Procedural unconscionability refers to the contractual bargaining process, whereas substantive unconscionability refers to unfair terms. The court must find evidence of both in an unfair bargaining process and unfair terms before invalidating a contract or clause as unconscionable.

Procedural unconscionability is a court's determination that the bargaining process was flawed. Procedural unconscionability is a finding of procedural abuses at the time of contract formation. A court may find procedural abuse if the printed terms of a form contract were hidden or if the plaintiff has no formal education or is unable to read the contract. Similarly, it is procedural abuse for a seller to trick an elderly, non-English-speaking customer into signing an unfair home improvement retail installment contract that is drafted in English.

Substantive unconscionability exists when the actual terms in a contract are unfair or oppressive. A significant price-cost disparity may be found to be substantively unconscionable. An example of this would be the sale of a $400 home freezer for $4,000. The basic test is whether the terms are so one-sided as to constitute oppression. Unconscionability requires one-sided terms combined with an unfair bargaining practice. Article 2A of the UCC on the lease of goods has adopted the concept of unconscionability. The trend of the law is to apply the concept of unconscionability to areas outside Article 2, such as to service contracts.

—*Michael L. Rustad*

See also Consumer protection laws; Contracts; Credit, consumer; Employment contracts.

Undergraduate preparation for law school

Getting into law school requires careful planning with special emphasis on advisement, course selection, a high grade point average, and a high score on the Law School Admission Test.

Prelaw students should seek a broad undergraduate education characterized by rigorous intellectual training involving relational, syntactical, and abstract thinking. This can be done only by completing a series of courses in a wide range of subjects from English to history to the natural sciences. While no single undergraduate major is recommended, students are advised to focus on academic areas in which they are interested and in which they do well, filling out the rest of their programs with courses that may be of value to them.

While the idea of "prelaw" activities has validity, the term should be used with caution, as it may have a negative effect on many law school admissions officers and committees who look for breadth in academic preparation and diversity in their student bodies. What is important is the mastery of basic skills and the acquisition of insight into human values and the human condition, with which lawyers must deal. Undergraduate courses in law should be avoided. Not only are such courses overly vocational; they also differ so much from the actual experiences gained in law school that they are of only marginal value. The reputation of undergraduate schools is also an important consideration. Are they accredited? What proportion of their faculties has terminal degrees? Do they have a good track record in getting their students into law school?

Skills, Grades, and Tests. Spoken and written words are the basis of law. Prelaw students should take courses that will enable them to speak clearly; comprehend, interpret, and analyze complex texts; expand their vocabularies; and write in a clear, expository manner. Many law schools require an application essay that becomes an important factor in the admissions process. Constant practice can lead to a marked improvement in both speaking and writing.

Students' grade point average (GPA) is very important. Most law schools require that students have at least a 3.5 grade point average. Law school admissions officers and committees analyze transcripts to determine if the courses students have taken have prerequisites and intellectual content and if they require rigorous application. A steady improvement in grades is desirable; a decline must be explained.

Along with a high GPA, preparing to achieve a high score on the Law School Admission Test (LSAT) is of great importance to prelaw students in their undergraduate education. All of the law schools accredited by the American Bar Association (ABA) require that students pass the LSAT, for it deals with the kind of thinking and mental activity associated with the successful study of law. Doing poorly on tests is not excused; law school is about test taking. The more selective the law school, the higher the required LSAT score. Many leading law schools use GPAs and LSAT scores to limit the numbers of applicants they admit. The LSAT, including its essay section, is a six-part test that lasts approximately four hours. It asks multiple-choice questions that assess logical and analytical reasoning and reading comprehension. The purpose of the test is to gauge persons' skills, not their knowledge. Two of its six parts, including the essay section, are not scored. The essay is sent to the law schools to which students apply. The LSAT can be repeated, but all scores are reported. Some law schools only consider the first score. The conditions under which the test is given and the nature of the test itself are important. Students are therefore advised to take trial tests repeatedly using old tests before taking the actual test. Ideally, taking the LSAT should be timed so that students have scores available before applying to law schools.

Advisement. Prelaw students should constantly seek advisement not only from prelaw advisors but also from professional organizations and from the law schools in which they might be interested. Some law schools permit and even encourage visits. Students should consider which law schools might be inclined to accept them and the areas of the law in which they hope to specialize. Some areas of the law are overcrowded, while some are more open. Fields such as patent law demand special skills. The

---

Undergraduate Preparation for Law School

More than 84,000 undergraduates who applied to law schools in 1994-1995 had undergraduate majors in these fields:

Social sciences:	47.6 percent
Arts and humanities:	19.7 percent
Business and management:	16.4 percent
Natural sciences:	4.6 percent
Engineering:	3.2 percent
Health professions:	1.1 percent
Computer sciences:	0.6 percent

Specific majors were:

Political science:	18.7 percent
English:	7.1 percent
Psychology:	4.8 percent
Criminal justice:	4.1 percent
Economics:	3.5 percent

availability of financial aid is another consideration. Above all, prelaw students should be realistic about assessing their capabilities. Some law schools admit less than 5 percent of applicants and others as many as 60 percent. An effective match between students and law schools should be of primary importance. The prestige of the law school and its ranking should be secondary. The American Bar Association does not rank the law schools it accredits but insists that they all adhere to its rigid standards.

Extracurricular Activities. Extracurricular activities can be of value if they are meaningful, involve commitment, and foster leadership qualities. They need not necessarily be related to law. Work experience should also be meaningful or justified by economic necessity. Involvement and commitment in these areas, however, should not serve to lower students' GPAs. Early in their academic careers, prelaw students should seek persons who know them, their work, and their specific achievements who might be willing to write meaningful recommendations.

Suggested Readings. *The Official Guide to U.S. Law Schools*, published by the Law School Admission Council (LSAC) in cooperation with the American Bar Association (ABA) and the Association of American Law Schools (AALS), is probably the most valuable reference work for prelaw students. It is the most thorough, accurate, and timely guide available to all 179 ABA approved law schools. Included are admissions requirements, program descriptions, salary and placement statistics, LSAT/GPA admissions profiles, facts for minority applicants, and finances. Other publications of the LSAC include *The Official LSAT Prep Series* of actual LSAT questions together with answer keys and *So You Want to Be a Lawyer*, containing information on ideal undergraduate preparation, how to choose a law school, how law schools choose students, and what law school admissions committees consider significant. Minority candidates should read *Thinking About Law School: A Minority Guide*. Other publications of value include Ronald Coleman's *The Princeton Review Pre-Law Companion* (New York: Random House, 1996), a concise overview by a veteran prelaw advisor of all aspects of prelaw activities, from curriculum planning to testing to applying to law school; Stephen Gillers' *Looking at Law School: A Student Guide, from the Society of American Law Teachers* (3d ed. New York: Dutton, 1990); and Craig Mayfield's *Reading Skills for Law Students* (Charlottesville, Va.: Michie, 1980). On the commercial level is *Barron's LSAT: How to Prepare for the Law School Admission Test* by J. Bobrow (Hauppauge, New York: Barron's Educational Series, 1996).

—*Nis Petersen*

See also Law School Admission Test; Law-school rankings; Legal education.

Unemployment insurance

Unemployment compensation is designed to provide financial assistance to individuals who are out of work through no fault of their own. To be eligible, claimants must be able to and be available for work.

In all fifty states and in the District of Columbia, eligibility requirements for unemployment insurance generally relate to a person's physical and mental capacity to perform remunerative work. Disqualification frequently results when individuals are terminated for employment-related misconduct.

Ability and Availability. In order to qualify for unemployment benefits claimants must be able to work and available for work. The availability requirement is a test to determine whether claimants would in fact be working were it not for their inability to find work that is appropriate for them. As long as individuals continue to look for work and are willing to accept suitable jobs, they are eligible for unemployment compensation. Although eligibility laws require that claimants be able to work, when they are presently unable to pursue their regular occupations, they do not lose their right to benefits if they are still able to engage in other remunerative employment. In most states, if an illness or disability precludes the performance of any gainful employment, affected claimants are ineligible for unemployment benefits. Such individuals may apply for either nonoccupational disability benefits or workers' compensation.

The unemployment statutes in all fifty states and the District of Columbia require that claimants demonstrate that they are ready and willing to work. These laws direct claimants to register at the appropriate public employment office. Although this provides some evidence of their availability, state employment offices usually require some additional indication that claimants are actively seeking work. This requirement is satisfied when claimants make reasonably diligent efforts each week to find suitable employment.

Eligibility and Ineligibility. The employment statutes in all fifty states and the District of Columbia have provisions that disqualify persons seeking unemployment benefits who have been recently terminated because of employment-related misconduct. Disqualifying conduct includes false statements on job applications, insubordination, profanity and violence, use of drugs or alcohol, poor work performance, and excessive absenteeism or tardiness.

A frequently litigated issue concerns the right of unemployed individuals to reject job offers that involve compensation significantly below that which they received in their previous positions. Unemployed persons who refuse to accept suitable employment may forfeit their right to receive benefits. While no definitive standard can be articulated, a position that pays a salary 16 to 20 percent below that previously earned by a claimant is likely to result in a finding that the proffered job is unsuitable. In such situations a claimant remains eligibile for unemployment compensation. Conversely, a 6 to 10 percent wage decrease is usually considered too insignificant to render a job unsuitable. Moreover, after claimants have had a reasonable period of time to locate work paying wages commensurate with those provided by their previous employment, they are normally expected to "lower their sights" and accept lower-paying jobs.

Ineligibility may also result when claimants are forced to stay home to care for young children or ill family members. In such situations these persons are deemed to have withdrawn from the active workforce. Nevertheless, claimants may take short vacations or enroll in training courses without losing their availability status.

Persons who relocate geographically while they are unemployed may face eligibility problems. This situation frequently arises when workers move to other regions to get married, to follow transferred spouses, or to find less expensive housing. Individuals who move to regions with as much potential for employment as the area they left are generally considered "available for work." Difficulties may arise, however, when persons relocate to communities in which there is no reasonable prospect of employment in their customary occupations.

Procedures for Claiming Unemployment Benefits. Individuals who are voluntarily or involuntarily out of work generally file claims for unemployment compensation in public employment offices. They must supply information about their recent past employment and the reason for their current unemployment. Their immediate past employer will have either filed a form indicating the reason for the claimant's loss of employment or will be sent a form requesting such information.

Once the claimant's file is complete, an employment agency deputy or claims examiner reviews the information to determine whether the claimant satisfies the eligibility requirements. In the vast majority of cases, claimants are determined to be eligible for benefits. However, if claimants are denied benefits, they may appeal the adverse decision. Also, when eligibility is determined, employers whose unemployment accounts are to be charged usually ask for agency review.

In most states, an initial appeal of an agency decision is considered by either a single referee, a commissioner, or a three-member tripartite board consisting of one management representative, one worker representative, and one neutral person. The reviewing parties examine copies of the existing files and they may accept additional oral and documentary evidence. Referees, commissioners, or review boards usually conduct informal, nonlegalistic hearings because the claimant and employers are usually not represented by attorneys. Nevertheless, the claimant and the employer may not only subpoena and examine witnesses but also explain and rebut adverse evidence.

After the hearing, the referee, commissioner, or review board notifies the claimant and employer in writing as to whether the initial eligibility determination has been sustained, modified, or reversed. Parties dissatisfied with the reviewer's decision may normally appeal the adverse decision to final administrative appeals bodies. After final administrative determinations have been reached, dissatisfied parties may seek judicial review in the appropriate state court.

Benefit Levels and Duration. In all fifty states and the District of Columbia, persons are only eligible for benefits if they earned at least a minimum amount of wages during the base period.

Generally, the base period is defined as the first four calendar quarters of the last five completed calendar quarters preceding the filing of an unemployment claim. The statutory minimum earnings during the base period range from a low of $150 in Hawaii to a high of $3,640 in Oklahoma. Most minimum earnings fall between $1,000 and $2,500. Forty-four states also require that those applying for benefits were employed during at least two of the calendar quarters in the base period.

Once an unemployed individual is determined to be eligible for benefits, an employment agency deputy or claims examiner determines the weekly benefit amount and the period of eligibility. States usually set weekly benefit amounts that range from 50 to 56 percent of applicants' average weekly earnings during the relevant calendar quarters. States also specify the minimum and maximum weekly benefit amounts available to unemployed individuals. These minimums range form $5 in Hawaii to $64 in Washington. The maximums range from $150 in Alabama to $444 in Massachusetts. Some states provide weekly benefit supplements based on the number of dependent children and spouses cared for by claimants. Fully covered claimants are generally entitled to a maximum of twenty-six weeks of benefits.

Suggested Readings. During the last two decades, many special interest groups have criticized the inadequate unemployment benefit levels available in most states. *Unemployment Compensation: Problems and Issues* (Washington, D.C.: Congressional Research Service, 1988) provides a comprehensive overview of these criticisms. To investigate each state's unemployment compensation programs, see the U.S. Department of Labor, *Comparison of State Unemployment Insurance Laws* (updated semiannually). Also, clear concise guidelines relevant to unemployment insurance laws and practices are generally available, free of charge, at state employment offices. For a general guide to unemployment insurance see Jose L. Portela, *Don't Lose Your Unemployment Benefits! A Handbook for Workers and the Unemployed* (New York: Apex Press, 1995). A history of unemployment insurance is presented in Saul J. Blaustein, Wilbur J. Cohen, and William Haber's *Unemployment Insurance in the United States: The First Half Century* (Kalamazoo, Mich.: W.E. Upjohn Institute for Employment Research, 1993).

—*W. Dene Eddings Andrews*

See also Employment at will; Health and disability insurance; Social Security; Workers' compensation.

Unethical conduct of attorneys

Attorneys who act inappropriately may be punished by the bar association or supreme court in the state in which they practice law.

In the United States admission to the practice of law and oversight of attorney conduct are matters supervised generally by the supreme courts of each state. In most states the supreme court remains the final authority in regulating admissions and attorney conduct, although the court may rely in part on the assistance of state bar associations. In practice, however, complaints concerning the conduct of lawyers should normally be directed to the state or local bar association, which generally plays the most important role in the initial investigation of and decisions concerning complaints.

Sanctions against attorneys for unethical conduct should be distinguished from other means of redress for inappropriate attorney behavior. The chief alternative avenues for such redress are criminal proceedings and civil lawsuits. Attorneys who violate the law in connection with their legal practice can find themselves subject to criminal sanctions. Similarly, attorneys who violate legal obligations owed to clients and other third parties can be sued for legal malpractice or a variety of other legal claims.

Varieties of Sanctions. The sanctions available to disciplinary authorities who regulate the conduct of lawyers vary from private reprimands to disbarment. For a relatively minor infraction disciplinary authorities may simply censure an attorney privately, informing him or her of the bar's verdict and warning against repeating the infraction. This private reprimand remains in the attorney's file, however, and might have a bearing on the severity of sanctions in future cases should further transgressions occur. For more serious cases, disciplinary authorities may move to a public reprimand, which informs other lawyers of the offending lawyer's ethical misconduct, generally by mentioning it in a legal publication such as the state bar association's monthly periodical. The next level of sanction is a suspension from the practice of law for some period of time, generally ranging from three months to five years. Finally, disciplinary authorities deal with the most severe ethical lapses by disbarring the offending attorney. Disbarment strips the attorney of the right to practice law in the state in question. In some cases, attorneys so disbarred may seek reinstatement to the bar after a period of time, normally specified in the original disbarment order. Reinstatement depends on whether the attorney demonstrates that the offending conduct is not likely to be repeated.

In the late twentieth century the traditional sanctions of reprimand, suspension, and disbarment were supplemented with other sanctions designed to educate offending lawyers. For example, disciplinary authorities sometimes dismiss complaints against lawyers for relatively minor infractions if the lawyers agree to attend a continuing legal education program on the subject of attorney ethics. Sometimes the right to undertake the practice of law again after a suspension or disbarment is linked to this kind of requirement. In addition, disciplinary authorities may occasionally make readmission to the bar after disbarment contingent on an erring lawyer's passing all or part of the state bar exam.

Ethical Rules. Beginning early in the twentieth century national and state bar associations attempted to set forth principles of legal ethics that would guide the conduct of lawyers and provide a basis for disciplining wayward attorneys. In 1983 the American Bar Association (ABA) proposed a set of ethical rules called the Model Rules of Professional Conduct. Since the ABA does not itself have authority to establish standards for legal ethics in each state, the Model Rules were simply a uniform collection of ethical principles proposed for adoption by the various state supreme courts. In fact, most states subsequently enacted some version of the Model Rules as their own, although many states modified them in some respects. A few states still operate under a predecessor set of ethics rules proposed by the ABA in the 1970's called the Model Code of Professional Responsibility.

Rules of legal ethics, whether the Model Rules or the older Model Code, attempt to set forth ethical principles to guide lawyers in dealing with the various ethical problems that occur in the practice of law. They define the various obligations that lawyers owe their clients, the courts, and third parties. Violation of these rules, which touch on matters as various as the kinds of fees lawyers may charge and their obligation to disclose the misconduct of their fellow lawyers, is the chief basis for sanctions against lawyers.

Sanctions for Other Types of Unethical Conduct. In the main lawyers receive sanctions for unethical conduct committed in their role as attorneys. Occasionally, however, disciplinary authorities sanction lawyers for ethical infractions that are not committed in the context of legal practice. For example, a lawyer might be sanctioned after being convicted of embezzlement or tax evasion. Lawyers may also be sanctioned for unethical business conduct, even if the conduct does not occur in connection with their practice of law.

The modern view—reflected, for example, in the ABA's Model Rules of Professional Conduct—is that lawyers should be disciplined only for conduct outside the scope of their practice under certain circumstances. According to the ABA's Model Rules, some kinds of illegal or unethical conduct may not reflect adversely on lawyers' fitness to practice law. Thus, even though private moral infractions, such as adultery, might be a crime in particular jurisdictions, this infraction does not necessarily mean that an attorney who engages in this conduct lacks the characteristics necessary to practice law. On the other hand, criminal offenses involving violence, dishonesty, or interference with the administration of justice would reflect adversely on a lawyer's fitness to practice law.

Suggested Readings. Among the many books cataloging the unethical practices of lawyers and suggesting possible remedies are Jethro K. Lieberman's *Crisis at the Bar: Lawyers' Unethical Ethics and What to Do About It* (New York: W. W. Norton, 1978), Donald E. DeKieffer's *How Lawyers Screw Their Clients: And What You Can Do About It* (New York: Barricade Books, 1995), and David W. Marston's *Malice Aforethought: How Lawyers Use Our Secret Rules to Get Rich, Get Sex, Get Even . . . And Get Away With It* (New York: W. Morrow, 1991). The late twentieth century witnessed a spate of books seeking to divine the roots of ethical failure in the legal profession. These include *Betrayed Profession: Lawyering at the End of the Twentieth Century* by Sol M. Linowitz with Martin Mayer (New York: Charles Scribner's

Sons, 1994), and Anthony T. Kronman's *The Lost Lawyer: Failing Ideals of the Legal Profession* (Cambridge, Mass.: Harvard University Press, 1993).

—*Timothy L. Hall*

See also Attorney-client relationship; Attorney trust accounts; Code of Professional Responsibility; Conflicts of interest; Disqualification of attorneys; Ethics; Grievance committees for attorney discipline; Model Rules of Professional Conduct.

Uniform laws

In order to eliminate differences between the laws of the U.S. states and to expedite dealings among the states, a national movement was created to establish uniform state laws.

The uniform law movement began when the Alabama State Bar Association recognized in 1881 that significant but unnecessary legal problems were created by wide variations in state laws involving interstate transactions or the movement of persons from one state to another. For example, wills that were valid in one state might have been invalid in another and sellers might have required different forms of contracts depending on where buyers lived.

Creating Uniform Laws. In 1889 the American Bar Association (ABA) decided to work for "uniformity of the laws" in the forty-four states. Within a year the New York legislature authorized the governor of New York to appoint three commissioners to explore the best way to effect uniformity of law among states, and the American Bar Association endorsed New York's action. The result was the first meeting of the Conference of State Boards of Commissioners on Promoting Uniformity of Law in the United States in 1892. By 1912 every state had appointed uniform law commissioners to what was thereafter known as the National Conference of Commissioners on Uniform State Laws. The U.S. Virgin Islands was the last jurisdiction to join, appointing its first commission in 1988.

The National Conference is a nonprofit, unincorporated association composed of state commissions on uniform laws from each state, the District of Columbia, the Commonwealth of Puerto Rico, and the U.S. Virgin Islands. Each jurisdiction determines its methods of appointment and the number of commissioners. Most commissioners are appointed by the governors of their respective states or by the state legislatures. The one requirement for the more than three hundred uniform law commissioners is that they be members of the bar in their jurisdictions. Some commissioners serve as state legislators while most are practitioners and some are judges and law professors. They serve for specific terms and receive no compensation for their work with the National Conference. The National Conference is largely funded by state appropriations. Expenses are apportioned among the states by means of an assessment based on population size. However, the research and drafting expertise employed by the Conference is donated by its commissioners. Commissioners devote thousands of hours—amounting in some cases to millions of dollars worth of time—to the development of uniform acts.

Work of the National Conference. The state commissions come together as the National Conference for the purpose of studying and reviewing the laws of the states to determine which areas of the law should be uniform. The commissioners then draft and propose for enactment specific statutes in areas of the law in which uniformity among the states is desirable. The National Conference can only suggest; no proposed statute is effective until a state legislature adopts it.

Since its founding, the National Conference has drafted more than two hundred uniform statutes on numerous subjects and in various fields of law, setting a uniform pattern for these subjects across the country. Uniform acts include the Uniform Probate Code, which protects the property of deceased persons; the Uniform Partnership Act, which is the basic law for a common form of doing business; and the Uniform Enforcement of Foreign Judgments Act, which ensures that court decisions in one state are recognized in another. In 1940 the National Conference turned to one of its most important efforts: offering comprehensive legal solutions to major commercial problems, resulting in the Uniform Commercial Code (UCC). The Uniform Commercial Code governs transactions involving the sale, lease, or financing of goods; negotiable instruments such as checks, promissory notes, and other methods of making payment; and letters of credit and transactions in securities. In short, the Code regulates matters essential to the economic development and well-being of the United States.

How Uniform Laws Are Developed. Each uniform law takes at least several years to develop. The process starts with a committee of the National Conference that investigates each proposed act and then reports to the Executive Committee of the Conference as to whether the subject warrants a draft uniform law. If the Executive Committee approves the proposal, a drafting committee of commissioners is appointed. Drafting committees meet throughout the year. Tentative drafts are not submitted to the entire National Conference until they have received extensive committee consideration. Drafting committees are assisted in their work by reporters, experts on the subject at hand who are usually appointed from academia, advisors from the American Bar Association, and observers from interested groups and organizations. Advisors and observers test the proposed statutes' workability under concrete circumstances so that they may aid the committees in drafting realistic, as opposed to theoretical, statutory rules. The process involves formulating a uniform consensus from collective experience on a national scale.

Draft acts are then submitted for initial debate to the entire National Conference at annual meetings. Each act must be considered section by section at not less than two annual meetings by all commissioners sitting as a Committee of the Whole. Once the Committee of the Whole approves an act, the act's final test is a vote by the jurisdictions in the National Conference. A majority of the jurisdictions present and no less than twenty jurisdictions must approve acts before they can be officially adopted as Uniform Acts.

At that point, a Uniform Act is officially promulgated for consideration by the states, the District of Columbia, Puerto Rico, and the U.S. Virgin Islands. Legislatures are urged to adopt Uniform Acts as written in order to "promote uniformity in law among the several states." Since each act has benefited from the extensive input by commissioners from each jurisdiction and often by suggestions from interested organizations or groups from different parts of the country, further tailoring is seldom necessary or desirable to accommodate the particular circumstances of individual states. The process by which Uniform Acts are proposed, drafted, and ultimately promulgated is designed to produce statutes that can be enacted without local variations.

When the drafting of such acts is completed, the commissioners are obligated to advocate their adoption in their home states. Normal resistance to anything "new" makes this a hard part of commissioners' job. However, the result is workable modern state law that helps keep the federal system alive.

The Importance of Uniform Laws. Uniform state laws simplify the legal life of businesses and individuals by providing rules and procedures that are consistent from state to state. Representing state governments and the legal profession, the National Conference of Commissioners on Uniform State Laws is a genuine confederation of state interests. It has sought to bring uniformity to the divergent legal traditions of fifty-three sovereign jurisdictions and has done so with significant success—so much success, in fact, that federal agencies have adopted proposals of the National Conference for federal regulations. Moreover, an executive branch white paper and the U.S. Congress have cited, and relied on, the work of the National Conference.

Suggested Readings. The definitive work on the National Conference of Commissioners on Uniform State Laws is by Walter Armstrong, *A Centennial History of the National Conference of Commissioners on Uniform State Laws* (Saint Paul, Minn.: West Publishing, 1991). Various uniform laws, such as the Uniform Commercial Code, are discussed in the American Bar Association's *Family Legal Guide* (Times Books, 1994).   —*Fred H. Miller*

See also Commercial litigation; Partnerships; Probate; Statute.

Unwed parents and rights of children

Laws pertaining to the rights of children of unwed parents vary widely from state to state, but children are generally entitled to visitation with and support from both biological parents.

A child may be born to unwed parents through a variety of circumstances: The father may not be free to marry the mother, the child may be conceived through rape or a chance encounter, either or both parents may be unwilling to marry the other, an unwed person may adopt a child, a child may be adopted or born to parents in a homosexual relationship, or a single woman may choose to conceive by donor insemination. Varying circumstances present different issues for parents.

There is no single standard of parents' responsibilities and rights in the United States. Laws vary from state to state, change in response to the changing definition of family, and can be interpreted in various ways by different judges. In most states, all biological fathers have the same rights, whether or not the parents are married. In all states, however, children have a right to visitation and financial support from each parent. A birth mother thus faces several issues when deciding to have a child without marrying the father.

Child Support and Visitation. If the father is aware of the child and acknowledges paternity, he can be required to pay child support, even if he and the mother have a written contract agreeing that he will not. If a parent later wants to collect child support from the noncustodial parent, state and federal governments provide parent locator services specifically for this purpose. (These cannot be used to collect alimony or other debts.) If the mother applies for public assistance, the state requires her to name the father and to seek to locate him in order to obtain child support from him. In addition, a 1992 federal law made it a felony for a parent to cross state lines to avoid paying child support. A signed contract between the parents, in which either parent waives child support, may be overturned in court if a judge rules that such support is in the child's best interest.

The noncustodial parent can demand visitation rights to see the child even if the parents have a written contract stipulating that the noncustodial parent has waived such rights. Since visitation is a right of the child, this generally will be granted, unless it can be proven that the noncustodial parent is a danger to the child. Even then, the noncustodial parent may be allowed to see the child if visits are supervised. If a mother tries to hide the existence of a child from the father, who later learns of it, a blood test establishing his paternity can override her efforts to keep him from participating in their child's life. Establishing paternity, however, can provide the child with health benefits, benefits related to a parent's service in the armed forces, and inheritance rights.

Legal experts often advise unwed parents to draft a contract defining a parenting plan, including their agreement on issues of visitation and child support, and to have this contract reviewed by an attorney. Although such a contract is not a binding agreement, if one parent later attempts to change the agreement, the court may take it into consideration when rendering a decision.

Donor Insemination. When a child is conceived through donor insemination, a contract is generally signed negating the donor's legal rights and responsibilities. In many states, a donor can be denied all rights to a child only if insemination was performed by a doctor and the mother was married to someone other than the donor. In the past, agencies usually destroyed information on donors, both to protect them from being sued for child support and to protect mothers' right to sole custody. More recently, however, many agencies have begun to keep records of donors' medical history for the child's later use. A small number of sperm banks have begun asking donors if they will allow children they have fathered to contact them when they have reached the age of majority. When a woman works with such a sperm bank, it is to her advantage to have such a contract reviewed by an attorney to ensure that her privacy and that of her child is protected.

Estates and Inheritances. An unwed parent of either sex needs to consider the question of estate planning. If one parent dies without having named a legal guardian for the child and an executor for the estate, the remaining biological parent generally is named the child's guardian and also has access to the child's inheritance.

On the other hand, in many states a mother cannot put a man's name on a child's birth certificate as the father unless the father is present at the time or has given his written consent. When no father is specified on the birth certificate, the father's name reads "unknown" or, if donor insemination was used, "anonymous donor." It is important that the mother consider what others will think when they read the child's birth certificate, which will be part of the child's public record for life.

The inheritance rights of children born to unwed parents are somewhat complex. A woman's child is her heir and will inherit from her if there is no will. However, if she has a will, the child must be mentioned by name to inherit. If paternity has been established, a child can inherit from the father if he has no will or if there is a will that refers to a "child" or "children." However, in many states children born out of wedlock cannot inherit from their grandparents unless they are specifically named in the will.

Suggested Readings. A clearly written and comprehensive book on legal matters affecting unwed (as well as divorced and separated) parents is Mimi E. Lyster's *Child Custody: Building Parenting Agreements That Work* (2d ed. Berkeley, Calif.: Nolo Press, 1996). It discusses parenting agreements, negotiating with the other parent, mediation and arbitration, and changes to agreements. It also includes information specific to a variety of nontraditional families and a chapter on federal and state laws on custody and visitation, with simple tables showing the main provisions in various states. Many books aimed at single mothers contain information that is also useful to unwed fathers. *Two of Us Make a World* by Prudence and Sherill Tippins (New York: Henry Holt, 1996) provides sample donor and coparenting agreements, a list of state child-support enforcement offices, recommended reading, and resources for single parents (mainly mothers). *Single Mothers by Choice* by Jane Mattes (New York: Random House, 1994) lists sperm banks that work with single women, adoption resources for single parents, and support groups, providing examples of two types of agreements with a known donor.

—*Irene Struthers Rush*

See also Adopted children's rights; Child abduction by parents; Child custody and support; Children's rights; Common-law marriage; Family law practice; Grandparents' rights; Parental responsibility for children; Paternity.

Usury

Charging a rate of interest on a loan in excess of a state's usury limit may lead to a legal determination that the loan is void.

In general terms, usury is the exaction of a rate of interest on a loan in excess of the amount allowed by law. Many states have enacted statutes regulating the percentage of interest that may be legally charged for the use of money. These statutes generally prohibit the taking of an amount of interest beyond the legal rate set in the statute. The harsh result of charging an excessive rate of interest is often the voiding of the loan entirely. This means that the person who has borrowed the money need not repay the balance on the loan and that the person who has lent it at a usurious interest rate goes unpaid. Finding this windfall to the borrower repugnant, some courts have ruled that the loan be "remade" at a rate of interest below that set in the usury statute.

Usury statutes are promulgated with a humanitarian purpose in mind by virtue of the police power that states may exercise for the protection of the public interest. Recognizing that borrowers are often powerless to resist the interest rates charged by moneylenders, legislatures pass usury statutes to protect needy borrowers. Although some legislators are uncomfortable about interfering in private contracts, statutory limits on the rate of interest a lender of money can charge are needed to protect borrowers from unconscionable moneylenders.

National banks are also covered by usury statutes. As a part of the general regulations governing banks, the National Bank Act (1863) prohibits national banks from charging or receiving usurious interest rates. This rate is generally determined by the greater of either the usury rate set by statute in the state in which the bank is located or at the rate in effect at the Federal Reserve Bank in the Federal Reserve District where the national bank is located. The consequences facing national banks that charge unlawful interest are set forth in the National Bank Act. This law provides for the forfeiture of the entire interest that has been agreed upon or, if the interest has already been paid, liability for double the amount of the interest paid.

In an attempt to provide national uniformity in the way states deal with usury and consumer credit issues, the National Conference of Commissioners on Uniform State Laws drafted the Uniform Consumer Credit Code (UCCC) in 1968. The UCCC is a comprehensive consumer credit protection act providing disclosure requirements, a ceiling on finance charges for consumer credit transactions, restrictions on creditors' rights, and the protection of buyers' and debtors' rights. One stated purpose of the UCCC is to simplify and modernize the laws governing retail installment sales, consumer credit, small loans, and usury. The law is designed to replace existing usury laws. Although states have the option of adopting the UCCC in whole or in part, a major benefit of national adoption would be uniform law and administrative rules in the areas of consumer credit and usury.

—*Helene Korbin*

See also Banking law; Consumer protection laws; Credit, consumer; Credit cards; Loans, personal.

V

Vagrancy

Vagrancy is a minor criminal charge with many different and often vague definitions, but generally it is aimed at pushing away "undesirable" persons from a community or otherwise controlling them.

Vagrancy laws, first enacted in fourteenth century England, made it a crime for serfs to wander from the feudal estates to which they were bonded. Since then the definition has become increasingly varied. In the United States vagrancy statutes have used as many as thirty different definitions, including status definitions that characterize persons as "rogues" and "drunkards," noncriminal conduct definitions that describe such behavior as "being idle" and "wandering," and criminal conduct definitions that describe such activities as "engaging in prostitution" or "gambling." Some of the more interesting definitions characterize persons as "jugglers," "pipers," "fiddlers," "habitual loafers," and "those frequenting places where alcoholic beverages are served." Those who have created vagrancy statutes have argued that the "wandering poor" must be controlled, that moral threats to the community must be repelled, and that socially acceptable work must be promoted. Such statutes have been criticized because they have been used to control and punish former slaves and striking workers and because they are effective in continually pushing "undesirables" from one community to another.

The crime of vagrancy is a minor offense, usually termed a misdemeanor or petty misdemeanor, which authorizes a fine or short jail term. It is often enforced through informal punishment, involving the arrest and jailing of vagrants and releasing them without charges the following day. For this reason, legal appeals have seldom been filed in vagrancy cases. In addition, vagrancy defendants are usually unable to afford legal counsel, while appeals expire due to short jail sentences. Some vagrancy statutes and the arrests based on those statutes have, however, been effectively challenged as violating constitutional protections. These legal challenges have led several states to drop their vagrancy laws or to develop more specific antiloitering or antibegging statutes.

There are several primary ways one might legally challenge an arrest or conviction for vagrancy, depending on the specific definition of vagrancy in force. A statute might be unconstitutionally vague because the definition does not inform a reasonable person what actions might be seen as criminal, such as acting in a lewd or wanton manner. A statute might be unconstitutionally arbitrary if it allows different police officers to formulate their own different definitions of what constitutes a crime. A statute might permit an improper exercise of police power by a local jurisdiction because it criminalizes an act or status that should not be criminalized. For example, some courts have said that merely because persons are addicted to gambling or alcohol does not provide a basis for criminalizing them. A vagrancy statute might also violate equal protection guarantees as well as prohibitions against slavery by forcing only poor people, but not rich people, to work. While some courts have found specific vagrancy statutes unconstitutional, in many cases other courts in different jurisdictions have ruled that similar vagrancy statutes are valid.

—*Peter Gregware*

See also Disorderly conduct; Loitering; Moral turpitude; Prostitution; Public nuisance.

Vandalism

Acts of the destruction of property such as breaking windows, damaging vehicles, or spray painting buses are all examples of the offense of vandalism.

Vandalism was previously punished by the crime of malicious mischief. To constitute vandalism the

Desecration of a cemetery is a form of vandalism. (James L. Shaffer)

property injured or destroyed had to be the property of another. States and municipalities have enacted a large number of statutes to curb vandalism. In many jurisdictions schools have an obligation to report any act of physical violence, trespass, vandalism, or property damage that occurs on school property. Many states provide that parents are vicariously responsible for the vandalism of an unemancipated minor. The purpose of this regulation is to control delinquent behavior or to compensate the victims of that behavior. Such statutes have been upheld on the grounds that they bear a rational relationship to the preservation and promotion of the public welfare.

A growing number of cities forbid the possession of spray paint in public buildings or facilities. In Minnesota a person may not deface, mar, or vandalize a sign or line marking the location of a pipeline. It is unlawful for any person to willfully break, carve upon, or harm the surfaces of caves in North Carolina. A growing number of jurisdictions have passed antivandalism statutes to combat a rising tide of hate crimes against persons, institutions, and property. The institutional vandalism statute of Illinois provides that a person may be punished for vandalism growing out of racial, color, creed, or religious bias. Vandalism is a crime increasingly associated with urban gang activities.

—*Michael L. Rustad*

See also Criminal law; Disorderly conduct; Graffiti; Hate crime statutes; Juvenile delinquency; Public nuisance; School law.

Vehicle licenses and registration

Before persons can legally drive motor vehicles, they must register them in the state in which they live and procure a license for them, which must be prominently displayed.

A vehicle is defined as a self-propelled unit that does not run on rails. Automobiles and trucks are primary examples. There are approximately 165 million registered automobiles in the United States. The total number of automobiles, trucks, motorcycles, motor homes, and off-road vehicles that travel the roads of the United States is enormous.

The registration of motor vehicles acknowledges ownership. In addition, registration and license fees are a sizable revenue source for states. Registration and licensing are state functions under the direction of the secretary of state, Department of Motor Vehicles, or similarly named office. A vehicle license is required by law before one can legally operate a motor vehicle. Possession of a registration certificate is proof that drivers or their designated alternates have the authority to operate the vehicle. Qualification varies from state to state and with the type of license. Vehicle registration is required at the time of vehicle purchase and must be available upon request to verify proof of ownership. Registration verification is necessary for renewal of a driver's license and the transfer of vehicle ownership to another party. Evidence of registration must be carried in the vehicle and a valid license plate must be attached to the outside, upon which tags are affixed showing current compliance. Each state designs its own license plate and, for an additional fee, personalized license plates may be purchased by drivers.

Vehicles owned and operated by the federal government, including military vehicles, have their own license plate designations. Likewise, vehicles owned by state and local governments have license plates especially designed for them. These are intended for such entities as state and local law-enforcement agencies, principal government officials, state governors, and city managers.

Drivers with special needs are identified by specific logos on their vehicle license plates. This is especially true of drivers with disabilities. The symbol of a wheelchair or other appropriate symbol indicates that a person may require special consideration—for example, the right to park in handicapped spaces nearest the entrances to public buildings and shopping centers.

In order to protect the environment, some states require that motor vehicles be inspected before registration is possible. Such inspections are generally performed by private auto workshops that issue a statement indicating that the vehicle has met the emission requirements set forth by the state and allowing the vehicle to be registered. Commercial vehicles, those used by businesses for transporting people or goods, require special registration procedures and fees. This category of vehicle includes trucks, buses, limousines, and trailers. The fee for these vehicles is generally determined by their weight and is higher for heavier vehicles.

—*Gordon A. Parker*

See also Automobile purchasing; Driving licenses; Personal property; Title.

Venue, change of

Moving of a trial to another district is known as change of venue.

"Venue" is defined as the place where a trial is held and the area from which citizens are to be selected as jurors. Both Article III of the U.S. Constitution and the Sixth Amendment require that a trial be held in "the State and district wherein the crime shall have been committed." In most states the "district" is usually the county where the crime was committed or, in civil cases, the place where the defendant resides. Federal courts are divided into judicial districts, which may cover a whole state or a portion of a state.

Change of venue requests are sometimes granted if the defendant can show that there is evidence of racial prejudice or the existence of a prejudicial atmosphere within a district that would make it unlikely that an impartial jury could be selected. Most requests, however, are the result of adverse pretrial publicity that jeopardizes a defendant's right to a fair trial. For example, in *Irvin v. Dowd* (1961) the U.S. Supreme Court ordered a new trial in a different district for a convicted mass murderer in Indiana on the grounds that extensive pretrial media coverage made it impossible to select an impartial jury that was not aware of the facts of the case and had not formed an opinion about the defendant's guilt.

—*Raymond Frey*

See also Juries; Jurisdiction; Trial publicity; Trials.

Verdict

The formal decision or finding made by a jury upon matters of fact submitted to them for deliberation and determination is known as a verdict.

In legal cases the court interprets the applicable law associated with a given case and explains the law to the jury. Based on the presented evidence the jury must determine the facts in the case and make a proper application of the law relating to those facts to arrive at a verdict. In general, the jury's verdict must be unanimous, but many states have modified the condition of unanimity, particularly in civil cases, so that the verdict can be rendered by a designated majority of the jury.

Verdicts may be either general or specific. A general verdict is that in which the jury pronounces "guilty" or "not guilty" and thus decides whether the plaintiff or the defendant wins the case. A general verdict is the verdict most often rendered in criminal cases. Moreover, in criminal cases the verdict must generally be unanimous and must be returned by the jury to the judge in open court. This verdict is based on every material fact submitted for the consideration of the jury. The court may also submit to the jury appropriate forms for a general verdict and, in some cases, a list of written questions concerning one or more of the relevant issues to the case that must be answered in the process of determining the verdict.

When the jury is asked by the court to answer specific questions of fact but leaves any decisions based on the law to the court, it is called a special verdict. The court often requires that the jury return a special verdict in the form of a special written finding upon each issue of fact, and the court determines if the defendant is guilty or not based on those answers. Civil cases may be decided by either a general or a special verdict.

When the verdict is presented in court, the defendant and all the jury members must be present. In most jurisdictions, the plaintiff or the defendant has the right to have the jury polled. If polled, each jury member is asked if the stated verdict is the one he or she favored. The verdict will not stand if the required number of jurors does not answer this question in the affirmative.

When the evidence conclusively dictates a clear verdict in favor of one of the litigants, the judge has the authority in many states to direct the jury to render a verdict in favor of either the plaintiff or the defendant. If it is evident to the court that a verdict is against the weight of the evidence, the court may order a new trial. However, in criminal cases, a verdict of acquittal is conclusive upon the prosecution (the state) so that the defendant will not be subjected to double jeopardy. However, in the event that the jury cannot reach a verdict, the defendant may be tried again.   —*Alvin K. Benson*

See also Acquittal; Conviction; Defendant; Directed verdict; Double jeopardy; Juries; Reasonable doubt; Testimony; Trials.

Victims' rights

In the 1980's and 1990's a growing concern with the rights of crime victims—in contrast to the more traditional concern with the rights of defendants—led to victims' rights legislation and programs at the state and federal levels.

The American criminal justice system has traditionally been concerned with ensuring the rights of defendants. Although justice is the ultimate objective, a number of legal provisions and procedures work to ensure that basic rights are afforded to the accused, even when the protection of such rights prevents speedy trials or conclusive decisions. For example, the exclusionary rule forbids the introduction of evidence that was obtained illegally, even when that evidence could conclusively prove a defendant's guilt. Increasing concern about crime rates and societal decline eventually caused such scrupulous attention to procedural over substantive justice to fall out of public favor.

The Victims' Rights Movement. Beginning in the 1980's a burgeoning victims' rights movement called attention to what it described as an "imbalanced system" that was more concerned with the rights of criminals than the rights of victims. The victims' rights movement argued that by focusing on justice for defendants and society at large the criminal justice system overlooks the emotional, legal, and physical needs of crime victims. Victims' rights organizations began to advocate a range of legal reforms and social programs to redress this presumed imbalance.

Although the victims' rights movement draws upon both conservative and liberal political values, it was greatly aided by the tough anticrime climate of Ronald Reagan's presidency. One of the most politically powerful organizations to promote victims' rights has been Mothers Against Drunk Driving (MADD), which is especially concerned with the rights of persons who have been injured by a drunk driver or who have lost a family member to a fatal drunk driving accident. Other victims' rights organizations have been concerned with different types of crimes. Many feminist groups have argued that the criminal justice system essentially "victimizes" rape victims a second time when they are required to recount their ordeals to skeptical police officers or insensitive judges. Some groups have been concerned with the rights of victims to be made aware of the imminent parole or release of their attackers. And still others have focused on the right of victims to be compensated for the physical and emotional injuries they sustain.

The victims' rights movement became enormously popular in the 1980's and 1990's. Public concern about violent crime was heightened by a number of dramatic incidents, including several well-publicized rapes and murders of young girls, the beating of a truck driver in Los Angeles during the riots that followed the first Rodney King trial, and the bombing of a federal building in Oklahoma City. Most indicators revealed that violent crime was actually declining in the United States, but public sensitivity to the issue created a political environment ripe for a "tough-on-crime" approach. Republican presidents Reagan and George Bush were able to capitalize on this mood, as were a number of Republican Congressional candidates who managed to secure a majority for their party in the House of Representatives in 1994.

Although Bush was defeated by Democrat Bill Clinton in 1992, this did not represent a blow to the anticrime and provictims' movements. Indeed, Clinton picked up these causes with vigor. For example, he proclaimed a National Crime Victims' Rights Week in April 1997 and made tougher criminal penalties a centerpiece of his social policies. In the 1990's the issue of victims' rights had become truly bipartisan, with both parties striving to demonstrate their sympathies for victims of crime.

As the victims' rights movement gathered momentum in the 1990's, its focus occasionally extended beyond the safety and fair treatment of crime victims. For example, the movement also became concerned with retribution as a "right" due to victims. Along these lines, some groups and legislators have worked to guarantee the right of families of murder victims to be present at the executions of the convicted killers. Some hitherto unsuccessful legislative proposals have fought for the right of such family members to physically cause the death sentence to be carried out by flipping a switch or other mechanism.

Although such extreme proposals have generally been deemed unnecessarily vengeful, a number of somewhat less controversial laws and programs have been established to promote victims' rights. These generally fall into two broad categories: victim assistance programs and victims' "bills of rights."

Victim Assistance Programs. The first victim assistance programs in the United States were created in the early 1970's. They tended to be located in large urban areas and focused primarily on sexual assault of women. These programs offered limited support services to women to whom the criminal justice system might seem intimidating and insensitive. Since that time, victim assistance programs have expanded in number and scope. By the 1990's victims programs were in place throughout the country, addressing not only victims of sexual assault but also child abuse, spousal battery, and other violent crimes.

Victim assistance programs typically offer services in three general areas: counseling and support, legal assistance, and public awareness and legislative reform. Counseling and support are perhaps the most common functions, helping victims to cope with post-traumatic stress disorder, rape trauma syndrome, and other conditions caused by assaults. Individual and group counseling, crisis intervention, medical referrals, and relocation services are some of the resources typically available. Programs also offer legal assistance to crime victims who testify, seek restraining orders, or otherwise face the criminal justice system. Services include orientation to the justice system and courtroom assistance. Finally, victim assistance services act as advocates for crime victims generally, raising public awareness of certain crimes and how to prevent them and advocating legislative reforms.

The federal government has promoted victim assistance programs through legislation and funding. The Federal Law Enforcement Assistance Administration funded the creation of model victim assistance programs in 1974. The Federal Victim and Witness Protection Act of 1982 established "fair treatment standards" for victims and witnesses of crimes. In that same year, President Reagan convened a Task Force on Victims of Crime. Two years later the Victims of Crime Act (VOCA) established a fund that provides grants to states to compensate crime victims and to state and local programs that provide direct assistance to crime victims and their families. In 1994 the Violent Crime Control and Law Enforcement Act augmented the VOCA fund and authorized funding of over $1 billion for fighting violence against women.

National nongovernmental organizations have also been established for promoting victims rights and victim assistance. Two advocacy groups were created: the National Organization for Victim Assistance (NOVA) in 1975 and the Victims' Assistance Legal Organization (VALOR) in 1981. In 1985 the National Victim Center was established to help promote the rights and needs of crime victims by working with thousands of local criminal justice and victim service organizations around the country.

Victims' Bills of Rights. Governmental efforts to bolster the rights of crime victims proliferated in the 1990's. In 1990 the U.S. Congress passed the Victims Rights and Restitution Act, commonly known as the Victims' Bill of Rights. This act focused on the right of crime victims to be present at the court proceedings against their alleged attackers and to be informed of the subsequent sentencing, incarceration, and parole or release of the convicted perpetrators. The U.S. Congress later enacted a number of other protections for crime victims, including legislation that required restitution payments.

The victims' rights movement has also sought to ensure the protection of victims' rights through constitutional amendments. As of the 1996 elections, twenty-nine states had amended their constitutions to include specific guarantees for crime victims. These "victims' bills of rights," as they are often called, guarantee persons certain legal rights, judicial standards, respect for privacy, and access to information. Most victims' bills of rights were approved by state voters by large margins. Nevertheless, despite their overwhelming popularity, some legal scholars and civil rights organizations have called such constitutional amendments an inappropriate and problematic means for addressing a complex societal issue. Some specific victims' rights amendments have been challenged as unconstitutional.

Notwithstanding such concerns, a bipartisan effort to enshrine victims' rights in the U.S. Constitution was launched in 1996 by Democratic senator Dianne Feinstein of California and Republican senator Jon Kyl of Arizona. Their Crime Victims Bill of Rights was supported by President Bill Clinton and his Republican opponent Bob Dole. The proposed constitutional amendment would guarantee a number of rights to victims of violent crime: the right to an order of financial restitution, the right to a speedy trial, the right to register objection to a proposed sentence or plea bargain, the right to attend the alleged perpetrator's trial and parole hearings, and the right to be apprised of the transfer, release, or escape of the convicted attacker.

Despite the proposed amendment's wide support, the legislation remained stalled in the Senate Judiciary Committee as of early 1998. Some speculated that it could again become a salient issue with the approach of the fall congressional elections. Others sought to continue promoting victims' rights through federal statutes.

Victims' Rights and Criminal Justice. The efforts to ensure victims' rights in the 1990's represented a shift away from the traditional focus in American jurisprudence on the rights of the accused and the convicted. The U.S. Constitution and legal system were founded on suspicions toward the powers of the state. Once a crime has been perpetrated, the criminal justice system has thus been more concerned with protecting individuals against the state than with the treatment of the victims. While few object to the desirability of evincing more compassion and sensitivity toward crime victims, the efforts to guarantee victims' rights through constitutional and statutory amendments raise difficult questions about jurisprudence and public policy. The quest for justice involves an uneasy balance among competing demands for societal order, governmental authority, individual liberty, equality under the law, penance, and humane treatment. The notion of victims' rights represents one side of that multifaceted concept.

Suggested Readings. A general treatment of victims' rights is provided in Debra J. Wilson's *The Complete Book of Victims' Rights* (Highlands Ranch, Colo.: ProSe Associates, 1995). A layperson's explanation of relevant legal issues is the focus of Margaret C. Jasper's *Victim's Rights Law* (Dobbs Ferry, N.Y.: Oceana, 1997). Leigh Glenn has produced a resource guide on victims' rights entitled *Victims' Rights: A Reference Handbook* (Santa Barbara, Calif.: ABC-Clio, 1997). The U.S. Department of Justice has put out a more specialized publication outlining the rights of victims of domestic violence. See *Know Your Rights: A Victim's Guide to the Domestic Violence Justice System* (Washington, D.C.: U.S. Department of Justice, 1997). For an overview of the victims' rights movement and its efforts to secure a victims' rights amendment see Kelly McMurry's "Victims' Rights Movement Rises to Power," *Trial* 33 (July, 1997). For a critique of the victims' rights amendment see Bruce Shapiro's "Victims and Vengeance: Why the Victims' Rights Amendment Is a Bad Idea," *The Nation* 264 (February 10, 1997). Eric Schlosser provides a detailed and hard-hitting case study of the emotions and thoughts of parents of murdered children and examines general issues of victims' rights and related policy issues. See "A Grief Like No Other," *The Atlantic Monthly* 280 (September, 1997). —*Steve D. Boilard*

See also Civil rights and liberties; Constitution, U.S.; Criminal justice system.

Visas, foreign

Permits required by U.S. citizens traveling to foreign countries are known as visas.

A visa is an official endorsement or stamp, usually placed in a passport, indicating that an officer of the nation to be visited has granted the traveler permission to enter. Few countries required visas or passports before the era of the two World Wars, when nationalistic animosities and suspicions of refugees motivated restrictions on visitors. How-

---

Entry Requirements for U.S. Visitors to Selected Countries

Caribbean and Latin America

Antigua and Barbuda: For stay of up to six months proof of U.S. citizenship and picture identification required, also return or onward transportation ticket

Argentina: Passport required but no visa needed for tourist stay of up to ninety days

Costa Rica: Passport or original U.S. birth certificate and photo identification and onward/return ticket required; tourist card for stay of up to ninety days issued at airport on arrival

Jamaica: Passport or original birth certificate and photo identification, onward/return ticket, and proof of sufficient funds required

Europe

France, Germany, and Italy: Passport required but no visa needed for stay of up to ninety days

Great Britain: Passport required but no visa for stay of up to six months

Poland: Passport valid for at least twelve months past date of entry required; no visa needed for stay of up to ninety days

Russia: Passport required; tourist visa requires three photos, confirmation from tourist agency in Russia, and visa processing fee

Asia and Africa

China: Passport and visa required. Transit visa required for stopping in China, even if traveler does not exit the plane or train; business travelers are required to obtain formal invitation from Chinese business contact

Egypt: Passport and visa required; tourist visa valid for three months, requires fee, one photo, and prepaid envelope for return of passport by certified mail

Israel: Passport, onward/return ticket, and proof of sufficient funds required; tourist visa valid for three months issued on arrival; requires two photos

Kenya: Passport and visa required; visa good for six months must be obtained in advance

South Africa: Passport required; tourist visa not required for stay of up to ninety days

---

Source: U.S. Department of State, "Foreign Entry Requirements," March, 1998.

ever, in the last half of the twentieth century, recognition of the economic benefits of tourism led to efforts to relax and simplify travel regulations. Foreign visas are normally issued by consulates located in major cities across the United States. Some countries, particularly those interested in attracting American tourists, delegate the task of issuing visas to travel offices or may even eliminate such formalities for short-term visitors.

Types of Visas. There are three main types of visas: diplomatic, official, and ordinary. Diplomatic visas identify holders as members of the diplomatic service, by custom exempt from the jurisdiction of the laws of the country to which they are assigned. Official visas identify government officers as deserving of special attention when traveling on official business. Ordinary visas cover a variety of situations. They may be temporary visitor's visas, granting permission to persons to enter and remain in a country for a few weeks or months, transient visas, permitting holders to remain only for as long as it takes to travel to their next destination, or student visas, valid only during the time the holders are in school. Some visas permit holders to work and live indefinitely in a country, while others specifically provide for immigrant status that enables persons to become naturalized citizens.

Visas as a Means of Control. Requiring entry visas and insisting on detailed application forms permits countries to screen out visitors they deem undesirable. Some countries also require exit visas for both foreigners and their own nationals, providing yet more barriers to travel.

Arab countries can be especially strict. Saudi Arabia does not grant tourist visas and at times has made it difficult for business and family visitors to receive exit permits.

During the Cold War, Communist-controlled countries and the United States used visa requirements to bar unwanted people and ideas. The Soviet Union and its satellites utilized entry visas to insulate their people from potentially subversive ideas and refused exit visas to dissidents, preventing them from leaving the country and contradicting the official propaganda positions of the state. The United States refused to grant visitor visas to people accused of having communist sympathies, even when they had been invited

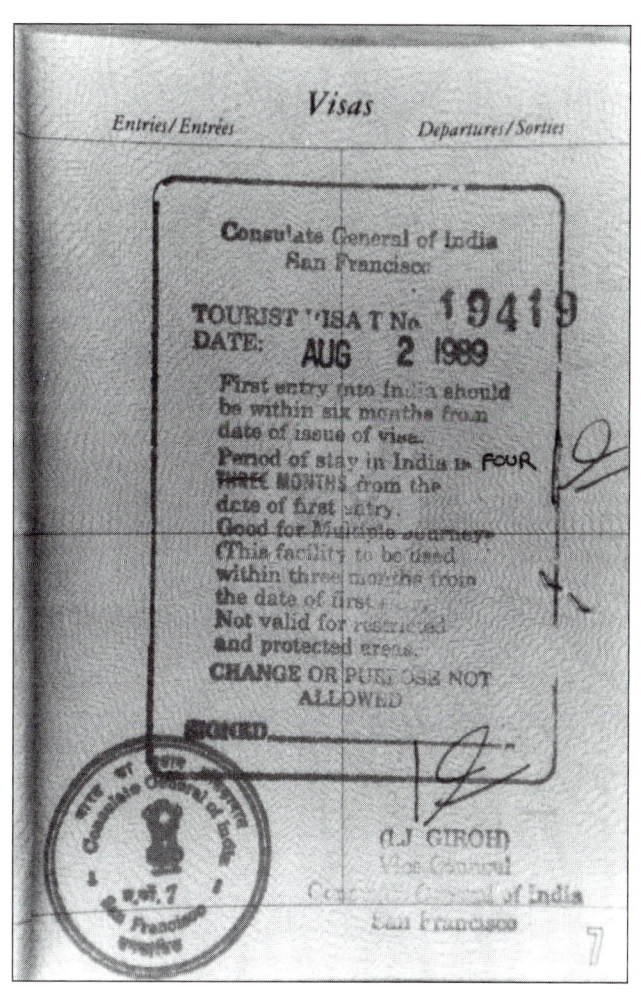

Indian visa stamped inside a U.S. passport. Most nations require visitors to carry passports bearing valid visas before they will admit them. (Ben Klaffke)

by U.S. organizations interested in hearing their views.

Provisions to Encourage Tourists. Countries in North and South America and in Western Europe have relatively simple procedures for U.S. citizens coming for short visits. Simplest of all are provisions for travel to Canada and Mexico. Persons making trips to Mexico for less than seventy-two hours that do not take them more than twenty kilometers beyond the border are not required to obtain entry permits. Tourist cards for stays of up to 180 days are easily available on proof of U.S. citizenship either with a passport or with a birth certificate and identification card containing a photograph. Canada formally asks for proof of citizenship for visits of up to 180 days, but tourists are more likely to need documents when reentering the United States from Canada than when going to Canada from the United States.

Few countries in the Caribbean require either visas or passports; proof of U.S. citizenship and a photo identification are sufficient. However, the State Department advises that passports, which have a photograph of the holder attached by the department, are the best possible identification. For example, cashing traveler's checks is always easier with a passport.

Most countries in Latin America and Western Europe still require passports as evidence of U.S. citizenship but waive the need for entry or exit visas. The movement to eliminate border controls between countries in the European Union further eases American travel on the continent. In contrast, Russia and some Asian and African countries require visas and insist on complicated formalities before issuing them.

As foreign entry regulations change on short notice, the State Department urges all travelers to check with the embassies or tourist offices of countries they wish to visit in order to be abreast of the latest provisions.

Suggested Readings. The State Department pamphlet "Foreign Entry Requirements," updated annually and also available on the department's Internet website http://travel.state.gov, is a thorough survey of foreign visa requirements. It is reprinted along with other government publications on travel in Gladson I. Nwanna's *Americans Traveling Abroad: What You Should Know Before You Go* (Baltimore, Md.: World Travel Institute Press, 1994). B. Sen's *A Diplomat's Handbook of International Law and Practice* (3d ed. Dordrecht, the Netherlands: Martinus Nijhoff, 1988) briefly examines the general principles of international law affecting the issuance of visas, while Graham H. Stuart's *American Diplomatic and Consular Practice* (2d ed. New York: Appleton-Century-Crofts, 1952) examines U.S. procedures. José D. Inglés's *Study of Discrimination in Respect of the Right of Everyone to Leave Any Country, Including His Own, and to Return to His Country* (New York: United Nations, 1963) describes how visa and passport requirements limit the ability of people to pursue what the United Nations has declared as the human right to travel. —*Milton Berman*

See also Canadian law; Foreign travel; Mexican travel; Passports; Visas, U.S.

Visas, U.S.

A visa issued by a U.S. consular officer is usually required of a noncitizen as a condition of entry into the United States.

United States immigration law provides a double buffer restricting noncitizen admission to the United States. With few exceptions, noncitizens must obtain visas issued by consular officers, State Department officials working in the noncitizens' countries. Without a visa, most noncitizens are summarily excluded from the United States by the Immigration and Naturalization Service (INS), a branch of the Justice Department. Even if noncitizens have visas, the INS can still deny them entry based on the INS's assessment of their eligibility to enter the United States. A visa is a travel document allowing noncitizens to travel to the United States and present themselves for admission. Although usually necessary for entry, it does not guarantee entry.

State Department consular officers issue two basic types of visas: immigrant visas, for those persons coming to the United States to become permanent resident aliens, and nonimmigrant visas, for those who plan to come to the United States temporarily for pleasure, work, or study. Most immigrant visas are distributed to persons who have family ties to persons in the United States and to persons who possess job skills needed by U.S. employers. Out of approximately 675,000 immigrant slots each year, 55,000 are issued by a lottery weighted in favor of individuals from countries with low levels of immigration to the United States.

Family Immigrant Visas. United States immigration policy favors noncitizens with certain family ties to persons in the United States. Children, spouses, and parents of United States citizens are called "immediate relatives" and receive the highest priority under the Immigration and Nationality Act of 1952, better known as the McCarran-Walter Act. To be considered a "child" for immigration purposes, a person must be under twenty-one years of age and unmarried. Unless they have undesirable traits, such as a criminal background, immediate relatives can obtain immigrant visas. The United States grants an unlimited number of immediate relative visas every year.

Other noncitizens seeking immigrant visas based on family ties are subject to an annual numerical quota, fluctuating between 226,000 and 480,000 annually. These visas are split into four categories for processing and numerical purposes: unmarried sons and daughters (grown unmarried children) of U.S. citizens; spouses, children, and unmarried sons and daughters of permanent resident aliens; married sons and daughters of U.S. citizens; and siblings of U.S. citizens. Because of the quotas placed on these categories of immigrants, backlogs develop. For example, there is about a ten-year wait to bring a sibling to the United States from Costa Rica.

Employment Immigrant Visas. United States immigration policy also favors industrious aliens who possess skills desired by or in short supply in the U.S. labor market. This policy conflicts with another policy, which seeks to protect the United States labor market. This tension is resolved in two ways: first, by placing numerical limits (approximately 140,000) on the number of these visas issued annually and, second, by imposing job offer and labor market tests on employment immigration, allowing noncitizens to receive an employment-based immigrant visa only if they have an offer of employment in the United States. Immigrants can meet this second condition only if there are no qualified U.S. workers able and willing to work in the jobs sought by immigrants, if employers pay prevailing wages, and if the hiring of aliens does not otherwise adversely affect the U.S. labor market.

If it is in the national interest, the attorney general's office may waive the job offer and labor market requirements for aliens who are members of professions for which an advanced degree is required or for aliens of exceptional ability. The job offer and labor market requirements are inapplicable to aliens with extraordinary abilities, as documented by sustained national or international acclaim, and to outstanding professors and researchers. The labor market test is also not applicable to certain multinational managers and executives engaged in intracompany transfers.

Nonimmigrant Business and Employment Visas. Many people seek to come to the United States temporarily to perform some type of work for an infinite variety of reasons. Some come for business meetings and others to market their goods. Still others come to perform warranty work or to start new businesses. Some noncitizens come to the United States temporarily as part of an intracompany transfer and others to enter the U.S. labor market for a temporary period of time, often in the hope of becoming permanent residents in the future.

U.S. law categorizes the variety of justifications for coming to the United States for business or employment purposes by offering different types of visas for different situations. For example, the B visa allows noncitizens to come to the United States for business meetings. The H visa, for temporary workers, raises the same concerns about protecting the U.S. labor market as employment-based immigrant visas. The tension is resolved in a similar fashion by imposing annual quotas on the number of H visas and by requiring a labor market test. In some situations, these quotas can be circumvented if aliens qualify for an L visa as company managers, executives, or employees who have specialized knowledge and come to the United States in an intracompany transfer. These quotas may also be circumvented if persons qualify for an E visa as the employees of treaty traders or treaty investors—persons who, pursuant to treaties between their countries and the United States, come to the United States to engage in substantial trade with their home countries or to develop and direct enterprises in which they have made a substantial investment.

Several million foreigners come to the United States as tourists every year on B visas. Additionally, several hundred thousand persons come to the United States to study or participate in cultural exchanges. Many of these people travel on F, J, or M visas. Foreign students at U.S. academic institutions have most likely traveled to the United States on F visas, which normally allow students to stay in the United States for the duration of their studies. J visas are used by students in special circumstances, such as when the U.S. government or a foreign government pays for students' education or when students come to the United States to acquire skills that are specifically needed in their native countries. In such instances, J visa holders may not apply for permanent residence in the United States until they have returned to their home countries for two years. M visas are used by vocational students and

U.S. Visa Categories

Family-based immigrant visas (all immigrant visa categories except the immediate relative category are subject to numerical restrictions)
Visas for Immediate relatives: spouses, children, and parents of U.S. citizens

- First preference: unmarried sons and daughters of U.S. citizens

- Second preference: spouses and the unmarried sons and daughters (including children) of permanent resident aliens

- Third preference: married sons and daughters of U.S. citizens

- Fourth preference: brothers and sisters of U.S. citizens

Employment-based immigrant visas

- First preference: "priority workers," which includes aliens of extraordinary ability, outstanding professors and researchers, and certain multinational executives and managers

- Second preference: aliens who are members of the professions holding advanced degrees and aliens of exceptional ability

- Third preference: skilled workers, professionals, and other workers

- Fourth preference: diverse group of "special immigrants," including certain religious ministers, retired U.S. employees, and former U.S. military personnel

- Fifth preference: aliens who come here to create employment opportunities by investing and engaging in a new commercial enterprise

Visas for diversity immigrants (aliens who win a lottery weighted in favor of aliens from country's and region's that have a low immigrant stream to the United States

Nonimmigrant visas (nonimmigrant visas are designated by the letter of the alphabet preceding the description; for example, an F Visa is a study visa)

- A. Ambassadors, public ministers, other foreign government officials, their spouses, children, and servants

- B. Temporary visitors for business or pleasure

- C. Aliens in transit

- D. Alien crewman

- E. Treaty traders, treaty investors, their spouses, and children

- F. Students attending an academic institution, their spouses, and children

- G. Representatives of foreign governments to international organizations, officers and employees of international organizations, and the spouses, children, and servants of such persons

- H. Temporary workers, including registered nurses, workers in "speciality occupations," agricultural workers, other workers, and the spouses, children, and servants of such persons

- I. Foreign media representatives, their spouses, and children

- J. Exchange visitors, including those participating in academic exchanges, their spouses, and children
- K. Fiancés of U.S. citizens
- L. Certain intracompany transferees, their spouses, and children
- M. Vocational students, their spouses, and children
- N. Officials of the North Atlantic Treaty Organization (NATO), their spouses, and children
- O. Aliens of extraordinary ability in certain fields, their spouses and children, and certain assistants
- P. Certain artists and entertainers, their spouses, and children
- Q. Aliens participating in certain international cultural exchanges
- R. Religious workers, their spouses, and children
- S. Certain aliens who, according to the attorney general or the secretary of state, possess critical reliable information concerning criminal or terrorist organizations and the spouses, unmarried sons and daughters (including children), and parents of such persons

are more restrictive because of the higher incidence of immigration fraud and abuse among vocational students.

Visa Processing. For most immigrant categories, visa processing begins with a visa petition filed with the INS by a petitioning employer or family member in the United States. The alien seeking an immigration benefit is considered the beneficiary of the petition. Once the INS has done its background work, the file is sent to a visa consular officer overseas for processing. Depending on the category, some nonimmigrant visas begin with petitions to the INS and others in the visa consular office.

Even if persons seeking a visa fit into one of the INS's immigrant or nonimmigrant categories, visa consular officers deny them visas if it is determined that the persons are inadmissable. Aliens can be held inadmissable on certain health-related grounds, because of prior abuse of U.S. immigration laws, because of certain criminal activity, on national security grounds, and because they may become an economic burden. Additionally, if visa consular officials doubt that nonimmigrants will leave the United States at the appointed time, such aliens can be denied visas.

To ensure that visa applicants qualify for admission to the United States, a personal interview with the visa consular office is often required. There is no judicial review of a denial of a visa application.

Suggested Readings. Several reference guides are available for those who seek more in-depth information on visas and entry into the United States. *Kurzban's Immigration Law Sourcebook: A Comprehensive Outline and Reference Tool* (6th ed. Washington, D.C.: American Immigration Law Foundation, 1998), by Ira Kurzban, provides a most comprehensive overview of U.S. immigration law and visas. Other resources include *Emigrating to the U.S.A.: A Complete Guide to Immigration, Temporary Visas, and Employment*, by Edward C. Beshara et al. (New York: Hippocrene Books, 1994), Carl Baldwin's *Immigracion Preguntas y Respuestas (Immigration Questions and Answers*, New York: Allworth, 1996), Henry Liebman's *The Immigration Handbook: For Work, Investment, Study and Retirement in the U.S.A.* (2d ed. Seattle, Wash.: Fairgreens, 1997), Sarah Ignatius's *Immigration Law and the Family* (New York: Clark Boardman Callaghan, 1995), and Howard David Deutsch's *Immigration the Easy Way* (Hauppauge, N.Y.: Barron's Educational Series, 1993). —*Michael A. Scaperlanda*

See also Adoption; Citizenship; Deportation; Divorce; Green cards; Immigration and Naturalization Service; Immigration law; Marriage; Passports; Visas, foreign.

Voting rights

The modern idea of representative democracy emphasizes that every adult citizen should have an equal opportunity to make meaningful choices in free elections.

Throughout American history, the growth of the democratic ideal has meant extending the right to vote to groups previously disfranchised, but only in the twentieth century has the right been extended broadly to African Americans, women, young adults, and the poor. Since 1971 noncitizens and convicted felons have been the only major groups not allowed to vote, although residents of the District of Columbia still have no voting representation in the U.S. Congress. Even with the establishment of broad suffrage rights, the voter turnout rate in the United States has remained low in comparison with other developed countries. Many reformers argue in favor of structural changes designed to make it more convenient for Americans to go to the polls.

The Right in the Constitution. During the American colonial period the right to vote was restricted to male property owners who were twenty-five years of age or older. One of the major themes of the American Revolution was the condemnation of taxation without representation, but the U.S. Constitution, as written in 1787, left it up to the states to determine the qualifications of voters. Although states had eliminated most property qualifications by the 1830's, the voting franchise was everywhere limited to male citizens. Before the Civil War of 1861 to 1865 many northern

African Americans fill the Fulton County courthouse in Atlanta, Georgia, during the Civil Rights era to register to vote. (AP/Wide World Photos)

states, including Abraham Lincoln's Illinois, did not allow free African Americans to vote.

The Fifteenth Amendment of 1870 stipulated that citizens could not be denied the right to vote because of "race, color, or previous condition of servitude." In spite of the amendment, however, state governments of the South used a combination of poll taxes, white primaries, the unequal enforcement of literacy requirements, and the refusal of local officials to register African American citizens to withhold the franchise from blacks. It was not until the passage of the Voting Rights Act of 1965 that the federal government really began to enforce the Fifteenth Amendment.

Following the Civil War women increasingly protested against their lack of political rights. Beginning with Wyoming in 1869 a number of western states extended the voting franchise to women, but the Supreme Court in 1875 ruled that the equal protection clause of the Fourteenth Amendment did not include a constitutional right to vote. Following decades of efforts by many determined women, the Nineteenth Amendment of 1920 guaranteed that the right to vote could not be denied because of sex. In contrast to the Fifteenth Amendment, none of the states tried to restrict enforcement of the Nineteenth Amendment.

The Twenty-Third Amendment of 1961 allowed residents of the District of Columbia to vote in presidential elections. The Twenty-Fourth Amendment of 1964 expanded the right of poor citizens to vote by making it unconstitutional to impose a poll tax as a voter qualification in federal elections. Although this amendment did not prohibit poll taxes in state elections, the Supreme Court in 1966 held that such taxes violated the principles of the Fourteenth Amendment. A few years later the Court ruled that one-year residency requirements were a violation of that amendment.

Until 1970 the voting age in many states was twenty-one years, but in that year the U.S. Congress passed a Voting Rights Act mandating that persons eighteen years old and older had the right to vote in federal, state, and local elections. The U.S. Supreme Court found that it was unconstitutional for the U.S. Congress to set the voting age for state and local elections, but the Twenty-Sixth Amendment, which was quickly ratified in 1971, established the age of eighteen as the legal voting age in all elections.

The Civil Rights Movement. Under the Jim Crow system, southern states maintained that political parties were private organizations that were not required to follow the nondiscriminatory mandates of the Fourteenth and Fifteenth Amendments. As late as 1935 the Supreme Court endorsed this theory, allowing parties in the South to exclude African Americans from voting in primary elections. Overruling its precedents in *Smith v. Allwright* (1944), the Court held that primary elections were an integral part of selecting candidates for public office, thus forbidding states from using the results of racially discriminatory primaries.

The Voting Rights Act of 1965 was a comprehensive law designed to enforce the guarantees of the Fifteenth Amendment. Aimed primarily at southern states, the law authorized the U.S. attorney general to appoint federal examiners to supervise registrations and elections when the Justice Department found evidence that states were likely guilty of racial discrimination. In addition, it prohibited literacy tests and required that all changes in state election laws be approved by the Justice Department. The law had a great impact on voting patterns in the South; within a few years the registration rates of southern African Americans were only slightly below that of whites. In 1975 the law was expanded to require bilingual ballots and to protect Hispanic Americans. In 1982 the law was strengthened and extended until the year 2007.

Fairness in Representation. As the U.S. population became more urbanized during the twentieth century, many state legislatures refused to redraw their electoral districts. As a result, the votes of rural residents sometimes counted more than ten times as much as those living in urban districts. In a series of cases culminating in *Reynolds v. Sims* (1964), the Supreme Court ruled that the Fourteenth Amendment mandated the regular reapportionment of state legislatures to produce representation based on the principle of "one-person, one vote." Henceforth, the voting power of some citizens could not be diluted so as to count for less than others.

In the early 1980's Supreme Court opinions recognized that one purpose of the Voting Rights Act was to promote African American officeholding, and the Court seemed to be sympathetic to the creation of electoral districts containing a majority of African American voters. In 1993 and 1995, however, the Supreme Court examined the constitutionality of extremely irregular districts drawn with this purpose in mind and decided that such districts were an unconstitutional form of "racial gerrymandering." States were allowed to take race into account when drawing district lines, but the use of race as the overriding motive was considered a violation of the equal protection clause. Since the Court's decisions meant a decrease in majority-minority congressional districts, it was expected that they would result in fewer African American officeholders.

Barriers to Voting. Voter registration, required in every state except North Dakota, has often discouraged people from voting. The National Voter Registration Act of 1993 was an attempt to force states to simplify the process. This act required that states permit persons to register to vote when obtaining or renewing their driver's licenses (called "motor-voters"), provide welfare and disability assistance to facilitate registration, and also allow registration by mail. Although critics feared that the law would increase election fraud, it apparently resulted in a significant increase in new registered voters for the election of 1996.

Many informed observers have suggested that voter participation would increase if voting were made easier. In most countries, elections are scheduled on Sundays or special holidays, but elections in the United States usually take place on working days, when some people find it almost impossible to go to the polls. Moreover, numerous elections are held on different dates for various federal, state, and local elections. Reformers argue that fewer elections would promote greater participation. Additional ways of making it more convenient to vote would include expanding the voting period to several days, allowing people to vote by mail (which was tried in Oregon in 1996), or even instituting computer voting over the Internet. Some countries, such as Belgium and Luxembourg, have laws that require citizens to vote, but such a policy would appear incompatible with American traditions of individual liberty.

Suggested Readings. For the decisions of the Supreme Court, see Ward Elliott's *The Rise of Guardian Democracy: The Supreme Court's Role in Voting Rights Disputes, 1845-1969* (Cambridge, Mass.: Harvard University Press, 1974) and Richard Claude's *The Supreme Court and the Electoral Process* (Baltimore: Johns Hopkins Press, 1970). David Garrow writes of a crusade for the right to vote in Selma, Alabama, in *Martin Luther King, Jr. and the Voting Rights Act of 1965* (New Haven, Conn.: Yale University Press, 1978). For the importance of this act see Chandler Davidson and Bernard Grofman's *Quiet Revolution in the South: The Impact of the Voting Rights Act, 1965-1990* (Princeton, N.J.: Princeton University Press, 1994). Elizabeth Frost and Kathryn Cullen provide a comprehensive account of the Nineteenth Amendment in *Women's Suffrage in America: An Eyewitness History* (New York: Facts on File, 1992). For the contemporary practice of voting, see William Flanigan and Nancy Zingale's *Political Behavior of the American Electorate* (Washington, D.C.: Congressional Quarterly, 1994) and Susan Tolchin's *The Angry Voter: How Voter Rage Is Changing the Nation* (Boulder, Colo.: Westview Press, 1996). —*Thomas T. Lewis*

See also Civil rights and liberties; Constitution, U.S.; Discrimination; Mexican American Legal Defense and Education Fund.

W

Warranties

A quality and performance guarantee, a product warranty is issued with commercial products.

A warranty is a seller's guarantee of the qualities or ownership of goods offered for sale. The warranty rights of a buyer are governed by state and federal law and vary from state to state. The principal source of warranty law is found in Article 2 of the Uniform Commercial Code (UCC), which is in effect in all U.S. states except Louisiana. There are two kinds of warranties: express and implied. Warranties are made by the seller and can be enforced by the buyer in a legal action for money damages.

Express and Implied Warranties. An express warranty arises when sellers describe their products or make statements about their products' qualities. Such statements may be made in advertising, in brochures, and in statements by the sellers' employees. A seller's statement that a car is "new" is a warranty. A statement that a used car has been driven 25,000 miles has been breached if the car has in fact been driven 40,000 miles. While factual statements about a product can give rise to warranty liability, a mere statement of opinion in vague language such as "this is a great car" is not a warranty.

Sellers who do not make any statements about their goods may nevertheless be liable if the goods are defective. They will be liable if the goods do not satisfy the requirements of an implied warranty. There are three types of implied warranties: the implied warranty of good title, the implied warranty of merchantability, and the implied warranty of fitness for a particular purpose.

When persons sell goods, they promise implicitly to buyers that a third person will not make a valid claim to those goods. Therefore, a seller who sells stolen goods breaches the warranty of good title. This title warranty becomes part of every sale unless a seller lets the buyer know that the seller does not claim good title.

A professional seller of goods is a merchant. When merchants sell goods, they make implied warranties that the merchandise will satisfy a reasonable buyer's expectations as to quality and performance. This type of warranty is known as the implied warranty of merchantability. A car dealer who delivers a car with defective brakes breaches an implied warranty of merchantability.

A third type of implied warranty arises if buyers tell sellers that they need the goods for a particular purpose. If the sellers know that the buyers are relying on the sellers to furnish satisfactory goods, there is an implied warranty that the goods recommended by the sellers will be suitable for the buyers' purposes.

Disclaimers and Limitations. The Uniform Commercial Code allows a seller to disclaim or exclude implied warranties in a sale of goods. The implied warranty of merchantability can be excluded if merchant sellers make written statements of their intention not to give the warranty. The written statement must mention the word "merchantability" and must be conspicuous. A conspicuous disclaimer is one which the buyer should notice. To exclude this implied warranty, a seller may state, for example: "No Implied Warranty of Merchantability."

A seller can also exclude the implied warranty of merchantability and fitness for a particular purpose by selling merchandise "as is." Used goods are often sold this way. If they are later found to be defective, the buyer may not have any rights against the seller. However, an "as is" disclaimer may not apply if the buyer or a third person is injured by a defective product.

It is more difficult for a seller to disclaim express warranties. However, if the buyer signs a written purchase agreement which prohibits the buyer from relying on any statements not included in the written agreement, the buyer may not be able to take advantage of promises made in presale statements by the seller's sales force.

If the seller is willing to give the buyer express or implied warranties, the Uniform Commercial Code permits the seller to limit a buyer's remedies if the product fails. Instead of money damages, the seller may limit the buyer to the repair or replacement of defective merchandise. A seller who offers repair or replacement as the only remedy for breach of warranty may avoid paying any money damages.

Written limitations on a buyer's right to recover damages from the seller are usually enforced. There is an exception when a product causes personal injuries to a buyer or a third person. A seller's attempt to exclude liability for personal injuries resulting from injuries caused by a defective product are usually unenforceable in a court of law.

State laws known as "lemon laws" may place additional burdens and restrictions on sellers who make express or implied warranties to consumers. For example, the seller who makes a repair warranty may be required to offer the repair at no charge, at a reasonably convenient location, and within a reasonable time. Such laws may allow the buyer to return the goods for a refund if the seller has failed to fix a problem with the merchandise after a reasonable number of attempts.

The Magnuson-Moss Warranty Act. In 1975 the U.S. Congress provided greater protection to consumers against deceptive warranties. The Magnuson-Moss Warranty Act covers manufacturers and other sellers who give written warranties on products normally used for personal, family, or household purposes. This act does not require a seller or manufacturer to give a written warranty. However, if a written warranty is offered, the act requires that it be written in simple language and made available to the consumer to read before the sale. A seller who offers a written warranty or service contract covered by the act may not disclaim implied warranties.

The principle purpose of the Magnuson-Moss Warranty Act is to make information available to consumers so that they may make better choices among competing products. The Federal Trade Commission (FTC) has issued regulations that require a seller who gives a written warranty to furnish the following types of information to the consumer: who can enforce the warranty; what is covered by the warranty; a statement of what the warrantor will do if the product is defective; how long the warranty will last; a statement of any limitation or exclusion of the consumer's right to recover damages; and what the consumer should do if the product is defective.

Warranty law is a complicated field. Persons who have purchased defective goods or been injured by defective products may be advised by lawyers as to whether or not they have any legal rights against the manufacturers or the stores at which they bought the merchandise.

Suggested Readings. Books written by lawyers for the layperson include Margaret C. Jasper's *The Law of Buying and Selling* (Dobbs Ferry, N.Y.: Oceana, 1996) and *The American Bar Association Guide to Consumer Law* (New York: Random House, 1977). For a good basic discussion of the Magnuson-Moss Warranty Act written for the layperson see *1975 Consumer Product Warranties Law with Explanations* (Chicago: Commerce Clearing House, 1975). The *Reader's Digest* has published *Consumer Advisor: An Action Guide to Your Rights* (rev. ed. New York: Reader's Digest Press, 1969), a book on a wide range of consumer protection issues, including the consumer's right to obtain credit and how to evaluate purchases ranging from goods and services to insurance and real estate. For up-to-date consumer information in ten categories (food, health, home, transportation, children, smart buying, product safety, money, education, and the environment) see the Federal Trade Commission's Web site: http://www.consumer.gov.

—*Susan J. Martin*

See also Commercial litigation; Lemon laws; Liability, civil and criminal; Product liability law.

Whistle-blowing

The reporting of official misconduct by an employee or other person is known as whistle-blowing.

Whistle-blowing is essentially the same as informing, except that the informant is in some way a member of an organization accused of or implicated in alleged misconduct. Typically, whistle-blowing occurs when an employee provides legally incriminating evidence against an employer or a fellow employee. In the political arena, less frequent but higher-profile instances of whistle-blowing have exposed alleged violations of public trust. Whistle-blowing also implies that the informant initiates a legal or public investigation.

Two significant issues make whistle-blowing

more specialized than informing. First, as a member of the organization accused of misconduct, the whistle-blower makes an ethical choice between loyalty to the organization and the laws of society. Second, as a member of the accused organization, the whistle-blower is potentially subject to reprisals by the organization.

In popular usage the term whistle-blowing is ambiguous. It may carry a pejorative meaning similar to that of a tattletale or it may imply a more positive sacrifice for a greater cause. Legal usage of the term whistle-blowing is closest to the latter. State and federal whistle-blowing laws are almost exclusively concerned with protecting the whistle-blower from retaliation from the accused organization. For example, the Civil Service Reform Act of 1978 protects federal employees who inform on the state bureaucracy from retaliation from their superiors. Protection against retaliation is also addressed under wrongful discharge laws.

Whistle-blowing laws typically protect informants who report health, safety, or financial misconduct. They generally authorize the courts to reinstate back pay, restore seniority and lost fringe benefits, and require reimbursement for litigation costs, attorney's fees, and fines. Some state statutes protect only employees who report safety violations that affect the community at large.

Whistle-blowing is sometimes a subordinate issue in high-profile court cases that test controversial laws or public policies. Frequently, whistle-blowing becomes an issue in civil rights and women's rights litigation over issues in the workplace.

Occasionally whistle-blowing has been the subject of controversial political issues. During the Vietnam era Daniel Ellsberg, an employee of the Pentagon, turned highly sensitive secret documents over to the news media. The documents, known as the "Pentagon Papers," undermined years of official public statements about the Vietnam War. The classified U.S. documents were printed in the *New York Times* and other newspapers. Public attention was divided between the revelations about U.S. foreign policy and the drama surrounding Ellsberg's ethical choice, on one hand, and the retaliatory actions of the U.S. government, on the other.

Another sensational instance of whistle-blowing in the political arena occurred in 1981, when President Ronald Reagan's budget director David Stockman told a journalist that the president's budget process was out of control. Stockman was considered the principle architect of Reagan's economic recovery program, and many feared his revelations threatened the stability of the U.S. economy. Republican leaders demanded Stockman's resignation, which he offered and Reagan refused.

The films *China Syndrome* (1979) and *Silkwood* (1983) are films that dramatize the experiences of employees who publicly expose their employers' illegal practices. In both films, the plots revolve around the protagonists' choice to publicize company misconduct and the companies' attempts to silence and penalize them. Both stories deal with corporate practices that ignore nuclear energy regulations and endanger public safety. *Silkwood* is based on the true story of Karen Silkwood, who was killed in a suspicious automobile accident before she was able to testify about dangerous practices at the plant where she worked. —*Thomas J. Roach*

See also Informants; Occupational health and safety; White-collar crime.

White-collar crime

Committed in the framework of legitimate businesses or enterprises, white-collar crimes result in substantial losses.

First coined by Edwin Sutherland in 1939, white-collar crime is a major concern among criminologists, policymakers, and the public. Although it includes acts by individuals, far more costlier violations are committed by organizational offenders within the corporate sector. Remedies may be pursued through administrative hearings, civil proceedings, or criminal prosecutions.

Nature of White-Collar Crime. The public first became acutely aware of white-collar, upper-class crime in the early 1900's. Novelists and investigative reporters, known as muckrakers, focused on corruption and crime committed by politicians, oil companies, and railroads magnates. Upton Sinclair's *The Jungle* (1906) exposed conditions so appalling in the meatpacking industry that federal regulatory laws were enacted after its publication. The first scholarly analysis of the problem by Sutherland in 1949 revealed that seventy of the country's largest corporations each averaged fourteen violations during their operating histories. Offenses included restraint-of-trade violations, patent infringements, unfair labor practices, advertising fraud, and illegal rebates. These and other widespread corporate illegalities, such as environmental violations and occupational safety infringements, are termed regulatory offenses, because investigation and enforcement are principally carried out by specific regulatory agencies.

Many states, like the federal government, have enacted legislation prohibiting white-collar crime. While some states have also established regulatory agencies, most place the role of investigation and enforcement in the hands of their offices of attorneys general. However, because of greater resources and jurisdictional flexibility, the federal government is more significantly involved in the overall regulation and prosecution of the problem. Regulation is the responsibility of such agencies as the Federal Trade Commission (FTC), the Environmental Protection Agency (EPA), the Occupational Safety and Health Administration (OSHA), and the Securities and Exchange Commission (SEC).

Several types of white-collar crimes are committed by individuals, small corporations, or organizations, ranging from employee theft, managed health-care fraud, and forgery to banking irregularities, obstruction of justice, and consumer fraud. Prosecuting crimes of this nature and offenses referred to the U.S. Justice Department by regulatory agencies are primarily the responsibility of the criminal justice system.

The Law and White-Collar Crime. There is no legally specific offense category termed "white-collar crime." These offenses are treated as violations of laws such as theft, fraud, and conspiracy, regardless of the perpetrator's occupational status. Nonetheless, numerous federal regulatory acts or statutes frequently provide the legal basis for controlling white-collar crime. Between 1890 (the Sherman Anti-Trust Act) and 1950 (the Celler-Kefauver Act) the U.S. Congress passed several antitrust laws designed to prevent restraint-of-trade and unfair competition by monopolies. Additional legislation has been aimed at a variety of other types of white-collar offenses. For example, the Pure Food and Drug Act (1906) and the National Traffic and Motor Vehicle Safety Act (1966) are intended to protect consumers from unsafe products, while the Occupational Safety and Health Act (1984) is meant to ensure safe workplaces. Sweeping concerns for the environment led to the Resource Conservation and Recovery Act (1976) and the Clean Air Act (1970) as means to deal with those who pollute the environment.

Various federal statutes are also commonly employed against white-collar crime. Title 18 United States Code makes it a crime to conspire to commit any offense against the United States or to defraud the United States or any of its agencies. This conspiracy statute is often central to the prosecution of many interstate white-collar crimes because, by definition, these offenses hinge on some degree of planning or preparation. Other important federal statutes also aimed at white-collar crime include those prohibiting mail fraud, wire fraud, false statements, false claims, and racketeering.

Regulation and Prosecution. Organizational white-collar crime is much more difficult to detect than conventional crime. Offenders are often politically and economically powerful enough to carry out hidden, elaborate, long-term schemes that escape public awareness. Despite these hindrances, regulatory agencies discover many violators as a result of media exposés, whistle-blowing by disgruntled employees, consumer complaints, and investigations conducted by occasional congressional committees and task forces.

Three options are available when agencies decide to pursue a case. First, an administrative hearing before a judge may be held. Although defendants may be represented by attorneys, the proceedings do not possess the same due process formalities as court trials. Sanctions may include cease-and-desist orders, special directives, licensing suspensions, or revocations and fines. All agency decisions may be appealed. Another alternative is for a regulatory agency to file a civil suit in federal court against an offender, such as a tort action. A trial may result in the awarding of compensatory or punitive financial penalties for losses, injuries, or damages caused by violators. This option has been increasingly pursued by private citizens acting as individuals or as a large category of plaintiffs in the form of class-action lawsuits. Civil verdicts are also subject to appeal. A regulatory agency's third option is to refer a case to the U.S. Justice Department for criminal prosecution instead of filing a civil lawsuit.

The criminal prosecution of white-collar crime occurs far less frequently than administrative hearings or civil actions. Nevertheless, prosecution is more likely to result when substantial evidence exists that criminal conduct is far reaching and has been committed by big offenders. The bulk of such prosecutions are carried out by the U.S. Attorney's Office of the Justice Department. The first major step is for a federal prosecutor to seek a required grand-jury indictment. Following the indictment and prior to the filing of formal charges, negotiations often take place in which the defendant agrees to plead guilty to lesser or fewer charges in return for favorable treatment at sentencing.

Depending on the strength of the evidence or to avoid going to trial, the prosecutor may be inclined to plea bargain. Instead of trying defendants, courts frequently allow those suspected of committing white-collar crimes to enter a plea of *nolo contendere* (no contest, or a plea that neither denies nor admits guilt). Thereby, defendants may be criminally punished but not subject to subsequent civil suits. Should negotiations fail, formal charges are filed and the case moves to trial in federal district court. A guilty verdict can result in a prison term, fine, or probation. Fines, probation, and mandatory community service are common outcomes of such trials. All convictions are subject to appeal.

Suggested Readings. The classic study of white-collar crime is Edwin H. Sutherland's *White Collar Crime* (New York: Holt, Rinehart and Winston, 1949). An excellent discussion of the relationship between law and white-collar crime may be found in Ellen S. Podgor's *White Collar Crime* (St. Paul, Minn.: West Publishing, 1993). General works covering the nature, investigation, prosecution, and punishment of white-collar crime include James William Coleman's *The Criminal Elite* (4th ed. New York: St. Martin's Press, 1998), David O. Friedrichs's *Trusted Criminals* (Belmont, Calif.: Wadsworth, 1996), and Jay S. Albanese's *White Collar Crime in America* (Englewood Cliffs, N.J.: Prentice-Hall, 1995). —*Henry W. Mannle*

See also Antitrust law; Asbestos litigation; Civil action; Class-action suits; Liability, civil and criminal; Plea bargain; Product liability law.

Wills

A will is a disposition by an individual of his or her property, intended to take effect after death.

A disposition of real property by will is termed a devise; a disposition of personal property by will is termed a bequest or legacy. The principal distinction between a will and any other type of conveyance is that a will takes effect only upon the death of the maker. A will is alterable by the maker, or testator, at any time during the testator's lifetime. Hence, during the testator's life beneficiaries under a will have no firm legal rights but merely an expectancy of an inheritance.

The common law of wills is founded on the original English Statute of Wills (1540) and cases decided thereunder. Common-law principals were subsequently embodied in statutes in most American jurisdictions, although the statutes frequently went beyond the common law or even reversed certain common-law doctrines.

A will appoints an executor to probate the estate, pay the bills, and distribute the property of the deceased. A will may also appoint a guardian or trustee, who could be the same person as the named executor, to have custody of the minor children of the deceased or to take care of finances for the surviving minor children.

If persons die without a will, their property is divided among their closest relatives according to the law of intestacy, which differs from state to state. In the event of a death without a will, an applicant must request to be administrator to distribute property according to the state's intestacy laws. Sometimes assets may be distributed differently by the laws of intestacy than the deceased would have wished. The estate may also be subject to more tax based on how the state distributes estate assets. Thus, to avoid the pitfalls of intestacy, a will functions as a cornerstone of most estate plans.

Requirements for Valid Wills. There are four main requirements in the formation of a valid will: The will must have been executed with testamentary intent, the testator must have had testamentary capacity at the time of execution, the execution must be free of fraud, duress, undue influence, or mistake, and the will must have been duly executed—that is, in compliance with statutory formalities.

Testamentary intent is a subjective test. It must always appear that the testator subjectively or personally intended the document or words to be his will. Testamentary intent consists of three elements: The testator must have intended to dispose of his property, he or she must have intended the disposition to occur only upon death, and he or she must have intended the instrument in question to accomplish the disposition. The requisite intent is a question of fact to be deduced from the examination of the will and the surrounding circumstances. Generally, it is presumed that a will that has been duly executed was executed with the requisite intent.

To make a valid will, the testator must have testamentary capacity, that is, must be of full age and sound mind and must act without undue influence by others. The age of majority is eighteen. A person's mental capacity for making a will is ordinarily tested at the time the will is executed and includes the understanding of the relationship between the testator and those who ought to be in his or her mind at the time of making a will, the understanding of the nature and extent of his or her property, the actual knowledge of the nature of the act of making a will, and the capacity to interrelate the previous factors and form an orderly scheme of disposition.

Fraud, undue influence, and duress are more accurately grounds for contesting a will that otherwise appears to be valid, although to be valid a will may not be executed while the testator is subject to any of these three situations.

The formalities of will execution vary somewhat from state to state, so that it is essential to know what formalities are required in the state in question at the time of the will's execution. Statutory and state-mandated requirements must be followed for the will to be duly executed. Standard formalities include subscription by the testator, the publication or declaration by the testator to the attesting witnesses that it is his or her will, both subscription and publication in the presence of at least two competent witnesses assembled to witness the execution, and the signing of the will by the witnesses attesting to subscription and publication in the presence of the testator and at his or her request.

Types of Wills. One type of will is the formal, or attested, will. By statute in the U.S. and in Great Britain, a will must be in writing, whether it disposes of real or personal property. A written will must be signed at the end; a testator unable to write may make an X, and such a mark is considered a valid signature. In the U.S. generally, two and in some states three persons must witness the will—that is, they must sign the will as witnesses to the signature of the testator. In most states the signing must be done in the presence of witnesses, and the testator must state that the document being signed is his or her will. The witnesses need not be acquainted with one another and may sign at the same time or at separate times, depending on the statutory requirements of the state in which the will is executed. Thus, the signature may, in most states, be written in the presence of one witness and acknowledged later by other witnesses.

Another form of will is the nuncupative will. Soldiers and sailors in combat may make valid oral wills, and in a number of jurisdictions in the U.S. an oral will is also valid when made by a testator during sickness that terminates in death. However, the verbal will must be made when, because of the apparent imminence of death, neither time nor opportunity exists to make a written will. The law usually provides that the contents of an oral will must be reduced to writing within six days after it was declared in the presence of the statutory number of witnesses, usually three. Such oral wills are termed nuncupative wills and may dispose only of personal property.

A third form of will is the holographic will, which is drafted entirely in the handwriting of the testator. This type of will may dispose of real or personal property or both. The statutes of some U.S. states recognize such wills as valid without formal execution or attestation if they are wholly written, dated, and signed by the testator's own hand. A holographic will is valid only if it complies literally with the controlling statute.

Attestation and Codicils. Two, and in some jurisdictions three, witnesses are required to attest to the signing of valid written wills. All witnesses to a will must be competent. A witness is considered incompetent if he or she is a beneficiary under the instrument—that is, if one of the necessary witnesses is a beneficiary, at common law, the will is void in its entirety. To remedy such a situation it has generally, although not universally, been provided by statute that a bequest to a subscribing witness shall be void and that the rest of the will shall otherwise be valid. Some statutes also provide for the saving of the subscribing witness's gift by voiding it only to the extent that it goes beyond what the subscribing witness would have taken from the estate had the will not been executed. In other words, if subscribing witnesses are beneficiaries, they are allowed to take only whatever they would receive legally in the absence of a will.

Witnesses must sign the will with an intent to attest to the facts witnessed. They must sign in the presence of the testator. An attestation clause, or a clause certifying the proper execution of the will, must usually be added after the testator's signature. It recites in detail the performance of the statutory requisites. Such a clause would be signed, sealed, published, and declared by the testator as his or her last will and testament in the presence of persons, who at the testator's request and in his or her presence and in the presence of each other have subscribed their names as witnesses.

A codicil is a testamentary instrument executed subsequent to the execution of a will and ordinarily intended as an amendment to the will. Thus, a codicil must alter, modify, or expand the provisions of the will in some manner. A codicil must be executed with the same formalities required for the execution of a will. However, the codicil does not have to be in the same form as the will it amends; hence a holographic codicil can alter a witnessed will and vice versa.

In addition to modifying, altering, or expanding the prior will as intended by the testator, a codicil may have either of three legal effects on the prior will: it may republish a prior valid will, it may incorporate by reference and thus validate a prior written will, or it may revive a previously revoked will that is still in existence.

Revocation and Probate. A will never operates until the testator's death. Thus, the testator retains the power to revoke the will at any time during his or her lifetime. The only exception to this occurs when two parties simultaneously make mutually irrevocable wills in which they name each other as their respective beneficiaries and expressly give up the right to revoke their wills. A testator may revoke his or her will by destroying it, either by burning or tearing it up, or by obliterating the signature. Any part or the whole of the will may be revoked by a codicil, or an amendment to the will, executed with the same statutory formalities as the will itself.

A valid later will revokes a prior will. Disposition of property by the testator before death, as by gift or sale, is not a revocation of the will, although its effect may be similar to one. By opera-

---

Will Provisions

Provisions in the approximate order in which they typically appear in wills.

- Basic identifying information regarding testator
- Declaration of domicile
- Revocation of prior wills and codicils
- Declaration of marital status
- Disposition of body
- Funeral directions
- Cemetery, masses, monument
- Payment of debts and taxes
- Tangible personalty
- Legacies
- Charitable bequests
- Real estate provisions
- Rights of surviving spouse
- Residue and remainder
- Children, including trusts or guardianships for minors, incompetent adult dependents, or beneficiaries
- Appointment and powers of fiduciaries
- Business interests
- Survivorship
- Disinheritance
- Clauses to avoid litigation
- Execution, self-proving affidavit

tion of law, marriage of the testator subsequent to the date of execution of the will revokes the will as to the surviving spouse or children, who are entitled to the same rights in the estate as if the testator had died intestate—that is, without leaving a will.

No disposition of an estate is made after the testator's death until the will is probated. The probate of a will is a court proceeding upon notice to the heirs and next of kin. Thus, probate is a public process that takes place according to procedures established in each state. During the probate process, probate fees are assessed, and probate can be costly depending on the state in which the will is to be probated. Probate can also be a lengthy process, although many states have enacted laws that have attempted to simplify the probate of both testamentary estates (ones in which there is a will) and intestate estates (ones in which there is no will to be found). Ancillary probate is the process by which each state accepts the will of another state's resident to convey the testator's title to his or her property within the state.

In many jurisdictions, a will can be made self-proving, which removes the need for witnesses to testify in any probate proceeding. The will is made self-proving by attaching an affidavit made by the witnesses as to the matters to which they would testify, such as the testator's identity, that the testator signed a document identified as a will, or that the witnesses believe the testator was of sound mind when making the will. To be self-proving, the witnesses and testator must sign both the will and the affidavit in appropriate places.

Challenges to Wills. A contest of a will may be brought to pose the issue of whether the document offered or admitted to probate is a valid will. The contestant may raise any matter tending to show that the will was not validly executed, that the testator lacked capacity, or any other defense to formation of the will, such as fraud, duress, or undue influence.

A will may be contested either at the time it is entered for probate or within whatever period of time thereafter as set by statute. The time period for will challenges (or contests or caveats) thus varies from state to state. A person is permitted to contest the will if and only if that person has a direct interest in the estate and will be economically benefited by setting the will aside. The statutes of each state must be consulted as to restrictions on a testator's disposition of his or her property by will. In many jurisdictions a will may not exclude a surviving spouse. The degree of participation of the spouse in the estate varies from state to state. Many jurisdictions, however, permit a person to exclude children from participation in the estate as long as the parent says specifically in the will that he or she is leaving out the children or leaving them a nominal sum.

Rules of Construction. Questions frequently arise about the construction of the terms of a will. The most important rule of construction is that the intention of the testator as it appears from the will shall be carried out whenever legally possible; when the will is ambiguous, the circumstances surrounding its execution may be examined in order to ascertain the testator's intentions.

Also important in the construction of wills is the classification of bequests or devises. There are four classes of testamentary gifts: specific, general, demonstrative, and residuary. Specific bequests or devises are gifts of particular items of either real or personal property that are capable of being identified and distinguished from all other property in the testator's estate. For example, a will may stipulate that a testator will leave a coin collection to a specific beneficiary.

General bequests or devises are gifts that are payable out of the general assets of the estate and do not require delivery of any specific thing or satisfaction from any designated portion of the testator's property. For example, a will may state that the testator wills $500 to a specific person.

A demonstrative bequest, which is usually in the form of money, is a bequest in which the testator wishes to be paid from a particular fund but which is payable from the general assets of the estate in the event that the fund designated is not sufficient. For example, a will may state that a particular person is to be paid a sum of money out of proceeds from the sale of an automobile.

Residuary gifts are gifts of the balance of the testator's real or personal property after specific, general, and/or demonstrative bequests (and claims against the estate) have been paid. If a specific bequest is made and the particular item is not in the estate at the time of death, the gift is adeemed by extinction. The gift fails entirely and the designated beneficiary receives nothing. Only specific bequests are affected this way. Courts usually classify gift as general rather than specific in order to avoid ademption. If the named bequest has been handled during the testator's lifetime by a gift to the beneficiary, the testamentary gift may be found to have been satisfied provided the testator is found to have intended that result. Ademption by satisfaction is recognized primarily with respect to gifts of money—hence, usually to general or residuary bequests and not to specific ones.

Classifying testamentary gifts also establishes the order of distribution for the gifts and the abatement thereof in case the assets in the estate are not sufficient to fully pay for all gifts made by the testator. Once the estate debts and expenses are paid, the bequests and devises under the will are generally distributed as follows: gifts to a surviving spouse, specific gifts (including demonstrative gifts to the extent that the specified fund exists from which the demonstrative gift is to be paid, general gifts (including demonstrative gifts to the extent that the specified fund does not exist), residuary gifts, and any intestate property.

Abatement is the process of reducing the testamentary gifts to beneficiaries because the estate is not sufficient to pay all estate obligations and the testamentary gifts. Abatement occurs in the reverse order from distribution. Within each class, gifts abate proportionately.

Suggested Readings. Donald J. Burris's *Layman's Law Guides: Protecting Your Assets* (Philadelphia, Pa: Chelsea House, 1997) is a handbook designed to help the layperson make informed decisions about estate planning. The book explains the four ways for property to pass from one person to another at death: intestate succession, joint tenancies, wills, and trusts. For each, the author poses an anecdotal introduction and discusses advantages and drawbacks. Jay H. Gingrich's *Wills Trusts and Estates* (Albany, N.Y.: Delmar, 1996) is a college paralegal textbook that goes beyond basic principles. It presents wills, estates, and trusts in a practical manner so that persons can handle common tasks and problems in this legal area. Steven Strauss's *Ask a Lawyer: Wills and Trusts* (New York: W. W. Norton, 1998) is part of a series on legal topics designed to give helpful advice in guiding the reader toward a personal estate plan. Daniel Sitarz's *Prepare Your Own Will* (Carbondale, Ill: Nova, 1991) is part of a legal self-help series. Designed as a guide and explanation of how to prepare a valid will without the aid of an attorney, it includes a sample fill-in-the-blank document and an appendix on "State Laws Relating to Wills." John C. Howell's *Writing a Will: the Citizens' Legal Guide* (Englewood Cliffs, N.J.: Prentice-Hall, 1981) is an early work designed to assist the layperson in writing a will without a lawyer. —*Diane S. Griffin*

See also Estates and estate planning; Executors; Intestate succession; Probate; Wills, holographic.

Wills, holographic

Written in the handwriting of the persons making them, holographic wills offer testators advantages but also present certain limitations.

Holographic wills are those written and signed in the handwriting of the testators (the persons making wills) but not formally attested to by witnesses. Because wills must normally be signed in the presence of witnesses to be legally valid, holographic wills are exceptions to this requirement. They are permitted by roughly half of the jurisdictions in the United States. The requirement that a holographic will must be in the handwriting of the testator is the most important factor in determining its validity. It is not sufficient that the will be personally prepared by the testator. For example, a will personally prepared by the testator on a typewriter or computer but not formally witnessed will fail to qualify as a holographic will since it is not in the handwriting of the testator.

Many states that accept holographic wills qualify their acceptance by imposing various special requirements. For example, some states require not only that the body of a holographic will be written in the testator's own hand, but that the will also contain the date written in the testator's hand. Some jurisdictions further require that the testator's signature appear at the end of the will, rather than at its beginning or in some other place. Others recognize the validity of a holographic will only if it has been stored among the testator's valuable papers. —*Timothy L. Hall*

See also Estates and estate planning; Executors; Wills.

Wiretap

A form of electronic surveillance, a wiretap permits persons to overhear a private conversation through a tapped telephone line without the knowledge or consent of at least one of the participants involved in the conversation.

With the invention of the telegraph and the telephone in the nineteenth century, it seemingly was inevitable that electronic surveillance capabilities would also become available before long. During the early 1860's various states enacted statutes that forbade the interception of telegraph messages. Police departments began to tap telephone lines in the 1890's. It is relatively easy for a wiretap to be placed on a telephone line. The line of a person under suspicion would have a tap run from it at the phone company's switching station. The "tap," or additional line, would then be connected to a listening device. In addition to listening to a suspect's conversations, authorities could also record them.

Law-enforcement officials argued that electronic surveillance was an indispensable tool in the fight against criminal activity, especially in the effective pursuit of persons thought to be involved in kidnapping, espionage, and organized crime. In 1928 the U.S. Supreme Court ruled in the landmark case of *Olmstead v. United States* that the use of wiretaps did not violate a person's Fourth Amendment rights against unreasonable searches and seizures. The police could not, however, trespass onto the property of a suspect. For the next forty years police officials could use wiretaps as long as trespassing was not necessary. In federal courts, evidence would be thrown out if it could be shown that the police had trespassed. In 1934 the Federal Communications Act made it clear that private citizens were prohibited from tapping messages or conversations.

In 1967 the Supreme Court reversed its opinion on wiretapping in the case of *Katz v. United States*. Instead of a territorial trespass approach to the validity of a wiretap, the Supreme Court concluded that if a person had a reasonable expectation of privacy, then authorities must obtain a warrant to use a wiretap. In Title III of the Omnibus Crime Control and Safe Streets Act of 1968, the U.S. Congress specified that wiretapping was illegal unless it was authorized by a judge and included a list of serious offenses, in which case electronic surveillance was legally permitted after a judicial warrant had been issued. The act also established that a wiretap could not last more than thirty days and that the person under surveillance had to be notified of the tap within ninety days of an application to authorize the surveillance or the completion of a successful interception.

In the 1986 Electronic Communications Privacy Act, Congress extended the protection against wiretapping to electronic mail. Known as the "Wiretap Act," it prohibited authorities from reading persons' e-mail. In 1991, 856 court-ordered wiretaps were approved by the appropriate federal or state agencies. In order to engage in wiretapping, law-enforcement personnel must show probable cause before a superior court judge, the attorney general, or the chief assistant attorney general of the criminal law division. Supreme Court justice Louis Brandeis made the classic argument against electronic surveillance in his 1928 dissent of the *Olmstead v. United States* case. He stated that a person should have the right "to be left alone" and that "The greatest dangers to liberty lurk in insidious encroachment by men of zeal, well-meaning but without understanding." Because of such technological advances as transistors, microcircuits, and lasers, electronic surveillance has become very efficient and extremely easy to accomplish. In 1998 Congress proposed to expand law enforcement's wiretapping authority. While Congress's efforts were applauded by the Federal Bureau of Investigation (FBI) and other police agencies, civil liberties organizations were appalled by the prospect of expanded wiretapping. —*Jeffry Jensen*

See also American Civil Liberties Union; Civil rights and liberties; Evidence; Federal Bureau of Investigation; Kidnapping; Privacy rights; Probable cause; Telephone law.

Witness protection programs

Government-directed witness protection programs ensure the safety of key witnesses during and after court proceedings.

Witness protection programs provide security for witnesses whose testimony is critical in important court proceedings. While some states have developed state-managed witness protection programs, the most frequently used program is the Federal Witness Protection Program. Since the Program's inception under Title V of the Racketeer Influenced and Corrupt Organization (RICO) statute, of 1970 as a tool to combat organized crime, more than five thousand witnesses have been part of the Witness Protection Program. Beyond providing for the safety of witnesses, the program also provides for the health, relocation, psychological welfare, and social adjustment of witnesses. Federal protection through the Witness Protection Program has been extended to provide protection for any witnesses and their families who are recommended to the Attorney General by a state U.S. attorney's office. After the program was evaluated by the Witness Security Review Committee in 1977, the Witness Security Reform Act, part of the Comprehensive Crime Control Act of 1984, was adopted to correct a number of deficiencies that existed in the original 1970 act.

A victim's compensation fund was established through an adjustment made to the Witness Protection Program by the Reform Act. This fund compensates persons or beneficiaries for death or physical injury that may occur during relocation. However, injuries that occur to witnesses cannot be used as a cause of action against the United States. Also, for those witnesses who are sentenced to and remain in prison, placement in one of the five protected witness units in special areas of federal penitentiaries is necessary. Located throughout the country, these units are operated by the Federal Bureau of Prisons.

Guidelines and Procedures. Before accepting witnesses in the Witness Protection Program, the attorney general considers the danger in which a community will be placed if a witness is relocated there. The safety of the town or region must be considered, because many of the witnesses in the program are criminals who, in exchange for revealing information, are provided with protection and a reduction in fines or prison time. However, the significance of witnesses' testimony may outweigh the danger in which the witnesses place the community. Witnesses and those close to them must have their criminal histories reviewed and pass a psychological examination.

If accepted into the program, the attorney general, with aid from the U.S. marshals, assists witnesses in a variety of ways. Witnesses may be provided with new identities, including new names and social security cards. Those involved in the program may then use the new information to obtain other pieces of identification, such as drivers' licenses. Consequently, witnesses' birth identities cease to exist in the public domain and the records of witnesses' birth identities are turned over to the marshals service.

Once the decision to relocate a witness is made, local law-enforcement officials are notified that there is a protected witness in their territory. A relocation inspector is provided to witnesses to help them adjust to their new locations and identities. The inspector advises the witnesses about improved living strategies, such as answering peoples' questions about the past. The witnesses are also provided with housing. For some, this may be a temporary safe house; for others, it may be a new permanent location. The transportation of previously owned household furniture and personal property to the witnesses' new locations may also be provided. However, the type of personal property relocated with the witnesses is regulated, because certain personal items could connect the witnesses to their previous identities.

The witnesses are provided with a stipend to meet basic living expenses. The amount and duration of the stipend are regulated by the attorney general. Once witnesses are able to support themselves, monetary aid ceases. They are also assisted with obtaining employment. While employment aid from the government entails paying for job training, government aid does not include providing false job résumés or references. Beyond these specific guidelines, witnesses generally are assisted in other ways that are necessary to achieve independence. The decision to reveal or not to reveal witnesses' identities or locations is made by the attorney general after weighing the danger to the witnesses, to the public, to the success of the program, and to the forthcoming trial. However, the attorney general must reveal any requested information if ordered to do so by the court.

Witness Agreement. Once approved for the program, witnesses must sign a Memorandum of Understanding with the attorney general. The Memorandum of Understanding includes the agreement to testify and to provide information related to the proceedings to appropriate law-enforcement officials. To provide for the safety of the community, protected witnesses must agree not to commit any crimes and to take necessary steps to avoid detection. The witnesses must comply with legal obligations and civil judgments and cooperate with reasonable requests of government employees who are involved in the protection process. Witnesses are allowed to designate persons to serve as their agents, who make a sworn statement regarding the witnesses' legal obligations, such as child custody and any outstanding debts. Witnesses are also advised to resolve the issue of child custody before entering the program, ensuring that their children's best interests are considered in making a decision. Protected witnesses must inform witness protection officials of probation and parole responsibilities, of other activities, and of their current addresses.

A Memorandum of Understanding is entered into with every individual in the protection program who is over eighteen years of age. Before completing the evaluation that determines whether witnesses qualify for the program, the attorney general may decide to provide protection to witnesses immediately. Immediate protection is necessary in situations in which the lack of immediate protection would harm the investigation. The attorney general also has the power to terminate the protection of the witnesses if the Memorandum of Understanding is breached or the witnesses provide false information. The decision to terminate protection is not open to judicial review.

Suggested Readings. A brief description of the Witness Protection Program can be found at the United States Marshals' Web site at http://www.usDoj.gov/marshals. This program is described in the website under "Marshals Service Missions" and "Witness Security." "The Invisible Family," by Robert Sabbag in the *New York Times Magazine* (February 11, 1996), provides a personal understanding of the Witness Protection Program and general information. A critical evaluation of the Witness Protection Program is contained in a seventeen-part series on protected witnesses by Bill Moushey in the *Pittsburgh Post-Gazette* (May, 1996). A more detailed discussion of the rights and obligations of witnesses and attorneys general is located at the Web site http://www.law.cornell.edu/uscode/, followed by a search for Title 18 Section 3521. The legislative history of the program and various legislative reform measures can be found in an article by Raneta J. Lawson in the *Arizona State Law Journal* (Tempe: Arizona State University College of Law, 1992). The Library of Congress Web site http://thomas.loc.gov/home/thomas.html contains the full text of the Comprehensive Crime Control Act of 1984. —*Kim Kochanek*

See also Marshals Service, U.S.; Testimony; Witnesses.

Witnesses

A witness is a person whose testimony under oath or affirmation is received as evidence in court or in a deposition.

The common law required that lay witnesses must speak only what they know first-hand and testify only as to facts. That is, they could not offer opinions, make inferences, or draw conclusions. The rule requiring first-hand personal knowledge has been preserved by the Federal Rules of Evidence (FRE). Because the meaning of the key terms "fact" and "opinion" is often unclear, the FRE have also liberalized the admissibility of lay opinions. Lay opinions are now allowed whenever they would be helpful, provided that they are rationally based on the witness's perceptions. The latter requirement simply means that the witness must have first-hand (personal) knowledge of the matter at issue. Thus, witnesses are allowed to say that a person was (or appeared to be) angry, kidding, dying, strong, sober, or drunk. Speed may be estimated, even sometimes in such terms as fast or slow. Other examples include, "It was a sturdy fence" and "The apple was rotten."

The requirement of first-hand knowledge should not be confused with the hearsay rule. If a witness states, "Jack shot Mary" but knows this only from others, the witness violates the first-hand personal knowledge rule. If the same witness in the same circumstances testifies that "Joe told me Jack shot Mary," the first-hand rule is not violated but the hearsay rule may be violated. Hearsay rules govern the admissibility of a declarant's out-of-court statements. Accordingly, hearsay may be recounted in court pursuant to an exception or exemption; in such instances, the lack of first-hand knowledge would affect the weight rather than the admissibility of the witness's testimony.

Incompetency or Disqualification of Witnesses. A competent witness is one who testifies to what he or she has seen, heard, or otherwise observed. Trial courts recognize two kinds of witness incompetencies, which result in automatic disqualification: the lack of personal knowledge and the failure to take the oath or affirmation regarding telling the truth.

In the past witnesses have been ruled incompetent because they have a personal interest in the case, past criminal convictions, drug or alcohol intoxication or addiction, a marital relationship with one of the involved parties, or mental incapacity. Moreover, persons who are too young may be disqualified as witnesses. Such matters are mainly deemed factors to consider for whatever they are worth in the realms of relevance and credibility.

Persons who are to be offered as witnesses are often subjected to a special series of questions (often outside the presence of the jury) to ascertain foundational facts. This series of questions is to determine whether prospective witnesses understand the duty to tell the truth, can distinguish fact from fantasy, and have the ability to communicate meaningfully with the jury. Children over six years old are rarely found to be incompetent. While state laws may differ, the FRE generally treat children, at least in principle, no different from other witnesses. These rules allow for the exclusion of child witnesses only for compelling reasons, which must be something other than mere age.

Witness Preparation and Sequestration. There are almost no formal limits on bona fide efforts to prepare a prospective witness for taking the witness stand. Thus, in preparing to testify, a witness may review documents, recordings, notes, and other pieces of documentation. The witness may also be rehearsed by attorneys but not prompted to tell an untruth.

In most jurisdictions there is a process called "sequestration," whereby witnesses may be prevented from listening to other testimony in the

Judge swears in a witness before she delivers her testimony. (James L. Shaffer)

case. Questions have arisen as to whether this bars trial witnesses from reading transcripts, attending depositions, listening to oral reports of what transpired at hearings, or watching televised portions of trials. The Oklahoma bombing trials of the late 1990's raised the question as to whether families of the deceased victims were permitted to view the trial if they planned to give "victim impact" statements at the death-penalty sentencing phase. The trial judge, upheld by the court of appeals, concluded that they could not. The U.S. Congress then legislated, specifically with retroactive effect, that such witnesses in such cases could view the trials.

Additionally, the FRE exempts from sequestration witnesses who are parties, the designated representatives of organizations that are parties, or essential persons, such as experts needed at counsel's table to assist the attorneys. This rule also requires the judge to enter a sequestration order upon an attorney's request or upon the judge's own motion. The judge's order serves to clarify the scope of witness sequestration in a particular case.

Procedure for Examining Witnesses. The basic pattern of a trial after jury selection and the opening statements of counsel is that the plaintiff presents his or her case through witnesses, documents, and other evidence. Then the defendant presents his or her case, which may consist of both denying facts asserted in the plaintiff's case and establishing affirmative defenses. A witness presented at either phase will normally be examined directly by the attorney presenting the witness, by the attorney from the opposing side during cross-examination, by the proponent to redirect examination and repair the damage caused during cross-examination, and finally by the opposing attorney in a second cross-examination to repair the damage of the proponent. In the absence of an exercise of the judge's discretion, repair is the only acceptable purpose of the last two sequences. Furthermore, repair may be severely limited or disallowed completely by the judge when the contribution of additional examination would be minimal. Further redirects and recrosses are always possible if necessary.

The order of presentation of witnesses in both civil and criminal trials is basically the same. The most significant difference is that the U.S. Constitution's Fifth Amendment privilege against self-incrimination prohibits the prosecution from calling criminal defendants to the stand as witnesses. In civil trials the plaintiff's lawyers often call defendants before other witnesses.

On direct examination attorneys usually must ask for and get yes-no or short answers. However, many jurisdictions give the judge discretion to permit extended narratives to the extent that they help develop the witness's testimony. Leading questions, those that suggest the answer, are generally improper on direct examination, with exceptions for forgetful, older, young, hostile, or adverse witnesses. In the case of forgetful, older, or young witnesses, leading questions serve a valid function in refreshing their memory or directing their attention. When lawyers call hostile or adverse witnesses to the stand, the danger that the witness will consciously or unconsciously acquiesce to the examiner's version of the truth is minimal, and leading questions are thus allowed. When witnesses are hostile to the examiner, the need for forcing them to answer the lawyer's questions is greater than the danger that leading questions present.

In common-law jurisdictions there are restrictions not only on leading questions but also on those deemed argumentative, misleading, compound, or otherwise multifaceted. The FRE treat these matters by reposing power in the judge to supervise witness examinations. Specifically, the FRE exhorts the judge to take reasonable measures to promote effectiveness and efficiency in ascertaining the truth and to protect witnesses from harassment or undue embarrassment.

There are two views as to the permissible scope of cross-examinations. The restrictive rule confines the cross-examiner to matters within the scope of direct examination. The wide-open rule allows any material issue in the case to be explored. The federal rules adopt the restrictive rule but allow the judge to make exceptions. Convenience of witnesses and trial efficiency often dictate that the judge exercise discretion regarding the proper scope of a witness's cross-examination.

Witnesses' Character and Credibility. By introducing personal testimony about a witness's character, it is possible to judge whether the witness has testified accurately, lied, or made a mistake; whether a person did or did not commit rape; whether a person was or was not careful; or whether a person turned a corner in an automobile in a particular way. However, such character-type propensity evidence is sometimes prejudicial, misleading, too time-consuming, or unfair. Accordingly, there is a general ban on the use of character-type propensity evidence unless it fits special rules for special exceptions. The exceptions are many.

It must be shown that reputation or character witnesses are familiar with the reputation of the person about whom they are testifying. Thus, in the case of reputation testimony, courts normally require that the witness and the subject have lived or done business in reasonable proximity to each other for a substantial period in the fairly recent past. Also, the reputation reported must be the subject's reputation in the relevant community and relatively current.

A prerequisite for the admissibility of personal opinions about another's propensities is that the person providing personal opinions had some substantial recent contact or relationship with the other person that would furnish a reasonable basis for a current opinion. Weaknesses in these foundational elements affect the weight rather than the admissibility of character-type propensity evidence. Rules of impeachment govern the efforts to test the opposing witnesses' credibility.

Everyone's Duty to Testify. Two kinds of witnesses may appear at a trial or deposition: ordinary lay witnesses or expert witnesses. A properly subpoenaed witness who fails to show up at the time and date specified is subject to arrest. Except for the reimbursement of costs of coming to court, ordinary witnesses may not be paid to testify. Because of the truth-seeking function of the court, parties and other witnesses can be compelled to give testimony, even if it is damaging to themselves or others. Accordingly, a person normally cannot prevent another person from disclosing confidences, secrets, or other matters. However, privileges are a narrow exception to these general rules. The privileges for confidential communications in the attorney-client, physician-patient, psychotherapist-patient, and husband-wife contexts are examples of such exceptions. Privileges operate to exclude relevant evidence in the name of some other social objective. Most true privileges are designed to promote certain kinds of relationships and particularly to promote confidential communications within these socially desirable relationships.

Suggested Readings. Elaborate treatments of judicial procedural matters that discuss witnesses include Paul Bergman and Sara J. Berman-Barnett's *Represent Yourself in Court: How to Prepare and Try a Winning Case* (2d ed. Berkeley Calif.: Nolo Press, 1998) and Paul Bergman's *Trial Advocacy in a Nutshell* (3d ed. St. Paul, Minn.: West Publishing, 1995). Both of these easy-to-read, helpful, and inexpensive paperbacks review the fundamentals of direct examinations and cross-examinations through numerous examples. *Bender's Forms of Discovery* (New York: Matthew-Bender; regularly updated) is a ten-volume treatise with sample questions for numerous kinds of cases, including product liability, employment discrimination, slip-and-fall, automobile accident, and breach of contract cases. This and similar lawyer "practice guides" are often available in the reference sections of public libraries. For a quick summary of the procedural rules involved in civil lawsuits, see Mary Kay Kane's *Civil Procedure in a Nutshell* (St. Paul, Minn.: West Publishing, 1996) and *Fundamentals of Litigation for Paralegals*, by Thomas Mauet and Marlene Maerowitz (3d ed. Boston: Little Brown, 1998). *Transcript Exercises for Learning Evidence*, by Paul Bergman (St. Paul, Minn.: West Publishing, 1992) contains various questions, answers, and judicial rulings from a variety of civil and criminal cases. This book is helpful for understanding the legal propriety of common objections. For discussions of the evidence rules on which common objections are based, see *Casenotes Law Outlines: Evidence*, by Kenneth Graham (Santa Monica, Calif.: Casenotes, 1996), and *Evidence: State and Federal Rules in a Nutshell*, by Paul F. Rothstein, Myrna Raeder, and David Crump (3d ed. St. Paul, Minn.: West Publishing, 1997).

—*W. Dene Eddings Andrews*

See also Advocate-witness rule; Cross-examination; Deposition; Objection; Perjury; Privileged communication; Subpoena; Testimony; Trials; Witnesses, expert.

Witnesses, expert

A person with specialized knowledge who testifies in court.

Generally speaking, witnesses are expected to provide testimony concerning only the facts of a case; they are not allowed to give personal opinions or their own interpretation of the facts. Expert witnesses are the exception; their task is specifically to provide opinions and interpretations concerning matters on which they have special training.

While there is no particular degree or set of credentials that qualify persons as expert witnesses, there are three criteria that are considered before allowing persons to offer opinion as part of their testimony. First, the topic under examination must be something that is not considered to be common knowledge—that is, it must be something about which a typical jury would not be knowledgeable. Such topics include, but are not limited to, specialized knowledge about medicine, firearms, engineering, psychology, or computer programming. Second, expert witness must be able to provide documentation of their expertise in the form of an advanced degree, professional certification, or proof of completion of specialized training that is officially recognized in their field. Third, the testimony of expert witnesses must be "relevant" and "valid"—that is, such witnesses must confine their opinions to the specifics of the case and to interpretations that are supported by science and other practitioners in the field. This criterion is often difficult to put into practice, partly because judges are often not able to assess the validity of opinions in fields other than law and partly because even experts may disagree on controversial subjects. The result is that a particular opinion may be considered acceptable and admissible in one court at one time but not in another court at another time.

Until 1993 the most commonly cited precedent for the admissibility of expert testimony was the 1923 case of *Frye v. United States*. In that case the court, in ruling on the admissibility of the results of a polygraph test, decided that expert opinion was only admissible if the scientific principle upon which it was based was "sufficiently established to have gained general acceptance in the particular field in which it belongs." In this case, the expert's testimony was not allowed. However, in the 1993 case of *Daubert v. Merrell Dow* the U.S. Supreme Court ruled on appeal that the "Frye test" was too strict. The intended effect of the judgment in *Daubert v. Merrell Dow* was to allow opinions based on newer, "cutting edge" research and technology to be heard in court, thereby allowing the legal system to keep pace with the rapid changes in science. An unavoidable, perhaps negative, consequence is that both expert testimony and judicial decisions regarding expert testimony are now less consistent than in the past. Particularly controversial areas include the domains of psychiatry, as in assessments of personal injury, violence-proneness, and insanity; eyewitness memory, especially in cases involving child witnesses and so-called "false memory"; and statistical probability, as in cases involving deoxyribonucleic acid (DNA) "fingerprinting" and class-action suits claiming discrimination or criminal negligence. —*Linda Mealey*

See also Evidence; Hearsay; Testimony; Witnesses.

Women in legal professions

Women are relatively well represented in the legal profession but have not yet progressed to management and prestige positions in proportion to their overall size in the population.

In the 1960's dramatic social and political changes increased the demand for lawyers. Movements for civil rights, women's rights, environmental protection, and consumer advocacy provided new areas of specialty. In 1972 the passage of Title IX of the Higher Education Act prohibited discrimination based on sex in student enrollment and faculty employment. Furthermore, the organization of legal work evolved. Solo legal practitioners were gradually replaced by larger firms. Changes in size, composition, structure, and function of the legal profession diminished the control previously exercised by the American Bar Association (ABA) and state bar associations.

Employment Statistics. Women accounted for less than 5 percent of law students in the United States in the 1960's, 26 percent in the mid-1970's, 40 percent in the mid-1980's, and 50 percent in the mid-1990's. On law school faculties, women filled 1.7 percent of full-time tenure-track faculty positions in 1967, 7.5 percent in 1976, and 16 percent in 1987. In addition, women in legal education taught in low-paying, low-visibility specialties, such as clinical instruction and legal writing. By contrast, women rarely achieved the prestigious, influential position of law school dean. In 1974, 3 percent of

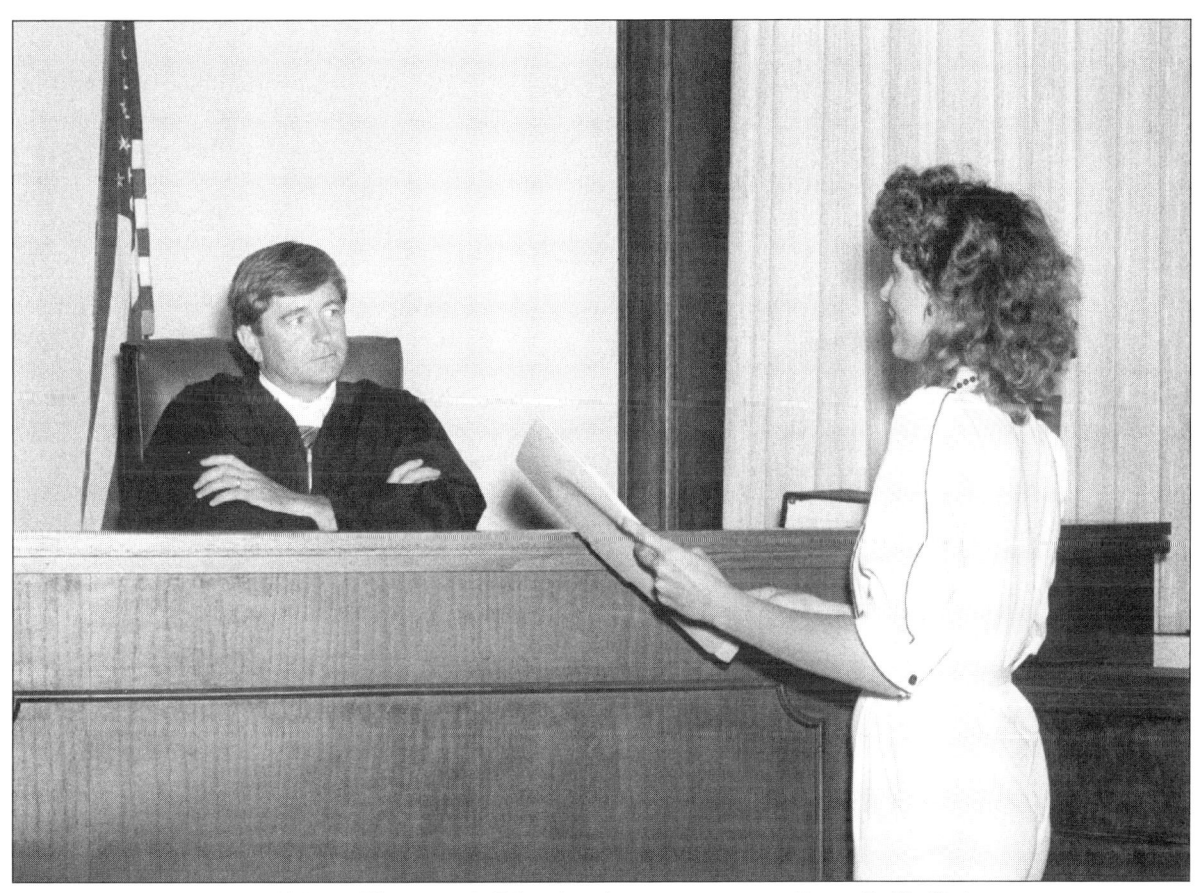

In 1994 only 25 percent of all American lawyers were women. (James L. Shaffer)

all law school deans were women and in 1987 6 percent.

In the workplace women accounted for less than 5 percent of lawyers in 1970, 12 percent in 1980, 20 percent in 1990, and 25 percent in 1994. In government law offices 25 percent of all managers are women while less than 15 percent are partners in private firms. Among the lawyers who entered private practice after 1970, 71 percent of women but only 48 percent of men did not become partners by 1984. Approximately 87 percent of all law firm partners today are males, while the number of female partners has increased by only 1 percent per year. A woman has a 39 percent less chance of becoming a partner than a man with comparable education and experience. Women who become partners do so about 26 percent more slowly than men. After taking into consideration nondiscriminatory composition effects, salary disparities due to discrimination constitute about 29 percent, or more than $12,000, annually. Men also receive higher raises when they are promoted. On average, male managing partners in medium-to-large firms earn nearly $84,000 more per year than male partners in small firms. By contrast, female managing partners in medium-to-large firms earn only $24,000 more than female partners in small ones.

Needed Changes. In law education, institutions must develop gender-sensitive hiring and promotion procedures to minimize alienation and increase women and minority representation. Because social events play an important role in an attorney's career advancement and a firm's ability to generate business, women students who lack mentors have difficulty learning the rituals of networking and cultivating client relationships. Even informal interactions, such as small talk, present women with a quandary: Friendly female lawyers may be misunderstood as sexually careless while serious women may be rejected as hostile. Thus, admission into law schools does not necessarily represent true equality of educational opportunity for women. Rather, fundamental changes must occur in faculty composition, pedagogy, institutional policies, and networking opportunities within legal education.

Many women lawyers work in a hostile environment, encountering deprecating and harassing behavior, such as sexist jokes and demeaning comments, which affect their morale, satisfaction, commitment, and their ability to represent clients effectively. Furthermore, women are not adequately represented in positions of real power and authority, clustering at the bottom rungs of prestige, income, and specialty fields, such as domestic relations, probate law, and trusts. All attorneys must have equal access to challenging work assignments, professional skills training, client contact, and meaningful evaluations and feedback. By ensuring the fair and equal allocation of resources, such as secretarial and support staffing, firms can demonstrate a commitment to diversity by holding management accountable for the professional advancement of women.

Because a legal career is frequently defined as total commitment to a workaholic schedule, including informal after-hours social events that may clash with women's personal responsibilities, law firms and corporations must develop more flexible models for career advancement. Thus, it is not enough to treat all people the same; rather, all people should be treated fairly, with respect for their differences, by developing objective, credible evaluation systems which ensure that the opportunities for development and advancement are determined by qualifications and merit.

Feminist lawyers have struggled to change employment discrimination law, challenging gender bias in legal reasoning and the ways it affects such diverse areas of law as contracts, family relations (domestic violence and child support law), and criminal sentencing (rape cases). By taking into consideration the reality of women's lives, feminist jurisprudence encourages a revision of law and legal process that embodies a more inclusive, less abstract, and more constructive worldview.

Professional Associations. The American Bar Association Commission on Women in the Profession assists and furthers the influence of women lawyers in the legal profession and the justice system, educating the profession through programs, policies, and publications. The National Association of Women Lawyers endorses women candidates for political office and the federal judiciary. The Multicultural Women Attorneys Network focuses on the impact of race, ethnicity, and gender on professional development and reports on gender barriers through statistical data, interviews, and anecdotes. The National Women Law Students' Association provides resources for improving the status of women in academic and professional settings, offering a forum for the exchange of ideas and a system of academic and professional support through mentoring. The National Organization for Women's Legal Defense and Education Fund, collaborating with the National Association of Women Judges, has designed a program to spotlight gender bias in the law, decision making, and courtroom interaction in state judicial systems. It also collects state-specific information on gender bias.

Suggested Readings. For a comprehensive overview of women in the legal professions, see Cynthia Fuchs Epstein's *Women in Law* (2d ed. Urbana: University of Illinois Press, 1993). Susan Ehrlich Martin and Nancy C. Jurik's *Doing Justice, Doing Gender: Women in Law and Criminal Justice Occupations* (Thousand Oaks, Calif.: Sage, 1996) examines the obstacles women face when dealing with police officers, lawyers, and correctional officers in the American justice system. For a discussion of the Australian jurisprudential community, see Margaret Thornton's *Dissonance and Distrust: Women in the Legal Profession* (Oxford, England: Oxford University Press, 1996). Issues concerning minority women lawyers can be found in *The Burdens of Both, the Privileges of Neither* (Chicago: American Bar Association, 1994). Statistical information is reported in Barbara A. Curran's *Women in the Law: A Look at the Numbers* (Chicago: American Bar Association, 1995), *Elusive Equality: The Experiences of Women in Legal Education* (Chicago: American Bar Association, 1996), and Valerie Fontaine's "Progress Report: Women and People of Color in Legal Education and the Legal Profession" in *Hastings Women's Law Journal* 6 (1995).

—*Sue Hum*

See also Affirmative action; American Bar Association; Attorney salaries; Law firm partners and associates; Law firm partnership tracks; Law firms; Law-school student demographics; Legal education.

Workers' compensation

A system to compensate workers for job-related accidents and occupational diseases.

Workers' compensation laws are a system to compensate employees who are injured, killed, or disabled on the job. The laws also cover occupational diseases. States have their own workers' compensation laws. There is no uniform federal law and the laws vary from state to state. There are also differences in the amounts of compensation to which injured workers are entitled. Workers' compensation statutes do not establish workplace safety standards under the federal Occupational Safety and Health Act of 1970.

All states have workers' compensation statutes. Maryland enacted the first such statute in 1902. Prior to the existence of these statutes, few workers were compensated for injuries or disabilities received on the job. The common law, which existed before the statutes, made it difficult for workers to recover any money from their employers for workplace injuries. Workers' injuries were seen to be the result of coworkers' negligence. Under the Fellow Servant Doctrine, the law did not impose liability on employers for negligent acts by coworkers, instead forcing injured workers to sue their supposedly negligent coworkers. Coworkers seldom had assets to compensate injured workers.

Workers' compensation statutes establish a state-sponsored administrative system. Employers generally pay for insurance to cover claims or pay for the claims themselves in self-insurance plans. In return, the workers' compensation system is the exclusive remedy available to workers for their injuries. This means that employees may not sue their employers or coemployees for a tort such as negligence, which might have caused their injuries.

Who Is Covered. State workers' compensation laws protect most workers. There are a few workers who are not covered under state workers' compensation statutes. Railroad employees, longshoremen, and sailors are covered by specific federal statutes.

Liability under the law is based on a death, injury, or disease "arising out of the course of employment." Accidents that occur at the workplace are covered under the statutes and injured employees are eligible for benefits under the law. Injuries that occur at home or while commuting to and from the place of employment are generally not covered.

Workers who are required to travel as a condition of their employment and are injured while traveling on business are eligible for benefits in most states. Employees traveling on employer business who deviate substantially from the business trip to conduct personal business are generally not eligible for compensation. Each state's law must be consulted for specifics.

How to Claim Workers' Compensation Benefits. Workers injured in workplace accidents must promptly file for benefits. Generally, claims are filed with employers. Employers refer claims to their insurers. If insurers accept the claims for payment, the employees may still face disputes as to the appropriateness of specific medical charges.

Insurers may also reject claims. For example, they may reject claims if they believe that workers' injuries did not arise out of the course of employment. They may also refuse claims if they believe their amounts are excessive or fraudulent.

The workers' compensation system provides a method for resolving disputes between injured employees and insurance companies or employers. Typically, employees hire an attorney in the event of contested claims. Disputes are resolved by a court that specializes in workers' compensation matters. Attorney fees are usually deducted from

---

When Workers' Compensation Attorneys Are Necessary

- When an injury occurs away from the worksite or under unusual circumstances that may require proof that it is work related

- When a person is suffering from a disease that is work related, such as lung disease

- When work-related injury causes permanent or temporary disablement

- When one disagrees with the amount the insurance company offers to pay

- When a claim is denied by the insurer

the amount of benefits awarded to employees in claims cases. Before retaining an attorney, injured employees should inquire about attorney fees.

Types of Benefits. Workers' compensation laws define the amounts of compensation to which employees are entitled for specific types of injuries. Claims are handled through an administrative system rather than by litigation under the tort system.

Workers' compensation statutes provide many types of benefits depending on the nature of the injury or disease. Employees injured in a work-related accident are eligible for payment of their medical bills as well as disability benefits if they cannot work due to their injuries.

Employees who are disabled in an accident or contract a disease arising out of the course of employment are entitled to disability income. Employees can be either temporarily or permanently disabled. Employees who are temporarily disabled are those whose injuries or illnesses are not severe enough to prevent their recovery and return to work. They receive temporary disability income while they are unable to work. Workers who are permanently disabled are those who are unable to fully return to work after their injuries or diseases. These workers are classified as either totally or partially disabled. Totally disabled workers are those whose injuries prevent them from working in the future. Such workers are eligible for 100 percent of the disability income benefits.

Employees classified as partially disabled are evaluated to determine how much their capacity to work has been reduced because of their injuries. For example, an injured employee who is assessed as 35 percent disabled because of a back injury will receive benefits amounting to 35 percent of the maximum amount.

Some specific kinds of injuries are termed "scheduled injuries." Scheduled injuries are generally permanent losses of the extremities. Workers' compensation statutes have a list or "schedule" of the amounts of compensation available for these types of injury. For example, if a person loses a finger in an accident, the schedule may indicate that the employee is entitled to two hundred weeks worth of benefits. If the employee loses two fingers, the scheduled compensation is established at a higher figure, such as three hundred weeks.

In scheduled injuries, the dollar amount of the weekly compensation depends on the wages of the injured employee prior to the injury. Workers who earned higher wages prior to their injuries are eligible for higher disability benefits than lower-paid workers. In addition, a maximum amount of benefits is established.

Suggested Readings. Persons must always consult the workers' compensation laws in their own states. Copies of state statutes are available at public libraries. Most state employment agencies publish informational pamphlets that are excellent sources of information on specific state provisions. A general overview of workers' compensation is found in Jack Hood, Benjamin Hardy, and Harold Lewis's *Workers' Compensation and Employee Protection Laws in a Nutshell* (St. Paul, Minn.: West Publishing, 1990). A good discussion of workers' compensation from the employers' perspective is found in Kenneth Sovereign's *Personnel Law* (3d ed. Englewood Cliffs, N.J.: Prentice-Hall, 1994) and Kenneth Wolff's *Understanding Workers' Compensation* (Rockville, Md.: Government Institutes, Inc., 1995). The issues from the perspective of injured employees is addressed by Lawrence White in *Human Debris: The Injured Worker in America* (New York: Seaview/Putnam, 1983).
—*Scott White*

See also Accidents and injuries; Common law; Occupational health and safety; Torts.

World Court

The reliance of the International Court of Justice on international law and its lack of enforcement mechanisms has prevented the establishment of a strong international legal forum.

The World Court, properly called the International Court of Justice, is the judicial organ of the United Nations (U.N.). It was formed after World War II to adjudicate disputes between countries. The origins of the court date back to the establishment of the Permanent Court of Arbitration during the Hague Conventions of 1899 and 1907. The Permanent Court of Arbitration was incorporated into the League of Nations in 1919 as the Permanent Court of International Justice. In 1945 the court was incorporated into the United Nations. Echoing the language of the Hague Conventions, the U.N. Charter observed that "in establishing the International Court of Justice, the United Nations hold before a war-stricken world the beacons of justice and law and offer the possibility of substituting orderly and judicial processes for the vicissitudes of war and the reign of brute force." The World Court continues to meet at the Hague in the Netherlands.

The U.N. Charter describes the World Court as the "principal judicial organ of the United Nations." All members of the United Nations are members of the World Court. The court is made up of fifteen judges elected by the General Assembly and the Security Council and drawn from different member states of the United Nations. The U.N. Charter also directs U.N. member states to select judges from "the main forms of civilization and of the principal legal systems in the world." Only member states, not individuals, may petition the court for adjudication of disputes. All states that are party to disputes brought before the World Court must consent to bringing their cases before the authority of the court. The World Court attempts to adjudicate disputes based on international laws, customs, treaties, and conventions.

The formulation of binding international legal norms in an international system composed of sovereign states has proved extremely difficult. Historically, states have preferred to obey international legal norms only when they reinforce and promote their own national security. Because the foundation of international law is based primarily on customs, observers note that the decisions of the World Court lack precedent and enforcement mechanisms. Because states embroiled in disputes may refuse to submit to the court's jurisdiction, issues defined by states as vital to national interests are rarely put before the court. Because of the unique nature of international law, the court has been used mainly as a forum to mediate disputes between members of the United Nations. While states are free to ignore formal judgments by the court, they often submit to mediation before the World Court in an attempt to prevent a formal World Court judgment against them.

Cold War tensions prevented the establishment of an active World Court after World War II. Between 1946 and 1975 only twenty-six cases that were brought before the World Court resulted in formal merit or nonmerit judgments. The United States, publicly a longtime supporter of the World Court, withdrew from the compulsory jurisdiction of the Court for two years to avoid adjudicating a dispute with Nicaragua over the mining of its harbors. In recent years attempts to expand the authority of the court have been met by opposition from influential members of the United Nations. Critics of the court have also noted the failure of the United Nations to bring to justice leaders of Cambodia, Rwanda, and the former Yugoslavia for their gross violations of human rights in the conduct of genocide.
—*Lawrence Clark*

See also Diplomatic immunity; International law; International tribunals.

Wrongful death

A death resulting from a willful act or negligence is wrongful death.

In wrongful death cases legal action is brought by a decedent's personal representative, surviving spouse, or next of kin on behalf of survivors who are seeking damages for loss of the support, services, or contributions they would have expected to receive from the decedent. Wrongful death statutes vary from state to state. Their common purpose, however, is to compensate the immediate dependent relatives for monetary losses caused by the death of the victim. Some states also permit recovery for deprivation of companionship, guidance, love, advice, and affection. Death statutes are civil in nature, and wrongful death actions may be brought for any wrongful act, intentional tort, negligence, or default that causes death. These actions are not proper for cases of breach of contract.

Historical Background. The Babylonian Code of Hammurabi included compensation for wrongful death. At common law, however, a right of recovery was denied for the death of one person killed by the negligence or wrongful act of another (dicta of Lord Ellenborough in *Baker v. Bolton*, 1808). This rule became the basis for the American common-law rule denying recovery for wrongful death in the absence of statute. Although Massachusetts courts of the colonial period had allowed compensation in death cases, the Supreme Judicial Court of Massachusetts followed *Baker* in 1848. Therefore, three basic rules existed at common law: If the tortfeasor (wrongdoer) died after committing a tort against a victim, the victim's claim died as well; if the victim died, the cause of action ended (except in actions for conversion or damage to personal property); there was no survival of a victim's claim after the victim's death and no claim of the victim's dependents against the tortfeasor for loss of support, grief, or sorrow. Most American statutes followed suit, limiting recovery to loss of pecuniary benefits.

Lord Campbell's Act of 1846 remedied prior injustices. Entitled "an act for compensating the families of persons killed by accidents," it provides that whenever the death of any person is caused by the wrongful act, neglect, or default of another, in such a manner as would have entitled the injured person to have sued had death not occurred, an action may be maintained if brought within twelve months after the death by the personal representative, for the benefit of the surviving spouse, parents, or children. The jury may award damages to be divided among the beneficiaries in such shares as the jury may determine in their verdict. Lord Campbell's Act, therefore, is significant in that it created a new cause of action based on defendant's wrongful act, limited recovery to certain named beneficiaries, and measured damages by the loss suffered by them.

Damages for Wrongful Death. The general measure of recovery is the value of the support, services, and contributions which the beneficiary might have expected to receive during the decedent's lifetime. Courts have also allowed consideration of a "hedonic" component of pecuniary loss, compensating for the loss of the pleasure of living. Since 1937 English courts have allowed separate recovery for the "loss of expectation of life." In 1976 the Supreme Court of Connecticut recognized an estate's cause of action to recover damages for loss of the ability to live and enjoy life's activities. The Seventh Circuit Court of Appeals in 1987 allowed expert testimony on the pecuniary value of life, recognizing that life has a measurable element consisting of the loss of the pleasure of living and that hedonic value encompasses the totality of a person's existence.

Involving speculation to a greater or lesser degree depending on matters such as life expectancy, income, character, habits, the health of the decedent, and past contributions to the family, the jury is given wide latitude in assessing damages. This is especially true in cases involving the death of a minor child (when the course of the future is highly speculative), a nonworking spouse, or an elderly or retired person. Most states also permit prenatal wrongful death actions, at least if the fetus had reached viability, to redress the wrong to the parents. There is also a tendency to find that the society, care, and attention of the decedent are "services" to the survivor with a financial value, which may be compensated.

Survival Statutes. Survival statutes continue the decedent's cause of action. These acts represent the estate's cause of action, one that the decedent would have brought had he or she lived, including pain and suffering minus expenses for maintenance during his or her lifetime. Included are medical and funeral expenses. Damages recovered by the estate in a survival action will be distributed according to the decedent's last will or according to the intestate statutes if the decedent had no will. Essentially, survival statutes continue the decedent's claim after death.

When a state's statutes provide for both a wrongful death and a survival action, they are two separate and distinct causes of action. Because survival statutes continue a decedent's cause of action, defenses such as contributory negligence, assumption of the risk, or consent may be asserted. Almost all courts say that a spouse's remarriage after a decedent's death should not reduce damages. Evidence that a surviving spouse has remarried is generally inadmissible as being irrelevant and prejudicial. The same reasoning prevails concerning evidence that a surviving spouse has adopted the decedent's minor child.

O. J. Simpson Civil Action. The most famous case of a wrongful death suit occurred in California. After former football star O. J. Simpson was acquitted in a 1994-1995 criminal trial for the killing of his ex-wife, Nicole, and Ron Goldman, a wrongful death action was commenced against Simpson to fix responsibility and assess damages for the death of Goldman and the assault on Nicole. There were four plaintiffs in the civil suit: Fred Goldman, individually; the estate of Ron Goldman; Sharon Rufo, individually (Goldman's natural mother); and the estate of Nicole Brown Simpson. Wrongful death and survival actions were filed.

In the survival action, had Goldman survived, he would have been able to sue his assailant for assault and battery and seek damages for injury and disfigurement plus punitive damages. Because he died, injury and disfigurement damages were moot, but punitive damages could be significant. Because he was deceased intestate (without a will), his personal representative could sue on his behalf. Any money recovered from the suit would have to be divided among his heirs (both parents). In the wrongful death claim, damages were sought for emotional support in the relationship between father and son. No claim was made for financial support in this case, but such a claim would have been proper on the theory that one day the child would have had a good job and supported his parents in their old age.

Goldman's mother filed her own claim for wrongful death, although she maintained no relationship with her son at the time of his death. The Nicole Brown Simpson estate also filed a survival claim for the battery that resulted in her death. Each minor child could conceivably bring a wrongful death claim against their father when they reach the age of majority.

Suggested Readings. Discussions of wrongful death exist in legal treatises such as William L. Prosser's *Handbook of the Law of Torts* (St. Paul, Minn.: West Publishing, 1941) and Dan B. Dobbs's *Handbook of the Law of Remedies* (St. Paul, Minn.: West Publishing, 1973). *Triumph of Justice: The Final Judgment on the Simpson Saga*, by Daniel Petrocelli with Peter Knobler (New York: Crown, 1998), is an exhaustive account of the O. J. Simpson civil trial detailing lawyer's insights, observations, and inside information. Elaine Lafferty's "The Inside Story of How O. J. Lost," *Time* (February 17, 1997) also contains an account of the civil trial. Stanley V. Smith's "Hedonic Damages in Wrongful Death Cases," *ABA Journal* (September 1, 1988) contains useful information on this element of damages. Stuart M. Speiser, Charles F. Krause, and Juanita M. Madole's *Recovery for Wrongful Death and Injury* (3d ed. Deerfield, Ill.: Clark Boardman Callaghan, 1992) details principles and cases in three volumes.

—*Marcia J. Weiss*

See also Civil action; Civil law; Damages; Torts.

Z

Zoning laws

Zoning laws regulate the use of real estate property by restricting a particular area of land to residential, commercial, industrial, or other uses.

Rules passed by local governments to regulate land and buildings in cities and towns have existed for much of the history of the United States. For example, in 1632 a town in Massachusetts allowed building construction only with the consent of the mayor. No buildings could be built on the outskirts of town until vacant areas in the town center had been filled. The first modern zoning laws date to 1916, when New York City established height and size controls for new buildings. The U.S. Supreme Court provided guidelines for zoning in a series of decisions in the 1920's and then generally ignored the issue for the next forty years.

Zoning Laws in the Early Twentieth Century. Prior to 1926 the Court upheld ordinances restricting the hours of operation of Chinese laundries in San Francisco but rejected a law forbidding putting laundries in wooden buildings. In 1900 the justices also agreed that New Orleans could designate only certain areas of the city for legal prostitution. From 1926 to 1928 the Supreme Court returned several key decisions concerning a local government's zoning rights. The most important case was *Village of Euclid v. Ambler Realty Co.* (1926), in which the Court decided that local governments could enact comprehensive zoning regulations. Zoning was held to be an exercise of the police power that gives states and local communities the right to promote and protect the safety of their citizens. After *Euclid*, zoning swept the nation. Under so-called Euclidian zoning, landscapes were divided into geometric patterns of use. Three kinds of zones were created: industrial, commercial, and residential. Under the ruling only residential use was exclusive; in other words, housing could be built in commercial zones and all uses were permitted in industrial zones. This type of zoning allowed for "administrative variance," whereby city officials could override zoning rules if the law created a unique hardship for an individual or business. It was out of the *Euclid* model that the Standard State Zoning Enabling Act of 1924 was issued by the Commerce Department. A suggested model for legislation but not law in itself, this act was adopted by all fifty states.

Since the 1920's the major change in zoning has been the number of different types of zones that have developed. Most cities have twenty to twenty-five types of zones rather than three. In most cases local governments have been given the power to zone, and very few state legislatures interfere with that power. Power is delegated under home rule provisions that are part of most state constitutions. Land use control power is based on the notion of home rule; communities should have the power to determine what can and cannot be built within their jurisdictions.

Reasonableness of Laws. Under recent Supreme Court rulings, zoning laws have to be reasonable, because they restrain the rights of private property owners. However, landowners cannot complain as long as zoning regulations are shown to be in the public interest and provide for the general welfare of the community. Zoning restrictions are required to meet the demands of the constitutional prohibition against taking private property for public use without just compensation. In 1994 the Supreme Court ruled in *Dolan v. City of Tigard* that cities and other municipalities cannot take land from private owners except through their power of eminent domain, which requires just compensation. Eminent domain is the right of the government to take private property for public use. This decision made it much more difficult for local governments to require of private builders that they give up part of their property to create accessways to lake shores, sidewalks, access roads, or parks.

Courts have rules that a zoning ordinance is illegal if it prevents a property owner from using it for any purpose for which it was reasonably adopted. What is reasonable depends on many factors, including, the location, size, and physical characteristics of the land or the character of the neighborhood in which it is located. Other factors to be considered are the effect of the ordinance on property values, the amount by which property values may be decreased, and what seems to be best for the community at large. An ordinance that was reasonable at one time may prove to be unreasonable as times change. The regulations are supposed to improve the quality of life of all people in the community rather than the welfare of a particular group. Since the 1920's courts have held that restrictions based solely on race or religion are invalid.

Zoning rules may restrict the types of buildings and the location of gas, telephone, and electrical lines. They may preserve the historical uniqueness of a neighborhood by limiting new construction or changes in existing structures. Rules may also establish and limit the size and height of buildings, the maximum or minimum numbers of rooms buildings may contain, the amount of floor space, and the minimum cost of buildings. Regulations may also establish minimum areas for front, rear, and side lots, off-street parking requirements, the number of buildings on a lot, and the number of units in a building that may be occupied. Neighborhoods may be restricted to single-family homes, multifamily apartment buildings, or townhouses. Usually special ordinances must be issued by the town government to construct schools, churches, hospitals, or charitable institutions in a district zoned for residential property.

Changing the Law. Only the legislative body empowered to enact zoning laws has the power to change or amend them. Usually, this cannot be done without public hearings. Zoning ordinances generally are not changed without approval of neighborhood residents. Local governments have broad powers to permit or prohibit certain property uses and may create whole areas in which only homes, stores, or industries may be built. If a building's use does not conform to a new ordinance but it has been standing in an area before the rule was passed, it has "legal nonconforming use." This means that the structure is protected by the U.S. Constitution unless it is abandoned or its ownership terminated. The property cannot be changed or taken away from its owner without just compensation. If it is destroyed by fire or flood, however, it cannot be rebuilt.

If property owners cannot meet the strict letter of a zoning regulation, they may ask enforcement officials for a variance. If the owners can prove that meeting the specific requirements would present a hardship for them, they can be granted a variation. This allows for a slight violation in zoning requirements. However, owners cannot create their own hardships by deliberately violating the law. If owners are not granted a variance and fail to make required changes to their property, they may be fined for each day the violation continues. Sometimes the fine is reduced if owners show a willingness to achieve the desired change in a reasonable time.

Suggested Readings. For a historical overview and detailed descriptions of U.S. Supreme Court cases, see Donald G. Hagman and Julian Conrad Juergensmeyer's *Urban Planning and Land Development Control Law* (2d ed. St. Paul, Minn.: West Publishing, 1986). For an expert's view consult Alexander Rathkopf's *The Law of Zoning* (3d ed., St. Paul, Minn.: West Publishing, 1987). Also of interest is Robert Anderson and Barry Roswig's *Planning Zoning and Subdivision: A Summary of Statutory Law in the Fifty States* (1966). The American Law Institute presents its recommendations in *A Model Land Development Code* (Philadelphia: American Law Institute, 1976).

—*Leslie V. Tischauser*

See also Building permits; Eminent domain; Home businesses; Landlords; Pets; Real estate law.

Important Federal Laws

The official compilation of federal laws, organized by subjects, is the United States Code (U.S.C.). Many libraries contain an annotated version of this code, which includes references to cases and other legal sources that interpret federal laws together with the laws themselves. This annotated version is known as the United States Code Annotated (U.S.C.A.). Copies of the United States Code may be found at several sites on the World Wide Web, including the FedLaw site operated by the Government Services Administration (http://www.legal.gsa.gov). The location of the United States Code within this Web site is http://www.legal.gsa.gov/fedfra1g.htm. In addition, the Cornell Law School, which maintains an immense and important collection of legal materials on the World Wide Web, also maintains a copy of the United States Code. The address for this copy is http://www.law.cornell.edu/uscode/. The most likely source for finding a hardcover copy of the U.S.C. or the U.S.C.A. is a public library or a law library. Most courthouses contain a law library that includes the U.S.C. or the U.S.C.A.

Organization of the United States Code. The code is organized into fifty sections, referred to as "titles," which correspond to fifty subjects: agriculture; aliens and nationality; arbitration; armed forces; bankruptcy; banks and banking; census; Coast Guard; commerce and trade; conservation; copyrights; crimes and criminal procedure; customs duties; education; flag and seal, seat of government, and the states; food and drugs; foreign relations and intercourse; general provisions; government organization and employees; highways; hospitals and asylums; Indians; Internal Revenue Code; intoxicating liquors; judiciary and judicial procedure; labor; mineral lands and mining; money and finance; National Guard; navigation and navigable waters; Navy (eliminated by the enactment of title 10); patents; patriotic societies and observations; pay and allowances of the uniformed services; Postal Service; the president; public buildings, property, and works; public contracts; public health and welfare; public lands; public printing and documents; railroads; shipping; surety bonds (repealed by the enactment of title 31); telegraphs, telephones, and radiotelegraphs; territories and insular possessions; transportation; the U.S. Congress; veterans' benefits; and war and national defense.

The titles of the United States Code are divided into chapters and the chapters into sections, but one need only know the title and the section of a particular law to find it.

Citations to the United States Code. When an act of Congress is incorporated into the code, the provisions of the act may be dispersed across several sections of the code, and these sections themselves may be scattered throughout several titles of the code. Thus, a given act may amend previously existing code sections, and its language might therefore be codified under the various sections it amends. These realities of legislative codification make it sometimes difficult to refer to a specific section of the code as locating a particular act. Whenever possible in the table below, the code reference is to the first of a series of sequential sections of the code or to some general statement of purpose of an act.

Table Coverage. The following table by no means exhaustively catalogs all federal laws. It is intended to refer the reader to some of the more important federal laws, to laws with relatively well-known popular names, and to laws of general interest to the public. Readers in need of a more comprehensive list of federal laws should consult the United States Code itself. A useful tool for looking up particular federal laws is the U.S.C. Table of Popular Names, which indexes federal laws according to the name generally given to the acts by which they became law. This table is included in the volumes of the U.S.C.A. and is available on the World Wide Web (http://www.law.cornell.edu/uscode/topn). The FedLaw Site of the General Services Administration (http://fedlaw.gsa.gov:80/intro2.htm) also includes a useful collection of federal laws organized by topic.

Abandoned Shipwreck Act (1988)	43 U.S.C. § 2101	Provides for federal control over the disposition of abandoned ships.
Acid Precipitation Act (1980)	42 U.S.C. § 8901	Establishes program to study acid rain.
Adamson Act (1916)	45 U.S.C. § 65	Establishes eight-hour day as basic definition of a day's work.
Administrative Procedures Act (1965)	5 U.S.C. § 500	Establishes procedures for federal administrative agencies to promulgate regulations and conduct hearings.
Age Discrimination Act (1975)	42 U.S.C. § 6101	Prohibits discrimination on the basis of age in programs or activities receiving federal financial assistance.
Age Discrimination in Employment Act (1967)	29 U.S.C. § 621	Prohibits arbitrary age discrimination in employment.
AIDS Housing Opportunity Act (1990)	42 U.S.C. § 12901	Provides resources and incentives for state and local governments to develop strategies to offer housing for victims of acquired immunodeficiency syndrome (AIDS) and their families.
American Folklife Preservation Act (1976)	20 U.S.C. § 2101	Establishes an American Folklife Center in the Library of Congress to preserve and present American folklife.
American Indian Religious Freedom Act (1978)	42 U.S.C. § 1996	Protects religious freedom of American Indians, Eskimos, Aleuts, and Native Hawaiians.
Americans with Disabilities Act (1990)	42 U.S.C. § 12101	Prohibits discrimination on the basis of disability in employment, programs and services provided by state and local governments, goods and services provided by private companies, and in commercial facilities.
Animal Welfare Act (1966)	7 U.S.C. § 2131	Provides humane treatment for various animals.
Anti-Injunction Law (1932)	29 U.S.C. § 101	Limits the ability of federal courts to issue injunctions in labor disputes.
Anti-Kickback Act (1986)	41 U.S.C. § 51	Prohibits kickbacks in federal contracts.
Antiquities Act (1906)	16 U.S.C. § 431	Provides for the protection and scientific investigation of historic and prehistoric ruins and objects of antiquity on lands owned or controlled by the Federal Government.
Archeological Resources Protection Act (1979)	16 U.S.C. § 470	Prohibits the removal, sale, receipt, and interstate transportation of archaeological resources obtained illegally from public or Native American lands.
Arms Export Control Act (1968)	22 U.S.C. § 2751	Regulates weapons exports.

Bald Eagle Protection Act (1940)	16 U.S.C. § 668	Prohibits wantonly possessing, selling, transporting, or trading bald or golden eagles, whether alive or dead, or eagle parts.
Bankruptcy Code (1978)	11 U.S.C. § 101	Generally regulates bankruptcy filings and rights.
Black Lung Act (1972)	30 U.S.C. § 938	Prohibits discrimination by mine operators against miners who suffer from pneumoconiosis, or black lung disease.
Buy American Act (1933)	41 U.S.C. § 10a	Establishes general policy for federal agencies to seek American-made products and supplies in making procurements.
Calder Act (1918)	15 U.S.C. § 261	Establishes times zones in the United States and daylight savings time.
Child Nutrition Act (1966)	42 U.S.C. § 1771	Establishes school breakfast programs.
Child Support Enforcement Act (1935)	42 U.S.C. § 651	Establishes a federal program of appropriations and support for the enforcement of child-support obligations.
Children's Bicycle Helmet Safety Act (1994)	15 U.S.C. § 6001	Establishes program to encourage the use of bicycle helmets by children under the age of sixteen.
Civil Action For Deprivation of Rights (1871)	42 U.S.C. § 1983	Allows persons whose constitutional rights have been violated to bring suit for redress.
Civil Justice Reform Act (1990)	28 U.S.C. § 471	Requires federal district courts to adopt plans to reduce expenses and delays.
Civil Rights Act (1866)	42 U.S.C. § 1982	Prohibits racial discrimination in real estate transactions.
Civil Rights Act (1964)	42 U.S.C. § 2000a	Prohibits discrimination in public accommodations, educational facilities, and employment on the basis of race, color, religion, or national origin.
Clayton Antitrust Act (1914)	15 U.S.C. § 12	Prohibits mergers or acquisitions that are likely to diminish economic competition.
Clean Air Act (1955)	42 U.S.C. § 7401	Establishes programs to control air pollution.
Clean Water Act (1948)	33 U.S.C. § 1251	Controls pollution in the nation's waterways.
Coastal Barrier Resources Act (1982)	16 U.S.C. § 3501	Restricts federal expenditures that have the effect of encouraging development of coastal barriers and their adjacent inlets, waterways, and wetlands.
Coastal Zone Management Act (1972)	16 U.S.C. § 1451	Creates program to manage and protect coastal zones.

Community Improvement Volunteer Act (1994)	40 U.S.C. § 276d	Establishes program to encourage volunteers to assist in the repair or construction of federally funded public buildings and public works.
Comprehensive Environmental Response, Compensation, and Liability Act (CERCLA) (1980)	42 U.S.C. § 9601	Provides for liability, compensation, cleanup, and emergency response relating to hazardous substances released into the environment and for the cleanup of inactive hazardous substances disposal sites; establishes a fund obtained from those who generate hazardous waste for use in cleanup and response actions of abandoned hazardous waste sites when no financially responsible parties can be found.
Consumer Credit Protection Act (Truth in Lending Act) (1968)	15 U.S.C. § 1501	Requires creditors to provide borrowers with information relevant to credit transactions.
Consumer Credit Protection Act (1968)	15 U.S.C. § 1601	Requires disclosure of credit terms to consumers and generally regulates consumer credit transactions.
Consumer Product Safety Act (1972)	15 U.S.C. § 2051	Provides for safety regulation of products.
Controlled Substances Act (1970)	21 U.S.C. § 801	Enacts comprehensive regulation of drugs.
Copyright Act (1947)	17 U.S.C. § 810	Protects and regulates the rights of the creators of original works.
Debt Collection Act (1982)	5 U.S.C. § 552a	Regulates debt collection practices.
Defense of Marriage Act (1996)	28 U.S.C. § 1738(c)	Provides that states are not required to recognize same-sex marriages performed in other states.
Drug-Free Workplace Act (1988)	41 U.S.C. § 701	Imposes drug-free workplace requirements on federal contractors and grant recipients.
Electronic Communications Privacy Act (1986)	24 U.S.C. § 2701	Protects the privacy of electronic communications.
Electronic Fund Transfer Act (1978)	15 U.S.C. § 1693	Regulates electronic transfers of funds.
Elementary and Secondary Education Act (1965)	20 U.S.C. § 6301	Provides federal support for public elementary and secondary education.
Emergency Wetlands Resources Act (1986)	16 U.S.C. § 3901	Promotes conservation of wetlands.
Employee Polygraph Protection Act (1988)	29 U.S.C. § 2001	Regulates use of polygraph tests by employers in businesses affecting commerce.
Employee Retirement Income Security Act (ERISA) (1974)	29 U.S.C. § 1001	Establishes federal program to assure the soundness of retirement plans.

Endangered Species Act (1973)	16 U.S.C. § 1531	Protects endangered species.
Equal Access Act (1984)	20 U.S.C. § 4071	Prohibits public secondary schools that receive federal financial assistance from denying access to school facilities to religious, political, or philosophical student groups when other noncurricular student groups are allowed access.
Equal Credit Opportunity Act (1974)	15 U.S.C. § 1691	Prohibits certain forms of discrimination on the basis of race, color, religion, national origin, sex or marital status, or age with regard to the provision of credit.
Equal Employment Opportunity Act (1972)	42 U.S.C. § 2000e	Prohibits employment discrimination on the basis of race, color, religion, sex, or national origin.
Equal Pay Act (1963)	29 U.S.C. § 201	Prohibits sex discrimination in pay given to employees.
Equal Rights Under the Law (1870)	42 U.S.C. § 1981	Protects individuals from discrimination based on race in making and enforcing contracts, participating in lawsuits, and giving evidence.
Ethics in Government Act (1978)	28 U.S.C. § 591	Regulates ethics of government officials.
Expedited Funds Availability Act (1987)	12 U.S.C. § 4001	Regulates availability of deposited funds at federally insured banks and other institutions.
Fair Credit Reporting Act (1970)	15 U.S.C. § 1681	Regulates credit reports.
Fair Debt Collection Practices Act (1977)	15 U.S.C. § 1692	Protects consumers from unfair debt collection practices.
Fair Housing Act (1968)	42 U.S.C. § 3601	Prohibits discrimination in housing transactions on the basis of race, color, religion, sex, familial status, or national origin.
Fair Labor Standards Act (1938)	29 U.S.C. § 201	Grants federal government power to regulate various matters relating to employment.
Fair Packaging and Labeling Act (1966)	15 U.S.C. § 1451	Provides for federal regulations of product labels and packaging.
Family and Medical Leave Act (1993)	29 U.S.C. § 2601	Provides employees with the right to take leave time to care for newborn children or sick family members.
Federal Arbitration Act (1947)	9 U.S.C. § 2	Provides for the enforcement of arbitration agreements.
Federal Deposit Insurance Act (1950)	12 U.S.C. § 1811	Establishes a federal insurance program for bank deposits.
Federal Employees' Compensation Act (1908)	5 U.S.C. § 8101	Provides compensation for federal workers injured, disabled, or killed in the course of their employment.

Federal Food, Drug, and Cosmetic Act (1938)	21 U.S.C. § 301	Regulates foods, drugs, and cosmetic products.
Federal Insecticide, Fungicide, and Rodenticide Act (1947)	7 U.S.C. § 136	Establishes requirements for the registration of insecticides, fungicides, and rodenticides.
Federal Insurance Contributions Act (1939)	26 U.S.C. § 3101	Establishes a tax on employees and employers to support Social Security benefits.
Federal Reserve Act (1913)	12 U.S.C. § 221	Establishes the Federal Reserve System for banks.
Federal Tax Lien Act (1966)	26 U.S.C. § 6321	Grants the federal government a lien to secure unpaid taxes.
Federal Tort Claims Act (1948)	28 U.S.C. § 2671	Permits suits against the federal government for harms inflicted upon citizens.
Federal Trade Commission Act (1914)	15 U.S.C. § 41	Establishes federal commission to oversee United States business practices.
Fish and Wildlife Conservation Act (1980)	16 U.S.C. § 2901	Establishes policy for federal agencies and departments to promote conservation of nongame fish and wildlife and their habitats.
Fishermen's Protective Act (1967)	22 U.S.C. § 1978	Restricts the import of fishery or wildlife products from countries that violate international environmental programs.
Food Stamp Act (1977)	7 U.S.C. § 2011	Provides welfare benefits for the purchase of food by indigent families.
Foreign Agents Registration Act (1938)	22 U.S.C. § 611	Requires that agents of foreign governments register with the United States.
Freedom of Access to Clinic Entrances Act (1994)	18 U.S.C. § 248	Prohibits the use of force or threats to hinder access to reproductive clinics or religious exercise at places of religious worship; prohibits damaging or destroying reproductive clinics or places of religious worship.
Freedom of Information Act (FOIA) (1966)	5 U.S.C. § 552	Allows public access to government information.
Goals 2000: Educate America Act (1994)	20 U.S.C. § 5801	Establishes program to encourage education reform.
Hazardous Materials Transportation Act (1974)	49 U.S.C. § 1801	Regulates transportation of hazardous materials in the United States.
Head Start Act (1981)	42 U.S.C. § 9831	Provides comprehensive health, educational, nutritional, social, and other services to economically disadvantaged children and their families.

Historic Sites Act (1935)	16 U.S.C. § 461	Authorizes the designation of national historic sites and landmarks.
Indian Child Welfare Act (1978)	25 U.S.C. § 1901	Seeks to protect the best interests of Native American children and to promote the stability and security of Native American tribes and families by establishing minimum federal standards for the removal of Native American children from their families and the placement of such children in foster or adoptive homes and by providing for assistance to Native American tribes in the operation of child and family service programs.
Individuals with Disabilities Education Act (1970)	20 U.S.C. § 1400	Guarantees a free public education to children with disabilities.
Insanity Defense Reform Act (1984)	18 U.S.C. § 20	Places on criminal defendants in federal courts the burden of proving the insanity defense when it is asserted as a defense to a criminal prosecution.
Insect Control Act (1937)	7 U.S.C. § 148	Authorizes the federal government to take steps to control outbreaks of insect pests and plant diseases.
Intelligence Identities Protection Act (1982)	50 U.S.C. § 421	Prohibits unauthorized disclosures of the identities of covert agents.
Internal Revenue Code (1954)	26 U.S.C. § 1	Enacts comprehensive laws relating to income taxes and deductions.
Jacob Wetterling Crimes Against Children and Sexually Violent Offender Registration Act (1994)	42 U.S.C. § 14071	Establishes procedures for registration of sexual offenders.
Jones Act (1915)	46 U.S.C. § 688	Allows recovery for injuries suffered at sea.
Juvenile Justice and Delinquency Prevention Act (1974)	42 U.S.C. § 5617	Creates system of federal training and support for state juvenile justice systems.
Labor-Management Relations Act (Taft-Hartley Act) (1947)	29 U.S.C. § 141	Regulates labor disputes.
Lanham Act (1946)	15 U.S.C. § 1051	Provides protection for registered trademarks.
Lobbying Disclosure Act (1995)	2 U.S.C. § 1601	Requires federal lobbyists to register and disclose their activities.
Longshore and Harbor Workers' Compensation Act (1927)	33 U.S.C. § 901	Provides compensation for employees injured in navigable waters of the United States.
McCarran-Ferguson Act (1945)	15 U.S.C. § 1011	Allows states to regulate and tax insurance companies.

Magnuson-Moss Warranty-Federal Trade Commission Improvement Act (1914)	15 U.S.C. § 45	Prohibits certain unfair business practices.
Mail Fraud Act (1948)	18 U.S.C. § 1341	Prohibits fraudulent schemes that use the U.S. mails.
Mann Act (1948)	18 U.S.C. § 2421	Prohibits travel across state lines to engage in criminal sexual activities.
Marine Mammal Protection Act (1972)	16 U.S.C. § 1361	Establishes a moratorium on the taking and importation of marine mammals and marine mammal products, with limited exceptions for scientific research.
Megan's Law (1996)	42 U.S.C. § 14071(e)	Authorizes release of information to the public concerning sex offenders.
Motor Vehicle Theft Act (1948)	18 U.S.C. § 2312	Punishes transportation of stolen cars in interstate or foreign commerce.
National Child Protection Act (1993)	42 U.S.C. § 5119	Establishes procedures for criminal background checks of child-care providers.
National Environmental Policy Act (1969)	42 U.S.C. § 4321	Establishes basic statement of policy concerning the nation's commitment to protect the environment.
National Firearms Act (1934)	26 U.S.C. § 5845	Regulates trade in firearms.
National Labor Relations Act (Wagner Act) (1935)	29 U.S.C. § 151	Establishes the right of workers to collectively bargain and join unions and generally regulates relations between management and labor.
Native American Graves Protection and Repatriation Act (1990)	25 U.S.C. § 3001	Provides for the protection of Native American and Native Hawaiian cultural items and establishes a process for the authorized removal of human remains, funerary objects, sacred objects, and objects of cultural patrimony from sites located on federal lands.
Occupational and Safety Health Act (OSHA) (1970)	29 U.S.C. § 651	Establishes system of regulations to protect employees.
Odometer Disclosure Act (1972)	49 U.S.C. § 32701	Prohibits tampering with vehicle odometers.
Oil Pollution Act (1990)	33 U.S.C. § 2701	Creates a provision for prevention of and response to oil spills.
Older Americans Act (1965)	42 U.S.C. § 3001	Establishes a program to assist in employment opportunities for elderly citizens.
Organic Foods Production Act (1990)	7 U.S.C. § 6501	Establishes national standards for the marketing of products claiming to be organically grown.

Paperwork Reduction Act (1980)	44 U.S.C. § 3501	Establishes procedures to minimize the paperwork burden for various persons resulting from the collection of information by or for the federal government.
Peace Corps Act (1961)	22 U.S.C. § 2501	Establishes the Peace Corp.
Pollution Prevention Act (1990)	42 U.S.C. § 13101	Establishes a policy of preventing pollution at its source whenever feasible.
Privacy Act (1974)	5 U.S.C. § 552a	Protects the privacy of personal information held by federal agencies.
Procurement Integrity Act (1988)	41 U.S.C. § 423	Regulates ethics and conflicts of interest in federal procurements.
Racketeer Influenced and Corrupt Organizations (RICO) statute (Organized Crime Control Act) (1970)	18 U.S.C. § 1961	Provides for criminal and civil punishments of racketeering and other illegal activities.
Rehabilitation Act (1973)	29 U.S.C. § 791	Promotes employment opportunities for handicapped individuals in federal jobs and in institutions and businesses that receive federal funds.
Roberts Act (1964)	40 U.S.C. § 701	Prohibits the acquisition or purchase of motor vehicles by the federal government unless they are equipped with passenger safety devices.
Robinson-Patman Anti-Discrimination Act (1914)	15 U.S.C. § 13	Prohibits anticompetitive price discrimination in commercial transactions.
Safe Drinking Water Act (1944)	42 U.S.C. § 300f	Establishes standards and policies to protect public health by ensuring safe drinking water.
Safe Homes for Women Act (1994)	18 U.S.C. § 2265	Makes it a crime to cross state lines in connection with domestic violence.
Securities Act (1933)	15 U.S.C. § 77a	Provides for the registration of and general regulation of securities.
Securities Exchange Act (1934)	15 U.S.C. § 78a	Establishes the Securities Exchange Commission and generally regulates security exchanges.
Service Contract Act (1965)	41 U.S.C. § 351	Establishes minimum wage and workplace safety requirements in federal contracts for services.
Sherman Act (1890)	15 U.S.C. § 1	Prohibits contracts, combinations, and conspiracies that unreasonably restrain interstate trade.
Small Business Act (1958)	15 U.S.C. § 631	Establishes a program to encourage the growth and support of small businesses.
Social Security Act (1935)	42 U.S.C. § 301	Provides for financial assistance to elderly citizens.

Speedy Trial Act (1974)	18 U.S.C. § 3161	Provides for speedy trials in federal criminal cases.
Standard Time Act (1918)	15 U.S.C. § 251	Establishes time zones in the United States.
Take Pride in America Act (1990)	16 U.S.C. § 4601	Establishes a program to instill in the public the importance of the appropriate use of and appreciation for federal, state, and local lands, facilities, and natural and cultural resources.
Toxic Substances Control Act (1976)	15 U.S.C. § 2601	Regulates toxic substances.
Truth in Negotiations Act (1950)	10 U.S.C. § 2301	Establishes competitive bidding requirements and other regulations pertaining to the procurement of services or supplies by a federal agency.
Truth in Savings Act (1991)	12 U.S.C. § 4301	Requires banks to disclose to depositors terms and conditions upon which interest is paid and fees are assessed.
Unfunded Mandates Reform Act (1995)	2 U.S.C. § 1501	Requires that the U.S. Congress, in passing federal laws, consider the financial impact of such laws on state, local, and tribal governments.
Victims of Child Abuse Act (1990)	42 U.S.C. § 13001	Establishes a federal program to support child-abuse prevention and punishment effects.
Victims of Crime Act (1984)	42 U.S.C. § 10601	Establishes a Crime Victims Fund to provide compensation to the victims of crimes.
Violence Against Women Act (1994)	42 U.S.C. § 3796gg	Provides definitions of, support for enforcement against, and remedies for a variety of forms of violence against women.
Voting Rights Act (1965)	42 U.S.C. § 1971	Prohibits racial discrimination in voting.
Walsh-Healey Public Contracts Act (1936)	41 U.S.C. § 35	Requires that federal government agencies and offices contract only with parties who satisfy minimum wage and maximum hour laws, child-labor requirements, and workplace safety requirements.
War Powers Resolution (1973)	50 U.S.C. § 1541	Attempts to facilitate congressional oversight and review of the U.S. president's commitment of armed forces in particular conflicts.

—Timothy L. Hall

Important U.S. Supreme Court Cases

Supreme Court cases appear in volumes referred to as "reporters." The official reporter for Supreme Court cases is a series referred to as the *United States Reports*, abbreviated in citations as "U.S." A typical citation to a Supreme Court case would be "250 U.S. 616," in which the first number represents the volume number from the *United States Reports* and the second the page on which the case begins. *United States Reports* does not contain the most recent Supreme Court cases. To find these, one must rely on other reporters. Perhaps the most well known of these is the *Supreme Court Reporter*, abbreviated in citations as "S.Ct." Citations to some of the last cases in this table include references to the *Supreme Court Reporter*.

Date	*Case*	*Citation*	*Decision*
1803	Marbury v. Madison	5 U.S. 137	The Court had the power of judicial review, that is, to determine the constitutionality of federal laws.
1810	Fletcher v. Peck	10 U.S. 87	The Court had authority to determine the constitutionality of state laws.
1819	Dartmouth College v. Woodward	17 U.S. 518	A state's attempt to revise the charter of a private college violated the contracts clause.
1819	Sturges v. Crowninshield	17 U.S. 122	A state law discharging previously existing debts violated the contracts clause.
1827	Ogden v. Saunders	25 U.S. 213	A state insolvency law did not violate the contracts clause when it applied only to contracts entered into subsequent to the law's passage.
1831	Cherokee Nation v. Georgia	30 U.S. 1	The Court lacked authority to hear a case brought by Cherokees because they were not a sovereign nation.
1833	Barron v. Baltimore	32 U.S. 243	The provisions of the Bill of Rights could only limit federal, not state, actions.
1837	Charles River Bridge Co. v. Warren Bridge Co.	36 U.S. 420	The contracts clause did not prevent a state from granting certain individuals the right to build and collect tolls from a bridge after already granting a similar right to other individuals to build a different bridge.
1857	Scott v. Sandford	60 U.S. 393	Blacks were not citizens of the United States and the U.S. Congress lacked authority to enact the Missouri Compromise.
1866	Ex parte Milligan	71 U.S. 2	The trial of civilians before a military tribunal was unconstitutional.
1873	Slaughterhouse Cases	83 U.S. 36	A state law that awarded a monopoly to one slaughterhouse did not violate the Fourteenth Amendment.

Date	Case	Citation	Decision
1879	Reynolds v. United States	98 U.S. 145	A federal antibigamy law did not violate free exercise rights of Mormons who wished to engage in the practice of polygamy.
1883	Civil Rights Cases	109 U.S. 3	Congress lacked authority under the Thirteenth and Fourteenth Amendments to enact a law prohibiting racial discrimination in inns and public conveyances.
1884	Hurtado v. California	110 U.S. 516	The Fourteenth Amendment's due process clause did not require a grand jury indictment in a state murder prosecution.
1895	In re Debs	158 U.S. 564	An injunction issued against strikers was a constitutional exercise of federal authority to remove obstructions to commerce.
1896	Plessy v. Ferguson	163 U.S. 537	A state law requiring separate railway facilities for African American and white passengers did not violate the equal protection clause.
1905	Lochner v. New York	198 U.S. 45	A state law that restricted the number of hours bakers could work interfered with freedom to contract and thus violated due process.
1908	Muller v. Oregon	208 U.S. 412	A state law that established maximum work hours for women was not unconstitutional.
1914	Weeks v. United States	232 U.S. 383	Evidence obtained in an illegal search may not be used in a subsequent criminal prosecution.
1915	Guinn v. United States	238 U.S. 347	A voter literacy requirement intended by a state to prevent African Americans from voting violated the Fifteenth Amendment.
1918	Hammer v. Dagenhart	247 U.S. 251	Congress lacked power under the commerce clause to prohibit interstate shipment of goods produced with child labor.
1919	Abrams v. United States	250 U.S. 616	Protest of U.S. policies involving Soviet Russia was not protected from punishment by the First Amendment.
1919	Schenck v. United States	249 U.S. 47	The prosecution of protests against the draft did not violate the First Amendment.
1921	Newberry v. United States	256 U.S. 232	Congress did not have power to limit campaign expenditures in primary elections.
1925	Gitlow v. New York	268 U.S. 652	The First Amendment did not prevent a state from punishing advocacy of the violent overthrow of government even if such advocacy did not immediately incite criminal action.
1925	Pierce v. Society of Sisters	268 U.S. 510	A state law requiring children to be educated in public schools violated due process.

Date	Case	Citation	Decision
1927	Buck v. Bell	274 U.S. 200	A state's sterilization of a mentally impaired female did not violate due process.
1927	Nixon v. Herndon	273 U.S. 536	A state law excluding African Americans from voting in Democratic primaries was unconstitutional.
1928	Olmstead v. United States	277 U.S. 438	So long as use of a wiretap did not require entry of private premises it was not an unreasonable search and seizure.
1931	Near v. Minnesota	283 U.S. 697	A state law prohibiting the publication of a newspaper that had printed defamatory articles violated the First Amendment.
1932	Powell v. Alabama	287 U.S. 45	Criminal defendants in rape cases are entitled to court-appointed attorneys.
1934	Home Building and Loan Association v. Blaisdell	290 U.S. 398	A state law declaring a moratorium on the repayment of mortgages did not violate the contracts clause.
1935	Grovey v. Townsend	295 U.S. 45	Limitation of state Democratic party membership to whites violated the equal protection clause
1936	Brown v. Mississippi	297 U.S. 278	The due process clause prohibited use of coerced confessions in state criminal prosecutions.
1936	Carter v. Carter Coal Co.	298 U.S. 238	Congress had no authority under the commerce clause to regulate labor conditions in the coal mining industry.
1937	Herndon v. Lowry	301 U.S. 242	Attempts to incite insurrection were not protected by the First Amendment.
1937	Palko v. Connecticut	302 U.S. 319	The double jeopardy limitation of the Fifth Amendment was not applicable to states.
1937	West Coast Hotel Co. v. Parrish	300 U.S. 379	The due process clause did not prevent a state from regulating the minimum wages for women and children.
1940	Chambers v. Florida	309 U.S. 227	The due process clause prohibited use of improperly obtained confessions.
1941	United States v. Classic	313 U.S. 299	Congress had authority to regulate primary elections when such elections were an important part of the election process for federal office.
1941	United States v. Darby	312 U.S. 100	Under the commerce clause, the U.S. Congress had authority to regulate wages and hours of workers who manufactured products shipped interstate.
1942	Wickard v. Filburn	317 U.S. 111	Congress had power under the commerce clause to regulate a farmer's consumption of wheat for personal use.

Date	Case	Citation	Decision
1943	Hirabayashi v. United States	320 U.S. 81	The equal protection clause did not prohibit a curfew law applicable to Japanese Americans during World War II.
1943	West Virginia State Board of Education v. Barnette	319 U.S. 624	The First Amendment prohibited schools from compelling Jehovah's Witness children to salute the flag and recite the pledge of allegiance.
1944	Korematsu v. United States	323 U.S. 214	The confinement of Japanese Americans in internment camps during World War II did not violate the equal protection clause.
1944	Smith v. Allwright	321 U.S. 649	The exclusion of African Americans from party primaries for state and national offices violated the Fourteenth and Fifteenth Amendments.
1946	Colegrove v. Green	328 U.S. 549	Federal courts had no authority to hear an action seeking to compel congressional redistricting since it was a political question.
1947	Adamson v. California	332 U.S. 46	A prosecutor in a state criminal proceeding did not violate due process by calling the jury's attention to a defendant's failure to testify.
1947	Everson v. Board of Education	330 U.S. 1	A state's reimbursement of parents for costs of transportation to parochial schools did not violate establishment clause.
1948	Shelley v. Kraemer	334 U.S. 1	The enforcement of a racially restrictive real estate covenant by a state court violated the Fourteenth Amendment.
1949	Wolf v. Colorado	338 U.S. 25	Due process did not require states to exclude illegally obtained evidence from use in criminal proceedings.
1950	Sweatt v. Painter	339 U.S. 629	A state's denial of admission for an African American applicant to the state law school violated equal protection.
1951	Dennis v. United States	341 U.S. 494	The criminal conviction of a speaker for advocating communism did not violate freedom of speech.
1954	Bolling v. Sharpe	347 U.S. 497	The District of Columbia's segregated public schools violated equal protection.
1954	Brown v. Board of Education	347 U.S. 483	State segregation of public schools violated equal protection.
1957	Roth v. United States	354 U.S. 476	Obscenity was not protected by the first amendment.
1957	Yates v. United States	354 U.S. 298	Freedom of speech prohibited government from prosecuting advocacy of forcible overthrow of government without proof of advocacy of specific acts to accomplish this end.

Date	Case	Citation	Decision
1958	Cooper v. Aaron	358 U.S. 1	It was a violation of equal protection to delay desegregation of public schools to avoid racial unrest.
1959	Barenblatt v. United States	360 U.S. 109	A contempt conviction of a witness before a congressional committee for refusal to testify concerning his beliefs and membership in a communist club did not violate the First Amendment.
1961	Mapp v. Ohio	367 U.S. 643	The Fourth Amendment's prohibition against use of evidence obtained as a result of an illegal search was applicable in state criminal proceedings.
1961	Scales v. United States	367 U.S. 203	The conviction of a criminal defendant for "active" membership in the Communist Party did not violate the First Amendment.
1962	Baker v. Carr	369 U.S. 186	A federal court had authority to hear an equal protection challenge to a state apportionment of legislative districts.
1962	Engel v. Vitale	370 U.S. 421	The establishment clause prohibited a state from composing and requiring the recitation of a nondenominational prayer in public schools.
1962	Robinson v. California	370 U.S. 660	The Eighth Amendment's cruel and unusual punishments clause prohibited classification of drug addiction as a crime.
1963	Abington School District v. Schempp	374 U.S. 203	The establishment clause prohibited recitations of the Lord's prayer and Bible readings in public schools.
1963	Gideon v. Wainright	372 U.S. 335	Due process required a state to provide an attorney to represent a defendant charged with a serious offense.
1963	Sherbert v. Verner	374 U.S. 398	The free exercise clause was violated by the refusal of a state to grant unemployment benefits to a Seventh Day Adventist fired for refusing to work on Saturday, her Sabbath.
1964	Escobedo v. Illinois	378 U.S. 478	A criminal defendant's right to counsel was violated by use of a confession obtained when he was a suspect and had been prevented from speaking with his attorney as he requested.
1964	Heart of Atlanta Motel v. United States	379 U.S. 241	Congress had power under the commerce clause to prohibit racial discrimination in privately owned places of public accommodation.
1964	Malloy v. Hogan	378 U.S. 1	The privilege against self-incrimination was applicable to state criminal proceedings.

Date	Case	Citation	Decision
1964	New York Times v. Sullivan	376 U.S. 254	The First Amendment required that a defamation claim against the press could only succeed in a case involving a public official if the press acted with actual malice.
1964	Reynolds v. Sims	377 U.S. 533	Equal protection required voting districts to be drawn up according to the "one person, one vote" standard.
1964	Wesberry v. Sanders	376 U.S. 1	Equal protection required that congressional districts not have substantial disparities in population.
1965	Griswold v. Connecticut	381 U.S. 479	A state law preventing married couples from using contraceptives violated the right of privacy.
1966	Harper v. Virginia Board of Elections	383 U.S. 663	The equal protection clause prohibited a state poll tax.
1966	Miranda v. Arizona	384 U.S. 436	State law-enforcement personnel were constitutionally required to inform suspects in police custody of their right to remain silent and to have counsel appointed.
1966	Sheppard v. Maxwell	384 U.S. 333	Excessive pretrial publicity violated a criminal defendant's right to a fair trial.
1967	In re Gault	387 U.S. 1	The privilege against self-incrimination and the right to counsel were applicable to criminal proceedings involving juveniles.
1967	Katz v. United States	389 U.S. 347	A wiretap on a telephone booth violated the Fourth Amendment's prohibition against unreasonable searches and seizures.
1967	Reitman v. Mulkey	387 U.S. 369	Equal protection was violated by a state constitutional provision that prohibited the state from interfering with racial discrimination by private individuals in sale or lease of property.
1968	Chimel v. California	395 U.S. 752	The Fourth Amendment allows law-enforcement personnel to perform a warrantless search incident to an arrest that may include arrestee's person and the area within his immediate control.
1968	Duncan v. Louisiana	391 U.S. 145	States are required by the due process clause to provide a trial by jury to persons charged with serious crimes.
1968	Green v. County School Board	391 U.S. 430	A school district could not satisfy its obligation to eliminate racial segregation by adopting a plan that allowed students to choose the school that they would attend.

Date	Case	Citation	Decision
1968	Harris v. United States	390 U.S. 234	Law-enforcement personnel conducting an otherwise legal warrantless search were entitled to seize objects in plain sight.
1968	Jones v. Alfred H. Mayer Co.	392 U.S. 409	Congress had authority under the Thirteenth Amendment to prohibit private acts of discrimination in housing sales.
1968	Terry v. Ohio	392 U.S. 1	The Fourth Amendment did not prohibit "stop and frisk" searches.
1968	United States v. O'Brien	391 U.S. 367	A federal law prohibiting destruction or mutilation of draft cards did not violate the First Amendment.
1968	Witherspoon v. Illinois	391 U.S. 510	A prosecutor in a murder case could not exclude potential jurors who expressed general objections to the death penalty.
1969	Alexander v. Holmes County Board of Education	396 U.S. 19	A public school district was required to desegregate its schools without further delay.
1969	Brandenburg v. Ohio	395 U.S. 444	A state may punish advocacy of illegal action only if the advocacy is directed toward inciting imminent lawless action and is likely to produce such action.
1969	Shapiro v. Thompson	394 U.S. 618	A durational residency requirement for the receipt of welfare benefits violated the right to relocate.
1969	Tinker v. Des Moines School District	393 U.S. 503	Freedom of speech protected the right of students to wear black armbands in protest of the Vietnam war.
1970	Brady v. United States	397 U.S. 742	The fact that a defendant feared receiving the death penalty and therefore pled guilty did not make the plea involuntary.
1970	Dandridge v. Williams	397 U.S. 471	A welfare law that imposed a maximum award per family without regard to family size did not violate the equal protection clause.
1971	Bivens v. Six Unknown Named Agents	403 U.S. 388	Victims of an illegal search could bring a civil suit against the federal officers who participated in the search.
1971	Graham v. Richardson	403 U.S. 365	The equal protection clause prevented a state from discriminating against aliens regarding eligibility for welfare benefits.
1971	Griffin v. Breckenridge	403 U.S. 88	Congress had power to punish racially motivated assaults on public highways.
1971	Griggs v. Duke Power Co.	401 U.S. 424	Congress could prohibit racial discrimination in employment and require that job tests be related to job skills.
1971	Lemon v. Kurtzman	403 U.S. 602	The establishment clause prohibited aid to parochial schools.

Date	Case	Citation	Decision
1973	Doe v. Bolton	410 U.S. 179	The right to an abortion was violated by state requirements that abortions be performed in hospitals, reviewed by other physicians, and limited to state residents.
1973	Frontiero v. Richardson	411 U.S. 677	A federal law that awarded military dependant benefits differently for males and females amounted to unconstitutional gender discrimination.
1973	Keyes v. School District No. 1	413 U.S. 189	District-wide desegregation remedies were permitted when one part of a district had engaged in segregation.
1973	Miller v. California	413 U.S. 15	Obscene materials could be prohibited by states.
1973	Roe v. Wade	410 U.S. 113	Laws restricting abortions violated a woman's right to an abortion, except as necessary to preserve the health of the mother after the first trimester of pregnancy or the life of the fetus after the second trimester.
1973	San Antonio Independent School District v. Rodriguez	411 U.S. 1	A state's partial reliance on local property taxes to fund public education did not violate equal protection.
1974	Milliken v. Bradley	418 U.S. 717	A federal court did not have authority to implement multi-district plans to integrate schools unless each district involved had engaged in purposeful segregation.
1976	Buckley v. Valeo	424 U.S. 1	Federal limits on amounts candidates for office could spend violated freedom of speech.
1976	Elrod v. Burns	427 U.S. 347	The First Amendment prevented public officials of one party from discharging non-civil service employees who were not members of that party when the employees were not in policy-making positions.
1976	Gregg v. Georgia	428 U.S. 153	The death penalty could not be imposed without consideration of the individual character of a defendant and the circumstances of the crime.
1976	Massachusetts Board of Retirement v. Murgia	427 U.S. 307	A state did not violate equal protection by establishing a mandatory retirement age for state police officers.
1976	Pasadena City Board of Education v. Spangler	427 U.S. 424	After official segregation has been remedied, a federal court lacked authority to order yearly adjustments to maintain racial balances in public schools.

Date	Case	Citation	Decision
1971	New York Times v. United States	403 U.S. 713	An injunction to prevent newspapers from publishing the Pentagon Papers would violate the First Amendment.
1971	Reed v. Reed	404 U.S. 71	A state law that gave preference to fathers over mothers as executors of their children's estates violated the equal protection clause.
1971	Santobello v. New York	404 U.S. 257	A defendant who entered a guilty plea based on a prosecutor's commitment to recommend a particular sentence was entitled to a remand when the prosecutor violated the commitment.
1971	Swann v. Charlotte-Mecklenburg Board of Education	402 U.S. 1	A district court had authority to make flexible use of racial quotas and could order busing to integrate a public school district that had previously segregated students by race.
1971	Tilton v. Richardson	403 U.S. 672	The establishment clause was not violated by a state's grant of construction funds to religious colleges for buildings to be used for secular purposes.
1972	Argersinger v. Hamlin	407 U.S. 25	The right to counsel applies to misdemeanor cases as well as felonies.
1972	Barker v. Wingo	407 U.S. 514	When a criminal defendant did not desire an immediate trial, the right to a speedy trial was not violated by delay of five years between arrest and trial.
1972	Dunn v. Blumstein	405 U.S. 330	Requirement that residents live in a location for a period of time to be eligible to vote violated equal protection.
1972	Eisenstadt v. Baird	405 U.S. 438	The equal protection clause was violated by a state law that permitted only married couples to purchase contraceptives.
1972	Furman v. Georgia	408 U.S. 238	In a death penalty case, the jury cannot be given complete discretion in the application of capital punishment.
1972	Lindsey v. Normet	405 U.S. 56	Summary eviction proceedings for tenants were permissible under the due process clause.
1972	Moose Lodge No. 107 v. Irvis	407 U.S. 163	A state's grant of a liquor license to a private club that practiced racial discrimination did not violate equal protection.
1972	Wisconsin v. Yoder	406 U.S. 205	The free exercise clause required that Amish parents be exempted from a state requirement that children attend high school after the eighth grade.

Date	Case	Citation	Decision
1976	Planned Parenthood v. Danforth	428 U.S. 52	A state law requiring certain women seeking an abortion to notify spouses or parents and requiring that physicians attempt to save the lives of aborted fetuses violated the right to an abortion.
1976	Runyon v. McCrary	427 U.S. 160	Federal law against racially discriminatory contracts prevented a private school from refusing to admit African American students.
1976	Washington v. Davis	426 U.S. 229	Requiring candidates for positions as police officers to take an aptitude test did not violate equal protection even though more African American than white candidates failed the test.
1977	Coker v. Georgia	433 U.S. 584	The cruel and unusual punishment clause prohibited the imposition of the death penalty for rape.
1977	Maher v. Roe	432 U.S. 464	A state was not required to pay for an indigent woman's non-therapeutic abortion.
1978	Regents of the University of California v. Bakke	438 U.S. 265	A state university could not use fixed racial quotas in determining medical school admissions but could consider race as one factor in deciding admissions.
1979	United Steelworkers of America v. Weber	443 U.S. 193	Affirmative action programs adopted voluntarily by employers did not violate federal laws against racial discrimination in employment.
1979	Vance v. Bradley	440 U.S. 93	Mandatory retirement for foreign service officials did not violate equal protection.
1980	Fullilove v. Klutznick	448 U.S. 448	A federal affirmative action program involving public works projects did not violate equal protection.
1980	Harris v. McRae	448 U.S. 297	A congressional restriction on the funding of medically necessary abortions did not violate the right to abortion.
1980	Rummel v. Estelle	445 U.S. 263	A life sentence imposed after a criminal defendant was found guilty of a third relatively minor offense was not unconstitutional.
1981	Rhodes v. Chapman	452 U.S. 337	Housing two prison inmates in a cell designed for one was not unconstitutional.
1981	Rostker v. Goldberg	453 U.S. 57	A federal law excluding women from the draft did not violate the equal protection clause.
1982	Hutto v. Davis	454 U.S. 370	The excessiveness of a sentence in relation to the crime was not unconstitutional.
1982	New York v. Ferber	458 U.S. 747	Freedom of speech did not protect depictions of children that were not obscene but were nevertheless pornographic.

Date	Case	Citation	Decision
1982	Plyler v. Doe	457 U.S. 202	Denial of public education to children of illegal aliens violated the equal protection clause.
1983	Mueller v. Allen	463 U.S. 388	The establishment clause did not prohibit parents of parochial children from taking advantage of a state income tax deduction for certain educational expenses.
1983	Solem v. Helm	463 U.S. 277	A state's imposition of a life sentence for the last of a series of nonviolent crimes constituted cruel and unusual punishment.
1984	Lynch v. Donnelly	465 U.S. 668	The inclusion of a nativity scene among other items in a Christmas display sponsored by a city did not violate the establishment clause.
1984	Massachusetts v. Sheppard	468 U.S. 981	The exclusionary rule did not apply to a search conducted by police officers who reasonably relied on the warrant, even if the search warrant was later found to be defective.
1984	Schall v. Martin	467 U.S. 253	It was not unconstitutional for a state to detain a suspect who posed a substantial risk of committing a serious crime before trial.
1984	United States v. Leon	468 U.S. 897	It was permissible to use illegally obtained evidence at trial if police had a search warrant and believed they were acting legally.
1985	New Jersey v. T.L.O.	469 U.S. 325	Public school students are protected against unreasonable searches and seizures by the Fourth Amendment.
1985	Tennessee v. Garner	471 U.S. 1	Police could not use deadly force to stop a fleeing felon except as necessary to prevent death or serious injury to bystanders.
1985	Wallace v. Jaffree	472 U.S. 38	A moment of silence statute enacted to restore prayer to public schools violated the establishment clause.
1986	Batson v. Kentucky	476 U.S. 79	Use of peremptory challenges by a prosecutor to exclude African Americans from a jury because of their race violated equal protection.
1986	Bowers v. Hardwick	478 U.S. 186	The right of privacy does not protect private, consensual homosexual conduct.
1986	Renton v. Playtime Theaters	475 U.S. 41	A local ordinance prohibiting adult theaters from operating near residential areas, churches, parks, or schools did not violate freedom of speech.
1986	Ford v. Wainwright	477 U.S. 399	It would be unconstitutional for a state to execute an insane prisoner.

Date	Case	Citation	Decision
1986	Thornburgh v. American College of Obstetricians and Gynecologists	476 U.S. 747	State informed consent and reporting requirements relating to abortions and a requirement that physicians attempt to preserve life of aborted fetuses violated the right to abortion.
1987	Edwards v. Aguillard	482 U.S. 578	A state law that required the teaching of "creation science" if evolution was taught violated the establishment clause.
1987	Illinois v. Krull	480 U.S. 340	The exclusionary rule does not prevent the use of illegally obtained evidence when a search was made in reasonable reliance upon a law authorizing warrantless administrative searches of vehicles.
1987	McCleskey v. Kemp	481 U.S. 279	Statistics revealing racial disparities in the imposition of the death penalty did not establish that the equal protection clause had been violated.
1987	Nollan v. California Coastal Commission	483 U.S. 825	A state's attempt to condition the award of a building permit on an owner's conveying an easement to the state across the owner's property violated the just compensation clause.
1987	Tison v. Arizona	481 U.S. 137	U.S. Constitution did not prohibit imposition of the death penalty for an accomplice to murder if the accomplice participated in a major way in the crime and displayed reckless indifference to human life.
1989	National Treasury Employees Union v. Raab	489 U.S. 656	Suspicionless drug testing of employees applying for drug interdiction positions was not unconstitutional.
1989	Richmond v. J. A. Croson Co.	488 U.S. 469	A municipal affirmative action program for construction contracts violated equal protection.
1989	Skinner v. Railway Labor Executives' Association	489 U.S. 602	It was not unconstitutional to require drug testing for railroad workers after major accidents.
1989	Stanford v. Kentucky	492 U.S. 361	The Eighth Amendment's cruel and unusual punishment clause did not necessarily prohibit the imposition of capital punishment for a crime committed while the defendant was a minor.
1989	Texas v. Johnson	491 U.S. 397	A state statute making it a crime to desecrate a flag violated the First Amendment.
1989	United States v. Monsanto	491 U.S. 600	Relying on a federal drug forfeiture statute, a court may order a pretrial freezing of a criminal defendant's assets even when the defendant seeks to use assets to pay an attorney.

Date	Case	Citation	Decision
1989	Wards Cove Packing Co. v. Atonio	490 U.S. 642	An employer accused of violating federal anti-discrimination law is allowed to rebut a showing that minorities were underrepresented in the workplace by demonstrating a reasonable business justification.
1989	Webster v. Reproductive Health Services	492 U.S. 490	A ban on the performance of abortions by state employees or in public facilities and a requirement that physicians perform a test to determine the viability of a fetus did not violate the right to an abortion.
1990	Employment Division v. Smith	494 U.S. 872	The free exercise clause did not require a state to exempt Native Americans who wished to use peyote in religious ceremonies from the effect of drug laws.
1990	Maryland v. Craig	497 U.S. 836	The testimony of a child witness in a sexual abuse case via closed circuit television does not necessarily violate a defendant's right to confront witnesses.
1990	Minnick v. Mississippi	498 U.S. 146	A confession obtained by forcing an individual to resume interrogation after consulting with an attorney was inadmissible.
1990	Osborne v. Ohio	495 U.S. 103	A law that punished the possession or viewing of child pornography did not violate freedom of speech.
1990	United States v. Eichman	496 U.S. 310	A federal law making it a crime to mutilate a United States flag violated freedom of speech.
1991	Arizona v. Fulminante	499 U.S. 279	The admission of an involuntary confession does not automatically require reversal of a criminal conviction when sufficient evidence besides the confession supports the conviction.
1991	Barnes v. Glen Theatre	501 U.S. 560	The First Amendment did prohibit a state from applying a public indecency law to prohibit nude dancing.
1991	Harmelin v. Michigan	501 U.S. 957	A state's imposition of a mandatory life sentence without parole did not amount to cruel and unusual punishment.
1991	Payne v. Tennessee	501 U.S. 808	The use of victim impact evidence during the sentencing phase of a capital murder case did not automatically constitute cruel and unusual punishment.
1991	Rust v. Sullivan	500 U.S. 173	Federal regulations that prohibit federally funded clinics from providing abortion counseling or referrals did not violate freedom of speech or the right to an abortion.

Date	Case	Citation	Decision
1992	Georgia v. McCollum	505 U.S. 42	The equal protection clause prevented a criminal defendant from using peremptory challenges to exclude potential jurors on the basis of their race.
1992	Lucas v. South Carolina Coastal Council	505 U.S. 1003	A zoning ordinance that prevented any economic use of property violated the takings clause.
1992	Planned Parenthood v. Casey	505 U.S. 833	A state law requiring spousal notification prior to an abortion violated the right to an abortion, but 24-hour waiting, informed consent, and reporting requirements did not violate this right.
1992	R.A.V. v. St. Paul	505 U.S. 377	A municipal ordinance prohibiting "hate speech" violated the First Amendment.
1992	United States v. Alvarez Machain	504 U.S. 655	It was permissible for a federal court to try a Mexican national forcibly kidnaped and brought to the United States.
1993	Church of the Lukumi Babalu Aye v. Hialeah	508 U.S. 520	Local laws enacted to prevent animal sacrifices by a religious group violated the free exercise clause.
1993	Shaw v. Reno	509 U.S. 630	A redistricting plan adopted solely to maximize minority voting strength may violate equal protection.
1993	Wisconsin v. Mitchell	508 U.S. 476	A law that provided more severe punishment for crimes motivated by racial hatred did not abridge freedom of speech.
1994	Board of Education of Kiryas Joel Village School District v. Grumet	512 U.S. 687	A state's creation of a school district to coincide with the boundaries of a religious enclave violated the establishment clause.
1994	City of Ladue v. Gilleo	512 U.S. 43	A city's general ban on residential signs violated freedom of speech.
1995	Adarand Constructors, Inc. v. Peña	515 U.S. 200	Federal affirmative action program must satisfy rigorous constitutional scrutiny.
1995	Rosenberger v. Rector & Visitors of the University of Virginia	515 U.S. 819	The refusal by a public university to allow a religious student organization the same right to have printing expenses reimbursed as enjoyed by other student organizations violated freedom of speech.
1995	United States v. Lopez	514 U.S. 549	Congress's attempt to regulate possession of firearms near schools exceeded its authority under the commerce clause.
1996	BMW of North America, Inc. v. Gore	517 U.S. 559	An award of $4 million in punitive damages, on the basis of $4,000 of actual damages, was grossly excessive and violated due process.

Date	Case	Citation	Decision
1996	Romer v. Evans	517 U.S. 620	A Colorado constitutional amendment that prohibited state laws designed to afford homosexuals protection against discrimination violated the equal protection clause.
1996	United States v. Armstrong	517 U.S. 456	African American criminal defendants charged with illegal possession of crack cocaine were not entitled to pretrial discovery concerning their claim that they were singled out for prosecution on the basis of their race without showing initially that the government had declined to prosecute similarly situated suspects of other races.
1996	United States v. Virginia	518 U.S. 515	A state's exclusion of women from a traditionally all-male military academy violated equal protection.
1997	City of Boerne v. Flores	117 S.Ct. 2157	Congress had no authority to protect religious believers from the unintended effects of state laws.
1997	Clinton v. Jones	117 S.Ct. 1636	The president of the United States is not immune from civil law suits while in office.
1997	Maryland v. Wilson	117 S.Ct. 882	A law-enforcement officer making a traffic stop may order passengers to get out of the car.
1997	Printz v. United States	117 S.Ct. 2365	Congress exceeded its authority under the commerce clause by requiring local law-enforcement officials to perform background checks on persons seeking to purchase guns.
1997	Reno v. ACLU	117 S.Ct. 2329	A federal law that attempted to regulate indecent material on the Internet violated the First Amendment.
1997	Washington v. Glucksberg	117 S.Ct. 2258	A state law prohibiting any individual from assisting the suicide of another did not violate due process.

—*Timothy L. Hall*

Legal Assistance Organizations

ETHNICITY- AND RELIGION-BASED ORGANIZATIONS

American-Arab Anti-Discrimination Committee (ADC)
4201 Connecticut Avenue NW, Suite 500
Washington, DC 20008

Founded in 1980, this grassroots organization represents Arab Americans, seeks to protect the rights of people of Arab descent, promotes and defends the Arab American heritage, and serves the needs of the Arab American community. The organization works through its Action Network and Media Monitoring Groups to end the stereotyping of Arabs in the media and discrimination against Arab Americans in employment, education, and politics.

American-Arab Relations Committee (AARC)
P.O. Box 416
New York, NY 10017

Founded in 1964, the AARC includes persons concerned about the goal of improving American Arab relations and the establishment of a peaceful and democratic Palestine. The AARC does not take stands on problems of the Arab world and inter-Arab relations or on domestic issues within the United States but opposes fascism, anti-Semitism, and Zionism with activities including picketing and demonstrations, filing lawsuits, and registering complaints with the Federal Communications Commission (FCC) about slanted portrayals of Arabs in the media.

American Israeli Civil Liberties Coalition (AICLC)
275 7th Avenue, Suite 1776
New York, NY 10001

Founded in 1981, the AICLC's objectives are to aid Israelis in educating other Israelis about civil liberties and to promote the practice of basic civil liberties such as freedom of religion, speech, press; due process in civil and criminal proceedings; equal protection under the law; academic freedom; and racial, ethnic, religious, and sexual equality. The AICLC serves as a source of financial and moral support, keeps Americans informed about the status of civil liberties in Israel, supports dialogue about civil liberties, and develops teacher-training programs.

Americans for Religious Liberty (ARL)
P.O. Box 6656
Silver Spring, MD 20916

Founded in 1980, the ARL is composed of individuals dedicated to preserving religious, intellectual, and personal freedom, the constitutional principle of separation of church and state, democratic secular public education, reproductive rights, and the Jeffersonian-Madisonian ideal of a pluralistic secular democracy.

Anti-Defamation League (ADL)
823 United Nations Plaza
New York, NY 10017

Founded in 1913, the ADL seeks to stop the defamation of Jewish people and to secure justice and fair treatment to all citizens. The ADL educates Americans about Israel, promotes better interfaith and intergroup relations, works against anti-Semitism, counteracts antidemocratic extremism, and strengthens democratic values and structures.

Asian American Center for Justice of the American Citizens for Justice
P.O. Box 2735
Southfield, MI 48037-2735

Founded in 1983, this organization works to eliminate discrimination and violence against Asian Americans by offering legal consultation and education, monitoring violence against Asians, and assisting local and county governments in developing affirmative action plans for recruiting Asian Pacific Americans.

Asian American Legal Defense and Education Fund (AALDEF)
99 Hudson Street
New York, NY 10013

Founded in 1974, the AALDEF includes attorneys, legal workers, and members of the community who seek to employ legal and educational methods to attack critical problems in Asian American communities by providing bilingual legal counseling and representation for people who cannot obtain access to legal assistance. Its areas of concern include immigration employment, voting rights, racially motivated violence against Asian Americans, environmental justice, and Japanese American redress.

Asian Law Alliance (ALA)
184 East Jackson Street
San Jose, CA 95112
Web site: http://scuish.scu.edu

The ALA is a nonprofit United Way agency that provides law services for the Asian Community by informing citizens of their legal rights and responsibilities and by helping to prevent legal problems for immigrants that have lived in the United States for short and long periods of time.

Catholic Interracial Council of New York (CIC)
899 10th Avenue
New York, NY 10019

Founded in 1934, the CIC works in cooperation with local parishes and governmental and voluntary groups to combat bigotry and discrimination and to promote social justice for all racial, religious, and ethnic groups.

Center for Democratic Renewal (CDR)
P.O. Box 50469
Atlanta, GA 30302

Founded in 1979, the CDR advocates federal prosecution of the Ku Klux Klan and other groups or individuals involved in racist violence by seeking to build public opposition to racist groups and their activities. The CDR assists victims of bigoted violence by working with trade unions, public officials, and religious, women's, civil rights, and grassroots organizations.

Center for the Advancement of the Covenant
San Francisco University Philosophy Department
1600 Holloway Avenue
San Francisco, CA 94132

Founded in 1992, this organization publicizes the United States ratification of the 1992 International Covenant on Civil and Political Rights and the rights it contains by organizing a network of nongovernmental organizations to work toward federal, state, and local government compliance with the Covenant.

Center for Third World Organizing (CTWO)
1218 East 21st Street
Oakland, CA 94606-3132

Founded in 1980, the CTWO provides training, issue analyses, and research to low-income minority organizations, including welfare, immigrant, and Native American rights groups, and monitors and reports on incidents of discrimination against people of color.

Chinese for Affirmative Action (CAA)
17 Walter U. Lum Place
San Francisco, CA 94108

Founded in 1969, the CAA includes individuals and corporations seeking equal opportunity for and the protection of the civil rights of Asian Americans. It works with the larger community to ensure fair treatment under the law in employment matters and has cooperated with state and local governmental agencies to help develop bilingual materials to aid Asian American job applicants. It also encourages the appointment and participation of Asian Americans on public boards and commissions.

Commission for Racial Justice (CRJ)
475 Riverside Drive, 16th Floor
New York, NY 10115

Founded in 1963, the CRJ is a racial justice agency representing the 1.7 million members of the United Church of Christ and promotes human rights programs and strategies to foster racial justice in African American, Third World, and other minority communities.

Commission for Social Justice (CSJ)
219 East Street NE
Washington, DC 20002

Founded in 1979, the CSJ serves as the antidefamation arm of the Order of Sons of Italy in America and monitors businesses, schools, and the media to combat negative portrayals of Italian Americans.

Cuban American Legal Defense and Education Fund (CALDEF)
2513 South Calhoun Street
Fort Wayne, IN 46807-1305

Founded in 1980, the CALDEF strives for equal treatment and opportunity for Cuban Americans and Hispanics in the fields of education, employment, housing, politics, and justice by discouraging negative stereotyping of Hispanics and works to educate the public about the plight of Cuban Americans and Latin Americans.

The Generation After (TGA)
P.O. Box 14, Homecrest Station
Brooklyn, NY 11229

Founded in 1979, the TGA includes individuals working to eradicate anti-Semitism by advocating human rights and social justice. Goals of the TGA are to accumulate and store data of neo-Nazi groups, such as their leaders names and addresses, to share such information with authorities to prevent violence that might be caused by such groups, and to monitor neo-Nazi newspapers in the United States.

Institute for First Amendment Studies (IFAS)
P.O. Box 589
Great Barrington, MA 01230

Founded in 1984, this organization of former members of fundamentalist churches and others is dedicated to the principle of the separation of church and state as provided for in the First Amendment to the U.S. Constitution. It monitors and reports on the activities of fundamentalist right-wing groups.

International Committee Against Racism (ICAR)
150 West 28th Street, Room 301
New York, NY 10001

Founded in 1973, the ICAR is dedicated to fighting against all forms of racism and to building a multiracial society by opposing racism in all its economic, social, institutional, and cultural forms by sponsoring on-the-job, community, college, and high-school workshops.

Mexican American Legal Defense and Education Fund (MALDEF)
634 South Spring Street, 11th Floor
Los Angeles, CA 90014
Web site: http://www.maldef.org

MALDEF was founded in 1968 following decades of discrimination and the violation of the civil rights of Mexican Americans. Its mission is to protect and promote the rights of the more than twenty-six million Latinos living in the United States.

National Alliance Against Racist and Political Repression (NAARPR)
11 John Street, Room 702
New York, NY 10038

Founded in 1973, the NAARPR is a coalition of political, labor, church, civic, student, and community organization dedicated to protecting people's right to organize. It seeks to mobilize people to unite in word and action against many forms of repression of human rights in the United States.

National Association for the Advancement of Colored People (NAACP)
4805 Mt. Hope Drive
Baltimore, MD 21215

Founded in 1909, the NAACP includes persons of all races and religions who believe in the objectives and methods of the NAACP to achieve equal rights through the democratic process and eliminate racial prejudice by removing racial discrimination in housing, employment, voting, schools, the courts, transportation, recreation, prisons, and business enterprises.

National Emergency Civil Liberties Committee (NECLC)
175 5th Avenue, Room 814
New York, NY 10010

Founded in 1951, the NECLC seeks to reestablish in full the traditional freedoms guaranteed under the U.S. Constitution and the Bill of Rights and stands uncompromisingly for civil liberties for everyone and every variety of descent.

National Urban League (NUL)
500 East 62nd Street
New York, NY 10021

Founded in 1910, the NUL is a voluntary nonpartisan community service agency of civic, professional, business, labor, and religious leaders with a staff of trained social workers and other professionals. The organization aims to eliminate racial segregation and discrimination in the United States and to achieve parity for African Americans and other minorities in every walk of American life.

People for the American Way (PFAW)
2000 M Street NW, Suite 400
Washington, DC 20036

Founded in 1980, the PFAW is a nonpartisan constitutional liberties organization of religious, business, media, and labor figures committed to reaffirming the traditional American values of pluralism, diversity, and freedom of expression and religion.

Protect Equality (PE)
6301 Rockhill Road, Suite 315
Kansas City, MO 64131

Founded in 1965, PE is a nationwide interfaith program enabling religious organizations, institutions, and others to support equal opportunity employers with their purchasing power.

Southern Christian Leadership Council (SCLC)
334 Auburn Avenue NE
Atlanta, GA 30303

Founded in 1957, the SCLC is a nonsectarian coordinating and service agency for local organizations seeking full citizenship rights, equality, and integration of African Americans in all walks of life in the United States. It subscribes to the philosophy of nonviolence.

Trade Union Leadership Council (TULC)
8670 Grand River Avenue
Detroit, MI 48204

Founded in 1957, the TULC includes primarily African American trade unionists in Michigan who seek to eradicate injustices perpetrated upon people because of race, religion, sex, or national origin. It also seeks increased leadership and job opportunities for African Americans.

OTHER ORGANIZATIONS

A. Philip Randolph Educational Fund (APREF)
1444 Eye Street NW, No. 300
Washington, DC 20005

Founded in 1964, the APREF seeks to eliminate prejudice and discrimination from all areas of life, educate individuals and groups on their rights and responsibilities, defend human and civil rights, and assist in the employment and education of the underprivileged.

Alliance for Justice (AFJ)
2000 P Street NW, Suite 712
Washington, DC 20036
e-mail: alliance@afj.org

The AFJ is a national association of environmental, civil rights, mental health, women's, children's, and consumer advocacy organizations. Since its inception in 1979, the Alliance has worked to advance the cause of justice for all Americans, strengthen the public interest community's ability to influence public policy, and foster the next generation of advocates.

American Association of Retired Persons (AARP)
601 East Street NW
Washington, DC 20049
Web site: http://www.aarp.org
e-mail: member@aarp.org

The AARP is a nonprofit, nonpartisan organization dedicated to helping older Americans achieve lives of independence, dignity, and purpose and assists retired persons with a variety of legal information.

American Association of University Women (AAUW) Legal Advocacy Fund
Department LAF.INT
1111 Sixteenth Street NW
Washington, DC 20036
Web site: http://www.aauw.org

The nation's largest legal fund that focuses solely on sex discrimination in higher education, the AAUW Legal Advocacy Fund provides funding and support for women seeking judicial redress for sex discrimination. Since 1981 the AAUW Legal Advocacy Fund has helped students, faculty, and administrators in higher education challenge discriminatory practices involving sexual harassment, denial of tenure or promotion, and inequality in women's athletics programs.

American Citizens for Justice (ACJ)
P.O. Box 2735
Southfield, MI, 48037-2735

The ACJ was founded in 1983 by Asian Pacific Americans and other individuals concerned with discrimination against ethnic groups. The ACJ works to combat and prevent racial intolerance, operates the Asian American Center for Justice, monitors legislation and law enforcement, works for civil rights in the areas of mental health, safety, health, and welfare, and promotes the teaching of Asian Pacific American history and culture.

American Civil Liberties Union (ACLU)
132 West 43rd Street
New York, NY 10036

Founded in 1920, the ACLU had 275,000 members and a staff of 125 in 1996. It champions the rights set forth in the Bill of Rights of the U.S. Constitution, such as freedom of speech, press, assembly, and religion; due process of law and fair trial; and equality before the law regardless of race, color, sexual orientation, national origin, political opinion, or religious belief. ACLU activities include litigation, advocacy, and public education. It sponsors litigation projects in such fields as women's rights, gay and lesbian rights, and children's rights.

American Prepaid Legal Services Institute (API)
541 Fairbanks Court
Chicago, IL 60611
Web site: http://www.abanet.org
e-mail: barbaramay@staff.abanet.org

The API supports insurance companies, prepaid legal plan sponsors and administrators, lawyers, and law firms with a concept similar to that of health insurance. Consumers pay a fixed premium in exchange for specified legal benefits that are used as needed.

Anti-Fascist Network
P.O. Box 4824
Omaha, NE 68104-0824

Founded in 1994 to ensure that the growth of government does not cancel out individual rights. This organization collects and researches information and its inaccuracy and misuse by any groups, organizations, or government agencies that irresponsibly use such inaccuracies to further their own goals at the expense of individual rights.

Association for the Sexually Harassed (ASH)
860 Manatawna Avenue
Philadelphia, PA 19128-1113

Founded in 1988, ASH includes employers, talk shows, attorneys, schools, victims of sexual harassment, and other interested organizations and individuals. It seeks to create national awareness of sexual harassment by providing experts for talk shows and mediation troubleshooting services to resolve sexual harassment problems between employees and employers. It also provides telephone counseling and consultation services.

Center for Constitutional Rights (CCR)
666 Broadway, 7th Floor
New York, NY 10012

Founded in 1966, the CCR is a legal and educational organization dedicated to advancing and protecting the rights guaranteed by the U.S. Constitution and the Universal Declaration of Civil Rights. The organization is committed to the creative use of law as a positive force for social change.

Children's Rights
132 West 43rd Street, 6th Floor
New York, NY 10036

Founded in 1995 with a staff of fifteen to fight for the rights of poor children who are dependent on government systems. Formerly called the Children's Rights Project of the American Civil Liberties Union (ACLU).

Citizens Against Lawsuit Abuse (CALA)
3128 Pacific Coast Highway, Suite 15
Torrance, CA 90505

CALA is a nonprofit, grassroots organization composed of Southern Californians dedicated to putting an end to lawsuit abuse. Their mission is to educate the public on the effects of lawsuit abuse in order to create a climate for reform of the U.S.

civil justice system. It educates the public about the direct costs of lawsuit abuse to consumers, taxpayers, and the state of California; it stimulates debate on the issue of civil justice reform and its process; and it serves as a watchdog over interest groups and persons who abuse the system for personal financial gain.

Citizens for a Better America (CBA)
P.O. Box 356
Halifax, VA 24558

Founded in 1975, the CBA includes churches and individuals united to create a better America by strengthening individual rights and serves as a public advocacy organization that lobbies for civil rights and environmental legislation.

Citizens' Commissions on Civil Rights (CCCR)
2000 M Street NW, Suite 400
Washington, DC 20036

Founded in 1982, the CCCR is a bipartisan organization of former federal cabinet officials concerned with achieving equality of opportunity. Its objectives are to monitor the federal government's enforcement of laws barring discrimination on the basis of race, sex, religion, ethnic background, age, or handicap, foster understanding of civil rights issues, and formulate constructive policy recommendations.

Citizens for Sensible Safeguards (CSS)
1742 Connecticut Avenue NW
Washington, DC 20009

Founded in 1995, the CSS involves a coalition of over 200 organizations concerned with environmental, educational, civil rights, disability, health, and social services issues and works to improve laws and safeguards that protect citizens.

Death with Dignity Education Center (DDEC)
P.O. Box 1238
San Mateo, CA 94401-0816

Founded in 1994, the DDEC is a diverse group of people who believe in the inherent right of persons to make their own choices about heath care and the end of life. The organization informs and educates the public about physician aid in dying so that people can make informed decisions.

Department of Civil Rights, AFL-CIO
815 16th Street NW
Washington, DC 20006

Founded in 1955, this staff arm of the American Federation of Labor-Congress of Industrial Organizations serves as an official liaison to women's and civil rights organizations and government agencies working in the field of equal opportunity. It helps to implement state and federal laws and AFL-CIO civil rights policies.

First Amendment Foundation (FAF)
1313 West 8th Street, Suite 313
Los Angeles, CA 90017

Founded in 1986, the FAF seeks to protect the rights of free expression of individuals and organizations and disseminates educational information on the First Amendment to the U.S. Constitution.

First Amendment Press (FAP)
8129 North 35th Avenue, No. 134
Phoenix, AZ 85051-5892

Founded in 1993, the FAP provides information on citizen's rights and alleged government misconduct, offers legal advice and solutions, conducts investigations, and maintains a speakers bureau.

Freedom of Expression Foundation (FOEF)
5220 South Marina Pacifica
Long Beach, CA 90803

Founded in 1983, the FOEF includes corporations, foundations, broadcasters, and publishers whose purpose is to provide information to the U.S. Congress and the public concerning freedom of speech as guaranteed by the First Amendment to the U.S. Constitution.

Freedom to Advertise Coalition (FAC)
2550 M Street NW, Suite 500
Washington, DC 20037

Founded in 1988, the FAC includes members of the American Advertising Federation, the American Association of Advertising Agencies, the Association of National Advertisers, the Magazine Publishers of American, the Outdoor Advertising Association of America, and the Point of Purchase Advertising Institute. These organizations have united to protect the rights of advertisers to "truthfully and nondeceptively advertise all legal products." The protection of the right of commercial free speech as guaranteed by the U.S. Constitution and opposition to proposed legislation that would ban or restrict tobacco, alcohol, and other legal product advertising are among its chief activities.

Judge David L. Bazelon Center for Mental Health Law
1101 15th Street NW, Suite 1212
Washington, DC 20005
e-mail: bazelon@nicom.com

Founded in 1972, this organization's purpose is to clarify, establish, and enforce the legal rights of people with mental and developmental disabilities by providing technical assistance and training to lawyers, consumers, providers of mental health and special education services, and policymakers at the federal, state, and local levels.

Lawyers' Committee for Civil Rights Under Law (LCCRUL)
1450 G Street NW, Suite 400
Washington, DC 20005

The LCCRUL operates through local communities of private lawyers to provide legal assistance to poor and minority groups living in urban areas in such fields as employment, voting rights, and housing discrimination.

Leadership Conference on Civil Rights (LCCR)
1629 K Street NW, Suite 1010
Washington, DC 20006

Founded in 1950, the LCCR is a coalition of national organizations working to promote the passage of civil rights, social, and economic legislation. It also seeks the enforcement of laws already on the books.

Media Coalition/Americans for Constitutional Freedom (MC/ACF)
1221 Avenue of the Americas, 24th Floor
New York, NY 10020

Founded in 1973, the MC/ACF includes trade associations united to defend the First Amendment right to produce and distribute books, magazines, recordings, video games, and videotapes. This organization also monitors censorship legislation at the federal and state levels.

National Academy of Elder Law Attorneys (NAELA)
1604 N. Country Road
Tucson, AZ 85716-3102
e-mail: accountladsit@naela.com

The NAELA supports practicing attorneys, law professors, and others interested in the provision of legal services to the elderly by providing technical expertise and education to the elderly and their families.

National Association to Protect Individual Rights (NAPIR)
5015 Gadsen
Fairfax, VA 22032-3411

Founded in 1991, the NAPIR conducts research on issues including information privacy and government budgeting and provides information to public officials and the press.

National Clearinghouse for Legal Services (NCLS)
205 W. Monroe
Chicago, IL 60606

The NCLS supports legal services attorneys and programs, private attorneys, law universities and libraries, court judges, and government organizations in providing information on case law with respect to issues related to poverty law and the consumer.

National Committee Against Repressive Legislation (NCARL)
1313 West 8th Street, Suite 313
Los Angeles, CA 90017

Founded in 1960, the NCARL promotes First Amendment Rights and opposes repressive laws and inquisitorial activities of government. Notable activities include reform of federal criminal laws and control of federal intelligence gathering agencies. The NCARL seeks to ban covert operations by the Central Intelligence Agency (CIA) and what the group feels is political spying and harassment by the Federal Bureau of Investigation (FBI).

National Institute for Citizen Education in the Law (NICEL)
711 G Street SE
Washington, DC 20003

The NICEL operates programs in law-related education in high schools and juvenile corrections settings to assist young people in becoming active, successful citizens.

National Legal Aid and Defender Association (NLADA)
1625 K Street NW, Suite 800
Washington, DC 20006-1604

The NLADA supports legal aid offices and public defender organizations representing indigent and individual members by providing technical and management assistance to local organizations offering legal services to poor persons involved with civil or criminal cases.

National Legal Center for the Medically Dependent and Disabled (NLCMDD)
1 South 6th Street
Terre Haute, IN 47808

The NLCMDD is a service organization working to defend the legal rights of indigent older and disabled persons in their quest for proper medical care.

National Resource Center for Consumers of Legal Services (NRCCLS)
6596 Main Street
P.O. Box 340
Gloucester, VA 23061

The NRCCLS supports legal programs in North America by serving as a clearinghouse while advising individuals and groups seeking to establish or evaluate legal service plans.

National Structured Settlements Trade Association (NSSTA)
1420 16th Street NW
Washington, DC 20036

The NSSTA supports structured settlement firms, life insurance companies, claims adjustors, attorneys, and other consultants involved in the tort process.

Pretrial Services Resource Center (PSRC)
1325 G Street NW, Suite 770
Washington, DC 20005

The PSRC provides criminal justice consulting services covering subjects such as data collection, jail overcrowding, and drug testing.

Southern Poverty Law Center (SPLC)
P.O. Box 2087
Montgomery, AL 36102

Founded in 1971, the SPLC seeks to protect and advance the legal and civil rights of poor people, regardless of race, through education and litigation. It does not accept fees from clients.

Southern Regional Council (SRC)
1900 Rhodes Haverty Building
134 Peachtree Street NW
Atlanta, GA 30303-1825

Founded in 1944, the SRC includes leaders in education, religion, business, labor, the community, and the professions interested in improving race relations and combating poverty in the South.

United States Privacy Council (USPC)
P.O. Box 15060
Washington, DC 20003

The USPC is composed of individuals and groups committed to strengthening the right to privacy in the United States by working to protect medical, insurance, and employee records, update legislation—including the Fair Credit Reporting Act, the Privacy Act of 1974, and the Electronic Communications Privacy Act—and improve public access to governmental information.

Volunteer Lawyers for the Arts (VLA)
1 E. 53rd Street, 6th Floor
New York, NY 10022

The VLA provides free legal services to artists and art organizations in art-related legal matters. It works to familiarize the legal profession and the arts community with legal problems that confront artists and provides them with available solutions.

Voters Telecomm Watch (VTW)
115 Pacific, No. 3
Brooklyn, NY 11201

Founded in 1994, the VTW works to protect individual electronic freedom and privacy and promote civil liberties in telecommunications by monitoring bills, positions, and voting records of elected officials, informing and alerting the public, and recommending legislation.

Western Center on Law and Poverty (WCLP)
3701 Wilshire Boulevard, Suite 208
Los Angeles, CA 90010

The WCLP provides legal counsel and representation to individuals and groups whose actions may effect change in institutions affecting the poor.

Workers' Defense League (WDL)
218 West 40th Street, Room 203-204
New York, NY 10018

Founded in 1936, the WDL is a labor-oriented human rights organization that provides counseling to workers on employment-related problems, conducts educational campaigns to defend and advance workers' rights, and maintains a speakers bureau.

—Daniel G. Graetzer

Legal Resources

The reality of legal research is that no single volume of books contains the whole law applicable to a particular person or circumstance. Rather, different governments and different branches within these governments create law, and the products of this multiple creative work are scattered across innumerable volumes. One of the professional skills of attorneys is the ability to navigate these multiple sources of legal authority, but interested laypersons may profit from understanding at least the broad contours of the legal terrain.

Primary Sources of the Law. The first major division of legal authority has to do with the divisions among federal, state, and local lawmaking authorities. Authorities at each of these levels create law, with the higher authority sometimes but not always displacing laws of the lower authority. For example, according to the supremacy clause of the U.S. Constitution, when the federal government creates laws inconsistent with those of state or local governments, the federal law prevails. However, federal laws frequently leave room for state and local laws on the same subject. As a consequence, a given situation may be subject to the law of one or all of these authorities, and legal researchers must be prepared to consult resources available for each.

Level	Branch	Chief Source of Legal Authority
Federal	Legislative (Congress)	United States Code or United States Code Annotated.
Federal	Executive branch	Executive orders and regulations enacted by federal departments and agencies and collected in the Code of Federal Regulations.
Federal	Judicial	Opinions in cases decided at the district court, court of appeals, and Supreme Court levels and collected in multivolume sets known as the *Federal Supplement*, *Federal Reporter*, and the *United States Reports*, respectively.
State	Legislative	Each state has a code of laws similar to the United States Code Annotated. Such codes include, for example, the Annotated California Code and the Code of Virginia Annotated.
State	Executive	State governors and other executive officials may produce executive orders comparable to those of the U.S. president. In addition, state administrative agencies generally promulgate regulations on a variety of subjects entrusted to them by state law.
State	Judicial	States have one or more levels of courts that produce published judicial opinions on questions of law. These opinions are collected in one or more "reporters," as they are called. In addition, West Publishing in St. Paul, Minnesota, a leading publisher of legal materials, collects opinions decided by the courts of states in various regions of the country into regional reporters, such as the *Pacific Reporter*, which includes cases decided by California and other western states, and the *Southern Reporter*, which includes cases decided by Mississippi courts and the courts of other southern states.

The second division of legal authority is among the various branches within government. Laws or legal rules may have their genesis in the legislative, executive, or the judicial branches of federal, state, or local governments. Legislatures create law in the form of statutes, which are ultimately collected in codes. Executives, at least at the federal level, create law in the form of executive orders or administrative regulations. Judicial branches create law in the form of case opinions and rules governing legal practice and procedure. Moreover, courts routinely interpret other legal materials, such as constitutions or statutes, and these interpretations are of sufficient importance that their content may be included in legal volumes containing constitutions or statutes. For example, a very common version of federal statutes is referred to as the United States Code Annotated and consists not only of statutes collected in the form of a code but also of references to case opinions that interpret the various provisions of the code.

Thus, a given legal problem may require that researchers consult legal authorities created by multiple branches of government within the federal, state, and local governmental systems. The following table attempts to summarize the key sources of legal authority for federal and state governments. In addition to the sources listed, the highest source of law for both federal and state governments is the U.S. Constitution. A copy of the U.S. Constitution is available in the United States Code Annotated and also at a number of sites on the World Wide Web, discussed below. In addition, state governments are subject to the authority of their respective state constitutions. Local governments produce laws as well in the form of municipal or county ordinances, but these laws generally lack the broad spectrum of lawmaking power as exercised by federal and state governments. Such laws enacted at the local level are generally available in local government offices and sometimes in public libraries.

Finding Primary Legal Sources. Primary legal sources, such as the United States Code and the various federal and state judicial opinions, are generally available from three sources. First, all the materials discussed in the preceding table are published as multivolume hardback series. Some public libraries have copies of such items as the United States Code Annotated and the annotated code for the relevant state. To find a more complete collection of primary sources of the printed type, one must generally gain access to a law library. Local courthouses are generally the most likely place to find a law library with the resources described above.

Second, all the sources above, and many more, may be accessed remotely from the two leading computer databases of the law profession: Westlaw and Lexis. These databases charge a subscription fee and per usage fees and are thus financially out of the range of most individuals other than lawyers.

Third, and perhaps most important, many primary legal sources are available free of charge on the World Wide Web. Individuals may access these sites either through personal or job-related Internet connections or through Internet connections made available in many public libraries. The following section describes some of the legal resources available on the Internet.

Online Resources. The following list contains a variety of World Wide Web resources relating to the law. One of the realities of the World Wide Web is that information sites sometimes change their locations and sometimes cease to exist altogether. Thus, readers may find that some addresses no longer work. It is impossible to briefly summarize the varieties of legal materials now available online, but two kinds of Web sites will be of most assistance to those interested in researching the law: sites that serve as indexes to legal resources generally and sites devoted to particular legal topics. The first list below contains the World Wide Web addresses of several general legal information sites on the Web.

ABA Legal Research Selected Starting Points
www.abanet.org/lawlink/home.html
Links to legal materials maintained by the American Bar Association (ABA).

ABA Network
www.abanet.org
Web site maintained by the American Bar Association (ABA) providing a variety of legal information for both lawyers and the public.

Alan Gahtan's Canadian Legal Resources
gahtan.com/lawlinks
Collection of Canadian legal resources.

American Law Resources On-Line
www.lawsource.com/also/usa.htm
Extensive collection of legal resources.

CataLaw
www.catalaw.com
Searchable index of legal information.

Center for Information Law and Policy
www.law.vill.edu
Collection of legal Web resources maintained by the Villanova Law School.

Counsel Quest
www.CounselQuest.com
Internet legal resources locator.

FedLaw
www.legal.gsa.gov
Web site maintained by the U.S. General Services Administration (GSA) devoted to legal resources useful to federal lawyers and employees.

Law Lists
www.lib.uchicago.edu/~llou/lawlists/info.html
A guide to electronic discussion groups concerning the law.

LawInfo Com
www.lawinfo.com
Referral site for lawyers and a variety of legal resources.

Legal Information Institute
www.law.cornell.edu
One of the Web's most exhaustive collections of legal materials maintained by the Cornell Law School.

Legal List
www.lcp.com/The-Legal-List
An outline of and introduction to legal resources on the Internet.

Library of Congress
lcweb.loc.gov/homepage/lchp_txt.html
Indexes to the holdings of the Library of Congress, on-line exhibits, and a variety of resources, including some legal materials.

Thomas
thomas.loc.gov
Detailed information about federal legislation maintained by the Library of Congress.

U.S. House of Representatives Internet Law Library
law.house.gov
General information source for federal law.

World Wide Web Virtual Library: Law
www.law.indiana.edu/law/v-lib/lawindex.html
General Web resources indexed by the Indiana University School of Law, Bloomington.

GOVERNMENT AGENCIES AND OFFICES

The next category of Web sites includes those maintained by various governmental agencies and offices that are generally devoted to a particular legal topic. Governmental agencies and offices frequently make available to the public legal information relevant to their operations.

Agriculture Department
14th and Independence Avenue SW
Washington, DC 20250
(202) 720-2791
www.usda.gov
Federal agency that supports agricultural production.

Bureau of Alcohol, Tobacco, and Firearms
650 Massachusetts Avenue NW
Washington, DC 20226
(202) 927-7777
www.atf.treas.gov/mailpage.htm
Collects taxes on and generally regulates alcohol, tobacco, and firearms.

Central Intelligence Agency
Public Affairs Staff
Central Intelligence Agency
Washington, DC 20505
(703) 482-0623.
www.odci.gov/cia
Provides intelligence information on issues relating to national security and conducts counterintelligence operations.

Consumer Product Safety Commission
East West Towers
4330 East West Highway
Bethesda, MD 20814
(301) 504-0580
www.cpsc.gov
Federal agency charged with protecting the public from unsafe products.

Customs Service
1301 Constitution Avenue, NW
Washington, DC 20229
(202) 927-1350
www.customs.ustreas.gov
Assesses and collects duties on imported goods.

Education Department
600 Independence Avenue SW
Washington, DC 20202-0498
(800) USA-LEARN
www.ed.gov
Federal agency that supports education in the United States.

Environmental Protection Agency
401 M Street SW
Washington, DC 20460
(202) 260-7963
www.epa.gov
Federal agency with responsibility for administering environmental laws.

Equal Employment Opportunity Commission
1801 L Street NW
Washington, DC 20507
(202) 663-4900
(800) 669-4000
www.eeoc.gov
Site operated by federal commission that enforces civil rights laws relating to employment.

Federal Bureau of Investigation (FBI)
J. Edgar Hoover Building
935 Pennsylvania Avenue NW
Washington, DC 20535-0001
(202) 324-3000
www.fbi.gov
Information on federal law enforcement.

Federal Trade Commission
CRC-240
Washington, DC 20580
(202) 382-4357
www.ftc.gov
Agency that registers complaints about credit reporting agencies and debt collection agencies and handles other issues relating to credit.

Fish and Wildlife Service
C Street NW
Washington, DC 20240
(202) 208-5634
www.fws.gov
Federal office with responsibility for conserving and enhancing fish and wildlife and their habitats.

Food and Drug Administration
5600 Fishers Lane
Rockville, MD 20857
(301) 443-1544
www.fda.gov
Federal agency with regulatory authority over food, cosmetics, and medicines.

Government Printing Office
Washington, DC 20402
(202) 783-3238
www.access.gpo.gov
Site of the government office that prints, binds, and distributes the publications of the U.S. Congress and the executive departments and offices of the federal government.

Health and Human Services Department
200 Independence Avenue SW
Washington, DC 20201
(202) 619-0257
www.os.dhhs.gov
Principal federal agency with responsibility for protecting health of citizens and providing essential services, especially to those of limited means.

Housing and Urban Development Department
451 7th Street SW
Washington, DC 20410
(202) 708-3600
www.hud.gov
Generally regulates housing matters in the United States.

Immigration and Naturalization Service
425 I Street NW
Washington, DC 20536
(202) 514-4316
www.ins.usdoj.gov

Source of information relating to becoming a U.S. citizen.

Internal Revenue Service
1111 Constitution Avenue NW
Washington, DC 20224
(800) 829-1040
www.irs.ustreas.gov

Determines, assesses, and collects taxes in the United States.

Justice Department
950 Pennsylvania Avenue NW
Washington, DC 20530-0001
(202) 514-2001
www.usdoj.gov

Chief arm of federal law enforcement.

Labor Department
200 Constitution Avenue, NW, Room S-1032
Washington, DC 20210
(202) 219-8211
www.dol.gov

Federal agency charged with enhancing job opportunities and ensuring the adequacy of workplaces.

National Park Service
1849 C Street NW
Washington, DC 20240
(202) 208-6843
www.nps.gov

Federal office that regulates the use and preservation of national parks.

Occupational Safety and Health Administration (in the Labor Department)
200 Constitution Avenue
Washington, DC 20210
(800) 321-6742 (for emergencies only)
www.osha.gov

Federal office with responsibility for preventing accidents and illnesses in the workplace.

Official Federal Government Web Sites (maintained by the Library of Congress)
lcweb.loc.gov/global/executive/fed.html
List of sites maintained by various federal agencies and offices.

Secret Service
1800 G Street N
Washington, DC 20223
(202) 435-5708

Protects the president of the United States and other public officials; investigates certain commercial crimes, including counterfeiting.

Securities and Exchange Commission
450 Fifth Street NW
Washington, DC 20549
(202) 942-7040
www.sec.gov

Federal agency with responsibility for administering federal securities laws and protecting investors.

Social Security Administration
Office of Public Inquiries
6401 Security Boulevard
Room 4-C-5 Annex
Baltimore, MD 21235
(800) 772-1213
www.ssa.gov

Federal office that administers the Social Security program.

State Department
2201 C Street NW
Washington, DC 20520
(202) 647-4000
www.state.gov

Chief agency for the implementation of U.S. foreign policy.

Treasury Department
1500 Pennsylvania Avenue NW
Washington, DC 20220
(202) 622-1100
www.ustreas.gov/menu.html

Federal agency that regulates currency, taxes, customs, and related matters.

White House
Washington, DC 20520

(202) 456-7041
www.whitehouse.gov/WH/Welcome-plain.html
Site providing a variety of information on the U.S. presidency.

LEGAL ORGANIZATIONS

Many nongovernmental organizations also provide information to the public on particular legal topics. The following list includes a number of such organizations.

ABA Center for Professional Responsibility
American Bar Association
541 North Fairbanks Court
Chicago, IL 60611-3314
(312) 988-5304
e-mail: ctrprofresp@abanet.org
Web site: www.abanet.org/cpr/home.html

Promotes the study and discussion of ethics relating to lawyers and judges.

Alliance for Justice
2000 P Street, NW, Suite 712
Washington, DC 20036
(202) 822-6070
e-mail: alliance@afj.org
Web site: www.afj.org

National association of environmental, civil rights, mental health, women's, children's and consumer advocacy organizations.

American Bar Association
750 N. Lake Shore Drive
Chicago, IL 60611
(312) 988-5000
e-mail: info@abanet.org
Web site: www.abanet.org

National association of lawyers.

American Inns of Court
127 South Peyton Street, Suite 201
Alexandria, Virginia 22314
(703) 684-3590
Web site: www.innsofcourt.org

Association of lawyers, judges, law teachers, and students dedicated to increasing professionalism in the practice of law.

Association of Trial Lawyers of America
1050 31st Street NW
Washington, DC 20007
(800) 424-2725
e-mail: help@atlahq.org.
Web site: www.atlanet.org

Association of plaintiffs' lawyers and others devoted to the cause of injured persons and other victims.

Better Business Bureau
Council of Better Business Bureaus, Inc.
4200 Wilson Boulevard, Suite 800
Arlington, VA 22203-1804
(703) 276-0100
Web site: www.bbb.org

Organization devoted to promoting fair and ethical business practices.

Conflict Resolution Center International
204 Thirty-seventh Street
Pittsburgh, PA. 15201-1859
(412) 687-6210
e-mail: crcii@conflictnet.org
Web site: www.conflictres.org

Organization that promotes nonviolent dispute resolution.

Electronic Privacy Information Center
666 Pennsylvania Avenue SE, Suite 301
(202) 544-9240
e-mail: info@epic.org
Web site: www.epic.org

Public interest research institute devoted to issues of privacy.

False Claims Act Legal Center
1220 19th Street NW, Suite 501
Washington, DC 20036
(800) 873-2573
e-mail: ams@taf.org
Web site: www.taf.org/taf

Organization that promotes whistle-blowers' suits against individuals and entities that have defrauded the U.S. government.

National Crime Prevention Council
1700 K Street NW, Second Floor
Washington, DC 20006-3817
(202) 466-6272

Web site: www.ncpc.org
National organization dedicated to crime prevention.

National Fraud Information Center
P.O. Box 65868
Washington, DC 20035
(800) 876-7060
e-mail: fraudinfo@psinet.com
Web site: www.fraud.org
Organization that assists consumers in obtaining advice about telephone solicitations and reporting possible telemarketing fraud to law-enforcement agencies.

National Lawyers Guild
558 Capp Street
San Francisco, CA 94110
(415) 285-5067
e-mail: nlgsf@igc.apc.org
Web site:
   www.emf.net/~cheetham/gnawld-1.html
National association of progressive lawyers.

National Organization for Victim Assistance
1757 Park Road NW
Washington, DC 20010
e-mail: nova@try-nova.org
Web site: www.try-nova.org
Nonprofit organization that seeks to further victims' rights.

National Paralegal Association
P.O. Box 406
Solebury, PA 18963
(215) 297-8333
e-mail: admin@nationalparalegal.org
Web site: www.nationalparalegal.org
Organization for paralegals and those interested in a paralegal career.

SELECTED RESEARCH CENTERS

The following is a list of selected centers devoted to research on particular topics. Since the titles of the centers reflect the centers' concentration, the list does not describe each organization. A few centers have e-mail addresses and/or Web sites, which have been included when available.

ABA Center on Children and the Law
1800 M Street, NW
Washington, DC 20036
(202) 331-2250
e-mail: ctrchildlaw@abanet.org
Web site: www.abanet.org/child

American Indian Law Center
P.O. Box 4456, Station A
Albuquerque, NM 87196
(505) 277-5462

Arizona State University Center for the Study of Law, Science, and Technology
College of Law
P.O. Box 877906
Tempe, AZ 85287-7906
(602) 965-2554
e-mail: rosalind.pearlman@asu.edu
Web site: www.asu.edu/law/lawscien.htm

California Center for Judicial Education and Research
2000 Powell Street, 8th Floor
Emeryville, CA 94608
(510) 450-3601

Center for Dispute Settlement
1666 Connecticut Avenue NW, Suite 501
Washington, DC 20009

Center for Information Technology & Privacy Law, John Marshall Law School
315 South Plymouth Court
Chicago, Illinois 60604
(312) 987-1419
e-mail: cil@jmls.edu
Web site: www.jmls.edu/info

Center for Law and Computers, Chicago-Kent College of Law
565 West Adams
Chicago, Illinois 60661
(312) 906-5300
e-mail: clc@chicagokent.kentlaw.edu
Web site: www.kentlaw.edu/clc

Center for Reproductive Law and Policy
120 Wall Street
New York, NY 10005
(212) 514-5534

Center for Women Policy Studies
2000 P Street NW, Suite 508
Washington, DC 20036
(202) 872-1770

College of William and Mary Institute of Bill of Rights Law
Marshal-Wythe School of Law
Williamsburg, VA 23185
(804) 221-3808
Web site: www.wm.edu/law/programs/bill_of_rights.htm

Columbia University Center for the Study of Human Rights
1108 International Affairs Building
New York, NY 10027
(212) 854-2479
e-mail: cshr@columbia.edu
Web site: www.columbia.edu/cu/humanrights

Crime Control Institute and Crime Control Research Corporation
1063 Thomas Jefferson Street, NW
Washington, DC 20007
(202) 337-2700

Florida State University Center for Employment Relations and Law
College of Law
Tallahassee, FL 32306
(904) 644-4287

Freedom Forum First Amendment Center
Vanderbilt University
1222 16th Avenue South
Nashville, TN 37212
(615) 321-9588
e-mail: info@fac.org
Web site: www.freedomforum.org

Georgetown University Anne Blaine Harrison Institute for Public Law
111 F. Street NW
Washington, DC 20001
(202) 662-9600

Harvard Legislative Research Bureau
Harvard Law School
Cambridge, MA 02138
(617) 495-4400

Judge David L. Bazelon Center for Mental Health Law
1101 15th Street NW, Suite 1212
Washington, DC 20005
(202) 467-5730

Loyola University of Chicago National Center for Freedom of Information Studies
820 North Michigan Avenue
Chicago, IL 60611
(312) 915-7095

Marine Law Institute University of Maine School of Law
246 Deering Avenue
Portland, Maine 04102
(207) 780-4474
e-mail: bbsmith@payson.usmacs.maine.edu
Web site: www.law.usm.maine.edu/mli/mli.htm

Marquette University National Sports Law Institute
1103 West Wisconsin Avenue
Milwaukee, WS 53233
(414) 288-5815
e-mail: munsli@vms.csd.mu.edu
Web site: www.mu.edu/law/sports/sports.htm#institute

Meiklejohn Civil Liberties Institute
P.O. Box 673
Berkeley, CA 94701-0673
(510) 848-0599
e-mail: mcli@igc.apc.org

N. Neal Pike Institute on Law and Disability, Boston University School of Law
765 Commonwealth Avenue
Boston, MA 02215
(617) 353-2904
e-mail: pikeinst@bu.edu
Web site: www.bu.edu/pike/home.html

National Center for Juvenile Justice
710 Fifth Avenue, Suite 3000
Pittsburgh, PA 15219-3000
(412) 227-6950
e-mail: ncjj2@nauticom.net
Web site: http://www.ncjj.org

National Center on Women and Family Law
799 Broadway, Room 402
New York, NY 10003
(212) 674-8200

National Council on Crime and Delinquency
684 Market Street, Suite 620
San Francisco, CA 94105
(415) 896-6223

National Immigration Law Center
1636 West 8th Street, Suite 215
Los Angeles, CA 90017
(213) 487-2531

National Women's Law Center
1616 P Street NW
Washington, DC 20036
202-328-5160
Web site: http://www.protectchoice.org/leadernwlc.html

Vermont Law School Environmental Law Center
Chelsea Street
South Royalton, VT 05068
(802) 763-8303
Web site: www.vermontlaw.edu/elc/elc.htm

—Timothy L. Hall

State Bar Associations

The lawyers in each state are organized into a statewide association that serves the interests of its members, the public, and the administration of justice. In many states membership in this bar association is mandatory—that is, a lawyer wishing to practice law in the state must be a member of the bar. In other states membership in the association is purely voluntary.

Bar associations generally supervise several matters of interest to the public. First, the state bar association in the state in which a lawyer practices is normally responsible for the professional discipline of the lawyer. Members of the public who believe that an attorney has acted unethically may make a complaint to the state bar association. In response, the bar typically investigates complaints and, in appropriate cases, brings disciplinary proceedings against a lawyer. Second, most state bar associations assist the public by referring people needing legal assistance to particular lawyers. Third, state bar associations often provide some form of legal education to the general public in the form of public lectures, telephone hotlines, pamphlets, and other services.

Alabama (11,500 members)
415 Dexter Avenue
Montgomery, AL 36104
Telephone: (334) 269-1515; fax: (334) 261-6310
e mail:info@alabar.org
Web site: http://www.alabar.org/

Alaska (3,278 members)
510 L Street, Suite 602
Anchorage, AK 99501
Telephone: (907) 272-7469; fax: (907) 272-2932
e-mail:alaskabar@alaskabar.org
Web site: http://www.alaskabar.org

Arizona (14,000 members)
111 West Monroe, Suite 1800
Phoenix, AZ 85003-1742
Telephone: (602) 252-4804; fax: (602) 271-4930
e-mail:azbar@azbar.org
Web site: http://www.azbar.org/

Arkansas (4,000 members)
400 West Markham
Little Rock, AR 72201
Telephone: (501) 375-4606, (800) 609-5668;
   fax: (501) 375-4901
e-mail:arkbar@ipa.net
Web site: http://www.arkbar.com

California (150,000 members)
555 Franklin Street
San Francisco, CA 94102-4498
Telephone: (415) 561-8200; fax: (415) 561-8228
Web site: http://www.calbar.org

Colorado (13,000 members)
1900 Grant Street, Ninth Floor
Denver, CO 80203
Telephone: (303) 860-1115; fax: (303) 894-0821
e-mail:cobar@cobar.org
Web site: http://www.cobar.org/

Connecticut (900 members)
101 Corporate Place
Rocky Hill, CT 06067-1894
Telephone: (860) 721-0025; fax: (860) 257-4125
e-mail:ctbar@ctbar.org
Web site: http://www.ctbar.org/

Delaware (2,500 members)
1201 Orange Street, Suite 1100
Wilmington, DE 19801
Telephone: (302) 658-5279; fax: (302) 658-5212
Web site: http://www.dsba.org

District of Columbia (66,000 members)
1250 H Street NW, 6th Floor
Washington, DC 20005
Telephone: (202) 737-1700; fax: (202) 626-3471
Web site: http://www.dcbar.org/

Florida (54,301 members)
650 Apalachee Parkway
Tallahassee, FL 32399-2300
Telephone: (850) 561-5600; fax: (850) 561-5827
e-mail:flabarwm@flabar.org
Web site: http://www.flabar.org

Georgia (25,500 members)
800 Hurt Building
50 Hurt Plaza
Atlanta, GA 30303
Telephone: (404) 527-8700; fax: (404) 527-8717
Web site: http://www.gabar.org/

Hawaii (5,900 members)
1136 Union Mall, PH 1
Honolulu, HI 96813
Telephone: (808) 537-1868; fax: (808) 521-7936
Web site: http://www.hsba.org/

Idaho (3,588 members)
525 West Jefferson Street
P.O. Box 895
Boise, ID 83701
Telephone: (208) 334-4500; fax: (208) 334-4515
Web site: http:state.id.us/isb

Illinois (33,000 members)
Illinois Bar Center
424 S. 2nd Street
Springfield, IL 62701
Telephone: (217) 525-1760; fax: (217) 525-0712
e-mail:info@illinoisbar.org
Web site: http://www.illinoisbar.org/

Indiana (10,500 members)
Indiana Bar Center
230 E. Ohio Street
Indianapolis, IN 46204-2119
Telephone: (317) 639-5465, (800) 266-2581;
    fax: (317) 266-2588
e-mail:isbaadmin@inbar.org
Web site: http://www.ai.org/isba/

Iowa (521 members)
East Locust Street, Floor 3
Des Moines, IA 50390-1939
Telephone: (515) 243-3179; fax: (515) 243-2511
Web site: http://www.iowabar.org/main.nsf

Kansas (6,200 members)
1200 Harrison Street
Topeka, KS 66601-1037
Telephone: (785) 234-5696; fax: (913) 234-381
e-mail:kbatech@ink.org
Web site: http://www.ink.org/public/cybar/

Kentucky (12,097 members)
514 West Main Street
Frankfort, KY 40601-1883
Telephone: (502)564-3795; fax: (502) 564-3225
e-mail:webmaster@kybar.org
Web site: http://www.kybar.org/

Louisiana (17,000 members)
601 Street Charles Avenue
New Orleans, LA 70130-3427
Telephone: (504) 566-1600; fax: (504) 566-0930
Web site: http://www.lsba.org

Maine (2,900 members)
124 State Street
P.O. Box 788
Augusta, ME 04332-0788
Telephone: (207) 622-7523; fax: (207) 623-0083
e-mail:info@mainebar.org
Web site: http://www.mainebar.org/

Maryland (17,300 members)
Maryland Bar Center
Baltimore, MD 21201
Telephone: (410) 685-7878, (800) 492-1964;
    fax: (410) 837-0518
e-mail:msba@msba.org
Web site: http://www.msba.org/

Massachusetts (19,000 members)
20 West Street
Boston, MA 02111
Telephone: (617) 338-0500; fax: (617) 338-0650

Michigan (31,000 members)
Michael Franck Building
306 Townsend Street
Lansing, MI 48933
Telephone: (517) 346-6300; fax: (517) 482-6248
e-mail:webmeister@michbar.org
Web site: http://www.michbar.org/

Minnesota (14,500 members)
514 Nicollet Mall, Suite 300
Minneapolis, MN 55402
Telephone: (612) 333-1183; fax: (612) 333-4927
e-mail:tgroshen@counsel.com
Web site: http://www.mnbar.org/

Mississippi (7,000 members)
643 North State Street
P.O. Box 2168
Jackson, MS 39225
Telephone: (601) 948-4471; fax: (601) 736-1713
e-mail:msbar@msbar.org
Web site: http://www.msbar.org/

Missouri (23,000 members)
P.O. Box 119
Jefferson City, MO 65102-0119
Telephone: (573) 635-4128; fax: (573) 635-2811
e-mail:mobar@mobar.org
Web site: http://www.mobar.org/

Montana (3,503 members)
46 N. Last Chance Gulch, #2A
Helena, MT 59601
Telephone: (406) 442-7660; fax: (406) 442-7763
Web site: http://www.montanabar.org

Nebraska (8,184 members)
635 S. 14th Street, 2nd Floor
Lincoln, NE 68501
Telephone: (402) 475-7091
e-mail:nsbasn01@nol.org
Web site: http://www.nebar.com

Nevada
600 E. Charleston Blvd.
Las Vegas, NV
Telephone: (702) 382-2200
e-mail: dsi@dynamic.dsi.org
Web site:
  http://www.dsi.org/statebar/nevada.htm

New Hampshire (4,651 members)
112 Pleasant Street
Concord, NH 03301
Telephone: (603) 224-6942; fax: (603) 224-2910
Web site: http://www.nh.com/legal/nhbar/

New Mexico (5,400 members)
5121 Masthead NE
P.O. Box 25883
Albuquerque, NM 87125
Telephone: (505) 797-6000; fax: (505) 843-8765
e-mail:lglstatebar@pop.nm.org
Web site: http://www.nmbar.org/

New Jersey
New Jersey Law Center
One Constitution Square
New Brunswick, NJ 08901-1500
Telephone: (732) 249-5000; fax: (732) 249-2815
Web site: http://www.njsba.com

New York (57,000 members)
One Elk Street
Albany, NY 12207
Telephone: (518) 463-3200; fax: (518) 463-8527
e-mail:mis@nysba.org

North Carolina (16,000 members)
P.O. Box 3688
Cary, NC 27519-3688
Telephone: (919) 677-0561, (800) 662-7407;
  fax: (919) 677-0761
e-mail:ncba@mail.barlinc.org
Web site: http://www.barlinc.org

North Dakota (1,800 members)
515 East Broadway, Suite 101
P.O. Box 2136
Bismarck, ND 58502
Telephone: (701) 255-1404; fax: (701) 224-1621

Ohio (24,000 members)
1700 Lake Shore Drive
P.O. Box 16562
Columbus, OH 43216-6562
Telephone: (614) 487-2050; fax: (614) 487-1008
Web site: http://www.ohiobar.org

Oklahoma (13,988 members)
P.O. Box 53036
1901 N. Lincoln
Oklahoma City, OK 73152
Telephone: (405) 524-2365; fax: (405) 524-1115

Oregon (12,500 members)
5200 S.W. Meadows Road
P.O. Box 1689
Lake Oswego, OR 97035-0889
Telephone: (503) 620-0222, (800) 452-8260;
  fax: (503) 684-1366
e-mail:info@osbar.org
Web site: http://www.osbar.org

Pennsylvania (28,000 members)
100 South Street
P.O. Box 186
Harrisburg, PA 17108-0186
Telephone: (717) 238-6715; fax: (717) 238-7182
e-mail:info@pabar.org
Web site: http://www.pabar.org

Rhode Island (4,500 members)
115 Cedar Street
Providence, RI 02903
Telephone: (401) 421-5740; fax: (401) 421-2703
e-mail:ribar@ribar.com
Web site: http://www.ribar.com

South Carolina (9,188 members)
950 Taylor Street, P.O. Box 608
Columbia, SC 29202
Telephone: (803) 799-6653; fax: (803) 799-4118
Web site: http://www.scbar.org

South Dakota (2,333 members)
222 East Capitol Avenue
Pierre, SD 57501-2596
Telephone: (605) 224-7554, (800) 952-2333;
    fax: (605) 224-0282
e-mail:tbarnett@sdbar.org
Web site: http://www.sdbar.org

Tennessee (7,500 members)
3622 West End Avenue
Nashville, TN 37205
Telephone: (615) 383-7421; fax: (615) 297-8058
e-mail:info@tba.org
Web site: http://www.tba.org/index.html

Texas (62,500 members)
1414 Colorado
Austin, TX 78711
Telephone: (512) 463-1463, (800) 204-2222;
    fax: (512) 463-1475
e-mail:76245.1564@compuserve.com
Web site: http://www.texasbar.com

Utah (6,500 members)
645 S. 200 East, #310
Salt Lake City, UT 84111
Telephone: (801) 531-9077; fax: (801) 531-0660
e-mail:info@utahbar.org
Web site: http://www.utahbar.org

Vermont (2,000 members)
P.O. Box 100
Montpelier, VT 05601
Telephone: (802) 223-2020; fax: (802) 223-1573
e-mail:bpaolin@vtbar.org
Web site: http://www.vtbar.org

Virginia (5,500 members)
707 E. Main Street, Suite 1500
Richmond, VA 23219-2803
Telephone: (804) 775-0500; fax: (804) 644-0052
e-mail:vsb@vsb.org
Web site: http://www.vsb.org

Washington (20,000 members)
2101 Fourth Avenue, Fourth Floor
Seattle, WA 98121-2330
Telephone: (206)727-8200; fax: (206) 727-8320
e-mail:barchief1@aol.com
Web site: http://www.wsba.org/

West Virginia (1,100 members)
2006 Kanawha Blvd., East
Charleston, WV 25311-2204
Telephone: (304) 558-2456; fax: (304) 558-2467
e-mail:pettyc@wvbar.org
Web site: http://www.wvbar.org/

Wisconsin (18,500 members)
402 W. Wilson Street
P.O. Box 7158
Madison WI 53707-7158
Telephone: (608) 257-3838; fax: (608) 257-5502
Web site: http://www.wisbar.org/home.htm

Wyoming (2,000 members)
500 Randall Avenue
Cheyenne, WY 82001
Telephone: (307) 632-9061; fax: (307) 632-3737
e-mail:wyobared@wyo.com
Web site: http://www.wyo.com

—Timothy L. Hall

Federal Law-Enforcement Agencies

DEPARTMENT OF AGRICULTURE

U.S. Forest Service Law Enforcement
14th and Independence Avenue SW
Washington, DC 20250
(703) 235-3440

There are 732 employees in law enforcement employed through headquarters in Washington, D.C., and nine regional offices: Juneau, Alaska; San Francisco, California; Lakewood, Colorado; Atlanta, Georgia; Missoula, Montana; Albuquerque, New Mexico; Portland, Oregon; Ogden, Utah; and Milwaukee, Wisconsin.

The U.S. Forest Service was originally established in 1905 under the Agriculture Department. The agency's special agents are directly charged with law-enforcement duties. Under Title XVI, section 559 of the U.S. Code, all forest officers have the authority to arrest individuals suspected of violating the law. Agents and officers of the U.S. Forest Service have law-enforcement responsibilities as spelled out under Title XVI, section 551, and Title XVIII, sections 641, 1361, 1852, and 1857, of the U.S. Code. They are also covered by the Assimilated Crimes Act, Title XVIII, section 13, of the U.S. Code and Title XXXVI of the Code of Federal Regulations.

DEPARTMENT OF DEFENSE

Defense Investigative Service
1340 Braddock Place
Alexandria, VA 22315
(703) 325-5324

DIS Agents are employed at five regional offices: Long Beach, California; Smyrna, Georgia; Cherry Hill, New Jersey; Irving, Texas; and Alexandria, Virginia. Extensive travel is involved.

The Defense Investigative Service was established on October 1, 1972, to eliminate duplication of effort by the investigative organizations of the various branches of the armed services. Agents conduct their investigations under the provisions of Executive Order 10450 and various statutes under Titles X and XVIII of the U.S. Code, the Code of Federal Regulations, and Department of Defense regulations.

Naval Investigative Service
Career Services Department
Washington, DC 20388

There are 1,200 agents employed at seven regional offices and three international offices: San Diego, California; San Francisco, California; Washington, D.C.; Pearl Harbor, Hawaii; New York, New York; Charleston, South Carolina; Norfolk, Virginia; London, England; Yosuka, Japan; and Subic Bay, the Philippines. Two years of overseas duty are expected, which may include a one-year tour of duty on a military vessel.

This investigative bureau was initially established in 1916 as a branch office of the Office of Naval Intelligence in New York City. Agents are authorized to carry firearms under Title X, section 1585, of the U.S. Code, and their arrest powers are granted under Title X, section 809. Other law-enforcement responsibilities are outlined under Title X, sections 807, 881, 890, 906, 918, 922, 932, and 936, of the U.S. Code.

DEPARTMENT OF THE INTERIOR

Bureau of Indian Affairs (BIA) Law Enforcement Division
1951 Constitution Avenue NW
Washington, DC 20245

Some 273 officers and investigators are employed through headquarters in Washington, D.C., and thirteen regional offices: Juneau, Alaska; Phoenix, Arizona; Window Rock, Arizona; Sacramento, California; Minneapolis, Minnesota; Billings, Montana; Albuquerque, New Mexico; Gallup, New Mexico; Anadarko, Oklahoma; Muskogee, Oklahoma; Portland, Oregon; Aberdeen, South Dakota; and Arlington, Virginia. Native American candidates are given preference in hiring by federal law.

The Indian Police service was formally created in 1878 to assist the U.S. Congress in asserting its constitutional authority to regulate commerce with Indians. The Reorganization Act of 1934 allowed

Indian tribes to establish tribal courts with tribal police. BIA officers and investigators have primary jurisdiction over criminal cases that occur on tribal lands, but the Federal Bureau of Investigation (FBI) is granted jurisdiction over the most serious crimes committed on reservations (particularly murder cases). BIA officers and investigators derive their arrest powers under Title XXV, section 36, and Title XVIII, section 3055, of the U.S. Code. They can administer oaths under Title XXV, section 36, and can investigate embezzlement cases under Title XVIII, section 1163. Individual states have the authority to enforce criminal statutes on Indian lands under Title XXV, section 1321, of the U.S. Code.

Bureau of Land Management Law Enforcement Division
18th and C Street NW
Washington, DC 20240
(202) 653-8815

Rangers and criminal investigators are employed through twelve regional offices: Anchorage, Alaska; Phoenix, Arizona; Sacramento, California; Lakewood, Colorado; Boise, Idaho; Billings, Montana; Reno, Nevada; Santa Fe, New Mexico; Portland, Oregon; Salt Lake City, Utah; Springfield, Virginia; and Cheyenne, Wyoming.

In addition to protecting public lands and mineral rights owned by the federal government, these law-enforcement officers are responsible for investigating violations of federal laws on these lands.

National Park Service
1849 C Street NW
Washington, DC 20240
(202) 208-5093

About 660 police officers and 1,500 rangers are employed through headquarters and three other personnel offices (Seasonal Employment Unit, U.S. Ranger Division, and U.S. Park Police) in Washington, D.C. Park police and rangers are required to live in government quarters for the most part, must meet rigorous physical demands of the job, and are expected to work frequent overtime in addition to working weekends, holidays, evenings, and during special events and emergencies as needed.

Legislation passed on August 26, 1916, and signed by President Woodrow Wilson established the procedure for designating and overseeing U.S. National Parks and Monuments. The General Authorities Act of 1974 granted law-enforcement powers to specific employees of the National Park Service. Park rangers and officers are granted law-enforcement authority under the provisions of several federal statutes, including Title XVI, section 10(b), and Title XXXVI, section 10, of the U.S. Code. The U.S. Park Police grew out of watch patrols established when the president's residence was built in the District of Columbia. It became known as the U.S. Park Police in May, 1919, and was placed under the control of the National Park Service in 1934. Its law-enforcement authority is derived from various statutes, including Title IV, section 4-201, chapter 2, of the District of Columbia Code. The agency has some jurisdiction in Maryland and Virginia under chapter 136, Public Law 447.

U.S. Fish and Wildlife Service Law Enforcement Division
1612 K Street NW
Washington, DC 20240
(703) 358-2120

About 620 agents and inspectors are employed through headquarters in Washington, D.C., and seven regional offices: Anchorage, Alaska; Denver, Colorado; Atlanta, Georgia; Hadley, Massachusetts; Twin Cities, Minnesota; Albuquerque, New Mexico; and Portland, Oregon.

The agency was founded in 1871 as the Commission of Fish and Fisheries. It later became the Bureau of Fisheries under the control of the Commerce Department. Special agents are involved in standard investigations and covert operations to enforce wildlife laws. Wildlife inspectors examine cargo containers, live animals, wildlife products, and documents at ports of entry to the United States, and they may seize shipments as evidence, participate in investigations, and testify in court. Agents and inspectors derive their enforcement authority under Titles XVI and XVIII of the U.S. Code, including Title XVIII, section 3504. Their responsibilities include the enforcement of the Lacy Act Amendments of 1981 (combining the Lacy Act of 1900 and the Black Bass Act), the Bald Eagle Act of 1940, the Migratory Bird Act of 1918, the Migratory Bird Hunting and Conservation Stamp Act, and the Airborne Hunting Act.

DEPARTMENT OF JUSTICE

Drug Enforcement Administration (DEA)
1100 I Street NW
Washington, DC 20537
(202) 307-4088, (800) 332-4288

Approximately 3,700 Special Agents are employed in offices in 170 U.S. cities and 74 duty posts in more than fifty foreign countries. Agents must be willing to accept assignments anywhere in the United States and may be assigned to tours of duty in foreign offices for two to three years.

The Bureau of Revenue initially had responsibility for enforcing the Harrison Narcotic Act of 1914, which imposed a tax on all narcotic drugs. The Bureau of Narcotics was later established under the control of the Treasury Department on June 14, 1930. It was transferred to the control of the Justice Department and was renamed the Bureau of Narcotics and Dangerous Drugs in 1965. On July 1, 1973, the agency was renamed the Drug Enforcement Administration as part of a planned reorganization of the federal government. From then on the U.S. Customs Service and Immigration and Naturalization (INS) officers were required to turn alleged drug offenders over to the DEA for investigation. Several federal statutes extend arrest powers and other law-enforcement responsibilities to DEA agents and investigators, including Title XXI, sections 878, 880, and 881 of the U.S. Code.

Federal Bureau of Investigation (FBI)
J. Edgar Hoover Building
10th Street and Pennsylvania Avenue NW
Washington, DC 20535
(202) 324-3000

About 9,800 special agents with 13,500 support personnel are employed at FBI headquarters and fifty-six field offices throughout the United States. Agents must be willing to accept assignments anywhere in the United States and may be given foreign assignments during their careers.

The agency was founded as the Bureau of Investigation in July, 1908. The FBI receives its general law-enforcement powers under Title XVIII, section 3052, of the U.S. Code. FBI agents investigate offenses covered under Title XVIII, sections 606, 641, 794, 872, 1001, 1073, 1201, and 1510, of the U.S. Code.

Federal Bureau of Prisons
320 First Street NW
Washington, DC 20534

More than 9,900 corrections officers are employed at seventy-one federal corrections facilities. They are employed and recruited through headquarters in Washington, D.C., and five regional offices: Dublin, California; Atlanta, Georgia; Kansas City, Missouri; Philadelphia, Pennsylvania; and Dallas, Texas.

Corrections officers are expected to be able to use force in subduing inmates who are armed and causing disturbances. The powers of these corrections officers are defined under Title XVIII, section 3050, of the U.S. Code. Other important sections of Title XVIII that apply to corrections officers include section 751 (making escaping from a federal representative or institution a felony offense), section 752 (making the assistance of an escapee a felony offense), section 753 (defining the criminal penalty for the attempted rescue of inmates), section 1114 (defining the criminal penalty for killing an officer or employee of a U.S. penal institution), and section 1792 (defining the powers granted for arresting mutineers and rioters within U.S. penal institutions).

Immigration and Naturalization Service (INS)
425 I Street NW
Washington, DC 20536
(202) 514-2690

More than 9,400 agents, inspectors, and officers, as well as 3,900 Border Patrol Agents are employed at key border crossings and ports of entry to the United States. Border Patrol Agents are expected to learn Spanish, since their first duty assignments are on the U.S.-Mexican border. The INS hires numerous "summer" inspectors to assist the agency during peak tourist times and to help cover for vacationing permanent staff members. INS law-enforcement personnel are employed and recruited through headquarters in Washington, D.C., and four regional offices: San Pedro, California; Twin Cities, Minnesota; Dallas, Texas; and Burlington, Vermont.

The Office of Commissioner of Immigration was established under the control of the State Department in 1864. The power to regulate immigration comes from Article VIII, section 1, of the U.S. Constitution. The agency became the Bureau of Immigration in 1895 under the control of the Treasury Department. Control was later transferred to the Commerce Department in 1903. The Immigration and Naturalization Service was formed on June 10, 1933, under control of the Labor Department before it was transferred to the Justice Department in 1940. The Border Patrol was founded in 1924. INS agents, inspectors, officers, and Border Patrol agents are responsible for enforcing the 1952 Immigration and Nationality Act (McCarran-Walter Act) and subsequent legislation concerning immigration. INS and Border Patrol personnel have arrest powers and search and seizure authority under Title VIII, section 1357, of the U.S. Code. Other statutes that apply include Title XVIII, sections 371, 911, 1001, 1425, 1426, and several other statutes under Titles VIII and XVIII of the U.S. Code.

U.S. Marshals Service
600 Army/Navy Drive
Arlington, VA 22202-4210
(202) 307-9065

Approximately 3,500 Deputy Marshals and administrative personnel are employed at 427 office locations in all ninety-four federal judicial districts. Deputy Marshals are expected to travel frequently for extended periods and must be willing to accept reassignment to other duty stations as necessary.

The Marshals Service was established under the Judiciary Act of 1789, and the first thirteen marshals were appointed by President George Washington. The agency was granted bureau status in 1974. U.S. Marshals derive their law-enforcement authority under Title XVIII, sections 111, 201, 333, 401, and 3053, of the U.S. Code. Other statutes that apply are found under Title XXVIII, sections 59 and 570.

DEPARTMENT OF THE TREASURY

Bureau of Alcohol, Tobacco, and Firearms (BATF)
650 Massachusetts Avenue NW
Washington, DC 20001
(202) 566-7321

More than 1,900 agents and investigators are employed and recruited through twenty-four regional offices.

The bureau's mission is to reduce the criminal use of firearms and explosives by enforcing federal laws concerning the distribution, possession, and use of these devices. The transport, sale, and distribution of alcohol and tobacco products is another key responsibility. BATF agents and investigators assist state, local, and foreign law-enforcement agencies to investigate illegal activities and ensure compliance with alcohol, tobacco, and firearms tax statutes. The bureau originally enforced the Volstead Act during Prohibition; it later became responsible for enforcing the Federal Alcohol Administration Act. In 1975, the ATF was given responsibility for enforcing violations of Public Law 95-575 involving the transportation and sale of contraband cigarettes. The bureau also has primary responsibility for enforcing the National Firearms and Transfer Record Act. BATF agents and investigators derive their arrest powers from Title XXVI, section 7608, of the U.S. Code. Other statutes that apply include Title XXVI, sections 7209, 7268, and 7271, and Title XVIII, sections 924 and 1202, of the U.S. Code

Bureau of Engraving and Printing Office of Police
301 14th Street SW
Washington, DC 20228
(202) 847-3458

Some 125 officers are employed to protect the bureau's employees, building, and equipment. They also provide security for the notes, certificates, postage stamps, and Treasury securities printed by the bureau.

The Bureau of Printing was established on July 11, 1862. The U.S. Secret Service Uniformed Force was divided in 1953, with some guards assigned to the Bureau of Engraving and Printing and others to the main Treasury building and annex.

Internal Revenue Service (IRS)
Criminal Investigation Division
1111 Constitution Avenue NW

Washington, DC 20224
(202) 622-5000

More than 3,600 agents and officers are employed and recruited through headquarters in Washington, D.C., and seven regional offices: San Francisco, California; Atlanta, Georgia; Chicago, Illinois; New York, New York; Cincinnati, Ohio; Philadelphia, Pennsylvania; and Dallas, Texas. These agents and officers operate out of sixty-two IRS districts throughout the United States.

The federal government's power to collect income tax was established under the Sixteenth Amendment to the U.S. Constitution in 1913 and was reinforced by the Revenue Act of 1913. Other revenue laws that have been passed by Congress are listed under Title XXVI of the U.S. Code. IRS revenue agents are responsible for investigating violations of federal tax laws, whereas IRS revenue officers are responsible for collecting delinquent taxes and seizing assets or property forfeited as a result of tax evasion or delinquency. IRS agents and officers derive their arrest powers under Title XXVI, section 7608(b)2, of the U.S. Code. Other statutes that apply include Title XXVI, sections 7201, 7203, 7206, 7602, and 7622.

U.S. Customs Service
1301 Constitution Avenue NW
Washington, DC 20229
(202) 927-2095

More than 10,000 agents, officers, inspectors, and pilots are employed by the U.S. Customs Service to ensure that all goods being imported and exported across U.S. borders do so in accordance with federal laws and regulations. They are employed and recruited through forty-eight regional offices.

Congressional authority to collect taxes was established in Article I, sections 3, 8, and 10, of the U.S. Constitution. Customs districts and officers were first established under the Tariff Act of 1789. The agency has been known as the U.S. Customs Service since 1973. Canine-enforcement officers train and work with dogs to enforce customs laws and regulations. Pilots must have a current commercial pilots license, pass a Class 1 physical examination, and meet required flight hours. Pilots provide air surveillance to crack down on illegal traffic crossing U.S. borders. Special agents are responsible for investigating customs crimes committed by various organized crime groups. The Customs Service hires numerous "summer" inspectors to assist the agency during peak tourist times and to help cover for vacationing permanent staff. Customs agents, investigators, inspectors, pilots, and officers derive their law-enforcement authority from various statutes, including Title XVIII, sections 201 and 3054, Title XIX, and Title XXVI, section 7607, of the U.S. Code.

U.S. Mint Office of Police
633 Third Street NW
Washington, DC 20220
(202) 874-6000

More than two hundred officers are responsible for maintaining security at the U.S. Mint offices in San Francisco, California; Denver, Colorado; West Point, New York; and Philadelphia, Pennsylvania. They also maintain security at the U.S. Bullion Depository at Fort Knox, Kentucky.

These police officers are charged with protecting the employees and the raw materials and coins they use and produce. The officers serve as armed guards and security officers but are not directly involved as criminal investigators in any incidents that occur at U.S. Mint offices.

U.S. Secret Service Personnel Division
1800 G Street NW
Washington, DC 20223
(202) 435-5708

Approximately 4,400 agents and uniformed officers are employed to provide physical security at the Treasury building and various other buildings and diplomatic missions in the Washington, D.C., area as well as at locations where official U.S. representatives are traveling abroad. Secret Service personnel investigate counterfeit schemes relating to coins, currency, government bonds, checks, stamps, credit and debit cards, false identification cards, mobile phone cloning, computer fraud, and other crimes involving Treasury securities and obligations of the federal government.

The division was created on July 5, 1865, to assist the U.S. Congress in asserting its authority to punish counterfeiters (Article I, section 8 of the U.S. Constitution). After John F. Kennedy's assassination, the Secret Service Division became a bureau within the Treasury Department and was renamed the U.S. Secret Service. Guards of the main Treasury building and annex became part of the Treasury Police Force under the Secret Service. Agents and officers derive their authority under Title XVIII, section 3056, of the U.S. Code. They also enforce the Presidential Protection Assistance Act of 1976 and Public Law 90-331, which extends protection to presidential candidates. Other statutes that apply include Title XVIII, sections 471, 472, 484, and 495. The Uniformed Division has duties that are enumerated under Title III, section 202.

DEPARTMENT OF VETERANS AFFAIRS (DOVA)

Office of Security and Law Enforcement
810 Vermont Avenue NW
Washington, DC 20420
(202) 273-4900

Some 2,300 Department of Veterans Affairs police officers provide security and law-enforcement services at 172 Veterans Affairs facilities throughout the United States. Units at each facility operate independently from the central office in Washington, D.C. Veterans are given special preference in hiring, and officers are expected to show respect to the disabled or impaired veterans with whom they work.

Members of the Security Service of the Veterans Affairs' Department of Medicine and Surgery have law-enforcement responsibilities enumerated under Title XXXVIII, section 218 of the U.S. Code.

INDEPENDENT AGENCIES

Environmental Protection Agency (EPA)
401 M Street SW
Washington, DC 20460
(202) 260-2090

Criminal investigators for the EPA are responsible for enforcing federal laws against environmental pollution and are employed and recruited through ten regional offices: San Francisco, California; Denver, Colorado; Atlanta, Georgia; Chicago, Illinois; Kansas City, Kansas; Boston, Massachusetts; New York, New York; Philadelphia, Pennsylvania; Dallas, Texas; and Seattle, Washington.

EPA Officers are responsible for investigating violations involving air, water, and land pollution. Some of the congressional legislation they are responsible for enforcing include the Water Quality Act of 1970, the Clean Air Amendments of 1970, the Federal Environmental Pesticide Control Act of 1972, the Federal Water Pollution Control Act Amendments of 1972, the Marine Protection, Research, and Sanctuaries Act of 1972, the Noise Control Act of 1972, the Safe Drinking Water Act of 1944, the Toxic Substances Control Act of 1976, and the Clean Water Act of 1977.

General Services Administration Federal Protective Service
18th and F Streets NW
U.S. Capitol Building
Washington, DC 20405
(202) 708-5082

More than seven hundred officers provide security and law-enforcement services at federal buildings and property throughout the United States. They are employed and recruited through eleven regional offices: San Francisco, California; Denver, Colorado; Washington, D.C.; Atlanta, Georgia; Chicago, Illinois; Boston, Massachusetts; Kansas City, Missouri; New York, New York; Philadelphia, Pennsylvania; Fort Worth, Texas; and Auburn, Washington.

Members of the Federal Protective Service derive their law-enforcement authority under Title XL, sections 318 and 319, of the U.S. Code.

Tennessee Valley Authority
400 West Summit Hill Drive
Knoxville, TN 37902
(615) 632-2101

Some 740 officers are employed by the Tennessee Valley Authority (TVA) to provide security services and protection for the natural resources, facilities, and employees that are part of the TVA's operations in producing electric power, regulating flood control channels, and developing forestry and wildlife resources.

The agency was established under the Tennessee Valley Authority Act of 1933 and is charged with protecting TVA property under the terms of this act. Officers have law-enforcement authority extended to them under the provisions of chapter 18 of the Code of Federal Regulations.

U.S. Postal Inspection Service
475 L'Enfant Plaza SW
Washington, DC 20260
(202) 268-4267

More than 3,500 inspectors and officers have jurisdiction over criminal investigations involving the security of the U.S. mails, postal service employees, and post office buildings. These inspectors and officers are employed and recruited through thirty regional offices in the continental United States and Puerto Rico.

The Postal Inspection Service is one of the oldest federal law-enforcement agencies, tracing its roots to the colonial postal system. In 1872 the U.S. Congress enacted the Mail Fraud Statute to combat a post-Civil War outbreak of swindles using the mails. Postal inspectors and police officers derive their authority to investigate mail fraud from Title XVIII, sections 711, 1341, 1701, 1707, 1709, and 3061(a), of the U.S. Code. They are empowered to investigate lottery fraud through the mail under Title XXXIX, section 3005.

JUDICIAL BRANCH

Administrative Office of the U.S. Courts (Human Resources Division)
1 Columbus Circle NE
Washington, DC 20544
(202) 273-1270

More than 3,700 probation officers are involved in investigations of defendants pending sentence. They also supervise federal offenders who are on probation or parole and conduct special investigations to assist the U.S. Parole Commission and the U.S. Bureau of Prisons. These officers are employed and recruited through various district offices that are part of the federal judiciary.

Although its functions existed earlier, this branch traces its origins to the establishment of the Division of Probation in 1940. Parole officers hold certain delegated powers under Title XVIII of the U.S. Code (especially sections 3654, 4203, and 4213) and the Code of Federal Regulations.

LEGISLATIVE BRANCH

U.S. Capitol Police
U.S. Capitol Building
119 D Street NW
Washington, DC 20510
(202) 224-9819

Approximately one thousand police officers are employed to provide security services for the U.S. Capitol Building and members and officers of the U.S. Congress and their families. Members of the U.S. Capitol Police force are assigned to several special divisions, including emergency response units, canine units, bicycle patrol units, and drug-enforcement units.

Officers of the Capitol Police Force derive their arrest authority under Title XL, section 212(a), of the U.S. Code. Under Public Law 143, passed by the 97th Congress, these officers can be assigned to protect members of Congress and their immediate family members.

QUASI OFFICIAL AGENCIES

Amtrak Police Department (National Railroad Passenger Corporation)
30th Street Station
Philadelphia, PA 19104
(215) 349-2812

More than three hundred officers provide security for Amtrak employees, passengers, and property. These police officers are often required to travel. They are employed and recruited through seven regional offices: Los Angeles, California; San Jose, California; Washington, D.C.; Chicago, Illinois; Boston, Massachusetts; New York, New York; Philadelphia, Pennsylvania.

Amtrak police officers are commissioned by both state and federal statutes to conduct criminal investigations connected with the Amtrak passenger railroad system.

Smithsonian Institution National Zoological Park Police
3001 Connecticut Avenue NW
Washington, DC 20008
(202) 673-4721

The National Zoological Park Police are responsible for providing security patrols on parkland in Washington, D.C., as well as at a conservation and research center located in Fort Royal, Virginia.

The National Zoological Park was created in

1890. The Smithsonian Institution was later authorized to employ special police officers under the provisions of Public Law 206, signed on October 24, 1951. The Park Police have enforcement powers as enumerated under Title XL, section 193(z), of the U.S. Code and are empowered to investigate specific violations listed under Title XL.

U.s. Inspector General Agencies

Departments of Agriculture, Commerce, Defense, Education, Energy, Health and Human Services, Housing and Urban Development, Interior, Justice, Labor, State, Transportation, Treasury, and Veterans Affairs; Agency for International Development (AID); Amtrak; Environmental Protection Agency (EPA); General Services Administration; National Aeronautics and Space Administration (NASA); Office of Personnel Management; Railroad Retirement Board; Small Business Administration; and the Tennessee Valley Authority (TVA).

More than four thousand agencies have Inspector General offices that maintain investigative staff members who work closely with other law-enforcement agencies.

—*Wendy Sacket*

Filmography

Much of what most Americans outside the legal professions know about these professions comes from viewing films and television programs. To help users understand relationships between art and reality, *Magill's Legal Guide* contains essays on media depictions of the legal professions. To further that aim, this filmography provides brief descriptions of films with legal themes. Titles are arranged under broad themes, which are organized alphabetically.

Attorneys

The Atlanta Child Murders (1985). Docudrama of the Wayne Williams murder case in Atlanta, with Jason Robards and Rip Torn giving riveting performances as opposing attorneys.

The Boys (1961). Investigating attorney uncovers the motives behind the crimes allegedly committed by four teenagers.

Body of Evidence (1993). Willem Dafoe plays a defense attorney involved in a torrid sexual relationship with a client (Madonna), who is accused of killing her lover.

The Burden of Proof (1992). This adaptation of a Scott Turow novel features a lawyer beset by a two-pronged dilemma: his wife's mysterious suicide and his brother-in-law's suspicious involvement in commodities trading that leads to a federal investigation.

Citizen Cohn (1992). James Woods gives an intense performance as Roy Cohn, an attorney notorious for his aggressive investigations of suspected communists for Senator Joseph McCarthy, whose name has become synonymous with smear campaigns to discredit Americans by calling them subversives.

Counsellor-at-Law (1933). An adaptation of an Elmer Rice play, with John Barrymore starring as a successful Jewish lawyer who confronts the cost of his rise from poverty, including his troubled marriage. An early and still effective look at the impact of legal careers on private lives.

Deep Cover (1992). Jeff Goldblum plays an eccentric lawyer who bumbles into an involvement in drug deals.

The Deliberate Stranger (1986). An effective dramatization of murderer Ted Bundy, a law student suspected of killing at least twenty-five women.

Guilty Conscience (1985). An egotistical lawyer (Anthony Hopkins) debates with himself about killing his wife in order to run off with his sexy mistress.

Man Under Suspicion (1984). A lawyer investigates a young girl's violent actions at a political rally and simultaneously probes the roots of fascism.

The Man Who Shot Liberty Valence (1962). In this classic by director John Ford, James Stewart plays a lawyer determined to establish the rule of law in the Wild West.

The Meanest Man in the World (1943). Jack Benny plays a lawyer who discovers that he can be successful only when he is nasty.

My Sweet Charlie (1970). A black lawyer (Al Freeman, Jr.) befriends an unwed white mother (Patty Duke) in rural Texas.

Shannon's Deal (1989). A Philadelphia attorney turned private investigator exposes an international drug deal. Noteworthy for John Sayles's realistic script.

True Confession (1937). A pathological liar (Carole Lombard) confesses to a murder she did not commit and has to be rescued by her lawyer-husband (Fred MacMurray). Remade as *Cross My Heart* (1946).

Young Mr. Lincoln (1939). Concentrates on Abraham Lincoln's early career as a lawyer.

The Young Philadelphians (1959). Paul Newman stars as a struggling attorney who schemes to be a success and to win a society girl (Barbara Rush).

Civil Rights

Separate but Equal (1991). A deft dramatization of *Brown v. Board of Education*, with Sidney Poitier playing Thurgood Marshall, Burt Lancaster as Marshall's conservative and articulate court opponent, and Richard Kiley in a bravura performance as Chief Justice Earl Warren.

Class Actions

Class Action (1991). Gene Hackman and Mary Elizabeth Mastrantonio play a father-daughter team of crusading, feisty attorneys who sue a negligent auto company.

Courtroom Comedy

Adam's Rib (1949). Starring Spencer Tracy and Katharine Hepburn and written by the husband-and-wife team of Garson Kanin and Ruth Gordon, this classic comedy pits a husband and wife against each other in a murder case. The adversarial relationship of attorneys is taken home with hilarious results.

Courtroom Drama

Anatomy of a Murder (1959). One of the greatest depictions of a murder trial, this film, set in a small Michigan town, details the battles between prosecuting and defense attorneys. This screen epic features fine performances by James Stewart and Arthur O'Connell, amplified by the flamboyant direction of Otto Preminger.

The Caine Mutiny (1954). Humphrey Bogart stars as Captain Queeg in this stunning dramatization of the court-martial of an unpopular officer. Based on a Herman Wouk novel that is itself reminiscent of Charles Nordhoff and James Hall's *Mutiny on the Bounty*. Remade for television in 1988.

Compulsion (1959). One of several films based on the 1924 murder trial of Richard Loeb and Nathan Leopold, who were convicted of killing a fourteen-year-old boy in Chicago. This cinemascopic version (starring Orson Welles, Dean Stockwell, and Bradford Dillman) is notable for its compelling treatment of courtroom testimony.

The Court-Martial of Billy Mitchell (1955). A depiction of the military genius who predicted Japan's attack on the United States, this film presents a complex portrait of the man and of the court-martial system. Rod Steiger plays a shrewd lawyer.

A Few Good Men (1992). A young Navy lawyer (Tom Cruise) investigates the case of two young Marines accused of murder. The film turns on the explosive confrontation between Cruise and Jack Nicholson, who plays the commanding officer intent on covering up what really happened.

Inherit the Wind (1960). Based on the famous 1925 trial of John Scopes, also known as the "monkey" trial, in which famous defense attorney Clarence Darrow (Spencer Tracy) defended a Tennessee schoolteacher's right to teach evolution against such famous figures as William Jennings Bryan (Fredric March). A 1988 remake is not nearly as compelling.

The Man Who Talked Too Much (1940). A riveting courtroom duel between two brothers (George Brent is the district attorney and William Lundigan the defense attorney). This is a remake of *The Mouthpiece* (1932), another remake of which was the film *Illegal* (1955).

Three Brave Men (1957). Set during the McCarthy period of the 1950's, this film depicts a lawyer (Ray Milland) who attempts to get a Navy clerk (Ernest Borgnine) reinstated after he is accused of being a communist. Based on Anthony Lewis's Pulitzer Prize-winning articles.

Witness for the Prosecution (1957). Based on an Agatha Christie play, this is a classic of courtroom suspense, starring Marlene Dietrich, Tyrone Power, Charles Laughton, and Elsa Lanchester.

Woman of Desire (1993). Robert Mitchum gives an impressive performance in court as a lawyer caught up in the murder of a playgirl's wealthy boyfriend.

Criminal Law

Penthouse (1933). Warner Baxter stars as a criminal lawyer on a campaign to bring down a crime boss. Remade as *Society Lawyer* (1939).

The People Against O'Hara (1951). A criminal lawyer (Spencer Tracy) reveals his unethical behavior during one of his cases.

Watched! (1972). Stacy Keach plays a former government lawyer who goes underground to expose a drug ring.

Death Penalty Cases

The Executioner's Song (1982). Tommy Lee Jones gives an award-winning performance as Gary Gilmore, who insists that Utah carry out its death sentence. Norman Mailer adapted his award-winning book into this riveting study of crime and the court system.

Just Cause (1995). A Harvard Law School professor (Sean Connery) takes up the cause of an African American man about to be executed for murder.

Defense Attorneys

Confessions: Two Faces of Evil (1994). James Earl Jones plays the defense attorney of two young men accused of killing a California cop. Based on a true-life story.

Count the Hours (1953). Macdonald Cary plays a convincing defense attorney who defends a migrant worker accused of a double murder.

Dummy (1979). Based on a real-life account, Paul Sorvino plays a court appointed deaf attorney defending a deaf-mute client accused of murder.

Eyewitness (1950). American defense lawyer (Robert Montgomery) duels with the British legal system while trying to represent his friend in a homicide case.

From the Hip (1987). A defense attorney (Judd Nelson) famous for his flamboyant and successful tactics in the courtroom is called upon to represent a client (John Hurt) accused of murder.

Guilty or Innocent: The Sam Sheppard Case (1975). Walter McGinn gives an effective performance as F. Lee Bailey, who defended the real-life Dr. Sheppard (a doctor accused of murdering his wife) at his retrial.

The Last Wave (1977). An Australian lawyer (Richard Chamberlain) defends an aborigine accused of murder.

The Lawyer (1970). Inspired by the real-life case of Dr. Sam Sheppard (who was accused of murdering his wife), Barry Newman plays a defense lawyer negotiating his way through legal procedure and battling an uncooperative client.

Marie (1985). Defense attorney Fred Thompson plays himself in this story of a Tennessee woman (Sissy Spacek) who blows the whistle on corruption in state government.

My Cousin Vinny (1992). Superbly acted tale of a Brooklyn attorney (Joe Pesci) who travels to the Deep South to defend a cousin accused of murder. Goes into detail about courtroom procedure.

The Tattered Dress (1957). Jeff Chandler plays a lawyer defending a society couple accused of murder.

They Won't Forget (1937). After an attractive student is murdered in a southern town, a northern lawyer (Claude Rains) is assigned to defend the accused man in a community more interested in protecting itself than in seeing justice done.

True Believer (1989). James Woods plays a former 1960's radical, now a jaded lawyer, who is goaded by his clerk (Robert Downey, Jr.) into action on behalf of a falsely imprisoned Asian American.

Twilight of Honor (1963). An older lawyer (Claude Rains) and younger one (Richard Chamberlain) team up to win a murder case.

The Unknown Man (1951). An unusual departure from most defense attorney scenarios, this film focuses on a lawyer (Walter Pigeon) who discovers his client is guilty and works out a way to reveal the truth.

When Every Day Was the Fourth of July (1978). A young girl pesters her father to defend a town handyman accused of homicide, even though the community is scornful of the lawyer's efforts.

District Attorneys

Boomerang! (1947). Elia Kazan directs a fine study of a prosecuting attorney investigating a murder case that begins with the rapid arrest of an innocent man.

Badge of the Assassin (1985). A New York City assistant district attorney, played with intensity by James Woods, tracks down a pair of cop killers.

The Big Easy (1987). Set in New Orleans, with an assistant district attorney (Ellen Barkin) investigating a local mob murder.

Legal Eagles (1986). An assistant district attorney (Robert Redford) becomes involved with a young, eccentric attorney (Debra Winger) and her weird client (Daryl Hannah).

The Mouthpiece (1932). A dedicated district attorney (Warren William) starts his career earnestly working for the people and then succumbs to slickness and corruption. Based on the real-life story of district attorney William Fallon.

Star Witness (1931). Walter Huston plays a district attorney who must cope with a frightened family that has witnessed a gangland killing.

State's Attorney (1932). John Barrymore stands out as a flamboyant district attorney.

The World Gone Mad (1932). A district attorney about to uncover a swindle is murdered and his successor investigates.

The Young Savages (1961). Burt Lancaster plays an idealistic district attorney determined to see justice done in a street gang slaying. A realistic, even brutal depiction of the criminal justice system.

Divorce

The Courtship of Andy Hardy (1942). Judge Hardy handles a divorce case.

Drugs

Shakedown (1988). A public defender (Peter Weller) teams up with an undercover cop (Sam Elliott) to combat illegal drug sales and distribution.

Estates

The Rothko Conspiracy (1983). Authentic, engrossing dramatization of the legal battle over Mark Rothko's estate, in which the daughter of the great expressionist painter took his executors to court.

Extortion

Big House, U.S.A. (1955). A brutal, realistic drama of Federal Bureau of Investigation (FBI) agents tracking down extortionists and kidnappers, starring Broderick Crawford and Ralph Meeker.

Experiment in Terror (1962). Glenn Ford gives a convincing performance as an agent from the Federal Bureau of Investigation (FBI) dealing with a bank clerk threatened by a violent extortionist.

Family Law

The Good Father (1987). Anthony Hopkins plays a lawyer who loses custody of a child and defends another person seeking to regain custody of his child. Simon Callow has a good role as an unscrupulous attorney.

Losing Isaiah (1995). A dedicated white Chicago social worker (Jessica Lange) rescues an African American baby from the trash (where he has been abandoned by his crack-addicted mother). Several years later, the reformed addict goes to court to reclaim her child.

Roe vs. Wade (1989). A dramatization of the landmark Supreme Court decision (1973) affirming a woman's right to have an abortion. Holly Hunter plays Roe, a feisty unmarried Texas woman, and Amy Madigan plays her young attorney.

Sarah and Son (1930). Fredric March plays a lawyer enlisted to help a woman (Ruth Chatterton) regain custody of a child that had been taken away from her many years earlier.

Immigration

Born in East L.A. (1987). A third-generation Latino man (Cheech Marin) is caught in an Immigration and Naturalization Service (INS) raid and is deported to Tijuana when he cannot produce identification.

Green Card (1990). Gerard Depardieu stars as an immigrant nominally married to Andie MacDowell. The two are forced to spend time together when Depardieu is investigated by the Immigration and Naturalization Service (INS).

Immunity

Lethal Weapon Two (1989). A smuggler hides behind his diplomatic immunity and is pursued by agents Danny Glover and Mel Gibson.

Jailhouse Lawyers

Doing Life (1986). Based on the real-life story of Jerry Rosenberg, a convicted murderer who became the first jailhouse attorney to escape execution. Rosenberg later became a negotiator for the rebellious prisoners at Attica prison in 1971.

Gideon's Trumpet (1980). A semiliterate Florida convict (Henry Fonda) petitions the U.S. Supreme Court and makes legal history. José Ferrer has a compelling role as Supreme Court justice Abe Fortas.

Judges

All God's Children (1980). Richard Widmark plays a judge who must decide on how to handle a forced busing case that is tearing apart his community. The social implications of the law are treated sensitively in this provocative drama.

Crimebroker (1993). Jacqueline Bisset plays a judge who is also a criminal mastermind.

Day of the Bad Man (1958). A courageous judge (Fred MacMurray) persists in his efforts to ensure that the execution of a convicted murderer be carried out in spite of efforts by the murderer's brother to rescue him.

Design for Scandal (1941). A reporter (Walter Pigeon) does a provocative story on a prominent female judge (Rosalind Russell).

First Monday in October (1981). Walter Matthau and Jill Clayburgh star in this comedy about the first woman Supreme Court justice. Sandra Day O'Connor was appointed to the Court just before this film was released.

Indict and Convict (1973). Myrna Loy gives a splendid performance as a female judge handling a case involving a junior district attorney accused of murdering his wife and her lover.

The Judge and the Assassin (1975). This French film is an insightful exploration of a judge's efforts to determine whether an accused murderer is shamming insanity.

Judge Hardy and Son (1939). Although most films in the Andy Hardy series show little of Judge's Hardy's work, this one does focus seriously on his efforts to help an aging couple facing eviction from their home.

Judge Horton and the Scottsboro Boys (1976). Arthur Hill plays an embattled southern judge trying to deal fairly with the famous 1931 case in which nine young African Americans were accused of raping a young woman.

Judge Priest (1934). Will Rogers gives a winning performance as a small-town judge whose sound judgment nevertheless proves to be controversial. Director John Ford remade this film in 1953 as *The Sun Shines Bright*, which he called his favorite film.

Judgment at Nuremberg (1961). Spencer Tracy presides as the American judge at the Nuremberg trials of Nazis for crimes against humanity. The nature of morality and the law are deeply probed in this film, which also features an outstanding performance by Maximilian Schell as a defense attorney.

The Life and Times of Judge Roy Bean (1972). Director John Huston may be the first filmmaker to have treated the law surrealistically. Certainly there is an element of parody in Paul Newman's performance as a self-appointed judge in the Wild West. Walter Brennan won his third Oscar award playing Judge Roy Bean in *The Westerner* (1940).

The Man from Colorado (1948). Glenn Ford plays a judge who twists the law to his tyrannical purposes in order to dominate the western territories.

Open Doors (1990). A judge (Gian Maria Volonte) presiding over a murder trial in fascist Italy probes what it means to judge another person and to uphold the law in a politically repressive country.

Judicial System

Beyond a Reasonable Doubt (1956). Dana Andrews plays a character pretending to be guilty of murder in order to get a first-hand look at the judicial system; he is subsequently unable to prove himself innocent.

Outrage! (1986). A defense attorney (Beau Bridges) takes the case of a father (Robert Preston) who admits to killing his daughter's rapist murderer and turns the trial into an attack on the judicial system.

Juries

Blind Vengeance (1990). White supremacists have murdered a father's only son, but when he brings them to justice, a jury acquits them and he seeks his own vengeance.

The Juror (1996). A somewhat far-fetched scenario in which an eager juror (Demi Moore) involved in the trial of a Mafia don is menaced by a Mafia thug who threatens to harm her friends and family if she votes guilty.

Ladies of the Jury (1932). A society matron creates chaos in the jury room during a murder trial.

Midnight (1934). A jury foreman is held responsible by both the press and his family for having sent a woman to the electric chair.

The Missing Juror (1944). An unknown killer avenges an innocent man executed for murder by murdering the jury.

Murder! (1930). Herbert Marshall stars in this early Alfred Hitchcock film about an actor sitting on a jury who holds out for the innocence of a woman accused of murder.

Murder Most Foul (1965). When Agatha Christie's famous detective, Miss Marple, sits on a jury and believes the defendant is innocent, she sets out to prove her case.

Swoon (1992). Another version of the murder case of Richard Loeb and Nathan Leopold—less compelling than *Compulsion* (1959), but nevertheless a stark and stimulating reenactment of the homophobic atmosphere that influenced the jury's deliberations.

Three for Jamie Dawn (1956). Jury members are pressured to return a not-guilty verdict.

Trial by Jury (1994). An exceptional dramatization of the jury process from the prosecutor's point of view, with telling scenes delving into the psychology of jurors.

Twelve Angry Men (1957). Sidney Lumet directs an all-star cast (Henry Fonda, Lee J. Cobb, Ed Begley, Jack Klugman, Martin Balsam, and E. G. Marshall) in a taut, riveting drama of a single juror who holds out against a bullying cohort of men bent on the conviction of a young man.

Kidnapping

The Lindbergh Kidnapping Case (1976). Accurate and riveting account of the celebrated kidnapping of the son of the aviator Charles Lindbergh.

Patty Hearst (1988). Natasha Richardson gives a solid performance as the newspaper heiress who was kidnapped by radicals and later placed on trial.

Law Enforcement

Black Widow (1986). An investigator (Debra Winger) from the justice department becomes obsessed with a woman (Theresa Russell) who marries men and then murders them.

The Blue Knight (1973). William Holden gives an award-winning performance as a Los Angeles street cop determined to bring a prostitute's killer to justice. Based on a Joseph Wambaugh novel notable for its authentic depiction of police procedures.

A Climate for Killing (1990). A small-town Arizona cop investigates a brutal murder but also has to contend with city officials questioning his investigation.

The Friends of Eddie Coyle (1973). A gritty drama about police corruption. Set in Boston, the film explores the seamy side of deals cops make with felons.

Internal Affairs (1990). Richard Gere is sensational as a corrupt cop investigated by an earnest Andy Garcia. A revealing look at the criminal justice system and at cops who make their own laws.

Prince of the City (1981). A true-life, documentary-like reconstruction of a New York City special investigations cop (Treat Williams) who informs on his buddies and finds himself more of a victim than a hero. Especially revealing are the interrogation scenes in which Williams watches his world collapse as he reveals more and more about law-enforcement corruption.

Serpico (1973). Based on the life story of a New York City undercover cop (played by Al Pacino), this film probes the corruption of the police force and the judicial system's efforts to reform it through Serpico's brave testimony.

Law Firms

The Firm (1993). A Harvard Law School graduate (Tom Cruise) confronts corruption in a big-name Memphis law firm.

Philadelphia (1993). Tom Hanks gives an Oscar-winning performance as a brilliant young lawyer afflicted with acquired immunodeficiency syndrome (AIDS). Because of his disease he is eased out of a posh Philadelphia law firm. Taking his former colleagues to court, Hanks's character reveals the inner workings and politics of high-priced law practices.

Law Students

Crime and Punishment, USA (1959). Loosely based on Fyodor Dostoevski's novel of the same name, George Hamilton plays a law student who becomes involved in robbery and murder.

Dealing (1972). A Harvard law student sets up a side business selling marijuana.

Handle with Care (1958) A law student investigates crime while his fellow students serve on a mock grand jury.

Joy in the Morning (1965). A law student (Richard Chamberlain) struggles through school and marriage in a small college town, where he fights against crude stereotyping and bigotry.

The Pelican Brief (1993). This adaptation of John Grisham's best-selling novel stars Julia Roberts as a law student with a theory about the assassination of two Supreme Court justices that puts her in great danger.

Run (1990). A city-wide manhunt for a law student who accidentally kills the son of a crime boss.

Tough as They Come (1942). A law student battles to reform a corrupt credit union.

True Colors (1991). Two law school students (John Cusack and James Spader) pursue diverging careers. One enters the Justice Department and is determined to fight injustice while the other pursues deal-making politics.

Young Man with Ideas (1952). A Montana lawyer moves to California and has trouble studying for the bar exam.

Legal Aid Attorneys

Nuts (1987). A rather nasty woman (Barbra Streisand) is assigned a legal aid attorney (Richard Dreyfuss), who works to win her right to stand trial for manslaughter while her family claims she is mentally incompetent.

Legal Corruption

And Justice for All (1979). Al Pacino plays a lawyer who battles a corrupt legal system in Maryland. Norman Jewison, a director drawn to social and political issues, satirizes the buying and selling of "justice" even as he lionizes a lawyer who bucks the system.

Carlito's Way (1993). Sean Penn plays a sleazy lawyer tied to a Puerto Rican ex-con played by Al Pacino. Director Paul Mazursky has an effective role as a judge.

Lawyer Man (1932). William Powell stars as an ambitious lawyer who is enmeshed both in womanizing and in dealings with corrupt politicians.

Mr. Ricco (1975). Dean Martin plays a corrupt

lawyer involved in racist murders, sex, and violence.

Night Court (1932). Walter Huston plays a corrupt judge who will stop at nothing to stop an investigation of himself, even if it means framing an innocent young couple.

Slightly Honorable (1940). Pat O'Brien and Broderick Crawford play two lawyers who uncover the corruption of a politician (Edward Arnold).

Smart Woman (1948). A determined lawyer (Brian Aherne) is determined to prosecute a crooked district attorney and other officials.

Legal Education

The Paper Chase (1973). It is freshman year at Harvard Law School, dominated by the crusty Professor Kingsfield, played with extraordinary aplomb by John Houseman. The role earned Houseman (better known as a theater producer) an Oscar and many choice roles, and it provided a generation of students with an insight into the exhilaration, boredom, and terror of law school and ambitious, aspiring attorneys.

Soul Man (1986). Not of the same high quality as *The Paper Chase*, this satire follows the desperate career of a young man who masquerades as an African American in order to qualify as a minority applicant to Harvard Law School.

Legal Procedure

To Kill a Mockingbird (1962). In an Oscar-winning performance, Gregory Peck plays a southern attorney defending an African American man accused of rape. This film (based on a popular novel) is unusual for a script that has Peck patiently explain to his children and their friends the details of legal procedure and the moral ramifications of the law.

Penalty Phase (1986). A fascinating film about a respected judge who allows a vicious killer to go free because his rights have been violated. A rare, searching study of the social and political pressures brought to bear on judges.

Reversal of Fortune (1990). A dramatization of the case of Claus von Bulow, who was accused of attempting to murder his wealthy wife. Ron Silver plays Harvard Law School professor Alan Dershowitz, famous for his ability to use legal procedure to reverse the convictions of his clients.

The Star Chamber (1983). Frustrated by legal procedures that too often permit the guilty to go free, a young judge (Michael Douglas), sets up his own alternative justice system. Although the working out of the premise is farfetched, the issues the film raises about so-called legal technicalities and how society responds to them are well dramatized.

Libel

Fear on Trial (1975). Based on the account of the efforts of attorney Louis Nizer (George C. Scott) to defend John Henry Faulk (William Devane), a writer blacklisted for being a communist.

The Trials of Oscar Wilde (1960). A respectful rendition of the libel suit writer Oscar Wilde brought against the Marquis of Queensberry.

Mafia Lawyers

Force of Evil (1948). John Garfield plays a crooked lawyer whose deals are complicated by his increasing greed.

The Godfather (1972) Robert Duvall gives a stunning performance as lawyer to the Corleone crime family.

The Godfather, Part II (1974). Duvall returns to his role as a mafia lawyer.

Party Girl (1958). Cult director Nicholas Ray probes the life of a crooked lawyer (Robert Taylor) and his efforts to free himself from the Chicago mob.

Negligence

The Verdict (1982). Paul Newman plays a down-and-out Boston attorney who redeems himself with a tenacious performance in a medical negligence case. Sidney Lumet's eloquent direction and David Mamet's screenplay make this an unusually revealing study of personalities and the law.

Parole

A Shadow in the Streets (1975). Tony LoBianco plays an ex-con who becomes a parole officer in an effort to rehabilitate himself. An unusually authentic view of the parole system.

Shockproof (1949). A parole officer (Cornell Wilde) falls in love with a parolee (Patricia Knight) in this effective *film noir*.

Personal Injury

The Fortune Cookie (1966). In an Oscar-winning performance, Walter Matthau plays a corrupt personal injury attorney who bilks insurance companies by exaggerating his clients' injuries.

Product Liability

The Good Fight (1992). A determined law professor (Christine Lahti) files suit against a tobacco company when her son's best friend develops mouth cancer.

Public Defenders

The Law (1974). Set in the public defender's office of a large city, an attorney (Judd Hirsch) pursues the case of a murdered football superstar.

Murder in the First (1995). A young lawyer (Christian Slater) from a public defender's office is assigned his first case: defending an Alcatraz prisoner who has killed a fellow inmate.

Real Estate

Leona Helmsley: The Queen of Mean (1990). Film that dramatizes the case of the New York real estate magnate who ran afoul of federal tax laws.

The Roof (1956). Renowned Italian director Vittorio De Sica's realistic study of a young couple who search for a home in housing-scarce postwar Rome and find one by taking advantage of a loophole in the law.

A Taxing Woman's Return (1990). A Japanese tax investigator ferrets out corruption among industrialists, gangsters, and politicians engaged in a conspiracy to inflate Tokyo real estate prices.

Slander

Action for Slander (1938). Clive Brook plays a cavalry officer accused of cheating at cards. Francis L. Sullivan gives a powerful performance as the lawyer who attempts to redeem his client's reputation.

Restless Disregard (1985). An inexperienced lawyer (Tess Harper) sues a newscaster (Leslie Neilsen) for defamation of character. Based on an actual suit brought against newsman Dan Rather for a report on the television program *60 Minutes*.

Supreme Court

Listen to Me (1989). Notable only for the film's climactic scene—a debate on abortion before the Supreme Court.

The Magnificent Yankee (1950). Informative biographical film that follows the career of Supreme Court justice Oliver Wendell Holmes. It all begins on a day in 1902, when Holmes and his wife come to Washington so that he can begin his career on the Court.

Savage (1973). Investigative reporters find compromising material on a nominee for the Supreme Court.

Women Lawyers

The Client (1994). In this fine adaptation of a John Grisham novel, Susan Sarandon plays a courageous attorney trying to protect a young boy from aggressive federal enforcement officials and a Mafia lawyer.

Criminal Behavior (1992). A tough attorney (Farrah Fawcett) is pursued by a killer.

Defenseless (1991). A defense attorney (Barbara Hershey) finds herself accused of killing her lover and is stalked by a killer at the same time.

Double Jeopardy (1992). Sela Ward plays a woman attorney defending her husband's ex-lover in a murder case.

Guilty as Sin (1993). An ambitious, competitive lawyer (Rebecca De Mornay) defends a womanizing client accused of murdering his wife.

Hanna K (1983). Jill Clayburgh plays an attorney caught between her Israeli ex-husband (a district attorney) and a Palestinian attempting to reclaim his home.

Jagged Edge (1985). An attorney (Glenn Close) defends and falls in love with a publishing magnate (Jeff Bridges), who is accused of murdering his wife. A superb combination of thriller and courtroom drama.

Music Box (1989). Jessica Lange plays an attorney who must defend her father who is charged with war crimes and threatened with deportation.

Other People's Money (1991). A Wall Street predator, Larry the Liquidator (Danny DeVito), does battle with a savvy attorney (Ann Miller).

Rage of Angels (1983). An ambitious lawyer (Jaclyn Smith) sleeps her way to the top of her profession, using powerful men who are one another's enemies.

Shame (1988). A motorcycle-riding lawyer takes on a town full of gang members who rape a sixteen-year-old girl.

—*Carl Rollyson*

Glossary

Note: entries preceded by asterisks are also included as essay topics.

Abandonment: Deliberately relinquishing an interest in property; deserting a spouse or child.

Abate: To decrease or terminate something.

Abstention: Decision by a federal court to refuse to consider a matter more properly addressed to a state court.

Abstract of title: Abbreviated history of the title to a piece of real estate, listing conveyances and encumbrances upon the property.

Abuse of discretion: Standard used by an appellate court to reverse actions of a lower court that are clearly erroneous.

Abuse of process: Improper use of a legal action after it has been filed.

Acceleration clause: Provision in a loan agreement that allows the lender to call the entire amount of the loan due when the borrower fails to comply with an obligation, such as the obligation to make timely payments.

Accessory: Person who assists in the commission of a crime in some secondary role.

*__Accomplice liability:__ Liability for intentionally assisting another in the commission of a crime.

Accused: Person charged with having committed a crime.

ACLU: American Civil Liberties Union.

*__Acquittal:__ The declaration at the conclusion of a trial that a criminal defendant is innocent.

Act of God: Event caused solely by natural forces.

Actionable: Providing grounds for a lawsuit.

Ad valorem tax: Tax based on the value of property owned or purchased.

*__Adultery:__ Voluntary sexual intercourse between a married person and someone other than that person's spouse.

*__Adversary system:__ System in which opposing parties rather than judges have chief responsibility for presenting evidence necessary to resolve a case.

*__Adverse possession:__ Means of acquiring title to property by occupying it openly for a lengthy period of time.

*__Advocate-witness rule:__ General prohibition against an attorney acting both as an advocate and a witness in the same case.

*__Affidavit:__ A sworn, written statement.

*__Affirmative action:__ Policies that single out particular minorities or women for beneficial treatment as a means of remedying past discrimination.

Affirmative defense: A specific defense against a claim other than a general denial of the facts contained in the charge—for example, self-defense as a defense to the charge of murder.

*__Age of majority:__ Age when a person is old enough to enter into a contract.

Aggravation: Circumstances of a crime that increase its seriousness in the view of the law.

Alias: Another name by which a person is known.

*__Alimony and maintenance:__ Payments that an individual is obligated to make to a former spouse for support.

Ambulance chaser: Lawyer or person working with a lawyer who attempts to contact an accident victim shortly after an accident for the purpose of representing the victim in a lawsuit.

*__American Association of Law Schools:__ Professional association of law schools in the United States.

*__American Bar Association:__ Largest national association of lawyers.

American Civil Liberties Union (ACLU): See appendix on legal assistance organizations.

*__American Inns of Court:__ Organization of attorneys, judges, law professors, and law students dedicated to the improvement of the legal profession.

*__Amicus curiae__ brief:__ Brief filed with a court by persons or organizations who are not parties to a case but are interested in the matter.

*__Amnesty:__ Pardon granted to persons guilty of a political crime.

*__Annotated codes:__ Copies of statutes organized by topic, accompanied by brief descriptions of cases referring to the statutes.

*__Annulment:__ Declaration that a transaction, most commonly a marriage, was never valid.

Anticipatory breach: Expressed intent to repudiate one's contractual obligation before the time for performing the obligation has arrived.

*Antitrust law: Law that protects commerce from unreasonable restraints and monopolies.
*Apparent authority: Authority of one person, the agent, to act for another, the principal, on the basis of indications by the principal suggesting that the agent has authority to act.
*Appeal: Request made to a higher court to review the decision of a lower court.
Appellant: Person who appeals a decision of one court to a higher court.
Appellee: Person whose victory in a lower court is appealed to a higher one by an appellant.
Appurtenance: Item attached to property of greater value, such as a fence to real estate.
*Arbitration: The submission of a dispute to a neutral third party with the agreement that this party's decision of the dispute will be binding.
Arm's length transaction: Transaction between unrelated parties pursuing their individual interests.
*Arraignment: Point in criminal proceeding when a person accused of a crime is brought before a court to be informed of the charges and to enter a plea.
*Arrest: To take a person into custody for the purpose of bringing the person to court on criminal charges.
*Arson: Unlawful burning of property.
Articles of incorporation: Formal documents filed with the state to form a corporation.
*Assault: The attempt or imminent threat to inflict bodily harm on another, even if such harm is not, in fact, inflicted.
Assessment: The determination of property's value for the purpose of taxation.
Assignment of error: Points made by a party appealing a case that specify errors made in a lower court.
*Assumption of risk: Defense used to escape a charge of negligence by asserting that an injured person knew of the risk of danger involved in some activity and voluntarily assumed such risk.
*Attachment: Legal procedure for taking possession of property as security for an anticipated judgment.
Attempt: Effort to commit a crime that may be punished even if the crime is not carried out.
Attestation: Act of witnessing the signing of a document and then signing the document as a witness.
*Attractive nuisance: Dangerous property to which children may be attracted.
Authenticate: To demonstrate an item's genuineness.

Bad faith: Dishonest conduct in dealings with another.
*Bail: Money or other property given to obtain the release from custody of a criminal defendant and to ensure that the defendant will subsequently appear in court.
Bail bond: Agreement by one party to procure the release of a criminal defendant specifying that the party will pay the bail amount should the defendant fail to appear in court.
*Bailiff: Person who keeps order in a courtroom.
*Bailment: Arrangement in which one party keeps another's property for some specified purpose, such as storage or repair.
Bait and switch: Dishonest business practice in which a seller advertises a particular product and then tries to sell consumers a higher-priced item when they arrive at the business.
*Bankruptcy: Legal proceeding that allows a person to obtain release from debts.
*Bar exams: Comprehensive tests of legal knowledge given to persons desiring to become lawyers.
Barrister: Trial lawyer in British trials.
Battery: The harmful touching of another.
*Bequest: Gift of personal property in a will.
Beyond a reasonable doubt: Degree of certainty required to convict a person accused of a crime.
*Bigamy: Crime of marrying another person when a previous marriage is still in effect.
Bill of attainder: Unconstitutional legislative action that singles out persons or groups for punishment without a trial.
*Bill of lading: Receipt given by the party who transports goods.
Bill of Rights: First ten amendments to the U.S. Constitution, which safeguard various individual liberties.
Bill of sale: Formal document conveying ownership of property.
*Billable hours: Hours an attorney spends working on a client's matter, for which the attorney bills an agreed upon hourly rate.

***Blackmail:** Attempt to extort money by threatening to inflict violence upon another or to expose another's wrongdoing.

***Black's Law Dictionary:** Foremost American dictionary of legal terms.

***Blue Book, The:** Book published by the *Harvard Law Review* containing standards for legal citation.

***Blue laws:** Laws that regulate business and entertainment activities on Sundays.

Blue sky law: Law that regulates sales of stocks or other securities for the protection of investors.

Bona fide: In good faith and without deception.

***Bond:** Instrument issued by a government or company promising to pay a certain rate of interest for a loan to a person who has loaned the government or company money.

Book value: The market value of property as reflected in accounting records.

***Boycott:** Refusal to do business with a party, normally in protest against that party's activities.

Breach of the peace: Criminal disturbance of public order.

***Bribery:** Attempt to influence a public person in the discharge of a public duty through offering the person something of value.

Brief: A concise statement of the facts and arguments in a case or a short summary of a matter.

***Burglary:** Entering a building with the purpose of committing a felony such as theft.

Business judgment rule: Doctrine that protects business managers from liability for mistakes when they act reasonably and honestly.

Capital crime: Crime punishable by death.

Capital gain: Profit made from the sale of a capital asset such as real estate.

Capital punishment: Punishment by death.

***Case law:** Law derived from the decisions of courts rather than from the actions of legislatures.

***Cause of action:** Grounds for bringing a claim against another party.

Caveat emptor: Latin phrase meaning "Let the buyer beware," signifying a buyer's responsibility for carefully inspecting goods sold, to protect the buyer from the consequences of a poor bargain.

Censorship: Restriction of speech on grounds of its asserted objectionableness.

***Certificate of deposit:** Document issued by a bank to verify the deposit of money with the bank.

Certiorari, writ of: Most commonly an application to the U.S. Supreme Court seeking review of a lower court decision.

***Chain of custody:** Account by one who offers physical evidence of the possession of the evidence from the moment it is discovered until it is offered in court.

Chain of title: History of transfers of a particular piece of property.

Chambers: Private office of a judge.

***Champerty:** Illegal payments by a person without a direct stake in a lawsuit to another person that allow the recipient to maintain the lawsuit.

Chancery court: Court that decides issues on general grounds of fairness rather than on precise rules of law.

Chattel: Personal as opposed to real property.

***Chattel paper:** A document that reflects a lien or mortgage in personal property.

***Check kiting:** Unlawful manipulation of two or more checking accounts to write worthless checks.

Churning: The abuse of a customer's confidence that occurs when a broker initiates transactions that are excessive in view of the type of account and the customer's expressed investing goals.

Circuit court: A court with jurisdiction over several districts or counties.

Circumstantial evidence: Secondary evidence from which a primary issue may be inferred.

Citation: An order issued by a court or law-enforcement officer requiring a person to appear in court.

Cite: To order someone to appear in court; to refer to legal authority in support of one's argument.

***Civil action:** Action brought for the redress of a wrong suffered by an individual or entity, as opposed to a criminal proceeding.

***Civil law:** Law relating to noncriminal matters; law deliberately implemented by a nation or state, as opposed to natural law.

Civil service: Employment in some branch of government other than the military.

***Class action suits:** Legal action brought on behalf of many individuals with a common interest by one or more representative plaintiffs.

Clemency: Reduction of a criminal sentence by the leniency of an executive official.

*Clerk of the court: Court official who maintains court records and files.

Close corporation: Corporation owned by a single individual or a few individuals.

*Cloud on title: Claim against property that casts doubt on the title of the property.

*Code of Professional Responsibility: Rules of legal ethics effective in many states from the early 1970's to the mid-1980's.

*Codes of civility: Rules adopted by courts or associations of lawyers to ensure that lawyers behave cordially in connection with lawsuits.

Codicil: Supplement to a will.

Coif, Order of: Legal honor society for students graduating in the top 10 percent of a law-school class.

Collateral: Property used as security for payment or performance of an obligation.

Collateral estoppel: Judicial doctrine providing that the resolution of issues litigated by parties in one case will thereafter be binding on them if raised in another case.

*Collective bargaining: The process of reaching agreement between employers and the representatives of employees regarding work-related matters.

Collusion: Secret agreement to commit fraud.

Commercial paper: Commercial documents that may be readily transferred from one party to another representing money or other things of value.

*Commitment, civil: Order sending a person to a mental institution.

*Common law: Law based on judicial decisions rather than legislative enactments.

*Common-law marriage: Agreement that is illegal in many states between a man and woman to live as husband and wife without participating in a formal ceremony or obtaining a marriage license.

*Community property: Property owned jointly by a husband and wife.

Comparative negligence: Doctrine comparing the negligence of a defendant and a plaintiff in a negligence action that allows the plaintiff to recover for damages that may be attributable to the defendant, even if the plaintiff was also partially negligent.

Compensatory damages: Damages that remedy an injury suffered, as opposed to punitive or nominal damages.

*Competency, legal: The capacity to understand and to act rationally.

Compulsory process: Right of a person charged with a crime to summon witnesses to court on his or her behalf.

Concurrent jurisdiction: Authority of two or more courts to hear the same case.

Concurring opinion: A judicial opinion in a case that agrees with the result reached by other judges but has different reasons for agreeing with this result.

*Confession: Admission of guilt.

Conjugal rights: Rights of married couples including companionship and sex.

*Consent decree: A court decree based on the agreement of the parties to a case.

Consequential damages: Damages not immediately caused by a loss but flowing secondarily from it, such as lost profits of a business destroyed by a flood.

*Consideration: The value given by each party to a contract.

*Consignment: Delivery of goods to one party to be sold on behalf of another.

*Conspiracy: Agreement among two or more parties to commit a criminal act.

*Contempt of court: Disobedience of a court order, or conduct that disrupts court proceedings or undermines the dignity of a court.

*Contingency fees: A fee payable to a lawyer only if the lawyer achieves a successful result in a case.

Continuance: Delay of court proceedings until some future date.

*Contract, breach of: The failure of a party to comply with the terms of an agreement.

*Conversion: Illegal taking of another's property without permission.

Conveyance: Transfer of an interest in property.

*Conviction: A final determination of guilt in a criminal proceeding, whether based on a trial or a guilty plea.

*Cooling-off period: Period during which a party can, in certain cases, rescind a contract.

*Copyright: Right of a writer or artist to control the use of created material for a period of time.

*Coroner: Public official charged with investigating the circumstances of violent or suspicious deaths.

Corporal punishment: Physical punishment.

***Corporate general counsel:** Attorney, often an employee of a corporation, who handles general legal affairs of the corporation.

***Corporations:** Entities created by law and treated as having identities distinct from the identities of their shareholders.

Corpus delicti: The body or substance of a crime, such as the corpse of a murder victim.

Corroborate: To support or confirm.

Cotenancy: Joint ownership of property.

Counterclaim: A claim made by a defendant in a lawsuit against a plaintiff.

***Counterfeiting:** The illegal copying of something and the passing off of the copy as an original.

***Court-awarded fees:** Attorneys fees provided to a prevailing party by law and assigned by a court.

***Court costs:** Expenses, excluding attorneys fees, of a lawsuit.

***Court-martial:** Proceeding to decide matters relating to the conduct of military personnel.

***Court reporter:** Individual who transcribes testimony in court proceedings.

***Covenant not to compete:** Agreement, normally by an employee or the seller of a business, not to engage in a competing business with the employer or the buyer of a business within a specified period of time.

***Credit record:** Record compiled by a credit bureau that details how an individual or company has handled credit obligations.

Creditor: Party to whom a debt is owed.

***Crime of passion:** Crime committed under the influence of strong emotion.

***Criminal intent:** A guilty or wrongful purpose.

Cross-claim: Claim made by a party against another party on the same side of a lawsuit.

***Cross-examination:** The questioning of a witness called on behalf of an opponent in a court or other legal proceeding.

***Cruel and unusual punishment:** Punishment forbidden by the Eighth Amendment to the U.S. Constitution that is disproportionate to a crime or otherwise excessive.

Culpable: Worthy of blame.

Damages: Monetary compensation awarded in a lawsuit to an injured party.

De minimus: Trivial or unimportant.

***Death certificate:** Official document declaring that an individual has died.

***Death row attorneys:** Attorneys who represent criminal defendants sentenced to death in appeals of their convictions.

***Declaratory judgment:** A court order stating the rights and liabilities of parties or rendering an opinion without otherwise awarding relief.

***Deed:** A written document that transfers rights in real property.

Deed of trust: A written document that grants a lender an interest in real property to secure a loan.

Defamation: The publication, either orally or in writing, of a statement that injuries another's reputation.

Default: A failure to perform some legal duty.

Default judgment: Judgment entered against a defendant in a civil case who fails to respond to a lawsuit.

***Defendant:** A person sued in a civil case or accused of having committed a crime in a criminal case.

Deficiency judgment: Judgment entered against a debtor for the amount of a debt still owing after a lender has used the debtor's collateral to reduce the debt partially.

Demand note: A promissory note payable when presented to the debtor rather than at a stated time in the future.

***Deportation:** The removal of a person from a country.

***Deposition:** Recorded questioning of a witness under oath prior to a trial.

Depreciation: Diminution in the value of property.

Derivative action: Lawsuit brought by a shareholder to enforce a claim or right of the corporation.

Devise: A gift by a will.

Dictum: Language in a judicial opinion that is not necessary to the decision.

***Dilatory tactics:** Attempts to delay or frustrate the progress of a legal proceeding.

Direct examination: Examination of a witness by the party who called the witness.

***Directed verdict:** A verdict rendered by a judge in favor of a criminal defendant or against a party in a civil action who has failed to present sufficient evidence to justify letting a jury determine a case.

***Discovery, pretrial:** Procedures for allowing parties to a court case to discover relevant information prior to the trial.

***Discrimination:** Treating persons or matters differently when no reasonable grounds exist for doing so.

***Dismissal:** The discontinuation of a case.

***Disorderly conduct:** Conduct that disturbs the peace.

Disposition: The transferring of something to the care of another; the final settlement of a legal issue.

Dissenting opinion: Opinion written by one or more judges who disagree with the result reached by a majority of judges in a case.

***District attorney:** The prosecuting attorney who represents the government within a particular judicial district.

***Divorce:** Termination of the marriage relationship.

Docket: Brief record of the proceedings in a case; also, the calendar of cases to be heard in a court.

Doctor of jurisprudence: The basic graduate degree necessary to practice law in the United States.

***Domicile:** A permanent home or residence.

***Double jeopardy:** A second prosecution for the same offense.

***Due process:** Fair and orderly treatment by law.

DUI: "Driving under the influence," or driving while intoxicated.

***Duress:** The use of threats or other exercises of power to force one to act against his or her will.

***Earnest money:** A down payment on a obligation, often forfeited if the party giving the down payment fails to perform the obligation.

***Easement:** The right to use another's property for a specific purpose.

***Embezzlement:** Unlawful appropriation of money or property held by one person in trust for another.

***Eminent domain:** The power of government to take property with just compensation for public purposes.

***Employment at will:** Employment relationship in which either the employer or employee may terminate the relationship for virtually any reason.

En banc: The determination of a case by all of the judges of a particular court.

Encroachment: Unlawful intrusion upon another's property, such as the erection of a fence on a portion of it.

Endorsement: The signature on a negotiable instrument, such as a check, that transfers the instrument to another party.

Enjoin: To command that something be done or not done.

***Entrapment:** Unlawful inducement of a person to commit a crime that would not have been committed except for the inducement.

***Equal protection of the law:** Constitutional requirement that persons similarly situated be accorded the same treatment.

Equity: Legal principles and procedures that emphasize the resolution of disputes according to general principles of fairness; also, the value of property minus any debts owed against it.

***Escrow:** The transfer of money or property to a third party to be held until the occurrence of a particular event.

***Eviction:** The forcing of a tenant to surrender possession of property.

Ex parte: A communication with only one side of a lawsuit.

***Exclusionary rule:** Rule that prevents the use of evidence in a criminal trial that was obtained illegally.

***Execution of judgment:** Enforcement of a judgment rendered by a court, normally by seizing and selling property of a person against whom the judgment has been entered.

***Executor:** The person appointed by a now-deceased person to handle the directives in a will.

Exemplary damages: Punitive damages; damages in excess of those needed to compensate an injury.

***Extortion:** Illegal use of threats to obtain money or property from another.

***Extradition:** The surrender by a U.S. state or foreign country of a person accused or convicted of a crime in another U.S. state or another country.

***Fair market value:** The price that property would bring if sold under ordinary circumstances.

FBI: Federal Bureau of Investigation.

Federal Bureau of Investigation (FBI). See list of federal law-enforcement agencies.

Fee simple: Property ownership that allows the

owner to dispose of the property without limitations.

*Felony: A serious crime, as distinguished from a misdemeanor.

*Fiduciary: Person with special obligation to act on another's behalf.

Fixture: Item of personal property that has become attached to real estate.

Force majeure: A natural or superior force, such as a flood or earthquake.

*Foreclosure: Termination of a party's property rights, generally by the holder of a mortgage.

*Forgery: Illegal creation or alteration of a document for a fraudulent purpose.

Forum non conveniens: Doctrine that allows a court to decline to hear a case if a court in a more convenient location can do so.

*Fraud: Intentional misrepresentation or distortion of facts.

Fraudulent conveyance: Conveyance of property by a debtor with the purpose of preventing a creditor from reaching the property.

*Future estate: An interest in land that does not include the right of present possession.

*Gag order: Court order preventing parties, attorneys, and others from discussing matters related to a case.

*Garnishment: Legal procedure used to seize money or wages of a party owing a debt or against whom a claim has been made.

*Grand jury: Group of citizens appointed to investigate possible crimes and to determine whether criminal indictments should be brought.

*Green cards: Documents evidencing permanent resident status in the United States.

Guaranty: The promise to perform another's obligation in the event that the person fails to perform it.

Guardian ad litem: Person appointed by a court to represent the interests of a child in a legal proceeding.

Guest statute: Law that prevents a nonpaying passenger in a motor vehicle from suing the driver in cases other than exceptional negligence.

*Habeas corpus, writ of: Application to a court to consider whether a person in custody is being held lawfully.

Habitability: The suitability of a dwelling to be lived in.

*Hate crime statutes: Laws that impose or increase penalties for crimes committed on the basis of particular prejudices, such as crimes motivated by racial hatred.

*Hearing: Legal proceeding other than a trial in which evidence is taken or legal arguments presented for a court to make some determination.

*Hearsay: Out-of-court statement offered to prove some matter in a legal proceeding.

*Holographic will: Handwritten will.

*Homestead: The dwelling in which a person lives and the surrounding land.

*Homicide: The killing of another person.

Hornbook: Relatively brief legal treatise on a particular subject.

Hung jury: A jury that cannot reach a verdict.

*Immunity: Freedom from having to fulfill some legal duty or from prosecution for a crime.

*Immunity, diplomatic: Freedom of diplomatic personnel from prosecution for crimes in the country in which they are posted.

Impanel: To select a jury.

Impeach: To discredit or accuse of wrongdoing.

Implead: To bring someone other than the original parties into a lawsuit.

In forma pauperis: To proceed as a pauper—that is, to proceed without having to pay normal legal costs.

Inalienable: Incapable of being transferred or given away.

Incorrigible: Not capable of reform.

Incriminate: To provide evidence that would implicate someone in having committed a crime.

Incumbrance: A mortgage, lien, or other claim against property.

*Indemnity: An agreement for one party to take on another's obligation or liability.

*Indictment: The accusation made by a grand jury that an individual has committed a crime.

Indigent: Poor.

Information: Accusation by a public official that an individual has committed a crime, used in many states as a counterpart to a grand jury indictment.

*Injunction: Order by a court for someone to do or not do something.

*Innocence, presumption of: Requirement that

government affirmatively prove that an individual has committed a crime.
*Inquest: Official investigation of whether a crime has occurred, especially in connection with a death.
INS: Immigration and Naturalization Service. See list of federal law-enforcement agencies.
Insolvency: The inability to pay debts as they become due.
*Insurance adjustor: An agent for an insurance company who investigates and settles claims on insurance policies.
Inter vivos: Transactions between parties who are living.
Interlocutory: Temporary or provisional.
Internal Revenue Service (IRS): See list of federal law-enforcement agencies.
Interrogatory: Questions submitted by one party to another to discover information relevant to a pending case.
*Intestate succession: Distribution of a deceased person's property in cases without a will.
Invitee: Someone invited onto the property of another.
IRS: Internal Revenue Service.

JD: Doctor of jurisprudence; the basic graduate degree necessary to practice law in the United States.
*Joint and several liability: Liability that allows an injured person to sue one or all the persons who contributed to the injury.
*Joint tenancy: Form of ownership in which two or more owners have equal rights in property.
Joint venture: A partnership for a particular business venture.
Judgment proof: Lacking assets that might be seized to satisfy a judgment.
*Judicial review: Authority of courts to review the constitutionality of legislative and executive actions.
*Jurisdiction: The authority of a court to hear and decide a particular case.
*Jurisprudence: Legal philosophy.
*Jury nullification: Verdict rendered by a jury in disregard of the law.
*Jury sequestration: Confinement of a jury during a trial or jury deliberations to prevent jury members from being influenced by contact with others.

Justifiable homicide: A permissible killing of another person, as in self-defense.
Juvenile delinquent: A minor who has committed a crime.

*Kidnapping: Unlawful detention of a person against the person's will.

*Landlord's lien: Interest of a landlord in property of a renter to secure payment of rental obligations.
*Larceny: The illegal taking of another's personal property.
Latent defect: Hidden defect.
*Law School Admission Test: Standardized test used by law schools to measure qualifications of potential law students.
Leading question: A question asked during the examination of a witness that suggests the answer desired.
*Lease: Agreement by which one party surrenders possession of property to another for the other's use during a specified period of time.
Legal tender: Currency that may be used to satisfy debts.
*Legalese: Technical legal language.
*Lemon laws: Laws that require automobile dealers or manufacturers to remedy defects in motor vehicles.
*Lesser included offense: A crime whose elements are necessarily proven by proof that a more serious crime has been committed.
Letters rogatory: Written requests from a court in one country to a foreign court requesting evidence or other legal assistance that is needed in a hearing or trial.
Lexis: Commercial computer database that includes a variety of legal and news sources.
Libel: A written defamation of one's character or reputation.
License: A right to do something that one would not otherwise be entitled to do.
*Lien: An interest in property to secure payment or performance of an obligation.
Limited partnership: A business venture in which one or more persons manage the venture and others, called limited partners, share in profits or losses without participating in management.
Lis pendens: A notice that property is subject to a lawsuit.

Litigation: A lawsuit, or a contest in court to enforce a right or to seek a remedy.
***Living will:** A written statement expressing a person's desire not to be kept alive by artificial means in the event of a serious illness or accident.
LLM: Master of laws, a graduate legal degree beyond the basic JD, or doctor of jurisprudence, degree.
***Loitering:** Standing idle or wandering about aimlessly.
***Long arm statute:** A law that allows a court in one state to exercise jurisdiction over a defendant in another.

Magistrate: A judicial official with authority to decide preliminary matters or minor cases.
Malfeasance: Wrongful or illegal conduct.
Malice aforethought: A predetermined intention to commit a wrongful act.
Malicious mischief: Spiteful destruction of personal property.
Malpractice: Misconduct by a professional such as an attorney or a physician.
Mandamus: A court order commanding some public official, court, or corporation to take certain action.
***Manslaughter:** The negligent or otherwise unlawful killing of a person without predetermined malice.
Maritime law: Law relating to the sea.
Market value: The value of property as reflected by the sale between a willing buyer and a willing seller.
***Martial law:** Control of civilians by a military authority.
***Mechanic's lien:** An interest granted in property to one who provides materials or services to another in connection with the property to ensure payment for such materials or services.
***Mediation:** Referral of a dispute to an objective third person, who attempts to help disputing parties reach a compromise.
***Medicaid:** Federal health insurance program.
***Medical examiner:** Public official charged with investigating the circumstances of suspicious or violent deaths.
***Medicare:** Federal health insurance program for persons sixty-five years of age or older.
Mens rea: Criminal intent.

***Minimum fee schedules:** Illegal agreements among lawyers that establish the lowest fee that any lawyer may charge for a particular service.
Minor: Person who has not reached the legal age of adulthood.
***Miranda rights:** Rights of criminal defendants when arrested.
***Misdemeanor:** A minor crime punishable by a fine or less than one year of imprisonment.
***Mistrial:** Termination of a trial because of misconduct or other unusual occurrence.
Mitigation of damages: Requirement that an injured person take reasonable steps to minimize the degree of injury.
Modus operandi: The way an action or crime is carried out.
***Moral turpitude:** Wrongful act involving dishonesty or depravity.
***Mortgage:** An interest in property given by a debtor to assure payment of a loan.
Motion: A request for some action directed to a court.
Murder: The killing of another person with malice aforethought.

Natural law: Legal principles derived from general moral intuitions rather than statutes or other law specifically enacted by some authority to make law.
Naturalization: The granting of citizenship rights to a foreigner.
***Negligence:** An unintentional failure to act with reasonable care.
***Negotiable instrument:** A document according to which one party makes an unconditional promise to another to pay a certain amount of money on demand or on a particular date.
Next of kin: Nearest relative by blood; person entitled to inherit from another according to an intestate succession statute.
***No-fault insurance:** Form of insurance for which a person who has suffered an injury makes a claim against his own insurance company rather than against the insurance company of the person at fault.
**Nolo contendere* plea:* A plea of a criminal defendant that neither denies nor admits guilt.
Nominal damages: Small or inconsequential damages awarded to a party who has been wronged but has suffered no actual damages.

***Nonprofit organizations:** Organizations whose profits are not distributed to the organization's owners, officers, or directors.
Nonrecourse: Obligation that does not expose the person obligated to personal liability even if the obligation is not satisfied.
Nonsuit: To dismiss a lawsuit.
***Notary public:** A person authorized by law to certify the signing of documents under oath.

***Objection:** A challenge to testimony or other evidence offered in court.
Obscenity: Patently offensive sexual material that lacks serious literary, artistic, political, or scientific value.
Obstruction of justice: Crime of interfering with the administration of justice such as by influencing a witness.
Of counsel: Part-time or temporary relationship of a lawyer to a law firm, in contrast to that of associates and partners.
Offer of proof: Means of preserving a record of evidence not admitted in a trial for consideration on appeal.
Open account: Unpaid account.
***Opinion:** Written statement by a judge or court summarizing facts, issues raised, and justification for the resolution of a case.
Ordinance: Law adopted by a local political body such as a city council.
Original jurisdiction: Authority of a court to make the initial determination of a particular issue, in contrast to appellate jurisdiction.
Overrule: To deny an objection in a case; to overturn the legal authority of a prior case.

***Palimony:** An award of support to one unmarried partner from another, similar to alimony.
***Pandering:** Encouraging another to engage in prostitution.
***Paralegal:** A nonlawyer with legal skills who works under the supervision of an attorney.
***Pardon:** The act of a president or governor exempting a person accused of a crime from punishment.
Parens patriae: Doctrine by which the state acts as surrogate parents when the biological parents are unable or unwilling to exercise parental authority.
***Parole:** Early release of a prisoner.

Parole evidence rule: Rule that forbids the introduction of oral testimony inconsistent with the terms of a written agreement.
***Partnership:** Form of business association in which owners share equally in profits and losses or as otherwise agreed upon.
***Patent:** Exclusive right granted by government to inventor to produce or sell invention for a period of time.
Patent defect: Defect in property that could be discovered by a reasonable inspection.
***Paternity:** Relationship of father to child.
Penal code: Collection of state or federal laws defining types of criminal conduct.
Peremptory challenge: Lawyer's objection to the seating of a particular person on a jury that need not be supported by specific reasons.
***Perjury:** False statement under oath.
***Personal property:** Property other than real estate.
***Personal recognizance:** Pretrial release of criminal defendant without bail on the basis of the defendant's promise to appear for trial.
Plain error rule: Rule allowing an appellate court to reverse a trial court proceeding even if the person appealing did not complain about the error at trial.
Plain view doctrine: Rule allowing law-enforcement personnel to seize items in plain view without a search warrant.
Plaintiff: One who brings a civil action.
***Plea:** Response of a criminal defendant to an indictment.
***Plea bargain:** Agreement between a prosecutor and a criminal defendant disposing of a criminal matter.
Pleadings: Documents filed by parties to a suit containing their claims and defenses regarding the suit.
Polling a jury: Asking each member of a jury whether he or she agrees with the jury verdict.
Polygraph: Machine used to conduct a lie detector test.
Positive law: Law created or enacted by an appropriate authority, in contrast to natural law.
Possession: Control of property.
Post mortem: Investigation after a death.
***Power of attorney:** A document granting one person authority to act on behalf of another.

Precedent: Case law that guides subsequent legal decisions.

Preemption: Constitutional doctrine that allows federal laws on a subject to override inconsistent state laws.

Preliminary hearing: A hearing used in cases not involving a grand jury indictment to determine whether there is probable cause to believe that an accused person has committed a crime.

Preliminary injunction: An order entered by a court at the beginning of a case to maintain the status quo during a trial.

Prenuptial agreement: A contract between anticipated spouses providing for the disposition of marital property in the event of divorce or death.

Preponderance of the evidence: Sufficient evidence to suggest that it is more likely than not that an asserted claim is true.

Pretrial conference: A conference between a judge and parties to a lawsuit after a case has been filed for the purpose of planning discovery and discussing the possibility of a settlement.

Price fixing: An illegal agreement between competitors establishing prices.

Prima facie **case:** True or valid on first view; evidence sufficient to prevail in a case absent some response from an opponent.

Privileged communication: Communication that may not be admitted into evidence in a judicial proceeding without the consent of the parties to the communication.

Pro bono legal work: Free legal services.

Pro rata : Proportionately.

Pro se: To represent oneself in a proceeding as opposed to being represented by an attorney.

Probable cause: Reasonable grounds for believing that an accused person has committed a crime.

Probate: Legal proceeding to establish whether a will is valid.

Probation: Early release of a criminal from prison.

Process: The legal procedure used by a court to obtain power over a particular person or property, such as a summons to appear in a case.

Promissory note: A written promise to pay the holder of a document a certain sum of money on demand or on a particular date.

Proof, burden of: The duty to prove a particular issue in a case.

Prosecutor: Lawyer, such as a district attorney, who represents the government in cases against persons accused of crimes.

Prostitution: The sale of sexual services.

Proximate cause: The legal cause of an injury.

Public defender: An attorney appointed by government to defend a person accused of a crime who cannot afford to hire a lawyer.

Public domain: Information or creative material not subject to copyright protection.

Public nuisance: Unlawful interference with a community's use of property.

Punitive damages: Damages in excess of those needed to compensate an injury; also known as exemplary damages.

Quitclaim deed: Conveyance of all of an owner's interest in property but not necessarily ownership free and clear of other possible claims.

Rape: Sexual intercourse with a person against the person's will.

Real property: Land and structures or items permanently attached to it.

Reasonable doubt: Standard of proof required in criminal cases; proof must be such as reasonably to preclude the possibility of innocence.

Receiving stolen property: The crime of accepting possession of property known to be stolen.

Recess: Temporary adjournment of legal proceedings.

Recidivism: The act of repeating a criminal offense.

Recusal: The disqualification of a judge from a legal case on the basis of objections of either party or at the judge's own request because of some prejudice or conflict of interest.

Redemption: The repurchase by a debtor within a specified period of property repossessed to satisfy a debt.

Release: To abandon a claim.

Remand: An order returning a proceeding for further action to a court that had originally heard it.

Remittitur: A court order reducing the amount of damages awarded by a jury.

Removal: Transfer of a case from one court to another, as from a state court to a federal court.

Repossession: A creditor's taking possession of collateral upon the debtor's failure to pay a debt.

Reprieve: To postpone the execution of a criminal sentence.

Res ipsa loquitor: Doctrine meaning literally "The thing speaks for itself," according to which an event is presumed to have been caused by the negligent conduct of another.

Res judicata: Doctrine that makes the resolution of a matter in one court conclusive of further attempts to relitigate the same matter.

Respondeat superior: Liability of an employer for acts of an employee committed during the course of employment.

Restitution: A legal remedy that seeks to restore property or money to the person from whom it was originally taken or obtained.

*****Restraining order, temporary:** Court order requiring or preventing some action for a short period of time until a more complete evaluation of the matter may be made by the court.

Restrictive covenant: Provision in a real estate document such as a deed limiting the use of real estate.

*****Retainer:** A fee for legal services paid in advance.

Reversible error: Significant error committed by a trial court justifying an appellate court to overrule the trial court's decision.

*****Robbery:** Violent taking of one's property within one's presence.

Satisfaction: Payment of a debt.

*****Search warrant:** A judicial order allowing law-enforcement personnel to enter and search a particular location.

*****Secured transaction:** A loan transaction in which the lender receives an interest in collateral to assure payment of the loan.

*****Self-defense:** Protection of one's person or property from attack by another.

Self-incrimination: Testimony by an individual that tends to suggest that the individual has committed a crime.

*****Sentencing:** The pronouncing of punishment on a person convicted of having committed a crime.

Service of process: Delivery to a defendant of a complaint or other documents representing the filing of a lawsuit against the defendant.

*****Sexual battery:** Sexual intercourse with one who, because of intoxication or other disability, is unable to consent to the intercourse.

*****Sexual harassment:** Unwarranted sexual advances of one person toward another.

*****Shareholder suit:** Suit by a shareholder of a corporation on behalf of the corporation.

*****Shoplifting:** A form of larceny in which a person intentionally conceals or possesses unpurchased merchandise either within or outside the premises of a store with the intent of converting the merchandise to his or her own use without paying for it.

Side bar: Discussions between a judge and attorneys in a case that cannot be heard by the jury or spectators.

Slander: Verbal statements that injure another's reputation.

*****Small claims court:** Civil courts with the power to decide cases involving only small amounts of money.

Sole proprietorship: Business owned by a single individual.

Solicitor general: Lawyer appointed by the president of the United States to represent the United States in cases before the U.S. Supreme Court.

Sovereign immunity: Doctrine that prevents suits against government unless the government has previously authorized such suits.

Special verdict: Verdict in which a jury responds to specific issues in a case.

Specific performance: Remedy for breach of contract that requires a breaching party to perform the obligation required by the contract.

*****Speedy trial requirement:** Right provided to criminal defendants by the Sixth Amendment to the U.S. Constitution guaranteeing that they be tried without excessive delay.

Standing: The right of a particular person to assert a claim in court.

Stare decisis: The principle that courts should generally follow the decisions of previous cases.

*****Statute:** Laws enacted by the legislative branch of government.

Statute of frauds: Legal requirement that certain contracts be in writing to be enforced.

*****Statute of limitation:** Statute setting forth a period of time in which a lawsuit must be filed.

Statutory rape: Crime of having sexual intercourse with an underage person even if the person consents.

***Stock certificate:** Document reflecting one's ownership share in a corporation.

Strict liability: Liability imposed without regard to whether one is at fault.

***Sublease:** A tenant's agreement with some third party for the party to possess all or a portion of leased property or goods.

Subornation of perjury: The crime of inducing another to commit perjury.

***Subpoena:** An order for a witness to appear in court to testify.

Subpoena duces tecum: An order for a witness to appear in court and to present to the court specified documents relevant to a case.

***Subrogation:** A legal right of one party to step into the shoes of another party and to assert that other party's claim.

***Summary judgment:** A judgment rendered by a court without a trial when the facts of a case are not in serious dispute.

***Summons:** Notice to a defendant that a lawsuit has been filed against him or her and a specification of the time at which the defendant must answer the claim.

Surety: A party who agrees to be liable for the obligation of another should the other default in performing the obligation.

***Tenancy in common:** Common ownership of property by two or more parties, each of which has the right to use the property.

Tender offer: Offer to shareholders of a corporation to purchase their share of stock in the corporation for a particular price.

***Test case:** A lawsuit brought to clarify or challenge some legal principle.

Testator: An individual who dies leaving a will.

***Testimony:** The statement made by a witness under oath in a legal proceeding.

***Theft:** The taking of a person's property without that person's consent.

Third party beneficiary: A person entitled to receive the benefit of a contract even though not a party to the contract.

***Three strikes laws:** Laws requiring life sentences for repeat criminal offenders.

***Title:** Ownership of property.

***Title search:** The examination of property records to determine the ownership of and claims against a piece of property.

***Tort:** A civil wrong committed by one party against another, excluding breaches of contract.

***Trade secret:** Confidential business information.

***Trademark:** A distinctive word or graphic used by a business to identify its product.

Transcript: Official record of a legal proceeding.

***Treason:** A rebellious action toward one's government.

***Trespass:** Interference with another's property rights.

***Truancy:** Failure of a student who is required to attend school to do so.

***Trust:** An arrangement by which one party holds property on behalf of another.

***Trust accounts, attorney:** Separate bank accounts maintained by attorneys for client funds.

***Trustee:** A person appointed to safeguard or manage another's property.

Trustee in bankruptcy: A person who assumes control of a debtor's property in a bankruptcy proceeding.

Ultra vires: Action taken in excess of those powers granted to an individual or entity.

***Unconscionable contracts:** Contracts that are grossly unfair to one of the bargaining parties.

Underwrite: To insure another against a particular loss or losses.

Undue influence: Inappropriate influence by one party over another.

***Usury:** The charging of excessive interest on a loan.

Vacate: To move out of property; also, to set aside or rescind a court order or decision.

***Vagrancy:** Idle wandering about and failure to work by a person who is able to do so.

***Vandalism:** Willful destruction of property.

Variance: Permission to use property in a manner otherwise prohibited by a zoning law.

Vendor: A seller.

Venire: The list of those summoned for jury duty.

***Venue, change of:** Transfer of the location of a lawsuit.

Verdict: The decision of a jury in a trial.

Vested: A presently existing right to something that is not contingent on the occurrence of a future condition.

Vicarious liability: The liability of one party for another party's actions or omissions.

Visa: Official permission to enter another country.
Void: Of no legal force.
Voir dire: The examination of potential jurors to determine their ability to serve on a jury or the preliminary examination of a witness to determine whether the witness is competent to testify.

Ward of the court: Person under the protection of the court, such as a child or a mentally infirm person.
Warrant: An order permitting an official to take some action, such as permitting law-enforcement personnel to arrest someone or search particular property.
***Warranty, product:** A promise that a product will have certain characteristics.
Warranty deed: A deed guaranteeing that the seller owns the property in question and that the property is free of any encumbrances other than those specifically referred to in the deed.
Westlaw: A commercial computerized legal database.
***Whistle-blowing:** Disclosure by an employee of an employer's wrongful conduct.

***White-collar crime:** Nonviolent crimes committed by business or banking professionals.
***Wills:** Documents setting forth parties' desires as to the disposition of their property upon their deaths.
***Wiretap:** Surreptitious monitoring of telephone conversations by law-enforcement officials.
***Witness:** A person who testifies to matters in a legal proceeding, whether orally or in writing.
***Witness, expert:** A person who offers testimony in a legal proceeding based on specialized knowledge of a subject.
***Workers' compensation:** Statutory arrangement to pay a worker for an injury suffered on the job, whether or not the injury was the fault of the worker.
Writ: A court's written command to do something.
***Wrongful death:** Statutory provision allowing the survivor of a person wrongfully killed by another's action to sue that other person for damages.

***Zoning laws:** Laws that divide localities into different areas and restrict land use in these areas.

Bibliography

Business and Commercial Law	1011
Civil Rights and Civil Liberties	1011
Consumer Law	1012
Courts and Judges	1012
Criminal Law and Procedures	1013
Employment Law	1013
Environmental Law	1014
Family Law	1014
General Legal Matters	1014
History, Biography, and Famous Trials	1015
Immigration Law	1016
Insurance and Personal Injury Law	1016
International Law	1016
Law Enforcement	1016
Legal Education	1016
Legal Practice	1017
Legal Reference and Research	1017
Legal Theory	1017
Medical Law	1018
Military Law	1018
Real Estate Law	1018
Tax Law	1018
Wills and Estate Law	1019

Business and Commercial Law

Adams, Paul. *One Hundred Fifty Five Legal Do's (and Don'ts) for the Small Business.* New York: J. Wiley & Sons, 1996.

Amernick, Burton A. *Patent Law for the Nonlawyer: A Guide for the Engineer, Technologist, and Manager.* 2d ed. New York: Van Nostrand Reinhold, 1991.

Dungan, Christopher Wright, and Donald Ridings. *Business Law.* New York: Barron's, 1990.

Frasier, Lynne Ann. *The Small Business Legal Guide.* Naperville, Ill.: Sourcebooks, 1996.

Hedglon, Mead. *How to Get the Best Legal Help for Your Business (At the Lowest Possible Cost).* New York: McGraw-Hill, 1992.

Holmes, Eric M., and Peter J. Shedd. *A Practical Guide to the Law of Secured Lending.* Englewood Cliffs, N.J.: Prentice-Hall, 1986.

Jackson, Thomas H. *The Logic and Limits of Bankruptcy Law.* Cambridge: Harvard University Press, 1986.

Jennings, Marianne, and Frank Shipper. *Avoiding and Surviving Lawsuits: The Executive Guide to Strategic Legal Planning for Business.* San Francisco: Jossey-Bass, 1989.

Milko, George, Kay Ostberg, and Theresa Meehan Rudy. *Everyday Contracts: Protecting Your Rights—a Step-by-Step Guide.* Rev. ed. New York: Random House, 1991.

Shenefield, John H., and Irwin M. Stelzer. *The Antitrust Laws: A Primer.* Washington, D.C.: AEI Press, 1993.

Sitarz, Daniel. *The Complete Book of Small Business Legal Forms.* Carbondale, Ill.: Nova, 1991.

Sobol, Richard B. *Bending the Law: The Story of the Dalkon Shield Bankruptcy.* Chicago: University of Chicago Press, 1991.

Steingold, Fred. *The Legal Guide for Starting and Running a Small Business.* 2d ed. Berkeley, Calif.: Nolo Press, 1995.

Walz, Michael K. *The Law and Economics: Your Rights as a Consumer.* Minneapolis, Minn.: Lerner, 1990.

Civil Rights and Civil Liberties

Adams, Arlin M., and Charles J. Emmerich. *A Nation Dedicated to Religious Liberty: The Constitutional Heritage of the Religion Clauses.* Philadelphia: University of Pennsylvania Press, 1990.

Alley, Robert S. *School Prayer: The Court, the Congress, and the First Amendment.* Buffalo, N.Y.: Prometheus Books, 1994.

Amar, Akhil Reed, and Alan Hirsch. *For the People: What the Constitution Really Says About Your Rights.* New York: Free Press, 1998.

Arons, Stephen. *Compelling Belief: The Culture of American Schooling.* New York: McGraw-Hill, 1983.

Ashmore, Harry S. *Hearts and Minds: The Anatomy of Racism from Roosevelt to Reagan.* New York: McGraw-Hill, 1982.

Bell, Derrick A. *And We Are Not Saved: The Elusive Quest for Racial Justice.* New York: Basic Books, 1987.

_____. *Faces at the Bottom of the Well: The Permanence of Racism.* New York: Basic Books, 1992.

Brill, Alida. *Nobody's Business: Paradoxes of Privacy.* Reading, Mass.: Addison-Wesley, 1990.

Carter, Stephen L. *Reflections of an Affirmative Action Baby.* New York: Basic Books, 1991.

Cruit, Ronald L. *Intruder in Your Home: How to Defend Yourself Legally with a Firearm.* New York: Stein & Day, 1983.

De Grazia, Edward. *Girls Lean Back Everywhere: The Law of Obscenity and the Assault on Genius.* New York: Random House, 1992.

Dill, Barbara. *The Journalist's Handbook on Libel and Privacy.* New York: Free Press, 1986.

Dworkin, Ronald M. *Life's Dominion: An Argument About Abortion, Euthanasia, and Individual Freedom.* New York: Knopf, 1993.

———. *Taking Rights Seriously.* Cambridge: Harvard University Press, 1977.

Eastland, Terry, and William J. Bennett. *Counting by Race: Equality from the Founding Fathers to Bakke and Weber.* New York: Basic Books, 1979.

Faux, Marian. *Roe v. Wade: The Untold Story of the Landmark Supreme Court Decision That Made Abortion Legal.* New York: Macmillan, 1988.

Foerstel, Herbert N. *Banned in the U.S.A.: A Reference Guide to Book Censorship in Schools and Public Libraries.* Westport, Conn.: Greenwood Press, 1994.

Garrow, David J. *Liberty and Sexuality: The Right to Privacy and the Making of Roe v. Wade.* New York: Macmillan, 1994.

Glasser, Ira. *Visions of Liberty: The Bill of Rights for All Americans.* New York: Arcade Publishing, 1991.

Hentoff, Nat. *Free Speech for Me—But Not for Thee: How the American Left and Right Relentlessly Censor Each Other.* New York: Harper Collins, 1992.

Hopkins, W. Wat. *Actual Malice: Twenty-five Years After Times v. Sullivan.* New York: Praeger, 1989.

Kalven, Harry, Jr. *A Worthy Tradition: Freedom of Speech in America.* Edited by Jamie Kalven. New York: Harper & Row, 1988.

Levy, Leonard W., ed. *Encyclopedia of the American Constitution.* New York: Free Press, 1986.

Lewis, Anthony. *Make No Law: The Sullivan Case and the First Amendment.* New York: Random House, 1991.

Meltzer, Milton. *The Bill of Rights: How We Got It and What It Means.* New York: Thomas Crowell, 1990.

Monk, Linda R. *The Bill of Rights: A User's Guide.* Alexandria, Va.: Close Up, 1991.

Sowell, Thomas. *Civil Rights: Rhetoric or Reality?* New York: William Morrow, 1984.

Strossen, Nadine. *Defending Pornography: Free Speech, Sex, and the Fight for Women's Rights.* New York: Scribner's, 1995.

Tribe, Laurence H. *Abortion: The Clash of Absolutes.* New York: W. W. Norton, 1990.

Urofsky, Melvin I. *A Conflict of Rights: The Supreme Court and Affirmative Action.* New York: Scribner's, 1991.

Williams, Patricia L. *The Alchemy of Race and Rights: The Diary of a Law Professor.* Cambridge: Harvard University Press, 1991.

Consumer Law

Drivon, Laurence E. *The Civil War on Consumer Rights.* With Bob Schmidt. Berkeley, Calif.: Conari Press, 1990.

Klein, David, Marymae E. Klein, and Douglas D. Walsh. *Getting Unscrewed and Staying That Way: The Sourcebook of Consumer Protection.* New York: Holt, 1993.

Lieberman, Marc R. *Your Rights as a Consumer: Legal Tips for Savvy Purchasing of Goods, Services, and Credit.* 2d ed. Hawthorne, N.J.: Career Press, 1994.

McGinn, Joseph C. *Personal Law: The Most Common Legal Problems and How to Solve Them.* Englewood Cliffs, N.J.: Prentice-Hall, 1982.

Sack, Steven Mitchell. *Don't Get Taken! How to Avoid Everyday Consumer Rip-offs.* Yonkers, N.Y.: Consumer Reports Books, 1993.

Taylor, Norman F., and Merrell G. Vannier. *Lemon Law: A Manual for Consumers.* Glendale, Calif.: Consumer Rights Center, 1991.

Courts and Judges

Forer, Lois G. *Money and Justice: Who Owns the Courts?* New York: Norton, 1984.

Feeley, Malcolm M. *Court Reform on Trial: Why Simple Solutions Fail.* New York: Basic Books, 1983.

Finkel, Norman J. *Commonsense Justice: Jurors' Notions of the Law.* Cambridge, Mass.: Harvard University Press, 1995.

Gould, Milton S. *The Witness Who Spoke with God and Other Tales from the Courthouse.* New York: Viking, 1979.

Hans, Valerie P., and Neil Vidmar. *Judging the Jury.* New York: Plenum Press, 1986.

Huber, Peter W. *Galileo's Revenge: Junk Science in the Courtroom.* New York: Basic Books, 1991.

Neely, Richard. *The Politics of State Courts.* New York: Free Press, 1988.

O'Brien, David M. *What Process Is Due? Courts and Science-Policy Disputes.* New York: Russell Sage Foundation, 1987.

Rehnquist, William H. *The Supreme Court: How It Was, How It Is.* New York: Quill, 1987.

Rosenberg, Gerald N. *The Hollow Hope: Can Courts Bring About Social Change?* Chicago: University of Chicago Press, 1991.

Rudy, Theresa. *Small Claims Court: Making Your Way Through the System—a Step-by-Step Guide.* Rev. ed. New York: Random House, 1990.

Sevilla, Charles M. *Disorder in the Court: Great Fractured Moments in Courtroom History.* New York: Norton, 1992.

Spence, Gerry. *With Justice for None.* New York: Time Books, 1989.

Strick, Anne. *Injustice for All.* New York: Putnam, 1977.

Tribe, Laurence H. *God Save This Honorable Court: How the Choice of Supreme Court Justices Shapes Our History.* New York: Random House, 1985.

Criminal Law and Procedures

Abramson, Leslie. *The Defense Is Ready: Life in the Trenches of Criminal Law.* With Richard Flaste. New York: Simon and Schuster, 1997.

Allison, Julie A. *Rape, the Misunderstood Crime.* Newbury Park, Calif.: Sage Publications, 1993.

Baker, Liva. *Miranda: The Crime, the Law, the Politics.* New York: Atheneum, 1983.

Bazelon, David L. *Questioning Authority: Justice and Criminal Law.* New York: Knopf, 1988.

Bedau, Hugo Adam. *The Death Penalty in America.* 3d ed. New York: Oxford University Press, 1982.

———, ed. *The Death Penalty in America: Current Controversies.* New York: Oxford University Press, 1997.

Burnham, David. *Above the Law: Secret Deals, Political Fixes, and Other Misadventures of the U.S. Department of Justice.* New York: Scribner, 1996.

Champion, Dean J. *The Roxbury Dictionary of Criminal Justice: Key Terms and Major Court Cases.* Los Angeles: Roxbury, 1997.

Dershowitz, Alan M. *The Best Defense.* New York: Random House, 1982.

Elikann, Peter T. *The Tough-on-Crime Myth: Real Solutions to Cut Crime.* New York: Insight Books, 1996.

Estrich, Susan. *Getting Away with Murder: How Politics Is Destroying the Criminal Justice System.* Cambridge, Mass.: Harvard University Press, 1998.

Ewing, Charles. *Battered Women Who Kill: Psychological Self-Defense as Justification.* Lexington, Mass.: Lexington Books, 1987.

Fletcher, George P. *A Crime of Self-Defense: Bernhard Goetz and the Law on Trial.* New York: Free Press, 1988.

———. *With Justice for Some: Victims' Rights in Criminal Trials.* Reading, Mass.: Addison-Wesley, 1995.

Friedman, Lawrence M. *Crime and Punishment in American History.* New York: Basic Books, 1993.

Ginsburg, William L. *Victims' Rights: A Complete Guide to Crime Victim Compensation.* Clearwater, Fla: Sphinx, 1994.

Jacob, Herbert. *Crime and Justice in Urban America.* Englewood Cliffs, N.J.: Prentice-Hall, 1980.

Kennedy, Randall. *Race, Crime, and the Law.* New York: Pantheon Books, 1997.

Kopel, David B., and Paul H. Blackman. *No More Wacos: What's Wrong with Federal Law Enforcement and How to Fix It.* Amherst, N.Y.: Prometheus Books, 1997.

Kramer, Rita. *At a Tender Age: Violent Youth and Juvenile Justice.* New York: Henry Holt, 1988.

Rothwax, Harold J. *Guilty: The Collapse of Criminal Justice.* New York: Random House, 1996.

Scheingold, Stuart A. *The Politics of Law and Order: Street Crime and Public Policy.* New York: Longman, 1984.

Weinreb, Lloyd L. *Denial of Justice: Criminal Process in the United States.* New York: Free Press, 1977.

Wexler, Richard. *Wounded Innocents: The Real Victims of the War Against Child Abuse.* Buffalo, N.Y.: Prometheus Books, 1990.

White, Bertha Rothe. *The Crimes and Punishment Primer.* Dobbs Ferry, N.Y.: Oceana, 1986.

Winslade, William J., and Judith Wilson Ross. *The Insanity Plea: The Uses and Abuses of the Insanity Defense.* New York: Scribner's, 1983.

Employment Law

Banta, William F. *AIDs in the Workplace: Legal Questions and Practical Answers.* Lexington, Mass.: Lexington Books, 1988.

Casey, Eileen L. *Maternity Leave: The Working Woman's Practical Guide to Combining Pregnancy, Motherhood, and Career.* Shelburne, Vt.: Green Mountain, 1992.

Chan, Anja Angelica. *Women and Sexual Harassment:*

A Practical Guide to the Legal Protections of Title VII and the Hostile Environment Claim. New York: Haworth Press, 1994.

Eisaguirre, Lynne. *Sexual Harassment: A Reference Handbook.* Santa Barbara, Calif.: ABC-Clio, 1993.

Joel, Lewin G. *Every Employee's Guide to the Law: Everything You Need to Know About Your Rights in the Workplace—and What to Do if They Are Violated.* Rev. ed. New York: Pantheon Books, 1996.

Olson, Walter K. *The Excuse Factory: How Employment Law Is Paralyzing the American Workplace.* New York: Martin Kessler, 1997.

Petrocelli, William, and Barbara Kate Repa. *Sexual Harassment on the Job.* Berkeley, Calif.: Nolo Press, 1992.

Rapoport, John D., and Brian L. P. Zevnik. *The Employee Strikes Back!* New York: Macmillan, 1989.

Sack, Steven Mitchell. *From Hiring to Firing: The Legal Survival Guide for Employers in the Nineties.* Merrick, N.Y.: Legal Strategies Publications, 1995.

Environmental Law

Foster, Kenneth R., David E. Bernstein, and Peter W. Huber, eds. *Phantom Risk: Scientific Inference and the Law.* Cambridge, Mass.: MIT Press, 1993.

Fumento, Michael. *Polluted Science: The EPA's Campaign to Expand Clean Air Regulations.* Washington, D.C.: AEI Press, 1997.

Grosse, W. Jack. *The Protection and Management of Our Natural Resources, Wildlife, and Habitat.* Dobbs Ferry, N.Y.: Oceana, 1992.

Patton-Hulce, Vicki. *Environment and the Law: A Dictionary.* Santa Barbara, Calif.: ABC-Clio, 1995.

Sagoff, Mark. *The Economy of the Earth: Philosophy, Law, and the Environment.* Cambridge, England: Cambridge University Press, 1988.

Wargo, John. *Our Children's Toxic Legacy: How Science and Law Fail to Protect Us from Pesticides.* New Haven: Yale University Press, 1996.

Wenner, Lettie McSpadden. *The Environmental Decade in Court.* Bloomington: Indiana University Press, 1982.

Wenz, Peter S. *Environmental Justice.* Albany: State University of New York Press, 1988.

Williams, Bruce Alan, and Albert R. Matheny. *Democracy, Dialogue, and Environmental Disputes: The Contested Languages of Social Regulation.* New Haven: Yale University Press, 1995.

Family Law

Fineman, Martha Albertson. *The Illusion of Equality: The Rhetoric and Reality of Divorce Reform.* Chicago: University of Chicago Press, 1991.

Friedman, Gary J. *A Guide to Divorce Mediation: How to Reach a Fair, Legal Settlement at a Fraction of the Cost.* New York: Workman, 1993.

Gillis, Phyllis L. *Days Like This: A Tale of Divorce.* New York: McGraw-Hill, 1986.

Glendon, Mary Ann. *The Transformation of Family Law: State, Law, and Family in the United States and Western Europe.* Chicago: University of Chicago Press, 1989.

Goldstein, Joseph, Anna Freud, Albert J. Solnit, and Sonja Goldstein. *In the Best Interests of the Child.* New York: Free Press, 1986.

Harwood, Norma. *A Woman's Legal Guide to Separation and Divorce in All Fifty States.* New York: Scribner's, 1985.

Horgan, Timothy J. *Winning Your Divorce: A Man's Survival Guide.* New York: Dutton, 1994.

Wallman, Lester, and Sharon McDonnell. *Cupid, Couples, and Contracts: A Guide to Living Together, Prenuptial Agreements, and Divorce.* New York: Master Media, 1994.

Wietzman, Lenore J. *The Marriage Contract: Spouses, Lovers, and the Law.* New York: Free Press, 1981.

Wilson, Carol Ann, and Edwin Schilling III. *The Survival Manual for Women in Divorce: One Hundred Eighty Two Questions and Answers.* Boulder, Colo.: Quantum Press, 1993.

Winner, Karen. *Divorced from Justice: The Abuse of Women and Children by Divorce Lawyers and Judges.* New York: ReganBooks, 1996.

General Legal Matters

Belli, Melvin M. *The Belli Files: Reflections on the Wayward Law.* Englewood Cliffs, N.J.: Prentice-Hall, 1983.

Christianson, Stephen G. *One Hundred Ways to Avoid Common Legal Pitfalls Without a Lawyer.* Secaucus, N.J.: Carol, 1992.

DuBoff, Leonard D. *The Law (in Plain English) for Writers.* 2d ed. New York: Wiley, 1992.

Fast, Julius, and Timothy Fast. *The Legal Atlas of the United States.* New York: Facts On File, 1997.

Ferguson, Robert A. *Law and Letters in American Culture.* Cambridge, Mass.: Harvard University Press, 1984.

Fischer, Louis. *School Law for Counselors, Psycholo-*

gists, and Social Workers. New York: Longman, 1985.

Friedman, Lawrence M. *American Law: An Introduction.* Rev. ed. New York: W. W. Norton, 1998.

Garry, Patrick M. *A Nation of Adversaries: How the Litigation Explosion Is Reshaping America.* New York: Plenum Press, 1997.

Haas, Carol. *Your Driving and the Law: A Crash Course in Traffic Tickets and Court, Auto Accidents and Insurance, and Vehicle-Related Lawsuits.* Bountiful, Utah: Horizon, 1991.

Helm, Alice K., ed. *The Family Legal Advisor: A Clear, Reliable, and Up-to-Date Guide to Your Rights and Remedies under the Law.* New York: Family Library, 1992.

Hill, Gerald N., and Kathleen Thompson Hill. *Real Life Dictionary of the Law: Taking the Mystery out of Legal Language.* Los Angeles: General, 1995.

Howard, Philip K. *The Death of Common Sense: How Law Is Suffocating America.* New York: Random House, 1994.

Jordan, Cora. *Neighbor Law: Fences, Trees, Boundaries, and Noise.* 2d ed. Berkeley, Calif.: Nolo Press, 1994.

Lehman, Godfrey D. *We the Jury: The Impact of Jurors on Our Basic Freedoms.* Amherst, N.Y.: Prometheus Books, 1997.

Moretti, Daniel S. *Animal Rights and the Law.* London: Oceana, 1984.

Niles, Gayle L. *Woman's Counsel: A Legal Guide for Women.* Denver, Colo.: Arden Press, 1984.

Pringle, Peter. *Cornered: Big Tobacco at the Bar of Justice.* New York: H. Holt, 1998.

Sack, Steven Mitchell. *The Working Woman's Legal Survival Guide.* Paramus, N.J.: Prentice-Hall, 1998.

Schwartz, Bernard. *A Book of Legal Lists: The Best and Worst in American Law with One Hundred Court and Judge Trivia Questions.* New York: Oxford University Press, 1997.

Shapiro, Fred R., and Jane Garry, eds. *Trial and Error: An Oxford Anthology of Legal Stories.* New York: Oxford University Press, 1998.

Strauss, Peter J., Robert Wolf, and Dana Shilling. *Aging and the Law.* Chicago: Commerce Clearing House, 1990.

Wolk, Stuart R., and William J. Luddy, Jr. *Legal Aspects of Computer Use.* Englewood Cliffs, N.J.: Prentice-Hall, 1986.

History, Biography, and Famous Trials

Aaseng, Nathan. *The O. J. Simpson Trial: What It Shows Us About Our Legal System.* New York: Walker, 1996.

Baker, Liva. *Justice from Beacon Hill: The Life and Times of Oliver Wendell Holmes.* New York: Harper Collins, 1991.

Bugliosi, Vincent. *No Island of Sanity—Paula Jones v. Bill Clinton: The Supreme Court on Trial.* New York: Ballantine, 1998.

Deutsch, Linda, and Michael Fleeman. *Verdict: The Chronicle of the O. J. Simpson Trial.* Kansas City, Mo.: Andrews and McMeel, 1995.

Greenberg, Jack. *Crusaders in the Courts: How a Dedicated Band of Lawyers Fought for the Civil Rights Revolution.* New York: Basic Books, 1994.

Hall, Kermit. *The Magic Mirror: Law in American History.* New York: Oxford University Press, 1989.

Kluger, Richard. *Simple Justice: The History of Brown v. Board of Education and Black America's Struggle for Equality.* New York: Knopf, 1975.

Knight, Alfred. *The Life of the Law: The People and Cases That Have Shaped Our Society, from King Alfred to Rodney King.* New York: Crown, 1996.

Larson, Edward J. *Summer for the Gods: The Scopes Trial and America's Continuing Debate over Science and Religion.* New York: Basic Books, 1997.

Novick, Sheldon M. *Honorable Justice: The Life of Oliver Wendell Holmes.* Boston: Little, Brown, 1989.

Paper, Lewis J. *Brandeis.* Englewood Cliffs, N.J.: Prentice-Hall, 1983.

Rembar, Charles. *The Law of the Land: The Evolution of Our Legal System.* New York: Simon & Schuster, 1980.

Rosenkranz, E. Joshua, and Bernard Schwartz, eds. *Reason and Passion: Justice Brennan's Enduring Influence.* New York: W. W. Norton, 1997.

Tushnet, Mark V. *Making Civil Rights Law: Thurgood Marshall and the Supreme Court, 1936-1961.* New York: Oxford University Press, 1994.

Urofsky, Melvin I. *Louis D. Brandeis and the Progressive Tradition.* Boston: Little, Brown, 1981.

Walker, Samuel. *In Defense of American Liberties: A History of the ACLU.* New York: Oxford University Press, 1990.

White, G. Edward. *Earl Warren: A Public Life.* New York: Oxford University Press, 1982.

Woodward, Bob, and Scott Armstrong. *The Brethren.* New York: Simon & Schuster, 1979.

Immigration Law

Harwood, Edwin. *In Liberty's Shadow: Illegal Aliens and Immigration Law Enforcement.* Stanford, Calif.: Hoover Institution Press, Stanford University, 1986.

Hite, Frederic C. *Aliens in the Workplace: An Employer's Guide to Immigration Law.* Boston, Mass.: Immigration Information Center, 1988.

Merritt, Nancy-Jo. *Understanding Immigration Law: How to Enter, Work, and Live in the United States.* 2d ed. Hawthorne, N.J.: Career Press, 1994.

Sloan, Irving J. *Law of Immigration and Entry to the United States of America.* 4th ed. New York: Oceana, 1987.

Insurance and Personal Injury Law

Asch, Peter. *Consumer Safety Regulation: Putting a Price on Life and Limb.* New York: Oxford University Press, 1988.

Mintz, Morton. *At Any Cost: Corporate Greed, Women, and the Dalkon Shield.* New York: Pantheon Books, 1985.

Olson, Walter K. *The Litigation Explosion: What Happened When America Unleashed the Lawsuit.* New York: Truman Talley, 1991.

Sugarman, Stephen D. *Doing Away with Personal Injury Law: New Compensation Mechanisms for Victims, Consumers, and Business.* New York: Quorum Books, 1989.

International Law

BenDaniel, David J., and Arthur H. Rosenbloom. *International M&A, Joint Ventures, and Beyond: Doing the Deal.* New York: John Wiley & Sons, 1997.

Bledsoe, Robert L. and Boleslaw A. Boczek. *The International Law Dictionary.* Santa Barbara, Calif.: ABC-Clio, 1987.

Falk, Richard, Friedrich Kratochwil, and Saul H. Mendlovitz, eds. *International Law: A Contemporary Perspective.* Boulder, Colo.: Westview Press, 1985.

McWhinney, Edward. *Conflict and Compromise: International Law and World Order in a Revolutionary Age.* New York: Holmes & Meier, 1981.

Moynihan, Daniel P. *On the Law of Nations.* Cambridge, Mass.: Harvard University Press, 1990.

Law Enforcement

Axelrod, Alan, and Charles Phillips. *Cops, Crooks, and Criminologists: An International Biographical Dictionary of Law Enforcement.* With Kurt Kemper. New York: Facts On File, 1996.

Cohen, Paul, and Shari Cohen. *Careers in Law Enforcement and Security.* New York: Rosen, 1990.

Denenberg, Barry. *The True Story of J. Edgar Hoover and the FBI.* New York: Scholastic, 1992.

Ferguson, Tom. *Modern Law Enforcement Weapons and Tactics.* 2d ed. Northbrook, Ill.: DBI Books, 1991.

McGee, Jim, and Brian Duffy. *Main Justice: The Men and Women Who Enforce the Nation's Criminal Laws and Guard Its Liberties.* New York: Simon & Schuster, 1996.

Philbin, Tom. *Cop Speak: The Lingo of Law Enforcement and Crime.* New York: J. Wiley, 1996.

Skolnick, Jerome H., and James J. Fyfe. *Above the Law: Police and the Excessive Use of Force.* New York: Free Press, 1993.

Smith, Elizabeth Simpson. *Breakthrough: Women in Law Enforcement.* New York: Walker, 1982.

Legal Education

Arnett, J. Robert, Arthur Coon, and Michael DiGeronimo. *From Here to Attorney: The Ultimate Guide to Excelling in Law School and Launching Your Legal Career.* Belmont, Calif.: Professional, 1993.

Arron, Deborah L. *What Can You Do with a Law Degree? A Lawyer's Guide to Career Alternatives Inside, Outside, and Around the Law.* Seattle: Niche Press, 1994.

Cooper, Cynthia L. *The Insider's Guide to the Top Fifteen Law Schools.* New York: Doubleday, 1990.

Deaver, Jeff. *The Complete Law School Companion: How to Excel at America's Most Demanding Post-Graduate Curriculum.* Rev. ed. New York: Wiley, 1992.

Frank, Steven J. *Learning the Law: Success in Law School and Beyond.* Secaucus, N.J.: Carol, 1992.

Lermack, Paul. *How to Get into the Right Law School.* 2d ed. Lincolnwood, Ill.: VGM Career Horizons, 1997.

Roth, George J. *Slaying the Law School Dragon: How to Survive—and Thrive—in First-Year Law School.* 2d ed. New York: Wiley, 1991.

Turow, Scott. *One L.* New York: Putnam, 1977.

Warner, Ralph E., Toni Ihara, and Barbara Kate

Repa. *Twenty-nine Reasons Not to Go to Law School*. 4th ed. Berkeley, Calif.: Nolo Press, 1994.

Legal Practice

Abramson, Jill, and Barbara Franklin. *Where They Are Now: The Story of the Women of Harvard Law 1974*. New York: Doubleday, 1986.

Altman, Mary Ann. *Life After Law: Second Careers for Lawyers*. Washington, D.C.: Wayne Smith, 1991.

Arron, Deborah L. *Running from the Law: Why Good Lawyers Are Getting out of the Legal Profession*. Berkeley, Calif.: Ten Speed Press, 1991.

Bartlett, Joseph W. *The Law Business: A Tired Monopoly*. Littleton, Colo.: Fred B. Rothman, 1982.

Couric, Emily. *The Trial Lawyers: The Nation's Top Litigators Tell How They Win*. New York: St. Martin's Press, 1988.

Deborah E. *Paralegal Practice and Procedure: A Practical Guide for the Legal Assistant*. 3d ed. Englewood Cliffs, N.J.: Prentice-Hall, 1994.

Glendon, Mary Ann. *A Nation Under Lawyers: How the Crisis in the Legal Profession Is Transforming American Society*. New York: Farrar, Straus & Giroux, 1994.

Granfield, Robert. *Making Elite Lawyers: Visions of Law at Harvard and Beyond*. New York: Routledge, Chapman and Hall, 1992.

Grutman, Roy. *Lawyers and Thieves*. New York: Simon & Schuster, 1990.

Harnett, Bertram. *Law, Lawyers, and Laymen: Making Sense of the American Legal System*. San Diego: Harcourt Brace Jovanovich, 1984.

Kronman, Anthony T. *The Lost Lawyer: Failing Ideals of the Legal Profession*. Cambridge, Mass.: Belknap Press of Harvard University Press, 1993.

Linowitz, Sol M. *Betrayed Profession: Lawyering at the End of the Twentieth Century*. With Martin Mayer. New York: Charles Scribner's Sons, 1994.

Margolick, David. *At the Bar: The Passions and Peccadilloes of American Lawyers*. New York: Simon & Schuster, 1995.

Marston, David W. *Malice Aforethought: How Lawyers Use Our Secret Rules to Get Rich, Get Sex, Get Even . . . And Get Away with It*. New York: W. Morrow, 1991.

Moll, Richard W. *The Lure of the Law and the Life Thereafter*. New York: Viking, 1990.

Munneke, Gary A. *Opportunities in Law Careers*. Lincolnwood, Ill.: VGM Career Horizons, 1994.

Nader, Ralph, and Wesley J. Smith. *No Contest: Corporate Lawyers and the Perversion of Justice in America*. New York: Random House, 1996.

Nossel, Suzanne, and Elizabeth Westfall. *Presumed Equal: What America's Top Women Lawyers Really Think About Their Firms*. Franklin Lakes, N.J.: Career Press, 1998.

Puccio, Thomas P. *In the Name of the Law: Confessions of a Trial Lawyer*. With Dan Collins. New York: W. W. Norton, 1995.

Ragano, Frank, and Selwyn Raab. *Mob Lawyer*. New York: Charles Scribner's Sons, 1994.

Schwartz, Laurens R. *What You Aren't Supposed to Know About the Legal Profession: An Expose of Lawyers, Law Schools, Judges, and More*. New York: SPI Books, 1993.

Stevens, Mark. *Power of Attorney: The Rise of the Giant Law Firms*. New York: McGraw-Hill, 1987.

Legal Reference and Research

Black, Henry Campbell. *Black's Law Dictionary: Definitions of the Terms and Phrases of American and English Jurisprudence, Ancient and Modern*. 6th ed. St. Paul, Minn.: West Publishing, 1990.

The Bluebook: Uniform System of Citation. 16th ed. Cambridge, Mass.: Harvard Law Review Association, 1996.

Corbin, John. *Find the Law in the Library: A Guide to Legal Research*. Chicago: American Library Association, 1989.

Elias, Stephen. *Legal Research: How to Find and Understand the Law*. 5th ed. Berkeley, Calif.: Nolo Press, 1997.

Evans, James H. *Law on the Net*. Berkeley, Calif.: Nolo Press, 1995.

Garner, Bryan A. *A Dictionary of Modern Legal Usage*. 2d ed. New York: Oxford University Press, 1995.

Herskowitz, Suzan. *Legal Research Made Easy*. Clearwater, Fla: Sphinx, 1995.

Mellinkoff, David. *Dictionary of American Legal Usage*. St. Paul, Minn.: West Publishing, 1992.

Shapiro, Fred R. *The Oxford Dictionary of American Legal Quotations*. New York: Oxford University Press, 1993.

Legal Theory

Adler, Mortimer Jerome. *We Hold These Truths: Understanding the Ideas and Ideals of the Constitution*. New York: Macmillan, 1987.

Berns, Walter F. *Taking the Constitution Seriously*. New York: Simon & Schuster, 1987.

Bernstein, Richard B. *Amending America: If We Love the Constitution So Much, Why Do We Keep Trying to Change It?* New York: Times Books, 1993.

Bork, Robert H. *The Tempting of America: The Political Seduction of the Law.* New York: Free Press, 1990.

Campos, Paul F. *Jurismania: The Madness of American Law.* New York: Oxford University Press, 1998.

Cantor, Norman F. *Imagining the Law: Common Law and the Foundations of the American Legal System.* New York: HarperCollins, 1997.

Cox, Archibald. *The Court and the Constitution.* Boston: Houghton Mifflin, 1987.

Howard, Philip K. *The Death of Common Sense: How the Law Is Suffocating America.* New York: Random House, 1994.

Irons, Peter H. *Brennan vs. Rehnquist: The Battle for the Constitution.* New York: Knopf, 1994.

Rawls, John. *Political Liberalism.* New York: Columbia University Press, 1993.

_____. *A Theory of Justice.* Cambridge: Belknap Press of Harvard University Press, 1971.

Medical Law

Barnett, Terry James. *Living Wills and More: Everything You Need to Ensure that All Your Medical Wishes Are Followed.* New York: Wiley, 1992.

Burris, Scott, ed. *AIDS Law Today: A New Guide for the Public.* 2d ed. New Haven, Conn.: Yale University Press, 1993.

Colen, B. D. *The Essential Guide to a Living Will: How to Protect Your Right to Refuse Medical Treatment.* New York: Prentice-Hall, 1991.

Isaac, Rael Jean, and Virginia C. Armat. *Madness in the Streets: How Psychiatry and the Law Abandoned the Mentally Ill.* New York: Free Press, 1990.

Palmer, Larry I. *Law, Medicine, and Social Justice.* Louisville, Ky.: Westminster/John Knox Press, 1989.

Rothman, David J. *Strangers at the Bedside: A History of How Law and Bioethics Transformed Medical Decision Making.* New York: Basic Books, 1991.

Sloan, Irving J. *The Right to Die: Legal and Ethical Problems.* New York: Oceana Publications, 1988.

Stolman, Marc D. *A Guide to Legal Rights for People with Disabilities.* New York: Demos, 1994.

Military Law

Howard, Michael, George J. Andreopoulos, and Mark R. Shulman, eds. *The Laws of War: Constraints on Warfare in the Western World.* New Haven: Yale University Press, 1994.

Kohn, Stephen M. *Jailed for Peace: The History of American Draft Law Violators, 1658-1984.* Westport, Conn.: Greenwood Press, 1986.

Musicant, Ivan. *The Banana Wars: A History of United States Military Intervention in Latin America from the Spanish-American War to the Invasion of Panama.* New York: Macmillan, 1990.

O'Hanlon, Michael E. *Saving Lives with Force: Military Criteria for Humanitarian Intervention.* Washington, D.C.: Brookings Institution Press, 1997.

Real Estate Law

Galaty, Fillmore W., Wellington J. Allaway, and Robert C. Kyle. *Modern Real Estate Practice.* 14th ed. Chicago, Ill.: Real Estate Education, 1996.

Irwin, Robert. *Buy and Sell Real Estate After the 1997 Tax Act: A Guide for Homeowners and Investors.* New York: J. Wiley, 1998.

Milko, George. *Real Estate: The Legal Side to Buying a House, Condo, or Co-op: A Step-by-Step Guide.* Rev. ed. New York: Random House, 1990.

Pombo, Richard, and Joseph Farah. *This Land Is Our Land: How to End the War on Private Property.* New York: St. Martin's Press, 1996.

Weaver, Jefferson Hane. *The Compact Guide to Property Law: A Civilized Approach to the Law.* St. Paul, Minn.: West Publishing, 1992.

Werner, Raymond J., and Robert Kratovil. *Real Estate Law.* 10th ed. Englewood Cliffs, N.J.: Prentice-Hall, 1993.

Tax Law

Barlett, Donald L., and James B. Steele. *America: Who Really Pays the Taxes?* New York: Simon & Schuster, 1994.

Birnbaum, Jeffrey H., and Alan S. Murray. *Showdown at Gucci Gulch: Lawmakers, Lobbyists, and the Unlikely Triumph of Tax Reform.* New York: Random House, 1987.

Burnham, David. *A Law unto Itself: Power, Politics, and the IRS.* New York: Random House, 1989.

Hoven, Vernon. *The Real Estate Investor's Tax Guide: What Every Investor Needs to Know to Maximize Profits.* 3d ed. Chicago, Ill.: Real Estate Education, 1998.

Kilpatrick, William A. *The Big Tax Lie.* New York: Simon & Schuster, 1986.

Schriebman, Robert S. *When You Can't Pay Your*

Taxes! How to Deal with the IRS. Homewood, Ill.: Dow Jones-Irwin, 1986.

Wills and Estate Law

Bove, Alexander A. *The Complete Book of Wills and Estates.* New York: H. Holt, 1989.

Daly, Eugene J. *Thy Will Be Done: A Guide to Wills, Taxation, and Estate Planning for Older Persons.* 2d ed. Amherst, N.Y.: Prometheus Books, 1994.

Ostberg, Kay. *Probate—Settling an Estate: A Step-by-Step Guide.* New York: Random House, 1990.

Plotnick, Charles, and Stephan R. Leimberg. *Keeping Your Money: How to Avoid Taxes and Probate Through Estate Planning.* New York: Wiley, 1987.

MAGILL'S LEGAL GUIDE

Topics by Subject Category

Arrest	XXIII	Legal Fees	XXVII
Attorneys	XXIII	Legal Forums	XXVII
Banking and Investments	XXIII	Legal Occupations	XXVII
Business	XXIV	Legal Practices	XXVIII
Civil Law Issues	XXIV	Legal Training	XXVIII
Constitutional Issues	XXIV	Medical and Health Issues	XXVIII
Contracts	XXIV	Military	XXVIII
Copyright, Patents, and Trademarks	XXV	Organizations and Government Agencies	XXVIII
Courtroom Procedure	XXV	Police	XXVIII
Crimes and Infractions	XXV	Procedural Matters	XXIX
Defendants	XXVI	Property Ownership and Renting	XXIX
Education	XXVI	The Public and the Legal Professions	XXIX
Employment	XXVI	Punishment	XXX
Ethics	XXVI	Taxes, Licenses, and Permits	XXX
Family Matters	XXVI	Vehicles and Travel	XXX
Foreign Travel and Business	XXVII	Wills and Estates	XXX
Insurance	XXVII		
Laws and Types of Laws	XXVII		

ARREST
Arraignment
Arrest
Bail
Certiorari, writ of
Confession
Defendant
Due process
Effective counsel
Entrapment
Evidence
Habeas corpus
Indictment
Innocence, presumption of
Law enforcement
Legal immunity
Legal services plans
Mexican travel
Personal recognizance
Plea
Police
Police detectives
Preliminary hearing
Probable cause
Proximate cause
Search warrant
Speedy trial requirement
State police
Stop and frisk
Subpoena
Suspect
Wiretap
Witnesses

ATTORNEYS
Advertising, legal
American Bar Association
Apparent authority
Attorney-client relationship
Attorney confidentiality
Attorney fee splitting
Attorney fees
Attorney salaries
Attorney sex with clients
Attorney trust accounts
Attorney types
Attorneys, court-appointed
Attorneys as fiduciaries
Bar associations
Death row attorneys
Disqualification of attorneys
District attorneys
Grievance committees for attorney discipline
Interest on attorney trust accounts
Law firm partners and associates
Law firm partnership tracks
Law firms
Legal clinics
Legal degrees
Liability of attorneys to nonclients
Military attorney
Personal injury attorneys
Pro bono legal work
Prosecutors
Public defenders
Solicitation of legal clients
Unauthorized practice of law
Unethical conduct of attorneys
Women in legal professions

BANKING AND INVESTMENTS
Banking law
Bankruptcy
Brokerage account
Canadian business law
Certificate of deposit
Check kiting
Credit, consumer
Credit cards

Credit record
Debt collection
Foreclosure
Intangible asset
Loans, business
Loans, personal
Mexican business law
Negotiable instrument
Retirement planning
Retirement plans
Secured transaction
Shareholder suit
Stock certificate
Stockholders
Usury

BUSINESS
Advertising, deceptive
Advertising, legal
Antitrust law
Automobile leasing
Automobile purchasing
Bankruptcy
Bill of lading
Boycott
Breach of contract
Broadcasting licenses
Business taxes
Canadian business law
Charitable contributions
Chattel paper
Consignment
Consumer protection laws
Contracts
Corporations
Covenant not to compete
Credit, consumer
Credit cards
Credit record
Debt collection
Door-to-door sales
Earnest money
Embezzlement
Export permits
Fair market value
Farming
Foreclosure
Franchise businesses
Fraud
Future estate

Gambling, legal
Home businesses
Import permits
Income taxes
Industrial espionage
Installment sales contract
Intangible asset
Internet
Lemon laws
Loans, business
Mail-order buying
Mechanic's lien
Mexican business law
Minimum wage laws
Nonprofit organizations
Partnerships
Property liability
Public accommodations
Repossession
Sales taxes
Secured transaction
Self-employment taxes
Service contracts
Shareholder suit
Small businesses
Stock certificate
Stockholders
Trade secret
Unconscionable contracts
Warranties
White-collar crime
Zoning laws

CIVIL LAW ISSUES
Accidents and injuries
Asbestos litigation
Automobile accidents
Breach of contract
Civil law
Conversion
Environmental legislation
Environmental practice
Joint and several liability
Negligence
Occupational health and
   safety
Personal injury law
Product liability
Torts
Workers' compensation

CONSTITUTIONAL ISSUES
Acquittal
Affirmative action
Age of majority
American Civil Liberties Union
Amnesty
Appeal
Civil law
Civil rights and liberties
Common law
Constitution, U.S.
Constitutions, state
Death penalty
Discrimination
Double jeopardy
Due process
Employment discrimination
Equal protection of the law
Fair housing law
Fifth Amendment
Freedom of information
   request
Freedom of press
Freedom of religion
Freedom of speech
Grand juries
Habeas corpus
Innocence, presumption of
Judicial review
Juries
Jury nullification
Law enforcement
Martial law
Miranda rights
Prisoners' rights
Race and the law
Religious institutions
Search and seizure, illegal
Search warrant
Speedy trial requirement
Victims' rights
Voting rights
Witness protection programs

CONTRACTS
Attorney fees
Breach of contract
Consideration
Contracts
Cosignatory

Topics by Subject Category

Covenant not to compete
Door-to-door sales
Duress
Earnest money
Employment contracts
Escrow
Foreclosure
Fraud
Home buying
Home selling
Installment sales contract
Lawsuits
Leases
Legalese
Living wills
Loans, business
Loans, personal
Mail-order buying
Mechanic's lien
Mortgages
Real estate listing agreements
Rental agreements
Secured transaction
Service contracts
Unconscionable contracts

COPYRIGHT, PATENTS, AND TRADEMARKS
Copyright
Fraud
Intangible asset
Patents
Public domain
Trade secret
Trademarks

COURTROOM PROCEDURE
Adversary system
Bailiffs
Burden of proof
Confession
Conflicts of interest
Court reporters
Cross-examination
Defendant
Directed verdict
Discovery
Due process
Effective counsel
Evidence

Exclusionary rule
Grand juries
Hearsay
Innocence, presumption of
Insanity defense
Judges
Juries
Jury duty
Jury nullification
Jury selection
Jury sequestration
Mistrial
Objection
Officers of the court
Plea
Plea bargain
Precedent
Probable cause
Prosecutors
Public defenders
Reasonable doubt
State judicial systems
Trials
Venue, change of
Witnesses
Witnesses, expert

CRIMES AND INFRACTIONS
Advertising, deceptive
Arrest, resisting
Arson
Assault and battery
Attractive nuisance
Bigamy
Blackmail
Breach of contract
Bribery
Burglary
Check kiting
Child abuse
Conspiracy
Counterfeiting
Crime of passion
Criminal intent
Criminal record
Defamation
Discrimination
Disorderly conduct
Drugs, illegal
Drunk driving

Duress
Embezzlement
Employment discrimination
Extortion
Felony
Forgery
Fraud
Gambling, illegal
Graffiti
Hit-and-run accident
Homicide
Ignorance of the law
Industrial espionage
Insurance fraud
Jaywalking
Juvenile delinquency
Kidnapping
Larceny
Libel
Loitering
Manslaughter
Medical malpractice
Misdemeanor
Moral turpitude
Negligence
Pandering
Perjury
Pickpocketing
Prostitution
Public nuisance
Rape
Reckless endangerment
Robbery
Search and seizure, illegal
Sexual battery
Sexual harassment
Shoplifting
Slander
Smuggling
Spousal abuse
Stalking
Theft
Treason
Trespass
Truancy
Unauthorized practice of law
Usury
Vagrancy
Vandalism

White-collar crime
Wrongful death

DEFENDANTS
Acquittal
Adversary system
Age of majority
Appeal
Arraignment
Arrest
Attorney-client relationship
Attorney fees
Burden of proof
Certiorari, writ of
Confession
Contempt of court
Conviction
Criminal record
Cross-examination
Defendant
Defendant self-representation
Defending the guilty
Dismissal
Double jeopardy
Due process
Effective counsel
Equal protection of the law
Ignorance of the law
Innocence, presumption of
Insanity defense
Legal services plans
Liability of attorneys to nonclients
Plea
Plea bargain
Principals (criminal)
Privileged communication
Public defenders
Reasonable doubt
Self-defense
Sentencing
Solicitation of legal clients
Verdict

EDUCATION
American Association of Law Schools
Home schooling
Law School Admission Test
Law-school rankings
Law-school student demographics
Law teaching
Legal education
School law
Study-abroad programs
Undergraduate preparation for law school

EMPLOYMENT
Collective bargaining
Employment at will
Employment contracts
Health and disability insurance
Income taxes
Labor law
Labor unions
Minimum wage laws
Pensions
Self-employment taxes
Social Security
Unemployment insurance
Whistle-blowing
Workers' compensation

ETHICS
Advertising, legal
Advocate-witness rule
Attorney confidentiality
Attorney sex with clients
Attorney trust accounts
Attorneys as fiduciaries
Code of Professional Responsibility
Codes of civility
Conflicts of interest
Defending the guilty
Dilatory tactics
Disqualification of attorneys
Ethics
Frivolous lawsuits
Grievance committees for attorney discipline
Impeachment of judges
Judicial bias
Judicial conduct code
Liability of attorneys to nonclients
Malpractice, legal
Model Rules of Professional Conduct
No-contact rule
Perjury
Privileged communication
Pro bono legal work
Solicitation of legal clients
Unauthorized practice of law
Unconscionable contracts
Unethical conduct of attorneys

FAMILY MATTERS
Abortion
Adopted children's rights
Adoption
Adultery
Age and the law
Age of majority
Bequests
Bigamy
Child abduction by parents
Child abuse
Child custody and support
Children's rights
Common-law marriage
Community property
Competency
Crime of passion
Divorce
Divorce mediators
Estate and gift taxes
Estates and estate planning
Family law practice
Foster parents
Funerals
Grandparents' rights
Home schooling
Inheritance tax
Intestate succession
Legal guardians
Marital separation
Marriage
Marriage, same-sex
Name changing
Nursing homes
Palimony
Parental divorce
Parental responsibility for children
Paternity

Topics by Subject Category

Patients' rights
Pets
Prenuptial agreements
Probate
Probation, juvenile
Stepparents
Surrogate parenting
Trusts
Unwed parents and rights of children
Victims' rights
Wills

FOREIGN TRAVEL AND BUSINESS
Automobile insurance
Canadian business law
Canadian law
Canadian travel
Citizenship
Deportation
Diplomatic immunity
Export permits
Extradition
Foreign travel
Green cards
Immigration and Naturalization Service
Immigration law
Import permits
International law
International tribunals
Mexican business law
Mexican law
Mexican travel
Passports
Study-abroad programs
Visas, foreign
Visas, U.S.

INSURANCE
Accidents and injuries
Asbestos litigation
Automobile accidents
Automobile insurance
Consumer protection laws
Environmental legislation
Health and disability insurance
Homeowner insurance
Hospitals

Insurance adjustors
Insurance fraud
Insurance law
Life insurance
Medicaid
Medicare
No-fault insurance
Nursing homes
Property liability
Social Security
Unemployment insurance
Workers' compensation

LAWS AND TYPES OF LAWS
Annotated codes
Antitrust law
Banking law
Blue laws
Broadcasting law
Canadian law
Case law
Civil law
Common law
Constitution, U.S.
Constitutions, state
Consumer protection laws
Criminal law
Environmental legislation
Fair housing law
Fifth Amendment
Fish and game laws
Gun laws
Hate crime statutes
International law
Labor law
Lemon laws
Long arm statute
Louisiana law
Maritime law
Martial law
Mexican law
Military law
Minimum wage laws
Product liability law
Real estate law
School law
Self-employment taxes
Space law
Statute
Statute of limitations

Substantive law
Superfund litigation
Telephone law
Three-strikes laws
Traffic law
Uniform laws
Zoning laws

LEGAL FEES
Attorney fee splitting
Attorney fees
Attorney salaries
Billable hours
Billing rates
Champerty and maintenance
Contingency fees
Court-awarded fees
Court costs
Litigation expenses
Minimum fee schedules
Retainers
Statutory fee ceilings

LEGAL FORUMS
Adversary system
Court-martial
Court types
Criminal justice system
Federal judicial system
Hearing
International tribunals
Juvenile criminal proceedings
Military tribunals
Small claims court
State judicial systems
Supreme Court, U.S.
Traffic court
Trials
World Court

LEGAL OCCUPATIONS
Attorney types
Attorneys, court-appointed
Bail bond agents
Bailiffs
Clerks of the court
Coroners
Corporate general counsel
Court reporters
Death row attorneys

District attorneys
Divorce mediators
Judges
Judicial appointments and elections
Judicial clerks
Judicial confirmation hearings
Law-student clerks
Legal secretary
Legislative counsel
Medical examiners
Military attorney
Notary public
Officers of the court
Paralegals
Parole officers
Personal injury attorneys
Police detectives
Private investigators
Prosecutors
Public defenders
Sheriffs
Women in legal professions

LEGAL PRACTICES
Administrative practice
Appellate practice
Commercial litigation
Corporate legal practice
Criminal prosecution
Environmental practice
Family law practice
Immigration law
Insurance law
Personal injury law
Public interest law
Tax law

LEGAL TRAINING
Bar exams
Black's Law Dictionary
Blue Book, The
Computerized legal databases
Law libraries
Law reviews
Law School Admission Test
Law-school rankings
Law-school student demographics
Law teaching

Legal degrees
Legal education
Legal honor societies
Legal treatises
Mock trials
Moot court
Study-abroad programs
Summer clerkships
Undergraduate preparation for law school

MEDICAL AND HEALTH ISSUES
Abortion
Accidents and injuries
Age and the law
AIDS-related problems
Alcohol
Asbestos litigation
Automobile accidents
Competency
Consumer protection laws
Coroners
Environmental legislation
Funerals
Health and disability insurance
Hit-and-run accident
Hospitals
Institutionalization
Insurance law
Life insurance
Living wills
Medicaid
Medical examiners
Medical malpractice
Medical records
Medical treatment, consent for
Medicare
Nursing homes
Occupational health and safety
Organ donation
Paternity
Patients' rights
Privacy rights
Right to die
Smoking and tobacco use
Social Security
Workers' compensation

MILITARY
Coast Guard, U.S.
Court-martial
Military attorney
Military law
Military police
Military tribunals
Treason

ORGANIZATIONS AND GOVERNMENT AGENCIES
American Association of Law Schools
American Bar Association
American Civil Liberties Union
American Inns of Court
Bar associations
Coast Guard, U.S.
Federal Bureau of Investigation
Immigration and Naturalization Service
Internal Revenue Service
Interpol
Labor unions
Marshals Service, U.S.
Mexican American Legal Defense and Education Fund
Military police
NAACP Legal Defense Fund
Police
Prison system
State police

POLICE
Arrest
Coast Guard, U.S.
Community-oriented policing
Confession
Entrapment
Federal Bureau of Investigation
Immigration and Naturalization Service
Informants
Interpol
Law enforcement
Marshals Service, U.S.
Military police
Police
Police detectives
Search and seizure, illegal

TOPICS BY SUBJECT CATEGORY

Search warrant
Sheriffs
Stakeout
State police
Stop and frisk
Subpoena
Suspect
Wiretap
Witnesses

PROCEDURAL MATTERS
Acquittal
Adversary system
Affidavit
Amicus curiae brief
Appeal
Arbitration
Arraignment
Arrest
Assumption of risk
Attachment
Bail
Burden of proof
Cause of action
Certiorari, writ of
Chain of custody
Civil action
Class-action suits
Confession
Consent decree
Contempt of court
Conviction
Cooling-off period
Court calendar
Court reporters
Cross-examination
Declaratory judgment
Defendant
Defendant self-representation
Deposition
Directed verdict
Dismissal
Double jeopardy
Due process
Effective counsel
Equal protection of the law
Evidence
Exclusionary rule
Execution of judgment
Gag order

Habeas corpus
Hearsay
Indictment
Injunction
Innocence, presumption of
Inquest
Insanity defense
Judgment proof
Jurisdiction
Lawsuits
Legal immunity
Lesser included offense
Mediation
Mistrial
Nolo contendere plea
Objection
Opinion
Personal recognizance
Plea
Plea bargain
Preliminary hearing
Principals (criminal)
Probable cause
Probation, adult
Probation, juvenile
Proximate cause
Release
Restraining order, temporary
Search warrant
Sentencing
Speedy trial requirement
Subpoena
Subrogation
Summary judgment
Summons
Test case
Testimony
Trial transcript
Venue, change of
Verdict
Witnesses
Witnesses, expert

PROPERTY OWNERSHIP AND RENTING
Building permits
Cloud on title
Community property
Deed
Easement

Eminent domain
Escrow
Eviction
Home buying
Home ownership
Home selling
Homeowner insurance
Homestead
Joint tenancy
Landlords
Landlord's lien
Leases
Marital property and debts
Mortgages
Personal property
Property liability
Property rights
Property taxes
Property types
Real estate law
Real estate listing agreements
Real property
Rent control
Rental agreements
Renters' rights
Subleases
Tenancy in common
Title
Title companies
Title search
Zoning laws

THE PUBLIC AND THE LEGAL PROFESSIONS
Advertising, legal
Community-oriented policing
Defending the guilty
Ethics
Films about the legal professions
Frivolous lawsuits
Legal clinics
Literature about the legal professions
Model Rules of Professional Conduct
Pro bono legal work
Solicitation of legal clients
Television courtroom programs

Television dramas about the
    legal profession

PUNISHMENT
Cruel and unusual punishment
Death penalty
Deportation
Dismissal
Extradition
Garnishment
Injunction
Parole
Parole officers
Prison system
Prisoners' rights
Probation, adult
Probation, juvenile
Sentencing
Verdict
Victims' rights

TAXES, LICENSES, AND PERMITS
Broadcasting licenses
Building permits
Business taxes
Copyright
Driving licenses
Estate and gift taxes
Export permits
Import permits
Income taxes
Inheritance tax
Patents
Pilot licenses
Property taxes
Sales taxes
Self-employment taxes
Tax law
Trademarks
Vehicle licenses and registration

VEHICLES AND TRAVEL
Accidents and injuries
Automobile accidents
Automobile insurance
Automobile leasing
Automobile purchasing
Canadian travel
Driving licenses
Foreign travel
Maritime law
Mexican travel
Pilot licenses
Traffic law
Traffic schools
Vehicle licenses and registration
Visas, foreign
Visas, U.S.

WILLS AND ESTATES
Executors
Family law practice
Intestate succession
Real estate law
Real estate listing agreements
Trustees
Trusts
Trusts, charitable
Wills
Wills, holographic

INDEX

AALS Directory of Law Teachers, 66
AALS Handbook, 66
AALS Newsletter, 66
Abortion, 1-4, 288, 740
Abortion Control Act (Pennsylvania), 2
Academy of Family Mediators, 277
Accessories, 345, 663, 690
Accidents and injuries, 4-8, 235
Accomplice liability, 8
Acquired immunodeficiency syndrome (AIDS), 33-36, 281, 328, 537, 697, 730, 994
Acquittal, 8-9
Act to Expedite the Strengthening of the National Defense, 323
Actus reus, 232, 550
Adams, John, 477, 487
Adarand Constructors v. Peña, 28
Administrative practice, 9-10
Admiralty law, 575
Adopted children's rights, 10-12
Adoption, 12-15, 331, 837
Adoption and Safe Families Act, 11
Adultery, 15-17
Adversary system, 17-19, 239, 243, 272, 313, 425; judges in, 17
Adverse possession, 19-20
Advertising, deceptive, 20-23, 196
Advertising, legal, 23-24
Advertising Age, 21
Advocate-witness rule, 25
Affidavit, 25-26, 852
Affirmative action, 26-29, 164, 186, 297, 523, 527, 540, 618; and Philadelphia Plan, 27; Title VII of, 26
African Americans, 159-161, 298, 307, 367, 394, 424, 526, 532, 559, 567, 618-619, 682, 703, 742-744, 780, 835, 908, 960, 962; and affirmative action, 27, 158, 526, 540; and AIDS, 35; arson attacks against, 62; and juries, 487, 745; and prison population, 694-695; and voting rights, 906-907. *See also* Racism
Age and the law, 29-32
Age Discrimination in Employment Act (ADEA), 29-30, 268, 296, 299-300, 809
Age of majority, 32-33, 147, 202, 358, 590
Agents, 51, 690

Agins v. City of Tiburon, 719
Agriculture Ammonia Institute-Rubber Manufacturers, 631
Agriculture Department, U.S., 195, 336-337, 354, 981
Aid to Families with Dependent Children (AFDC), 584, 808, 810
Air bags, 195
Air Force, U.S., 218, 380, 603-604
Air Pollution Control Act, 303
Airborne Hunting Act, 983
Alcohol, 36-38, 237, 287, 358, 456, 600, 644-645, 710-711, 779, 805, 837, 886, 894, 965; and automobile accidents, 100, 133; driving under the influence of, 232, 283-284, 286, 865; and incompetency, 202, 590, 746, 748, 790; and legal drinking age, 33, 235, 715, 921; prohibited sale of, 111, 382, 394, 515, 807; and taxes, 775, 804. *See also* Blue laws
Alcohol Administration Act, 984
Alcohol beverage commissions (ABC), 38
Alibrandi, Martina N., 110
Alien and Sedition Acts, 367
Alimony, 39-41, 47, 222, 273, 275, 331-332, 756, 770
Allen, E. C., 569
Allied Control Council, 460
Alternative dispute resolution, 54, 68, 171, 533, 583, 623, 703
Alzheimer's disease, 771
Amendments, Constitutional. *See* Constitutional amendments
American Arbitration Association, 54, 171, 533, 584
American Association of Franchisees and Dealers, 363
American Association of Law Libraries, 521
American Association of Retired Persons (AARP), 29
American Bar Association (ABA), 23, 41-43, 68, 103, 241, 333, 446, 463, 470, 521, 527, 546, 639, 736, 843, 846, 924, 926, 969; Committee on Ethics and Professional Responsibility of, 23; and the death penalty, 252; and legal advertising, 24; and legal

education, 79, 524-526, 528-529, 537-538, 540, 884-885; and legal ethics, 71, 73, 78, 85, 138, 167-168, 185-186, 263, 314, 472, 476, 613, 623, 625, 663, 888; and legal fees, 75; Litigation and Business Law Sections, 171; and pro bono legal work, 704; and uniform laws, 15, 570, 889. *See also* Bar associations
American Civil Liberties Union (ACLU), 43-44, 81, 369, 373, 377, 461, 697-698, 835, 852, 963
American Civil Liberties Union v. Reno, 461
American Conference of Governmental Industrial Hygienists, 631
American Federation of Labor (AFL), 503, 506
American Federation of Labor-Congress of Industrial Organizations (AFL-CIO), 506, 964
American Friends Service Committee, 430
American Humane Society, 141
American Immigration Lawyers Association (AILA), 435
American Inns of Court, 44-45, 544
American Institute of Architects, 533
American Institute of Real Estate Appraisers, 417
American Intellectual Property Law Association, 103
American Land Title Association, 857
American Law Institute, 232, 422
American Library Association, 461
American Medical Association (AMA), 1, 141
American National Standards Institute, 631
American Patriot Network, 175
American Petroleum Institute, 631
American Revolution, 153, 370, 471, 598, 782, 795
American Society for Testing Materials, 631
American Society of Agricultural Engineers, 631
American Society of Appraisers, 417
American Society of Home Inspectors, 408
American Society of Mechanical Engineers, 631

XXXI

American Stock Exchange, 120, 826
American Telephone and Telegraph Co. v. United States, 48
American Telephone and Telegraph Company (AT&T), 844-845
American Tobacco Company, 50
American Welding Society, 631
Americans with Disabilities Act (ADA), 164, 268, 296, 299-300, 701
Amicus curiae brief, 45, 434
Amish, 371, 413, 780
Amnesty, 45-46
Anglim, Christopher Thomas, 170
Animal Welfare Act, 672
Annotated codes, 46-47
Annulment, 47, 272, 578
Anticounterfeiting Consumer Protection Act, 215
Anti-Defamation League of the B'nai B'rith, 399
Anti-Drug Abuse Act (1986), 281-282
Anti-Injunction Act (Norris-LaGuardia Act), 503, 508
Anti-Kickback Act, 365
Anti-Terrorism and Effective Death Penalty Act (AEDPA), 259
Antitrust law, 48, 50-51, 113, 210, 213, 822. *See also* Clayton Anti-Trust Act; Sherman Anti-Trust Act
Apparent authority, 51
Appeal, 51-52
Appellate courts, 134, 222-223, 343
Appellate practice, 52-54, 156, 874
Appleseed Centers for Law and Justice, 739
Aptheker v. Secretary of State, 651
Arab League, 113
Arabs, 959
Arbitration, 54-56, 171, 533, 583
Archer, Charles W., 242
Archimedes, 652
Armed Forces Police, 605
Arms Export Control Act, 323
Army, U.S., 190, 218, 380, 603-604
Army Criminal Investigation Division, 603-604
Arraignment, 56
Arrest, 56-60, 83, 92, 182-183, 237, 271, 285, 287, 301, 445, 513, 684, 695, 706, 726, 816, 820, 839; resisting arrest, 61. *See also* False arrest
Arson, 61-63, 340, 345, 422
Articles of Confederation; amendment process, 191
Asahara Shoko, 342

Asbestos, 6, 303, 305, 469, 632; litigation, 63-64
Asbestos Hazardous Emergency Response Act, 64
Asian American Bar Association (Arizona), 703
Asian American Center for Justice, 963
Asian Americans, 153, 526-527, 743, 959-960
Assault and battery, 64-65, 236, 345
Association of American Law Schools (AALS), 65-66, 529, 538, 540
Association of Immigration and Nationality Lawyers, 435
Association of Immigration Attorneys (AIA), 435
Assumption of risk, 66
Asylum, 260, 326, 434
Atomic Energy Act (1946), 323
Atomic Energy Act (1954), 323
Attachment, 67
Attica prison uprising, 691
Attorney-client relationship, 67-70, 85, 315, 551
Attorney confidentiality, 71-72. *See also* Confidentiality
Attorney fee splitting, 72-73
Attorney fees, 73-75, 275, 563, 811. *See also* Retainers
Attorney general, 80, 240, 530, 919
Attorney salaries, 75-77
Attorney sex with clients, 77
Attorney trust accounts, 77-79
Attorney types, 79-82
Attorneys, court-appointed, 82-85
Attorneys as fiduciaries, 85. *See also* Fiduciaries
Attractive nuisance, 85-86
Augustus, John, 710
Australia, 173, 607, 644, 681
Automobile accidents, 86-87
Automobile insurance, 87-88. *See also* Insurance law
Automobile leasing, 88
Automobile purchasing, 88-90
Azidothymidine (AZT), 35

Bachelor of laws degree (LLB), 537-538
Baehr v. Lewin, 268, 580
Baehr v. Miike, 580
Bail, 91-93, 237, 646, 670
Bail bond agents, 93
Bail Reform Act, 92, 281
Bailey, F. Lee, 991
Bailiffs, 93-94, 490

Bailment, 94-95, 534
Bait-and-switch advertising, 22
Bajakajian v. United States, 719
Baker & McKenzie, 76, 518
Baker v. Bolton, 929
Bald Eagle Act, 982
Baldwin, Joseph G., 556
Baldwin, Simeon A., 42
Ball, John, 559
Ballard, Gary, 370
Balloon payments, 88
Bank Holding Company Act, 96-98
Bank Insurance Fund (BIF), 95
Banking Act, 96
Banking law, 95-98
Bankruptcy, 98-103, 157, 172, 230, 336, 363, 412, 469
Bankruptcy Act, 99
Bankruptcy Reform Act, 99
Bar associations, 103-104, 977-980. *See also* American Bar Association (ABA)
Bar exams, 104-105, 174
Barker v. Wingo, 813
Barristers, 79
Bastard Nation, 11
Bates v. State Bar of Arizona, 22, 24
Batson v. Kentucky, 745
Belgium, 908
Bell, Alexander Graham, 844
Bell System, 844
Bell v. Wolfish, 695
Benét, Steven Vincent, 557
Bequests, 105-106. *See also* Wills
Better Business Bureau, 21, 570
Bhopal, India, 7, 211
Bible, 183, 373; New Testament, 720; Old Testament, 99, 720
Bigamy, 106-107
Bill of lading, 107-108
Bill of Rights, English, 173, 244, 398
Bill of Rights, U.S., 43, 82, 133, 152, 158-159, 189-190, 192-193, 251, 288, 347, 368, 378, 391, 442, 697, 699, 961, 963
Billable hours, 108
Billing rates, 108-109
Birth control, 149, 852
Black, Henry Campbell, 110
Black, Hugo, 375
Black Bass Act, 982
Black Lawyers Association (Massachusetts), 703
Black lung disease, 6
Blackmail, 77, 109, 324, 792. *See also* Extortion
Blackmun, Harry A., 2

INDEX

Black's Law Dictionary, 110
Blackstone, Sir William, 173, 540, 547
Blue Book, The, 110-111, 463
Blue laws, 111-112
Board of Immigration Appeals, 434
Boddie v. Connecticut, 273
Boerne v. Flores, 372
Bona fide occupational qualification (BFOQ), 298
Bonaparte, Charles J., 339
Bond, 112-113
Booth, John Wilkes, 188
Borden, Lizzie, 559
Border Patrol, 429-430, 984
Bork, Robert, 44
Bourne v. Flores, 760
Bowers v. Hardwick, 268, 700
Boycott, 113, 504
Brady Handgun Violence Prevention Act, 395
Brandeis, Louis, 174, 918
Breach of contract, 70, 113-115, 246-247, 266, 295, 447, 531, 590, 594, 665, 929. *See also* Contracts
Brennan, William, 367
Breyer, Stephen, 9
Bribery, 115-117, 442
Brinegar v. United States, 705
British Empire, 678
British North America Act, 131-132
Broadcasting law, 117-119
Broadcasting licenses, 119-120
Brobeck, Phleger & Harrison L.L.P., 76
Brokerage account, 120-121
Bronston v. United States, 662
Brougham, Lord Henry Peter, 634
Brown v. Board of Education, 160-161, 267, 307, 532, 618, 697, 742, 780, 834-835, 989
Bryan, William Jennings, 990
Buckley v. Valeo, 686
Budget Reconciliation Act, 658
Building codes, 122
Building permits, 122
Bulow, Claus von, 847, 995
Bundy, Ted, 989
Burden of proof, 122-123
Bureau of Alcohol, Tobacco, and Firearms (BATF), 36, 395, 437, 456, 515, 685
Bureau of Biological Survey, 354
Bureau of Fisheries, 354
Bureau of Immigration Appeals (BIA), 260
Bureau of Labor Statistics, 631

Bureau of Narcotics and Dangerous Drugs, 983
Bureau of Printing, 984
Bureau of Prisons, U.S., 694, 987
Bureau of Professional Responsibility (Pennsylvania), 821
Bureau of Revenue, 983
Burger, Warren, 45
Burger King, 361
Burglary, 123-125, 345, 422, 497, 726
Bush, George, 898
Business taxes, 125-127
Business, Transportation, and Housing Agency, 820
Busing, 28, 713, 780

Cable Communications Act, 854
Calder, Ronald, 325
California Family Law Act, 273
California v. Cabazon Band of Mission Indians, 385
Cambodia, 929
Camden, Charles Pratt, 173
Canada Act, 131
Canada Business Corporations Act (CBCA), 128
Canadian Bar Association, 315
Canadian business law, 128-130
Canadian-controlled private corporations (CCPCs), 129
Canadian Criminal Code, 386
Canadian Environmental Protection Act (CEPA), 130
Canadian law, 131-133, 173, 252, 681, 901
Canadian National Railway (CNR), 134
Canadian Pacific Railway (CPR), 134
Canadian travel, 133-134
Capital punishment. *See* Death penalty
Capitol Police, U.S., 987
Capote, Truman, 561
Cárdenas, Cuauhtémoc, 597
Cardozo, Benjamin, 442, 781
Cardozo Studies in Law and Literature, 522
Carlin, George, 369
Caroline, queen of England, 634
Carroll v. United States, 706
Case law, 45, 57, 130, 134-136, 156, 174, 199, 331, 508, 546, 597, 867. *See also* Common law; Precedent
Cause of action, 136
Celex, 181
Celler Kefauver Act, 912
Censorship, 44, 366-370, 375

Centers for Disease Control and Prevention (CDC), 208
Central America, 430, 432, 435
Central Intelligence Agency (CIA), 341, 365, 965
Certificate of deposit, 121, 136-137
Certiorari, writ of, 52, 137, 475, 834
Chain of custody, 137
Challenger, 366
Champerty and maintenance, 138
Charitable contributions, 138-139
Charter of Rights and Freedoms (Canada), 131-133
Chattel paper, 121, 139
Check kiting, 139-140
Chevron, U.S.A., Inc. v. Natural Resources Defense Council, 10
Child abduction by parents, 140
Child abuse, 140-144, 391
Child Abuse Prevention and Treatment Act, 141, 144
Child custody and support, 17, 40, 47, 75, 140, 144-148, 222, 273, 275-276, 331, 334, 361, 392, 398, 501, 689, 824, 920
Child Custody Jurisdiction and Enforcement Act, 392
Child labor, 336
Child Welfare Act, 15
Child Welfare League of America, 11
Children born out of wedlock, 148, 892
Children's Bill of Rights, 149
Children's rights, 44, 148-150
Children's Television Act, 118
China, 252, 437, 652
Chinese Americans, 742
Christian Coalition, 149
Christian Scientists, 642
Christianity, 852
Chronicle of Higher Education, 520
Church Arson Bill, 62
Church of Jesus Christ of Latter-day Saints (Mormons), 106, 297, 371, 758
Churchill, Winston, 557
Citizenship, 150-153, 159, 259
City of Richmond v. Croson, 20
Civil action, 153-156
Civil Code (Louisiana), 568
Civil code law, 157
Civil law, 156-158, 174, 235, 257, 265, 551, 831
Civil Rights Act (1866), 328
Civil Rights Act (1964), 163, 267-268, 296, 325, 732, 791; and affirmative action, 26

XXXIII

Civil Rights Act (1968), 267, 328
Civil Rights Act (1991), 296-297, 299-300, 791
Civil rights and liberties, 158-164, 307, 391, 683, 701, 924, 960, 964
Civil Rights Commission, U.S., 742
Civil Rights Law (1871), 697
Civil Rights movement, 618, 907
Civil Rights of Institutionalized Persons Act, 697
Civil Service Reform Act, 505, 602, 911
Civil War, 158, 191, 328, 398, 581-582, 640, 742, 804, 852, 906
Claiborne, Harry, 436
Class-action suits, 164-165
Clayton Anti-Trust Act, 48, 113, 247, 503
Clean Air Act, 9, 63, 303, 833, 912
Clean Air Amendments, 986
Clean Water Act, 303-304, 338, 833, 986
Clerks of the court, 81, 165
Clinical Law Review, 66
Clinton, Bill, 3, 11, 28, 69, 207, 252, 259, 516, 571, 607, 805, 815, 898-899
Cloud on title, 165-166
Coase, Ronald, 523
Coast Guard, U.S., 166-167, 218-219, 603-604
Cobb, Irvin S., 557
Code of Federal Regulations, 336, 434, 463
Code of Professional Responsibility, 73, 85, 167, 393
Code pleading, 136
Codes of civility, 167-168
Codicils, 915
Cohabitation, 331
Cohen v. California, 377
Cohn, Roy, 989
Coke, Edward, 175, 540, 547
Cold War, 459, 651, 901, 929
Collateral, 139, 338, 448, 552, 566, 614, 616, 752-753, 783-784
Collateral estoppel, 279-280
Collective bargaining, 168-170, 295, 503, 505, 507, 660
Collins, Robert, 437
Color of title, 19
Colquhoun, Patrick, 680
Commerce Department, U.S., 354, 429, 932, 984
Commercial law, 104
Commercial litigation, 170-173

Commission on Medical Malpractice, 668
Common law, 1, 22, 61-62, 64, 87, 90, 94, 113, 123, 131, 135-136, 144, 156, 173-175, 345, 362, 394, 442, 510, 615, 619, 623, 690, 700, 767, 862-863, 927, 929. *See also* Case law; Precedent
Common-law marriage, 107, 175-176, 577
Commonwealth v. Feigenbaum, 270
Commonwealth v. Hunt, 503, 506
Communications Act, 117-119
Communications Decency Act (CDA), 369, 386, 461
Communism, 151, 431, 651
Communist Party, 505
Community-oriented policing, 176-177
Community property, 177-180, 275, 331, 568
Competency, 180
Competition Act (Canada), 129-130
Competition Bureau (Canada), 129
Competition Tribunal (Canada), 130
Competitive Equality in Banking Act (CEBA), 97
Comprehensive Crime Control Act, 919
Comprehensive Drug Abuse Prevention and Control Act (Controlled Substances Act), 280
Comprehensive Environmental Response, Compensation, and Liability Act (CERCLA), 304, 833
Compressed Gas Association, 631
Computerized legal databases, 181
Confederacy, 581, 640
Confession, 181-183
Confidentiality, 18, 31, 34, 54, 69-70, 171, 226, 316, 588, 634, 657, 663, 701-702, 705, 923. *See also* Attorney confidentiality
Conflicts of interest, 183-186; and judges, 184, 186
Congress, U.S.: House of Representatives, 190, 328, 436, 549, 834, 898; Senate, 190, 220, 240, 282, 328, 476, 549, 834
Congress of Industrial Organizations (CIO), 506
Connolly, M. J., 110
Consent decree, 186
Conservation Reserve Program (CRP), 338
Consideration, 187, 201
Consignment, 187-188

Consignment Sales Act (Utah), 187
Consolidated Farm Service Agency (CFSA), 337
Consolidated Omnibus Budget Reconciliation Act (COBRA), 402
Conspiracy, 188
Constitution, U.S., 9, 32, 46, 56, 91, 110, 158, 188-193, 205, 222-223, 249, 270, 291, 294, 325, 343, 384, 398-399, 442, 470, 476, 487, 515, 568, 581, 603, 609, 640, 644, 777, 834, 870, 896, 899; and Articles of Confederation, 191; equal protection clause, 307; Obscenity, 119
Constitutional amendments: First Amendment, 7, 23-24, 35, 43, 113, 117, 119, 160, 185, 190, 257, 366-367, 369-375, 377, 386, 461, 567, 671, 686-687, 697, 700, 756, 758-759, 778, 780, 811, 845, 961, 964-965; Second Amendment, 173, 190, 395, 718, 785; Fourth Amendment, 173, 190, 283, 320, 673, 697, 699, 705-706, 718, 778, 781-782, 828, 918; Fifth Amendment, 78, 153, 173, 181, 236, 279, 288, 320, 347-348, 390-391, 393, 493, 496-497, 545, 551, 651, 697, 699, 718-719, 922; Sixth Amendment, 74, 81-82, 153, 190, 236, 286, 393, 483, 487, 734, 789, 813, 830, 846, 872, 875, 896; Seventh Amendment, 173, 190, 478, 483, 875; Eighth Amendment, 91-92, 190, 244-245, 250, 497, 698, 719, 855; Ninth Amendment, 191; Tenth Amendment, 191, 512, 776; Thirteenth Amendment, 191; Fourteenth Amendment, 1, 28, 43, 113, 150, 152, 159-164, 191, 236, 279, 286, 288, 296, 307, 325, 371, 442, 493, 496, 511, 545, 697-699, 742, 771, 780, 813, 907; Fifteenth Amendment, 191, 907; Sixteenth Amendment, 456; Eighteenth Amendment, 36-37; Nineteenth Amendment, 191, 267, 907; Twenty-first Amendment, 33, 36-38; Twenty-third Amendment, 907; Twenty-sixth Amendment, 33, 907
Constitutions, state, 192-194
Consumer Credit Protection Act (Truth in Lending Act), 20, 197, 226, 229, 231, 387, 409, 411, 566
Consumer Protection Acts, 90

Index

Consumer protection laws, 194-198
Consumers' Union, 21
Contempt of court, 198-199
Contingency fees, 199, 823
Contracts, 87, 104, 157, 171, 174, 180, 187, 199-203, 213, 235, 295, 363, 407, 716, 725, 761-762, 862, 882; bilateral, 200; capacity, 201; enforceability, 202; expressed, 200; and fraud, 202; implied, 200; legality of, 202; mailbox rule, 201; mirror-image rule, 201; option, 201; reasonableness of, 201-202; and remedy, 203; rescission of, 202; statute of limitations, 203; unilateral, 200. *See also* Breach of contract; Consideration
Controlled Substances Act, 280
Conversion, 68, 203-204, 673, 858
Conviction, 204
Cooling-off period, 204-205
Cooper, James Fenimore, 556
Cooper v. Pate, 697
Copyright, 172, 178, 205-207, 482, 719, 724, 736, 855
Copyright Act, 206, 737
Copyright Office, U.S., 864
Cornell's Legal Information Institute, 181
Cornwell, Patricia, 559
Coroners, 208, 446
Corporal punishment, 142, 787
Corporate general counsel, 208-209
Corporate legal practice, 209-211
Corporations, 82, 100, 125, 138, 165, 209, 211-214, 378, 440, 794-795, 799, 825-826, 840
Corrupt motive doctrine. *See* Conspiracy
Cosby, Bill, 324
Cosignatory, 214-215
Cosmos 954, 812
Couch on Insurance, 547
Counterfeiting, 215-216, 464, 515
Court-awarded fees, 216-217
Court calendar, 217
Court costs, 217, 218
Court of International Trade, U.S., 223
Court reporters, 221
Court types, 221-224; appellate courts, 222-223, 343; administrative law courts, 135; bankruptcy courts, 223; chancery courts, 222; Claims Court, U.S., 344; Court of Appeals for the Armed Forces, 220; Court of Federal Claims, U.S., 224; Court of International Trade, U.S., 344; Court of Military Appeals, U.S., 224, 344, 606; Court of Veterans Appeals, 224; courts of record, 222; criminal courts, 222; district courts, 223, 343; equity courts, 222; family law courts, 223; federal district courts, 134; juvenile courts, 132, 223, 491, 493-494, 496-497, 817; municipal courts, 135, 222, 343; night court, 222; probate courts, 154, 222, 312, 323, 482, 802; superior courts, 222; Tax Court, U.S., 224

Court-martial, 218-220, 603-604
Covenant not to compete, 224-225
Covenants, conditions, and restrictions (CC&Rs), 410
Covington & Burling, 518
Cravath Swain & Moore, 518
Credit, consumer, 197, 225-227
Credit cards, 215, 227-230, 360
Credit Practices Rule, 226
Credit record, 229-231
Credit Reporting Act, 197, 700
Crime Control Act, 281
Crime Control and Law Enforcement Act, 451
Crime of passion, 231-232
Crime Victims Bill of Rights, 899
Criminal intent, 232-233
Criminal Justice Information Services (CJIS), 242
Criminal justice system, 183, 233-236, 239
Criminal law, 104, 157, 174, 235-239, 257, 265, 551, 639, 831
Criminal prosecution, 239-241
Criminal record, 241-243
Crofton, Sir Walter, 644
Cross-examination, 243-244, 258, 288, 318, 403, 853
Cruel and unusual punishment, 152, 190, 250, 288
Cruikshank v. United States, 395
Cruzan v. Director, Missouri Department of Health, 563, 700
Cuba, 358, 438, 652
Cuban Americans, 961
Curtis, H. K., 569
Customs Office, U.S., 344
Customs Service, U.S., 437, 685, 807, 983

Daley, Richard, 682
Dalkon Shield, 172

Damages, 203, 246-248, 365, 441, 453, 467, 531, 551, 858, 861, 930
Darrow, Clarence, 990
Darwin, Charles, 852
Daubert v. Merrell Dow, 924
Davis-Bacon Act, 508, 607
Death certificate, 248-249
Death penalty, 249-253, 322, 327, 399, 423, 491, 606, 871
Death row attorneys, 253-254
Death with Dignity Act, 772
Debt collection, 254-255
Declaratory judgment, 255-256
Deed, 256, 755, 761, 855
Defamation, 256-257, 797-798
Defendant, 257-258
Defendant self-representation, 258
Defending the guilty, 258-259
Defense Department, U.S., 729
Defense of Marriage Act (DOMA), 578, 580
Democratic-Republican Party, 477
Denmark, 579
Deoxyribonucleic acid (DNA), 924; and evidence, 137; and forensic investigation, 585; and paternity, 17, 656
Deportation, 46, 243, 259-262
Deposition, 154, 221, 262-263, 563, 852
Depository Institutions Deregulation and Monetary Control Act (DIDMCA), 97
Diagnosis-related-groups (DRG) system, 400
Dilatory tactics, 263
Diplomatic immunity, 264
Direct Marketing Association (DMA), 570-571
Directed verdict, 264-265
Disbarment, 888
Discovery, 17, 26, 154, 265-266
Discrimination, 82, 133, 161, 164, 193, 266-269, 510, 537, 618, 657, 703, 727-728, 731-732, 764, 960, 962; age, 268; in the military, 268; racial, 165, 267, 296, 298, 523, 732, 742-744, 907; religious, 267, 296, 298; sexual, 163, 165, 266-268, 296, 298, 743. *See also* Employment discrimination
Dismissal, 269
Disorderly conduct, 269-270
Disqualification of attorneys, 270
District attorneys, 76, 239, 271-272. *See also* Prosecutors
Division of Biological Survey, 354

XXXV

Divorce, 16, 39-41, 47, 82, 132, 140, 144, 146, 148, 176-179, 222, 235, 272-277, 331-334, 391, 501, 566, 575, 578-579, 596, 688, 756, 824; equitable distribution of property in, 274; no-fault divorce, 273. *See also* Community property
Divorce mediators, 277
Divorce Reform Law (New York), 273
DNA. *See* Deoxyribonucleic acid
Dolan v. City of Tigard, 932
Dole, Bob, 899
Domestic violence, 65, 814
Domestic Violence Hotline, 815
Domicile, 278
Don't Forget Me Society, 11
Door-to-door sales, 196, 226, 278-279
Double jeopardy, 9, 190, 236, 279-280, 347, 662
Douglas, William O., 375, 437
Douglas Corp. v. Green, 298
Draft Act, 728
Dreiser, Theodore, 561
Driver's Privacy Protection Act, 817
Driving licenses, 280, 286-287, 600
Driving School Association of America (DSAA), 870
Drug Enforcement Administration (DEA), 282, 341, 515, 685
Drug testing, 283, 646, 699
Drugs, illegal, 245, 280-283, 340, 430, 464, 515, 597, 599, 611, 617, 637, 645, 653, 680, 692, 710, 725, 728, 744, 779, 806-807
Drunk driving, 283-288, 358, 866-867, 898
Drunkenness, public, 599, 611
Ducks Unlimited, 356
Due process, 153, 190-191, 288, 307, 698, 700, 771
Duncan v. Kahanamoku, 218, 582
Dunne, Dominick, 562
Duress, 288-289
Durham test, 446

Earnest money, 290
Easement, 20, 165, 290-291, 857
Economic Espionage Act, 442, 854
Edmunds Act, 106
Edmunds-Tucker Act, 106
Education Department, U.S., 413, 537
Effective counsel, 291-292
Eighteenth Amendment. *See* Constitutional amendments
Eighth Amendment. *See* Constitutional amendments
Eisenhower, Dwight D., 470

Electronic Communications Privacy Act (Wiretap Act), 918
Electronic Fund Transfers Act, 229
Elixir Sulfanilimide, 6
Elizabeth I, queen of England, 795
Ellenborough, Lord, 929
Ellsberg, Daniel, 911
Embezzlement, 292-293, 364, 854
Emergency Planning and Community Right-to-Know Act, 304
Eminent domain, 294, 932
Employee Retirement Income Security Act (ERISA), 171, 440, 768
Employment at will, 294-295
Employment contracts, 295-296
Employment discrimination, 296-300. *See also* Discrimination
Employment Division, Department of Human Resources v. Smith, 372, 759
Employment Retirement Income Security Act (ERISA), 658-661
Endangered Species Act (ESA), 304, 355
Endangered Species Conservation Act, 355
Endangered Species Preservation Act, 355
Engel v. Vitale, 373
Entick v. Carrington, 782
Entrapment, 116, 236, 301
Environmental Law, 547
Environmental legislation, 301-305, 338, 348
Environmental Pesticide Control Act, 339, 986
Environmental Policy Act, 302
Environmental practice, 305-307
Environmental Protection Agency (EPA), 9, 63, 80, 302, 304-305, 354, 437, 633, 833, 912
Equal Access Act, 373
Equal Credit Opportunity Act, 226, 229, 231, 268, 330
Equal Employment Opportunity Commission (EEOC), 26, 29, 186, 296-297, 299, 742, 793
Equal Pay Act, 268, 296
Equal protection of the law, 81, 307, 744, 907. *See also* Constitution, U.S.
Equal Rights Amendment (ERA), 163, 268
Erie Railroad Co. v. Tompkins, 174
Escrow, 308-309, 409, 768
Espionage, 374, 870, 918. *See also* Industrial espionage
Establishment clause, 370, 373, 759

Estate and gift taxes, 309-310, 842
Estates and estate planning, 310-312, 482, 639, 881
Estes v. Texas, 846
Ethics, 68-69, 72, 74, 167, 313-317, 332, 606, 623, 736, 887-889
Ethics in Government Act, 184
European Union, 902
Euthanasia, 424, 740, 771-772
Everson v. Board of Education, 780
Eviction, 317-318
Evidence, 318-321, 873, 875, 910
Evolution, theory of, 43, 852
Ex parte Milligan, 218, 582, 606
Exclusionary rule, 321
Exclusive Economic Zones (EEZ), 576
Exclusive provider organization (EPO), 402
Execution of judgment, 321-322
Executors, 322-323. *See also* Wills
Export Administration Act (EAA), 113, 323
Export Control Act, 323
Export permits, 323
Extortion, 109, 323-325. *See also* Blackmail
Extradition, 325-327, 807
Extradition Act, 326
Exxon oil spill, 172, 211

Fair Credit Billing Act, 229, 231
Fair Credit Reporting Act, 197, 226, 229-230, 966
Fair Debt Collection Practices Act (FDCPA), 197, 226, 229, 231, 255, 552, 566
Fair employment practices laws (FEPs), 792
Fair Housing Act, 328-330
Fair Housing Amendments Act, 328
Fair housing law, 328-330
Fair Labor Standards Act, 336, 508, 607
Fair market value, 330
Fair Packaging and Labeling Act (Truth in Packaging Act), 20, 196
Fairness Doctrine, 119
Fallon, William, 991
False arrest, 58, 669, 797
False Claims Act, 364
False imprisonment, 797
Family court, 144
Family Education Rights and Privacy Act, 700
Family Farmer Bankruptcy Act, 336
Family law practice, 331-334, 639

INDEX

Family Support Act, 148
Farm Credit Banks, 337
Farm Service Agency, 338
Farming, 334-339
Fathers' rights, 333
Faulk, John Henry, 995
Federal Agricultural Mortgage Corporation, 335
Federal Aiding and Abetting statute, 8
Federal Alcohol Administration Act, 36
Federal Aviation Administration (FAA), 675-676
Federal Bankruptcy Code, 412
Federal Bar Association, 103
Federal Bureau of Investigation (FBI), 116, 240, 242, 327, 339-342, 360, 364-365, 443, 470, 501, 515, 617, 679-680, 685, 773, 814, 821, 918, 965, 982 983
Federal Bureau of Prisons, 430, 919
Federal Coal Mine Health and Safety Act, 633
Federal Communications Act, 918
Federal Communications Commission (FCC), 9, 21, 38, 117, 119-120, 223, 369, 959
Federal Communications Commission Act, 21
Federal Communications Law Journal, 522
Federal Computer Fraud and Abuse Act, 617
Federal Consumer Leasing Act, 88
Federal Deposit Insurance Corporation (FDIC), 95-96, 197, 831
Federal Deposit Insurance Corporation Improvement Act (FDICIA), 98
Federal Drug Administration (FDA), 570, 805
Federal Election Campaign Act, 685
Federal Election Commission (FEC), 685
Federal Firearms Act, 395
Federal Food, Drug, and Cosmetic Act, 21
Federal Funeral Industry Practices Revised Rule, 379
Federal Home Loan Bank Board, 98
Federal Housing Administration (FHA), 615-616
Federal Insurance Contributions Act, 809
Federal judicial system, 343-344

Federal Law Enforcement Assistance Administration, 898
Federal law-enforcement agencies, 981-988
Federal laws, 934-943
Federal Register, 463
Federal Reserve Bank, 753
Federal Reserve Board, 96, 197
Federal Reserve System (FRS), 95, 197
Federal Rules of Civil Procedure (FRCP), 136, 218, 378
Federal Rules of Evidence (FRE), 318, 403, 702, 920, 922
Federal Savings and Loan Insurance Corporation (FSLIC), 95, 97
Federal Securities Act, 197
Federal Securities Exchange Act, 197
Federal Tort Claims Act, 602
Federal Trade Commission (FTC), 20, 22, 24, 196, 204, 214, 226, 231, 278-279, 362, 364, 379-380, 447, 570-571, 910, 912
Federal Trade Commission Act, 20, 22, 279
Federal Unemployment Tax Act, 810
Federal Uniform Child Custody Jurisdiction Act, 140
Federal Water Pollution Control Act, 302
Federal Witness Protection Program, 919
Federalist Party, 477
Federalist Society, 529
Federation of Organized Trades and Labor Unions, 506
Feinstein, Dianne, 899
Fellow Servant Doctrine, 927
Felony, 56, 61, 124, 222, 235, 242, 287, 344-346, 391, 404, 422, 488, 568, 637, 688, 691, 703, 711, 729, 756, 855
Felony Murder Rule, 61
Feminism, 133, 232, 333, 730, 898, 926
Fiduciaries, 69, 77, 85, 171, 347, 877
Fifteenth Amendment. *See* Constitutional amendments
Fifth Amendment. *See* Constitutional amendments
Films about the legal professions, 348-353, 989-996
Financial Reform Recovery and Enforcement Act (FIRREA), 98
FindLaw, 181
Fingerprinting, 242, 684, 781

First Amendment. *See* Constitutional amendments
Fish and game laws, 353-356
Fish and Wildlife Service, U.S., 354-355
Fish Commission, U.S., 354
Florio, James, 723
Food and Drug Administration (FDA), 6, 9, 21, 195-196, 437
Food, Drug, and Cosmetic Act, 6
Food Security Act, 338
Food stamps, 31
Ford, Gerald R., 46, 437, 505, 640
Ford Foundation, 739
Ford v. Wainwright, 252
Foreclosure, 356-357, 447
Foreign Bank Supervision and Enhancement Act, 98
Foreign travel, 357-360
Forest Service, U.S., 981
Forgery, 360, 912
Fortas, Abe, 992
Foster parents, 360-361
Fouché, Joseph, 679
Fourteenth Amendment. *See* Constitutional amendments
Fourth Amendment. *See* Constitutional amendments
France, 174, 222, 252, 508, 606
Franchise Act (New Jersey), 363
Franchise businesses, 361-363
Franchise Investment law (California), 363
Franchise Rule, 364
Franklin, Benjamin, 569
Fraud, 22, 90, 140, 363-365, 371, 451, 500, 619, 622, 628, 761-762, 854, 912
Freedman's Bureau, 703
Freedom of Access to Clinic Entrances Act (FACE), 4, 817
Freedom of assembly, 35, 567, 697
Freedom of expression, 367, 778
Freedom of Information Act, 365
Freedom of information request, 365-366
Freedom of press, 7, 23, 153, 160, 288, 366 370, 697, 700
Freedom of religion, 133, 153, 288, 370-373
Freedom of speech, 23, 43, 117, 119, 133, 153, 160, 185, 257, 288, 374-375, 377-378, 697, 719, 811
Freud, Sigmund, 495
Frivolous lawsuits, 378
Frye v. United States, 924
Fugitive Slave Act, 580

XXXVII

Funerals, 378-380
Furman v. Georgia, 249-250
Future estate, 380-381

Gag order, 382
Gambling, illegal, 340, 382-384
Gambling, legal, 384-387, 576
Gardner, Erle Stanley, 558
Garn-St. Germain Depository Institutions Act (DIA), 97
Garnishment, 94, 102, 387, 566, 803
Gay rights, 44. *See also* Homosexuals
General Accounting Office (GAO), 587
General Agreement on Tariffs and Trade (GATT), 576, 654
General Authorities Act, 982
General Motors, 195
General Services Administration (GSA), 749, 970
Geneva Conventions, 461
German Legal Aid Society, 703
Germany, 174, 252
Gerrymandering, 908
Gerst, Maggie, 641
Gideon v. Wainwright, 82, 703, 734
Gillars, Mildred, 871
Gilmore, Gary, 561, 990
Ginsburg, Martin, 842
Ginsburg, Ruth Bader, 3
Gitlow v. New York, 43, 375, 837
Glass Steagal Wall, 96
Goldfarb v. Virginia State Bar, 606
Goldman, Ron, 551, 930
Gompers, Samuel, 503, 506
Government Accounting Office (GAO), 451
Graffiti, 388-390
Grain Inspection Service, 337
Grain Standards Act, 337
Grand jury, 237, 390-391, 441, 446, 852-853
Grandparents' rights, 391-392
Gray, Horace, 475
Great Britain, 67, 99, 128, 157, 252, 294, 391, 707; and common law, 157, 421, 442, 568; and coroners, 208; *habeas corpus* in, 398; misdemeanors in, 611; mortgages in, 614; policing in, 176, 678, 681, 795; study-abroad programs in, 829; trials in, 478, 491, 873; trusts in, 877; and vagrancy laws, 894
Great Depression, 36, 197, 249, 384, 504, 558, 615-616, 644
Greeks, 140, 150, 652
Green cards, 392-393, 432-433

Greenman v. Yuba Power Products, Inc., 716
Gregg v. Georgia, 249-250
Grievance committees for attorney discipline, 393
Griffin v. Illinois, 873
Griswold v. Connecticut, 699, 852
Groome, John C., 819
Grotius, Hugo, 458-459, 575
Guam, 224, 630, 810
Gun Control Act, 395
Gun laws, 393-397. *See also* Self-defense

Habeas corpus, 204, 220, 251, 292, 326, 398-399, 581, 599
Hague Conventions, 928
Hague v. CIO, 375
Haiti, 261
Hamas, 342
Hamilton, Alexander, 37, 487, 685
Hammurabi, Code of, 929
Hand, Learned, 562
Harlan, John M., 377
Harris v. Forklift Systems, Inc., 791
Harrison Narcotic Act, 983
Harriss v. United States, 238
Harter Act, 107
Hastings, Alcee, 436
Hate crime statutes, 399
Hazardous and Solid Wastes Amendment, 304
Hazardous substances, 130, 437, 632, 833
Hazelwood School District v. Kuhlmeier, 779
Hazen Paper Co. v. Biggins, 268
Health and disability insurance, 399-403
Health and Human Services Department, U.S., 280, 437
Health Care Financing Administration (HCFA), 584, 808, 810
Health Insurance Portability and Accountability Act (Kennedy-Kassebaum Act), 363, 402
Health Maintenance Organization (HMO), 401
Hearing, 403
Hearsay, 403
Hearsay rule, 920
Heart of Atlanta Motel v. United States, 732
Helmsley, Leona, 996
Henry, Patrick, 556

Hicks, Stephen C., 110
Higher Education Act, 924
Highway Patrol (California), 820-821
Hill, Anita, 296
Hinckley, John W., 446
Hippocratic oath, 588, 771
Hispanics, 158, 430, 526, 540, 592, 694, 743-744, 907; and AIDS, 35. *See also* Mexican Americans
Hit-and-run accident, 404
Holmes, Oliver Wendell, 374-375, 547, 657, 837, 996
Holy Roman Empire, 458
Home businesses, 404-407
Home buying, 407-410
Home Mortgage Disclosure Act, 330
Home ownership, 410-413
Home School Legal Defense Association, 415
Home schooling, 413-415
Home selling, 415-418
Home Solicitation Trade Practices Rule, 205
Homeowner insurance, 418-420
Homestead, 420-421
Homestead Act, 725
Homicide, 208, 345, 421-425, 561, 574, 726
Homosexuals, 35, 44, 268, 578-580, 891
Hoover, J. Edgar, 339
Hospitals, 425-427
House of Representatives. *See* Congress, U.S.
Housing and Urban Development Department (HUD), 330, 616
Hubble Space Telescope, 365
Human immunodeficiency virus (HIV), 33-35, 537, 577, 697, 729. *See also* Acquired immunodeficiency syndrome (AIDS)
Humane Society, 673
Hung jury, 236
Hunter, Evan (Ed McBain), 559
Hurtado v. California, 391, 442
Hyatt Legal Plans, 546

Ignorance of the law, 428
Illegal Immigration Reform and Immigrant Responsibility Act (IIRIRA), 260, 430, 432
Immigrants, 394, 431, 434, 557, 903
Immigration and Nationality Act (McCarran-Walter Act), 431, 433, 902, 984

Index

Immigration and Naturalization Service (INS), 15, 151, 153, 243, 260, 392, 428-431, 434, 515, 614, 759, 902, 905, 983
Immigration law, Canadian, 132
Immigration law, U.S., 431-436
Immigration Marriage Fraud Act, 433
Immigration Reform and Control Act (IRCA), 432
Impeachment, 834
Impeachment of judges, 436-437, 470
Import permits, 437-438
In re Gault, 496-497
In re Winship, 497
Income taxes, 438-441, 456, 757, 842
Indecency, 117, 119
Indemnity, 441
Independent Insurance Agents of America, 87
Indian Gaming Regulatory Act (IGRA), 384-386
Indian Police, 981
Indictment, 441-442
Individual retirement account (IRA), 121, 768-770
Individuals with Disabilities Education Act (IDEA), 268
Industrial espionage, 442-443
Industrial Revolution, 630, 666, 713
Industrial Workers of the World (IWW), 506
Industry Canada, 129
Infanticide, 140
Informants, 443-444
Infraction, 56, 217-218, 466, 611, 865-866, 887
Inheritance tax, 444, 879
Injunction, 222, 444-445
Innocence, presumption of, 445-446
Innocent III, 873
Inquest, 446
Insanity defense, 446-447
Installment sales contract, 195, 447-448
Institute of Makers of Explosives, 631
Institutionalization, 180, 448-449
Insurance adjustors, 449-450
Insurance defense, 450-451
Insurance fraud, 451. *See also* Fraud
Insurance law, 452-454. *See also* Automobile insurance
Insurance Research Council, 451
Insurance triangle, 454-455
Insurgents v. United States, 37
Intangible asset, 455
Integration, 780

Intellectual property, 172, 205, 462, 719. *See also* Copyright
Interest on attorney trust accounts, 455
Interest on Lawyers Trust Account programs (IOLTA), 78, 455
Interior Department, U.S., 304, 354
Internal Revenue Bureau, 456
Internal Revenue Code, 36, 126, 438, 625, 786-787, 799, 808, 840
Internal Revenue Service (IRS), 9-10, 80, 126, 138, 224, 310, 372, 398, 406, 439-440, 456-457, 463, 515, 552, 625, 685, 786, 800, 808, 822, 841
International AntiCounterfeiting Coalition (IACC), 216
International Banking Act, 96
International Business Machines (IBM), 864
International Center for Settlement of Investment Disputes, 598
International Chamber of Commerce, 594
International Convention for the Unification of Certain Rules of Law relating to Bills of Lading, 108
International Court of Justice, 929. *See also* World Court
International Ice Patrol, 166
International law, 457-460
International Maritime Organization (IMO), 576
International Military Tribunal, 460
International Trade Commission, 863
International tribunals, 460-461
International Union, United Auto Workers v. Johnson Controls, 298
Internet, 227, 369, 386, 461-463, 520, 522-523
Interpol, 215, 463-464, 515
Interstate commerce, 195, 338, 395, 451, 508, 638, 722, 730, 863
Interstate Commerce Commission (ICC), 196, 515
Interstate succession, 464-465, 917
Interstate Stalking Punishment Act, 817
Intestate succession, 464-465, 917
Iota Tau Tau, 544
Iran, 252, 358, 438, 652
Iraq, 252, 261, 358, 438, 652
Ireland, 678, 681, 819
Irvin v. Dowd, 896
Israel, 113
Italy, 652

Jackson, Andrew, 653
Jackson, Robert Houghwout, 232
Jacobson v. United States, 301
James, Kay, 386
James I, king of England, 653, 803
Japan, 221, 342
Japanese Americans, 43, 153, 581, 703, 960
Jaywalking, 466, 611
Jefferson, Thomas, 370, 437, 487, 756; and *Marbury v. Madison*, 477
Jehovah's Witnesses, 642, 852
Jews, 44, 370, 372, 399, 557, 671, 959
Jim Crow, 907
John laws, 728
Johnson, Andrew, 46
Johnson, Gregory Lee, 378
Johnson, Lyndon B., 26, 328-329, 566, 704
Johnston Island, 630
Johnston v. Atlanta Humane Society, 671
Joint and several liability, 466
Joint tenancy, 19, 466-467, 851
Jones, Elaine, 618
Jones Act, 576
Jones, Day, Reavis, and Pogue, 518
Jones-Randall Bill, 37
Journal of Air Law, 522
Journal of Law and Contemporary Problems, 522
Journal of Law and Economics, 522
Journal of Legal Education, 66
Journal of Legal Studies, 523
Journal of Online Law, 522
Judges, 467-469; impeachment of, 436-437, 470
Judgment proof, 469-470
Judicial appointments and elections, 470-479
Judicial bias, 472-475
Judicial clerks, 475-476, 525
Judicial conduct code, 476
Judicial confirmation hearings, 476
Judicial Improvements Act, 644
Judicial review, 477-478; and *Marbury v. Madison*, 477
Judiciary Act, 91, 580, 984
Judiciary Act (1789); and *Marbury v. Madison*, 477
Juries, 478-481
Juris doctor (JD), 75, 537-538
Jurisdiction, 481-482
Jurisprudence, 482-483
Jury duty, 483-484, 486
Jury nullification, 486-487
Jury selection, 487-490
Jury sequestration, 490

XXXIX

Jus sanguinis, 150
Jus soli, 150
Justice Department, U.S., 23, 80, 101, 240, 305, 339, 515, 530, 725, 815, 822, 833, 844, 912-913, 983
Juvenile criminal proceedings, 490-493; and *In re Gault*, 497
Juvenile delinquency, 494-499
Juvenile justice; and *In re Gault*, 496

K., Gregory, 640
Kaeser v. Zoning Board of Appeals of Town of Stratford, 671
Kastigar v. United States, 391
Katz v. United States, 918
Katzenbach v. McClung, 732
Keeton, Page, 547
Kennedy, John F., 505, 985
Kent, James, 541, 547
Kent v. Dulles, 651
Kent v. United States, 496
Kentucky v. Dennison, 325
Keogh plans, 768, 770
Kessler, David A., 805
Kevorkian, Dr. Jack, 771
Kidnapping, 140, 188, 345, 500-502, 601, 846
King, Dr. Martin Luther, Jr., 329, 365
King, Rodney, 682, 898
Klopfer v. North Carolina, 813
Koon, Stacey, 682
Korean War, 605
Kronman, Anthony, 518
Ku Klux Klan, 161, 398, 568
Kutak, Robert J., 167
Kyl, Jon, 899

Labeling, 196
Labor Department, U.S., 170, 429, 607; Office of Federal Contract Compliance (OFCC), 26; Office of Federal Contract Compliance Programs (OFCCP), 28
Labor law, 157, 213, 503-506, 508
Labor-Management Relations Act (Taft-Hartley Act), 169, 504-505, 508
Labor-Management Reporting and Disclosure Act (Landrum-Griffin Act), 505, 509
Labor unions, 54, 67, 168, 170, 340, 503-510, 592, 596, 962
Lacey, John, 354
Lacey Act, 354, 982
LaFave, W. R., 547
La Guardia, Fiorello, 709

Landlords, 510-511, 536, 761-763. *See also* Rental agreements; Renters' rights
Landlord's lien, 511
Landrum-Griffin Act. *See* Labor-Management Reporting and Disclosure Act
Langbein, John H., 523
Langdell, Christopher Columbus, 529
Lanham Act, 863-864
Lanham Trademark Act, 20
Lanni, J. Terrance, 386
Larceny, 188, 293, 345, 364, 496-497, 512, 557, 674, 710, 726, 797, 854
Latin America, 386, 679, 681, 759, 902
Law and Contemporary Problems, 522
Law enforcement, 512-516
Law Enforcement Assistance Administration (LEAA), 516
Law Enforcement Training Center, 516
Law firm partners and associates, 516-517
Law firm partnership tracks, 517-518
Law firms, 518
Law libraries, 519-521
Law of the Sea convention, 575-576
Law reviews, 521-524
Law School Admission Council (LSAC), 524-525
Law School Admission Service (LSAS), 540
Law School Admission Test (LSAT), 524-525, 540, 883-884
Law-school rankings, 524-525
Law-school student demographics, 525-527
Law-student clerks, 527-528
Law teaching, 528-530
Lawphone, 546
Lawsuits, 530-533
Leases, 336, 510, 534-536, 673, 725, 761, 765. *See also* Subleases
Lee, Harper, 558
Legal Aid Society of New York, 703
Legal assistance organizations, 959-967
Legal clinics, 536-537
Legal degrees, 537-539
Legal education, 539-543. *See also* Summer clerkships; Undergraduate preparation for law school
Legal guardians, 543-544
Legal honor societies, 544-545
Legal immunity, 545
Legal resources, 968-976

Legal secretary, 545-546
Legal Services Corporation (LSC), 703-704
Legal services plans, 546
Legal Services Program (LSP), 704
Legal treatises, 546-547
Legalese, 547-548
Legislative counsel, 548-549
Legum magister (LLM), 538, 842-843
Lemon laws, 549-550, 790, 910
Leopold, Nathan, 990, 993
Lesser included offense, 550-551
Lewin, John, 580
Lewinsky, Monica, 571
Lewis v. United States, 875
Lexis, 181, 438, 520, 522
Liability, civil and criminal, 551
Liability Convention, 812
Liability of attorneys to nonclients, 551-552
Libel, 367, 369, 545, 552, 798
Library of Congress, 970; Copyright Office of, 206
Libya, 358, 438
Lien, 165, 254, 511, 552-553
Life insurance, 553-555
Limited liability company (LLC), 126-127, 212-213, 440, 799-801, 840
Limited liability partnership (LLP), 800
Lincoln, Abraham, 99, 188, 398, 557, 581, 907, 989
Lindbergh, Charles, 846
Literature about the legal professions, 555-559, 561-562
Litigation expenses, 562-563
Little FTC Acts. *See* Unfair or deceptive acts or practices (UDAP) statutes
Living wills, 30, 563-564
Loans, business, 564-565
Loans, personal, 565-567
Lochner v. New York, 477
Locke, John, 785
Loeb, Richard, 990, 993
Loewe v. Lawlor, 687
Loitering, 567, 611
London Metropolitan Police (LMP), 176, 678, 683-684
Long arm statute, 567-568
Lord Campbell's Act, 930
Lottery, 384
Louisiana law, 173, 568, 909
Low Countries, 681
Lundman v. McKown, 642
Luxembourg, 908

INDEX

Lyng v. Northwest Indian Cemetery Protective Association, 758

McBain, Ed. *See* Hunter, Evan
McCarran-Ferguson Act, 418, 452
McCarran-Walter Act. *See* Immigration and Nationality Act
McCarthy, Joseph R., 375, 989-990
McCleskey v. Kemp, 252, 745
McCorvey, Norma, 1
McFadden Act, 96-98
Mack v. United States, 395
McKeiver v. Pennsylvania, 497
McKennon v. Nashville Banner Publishing Co., 999
McNaughton test, 446
Macon B. Allen Civil Rights Clinic (Boston), 703
Maconochie, Alexander, 644
Macy, R. H., 569
Madison, James, 190-191, 370; and *Marbury v. Madison*, 477
Magnuson-Moss Warranty Act, 20, 89, 570, 883, 910
Mail Fraud Act, 365
Mail Order Action Line, 571
Mail order buying, 569-572
Mailer, Norman, 561
Maintenance, alimony and, 39-41
Major League Baseball Players Association, 507
Mala in se, 235
Mala prohibita, 235
Malpractice, legal, 551, 572-573
Malpractice, medical, 667
Mann Act, 638, 730
Manslaughter, 345, 421-423, 573-574, 772
Mapp v. Ohio, 321, 781
Maquiladora program, 594
Marbury, William, 477
Marbury v. Madison (1803), 477
Marine Corps, U.S., 218, 380, 603-604
Marine Protection, Research, and Sanctuaries Act, 303, 986
Marital property and debts, 574-575
Marital separation, 39, 144, 146, 179, 331, 575
Maritime law, 575-577
Maritime Law Association, 103
Marriage, 47, 106-107, 132, 147, 175-178, 272-273, 331, 575, 577-579, 688-689
Marriage, same-sex, 579-580
Marshall, John, 477; and *Marbury v. Madison*, 477
Marshall, Thurgood, 618, 837, 989

Marshals Service, U.S., 515, 580-581
Martial law, 581-582
Marvin, Lee, 637
Marvin v. Marvin, 637
Massachusetts Board of Retirement v. Murgia, 29
Matera, Lia, 558
Maternal and Child Health and Crippled Children's Services, 808
May Act, 728
Mechanic's lien, 552, 582-583
Mediation, 171, 533, 583-584
Medicaid, 31, 400, 584-585, 703, 808, 810
Medical Examiner and Coroner Information Sharing Program (MECISP), 208
Medical examiners, 585
Medical malpractice, 586-588
Medical records, 588-589
Medical treatment, consent for, 589-591
Medicare, 31, 400, 591, 786, 808-809
Medicare Catastrophic Coverage Act, 31
Medicare Supplementary Medical Insurance (SMI), 808
Medications, 195
Melville, Herman, 556
Menendez brothers, 562
Mens rea, 232, 235
Merchant Marine Act (1920), 576
Merchant Marine Act (1936), 576
Meritor Savings Bank v. Vinson, 791
Mexican Agrarian Code, 593
Mexican American Legal Defense and Education Fund (MALDEF), 592
Mexican American War, 596
Mexican Americans, 153, 526, 592, 742, 961
Mexican business law, 592-596
Mexican Civil Code, 593, 596
Mexican Federal Labor Law, 595
Mexican Foreign Investment Law, 597-598
Mexican law, 596-599
Mexican Revolution, 593
Mexican travel, 599-601
Mexico, 327, 342, 430, 501, 803, 901
Middle East, 803
Migratory Bird Act, 982
Migratory Bird Hunting and Conservation Stamp Act, 983
Miike, Lawrence, 580
Military attorney, 602
Military justice, 605

Military law, 240, 602-605
Military police, 604-605
Military tribunals, 605-606
Miller v. California, 368
Miller v. Texas, 395
Miller v. United States, 395
Minimum fee schedules, 606
Minimum wage laws, 606-608
Miranda rights, 347, 608-610, 866. See also *Miranda v. Arizona*
Miranda v. Arizona, 58, 182, 608, 610. *See also* Miranda rights
Misdemeanor, 56, 235, 610-611, 729, 755, 797, 816
Misfeasance, 667
Misrepresentation, 364
Missouri Compromise, 852
Missouri Plan, 471
Mistrial, 611-612, 874
Mobil Oil, 361
Mock trials, 45, 612-613
Model Code of Judicial Conduct, 186, 476
Model Code of Professional Conduct, 704
Model Code of Professional Responsibility, 24, 314, 888
Model Drug Paraphernalia Act, 282
Model Penal Code, 110, 232, 422, 447, 637
Model Rules of Judicial Conduct, 472-474
Model Rules of Professional Conduct, 71-73, 78, 85, 138, 167-168, 185, 263, 314, 613, 623, 634, 705, 888
Model Rules of Professional Responsibility, 315-316. *See also* Code of Professional Responsibility
Molly Maguires, 506
Mondale, Walter, 141
Money market deposit account (MMDA), 97
"Monkey" trial, 43, 350, 852, 990
Monogamy, 106-107
Moon Treaty, 812
Moore, Jason, 641
Moot court, 541, 544, 613
Moral turpitude, 613-614
Morgenthau, Hans, 459
Morissette v. United States, 232
Mormons. *See* Church of Jesus Christ of Latter-day Saints
Mortgages, 165, 335, 356, 411-412, 417, 564, 614-617, 753, 856
Mothers Against Drunk Driving (MADD), 898

XLI

Moyer v. Peabody, 582
Mugging, 773
Multicultural Women Attorneys Network, 926
Multiple jurisdiction offenses, 617
Murder, 345, 422, 446, 557, 573, 726, 771

NAACP Legal Defense and Educational Fund, 618
NAACP v. Claiborne Hardware Co., 113
Nader, Ralph, 194, 739
Name changing, 619-620
Napoleon I (Bonaparte), 156, 679
Napoleonic Code, 132, 173-174, 568, 599
National Advertising Review Board, 21
National Aeronautics and Space Administration (NASA), 366
National Association for the Advancement of Colored People (NAACP), 618, 835, 852, 961; *NAACP v. Claiborne Hardware Co.*, 113
National Association of Attorneys General, 240
National Association of Medical Examiners (NAME), 585
National Association of Public Insurance Adjustors (NAPIA), 450
National Association of Social Workers, 11
National Association of Women Judges, 926
National Association of Women Lawyers, 926
National Bank Act, 228, 892
National Center of Child Abuse and Neglect (NCCAN), 141, 144
National Commission on Children, 642
National Conference of Commissioners on Uniform State Laws, 11, 15, 42, 570-571, 862, 889-890, 892
National Credit Union Administration (NCUA), 197
National Crime Information Center, 685, 821
National Criminal Justice Commission, 693-694
National District Attorneys Association, 240
National Education Association (NEA), 507

National Electrical Manufacturers Association, 631
National Environmental Policy Act (NEPA), 302, 602
National Fire Protection Association, 631
National Firearms Act (NFA), 395
National Firearms and Transfer Record Act, 984
National Gambling Impact Study Commission, 386
National Guard, 218, 581
National Highway Traffic Safety Administration (NHTSA), 87
National Incident Study of Neglect (NIS), 144
National Institute of Justice, 816
National Institute of Occupational Safety and Health (NIOSH), 632
National Labor Board, 504
National Labor Relations Act (Wagner Act), 504-505, 508
National Labor Relations Board (NLRB), 169-170, 223, 504, 508
National Labor Union, 506
National Law Journal, 529
National Lawyers' Guild (NLG), National Immigration Project of the, 435
National Marine Fisheries Service, 354
National Organ Transplant Act (NOTA), 635
National Organization for Victim Assistance (NOVA), 899
National Pollutant Discharge Elimination System (NPDES), 302
National Resource Center for Consumers of Legal Services, 546
National Sheriffs' Association (NSA), 796
National Sheriff's Institute (NSI), 796
National Socialist Party v. Village of Skokie, 377
National Traffic and Motor Vehicle Safety Act, 912
National Transportation Safety Board, 6
National Treasury Employees Union v. United States, 185
National Victim Center, 899
National Violence Against Women Survey, 816
National Voter Registration Act, 908
National Wildlife Federation, 739
National Wildlife Refuge System, 354

National Women Law Students' Association, 926
Nationwide Insurance Enterprise, 451
Native Americans, 15, 370, 372, 383, 526-527, 540, 758, 803, 819, 960
Native wine laws, 38
Natural Resources Conservation Service, 338-339
Naturalization, 151, 153
Naval Investigation Service, 603-604
Navy, U.S., 166, 190, 218-219, 380, 603-604
Nazis, 375, 434, 460, 871, 961, 993
Negligence, 86-87, 232, 364, 423, 620-621, 665-667, 673, 716-717, 726, 861, 929-930
Negotiable instrument, 289, 621-622
Neighbor problems, 623
The Netherlands, 579
New Deal, 504
New Jersey v. T.L.O., 778
New York Society for the Prevention of Cruelty to Children, 141
New York Stock Exchange, 120, 533, 826
New York Times v. Sullivan, 367
New Zealand, 173, 607, 681
Nicaragua, 261, 459, 929
Nigeria, 252
Night court, 623
Nineteenth Amendment. *See* Constitutional amendments
Ninth Amendment. *See* Constitutional amendments
Nix v. Whiteside, 663
Nixon, Richard M., 26, 46, 355, 367, 391, 505, 630, 640, 668, 685
Nixon, Walter, 436
Nizer, Louis, 995
No-contact rule, 623-624
No-fault divorce. *See* Divorce
No-fault insurance, 624, 665
Noble Order of the Knights of Labor, 506
Noise Control Act, 986
Nolan, Joseph R., 110
Nolan-Haley, Jacqueline M., 110
Nollan v. California Coastal Commission, 719
Nolo contendere plea, 624-625, 676-677, 913
Nonfeasance, 667
Nonprofit organizations, 625-627
Non-Resident Violator Compact, 866
Norris, Frank, 557
Norris-LaGuardia Act. *See* Anti-Injunction Act

INDEX

North American Agreement on Environmental Cooperation, 598-599
North American Free Trade Agreement (NAFTA), 593-594, 596-599
North Korea, 358, 438, 652
Northern Mariana Islands, 224
Norway, 579
Notary public, 627-628
Nuclear Regulatory Commission, 633
Nuremberg Trials, 460-461, 993
Nursing Home Reform Act, 31
Nursing homes, 628-629

Objection, 630
Obscenity, 117, 119, 368-369
Occupational health and safety, 630-634
Occupational Safety and Health Act, 303, 912, 927
Occupational Safety and Health Administration (OSHA), 303, 337, 339, 630-632, 782, 912
O'Connor, Sandra Day, 2
O'Donnell, Lillian, 559
Office of Economic Opportunity (OEO), 704
Office of Economic Ornithology, 354
Office of Foreign Assets Control Regulations, 438
Office of the Comptroller of the Currency (OCC), 95-96
Office of Thrift Supervision (OTS), 98
Office of Violence Against Women, 815
Officers of the court, 634
Oil Pollution Act, 576
Old-Age, Survivors, and Disability Insurance (OASDI), 786, 808
Older Workers Benefit Protection Act (OWBPA), 661
Olmstead v. United States, 918
Omnibus Crime Control and Safe Streets Act, 700, 918
Opinion, 634-635
Order of Barristers, 544
Order of Sons of Italy, 960
Order of the Coif, 544
Oregon Adoptive Rights Association, 11
Organ donation, 635-636
Organization of Petroleum Exporting Countries (OPEC), 48
Organized Crime Control Act. *See* Racketeer Influenced and Corrupt Organizations (RICO) statute
Ornitz, Samuel, 557
Otis, James, 782
Outer Continental Shelf Lands, 630
Outer Space Treaty, 812

Pacific Islanders, 526-527
Pacific Legal Foundation, 739
Pacifica Broadcasting v. FCC, 369
Packers and Stockyards Act, 337
Palestinians, 342, 959
Palimony, 637
Pandering, 637-638
Papachristou v. City of Jacksonville, 238
Paralegals, 516, 638-640
Pardon, 640
Parens patriae, 144, 491, 493-494
Parental divorce, 640-641
Parental Kidnapping Prevention Act, 140
Parental responsibility for children, 641-643
Park Police, U.S., 982
Parole, 234, 421, 643-646
Parole Commission, U.S., 987
Parole Commission Phaseout Act, 644
Parole officers, 233, 646-647
Partnerships, 126, 440, 647-650, 799, 840
Passports, 133, 358, 650-652
Patent and Trademark Office, U.S., 653, 864
Patent Court, 105
Patent Law, 653
Patents, 172, 178, 455, 482, 652-655, 724, 736, 855
Paternity, 17, 641, 655-656, 660, 891-892
Patient Self-Determination Act (PSDA), 563, 590, 658, 771
Patient's Bill of Rights, 589
Patients' rights, 656-658
Paul, Randolph, 842
Pawnbrokers, 567
Peacock case, 232
Pearson, Edmund, 559
Peel, Robert, 176, 678, 683
Pennypacker, Samuel W., 819
Pennzoil, 172
Pension Benefit Guaranty Corporation, 31
Pensions, 575, 658-662
Pentagon Papers, 367, 911
People by Koppell v. Alamo Rent-A-Car, 32
Perishable Agricultural Commodities Act (PACA), 337
Perjury, 72, 557, 662-663
Permanent Court of Arbitration, 928
Personal injury attorneys, 82, 663-665
Personal injury law, 665-669
Personal injury protection (PIP), 87
Personal property, 254, 419, 447, 552, 669-670, 725, 749
Personal recognizance, 670-671
Pesticides, 339
Pets, 623, 671-674, 763, 830
Phi Alpha Delta, 544
Phi Delta Phi, 544
Philadelphia Plan, 27
Philippine Constabulary, 819
Philippines, 398, 678
Phillips Petroleum, 7
Phillips v. Washington Legal Foundation, 78, 455
Physician-assisted suicide. *See* Euthanasia
Pickering v. Board of Education, 779
Pickpocketing, 601, 674
Pilot licenses, 674-676
Pinkertons, 701
Planned Parenthood, 852
Planned Parenthood of Southeastern Pennsylvania v. Casey, 2
Plea, 676-677
Plea bargain, 183, 238, 272, 287, 677-678, 873
Plessy v. Ferguson, 160, 780
Poindexter, Joseph, 581
Police, 56-57, 61, 116, 176, 233, 443, 513-514, 608, 678-683, 725, 728, 745, 781, 807, 816, 828-829, 839, 876, 918. *See also* Community-oriented policing; State police
Police detectives, 683-685
Police review boards, 176
Political campaign contributions, 685-686
Pollock v. Farmers' Loan & Trust Co., 456
Pollution: of air, 303; by toxic chemicals, 303; of water, 302
Polygamy, 106, 434, 758
Pomerene Bills of Lading Act, 107
Pornography, 301, 368, 386
Posse Comitatus Act, 605
Post, Melville Davisson, 558
Postal Service, U.S., 21, 196, 365, 515, 569-571
Powderly, Terence V., 506
Powell, Laurence, 682
Power of attorney, 686-687

XLIII

Precedent, 22, 157, 174, 687. *See also* Case law; Common law
Preferred provider organization (PPO), 402
Pregnancy Discrimination Act, 268, 296
Preliminary hearing, 687-688
Prenuptial agreements, 202, 312, 331-332, 688-689
Pre-Paid Legal Services, 546
Preventive detention, 92
Principals (criminal), 345, 689-690
Principals and agents, 51, 690
Printer's Ink, 21
Printz v. United States, 395
Prison system, 691-695
Prisoners' rights, 695-699
Privacy Act, 700, 966
Privacy rights, 1, 44, 149, 265, 288, 699-701
Private investigators, 701-702
Privileged communication, 702-703
Pro bono legal work, 108, 373, 435, 703-705, 736
Probable cause, 237, 705-707, 839
ProBAR, 435
Probate, 165, 707-709, 916, 926
Probation, 234; adult, 710-713; juvenile, 713-715
Product liability law, 5, 172, 194, 716-717
Program of State Governments, 141
Progressive Era, 354, 471, 557
Prohibition, 33, 36-37, 349, 706, 804
Property liability, 717-718
Property rights, 718-720
Property taxes, 19, 407, 720-724, 750, 757-758, 857. *See also* Tax law
Property types, 724-725. *See also* Personal property; Real property
Proposition 227 (Unz initiative), 592
Prosecutors, 56-57, 76, 80, 239-240, 271, 287, 498, 677, 688, 725-728, 814
Prosser, William L., 547
Prosser and Keeton on Torts, 547
Prostitution, 340, 496, 597, 637, 728-730
Protestant Reformation, 720
Provenzio, Anthony, 642
Provenzio, Susan, 642
Provincial courts (Canada), 132
Provost marshals, 605
Proximate cause, 730-731
Psychoanalysis, 495
Public accommodations, 731-733
Public defenders, 74, 733-736

Public domain, 736-737, 919
Public Health Cigarette Smoking Act, 804
Public interest law, 737-740
Public nuisance, 740
Public school, 373, 413, 642, 777, 779-780. *See also* School law
Puerto Ricans, 526
Puerto Rico, 224, 259, 325-326, 340, 630, 810, 889-890
Puerto Rico v. Branstad, 325
Puffery, 20
Pure Food and Drug Act, 912
Purkett v. Elem, 745

Qualified Thrift Lender Test (QTL), 98
Quarles v. New York, 182
Quebec, 131-132, 173
Quebec Act, 131
Quill Corporation v. North Dakota, 776
Quitclaim deed, 741

Race and the law, 742-745
Racism, 251-252, 394, 523. *See also* African Americans Civil Rights Acts; Civil rights and liberties
Racketeer Influenced and Corrupt Organizations (RICO) statute (Organized Crime Control Act), 172, 365, 515, 919
Railway Labor Act, 504, 508
Raleigh, Sir Walter, 803
Randall, Margaret, 259
Rape, 64, 345, 422, 500, 745-749, 814. *See also* Sexual battery
Reagan, Ronald, 281, 446, 692, 897-899, 911
Real estate law, 639, 749-753
Real estate listing agreements, 753-754
Real Estate Settlement Procedures Act (RESPA), 409
Real property, 104, 128, 166, 254, 322, 330, 334, 616, 669, 724-725, 741, 749, 752, 754-755, 761
Reasonable doubt, 755
Reckless endangerment, 755-756
Reconstruction, 150, 328
Rector, Ricky Ray, 252
Red Lion Broadcasting Co. v. Federal Communications Commission (F.C.C.), 369
Red Scare, 651
Reeve, Tapping, 541
Reformation, 174
Refugees, 431-432, 434

Regents of the University of California v. Bakke, 28
Registration Convention, 812
Rehabilitation Act, 268
Rehabilitative support, 756
Rehnquist, William, 2, 835
Release, 756
Religion. *See* Freedom of religion
Religious Freedom Restoration Act (RFRA), 372, 759
Religious institutions, 756-760
Reno v. American Civil Liberties Union, 369
Rent control, 510, 760-761, 766
Rental agreements, 761-764
Renters' rights, 764-766. *See also* Eviction; Landlords
Repossession, 766-767
Republican Party, 355, 378, 911
Rescission, 365
Rescue Agreement, 812
Residential Landlord and Tenant Act, 762
Resisting arrest, 61
Resolution Trust Corporation (RTC), 98
Resource-based relative value scale (RBRVS), 400
Resource Conservation and Recovery Act, 304, 912
Restatement of Torts, 862
Restatements of the Law, 110
Restraining order, temporary, 767
Retail installment sales acts (RISAs), 447
Retainers, 767-768
Retirement Equity Act (REA), 660, 768
Retirement planning, 768-770
Retirement plans, 770
Reverse discrimination, 28
Revised Model Business Corporation Act (RMBCA), 800
Revised Model Nonprofit Corporation Act, 625
Revised Uniform Deceptive Trade Practices Act, 570
Reynolds v. Sims, 907
Reynolds v. United States, 371, 758
Rhodes v. Chapman, 695
Riegle-Neal Interstate Banking and Branching Efficiency Act, 96, 98
Right to die, 771-773
Right to Financial Privacy Act, 700
Right-to-work laws, 170
River and Harbor Act (RHA), 301

Robbery, 324, 345, 422, 496, 500, 674, 690, 711, 725, 773-774, 854
Robertson, Pat, 386
Robinson-Patman Act, 50
Rodgers, W. H., Jr., 547
Roe v. Wade, 1-3, 288, 478, 700, 834
Roman Catholic Church, 47, 372
Roman law, 67, 140, 150, 156, 599, 614
Rome, 482
Romer v. Evans, 268
Roosevelt, Franklin D., 504, 581, 728
Roosevelt, Theodore, 50, 195, 607
Rosenberg, Ethel, 870
Rosenberg, Julius, 870
Ross v. United States, 706
Roth, William, 769-770
Royal Irish Constabulary (RIC), 678, 819
Rufo, Sharon, 930
Rules of Federal Civil Procedure, 164
Rules of Professional Conduct, 85, 663
Russia, 342, 650
Rwanda, 929

Safe Drinking Water Act, 303, 986
St. Mary's Honor Center, et al., v. Hicks, 298
Salerno v. United States, 92
Sales taxes, 440, 571, 757, 775-776
Salinas, Carlos, 593, 597
Salomon v. Salomon & Co., 129
Samoa, 630
San Antonio Independent School District v. Rodriguez, 723, 837
Sanders, Lawrence, 559
Sandoval v. California, 755
Santería, 372
Saudi Arabia, 901
Savings Association Insurance Fund (SAIF), 95
Savings Incentive Match Plan for Employees (SIMPLE), 770
Scandinavia, 681
Schaeffer, Rebecca, 816
Schenck v. United States, 374
Schnapp v. Lefkowitz, 671
Schober, Johann, 463
School law, 776-781. *See also* Home schooling; Public school
Scientiae juridicae doctor (SJD), 538
Scientology, Church of, 759
Scopes, John T., 43, 350, 852, 990
Scott, Scott, 852
Scott v. Sandford, 852
Search and Seizure, 547

Search and seizure, illegal, 153, 190, 284, 288, 320, 673, 699, 705, 718, 778, 781-782, 918. *See also* Search warrant
Search warrant, 782-783, 839. *See also* Search and seizure, illegal
Sears, Richard, 569
Second Amendment. *See* Constitutional amendments
Secret Service, U.S., 215
Secured transaction, 157, 783-785
Securities Act, 172, 625
Securities and Exchange Commission (SEC), 21, 120, 197, 912
Security agreement, 139
Segregation, 81, 160-161, 307, 780, 962
Selective Service, 393
Self-defense, 236, 785
Self-employment taxes, 785-787
Self-incrimination, 922
Seminole Tribe of Florida v. Florida, 386
Senate, U.S.. *See* Congress, U.S.
Sentencing, 787-789
Sentencing Commission, U.S., 282
Sentencing Reform Act, 282, 644
Separate but equal doctrine, 267. *See also Plessy v. Ferguson*
Separate property, 178
Service contracts, 789-790
Seventh Amendment. *See* Constitutional amendments
Sex education, 149
Sexual abuse, 141-142, 641
Sexual battery, 500, 726, 748, 790-791. *See also* Assault and battery; Rape
Sexual harassment, 163, 210, 325, 523, 791-794, 963
Shareholder derivative suit, 213
Shareholder suit, 794-795
Sheinbein, Samuel, 327
Shephard's Citations, 45
Sheppard, Sam, 991
Sherbert v. Verner, 371
Sheriffs, 795-797
Sherman Anti-Trust Act, 48, 50, 119, 503, 556, 687, 912. *See also* Antitrust law
Sherman v. United States, 301
Shipping Act, 576
Shoplifting, 496, 797-798
Silkwood, Karen, 911
Simplified Employee Pension Plan (SEP), 406
Simpson, Nicole, 551, 930

Simpson, O. J., 279, 487, 551, 562, 684, 848, 930
Sinclair, Upton, 194-195, 911
Sixteenth Amendment. *See* Constitutional amendments
Sixth Amendment. *See* Constitutional amendments
Skadden, Arps, Slate, Meagher, and Flom, 518
Slander, 552, 798. *See also* Libel
Slavery, 153, 191, 556, 580, 742, 806, 852
Small Business Administration (SBA), 800-801
Small Business Job Protection/Minimum Wage Increase Act, 607, 770
Small businesses, 798-802
Small claims court, 802-803
Smith v. Allwright, 907
Smoking and tobacco use, 803-806, 837
Smuggling, 464, 806-808
Social Security, 31, 125, 147, 177-178, 456, 554, 577, 591, 758, 786, 808-811, 972; and Old-Age, Survivors, and Disability Insurance (OASDI), 31; Unemployment Compensation, 808
Social Security Act, 141, 584, 591, 808, 810
Social Security Administration (SSA), 31, 380, 463, 808, 810
Social Services for Adults and Children, 808
Socialist Labor Party, 506
Socialist Party, 43, 506
Society for the Prevention of Pauperism, 494
Society of Automotive Engineers, 631
Solario v. United States, 603
Solicitation of legal clients, 811-812. *See also* Advertising, legal
Solicitors, 79
Sontag, Deborah, 243
South Africa, 252
Soviet Union, 323, 459, 606, 812, 870, 901
Space law, 812
Spain, 174, 596
Spanish-American War, 312
Spanish law, 177
Speakeasies, 37
Special Library Association, 521
Speech and press, freedom of, **376**
Speedy Trial Act, 813
Speedy-trial requirement, 813

Spousal abuse, 331, 813-816
Sputnik I, 812
Stack v. Boyle, 91-92
Stakeholders, 827
Stakeout, 816
Stalking, 816-817
Standard Oil, 50
Standard State Zoning Enabling Act, 932
Standards for Criminal Justice, 241
Standards of Training for Competency of Watchstanding (STCW), 576
Star Chamber (Great Britain), 173
Stare decisis, doctrine of, 47, 131, 134-135, 157, 174, 344
Starr, Kenneth, 571
State bar associations, 977-980
State Department, U.S., 652, 902
State judicial systems, 817-818
State police, 818-822
State v. Meyer, 270
Statute, 822
Statute of Frauds, 761
Statute of limitations, 203, 822-823
Statute of Monopolies (Great Britain), 50
Statute of Wills (Great Britain), 913
Statutory fee ceilings, 823
Statutory rape, 748
Stephens, Uriah S., 506
Stepparents, 824-825
Stock certificate, 825-826
Stockholders, 210, 212, 690, 826-828
Stockman, David, 911
Stone, Harlan Fiske, 687
Stop and frisk, 828-829
Story, Joseph, 547
Stowe, Harriet Beecher, 556
Stradivari, Antonio, 652
Strickland v. Washington, 292
Strikebreaking, 168, 580
Strikes, 169, 503-507, 557, 593, 596, 819, 894
Study-abroad programs, 829
Subleases, 762, 829-830. *See also* Leases; Rental agreements
Subpoena, 830-831
Subrogation, 831
Substantive law, 831-832
Sudden infant death syndrome (SIDS), 208
Summary judgment, 832
Summer clerkships, 832. *See also* Legal education
Summons, 833
Super NOW accounts, 97

Superfund law. *See* Comprehensive Environmental Response, Compensation, and Liability Act
Superfund litigation, 304, 306, 833-834
Supplemental Security Income (SSI), 31, 584, 808, 810. *See also* Social Security
Supremacy clause, 968
Supreme Court, U.S., 163, 193, 220, 222-223, 343, 834-837, 866; and abortion, 1-2, 700; and adoption, 11; and affirmative action, 28, 743; cases, 944-958; and citizenship, 152, 158; and civil rights, 58, 72, 81-82, 113, 159, 161, 182, 185, 244, 288, 292, 307, 347, 369, 378, 461, 609, 663, 699, 734; and the death penalty, 249-250, 253, 423; and education, 642, 777; and euthanasia, 590; and immigrants, 150; judicial review and, 477; juvenile justice and, 496; and labor law, 169, 508; and presidency, 477; and zoning laws, 932
Supreme Court of Canada, 132
Supreme Truth, 342
Surrey, Stanley, 842
Surrogate parenting, 837-838
Suspect, 838-839
Sutherland, Edwin, 911
Sutherland, Pamela K., 77
Sweden, 579
Swift v. Tyson, 174

Taft-Hartley Act (Labor-Management Relations Act), 169, 504, 505, 508
Taney, Roger, 852
Task Force on Victims of Crime, 899
Tax Court, U.S., 439, 841
Tax law, 82, 121, 129, 138, 157, 209, 213, 338, 383, 387, 406, 411, 456, 759, 800, 822, 840-844. *See also* Business taxes; Estate and gift taxes; Estates and estate planning; Income taxes; Inheritance tax; Internal Revenue Service
Tax Reform Act, 312, 660, 768, 842
Tax Relief Act, 786
Taxpayer Relief Act, 769-770
Telecommunications Act, 117-120
Telemarketing Sales Rules, 364
Telephone Consumer Protection Act, 571
Telephone law, 844-846
Television courtroom programs, 846-848

Television dramas about the legal profession, 848-851
Tenancy in common, 851
Tennessee v. Scopes, 852
Tennessee Valley Authority (TVA), 988
Tennessee Valley Authority Act, 986
Tenth Amendment. *See* Constitutional amendments
Tenure, 779-780, 963
Terrorism, 342, 357-358, 398, 500, 581, 680
Terry, Luther L., 804
Terry v. Ohio, 829
Test case, 851-852
Testimony, 852-853
Texas Monthly v. Bullock, 757
Texas Rangers, 819
Texas v. Johnson, 378
Thalidomide, 1, 6, 195
Thames, Richard, 680
Theft, 853-854
Thirteenth Amendment. *See* Constitutional amendments
Thirty Years' War, 458
Thomas, Clarence, 296
Thomas, Frederick W., 556
Thompson, Fred, 991
Three-strikes laws, 245, 646, 855
Thurmond, Strom, 399
Tinker, John, 778
Tinker, Mary Beth, 778
Tinker v. Des Moines Independent Community School District, 778
Title, 855-856
Title companies, 856-857
Title insurance, 166
Title search, 857
Tocqueville, Alexis de, 470, 483, 691
Torts, 57, 87, 104, 157, 171-172, 174, 203, 213, 305-306, 363, 568, 602, 665, 700, 716, 756, 857-858, 860-862, 927
Toxic Substances Control Act, 303, 986
Trade secret, 172, 767, 862-863
Trademarks, 172, 455, 462, 482, 863-865
Trading with the Enemy Act, 323
Traffic court, 865-866
Traffic law, 513, 866-868
Traffic schools, 868, 870
Transportation Department, U.S., 166
Treason, 152, 515, 870-871
Treasury Department, U.S., 36, 95, 98, 215, 339, 429, 437, 456, 515, 548, 842, 983-985

Index

Treaty of Westphalia, 458
Trespass, 124, 551, 611, 673, 767, 858, 871
Trial publicity, 871-872
Trial transcript, 872-873
Trials, 873-876; Rambo litigation tactics, 17; trial by ambush, 17, 262, 563
Trout Unlimited, 356
Truancy, 876-877
Trust Territory of the Pacific Islands, 630
Trustees, 171, 336, 877
Trusts, 138, 183, 310, 363, 639, 709, 855, 877-881, 926; charitable, 881
Truth in Lending Simplification and Reform Act, 566
Turkey, 650
Turow, Scott, 558
Twenty-first Amendment. *See* Constitutional amendments
Twenty-sixth Amendment. *See* Constitutional amendments
Twenty-third Amendment. *See* Constitutional amendments

Unauthorized practice of law, 882
Unconscionable contracts, 762, 882-883
Undergraduate preparation for law school, 883-885. *See also* Legal education
Underwriters Laboratories, 631
Unemployment Compensation Act, 336
Unemployment insurance, 885-887
Unethical conduct of attorneys, 887-889
Unfair labor practices, 170
Unfair or deceptive acts or practices (UDAP) statutes, 22
Unfair Trade Practices Act, 90
Unified Network for Organ Sharing (UNOS), 635
Uniform Code of Military Justice (UCMJ), 218-219, 602-603, 605-606. *See also* Military law
Uniform Commercial Code (UCC), 88, 126, 130, 171-172, 187, 199, 228, 293, 337, 361, 364, 462, 551, 571, 582, 783, 790, 826, 883, 889, 909; Statute of Frauds of, 364
Uniform Consumer Credit Code (UCCC), 90, 892
Uniform Controlled Dangerous Substances Act, 280

Uniform Crime Victims Reparations Act, 63, 502
Uniform Customs and Practices for Documentary Credits, 594
Uniform Enforcement of Foreign Judgments Act, 889
Uniform Franchise Offering Circular, 363
Uniform Gifts to Minors Act, 312
Uniform Interstate Family Support Act (UIFSA), 147
Uniform laws, 889-890
Uniform Partnership Act (UPA), 647, 889
Uniform Pre-Marital Agreement Act, 688
Uniform Probate Code, 889
Uniform Residential Landlord and Tenant Act, 761
Uniform Trade Secrets Act (UTSA), 862
Uniform Transfers to Minors Act, 312
Union Carbide Corporation, 7, 211
United Auto Workers (UAW), 506
United Church of Christ, 960
United Electrical Workers, 507
United Food and Commercial Workers (UFCW), 507
United Nations (U.N.), 149, 459-460, 575, 928
United Nations Commission on International Trade Law, 598
United Nations Convention on the Carriage of Goods by Sea (Hamburg Rules), 108
United Nations Convention on the Rights of the Child, 149
United States Code, 46, 463
United States Code Annotated, 47
United Steelworkers of America v. Weber, 297
Universal Declaration of Civil Rights, 963
Universal Declaration of Human Rights, 651
Unwed parents and rights of children, 890-892
Use tax, 571
USSC+, 181
Usury, 226, 892-893

V-chip, 119
Vacco v. Quill, 772
Vagrancy, 894
Value-added tax (VAT), 125, 438, 440, 775-776
Vandalism, 270, 441, 894-895

Vehicle licenses and registration, 895-896
Vehicular Control Module (Mexico), 600
Vehicular homicide, 867
Venue, change of, 896
Verdict, 896-897
Verdugo-Urquidez v. United States, 395
Versace, Gianni, 562
Veteran Affairs Department, 616
Veterans, 31, 138, 380
Veterans Administration (VA), 380, 616
Veterans Benefits Administration, 31
Via Rail Canada, 134
Victim and Witness Protection Act, 898
Victims' Assistance Legal Organization (VALOR), 899
Victims' Bill of Rights, 899
Victims of Crime Act (VOCA), 899
Victims' rights, 897-900
Vietnam War, 33, 46, 371, 640, 728, 778, 911
Village of Euclid v. Ambler Realty Co., 932
Vinson, Frederick Moore, 91
Violence Against Women Act, 815-816
Violent Crime Control and Law Enforcement Act, 395, 815, 899
Virgin Islands, 224, 630, 810, 889-890
Visas, Canadian, 133-134
Visas, foreign, 900-902
Visas, U.S., 432, 902-903, 905
Voir dire, 486, 488-489
Volstead Act, 37
Voting rights, 191, 597, 618, 906-908, 965
Voting Rights Act, 267, 907

Wake Island, 630
Wales, 173, 678, 681
Walsh-Healey Act, 633
Walz v. Tax Commission, 757
Wanamaker, John, 569
Wapner, Joseph, 848
War crimes, 259
War on Drugs, 70, 280-282, 692, 735
War on Poverty, 704
Ward, Aaron Montgomery, 569
Warranties, 22, 89, 909-910
Warranty of habitability, implied, 763
Warranty of quiet enjoyment, implied, 763
Warren, Earl, 375, 496, 813, 989
Warsaw Convention, 357
Wartime Food Control Bill, 37

Washington, George, 569, 653, 803, 984
Washington Post, 367
Washington v. Glucksberg, 772
Water Pollution Control Act, 302-303, 986
Water Quality Act, 302, 986
Watergate, 391, 685
Watterston, George, 556
Webb-Kenyon Law, 37
Webster v. Reproductive Health Services, 2
Wechler, Herbert, 523
Weeks v. United States, 321, 781
Wellington, Duke of, 683
Welsh v. United States, 371
Wendt, Gary C., 275
Wendt, Lorna J., 275
Wendt v. Wendt, 275
West Indies, 803
Westlaw, 181, 438, 520, 522
Wheeler-Lea Act, 20
Whiskey Rebellion, 37, 46
Whistle-blowing, 295, 910-912
White, Byron R., 2
White-collar crime, 340, 911-913
White Slave Traffic Act, 638, 730
Whitman, Christine, 723
Wigmore on Evidence, 547
Wildlife and Sportsfishing Restoration Act (Pittman-Robertson Act), 354
William the Conqueror, 795
Williams, Wayne, 989
Williams-Steiger Occupational Safety and Health Act, 630
Williams v. United States, 390
Williston on Contracts, 547
Wills, 82, 105, 179-180, 222, 311-312, 322, 363, 482, 725, 856, 880, 913-917. *See also* Bequests; Intestate succession; Living wills
Wills, holographic, 917
Wilson, James, 541
Wilson, O. W., 682
Wilson, Woodrow, 37, 982
Wiretap, 918
Wisconsin v. Yoder, 642, 780
Witness protection programs, 918-920
Witness Security Program, 581
Witness Security Reform Act, 919
Witness Security Review Committee, 919
Witnesses, 243, 262, 265, 272, 288, 313, 318-319, 563, 853, 873, 919-923
Witnesses, expert, 180, 320, 923-924
Wolf v. Colorado, 781
Women in legal professions, 924-926
Women's Legal Defense and Education Fund, 926
Women's rights, 267
Woodward, Louise, 562
Workers' compensation, 6, 336, 927-928
World Court, 459, 928-929
World War I, 37, 323, 459, 463, 650
World War II: and atomic secrets, 870; and conscientious objectors, 371; and the death penalty, 249; and internment of Japanese Americans, 153, 703; and military courts, 606; and Nazis, 259, 434, 460, 871; and suspension of *habeas corpus*, 398
Wrongful death, 929-931
Wythe, George, 528, 541

Yoder v. Wisconsin, 371, 413
Yugoslavia, 438, 929

Zemel v. Rusk, 652
Zoning Commission of the Town of Danbury v. Peter Grandieri et al., 671
Zoning laws, 405, 758, 932-933